THE OFFICIAL PRICE GUIDE TO COLLECTIBLE ROCK RECORDS

BY RANDAL C. HILL

FIRST EDITION

HOUSE OF COLLECTIBLES, ORLANDO, FLORIDA 32811

DEDICATION

To my wife Sue
To my children,
Scott and Kathleen

Published by the: House of Collectibles, Inc.
773 Kirkman Road, No. 120
Orlando, FL 32811

Printed in the United States of America

Library of Congress Catalog Card Number: 78-72032

ISBN: 0-87637-105-5

Questions, comments, corrections and suggestions are gladly welcomed. Write:
Randal C. Hill
P. O. Box 1921
Covina, CA 91722

THE OFFICIAL PRICE GUIDE TO COLLECTIBLE ROCK RECORDS

TABLE OF CONTENTS

ACKNOWLEDGEMENTS

Inside color photography by Jon Edwards

Jon Edwards Creative Photography
(213) 448-3587

All photos, records and covers courtesy of
Alan C. Lungstrum

Clark Records and Photos
P. O. Box 1062
West Covina, CA 91793

Special thanks to John A. Singleton of
Sun International Corp.

Special appreciation is given to the following folks who helped shape the final product:

Dave Antrell
Bill Berry
Jan Berry
Freddy Cannon
Jim Cooprider
Jim Courneya
Jan-Erik Ekblom
Bill Griggs
John Harrell
Frank M. Kisko
Donald Kuhn
Alan Clark Lungstrom
Mark Plummer
Steve Propes
Don Spears
Darryl Stolper
Dean Torrence
Tom Wenzel
Bobby Vee

And a special thanks to John Schell

ABOUT THE AUTHOR

Randal C. Hill is an English teacher at a southern California high school. An impressionable junior-high student when 1955 brought Bill Haley, Little Richard, Chuck Berry and Fats Domino into his life, Hill never lost his love for or an interest in the early rock-and-roll sound and its consequent recordings. He worked part time as a disc jockey during his college days. Now a frequenter of garage sales and thrift stores, perseverence paid off when he found a VG copy of "The Surfer Moon" by Bob and Sheri at a local thrift store. The disc, the most highly sought-after Brian Wilson-rated single, cost Hill ten cents.

His record collection numbers 3,000 singles and "a few hundred" albums.

He is also the author of three educational workbooks—on rock, soul and country music—geared for the remedial adolescent reader.

INTRODUCTION

The raucous novelty of rock-and-roll was dismissed by adults of the mid-1950's as an irritating fad. And even though that greasy Southern kid named Presley proved a catalyst between "race music" and adolescent-oriented "be-bop", his days were surely numbered! Thus spake the all-knowing adults trying to deal with a force far beyond their control.

Elvis opened the floodgates, and previously suppressed black artists such as Chuck Berry, Fats Domino and Little Richard burst forth to become a stable of nearly every (white) teenager's musical diet. Crude, unrefined, but at least refreshing in its newness, rock-and-roll of the 1950's was ushered out by the Holly/Valens/Bopper tragedy and rock went into limbo. Elvis returned from Germany shorn of his sideburns and sensuality. While good individual records came and went, it was to take a sun-bleached California family called the Beach Boys (only the drummer, Dennis, surfed) to pump some adrenalin into the limp mass of rock-and-roll.

And just as rock enthusiasts around the world started becoming jaded by songs about surfing, hot rods and summertime love, along came a cocky Liverpool bar band playing Chuck Berry riffs and maintaining that someday they would be "bigger than Elvis". The British invasion offered freshness once again, even though that initial novelty was only rehashed 1950s music.

But the later 1960s proved to be turbulent, and rock-and-roll gave way to "rock music", due chiefly to the ***Sergeant Pepper*** album. While regarded as the most creative rock effort by any group, ***Seageant Pepper's*** sophisticated psychedelia stuck a death knell to rock-and-roll and hardly anyone mourned its passing—then.

With the coming of the 1970s, the war in Vietnam wound down, Elvis returned to the stage but this time to pot-bellied, middle-aged and middle-classed Las Vegas audiences. The most notable solo stars of the early and mid-1970s were Elton John and Peter Frampton—hardly in the Elvis category. And as the current decade draws to a close, there have been painfully few artists who have generated even the excitement of the mid-1960s, let alone the frenzied rawness of the 1950's. (Bruce Springsteen stands as a notable exception.)

In 1977 Americans spent $3,5000,000,000 on recorded music—a 28% jump from the previous year. Rock has now achieved widespread acceptance. But the thrill of early rock-and-roll—from the pre-Elvis years to the close of the Beatle era—was/is lacking. The Presleys and Hollys and Berrys have now been replaced by the Framptons and Manilows and Gibbs.

Some people want to relive those thrilling days of yesteryear.

There is no better way to do this than through the collecting of good old rock-and-roll records. The past few years have seen an ever-increasing number of collectors—both young and old—who find delight in the search and fulfillment in the find of that "special" disc, whether to fill a gap in a dog-eared "want list" or simply to revive a hazy segment of the past that only the playing of an "oldie" can conjure up.

Are you a record collector?

If not, do you want to become one?

If you have read to this point, you at least have shown the curiosity to see what this publication is all about.

It's about collecting rock-and-roll records.

It's about what you ***should*** be paying for these desirable discs.

It's about time you thought about this exciting and (as you'll see) profitable hobby.

HOW TO START A COLLECTION

The would-be collector should know himself in terms of his interests. Does he seek every recorded piece of was by Presley or the Beatles or the Rolling Stones? Does he wish to know just about everything in the world of early r & b? (Steve Propes' ***Those Oldies But Goodies*** [Collier-Macmillian, $1.95 would fill that bill.) Does he wish to "run" the entire Philles (hard but not impossible) or Sun (good luck) catalog? Does he want a mint-condition copy of every disc that found a slot in the Top 10? Or the Top 100?

Once he knows where he is headed, the novice can begin to take part in the excitement of being a collector of rock records. (Whatever the case may be, this text will provide helpful buying and selling information to both the beginning and experienced collector.)

Next comes the search that never ends. First of all, forget about your local record store, interested in pushing only the current "in" material. Do, however, become familiar with local thrift stores and visit them often. And watch newspapers for garage sales.

Sorting through stacks of thrift-store or garage-sale records is hardly the "outsider's" idea of a pleasant or profitable way of spending your weekend time. But to the esthete, the possibility of finding a disc of note provides the continuing incentive when hours, days, weeks or months have yielded little of value. Something in the avid collector drives him on . . . and on . . .

Some collectors prefer the convenience of at-home buying and selling through published lists. If you're inclined to become involved in record auctions, write Record Exchanger, Box 2144, Anaheim, CA 92804, and ask to be put on their mailing list. By the way, never bid on records you aren't able to pay for. If you do win records, pay for them immediately and keep a good name for yourself.

Goldmine is the periodical bible for the record collector. It costs $10 a year and is available through Arena Magazine Co., Box 61, Fraser, MI 48026. This publication includes interviews, a variety of columns, several pages of auction sales and want lists and notations of forthcoming record shows and conventions.

INVESTING AND FUTURE TRENDS

While coin, stamp and even beer-can collecting carries a certain stamp of "respectability", there are those (again, "outsiders") who still see the compulsive accumulating of rock discs as a waste of time and money. In reality, it is neither.

There is one hard-and-fast rule each collector should know:

NO IN-DEMAND ROCK RECORD WILL EVER DEPRECIATE IN VALUE!

"Heartbreak Hotel" sold a million copies and carries a 1956 price tag of 89¢. Today that same single in mint condition should bring $5.00. In 1964 "I Want To Hold Your Hand" was priced likewise, also hit the peak of the rock charts and today is worth three times the original price. This illustration serves to point out a pair of concepts to remember about collecting rock-and-roll records:

1. A disc doesn't have to be obscure to be worth money.
2. The ***condition*** of a collectible disc is of utmost importance.

Even certain best-sellers kept in good condition become valuable in time, as the two examples above show. Perhaps it hurts to think you must now pay several dollars for the same record you could have had at one time for less than a dollar—or ***did*** have—but played it to death, kept it unsleeved and ended up using it as a drinking-glass coaster or a Frisbee. More and more collectors are putting their discs on tape, therefore subjecting them to but one play, and storing them, always in sleeves and sometimes in plastic envelopes as well.

Guidelines have been drawn—certain r & b discs, records by Presley, Holly, Berry, Domino, etc., have become valuable—on their ***original labels*** and in ***very good-to-mind condition.*** If you have access to such discs through family or friends, garage sales, thrift stores or swap meets, glom onto whatever you can. You won't be sorry.

For the future? Get ahold of ***early*** (pre-mass popularity) recordings by Linda Ronstadt, Elton John, Fleetwood Mac. Common now? Pretty much. In the future? No—and worth a lot more then!

It is also worthwhile picking up duplications of desirable rock records. They will undoubtedly come in handy later for selling or—better yet—trading. That "double" you possess may be just what a fellow collector has been avidly seeking for a long time . . .

CARE, STORING AND DISPLAYING

The cardinal rule for storing singles is to keep them in paper sleeves and plastic as well if you've got a "money" record. Clean the disc first with a soft cloth and rubbing alcohol. (This process ***ruins*** 78's, though; cleanse them with a mild liquid detergent and lukewarm water.) Albums, also cleaned with alcohol, should be stored in the jacket ***and*** with a paper inner sleeve turned up so the disc doesn't roll out of the jacket and break. Singles, EPs and albums should always be stored upright, never stacked one upon another.

Label stickers can often be removed with a droplet of water and prolonged light rubbing. The result should be no damage at all to the record's label. Non-soluble stickers, however, are another story, just as are felt-penned names across labels that can drive the collector-owner of a near-virgin disc wild with rage. These scrawled statements of ownership, as with the permanent stickers, lessen the value of a collectible disc.

Records are best stored in a room of moderate temperature. Heat is a record's worst enemy, as you undoubtedly found out the first time you left records on a parked seat during the summertime.

Doubles or records that look good but play poorly can be put to good use as wall hangings. If guns, paintings or animal heads can serve as decorations, why not records of certain artists in which you are interested or labels you may find to your liking?

CONDITION

By actual definition, a record is Mint ***only*** if it has never been played. Unless you are dealing in store-stock merchandise, this definition has been stretched (out of necessity) by nearly every collector.

This book deals with prices for two grades:

MINT-unplayed or played a minimum of times so as to produce no scratches, label blemishes or audible surface noise.

VG (Very Good)-a well-cared-for record, usually stored in a sleeve or jacket since first bought, with ***some*** scratches and surface noise but not enough to detract aurally or visually. More specific grading uses the symbols + and −. (For example, a M− record is slightly better than a VG+ one.)

Grading with any record less than unplayed (mint) is subjective. Practice in grading discs doesn't make perfect but experience ***is*** the best teacher. Be particular in buying and honest in selling. An unhappy customer warrants an immediate refund. If you're the seller, it is better to undergrade than to label a record's condition better than it really it.

HOW TO USE THIS BOOK

As a record collector, you will undoubtedly never complete your collection—nor would you especially want to! (What's to strive for if that happens!) Even if your tastes runs to specific areas of interest—rockabilly, surf instrumentals, early r & b—or even particular artists (Elvis, Buddy Holly, the Beatles), there is always something else to get—a reissue single, another obscure picture sleeve, an actual autograph by the artist, an acetate pressing.

Those items of interest are not included in this book.

Here you will find the rudiments—commercially released singles, EPs and albums that have proven to have universal interest among collectors of rock-and-roll records. There is a smattering of early rhythm-and-blues, some rockabilly, a few soul discs. And there is a complete Sun singles discography, complete with prices and chart ratings. But chiefly this book is about rock; that is, rock-and-roll before it became the formula-perfect, semi-computerized, multi-tracked and somewhat sterile mass product it is today.

Collectors have been buying, selling and trading collectible discs of this particular art form long enough to have established a somewhat specific value for each and every disc.

In the end, of course, the price of any collectible rock item is subjective. If you are a Beach Boys collector and someone offers you a mint copy of "Surfin" on X for a firm $100 and you pay it, does this mean that you have set a precedent and that all such items will now go for $100?

No. It only means that you paid nearly twice what you should have for that record. There is no doubt that someday an X version of "Surfin' " *will* be worth $100—but it isn't now.

The value of a record is determined by how badly you want it and how much you are will to pay for it—"whatever the traffic will bear".

This book will hopefully clear the air about some highly overpriced records. Some, of course, are legitimately high . . . they are in demand and quantity is scarce.

LISTINGS

Artists in this book are listed in alphabetical order. Each release or series of releases is preceded by the name of the label on which the artist recorded. Records are listed chronologically.

ISSUE NUMBERS

In addition to song titles and the names of record labels, each disc featured in this guide is also shown with an issue number. This series of digits — anywhere from two to six numbers — identifies the sequence of record releases from each particular outfit.

Issue numbers can be used to establish dates when certain records were issued. For example, if a collector has a copy of the Four Seasons' "Walk Like a Man" (Vee Jay 485), he would possibly know that Vee Jay 485 was an early 1963 release. Therefore, he could establish that the Beatles' first American Vee Jay release of "Please Please Me" (Vee Jay 498) came shortly afterwards, during the first half of 1963 and nearly a year before they achieved mass popularity early in 1964.

Each record listed in this book is a 45 rpm single unless marked as an EP (extended-play single) or album. Prices for EPs and albums are ***with covers in good condition.*** A number in parentheses indicates the highest position that a particular single reached on ***Billboard's*** Hot 100 chart for pop (i.e., rock) singles. No parentheses on a line listing a single's title means that the disc never sold enough copies to break that mystical barrier and is probably (but not always) more rare than a single that was a chart winner.

ISSUE #	LABEL	ARTIST/TITLE	VG	MINT
		ACADEMICS		
□100	ANCHO	AT MY FRONT DOOR/DARLA MY DARLIN'	5.00	8.00
□101		HEAVENLY LOVE/TOO GOOD TO BE TRUE	6.00	10.00
		JOHNNY ACE		
□107	DUKE	CROSS MY HEART/ANGEL	3.00	5.00
□112		THE CLOCK/ACE'S WILD	3.00	5.00
□136		PLEDGING MY LOVE/NO MONEY(17)	2.50	5.00
		LINK ADAMS		
□111	A-OKAY	ANGEL OR NOT/LONELY TEEN	3.50	6.00
		NICKY ADDEO		
□200	SAVOY	GLORIA/BRING BACK YOUR HEART	7.00	12.00
□200		GLORIA/BRING BACK YOUR HEART (colored wax)	12.00	20.00
□104	SELSOM	OVER THE RAINBOW/FOOL #2	12.00	20.00
		ADMIRATIONS		
□71521	MERCURY	THE BELLS OF ROSA RITA/LITTLE BO-PEEP	5.00	8.00
□71883		TO THE AISLE/HEY SENORITA	12.00	20.00
		JEWEL AKENS		
		SEE: FOUR DOTS, JEWEL AND EDDIE		
□6716	MINASA	DANCING JENNY/WEE BIT MORE OF YOUR LOVIN'	1.75	3.00
□5007	CAPEHART	THE DANCING MASHED POTATOES/ WEE BIT MORE OF YOUR LOVIN'	1.75	3.00
□2005	RTV	OVER AND OVER/MUSIC BOX	1.75	3.00
		STEVE ALAIMO AND THE REDCOATS		
□6064	MARLIN	I WANT YOU TO LOVE ME/BLUE SKIES	5.00	8.00
□6067		SHE'S MY BABY/SHOULD I CALL	4.00	7.00
□6445	DICKSON	BLUE FIRE/MY HEART NEVER SAID GOODBYE	4.00	7.00
		ARTHUR ALEXANDER		
□16309	DOT	YOU BETTER MOVE ON/ A SHOT OF RHYTHM AND BLUES (24)	1.25	2.50
□16357		WHERE HAVE YOU BEEN (ALL MY LIFE)/ SOLDIER OF LOVE (58)	1.50	3.00
□16387		ANNA/I HANG MY HEAD AND CRY (68)	1.75	3.00
□16425		YOU'RE THE REASON/GO HOME GIRL	1.25	2.00
□10454		DREAM GIRL/I WONDER WHERE YOU ARE TONIGHT	1.25	2.00
□16509		PRETTY GIRLS EVERYWHERE/BABY BABY	1.25	2.00
□16554		KEEP HER GUESSIN'/WHERE DID SALLY GO?	1.25	2.00
□16616		BLACK KNIGHT/OLE JOHN AMOS	1.25	2.00
□16737		DETROIT CITY/YOU DON'T CARE	1.25	2.00
		ARTHUR ALEXANDER—ALBUM		
□3434 (M)	DOT	YOU BETTER MOVE ON	5.00	8.00
□25434 (S)		YOU BETTER MOVE ON	6.00	10.00
		DAVIE ALLEN AND THE ARROWS		
□101	CUDE	WAR PATH/BEYOND THE BLUE (Davie Allen)	6.00	10.00
□3223	MARC	WAR PATH/BEYOND THE BLUE (Davie Allen)	3.00	5.00
□1	SIDEWALK	APACHE '65/BLUE GUITAR	3.00	5.00
□116	TOWER	APACHE '65/BLUE GUITAR (64)	1.50	2.50
□133		MOON DAWG '65/DANCE THE FREDDIE	1.75	3.00

ISSUE #	LABEL	ARTIST/TITLE	VG	MINT
□142		BABY RUTH/I'M LOOKING OVER A FOUR LEAF CLOVER	1.25	2.00
□150		SPACE HOP/GRANNY GOOSE	1.25	2.00
□267		THEME FROM THE WILD ANGELS/U. F. O. (99)	1.25	2.00
□295		BLUE'S THEME/BONGO PARTY (37)	1.00	2.00
□341		DEVIL'S ANGELS/CODY'S THEME (97)	1.25	2.00
□381		BLUE RIDES AGAIN/CYCLE-DELIC	1.25	2.00
		DAVIE ALLEN AND THE ARROWS—ALBUMS		
□5002 (M)	*TOWER*	APACHE '65	3.50	6.00
□5002 (S)		APACHE '65	4.50	8.00
□5078 (M)		BLUE'S THEME	3.00	5.00
□5078 (S)		BLUE'S THEME	4.00	7.00
□5094 (M)		THE CYCLE-DELIC SOUNDS OF DAVIE ALLEN AND THE ARROWS	3.00	5.00
□5094 (S)		THE CYCLE-DELIC SOUNDS OF DAVIE ALLEN AND THE ARROWS	4.00	7.00
		LEE ALLEN AND HIS BAND		
□1027	*EMBER*	WALKIN' WITH MR. LEE/PROMENADE (54)	1.50	3.00
□1031		STROLLIN' WITH MR. LEE/BOPPIN' AT THE HOP	1.75	3.00
□1039		TIC TOC/CHUGGIN' (92)	1.75	3.00
□1047		JIM JAM/SHORT CIRCUIT	1.75	3.00
□1057		CAT WALK/CREOLE ALLEY	1.75	3.00
		LEE ALLEN AND HIS BAND—EP		
□103	*EMBER*	WALKIN' WITH MR. LEE	5.00	8.00
		LEE ALLEN AND HIS BAND—ALBUM		
□200 (M)		WALKIN' WITH MR. LEE	18.00	30.00
		RICHIE ALLEN		
□5683	*IMPERIAL*	STRANGER FROM DURANGO/REDSKIN (90)	1.50	2.50
□5720		HAUNTED GUITAR/IN A PERSIAN WORLD	1.50	2.50
□5846		COMIN' BACK TO YOU/MR. HOBBS THEME	1.25	2.00
□5917		BUTTERSCOTCH/SUNDAY PICNIC	1.25	2.00
□5984		BALLAD OF THE SURF/THE QUIET SIDE	1.50	2.50
		RICHIE ALLEN—ALBUMS		
□9229 (M)	*IMPERIAL*	THE RISING SURF	7.00	12.00
□9243 (M)		SURFER'S SLIDE	7.00	12.00
		ARVIE ALLENS (RITCHIE VALENS)		
□4111	*DEL-FI*	FAST FREIGHT/BIG BABY BLUES	3.00	5.00
		ALLEY CATS		
□108	*PHILLES*	PUDDIN' 'N TAIN/FEEL SO GOOD (43)	2.50	4.00
		HERBIE ALPERT		
□700	*CAROL*	SWEET GEORGIA BROWN/VIPER'S BLUES	2.50	4.00
		HERBIE ALPERT SEXTET		
□34036	*ALTAIRS*	SUMMER SCHOOL/HULLY GULLY	2.50	4.00
□803	*AMY*	IF YOU LOVE ME/GROOVY TIME	3.50	6.00
		AMERICA		
□5001	*AMERICAN INTERNATIONAL*	DON'T FORGET ABOUT ME/DON'T MAKE ME OVER	2.50	4.00
		AMERICAN SPRING (HONEYS)		
		PRODUCER: BRIAN WILSON		
□45834	*COLUMBIA*	SHYIN' AWAY/FALLIN' IN LOVE	7.00	12.00

ISSUE #	LABEL	ARTIST/TITLE	VG	MINT
		LEE ANDREWS AND THE HEARTS		
☐102	MAINLINE	LONG LONELY NIGHTS/THE CLOCK	20.00	30.00
☐1665	CHESS	LONG LONELY NIGHTS/THE CLOCK (45)	2.00	3.50
☐1675		TEAR DROPS/THE GIRL AROUND THE CORNER (20)	1.75	3.00
☐1000	ARGO	TEAR DROPS/THE GIRL AROUND THE CORNER	3.50	6.00
		ANGELS		
☐107	CAPRICE	'TIL/A MOMENT AGO (14)	1.25	2.50
☐112		CRY BABY CRY/THAT'S ALL I ASK OF YOU (38)	1.25	2.50
☐116		EVERBODY LOVES A LOVER/BLOW, JOE	1.25	2.00
☐118		I'D BE GOOD FOR YOU/YOU SHOULD HAVE TOLD ME	1.25	2.00
☐121		A MOMENT AGO/COTTON FIELDS	1.25	2.00
☐1834	SMASH	MY BOYFRIEND'S BACK/(LOVE ME) NOW (1)	.75	2.00
☐1854		I ADORE HIM/THANK YOU AND GOODNIGHT (25)	1.00	2.00
☐1870		WOW WOW WEE/SNOWFLAKES AND TEARDROPS (41)	1.25	2.00
☐1885		LITTLE BEATLE BOY/JAVA	1.50	2.50
☐1915		DREAM BOY/JAMAICA JOE	1.25	2.00
☐1931		THE BOY FROM 'CROSS TOWN/ A WORLD WITHOUT LOVE	1.25	2.00
		ANGELS—ALBUMS		
☐1001 (M)	CAPRICE	AND THE ANGELS SING	6.00	10.00
☐1001 (S)		AND THE ANGELS SING	7.00	12.00
☐27039 (M)	SMASH	MY BOYFRIEND'S BACK	5.00	8.00
☐67039 (S)		MY BOYFRIEND'S BACK	6.00	10.00
☐27048 (M)		A HALO TO YOU	5.00	8.00
☐67048 (S)		A HALO TO YOU	6.00	10.00
		ANIMALS		
☐13242	MGM	GONNA SEND YOU BACK TO WALKER/ BABY LET ME TAKE YOU HOME (57)	1.50	2.50
☐13264		HOUSE OF THE RISING SUN/ TALKING 'BOUT YOU (1)	1.00	2.00
☐13274		I'M CRYING/TAKE IT EASY BABY (19)	1.00	2.00
☐13298		BOOM BOOM/BLUE FEELING (43)	1.00	2.00
☐13311		DON'T LET ME BE MISUNDERSTOOD/ CLUB A GO GO	.75	2.00
☐13339		BRING IT ON HOME/FOR MISS CAULKER (32)	1.00	2.00
☐13382		WE GOTTA GET OUT OF THIS PLACE/ I CAN'T BELIEVE IT (13)	.75	2.00
☐13414		IT'S MY LIFE/I'M GOIN TO CHANGE THE WORLD (23)	1.00	2.00
☐13468		INSIDE-LOOKING OUT/YOU'RE ON MY MIND (34)	1.00	2.00
☐13514		DON'T BRING ME DOWN/CHEATING (12)	.75	2.00
☐13582		SEE SEE RIDER/SHE'LL RETURN IT (10)	.75	2.00
☐13636		HELP ME GIRL/THAT AIN'T WHERE IT'S AT (29)	1.00	2.00
☐13721		WHEN I WAS YOUNG/A GIRL NAMED SANDOZ (15)	.75	2.00
☐13769		SAN FRANCISCAN NIGHTS/GOOD TIMES (9)	.75	2.00
☐13868		MONTEREY/AIN'T THAT SO (15)	.75	2.00
☐13917		ANYTHING/IT'S ALL MEAT (80)	1.00	2.00
☐13939		SKY PILOT (PT. 1)/(PT. 11) (14)	.75	2.00
☐14013		WHITE HOUSES/RIVER DEEP-MOUNTAIN HIGH (67)	1.00	2.00
		ANIMALS—ALBUMS		
☐4264 (M)	MGM	THE ANIMALS	3.50	6.00
☐4264 (S)		THE ANIMALS	4.50	8.00

ISSUE #	LABEL	ARTIST/TITLE	VG	MINT
□ 4281 (M)		THE ANIMALS ON TOUR	3.00	5.00
□ 4281 (S)		THE ANIMALS ON TOUR	4.00	7.00
□ 4305 (M)		ANIMAL TRACKS	3.00	5.00
□ 4305 (S)		ANIMAL TRACKS	4.00	7.00
□ 4324 (M)		THE BEST OF THE ANIMALS	3.00	5.00
□ 4324 (S)		THE BEST OF THE ANIMALS	4.00	7.00

PAUL ANKA

Born in Canada on July 30, 1941, Paul Anka cut his first single during a vacation trip to southern Califronia. A year later he flew to New York City, where he met ABC-Paramount arranger Don Costa. Paul played Costa a tape of "Diana", a song Anka had written based on a previous infatuation with an older baby-sitter he once had. A smash hit before Anka turned sixteen, "Diana" went on to sell 8,000,000 singles and become the world's third-largest-selling rock record.

Numerous Top 10 hits followed, including "Lonely Boy", supposedly written about Annette Funicello. In 1962 Anka signed with RCA Records but his career declined shortly afterwards. No problem, though. Anka had become a millionaire at twenty through the shrewd buying of apartment houses. His career was briefly revitalized during the mid-1970s by such songs as "You're Having My Baby".

PAUL ANKA

ISSUE #	LABEL	ARTIST/TITLE	VG	MINT
☐ 472	***RPM***	I CONFESS/BLAU-WILE DEVEEST FONTAINE (with the Jacks)	15.00	25.00
☐ 9831	***ABC-PARAMOUNT***	DIANA/DON'T GAMBLE WITH LOVE (2)	2.00	4.00
☐ 9855		I LOVE YOU BABY/ TELL ME THAT YOU LOVE ME (97)	1.75	3.00
☐ 9880		YOU ARE MY DESTINY/ WHEN I STOP LOVING YOU (7)	1.50	3.00
☐ 9907		CRAZY LOVE/LET THE BELLS KEEP RINGING (19)	1.50	3.00
☐ 9937		MIDNIGHT/VERBOTEN (69)	1.75	3.00
☐ 9956		JUST YOUNG/SO IT'S GOODBYE (80)	1.75	3.00
☐ 9987		MY HEART SINGS/THAT'S LOVE (15)	1.50	3.00
☐ 10011		I MISS YOU SO/LATE LAST NIGHT (33)	1.75	3.00
☐ 10022		LONELY BOY/YOU WAY (1)	1.50	3.00
☐ 10040		PUT YOUR HEAD ON MY SHOULDER/ DON'T EVER LEAVE ME (2)	1.50	3.00
☐ 10064		IT'S TIME TO CRY/ SOMETHING HAS CHANGED ME (94)	1.75	3.00
☐ 10082		PUPPY LOVE/ADAM AND EVE (2)	1.50	3.00
☐ 10106		MY HOME TOWN/SOMETHING HAPPENED (8)	1.50	3.00
☐ 10132		HELLO YOUNG LOVERS/ I LOVE YOU IN THE SAME OLD WAY (23)	1.75	3.00
☐ 10147		SUMMER'S GONE/I'D HAVE TO SHARE (11)	1.50	3.00
☐ 10163		I SAW MOMMY KISSING SANTA CLAUS/ RUDOLPH THE RED-NOSED REINDEER	2.50	4.00
☐ 10168		THE STORY OF MY LOVE/ DON'T SAY YOU'RE SORRY (16)	1.50	3.00
☐ 10169		IT'S CHRISTMAS EVERYWHERE/ RUDOLPH THE RED-NOSED REINDEER	2.50	4.00
☐ 10194		TONIGHT MY LOVE TONIGHT/ I'M JUST YOUR FOOL ANYWAY (13)	1.50	3.00
☐ 10220		DANCE ON LITTLE GIRL/I TALK TO YOU (10)	1.50	3.00
☐ 10239		CINDERELLA/KISSIN' ON THE PHONE (35)	1.50	2.50
☐ 10279		LOVELAND/THE BELLS AT MY WEDDING	1.50	2.50
☐ 10282		THE FOOL'S HALL OF FAME/ FAR FROM THE LIGHTS OF TOWN	1.50	2.50
☐ 10311		I'D NEVER FIND ANOTHER YOU/UH HUH	1.50	2.50
☐ 10338		I'M COMING HOME/CRY (94)	1.50	2.50
☐ 7977	***RCA***	LOVE ME WARM AND TENDER/ I'D LIKE TO KNOW (12)	1.25	2.50
☐ 8030		A STEEL GUITAR AND A GLASS OF WINE/ I NEVER KNEW YOUR NAME (13)	1.25	2.50
☐ 8068		EVERY NIGHT/THERE YOU GO (46)	1.25	2.00
☐ 8097		ESO BESO/GIVE ME BACK MY HEART (19)	1.00	2.00
☐ 8115		LOVE/CRYING IN THE WIND (26)	1.25	2.00
☐ 8170		REMEMBER DIANA/AT NIGHT (39)	1.50	2.50
☐ 8195		HELLO JIM/YOU'VE GOT THE NERVE TO CALL THIS LOVE (97)	1.25	2.00
☐ 8237		WONDROUS ARE THE WAYS OF LOVE/ HURRY UP AND TELL ME	1.25	2.00
☐ 8272		DID YOU HAVE A HAPPY BIRTHDAY?/ FOR NO GOOD REASON AT ALL (89)	1.25	2.00

LATER RCA SINGLES ARE WORTH UP TO $1.50 MINT

ISSUE #	LABEL	ARTIST/TITLE	VG	MINT
		PAUL ANKA—ALBUMS		
☐ 240 (M)	ABC-PARAMOUNT	PAUL ANKA	12.00	20.00
☐ 296 (M)		MY HEART SINGS	8.00	15.00
☐ 323 (M)		PAUL ANKA SINGS HIS BIG 15	8.00	15.00
☐ 347 (M)		SWINGS FOR YOUNG LOVERS	7.00	12.00
☐ 347 (S)		SWINGS FOR YOUNG LOVERS	8.00	15.00
☐ 353 (M)		ANKA AT THE COPA	7.00	12.00
☐ 353 (S)		ANKA AT THE COPA	8.00	15.00
☐ 360 (M)		IT'S CHRISTMAS EVERYWHERE	8.00	15.00
☐ 360 (S)		IT'S CHRISTMAS EVERYWHERE	10.00	18.00
☐ 371 (M)		STRICTLY INSTRUMENTAL	7.00	12.00
☐ 371 (S)		STRICTLY INSTRUMENTAL	8.00	15.00
☐ 390 (M)		PAUL ANKA SINGS HIS BIG 15, VOL. 2	7.00	12.00
☐ 390 (S)		PAUL ANKA SINGS HIS BIG 15, VOL. 2	8.00	15.00
☐ 409 (M)		PAUL ANKA SINGS HIS BIG 15, VOL. 3	8.00	15.00
☐ 409 (S)		PAUL ANKA SINGS HIS BIG 15, VOL. 3	10.00	18.00
☐ 2502 (M)	RCA	YOUNG, ALIVE AND IN LOVE	6.00	10.00
☐ 2502 (S)		YOUNG, ALIVE AND IN LOVE	7.00	12.00
☐ 2575 (M)		LET'S SIT THIS ONE OUT	6.00	10.00
☐ 2575 (S)		LET'S SIT THIS ONE OUT	7.00	12.00
☐ 2614 (M)		OUR MAN AROUND THE WORLD	6.00	10.00
☐ 2614 (S)		OUR MAN AROUND THE WORLD	7.00	12.00
☐ 2691 (M)		21 GOLDEN HITS (redone)	3.50	6.00
☐ 2691 (S)		21 GOLDEN HITS (redone)	4.50	8.00

PAUL ANKA, JOHNNY NASH, GEORGE HAMILTON IV

| ☐ 9974 | ABC-PARAMOUNT | THE TEN COMMANDMENTS/ IF YOU LEARN TO PRAY (29) | 2.50 | 4.00 |

ANNETTE

Utica, New York, was the hometown of Annette Funicello. She was born there October 22, 1942, although shortly thereafter she and her family trekked to southern California. In October of 1955—just before entering her teen years—Annette auditioned for Walt Disney's Mouseketeers. Winning a spot on "The Mickey Mouse Club", Annette soon drew more fan mail than any other Mouseketeer.

In 1958 Disney gave Annette a chance to try her luck in the recording studio. Her third single for the Disneyland label was "Tall Paul", supposedly about Paul Anka (who is actually rather short). The song shot to the Top 10, thanks in part to Annette's appearances on Dick Clark's "American Bandstand" as well as "The Mickey Mouse Club". Annette later signed with Vista Records—also a part of the Disney empire—where she scored with a trio of Top 20 singles.

During the mid-1960s Annette starred in teen-oriented movies with the likes of Frankie Avalon and Fabian. Now married to Jack Gilardi, her former manager, Annette is a housewife with three children in southern California's San Fernando Valley.

ISSUE #	LABEL	ARTIST/TITLE	VG	MINT
		ANNETTE		
☐ 102	***DISNEYLAND***	HOW WILL I KNOW MY LOVE/ DON'T JUMP TO CONCLUSIONS	3.50	6.00
☐ 114		THAT CRAZY PLACE FROM OUTER SPACE/ GOLD DUBLOONS AND PIECES OF EIGHT	3.00	5.00
☐ 118		TALL PAUL/MA, HE'S MAKING EYES AT ME (7)	1.50	3.00
☐ 758		HOW WILL I KNOW MY LOVE/ ANNETTE (Jimmy Dodd)	2.50	4.00
☐ 336	***VISTA***	JO-JO THE DOG-FACED BOY/LOVE ME FOREVER (73)	1.75	3.00
☐ 339		LONELY GUITAR/WILD WILLIE (50)	1.75	3.00
☐ 344		MY HEART BECAME OF AGE/ESPECIALLY FOR YOU	1.75	3.00
☐ 349		FIRST NAME INITIAL/ MY HEART BECAME OF AGE (20)	1.25	2.50
☐ 354		O DIO MIO/IT TOOK DREAMS (10)	1.25	2.50
☐ 359		TRAIN OF LOVE/TELL ME WHO'S THE GIRL (36)	1.50	2.50
☐ 362		PINEAPPLE PRINCESS/LUAU CHA CHA CHA (11)	1.25	2.50
☐ 369		TALK TO ME BABY/I LOVE YOU BABY (92)	1.50	2.50
☐ 374		DREAM BOY/PLEASE, PLEASE SIGNORE (87)	1.50	2.50
☐ 388		DREAMIN' ABOUT YOU/THE STRUMMIN' SONG	1.25	2.00
☐ 392		THAT CRAZY PLACE FROM OUTER SPACE/ SEVEN MOONS	1.25	2.00
☐ 394		THE TRUTH ABOUT YOUTH/I CAN'T DO THE SUM	1.25	2.00
☐ 400		MY LITTLE GRASS SHACK/HUKILAU SONG	1.25	2.00
☐ 405		HE'S MY IDEAL/MR. PIANO MAN	1.25	2.00
☐ 407		BELLA BELLA FLORENCE/CANZONE D'AMORE	1.25	2.00
☐ 414		TEENAGE WEDDING/WALKING AND TALKING	1.25	2.00
☐ 427		TREAT HIM NICELY/PROMISE ME ANYTHING	1.25	2.00
☐ 431		MERLIN JONES/THE SCRAMBLED EGGHEAD	1.25	2.00
☐ 432		CUSTOM CITY/REBEL RIDER	1.50	2.50
☐ 433		MUSCLE BEACH PARTY/I DREAM ABOUT FRANKIE	1.50	2.50
☐ 436		BIKINI BEACH PARTY/THE CLYDE	1.50	2.50
☐ 437		THE WAH WATUSI/THE CLYDE	1.50	2.50
☐ 438		SOMETHING BORROWED, SOMETHING BLUE/ HOW WILL I KNOW MY LOVE	1.25	2.00
☐ 440		THE MONKEY'S UNCLE/HOW WILL I KNOW MY LOVE	2.50	4.00
		(VISTA 440 FEATURES BACKUP BY THE BEACH BOYS)		
☐ 442		BOY TO LOVE/NO ONE COULD BE PROUDER	1.25	2.00
☐ 450		NO WAY TO GO BUT UP/CRYSTAL BALL	1.25	2.00
☐ 802		LET'S GET TOGETHER/THE PARENT TRAP	1.50	2.50
☐ 9828	***EPIC***	BABY NEEDS ME NOW/MOMENT OF SILENCE	2.50	4.00
☐ 326	***TOWER***	WHAT'S A GIRL TO DO/ WHEN YOU GET WHAT YOU WANT	2.50	4.00
		ANNETTE—EPs		
☐ 04	***DISNEYLAND***	TALL PAUL	8.00	15.00
☐ 69		MICKEY MOUSE CLUB-ANNETTE	6.00	10.00
		ANNETTE—ALBUMS		
☐ 3301 (M)	***VISTA***	ANNETTE	12.00	20.00
☐ 3302 (M)		ANNETTE SINGS ANKA	8.00	15.00
☐ 3303 (M)		HAWAIIANETTE	8.00	15.00
☐ 3304 (M)		ITALIANETTE	8.00	15.00
☐ 3305 (M)		DANCE ANNETTE	7.00	12.00
☐ 3309 (M)		THE PARENT TRAP	7.00	12.00
☐ 3312 (M)		ANNETTE-THE STORY OF MY TEENS	7.00	12.00

ISSUE #	LABEL	ARTIST/TITLE	VG	MINT
□3314 (M)		MUSCLE BEACH PARTY	8.00	15.00
□3316 (M)		ANNETTE'S BEACH PARTY	8.00	15.00
□3320 (M)		ANNETTE ON CAMPUS	6.00	10.00
□3324 (M)		ANNETTE AT BIKINI BEACH	7.00	12.00
□3325 (M)		ANNETTE'S PAJAMA PARTY	6.00	10.00
		AQUANAUTS		
□1005	*SAFARI*	BOMBARA/RUMBLE ON THE DOCKS	3.00	5.00
		AQUA-NITES		
□1000	*ASTRA*	LOVER DON'T YOU WEEP/CARIOCA	12.00	20.00
□2001		LOVER DON'T YOU WEEP/CHRISTI	8.00	15.00
		AQUATONES		
□1001	*FARGO*	YOU/SHE'S THE ONE FOR ME (21)	2.50	4.00
□1002		SAY YOU'LL BE MINE/SO FINE	3.00	5.00
□1003		OUR FIRST KISS/THE DRIVE-IN	3.00	5.00
□1005		MY ONE DESIRE/MY TREASURE	3.00	5.00
□1015		EVERY TIME/THERE'S A LONG LONG TRAIL	3.00	5.00
□1016		CRAZY FOR YOU/WANTED	3.00	5.00
□1111		MY DARLING/FOR YOU, FOR YOU	3.00	5.00
		AQUATONES—ALBUM		
□3001 (M)	*FARGO*	THE AQUATONES SING	20.00	35.00
		ARCADES		
□116	*JOHNSON*	FINE LITTLE GIRL/MY LOVE	2.50	4.00
□2015	*GUYDEN*	BLACKMAIL/JUNE WAS THE END OF AUGUST	2.50	4.00
		VANCE ARNOLD (JOE COCKER)		
□40255	*PHILLIPS*	I'LL CRY INSTEAD/THOSE PRECIOUS WORDS	3.00	5.00
		ARROGANTS		
□6226	*LUTE*	MIRROR MIRROR/CANADIAN SUNSET	3.50	6.00
□200	*VANESS*	TAKE LIFE EASY/STONE BROKE	2.50	4.00
□12184	*BIG A*	MAKE UP YOUR MIND/TOMBOY	2.50	4.00
		DEL ASHLEY (DAVID GATES)		
□103	*PLANETARY*	LITTLE MISS STUCK-UP/THE BRIGHTER SIDE	3.00	5.00
		ASSOCIATION		
□5505	*JUBILEE*	BABE, I'M GONNA LEAVE YOU/ CAN'T YOU HEAR ME CALL YOUR NAME	2.50	4.00
□730	*VALIANT*	ONE TOO MANY MORNINGS/FORTY TIMES	1.50	2.50
		ASTRONAUTS		
□459	*JAN ELL*	GENEVA TWIST/TAKE 17	2.50	4.00
□100	*LUNEY*	RIDGE ROUTE/BLAST OFF	2.50	4.00
□1000	*VANRUS*	SKI LIFT/BLUES BEAT	2.50	4.00
□8194	*RCA*	BAJA/ KUK (94)	1.50	2.50
□8224		HOT DOGGIN'/EVERYONE BUT ME	1.25	2.00
□8298		SURF PARTY/COMPETITION COUPE	1.25	2.00
□8364		SWIM LITTLE MERMAID/GO FIGHT FOR HER	1.00	2.00
□8419		RIDE THE WILD SURF/AROUND AND AROUND	1.25	2.00
		LATER RCA SINGLES ARE WORTH UP TO $1.50 MINT		
		ASTRONAUTS—ALBUMS		
□2760 (M)	*RCA*	SURFIN' WITH THE ASTRONAUTS	4.00	7.00
□2760 (S)		SURFIN' WITH THE ASTRONAUTS	5.00	9.00
□2782 (M)		EVERYTHING IS A-OK	3.50	6.00

ISSUE #	LABEL	ARTIST/TITLE	VG	MINT
□ 2782 (S)		EVERYTHING IS A-OK	4.50	8.00
□ 2858 (M)		COMPETITION COUPE	3.50	6.00
□ 2858 (S)		COMPETITION COUPE	4.50	8.00
		AUDREY		
□ 104	*PLUS*	DEAR ELVIS (PAGE 1) (PAGE 2) (87)	10.00	18.00

FRANKIE AVALON

Frankie Avalon (real name Avalonne) first saw life in Philadelphia on September 18, 1940. Originally he wished to someday become a reknowned boxer. Then he saw a movie entitled "Young Man With a Horn". That did it. Avalon switched his future ambition to that of trumpeteer. His father purchased a trumpet, and Avalon cut a pair of 1952 singles on which he played his trumpet. He was eleven years old at the time.

As a teenager Avalon signed with Chancellor Records. His first two singles bombed, but his third attempt was a smash hit—and somewhat of a fluke. Frankie held his nose and sang while horsing around, waiting for the final rehearsal of "DeDe Dinah". The producer correctly sensed that the gimmick might provide Chancellor with a novelty hit.

After No. 1 singles like "Venus" and "Why" Frankie's career faded; however, he later resurfaced in several beach-party movies during the 1960s. Today he, his wife (a former dental assistant) and their eight children live in Hollywood. A disco version of "Venus" pumped some temporary life into Avalon's career in 1976.

ISSUE #	LABEL	ARTIST/TITLE	VG	MINT
		FRANKIE AVALON		
☐0006	X	TRUMPET SORRENTO/THE BOOK	6.00	10.00
☐0026		TRUMPET TARANTELLA/DORMI, DORMI	6.00	10.00
		(X LABELS READ "BY 11 YEAR OLD FRANK AVALON")		
☐1004	CHANCELLOR	CUPID/JIVIN' WITH THE SAINTS	4.00	7.00
☐1006		TEACHER'S PET/SHY GUY	3.50	6.00
☐1011		DEDE DINAH/OOH LA LA (7)	1.50	3.00
☐1016		YOU EXCITE ME/DARLIN' (49)	1.75	3.00
☐1021		GINGERBREAD/BLUE BETTY (9)	1.50	3.00
☐1026		I'LL WAIT FOR YOU/WHAT LITTLE GIRL (8)	1.50	3.00
☑1031	5	VENUS/I'M BROKE (1)	1.25	2.50
☐1036		BOBBY SOX TO STOCKINGS/ A BOY WITHOUT A GIRL (8)	1.25	2.50
☐1040		JUST ASK YOU HEART/TWO FOOLS (7)	1.25	2.50
☐1045		WHY/SWINGIN' ON A RAINBOW (1)	1.25	2.50
☐1048		DON'T THROW AWAY ALL THOSE TEARDROPS/ TALK TALK TALK (22)	1.25	2.00
☐1052		WHERE ARE YOU/TUXEDO JUNCTION (32)	1.25	2.00
☐1056		TOGETHERNESS/DON'T LET LOVE PASS ME BY (26)	1.25	2.00
☐1065		A PERFECT LOVE/THE PUPPET SONG (47)	1.25	2.00
☐1071		ALL OF EVERYTHING/CALL ME ANYTIME (70)	1.25	2.00
☐1077		GOTTA GET A GIRL/WHO ELSE BUT YOU (82)	1.25	2.00
☐1081		THE SUMMER OF '61/ VOYAGE TO THE BOTTOM OF THE SEA	1.50	2.50
☐1087		TRUE TRUE LOVE/MARRIED (90)	1.25	2.00
☐1095		SLEEPING BEAUTY/THE LONELY BIT	1.00	1.50
☐1101		AFTER YOU'VE GONE/ IF YOU DON'T THINK I'M LEAVING	1.00	1.50
☐1107		YOU ARE MINE/PONCHINELLA	1.00	1.50
☐1114		VENUS/I'M BROKE (reissue)	.75	1.25
☐1115		A MIRACLE/DON'T LET ME STAND IN YOUR WAY	1.00	1.50
☐1125		WELCOME HOME/DANCE BOSSA NOVA	1.00	1.50
☐1131		MY EX-BEST FRIEND/FIRST LOVE NEVER DIES	1.00	1.50
☐1134		COME FLY WITH ME/GIRL BACK HOME	1.00	1.50
☐1135		CLEOPATRA/HEARTBEATS	1.00	1.50
☐1139		BEACH PARTY/DON'T STOP NOW	1.00	1.50
		FRANKIE AVALON—EPs		
☐A-5001	CHANCELLOR	FRANKIE AVALON, VOL. 1	3.00	5.00
☐B-5001		FRANKIE AVALON, VOL. 2	3.00	5.00
☐C-5001		FRANKIE AVALON, VOL. 3	3.00	5.00
☐A-5002		THE YOUNG FRANKIE AVALON	3.00	5.00

ISSUE #	LABEL	ARTIST/TITLE	VG	MINT
☐ B-5002		THE YOUNG FRANKIE AVALON	3.00	5.00
☐ C-5002		THE YOUNG FRANKIE AVALON	3.00	5.00
☐ A-5004		SWINGIN' ON A RAINBOW	2.50	4.00
☐ B-5004		SWINGIN' ON A RAINBOW	2.50	4.00
☐ C-5004		SWINGIN' ON A RAINBOW	2.50	4.00
		FRANKIE AVALON—ALBUMS		
☐ 5001 (M)	*CHANCELLOR*	FRANKIE AVALON	8.00	15.00
☐ 5002 (M)		THE YOUNG FRANKIE AVALON	7.00	12.00
☐ 5004 (M)		SWINGIN' ON A RAINBOW	7.00	12.00
☐ 5009 (M)		AVALON AND FABIAN	8.00	15.00
☐ 5011 (M)		SUMMER SCENE	7.00	12.00
☐ 5018 (M)		A WHOLE LOTTA FRANKIE (greatest hits)	6.00	10.00

B

ISSUE #	LABEL	ARTIST/TITLE	VG	MINT
		BABY RAY AND THE FERNS (FRANK ZAPPA)		
☐ 1378	*DONNA*	THE WORLD'S GREATEST SINNER/ HOW'S YOUR BIRD	6.00	10.00
		KENNY BAKER		
☐ 541	*ORBIT*	GOODBYE LITTLE STAR/I'M GONNA LOVE YOU	5.00	8.00
		LAVERN BAKER		
☐ 1047	*ATLANTIC*	TWEEDLE DEE/TOMORROW NIGHT (22)	2.00	4.00
☐ 1057		BOP TING-A-LING/THAT'S ALL I NEED	2.50	4.00
☐ 1104		I CAN'T LOVE YOU ENOUGH/STILL (48)	1.50	3.00
☐ 1116		JIM DANDY/TRA LA LA (22)	1.50	3.00
☐ 1136		JIM DANDY GOT MARRIED/GAME OF LOVE (76)	1.25	2.50
☐ 2007		I CRIED A TEAR/DIX-A-BILLY (6)	1.00	2.00
☐ 2021		I WAITED TOO LONG/YOU'RE TEASIN' ME (33)	1.00	2.00
☐ 2033		SO HIGH, SO LOW/IF YOU LOVE ME (52)	1.00	2.00
☐ 2099		SAVED/DON JUAN (37)	1.00	2.00
☐ 2167		SEE SEE RIDER/STORY OF MY LOVE (34)	1.00	2.00
		MARTY BALIN		
		SEE: JEFFERSON AIRPLANE		
☐ 9146	*CHALLENGE*	NOBODY BUT YOU/YOU MADE ME FALL	6.00	10.00
☐ 9156		I SPECIALIZE IN LOVE/YOU'RE ALIVE WITH LOVE	6.00	10.00
		BALLADS		
☐ 5028	*FRANWIL*	BEFORE YOU FALL IN LOVE/BROKE	6.00	10.00
		HANK BALLARD AND THE MIDNIGHTERS		
☐ 5171	*KING*	THE TWIST/TEARDROPS ON YOUR LETTER (28)	1.50	3.00
		(ORIGINAL VERSION)		
☐ 5195		KANSAS CITY/I'LL KEEP YOU HAPPY (72)	1.50	2.50
☐ 5341		FINGER POPPIN' TIME/ I LOVE YOU, I LOVE YOU SOOO (7)	1.00	2.00
☐ 5400		LET'S GO, LET'S GO, LET'S GO/ IF YOU'D FORGIVE ME (6)	1.00	2.00

ISSUE #	LABEL	ARTIST/TITLE	VG	MINT
☐ 5430		THE HOOCHI COOCHI COO/		
		I'M THINKING OF YOU (23)	1.00	2.00
☐ 5459		LET'S GO AGAIN/DEEP BLUE SEA (39)	1.25	2.00
☐ 5491		THE CONTINENTAL WALK/WHAT IS THIS I SEE? (33)..	1.00	2.00
☐ 5510		THE SWITCH-A-ROO/THE FLOAT (26)	1.00	2.00
☐ 5535		KEEP ON DANCING/NOTHING BUT GOOD (49)	1.00	2.00

HANK BALLARD AND THE MIDNIGHTERS—EPs

☐ 435	*KING*	SINGIN' AND SWINGIN', VOL. 1	3.00	6.00
☐ 451		SINGIN' AND SWINGIN', VOL. 2	3.00	6.00

HANK BALLARD AND THE MIDNIGHTERS—ALBUMS

☐ 541 (M)	*KING*	THEIR GREATEST JUKE BOX HITS	8.00	15.00
☐ 581 (M)		HANK BALLARD AND THE MIDNIGHTERS	7.00	12.00

BARBARIANS

☐ 290	*JOY*	HEY LITTLE BIRD/YOU'VE GOT TO UNDERSTAND ...	3.00	5.00
☐ 3308	*LAURIE*	ARE YOU A BOY OR ARE YOU A GIRL/		
		TAKE IT OR LEAVE IT (55)	1.25	2.50
☐ 3321		SUSIE Q/WHAT THE NEW BREED SAY	1.00	2.00
☐ 3326		MOULTY/I'LL KEEP ON SEEING YOU (90)	1.00	2.00

BARBAROSO AND THE HISTORIANS

☐ 110	*JADE*	ZOOM/WHEN I FALL IN LOVE	5.00	8.00

ANNETTE BARD
SEE: TEDDY BEARS

☐ 5643	*IMPERIAL*	WHAT DIFFERENCE DOES IT MAKE?/ALIBI	3.50	6.00

STEVE BARRI
SEE: FANTASTIC BAGGIES

☐ 1003	*RONA*	DOWN AROUND THE CORNER/PLEASE LET IT BE YOU ..	2.50	4.00
☐ 1004		THE STORY OF THE RING/I WANT YOUR LOVE	2.50	4.00
☐ 1005		TWO DIFFERENT WORLDS/		
		DON'T RUN AWAY FROM LOVE	2.50	4.00
☐ 1006		WHENEVER YOU KISS ME/NEVER BEFORE	2.50	4.00

BARRIES

☐ 102	*VERNON*	WHY DON'T YOU WRITE ME/MARY-ANN	6.00	10.00
☐ 1101	*EMBER*	TONIGHT TONIGHT/MARY-ANN	5.00	8.00

BARRY AND THE TAMERLANES

☐ 6004	*VALIANT*	I WONDER WHAT SHE'S DOING TONIGHT/		
		DON'T GO (21)	1.25	2.50
☐ 6040		ROBERTA/BUTTERFLY	1.50	2.50
☐ 6046		LUCKY GUY/I DON'T WANT TO BE YOUR CLOWN ...	1.50	2.50
☐ 6050		A DATE WITH JUDY/PRETTY THINGS	1.50	2.50
☐ 6059		DON'T CRY CINDY/GEE	1.50	2.50

BARRY AND THE TAMERLANES—ALBUM

☐ 406 (M)	*VALLIANT*	I WONDER WHAT SHE'S DOING TONIGHT	6.00	10.00

JEFF BARRY

☐ 7477	*RCA*	IT'S CALLED ROCK AND ROLL/HIP COUPLES	8.00	15.00
☐ 7797		LONELY LIPS/FACE FROM OUTER SPACE	8.00	15.00
☐ 7821		ALL YOU NEED IS A QUARTER/TEEN QUARTET	8.00	15.00
☐ 31037	*DECCA*	IT WON'T HURT/NEVER NEVER	5.00	8.00
☐ 31089		WHY DOES THE FEELING GO AWAY/LENORE	5.00	8.00

ISSUE #	LABEL	ARTIST/TITLE	VG	MINT
		JOE BARRY		
☐ 144	*JIN*	I'M A FOOL TO CARE/I GOT A FEELING	3.50	6.00
☐ 1702	*SMASH*	I'M A FOOL TO CARE/I GOT A FEELING (24)	1.00	2.00
		LEN BARRY		
☐ 303	*CAMEO*	JIM DANDY/DON'T COME BACK	1.50	3.00
☐ 318		HEARTS ARE TRUMP/LITTLE WHITE HOUSE	1.50	3.00
☐ 969	*PARKWAY*	HEARTS ARE TRUMP/LITTLE WHITE HOUSE	1.25	2.50
☐ 72299	*MERCURY*	LET'S DO IT AGAIN/HAPPY DAYS	1.25	2.50
☐ 31788	*DECCA*	LIP SYNC (TO THE TONGUE TWISTERS)/ AT THE HOP '65 (84)	1.50	2.50
☐ 31827		1-2-3/BULLSEYE (2)	.75	2.00
		LEN BARRY—ALBUMS		
☐ 1082 (M)	*CAMEO*	LEN BARRY SINGS WITH THE DOVELLS	5.00	8.00
☐ 4720 (M)	*DECCA*	1-2-3	3.00	5.00
☐ 74720 (S)		1-2-3	4.00	7.00
		BAY CITY ROLLERS		
☐ 45169	*BELL*	KEEP ON DANCING/ALL RIGHT	1.75	3.00
		BAYMEN		
☐ 6000	*MERRI*	BONZAI/DAYBREAK	5.00	8.00
		BAYSIDERS		
☐ 19366	*EVEREST*	OVER THE RAINBOW/MY BONNIE	1.75	3.00
☐ 19386		LOOK FOR THE SILVER LINING/TREES	1.75	3.00
☐ 19393		THE BELLS OF ST. MARY'S/ COMIN' THROUGH THE RYE	1.75	3.00
		BAYSIDERS—ALBUM		
☐ 5124 (M)	*EVEREST*	OVER THE RAINBOW	10.00	18.00
		B. BUMBLE AND THE STINGERS		
☐ 140	*RENDEZVOUS*	BUMBLE BOOGIE/SCHOOL DAY (21)	1.25	2.50
☐ 151		BOOGIE WOOGIE/NEAR YOU (89)	1.50	2.50
☐ 160		BEE HIVE/CARAVAN	1.50	2.50
☐ 166		NUT ROCKER/NAUTILUS (23)	.75	2.00
☐ 174		ROCKIN' ON-'N'-OFF/MASHED #5	1.00	2.00
☐ 179		APPLE KNOCKER/THE MOON AND THE SEA	1.00	2.00
☐ 182		DAWN CRACKER/SCALES	1.00	2.00
☐ 192		BABY MASH/NIGHT TIME MADNESS	1.00	2.00

BEACH BOYS

They began as Kenny and the Cadets, a garage band from the Los Angeles suburb of Hawthorne. A name change came later when Dennis Wilson (the only Wilson who surfed) convinced brother Brian that surfing was bound to be the next southern California fad. That did it; they became the Beach Boys. "Surfin' " gained only minimal nationwide attention and sales.

The Beach Boys signed with Capitol and their first effort set the pace for the Beach Boys' first few hit singles, a systematic formula of teen songs about surfing and hot cars.

The Beach Boys were one of the few American groups to withstand the 1964 British invasion, although Brian Wilson had at one time dismissed the Beatles as a "one-shot novelty group".

Though considered ancient for a rock band, the Beach Boys are still together, still touring and still recording. Brian "retired" during the late 1960s due to hearing and drug problems but today occasionally appears onstage during concerts.

ISSUE #	LABEL	ARTIST/TITLE	VG	MINT
		BEACH BOYS		
□301	***X***	SURFIN'/LUAU	35.00	60.00
□301	***CANDIX***	SURFIN'/LUAU (without "Era Sales" on label)	18.00	30.00
□301		SURFIN'/LUAU (with "Era Sales" on label)	12.00	20.00
□331		SURFIN'/LUAU (75)	18.00	30.00
□4777	***CAPITOL***	SURFIN' SAFARI/409 (14)	2.00	3.50
□4880		TEN LITTLE INDIANS/COUNTY FAIR (49)	3.00	5.00
□4932		SURFIN' U.S.A./SHUT DOWN (3)	1.50	3.00
□5009		SURFER GIRL/LITTLE DEUCE COUPE (7)	1.50	3.00
□5069		BE TRUE TO YOUR SCHOOL/IN MY ROOM (6)	1.50	3.00
□5096		LITTLE SAINT NICK/THE LORD'S PRAYER	3.00	5.00
□5118		FUN, FUN, FUN/WHY DO FOOLS FALL IN LOVE (5)	1.50	3.00
□5174		I GET AROUND/DON'T WORRY BABY (1)	1.50	3.00
□5235		WHEN I GROW UP/SHE KNOWS ME TOO WELL (9)	1.50	3.00
□5306		DANCE, DANCE, DANCE/ THE WARMTH OF THE SUN (8)	1.50	3.00
□5312		THE MAN WITH ALL THE TOYS/BLUE CHRISTMAS	2.50	5.00
□5372		DO YOU WANNA DANCE?/ PLEASE LET ME WONDER (12)	1.50	3.00
□5395		HELP ME RHONDA/KISS ME BABY (1)	1.25	2.50
□5464		CALIFORNIA GIRLS/LET HIM RUN WILD (3)	1.25	2.50
□5540		THE LITTLE GIRL I ONCE KNEW/ THERE'S NO OTHER (20)	1.25	3.00
□5561		BARBARA ANN/GIRL DON'T TELL ME (2)	1.00	2.50
□5602		SLOOP JOHN B/YOU'RE SO GOOD TO ME (3)	1.00	2.50
□5676		GOOD VIBRATIONS/LET'S GO AWAY FOR AWHILE (1)	1.00	2.50
□5706		WOULDN'T IT BE NICE/GOD ONLY KNOWS (8)	1.00	2.50
□2028		WILD HONEY/WIND CHIMES (31)	1.25	2.50
□2068		DARLIN'/HERE TODAY (19)	1.25	2.50
□2160		FRIENDS/LITTLE BIRD (47)	1.25	3.00
□2239		DO IT AGAIN/WAKE THE WORLD (20)	1.00	3.00
□2360		BLUEBIRDS OVER THE MOUNTAIN/ NEVER LEARN NOT TO LOVE (61)	1.50	3.00
□2432		I CAN HEAR MUSIC/ALL I WANT TO DO (24)	1.25	3.00
□2530		BREAK AWAY/CELEBRATE THE NEWS (63)	3.00	5.00
□2765		COTTON FIELDS/THE NEAREST FARAWAY PLACE	6.00	10.00
□2937		SALT LAKE CITY/AMUSEMENT PARKS U.S.A. (promotional)	75.00	150.00
□	***CAPITOL CUSTOM***	BOOGIE WOOGIE/SPIRIT OF AMERICA	40.00	70.00
□1001	***BROTHER***	HEROES AND VILLAINS/YOU'RE WELCOME (12)	1.25	3.00
□1002		GETTIN' HUNGRY/DEVOTED TO YOU	2.50	4.00
□0894	***REPRISE***	ADD SOME MUSIC TO YOUR DAY/ SUSIE CINCINATTI (64)	1.75	3.00
□0929		THIS WHOLE WORLD/SLIP ON THROUGH	2.50	4.00
□0957		TEARS IN THE MORNING/IT'S ABOUT TIME	2.50	4.00
□0998		COOL, COOL WATER/FOREVER	2.50	4.00
□1015		LONG PROMISED ROAD/DEIRDRE	2.50	4.00
□1047		LONG PROMISED ROAD/TILL I DIE (89)	2.00	3.50
□1058		SURF'S UP/DON'T GO NEAR THE WATER	2.50	4.00
□1091		CUDDLE UP/YOU NEED A MESS OF HELP TO STAND ALONE	5.00	8.00
□1101		MARCELLA/HOLD ON, DEAR BROTHER	2.50	4.00
□1138		SAIL ON SAILOR/ONLY WITH YOU (79)	2.00	3.50

ISSUE #		LABEL	ARTIST/TITLE	VG	MINT
□ 1156			CALIFORNIA SAGA/FUNKY PRETTY (84)	2.00	3.50
□ 1321			CHILD OF WINTER/SUSIE CINCINNATI	6.00	10.00
□ 1325			SAIL ON SAILOR/ONLY WITH YOU (49)	1.75	3.00
□ 66016		*ODE*	WOULDN'T IT BE NICE/ THE TIMES THEY ARE A-CHANGIN'	4.00	7.00

BEACH BOYS—EP

ISSUE #		LABEL	ARTIST/TITLE	VG	MINT
□ 5267		*CAPITOL*	FOUR BY THE BEACH BOYS (44)	7.00	12.00

BEACH BOYS—ALBUMS

ISSUE #		LABEL	ARTIST/TITLE	VG	MINT
□ 1808	(M)	*CAPITOL*	SURFIN' SAFARI	4.00	7.00
□ 1890	(M)		SURFIN' U.S.A.	4.00	7.00
□ 1981	(M)		SURFER GIRL	4.00	7.00
□ 1998	(M)		LITTLE DEUCE COUPE	4.00	7.00
□ 2027	(M)		SHUT DOWN, VOL. 2	4.00	7.00
□ 2110	(M)		ALL SUMMER LONG	4.00	7.00
□ 2164	(M)		THE BEACH BOYS' CHRISTMAS ALBUM	5.00	8.00
□ 2198	(M)		THE BEACH BOYS' CONCERT	4.00	7.00
			(STEREO VERSIONS OF THE ABOVE HAVE THE SAME VALUE)		
□ 2269	(M)		THE BEACH BOYS TODAY!	4.00	7.00
□ 2269	(S)		THE BEACH BOYS TODAY!	3.50	6.00
□ 2354	(M)		SUMMER DAYS (AND SUMMER NIGHTS)	4.00	7.00
□ 2354	(S)		SUMMER DAYS (AND SUMMER NIGHTS)	3.50	6.00
□ 2398	(M)		THE BEACH BOYS' PARTY	3.50	6.00
□ 2398	(S)		THE BEACH BOYS' PARTY	3.00	5.00
□ 2458	(M)		PET SOUNDS	3.50	6.00
□ 2458	(S)		PET SOUNDS	3.00	5.00
□ 2545	(S)		BEST OF THE BEACH BOYS, VOL. 1	3.00	5.00
□ 2706	(S)		BEST OF THE BEACH BOYS, VOL. 2	3.00	5.00
□ 2859	(S)		WILD HONEY	3.50	6.00
□ 2891	(S)		SMILEY SMILE (black Capitol label)	60.00	100.00
□ 2893	(S)		STACK-O-TRACKS (with book)	25.00	40.00
□ 2893	(S)		STACK-O-TRACKS (without book)	18.00	30.00
□ 2895	(S)		FRIENDS	3.50	6.00
□ 2945	(S)		BEST OF THE BEACH BOYS, VOL. 3	3.00	5.00
□ 9001	(S)	*BROTHER*	SMILEY SMILE (reissue of rare Capitol album)	5.00	8.00

BEACH BUMS

SEE: BOB SEGER

ISSUE #		LABEL	ARTIST/TITLE	VG	MINT
□ 1010		*ARE YOU KIDDING ME?*	BALLAD OF THE YELLOW BERET/FLORIDA TIME	6.00	10.00

BEATLES

In 1956 John Lennon was so overwhelmed by Elvis Presley that he decided to form his own band. They were called the Quarrymen, as they all attended Quarry Bank School in Liverpool, England. An unsuccessful rock quartet, the Quarrymen began to lose less-dedicated members. Paul McCartney, rejected at first for being too young, was later allowed to join when John decreed that Paul bore a strong resemblance to Elvis. Soon George Harrison, a friend of Paul's, entered the picture.

They endured several name changes including the Four Everlys, Johnny and the Moondogs, and the Beat Brothers. Finally they settled on the name Beatles, after Buddy Holly's Crickets group. Drummer Pete Best was fired, reportedly over jealousy from John and Paul. (Best got the most attention from the Liverpool ladies.) A less handsome Richard Starkey (Ringo Starr) took Best's place. Today Pete Best toils as a Liverpool baker.

After backing rocker Tony Sheridan, the Beatles came on their own with an original "Love Me Do" after rejecting "How Do You Do It", later a hit for Gerry and the Pacemakers. The Beatles are hailed as rock's consummate group, thanks chiefly to the writing team of Lennon-McCartney and the band's amazing ability to create diverse rock styles and prove themselves masters of each.

BEATLES

SEE: TONY SHERIDAN AND THE BEAT BROTHERS

ISSUE #	LABEL	ARTIST/TITLE	VG	MINT
□498	***VEE JAY***	PLEASE PLEASE ME/ASK ME WHY	60.00	100.00
□522		FROM ME TO YOU/THANK YOU GIRL	15.00	25.00
□581		FROM ME TO YOU/PLEASE PLEASE ME (3)	2.00	4.00
□587		DO YOU WANT TO KNOW A SECRET?/ THANK YOU GIRL (2)	1.75	3.50
□4152	***SWAN***	SHE LOVES YOU/I'LL GET YOU (white label)	25.00	40.00
□4152		SHE LOVES YOU/I'LL GET YOU (black label) (1)	1.50	3.00
□4182		SIE LIEBT DICH/I'LL GET YOU (97)	12.00	20.00
□9001	***TOLLIE***	TWIST AND SHOUT/THERE'S A PLACE (2)	2.00	4.00
□9008		LOVE ME DO/P.S., I LOVE YOU (1)	2.00	4.00
□13213	***MGM***	MY BONNIE/THE SAINTS (26)	3.00	5.00
□13227		WHY/CRY FOR A SHADOW (88)	6.00	10.00
□6302	***ATCO***	SWEET GEORGIA BROWN/TAKE OUT SOME INSURANCE ON ME	6.00	10.00
□0308		AIN'T SHE SWEET/NOBODY'S CHILD (19)	2.00	3.50
☑5112 10	***CAPITOL***	I WANT TO HOLD YOUR HAND/ I SAW HER STANDING THERE (1)	1.50	3.00
□5150		CAN'T BUY ME LOVE/YOU CAN'T DO THAT (1)	1.50	3.00
□5222		A HARD DAY'S NIGHT/ I SHOULD HAVE KNOWN BETTER (1)	1.50	3.00
□5234		I'LL CRY INSTEAD/I'M HAPPY JUST TO DANCE WITH YOU (25)	1.75	3.50
□5235		AND I LOVE HER/IF I FELL (12)	1.75	3.50
□5255		MATCHBOX/SLOW DOWN (17)	1.75	3.50
□5327		I FEEL FINE/SHE'S A WOMAN (1)	1.50	3.00
□5371		EIGHT DAYS A WEEK/I DON'T WANT TO SPOIL THE PARTY (1)	1.50	3.00
□5407		TICKET TO RIDE/YES IT IS (1)	1.50	3.00
□5476		HELP/I'M DOWN (1)	1.50	3.00
□5498		YESTERDAY/ACT NATURALLY (1)	1.50	3.00
□5555		WE CAN WORK IT OUT/DAY TRIPPER (1)	1.50	3.00
□5587		NOWHERE MAN/WHAT GOES ON (3)	1.25	2.50
□5651		PAPERBACK WRITER/RAIN (1)	1.25	2.50
□5715		YELLOW SUBMARINE/ELEANOR RIGBY (2)	1.25	2.50
□5810		PENNY LANE/STRAWBERRY FIELDS FOREVER (1)	1.25	2.50
□5904		ALL YOU NEED IS LOVE/ BABY YOU'RE A RICH MAN (1)	1.25	2.50
□2056		HELLO GOODBYE/I AM THE WALRUS (2)	1.25	2.50
□2138		LADY MADONNA/THE INNER LIGHT (4)	1.25	2.50
□2276	***APPLE***	HEY JUDE/REVOLUTION (1)	1.00	2.00
□2490		GET BACK/DON'T LET ME DOWN (1)	1.00	2.00
□2531		THE BALLAD OF JOHN AND YOKO/ OLD BROWN SHOE (8)	1.00	2.00
□2654		COME TOGETHER/SOMETHING (1)	1.00	2.00
□2764		LET IT BE/YOU KNOW MY NAME (LOOK UP MY NUMBER) (1)	1.00	2.00
□2832		THE LONG AND WINDING ROAD/FOR YOU BLUE (1)	1.00	2.00

BEATLES—EPs

ISSUE #	LABEL	ARTIST/TITLE	VG	MINT
□18901	***VEE JAY***	SOUVENIR OF THEIR VISIT TO AMERICA	20.00	30.00
□2121	***CAPITOL***	FOUR BY THE BEATLES (92)	25.00	40.00
□5365		4 - BY THE BEATLES (68)	18.00	30.00

ISSUE #	LABEL	ARTIST/TITLE	VG	MINT
		BEATLES—ALBUMS		
☐ DX 30 (M)	*VEE JAY*	BEATLES VS. THE FOUR SEASONS	18.00	30.00
☐ DX 30 (S)		BEATLES VS. THE FOUR SEASONS	40.00	70.00
☐ PRO 202 (M)		HEAR THE BEATLES TELL ALL	15.00	25.00
☐ 1062 (M)		INTRODUCING THE BEATLES (album photos on back)	35.00	60.00
☐ 1062 (S)		INTRODUCING THE BEATLES (album photos on back)	70.00	120.00
☐ 1062 (M)		INTRODUCING THE BEATLES (with "Love Me Do")	8.00	15.00
☐ 1062 (S)		INTRODUCING THE BEATLES (with "Love Me Do")	18.00	30.00
☐ 1062 (M)		INTRODUCING THE BEATLES (with "Please Please Me")	7.00	12.00
☐ 1062 (S)		INTRODUCING THE BEATLES (with "Please Please Me")	15.00	25.00
☐ 1085 (M)		THE BEATLES AND FRANK IFIELD (ON STAGE)	175.00	300.00
☐ 1085 (S)		THE BEATLES AND FRANK IFIELD (ON STAGE)	300.00	500.00
		(ABOVE ALBUMS FEATURE A PAINTED BEATLE PORTRAIT)		
☐ 1085 (M)		THE BEATLES AND FRANK IFIELD (ON STAGE)	8.00	15.00
☐ 1085 (S)		THE BEATLES AND FRANK IFIELD (ON STAGE)	15.00	25.00
		(ABOVE ALBUMS FEATURE A DRAWING OF AN OLD MAN)		
☐ 1092 (M)		SONGS, PICTURES AND STORIES OF THE BEATLES	7.00	12.00
☐ 4215 (M)	*MGM*	THE BEATLES WITH TONY SHERIDAN AND GUESTS	8.00	15.00
☐ 4215 (S)		THE BEATLES WITH TONY SHERIDAN AND GUESTS	18.00	30.00
☐ 601 (M)	*CLARION*	THE AMAZING BEATLES	7.00	12.00
☐ 601 (S)		THE AMAZING BEATLES	9.00	16.00
☐ 69 (M)	*SAVAGE*	THE SAVAGE YOUNG BEATLES	8.00	15.00
☐ 563 (M)	*METRO*	THIS IS WHERE IT STARTED	6.00	10.00
☐ 563 (S)		THIS IS WHERE IT STARTED	7.00	12.00
☐ 2047 (M)	*CAPITOL*	MEET THE BEATLES (brown lettering)	6.00	10.00
☐ 2080 (M)		THE BEATLES' SECOND ALBUM	5.00	8.00
☐ 2108 (M)		SOMETHING NEW	4.00	7.00
☐ 2222 (M)		THE BEATLES STORY	5.00	8.00
☐ 2228 (M)		BEATLES '65	3.50	6.00
☐ 2309 (M)		THE EARLY BEATLES (reissue of Vee Jay material)	3.50	6.00
☐ 2358 (M)		BEATLES VI	3.50	6.00
☐ 2368 (M)		HELP!	3.50	6.00
☐ 2442 (M)		RUBBER SOUL	3.50	6.00
		(STEREO VERSIONS OF THE ABOVE HAVE THE SAME VALUE)		
☐ 2553 (M)		YESTERDAY AND TODAY (butcher cover-never covered)	175.00	300.00
☐ 2553 (S)		YESTERDAY AND TODAY (butcher cover-never covered)	300.00	500.00
☐ 2553 (M)		YESTERDAY AND TODAY (butcher cover-peeled well)	50.00	80.00
☐ 2553 (S)		YESTERDAY AND TODAY (butcher cover-peeled well)	80.00	150.00
☐ 2553 (M)		YESTERDAY AND TODAY (standard cover with trunk)	3.50	6.00
☐ 2576 (M)		REVOLVER	3.50	6.00
		(STEREO VERSIONS OF ABOVE TWO HAVE THE SAME VALUE)		
☐ 2653 (M)		SERGEANT PEPPER'S LONELY HEARTS CLUB BAND	4.50	8.00
☐ 2653 (S)		SERGEANT PEPPER'S LONELY HEARTS CLUB BAND	3.50	6.00
☐ 2835 (M)		MAGICAL MYSTERY TOUR	4.50	8.00
☐ 2835 (S)		MAGICAL MYSTERY TOUR	3.50	6.00
☐ 3366 (M)	*UNITED ARTISTS*	A HARD DAY'S NIGHT	3.50	6.00
☐ 6366 (S)		A HARD DAY'S NIGHT	4.00	7.00

ISSUE #	LABEL	ARTIST/TITLE	VG	MINT
□100 (S)	*APPLE*	CHRISTMAS FAN CLUB ALBUM	18.00	30.00
□101 (S)		THE BEATLES (the white album)	5.00	8.00
□153 (S)		YELLOW SUBMARINE	3.50	6.00
□383 (S)		ABBEY ROAD	3.50	6.00
		BEAU BRUMMELS		
□8	*AUTUMN*	LAUGH LAUGH/STILL IN LOVE WITH YOU BABY (15)	.75	2.00
□10		JUST A LITTLE/THEY'LL MAKE YOU CRY (8)	.75	2.00
□16		YOU TELL ME WHY/I WANT YOU (38)	.75	2.00
□20		DON'T TALK TO STRANGERS/IN GOOD TIME (52)	.75	2.00
□24		GOOD TIME MUSIC/SAD LITTLE GIRL (97)	.75	2.00
		BEAU BRUMMELS—ALBUMS		
□103 (M)	*AUTUMN*	INTRODUCING THE BEAU BRUMMELS	4.00	8.00
□104 (M)		THE BEAU BRUMMELS, VOL. 2	3.50	7.00
		BEAU-MARKS		
□1032	*TIME*	ROCKIN' BLUES/OH JOAN	2.50	4.00
□5017	*SHAD*	CLAP YOUR HANDS/DADDY SAID (45)	1.50	3.00
□5021		'CAUSE WE'RE IN LOVE/BILLY WENT A-WALKING	1.75	3.00
□70029	*PORT*	LOVELY LITTLE LADY/LITTLE MISS TWIST	1.75	3.00
□5035	*RUST*	CLASSMATE/SCHOOL IS OUT	1.75	3.00
□5051		TENDER YEARS/I'LL NEVER BE THE SAME	1.75	3.00
		JIMMY BEAUMONT		
		SEE: SKYLINERS		
□112	*MAY*	EV'RYBODY'S CRYIN'/CAMERA (100))	2.00	3.50
□115		I SHOULDA LISTENED TO MAMA/JUAREZ	1.75	3.00
□120		NEVER SAY GOODBYE/I'M GONNA TRY MY WINGS	1.75	3.00
□136		I'LL ALWAYS BE IN LOVE WITH YOU/ GIVE HER MY BEST	1.75	3.00
□3007	*GALLANT*	PLEASE SEND ME SOMEONE TO LOVE/ THERE IS NO OTHER LOVE	1.75	3.00
□607	*COLPIX*	THE END OF A STORY/BAION RHYTHMS	1.75	3.00
□510	*BANG*	TELL ME/I FEEL I'M FALLING IN LOVE	1.75	3.00
□525		I NEVER LOVED HER ANYWAY/ YOU GOT TOO MUCH GOIN' FOR YOU	1.75	3.00
		BEEFEATERS (BYRDS		
□45013	*ELEKTRA*	PLEASE LET ME LOVE YOU/DON'T BE LONG	15.00	25.00
		BEL-AIRES		
□30631	*DECCA*	MY YEARBOOK/ROCKIN' AND STROLLIN'	6.00	10.00
		BEL-AIRES		
□5034	*ARVEE*	MR. MOTO/LITTLE BROWN JUG	1.50	3.00
□54	*TRIUMPH*	KAMI-KAZE/VAMPIRE	1.50	3.00
□107	*LUCKY TOKEN*	BAGGIES/CHARLIE CHAN	1.50	3.00
		BELL NOTES		
□1004	*TIME*	I'VE HAD IT/BE MINE (6)	1.25	3.00
□1010		OLD SPANISH TOWN/SHE WENT THAT-A-WAY (76)	1.75	3.00
□1013		THAT'S RIGHT/BETTY DEAR	1.75	3.00
□1015		YOU'RE A BIG GIRL NOW/DON'T ASK ME WHY	1.75	3.00
□1017		WHITE BUCKSKIN SNEAKERS AND CHECKERBOARD SOCKS/NO DICE	1.75	3.00
		BELL NOTES—EP		
□100	*TIME*	I'VE HAD IT	6.00	10.00

ISSUE #	LABEL	ARTIST/TITLE	VG	MINT
		TONY BELLUS		
□023	*NRC*	ROBBIN' THE CRADLE/VALENTINE GIRL (25)	1.25	2.50
□035		HEY LITTL DARLIN'/ONLY YOUR HEART	1.25	2.00
□051		THE ECHO OF AN OLD SONG/THE END OF MY LOVE	1.00	2.00
		TONY BELLUS—ALBUM		
□8 (M)	*NRC*	ROBBIN' THE CRADLE	15.00	25.00
		BELMONTS		
□3080	*LAURIE*	WE BELONG TOGETHER/SUCH A LONG WAY	5.00	8.00
□1000	*SURPRISE*	TELL MY WHY/SMOKE FROM YOUR CIGARETTE	8.00	15.00
□500	*SABRINA*	TELL MY WHY/SMOKE FROM YOUR CIGARETTE (18)	1.5	3.00
□501		DON'T GET AROUND MUCH ANYMORE/ SEARCHING FOR A NEW LOVE (57)	1.75	3.00
□502	*SABINA*	I NEED SOMEONE/THAT AMERICAN DANCE (75)	1.75	3.00
□503		I CONFESS/HOMBRE	1.75	3.00
□505		COME ON LITTLE ANGEL/HOW ABOUT ME? (28)	1.50	3.00
□507		DIDDLE-DEE-DUM/FAREWELL (53)	1.50	3.00
□509		ANN-MARIE/ACCENTUATE THE POSITIVE (86)	1.75	3.00
□513		WALK ON BY/LET'S CALL IT A DAY	1.75	3.00
□517		MORE IMPORTANT THINGS TO DO/ LET'S CALL IT A DAY	1.75	3.00
□519		C'MON EVERYBODY/WHY	5.00	8.00
□521		NOTHING IN RETURN/SUMMERTIME TIME	5.00	8.00
□809	*UNITED ARTISTS*	I DON'T KNOW WHY/SUMMERTIME	3.00	5.00
□904		(THEN) I WALKED AWAY/TODAY MY LOVE HAS GONE AWAY	3.00	5.00
□966		I GOT A FEELING/TO BE WITH YOU	3.00	5.00
□5007		COME WITH ME/YOU'RE LIKE A MYSTERY	2.50	4.00
		BELMONTS—ALBUM		
□5001 (M)	*SABINA*	CARNIVAL OF HITS	8.00	15.00
		BELVEDERES		
□217	*BATON*	COME TO ME BABY/PEPPER-HOT BABY	3.50	6.00
□009	*TREND*	LET'S GET MARRIED/WOW WOW, MARY MARY	3.00	5.00
		BOYD BENNETT		
□1413	*KING*	WATERLOO/I'VE HAD ENOUGH	6.00	10.00
□1432		POISON IVY/YOU UPSET ME BABY	5.00	8.00
□1443		BOOGIE AT MIDNIGHT/EVERLOVIN'	5.00	8.00
□1470		SEVENTEEN/LITTLE OLD YOU-ALL (5)	3.00	6.00
□1475		TENNESSEE ROCK AND ROLL/00-00-00	2.75	5.00
□1494		MY BOY FLAT-TOP/ BANJO ROCK AND ROLL (39)	2.00	4.00
		PRICES ABOVE ARE FOR MAROON LABELS; SECOND-PRESS BLUE LABELS ARE WORTH HALF		
		BOYD BENNETT—EPs		
□337	*KING*	ROCK AND ROLL WITH BOYD BENNETT	6.00	10.00
□383		ROCK AND ROLL WITH BOYD BENNETT	6.00	10.00
		BOYD BENNETT—ALBUM		
□594 (M)	*KING*	BOYD BENNETT	15.00	25.00
		JOE BENNETT AND THE SPARKLETONES		
□9837	*ABC-PARAMOUNT*	BLACK SLACKS/BOPPIN' ROCK BOOGIE (17)	1.50	3.00
□9867		PENNY LOAFERS AND BOBBY SOCKS/ROCKET (43)	1.50	3.00
□9885		COTTON PICKIN' ROCKER/I DIG YOU BABY	1.50	2.50

ISSUE #	LABEL	ARTIST/TITLE	VG	MINT
□9929		WE'VE HAD IT/LITTLE TURTLE	1.50	2.50
□9959		LATE AGAIN/DO THE STOP	1.50	2.50
□10659		RUN RABBIT RUN/WELL-DRESSED MAN	1.25	2.00
□537	***PARIS***	WHAT THE HECK/BOYS DO CRY	1.25	2.00
□542		ARE YOU FROM DIXIE?/BEAUTIFUL ONE	1.25	2.00
		RON BENNETT		
□1	***TA-RAH***	MY ONLY GIRL/DINGLE DANGLE DOLL	3.00	5.00
		RON BERNARD		
□105	***JIN***	THIS SHOULD GO ON FOREVER/ PARDON, MR. GORDON	5.00	8.00
□5327	***ARGO***	THIS SHOULD GO ON FOREVER/ PARDON, MR. GORDON (20)	1.00	2.50
		ROD BERNARD—ALBUM		
□4007 (M)	***JIN***	ROD BERNARD	7.00	12.00

CHUCK BERRY

He was born Charles Edward Anderson Berry on October 18, 1926. As one of six children, Chuck sang in a church choir during his adolescent years. Encouraged by a St. Louis music teacher, Berry purchased a six-string Spanish guitar but soon graduated to an electric instrument.

After high school Chuck earned a degree from Poro Junior College. He then became a hairdresser by day and played and sang in his Chuck Berry Combo at night. During a Chicago vacation, Berry sat in with bluesman Muddy Waters. Muddy was so impressed by the Missouri native that he insisted Chuck meet Leonard Chess, the owner of Chess Records. Berry auditioned a song called "Ida Red", which he later changed to "Maybellene". (Berry's previous profession as a hairdresser supposedly helped supply the name from the eyebrow pencil.) "Maybellene" became a mid-1950s classic, the first of many for Berry.

Long heralded as rock's ultimate pioneer and creator, Chuck Berry recorded a number of rocking standards but never hit the No. 1 spot until 1972 with the novelty "My Ding-A-Ling".

ISSUE #	LABEL	ARTIST/TITLE	VG	MINT
		CHUCK BERRY		
□ 1604	*CHESS*	MAYBELLENE/WEE WEE HOURS (5)	2.50	5.00
□ 1610		THIRTY DAYS/TOGETHER	3.50	6.00
□ 1615		NO MONEY DOWN/THE DOWNBOUND TRAIN	3.50	6.00
□ 1626		ROLL OVER BEETHOVEN/DRIFTING HEART (29)	3.00	5.00
□ 1635		TOO MUCH MONKEY BUSINESS/ BROWN EYED HANDSOME MAN	3.50	6.00
□ 1645		YOU CAN'T CATCH ME/HAVANA MOON	3.00	5.00
□ 1653		SCHOOL DAY/DEEP FEELING (5)	2.00	4.00
□ 1664		OH BABY DOLL/LAJUNDA (57)	2.50	4.00
		(ABOVE ISSUES FEATURED THE SILVER-AND-BLUE CHESS-TOP LABELS)		
□ 1671		ROCK AND ROLL MUSIC/BLUE FEELING (8)	1.75	3.50
□ 1683		SWEET LITTLE SIXTEEN/REELIN' AND ROCKIN' (2)	1.75	3.50
□ 1691		JOHNNY B. GOODE/AROUND AND AROUND (8)	1.75	3.50
□ 1697		BEAUTIFUL DELILAH/VACATION TIME (81)	1.75	3.00
□ 1700		CAROL/HEY PEDRO (18)	1.50	3.00
□ 1709		SWEET LITTLE ROCK AND ROLL/JOE JOE GUN (47)	1.50	3.00
□ 1714		MERRY CHRISTMAS BABY/RUN RUDOLPH RUN (71)	1.75	3.00
□ 1716		ANTHONY BOY/THAT'S MY DESIRE (60)	1.75	3.00
□ 1722		LITTLE QUEENIE/ALMOST GROWN (32)	1.50	3.00
□ 1729		BACK IN THE U.S.A./MEMPHIS, TENNESSEE (37)	1.50	3.00
□ 1736		CHILDHOOD SWEETHEART/BROKEN ARROW	1.50	2.50
□ 1747		TOO POOPED TO POP/LET IT ROCK (42)	1.25	2.50
□ 1754		BYE BYE JOHNNY/WORRIED LIFE BLUES	1.50	2.50
□ 1763		MAD LAD/I GOT TO FIND MY BABY	1.50	2.50
□ 1767		JAGUAR AND THE THUNDERBIRD/ OUR LITTLE RENDEZVOUS	1.25	2.00
□ 1779		LITTLE STAR/I'M TALKING ABOUT YOU	1.25	2.00
□ 1799		GO GO GO/COME ON	1.25	2.00
□ 1853		I'M TALKING ABOUT YOU/DIPLOMA FOR TWO	1.25	2.00
□ 1866		SWEET LITTLE SIXTEEN/MEMPHIS (reissue)	.75	1.50
□ 1883		NADINE/ORANGUTANG (23)	1.00	2.00
□ 1898		NO PARTICULAR PLACE TO GO/YOU TWO (10)	1.00	2.00
□ 1906		YOU NEVER CAN TELL/BRENDA LEE (14)	1.00	2.00
□ 1912		LITTLE MARIE/GO BOBBY SOXER (54)	1.25	2.00
□ 1916		PROMISED LAND/THINGS I USED TO DO (41)	1.00	2.00
□ 1926		DEAR DAD/LONELY SCHOL DAYS (85)	1.25	2.00

LATER CHESS SINGLES ARE WORTH UP TO $1.50 MINT

ISSUE #	LABEL	ARTIST/TITLE	VG	MINT
		CHUCK BERRY—EPs		
☐5118	*CHESS*	AFTER SCHOOL SESSION	6.00	10.00
☐5119		ROCK AND ROLL MUSIC	6.00	10.00
☐5121		SWEET LITTLE SIXTEEN	5.00	8.00
☐5124		PICKIN' BERRIES	5.00	8.00
		ADD $5.00 PER EP FOR SILVER-TOP LABELS		
		CHUCK BERRY—ALBUMS		
☐1426 (M)	*CHESS*	AFTER SCHOOL SESSION	8.00	15.00
☐1432 (M)		ONE DOZEN BERRYS	7.00	12.00
☐1435 (M)		CHUCK BERRY IS ON TOP	6.00	10.00
☐1448 (M)		ROCKIN' AT THE HOPS	6.00	10.00
☐1456 (M)		MORE JUKE BOX HITS	6.00	10.00
☐1465 (M)		MORE CHUCK BERRY	6.00	10.00
		JAN BERRY		
		SEE: JAN AND ARNIE, JAN AND DEAN		
☐6101	*RIPPLE*	TOMORROW'S TEARDROPS/ MY MIDSUMMER NIGHT'S DREAMS	12.00	20.00
☐55845	*LIBERTY*	THE UNIVERSAL CROWD/ I CAN'T WAIT TO LOVE YOU	2.50	4.00
☐66023	*ODE*	MOTHER EARTH/BLUE MOON SHUFFLE	5.00	8.00
☐66034		DON'T YOU JUST KNOW IT/ BLUE MOON SHUFFLE (Jan)	4.00	7.00
☐66050		TINSEL TOWN/BLOW UP MUSIC (1 Jan 1)	3.50	6.00
☐66111		FUN CITY/TOTALLY WILD	3.00	5.00
☐66120		SING SANG A SONG/SING SANG A SONG	3.00	5.00
		ROD BERRY AND THE BEL RAVES		
☐1001	*DREEM*	WHAT A DOLLY/HOT ROD (Lou Berry)	50.00	80.00
☐169	*20TH FOX*	WHAT A DOLLY/HOT ROD (Lou Berry)	30.00	50.00
		PETER BEST (EX-BEATLE)		
☐800	*ORIGINAL BEATLES DRUMMER*	(I'LL TRY) ANYWAY/I WANNA BE THERE	6.00	10.00
☐711	*MR. MASTRO*	I CAN'T DO WITHOUT YOU/KEYS TO MY HEART	6.00	10.00
☐712		I'M BLUE/CASTING MY SPELL	6.00	10.00
☐391	*CAMEO*	BOYS/KANSAS CITY	5.00	8.00
		PETER BEST—ALBUM		
☐71 (M)	*SAVAGE*	BEST OF THE BEATLES	15.00	25.00

BIG BOPPER

The Big Bopper, whose real name was Jape Richardson, had just turned 24 when he died in 1959. That accident in an Iowa pasture ended his life but established the Big Bopper forever in rock-and-roll history. Though he had only one Top 10 hit—"Chantilly Lace"—Jape Richardson was a man of many talents, including that of a songwriter for others. "Running Bear" by Johnny Preston was a No. 1 hit penned by Richardson, who is heard making the Indian calls on the record.

A native of Sabine Pass, Texas, where he was born on October 24, 1934, Richardson went by the initial J. P. as he disliked his real name. While in college he found work as a part-time disc jockey. He became an instant success with his jovial bass delivery and soon became a top name on Beaumont's station KTRM.

He cut the single of "Chantilly Lace" on the Texas-based D label. The master was then released to Mercury Records, which had a larger distribution budget. When the single rocketed to the Top 10, Richardson took a leave of absence to go on a midwestern winter tour with Buddy Holly, Ritchie Valens, Dion and the Belmonts, and Frankie Sardo. The rest is history.

ISSUE #		LABEL	ARTIST/TITLE	VG	MINT
			BIG BOPPER		
			SEE: JAPE RICHARDSON		
□1008		D	CHANTILLY LACE/PURPLE PEOPLE EATER MEETS THE WITCH DOCTOR	15.00	25.00
□71343		MERCURY	CHANTILLY LACE/PURPLE PEOPLE EATER MEETS THE WITCH DOCTOR (6)	1.25	2.50
□71375			BIG BOPPER'S WEDDING/ LITTLE RED RIDING HOOD (38)	1.50	3.00
□71416			WALKING THROUGH MY DREAMS/ SOMEONE WATCHING OVER YOU	3.00	5.00
□71451			IT'S THE TRUTH, RUTH/ THAT'S WHAT I'M TALKING ABOUT	3.50	6.00
□71482			PINK PETTICOATS/THE CLOCK	3.50	6.00
			BIG BOPPER—ALBUM		
□20402	(M)	MERCURY	CHANTILLY LACE	30.00	50.00
			BILLY AND LILLIE		
□4002		SWAN	LA DEE DAH/THE MONSTER (9)	1.00	2.50
□4005			HAPPINESS/CREEPIN', CRAWLIN', CRAWLIN' (56)	1.25	2.50
□4011			HANGIN' ON TO YOU/THE GREASY SPOON	1.25	2.00
□4020			LUCKY LADYBUG/I PROMISE YOU (14)	1.00	2.50
□4030			TUMBLED DOWN/ALOYSIUS HORATION THOMAS THE CAT	1.25	2.00
□4036			BELLS, BELLS, BELLS/HONEYMOONIN'	1.25	2.00
□4042			TERRIFIC TOGETHER/SWAMPY	1.25	2.00
□4051			FREE FOR ALL/THE INS AND OUTS (OF LOVE)	1.25	2.00
□4058			OVER THE MOUNTAIN, ACROSS THE SEA/ THAT'S THE WAY THE COOKIE CRUMBLES	1.50	2.50
□4069			AIN'T COMIN' BACK TO YOU/BANANAS	1.25	2.00
			BILL BLACK'S COMBO		
□2018		HI	SMOKIE (PT. I)/(PT. II) (17)	1.00	2.50
□2021			WHITE SILVER SANDS/THE WHEEL (9)	1.00	2.00
□2022			JOSEPHINE/DRY BONES (18)	1.00	2.00
□2026			DON'T BE CRUEL/ROLLIN' (11)	1.00	2.00
□2027			BLUE TANGO/WILLIE (16)	1.00	2.00
□2028			HEARTS OF STONE/ROYAL BLUE (20)	1.00	2.00
□2036			OLE BUTTERMILK SKY/YOGI (25)	1.00	2.00
□2038			MOVIN'/HONKY TRAIN (41)	1.00	2.00
□2042			TWIST-HER/MY GIRL JOSEPHINE (26)	1.00	2.00
			LATER HI SINGLES ARE WORTH UP TO $1.50 MINT		
			BILL BLACK'S COMBO—EPs		
□22001		HI	SMOKIE	3.50	6.00
□22002			SOLID AND RAUNCHY	3.00	5.00
□22003			THAT WONDERFUL FEELING	2.50	5.00
			BILL BLACK'S COMBO—ALBUMS		
□12001	(M)	HI	SMOKIE	7.00	12.00
□12003	(M)		SOLID AND RAUNCHY	6.00	10.00
□12005	(M)		MOVIN'	3.50	6.00
□12005	(S)		MOVIN'	4.50	8.00
			JACK BLACK		
			SEE: JAY BLACK AND THE AMERICANS		
□50166		UNITED ARTISTS	WHAT WILL MY MARY SAY/RETURN TO ME	1.75	3.00

ISSUE #	LABEL	ARTIST/TITLE	VG	MINT
		BILLY BLAND		
☐1022	*OLD TOWN*	CHICKEN HOP/OH, YOU FOR ME	1.50	2.50
☐1035		IF I COULD BE YOUR MAN/I HAD A DREAM	1.50	2.50
☐1076		LET THE LITTLE GIRL DANCE/SWEET THING (7)	1.00	2.00
☐1082		YOU WERE BORN TO BE LOVED/PARDON ME (94)	1.25	2.00
☐1088		HARMONY/MAKE BELIEVE LOVER (91)	1.25	2.00
		MARCIE BLANE		
☐120	*SEVILLE*	BOBBY'S GIRL/TIME TO DREAM (3)	.75	2.00
☐123		WHAT DOES A GIRL DO/HOW CAN I TELL HIM (82)	1.00	2.00
☐126		LITTLE MISS FOOL/RAGTIME SOUND	1.25	2.00
☐128		YOU GAVE MY NUMBER TO BILLY/TOLD YOU SO	1.25	2.00
☐133		BOBBY DID/AFTER THE LAUGHTER	1.25	2.00
☐137		SHE'LL BREAK THE STRING/THE HURTIN' KIND	1.25	2.00
		BLENDAIRS		
☐252	*TIN PAN ALLEY*	MY LOVE IS JUST FOR YOU/REPETITION	5.00	8.00
		BLENDERS		
☐114	*WITCH*	DAUGHTER/EVERYBODY'S GOT A RIGHT (61)	1.25	2.50
☐117		BOYS THINK (EVERY GIRL'S THE SAME)/ SQUAT AND SQUIRM	1.25	2.00
		BLOCKBUSTERS		
☐725	*CRYSTALLETTE*	HI HON/BOOGIE BOP	3.00	5.00
		BLOSSOMS		
		FEATURED: DARLENE LOVE		
☐3822	*CAPITOL*	HE PROMISED ME/MOVE ON	1.50	2.50
☐3878		HAVE FAITH IN ME/LITTLE LOUIE	1.50	2.50
☐4072		BABY DADDY-O/NO OTHER LOVE	1.50	2.50
☐9109	*CHALLENGE*	SON-IN-LAW/I'LL WAIT (79)	1.25	2.00
☐0436	*REPRISE*	GOOD GOOD LOVIN'/ THAT'S WHEN THE TEARS START	1.25	2.00
☐13964	*MGM*	TWEEDLE DEE/YOU GOT ME HUMMIN'	1.25	2.00
		BLUE JAYS		
☐2008	*MILESTONE*	LOVER'S ISLAND/YOU'RE GONNA CRY (31)	1.25	2.50
☐2009		TEARS ARE FALLING/TREE TOP LEN	1.50	2.50
		BLUESOLOGY		
		FEATURED: ELTON JOHN		
☐594	*FONTANA*	COME BACK BABY/TIMES ARE GETTING TOUGHER	12.00	20.00
☐668		EVERY DAY I HAVE THE BLUES/MR. FRANTIC	12.00	20.00
☐56195	*POLYDOR*	JUST A LITTLE BIT/SINCE I FOUND YOU BABY	10.00	18.00
		ALL OF THE ABOVE ARE BRITISH RELEASES		
		BOB AND SHERI		
☐101	*SAFARI*	THE SURFER MOON/HUMPTY DUMPTY	200.00	300.00
		THIS WAS BRIAN WILSON'S FIRST PRODUCTION - 1961		
		BOB B. SOXX AND THE BLUE JEANS		
☐107	*PHILLES*	ZIP-A-DEE-DOO-DAH/FLIP AND NITTY (8)	1.25	2.50
☐110		WHY DO LOVERS BREAK EACH OTHER'S HEARTS/ DR. KAPLAN'S OFFICE (38)	1.50	3.00
☐113		NOT TOO YOUNG TO GET MARRIED/ANNETTE (63)	1.75	3.00

BOBBETTES

Once a New York City man was intrigued by a group of singing neighbors. All twelve and thirteen, the female quintet was known as the Bobbettes. They were then students at New York's P. S. 109. They also had a crush on their handsome young principal, whose name was Mr. Lee. The young ladies had composed a song about their idol and often sang it on the streets. Their neighbor felt the girls had great potential, so he encouraged them to hone "Mr. Lee" to perfection and try to record it.

Later, the neighbor arranged an audition at Atlantic Records. As a result the Bobbettes were given the chance to cut their catchy novelty tune. Backed by the infectious chalypso "Look At the Stars", the rocking "Mr. Lee" soon became a million seller and made the Bobbettes instant (if temporary) record stars.

A later Atlantic follow-up of "I Shot Mr. Lee" did nothing, so the master was released on the small Triple-X label. That song managed to make the Top 100, but sales didn't approach that of "Mr. Lee." A third minor chart single—"Have Mercy Baby"—failed to establish the Bobbettes as consistent hitmakers.

ISSUE #	LABEL	ARTIST/TITLE	VG	MINT
		BOBBETTES		
□1144	***ATLANTIC***	MR. LEE/LOOK AT THE STARS (6)	1.25	2.50
□2069		I SHOT MR. LEE/UNTRUE LOVE	1.75	3.00
□104	***TRIPLE-X***	I SHOT MR. LEE/BILLY (52)	1.50	2.50
□106		HAVE MERCY BABY/DANCE WITH ME, GEORGIE (66)	1.50	2.50

ISSUE #	LABEL	ARTIST/TITLE	VG	MINT
		BOBOLINKS		
☐573	*KEY*	ELVIS PRESLEY'S SERGEANT/ YOUR COTTON PICKIN' HEART	3.50	6.00
		BOBSLED AND THE TOBOGGANS		
		FEATURED: BRUCE JOHNSTON		
☐400	*CAMEO*	HERE WE GO/SEA AND SKI	2.50	4.00
		GARY U.S. BONDS		
☐1003	*LEGRAND*	NEW ORLEANS/PLEASE FORGIVE ME (6)	1.00	2.50
☐1005		NOT ME/GIVE ME ONE MORE CHANCE	1.75	3.00
☐1008		QUARTER TO THREE/TIME OLD STORY (1)	.75	2.00
☐1009		SCHOOL IS OUT/ONE MILLION TEARS (5)	.75	2.00
☐1012		SCHOOL IS IN/TRIP TO THE MOON (28)	1.00	2.00
☐1015		DEAR LADY TWIST/HAVIN' SO MUCH FUN (9)	.75	2.00
☐1018		TWIST TWIST SENORA/FOOD OF LOVE (9)	.75	2.00
☐1019		SEVEN DAY WEEKEND/GETTIN' A GROOVE (27)	1.00	2.00
☐1020		COPY CAT/I'LL CHANGE THAT TOO (92)	1.25	2.00
☐1022		I DIG THIS STATION/MIXED UP FACULTY	1.25	2.00
☐1025		DO THE LIMBO WITH ME/ WHERE DID THAT NAUGHTY GIRL GO	1.25	2.00
		LATER LEGRAND SINGLES ARE WORTH UP TO $2.00 MINT		
		GARY U.S. BONDS—ALBUMS		
☐3001 (M)	*LEGRAND*	DANCE TILL QUARTER TO THREE	6.00	10.00
☐3002 (M)		TWIST UP CALYPSO	5.00	8.00
☐3003 (M)		THE GREATEST HITS OF GARY U.S. BONDS	5.00	8.00
		BONNEVILLES		
☐103	*MUNICH*	LORRAINE/ZU ZU	4.00	7.00
		BONNIE AND THE TREASURES		
		FEATURED: RONNIE SPECTOR		
☐5005	*PHI DAN*	HOME OF THE BRAVE/OUR SONG (77)	2.50	4.00
		BONNIE SISTERS		
☐328	*RAINBOW*	CRY BABY/BROKEN HEART (35)	1.50	3.00
☐333		WANDERING HEART/TRACK THAT CAT	1.50	2.50
		SONNY BONO AND LITTLE TOOTSIE		
☐733	*SPECIALTY*	COMIN' DOWN THE CHIMNEY/ONE LITTLE ANSWER	2.50	4.00

PAT BOONE

While less a legend than Presley, Charles Boone (Pat is a middle name) is still a 1950s institution. He was born in Nashville, Tennessee, on June 1, 1934. Pat is a direct descendant of Daniel Boone and was a three-letter athlete as well as student-body president during his high-school days. Shortly after graduation he married another Nashville native, Shirley Foley, a daughter of country star Red Foley.

As a teenager, Boone won a recording contract with Nashville's small Republic label. Nothing from those studio dates was a success. Boone later enrolled in a Nashville college but soon transfered to North Texas State. During that time he won first place on "Ted Mack's Amateur Hour." A disc-jockey pal of Boone's introduced the clean-cut college student to Dot Records owner Randy Wood. While Boone prefered ballads—his real forte—Wood insisted that Boone "cover" r & b hits of the day. Those insipid singles made Boone's name known, and his record sales rivaled Presley's during the later 1950s. Pat was later allowed the shift to ballads, where he found even greater success.

ISSUE #	LABEL	ARTIST/TITLE	VG	MINT
		PAT BOONE		
☐7062	***REPUBLIC***	REMEMBER TO ME MINE/ HALFWAY CHANCE WITH YOU	5.00	8.00
☐7084		I NEED SOMEONE/LOVING YOU MADLY	4.00	7.00
☐7119		I NEED SOMEONE/MY HEART BELONGS TO YOU	3.50	6.00
☐15338	***DOT***	TWO HEARTS/TRA LA LA (16)	2.00	4.00
☐15377		AIN'T THAT A SHAME/ TENNESSEE SATURDAY NIGHT (2)	1.50	3.00
☐15422		AT MY FRONT DOOR/NO OTHER ARMS (7)	1.50	3.00
☐15435		GEE WHITTAKERS/TAKE THE TIME (27)	1.75	3.50
☐15433		TUTTI FRUITTI/I'LL BE HOME (5)	1.50	3.00
☐15457		LONG TALL TALLY/JUST AS LONG AS I'M WITH YOU (18)	1.50	3.00
☐15472		I ALMOST LOST MY MIND/ I'M IN LOVE WITH YOU (1)	1.25	2.50
LATER DOT SINGLES ARE WORTH UP TO $1.50 MINT WITH ONE EXCEPTION:				
☐16658		LITTLE HONDA/BEACH GIRL (Brian Wilson Production)	2.50	4.00
		PAT BOONE—EPs		
☐1049	***DOT***	PAT BOONE	1.50	3.00
☐1053		PAT ON MIKE	1.50	3.00
☐1054		FRIENDLY PERSUASION	2.00	4.00
☐1064		TUTTI FRUITTI	1.75	3.50
		PAT BOONE—ALBUMS		
☐3012 (M)	***DOT***	PAT ON MIKE	3.00	6.00
☐3030 (M)		HOWDY	2.50	5.00
☐3050 (M)		PAT	2.50	5.00
☐3071 (M)		PAT'S GREATEST HITS	3.00	6.00
		BOP-CHORDS		
☐2601	***HOLIDAY***	CASTLE IN THE SKY/MY DARLING, TO YOU	10.00	18.00
☐2603		WHEN I WOKE UP THIS MORNING/I REALLY LOVE HER	8.00	15.00
☐2608		BABY/SO WHY	7.00	12.00
		JIMMY BOWEN		
☐797	***TRIPLE D***	I'M STICKIN' WITH YOU/ PARTY DOLL (Buddy Knox)	30.00	50.00
☐4001	***ROULETTE***	I'M STICKIN' WITH YOU/EVER-LOVIN' FINGERS (14)	1.75	3.50
☐4010		WARM UP TO ME BABY/I TRUSTED YOU (57)	1.50	3.00
☐4017		DON'T TELL ME YOUR TROUBLES/ EVER SINCE THAT NIGHT	1.75	3.00
☐4023		CROSS OVER/IT'S SHAMEFUL	1.75	3.00
☐4083		BY THE LIGHT OF THE SILVERY MOON/ THE TWO-STEP (50)	1.25	2.50
☐4102		MY KIND OF WOMAN/BLUE MOON	1.50	2.50
☐4122		ALWAYS FAITHFUL/WISH I WERE TIED TO YOU	1.50	2.50
☐4175		YOU'RE JUST WASTING YOUR TIME/ WALKING ON AIR	1.50	2.50
☐4224		YOUR LOVING ARMS/OH YEAH, OH YEAH	1.50	2.50
		JIMMY BOWEN—EP		
☐302	***ROULETTE***	JIMMY BOWEN	6.00	10.00
		JIMMY BOWEN—ALBUM		
☐25004 (M)	***ROULETTE***	JIMMY BOWEN	15.00	25.00

ISSUE #	LABEL	ARTIST/TITLE	VG	MINT
		DAVID BOWIE		
☐5815	*WARNER BROTHERS*	CAN'T HELP THINKING ABOUT ME/ AND I SAY TO MYSELF	12.00	20.00
☐85009	*DERAM*	RUBBER BAND/THERE IS A HAPPY LAND	7.00	12.00
☐85016		LOVE YOU TILL TUESDAY/DID YOU HAVE A DREAM?	7.00	12.00
☐72949	*MERCURY*	SPACE ODDITY/WILD-EYED BOY FROM FREECLOUD	5.00	8.00
☐73075		MEMORY OF A FREE FESTIVAL (PT. 1)/(PT. 11)	6.00	10.00
☐0605	*RCA*	CHANGES/ANDY WARHOL (66)	1.50	2.50
☐0719		STARMAN/SUFFRAGETTE CITY (65)	1.50	2.50
☐0838		THE JEAN GENIE/HANG ON TO YOURSELF (71)	1.50	2.50
☐0876		SPACE ODDITY/THE MAN WHO SOLD THE WORLD (15)	1.00	2.00
		DAVID BOWIE—ALBUMS		
☐16003 (M)	*DERAM*	DAVID BOWIE	15.00	25.00
☐18003 (S)		DAVID BOWIE	18.00	30.00
☐61246 (M)	*MERCURY*	MAN OF WORDS, MAN OF MUSIC	12.00	20.00
☐61325 (M)		THE MAN WHO SOLD THE WORLD	8.00	15.00
		TOMMY BOYCE		
☐16117	*DOT*	GIVE ME THE CLUE/GYPSY SONG	2.00	3.50
☐7976	*RCA*	ALONG CAME LINDA/YOU LOOK SO LONELY	2.00	3.50
☐8025		COME HERE JO-ANN/THE WAY I USED TO	2.00	3.50
☐8074		I'LL REMEMBER CAROL/TOO LATE FOR TEARS (80)	1.75	3.00
☐8126		HAVE YOU HAD A CHANGE OF HEART/ SWEET LITTLE BABY	1.75	3.00
☐8208		DON'T BE AFRAID/A MILLION THINGS TO SAY	1.50	2.50
		BOYFRIENDS (5 DISCS)		
☐569	*KAPP*	LET'S FALL IN LOVE/OH LANA	8.00	15.00
		JAN BRADLEY		
☐1044	*FORMAL*	MAMA DIDN'T LIE/LOVERS LIKE ME	3.50	6.00
☐1845	*CHESS*	MAMA DIDN'T LIE/LOVERS LIKE ME (14)	1.00	2.00
		BREAKAWAYS		
☐10526	*LONDON*	THAT BOY OF MINE/HERE SHE COMES	2.50	4.00
☐323	*CAMEO*	HE DOESN'T LOVE ME/THAT'S HOW IT GOES	1.75	3.00
		BREAKERS		
☐1001	*VRANA*	KAMI-KAZE/SURF BREAKERS	1.75	3.00
☐14	*IMPACT*	SURFIN' TRAGEDY/SURF BIRD	1.75	3.00
		DONNIE BROOKS		
☐3004	*ERA*	LIL' SWEETHEART/IF YOU'RE LOOKIN'	1.50	2.50
☐3007		SWAY AND MOVE WITH THE BEAT/WHITE ORCHID	1.50	2.50
☐3014		THE DEVIL AIN'T A MAN/HOW LONG?	1.50	2.50
☐3018		MISSION BELL/DO IT FOR ME (7)	.75	2.00
☐3028		DOLL HOUSE/ROUND ROBIN (31)	1.00	2.00
☐3042		MEMPHIS/THAT'S WHY (90)	1.25	2.00
		LATER ERA SINGLES ARE WORTH UP TO $1.50 MINT		
		DONNIE BROOKS—ALBUM		
☐105 (M)	*ERA*	THE HAPPIEST	4.00	7.00
		RUTH BROWN		
☐986	*ATLANTIC*	MAMA, HE TREATS YOUR DAUGHTER MEAN R & B BLUES	3.00	5.00
☐1044		SOMEBODY TOUCHED ME/MAMBO BABY	2.50	4.00

ISSUE #	LABEL	ARTIST/TITLE	VG	MINT
☐1125		LUCKY LIPS/MY HEART IS BREAKING OVER YOU (26)	1.50	3.00
☐1197		THIS LITTLE GIRL'S GONE ROCKIN'/WHY ME (24)	1.50	3.00
		BRUCE AND JERRY		
		FEATURED: BRUCE JOHNSTON		
☐1003	*ARWIN*	I SAW HER FIRST/TAKE THIS PEARL	3.50	6.00
		BRUCE AND TERRY		
		FEATURED: BRUCE JOHNSTON, TERRY MELCHER		
☐42956	*COLUMBIA*	CUSTOM MACHINE/MAKAHA AT MIDNIGHT (85)	2.00	3.50
☐43055		SUMMER MEANS FUN/YEAH! (72)	1.75	3.00
☐43238		I LOVE YOU MODEL T/CARMEN	2.00	3.50
☐43378		FOUR STRONG WINDS/RAINING IN MY HEART	2.00	3.50
☐43479		COME LOVE/THANK YOU BABY	2.00	3.50
☐43582		DON'T RUN AWAY/IT'S ALRIGHT NOW	2.00	3.50
		BILLY BRYAN (GENE PITNEY)		
☐351	*BLAZE*	GOING BACK TO MY LOVE/CRADLE OF MY ARMS	2.50	4.00
		BUBBLE PUPPY		
☐128	*INTERNATIONAL ARTISTS*	HOT SMOKE AND SASSAFRASS/LONELY (14)	1.00	2.00
☐133		IF I HAD A REASON/BEGINNINGS	1.50	2.50
☐136		DAYS OF OUR TIME/THINKIN' ABOUT THINKIN'	1.75	3.00
☐138		WHAT DO YOU SEE/HURRY SUNDOWN	1.75	3.00
		BUBBLE PUPPY—ALBUM		
☐10 (M)	*INTER-NATIONAL ARTISTS*	A GATHERING OF PRMISES	7.00	12.00
		BUCHANAN AND GOODMAN		
☐101	*RADIOACTIVE*	THE FLYING SAUCER (PT. 1)/(PT. 11)	7.00	12.00
☐101	*LUNIVERSE*	THE FLYING SAUCER (PT. 1)/(PT. 11) (7)	2.50	5.00
☐102		BUCHANAN AND GOODMAN ON TRIAL/CRAZY (80)	4.00	7.00
☐103		THE BANANA BOAT STORY/THE MYSTERY	5.00	8.00
☐105		FLYING SAUCER THE 2ND/MARTIAN MELODY (19)	2.50	5.00
☐107		SANTA AND THE SATELLITE (PT. 1)/(PT. 11) (32)	2.50	5.00
☐108		THE FLYING SAUCER GOES WEST/ SAUCER SERENADE	5.00	8.00
☐500	*COMIC*	FLYING SAUCER THE 3RD/THE CHA CHA LESSON	5.00	8.00
☐301	*NOVELTY*	FRANKENSTEIN OF '59/FRANKENSTEIN RETURNS	3.50	6.00
		BUCHANAN AND GOODMAN—ALBUM		
☐716 (M)	*BUCHANAN AND GOODMAN*	THE FLYING SAUCER STORY, VOL. 1	15.00	25.00
		BUCKINGHAMS		
		SEE: CENTURIES, FALLING PEBBLES		
☐4618	*SPECTRA-SOUND*	SWEETS FOR MY SWEET/BEGINNER'S LOVE	3.50	6.00
☐844	*U.S.A.*	DON'T WANT TO CRY/I'LL GO CRAZY	2.00	3.50
☐848		I CALL YOU NAME/MAKIN' UP AND BREAKIN' UP	1.75	3.00
☐860		KIND OF A DRAG/YOU MAKE ME FEEL SO GOOD (1)	.75	2.00
☐869		LAWDY MISS CLAWDY/ MAKIN' UP AND BREAKIN' UP (41)	1.00	2.00
		BUCKINGHAMS—ALBUM		
☐107 (M)	*U.S.A.*	KIND OF A DRAG	4.00	7.00

ISSUE #	LABEL	ARTIST/TITLE	VG	MINT
		BUDDIES (TOKENS)		
☐102	*SWING*	ON THE GO/MY ONLY FRIEND	2.00	3.50
		BUDDY AND THE FADS		
☐1001	*MOROCCO*	WON'T YOU LOVE ME?/IS IT JUST A GAME?	7.00	12.00
		BUFFALO REBELS (ROCKIN' REBELS)		
☐0095	*MAR-LEE*	DONKEY WALK/BUFFALO BLUES	2.50	4.00
☐0096		THEME FROM REBEL/ANY WAY YOU WANT ME	2.50	4.00

BUFFALO SPRINGFIELD

A rock critic once called Buffalo Springfield "the group too good to stay together." The reason was some of its members—Neil Young, Stephen Stills, Jim Messina, Ritchie Furay.

The band formed in 1966 in Los Angeles. During a traffic jam at a record company parking lot, two folk singers—Stills and Furay—began talking with two Canadians—Neil Young and Bruce Palmer. The latter duo had motored from Canada in a hearse and were seeking studio work in southern California. Buffalo Springfield became the new group's name; it was taken from a certain tractor model made by the Caterpillar company.

Buffalo Springfield's first two singles failed to sell, although they did receive FM airplay. With their third single the band saw success, and Buffalo Springfield was on its way. The group was critically acclaimed but, following numerous drug busts and a diffusion of musical directions, the band broke up a year later. While together, though, Buffalo Springfield provided some of the best folk-rock music of the mid-1960s.

ISSUE #	LABEL	ARTIST/TITLE	VG	MINT
		BUFFALO SPRINGFIELD		
□6428	ATCO	NOWADAYS CLANCY CAN'T EVEN SING/ GO AND SAY GOODBYE	1.50	2.50
□6452		BURNED/EVERBODY'S WRONG	1.50	2.50
□6459		FOR WHAT IT'S WORTH/DO I HAVE TO COME RIGHT OUT AND SAY IT (7)	.75	2.00
□6499		BLUEBIRD/MR. SOUL (58)	1.00	2.00
□6519		ROCK 'N' ROLL WOMAN/ A CHILD'S CLAIM TO FAME (44)	1.00	2.00
□6545		EXPECTING TO FLY/EVERYDAYS (98)	1.25	2.00
□6572		UNO-MUNDO/MERRY-GO-ROUND	1.25	2.00
□6602		KIND WOMAN/SPECIAL CARE	1.25	2.00
□6615		ON THE WAY HOME/FOUR DAYS GONE	1.25	2.00
		DORSEY BURNETTE		
□188	ABBOTT	THE DEVIL'S QUEEN/LET'S FALL IN LOVE	2.50	4.00
□16	CEE JAM	BERTHA LOU/'TIL THE LAW SAYS STOP	2.50	4.00
□5561	IMPERIAL	TRY/YOU CAME AS A MIRACLE	1.75	3.00
□5597		LONELY TRAIN/MISERY	1.75	3.00
□5668		WAY IN THE MIDDLE OF THE NIGHT/YOUR LOVE	1.75	3.00
□5987		CIRCLE ROCK/HOUSE WITH A TIN ROOFTOP	1.75	3.00
□3012	ERA	TALL OAK TREE/JUAREZ TOWN (23)	1.00	2.50
□3019		HEY LITTLE ONE/BIG ROCK CANDY MOUNTAIN (48)	1.25	2.50
□3025		THE GHOST OF BILLY MALOO/RED ROSES	1.25	2.00
□3033		THE RIVER AND THE MOUNTAIN/THIS HOTEL	1.25	2.00
□3041		(IT'S NO) SIN/HARD ROCK MINE	1.25	2.00
□3045		GREAT SHAKIN' FEVER/THAT'S ME WITHOUT YOU	1.25	2.00
		DORSEY BURNETTE—ALBUM		
□102 (M)	ERA	TALL OAK TREE	5.00	8.00

JOHNNY BURNETTE

On August 1, 1964, newspapers around the nation carried a small news item that a rock-and-roll singer had died in a water-skiing accident in northern California. No headlines were made by the event, but the death of Johnny Burnette was of great sadness to those familiar with the foundations of early rockabilly music.

He was born in Memphis, Tennessee, on March 25, 1934. As a youngster Burnette took up boxing and was good enough to win the Golden Gloves award. Still, Johnny possessed an even greater interest—music. He finally succumbed to his desires and formed the Johnny Burnette Trio, which featured Johnny, his brother Dorsey and mutual friend Paul Burlison. They all worked during the day for the Crown Electric Company, which employed another Memphis local, Elvis Presley.

After winning on "Ted Mack's Amateur Hour" the trio signed with Coral Records. "The Train Kept A Rollin' " became a Memphis hit. But eventually the band broke up and Burnette went on his own. Johnny finally saw major success with his sixth single, "Dreamin' ". He then recorded two other smash hits for Liberty Records. Burnette's career declined, but he stayed involved in the music business until his untimely death at age thirty.

ISSUE #	LABEL	ARTIST/TITLE	VG	MINT
		JOHNNY BURNETTE		
□ 44001	*FREEDOM*	I'M RESTLESS/KISS ME	3.50	6.00
□ 44011		GUMBO/ME AND THE BEAR	3.50	6.00
□ 44017		SWEET BABY DOLL/I'LL NEVER LOVE AGAIN	3.50	6.00
□ 55222	*LIBERTY*	SETTIN' THE WOODS ON FIRE/KENTUCKY WALTZ	1.75	3.00
□ 55243		DON'T DO IT/PATRICK HENRY	1.75	3.00
□ 55258		DREAMIN'/CINCINNATI FIREBALL (11)	1.00	2.50
□ 55285		YOU'RE SIXTEEN/I BEG YOUR PARDON (8)	1.00	2.50
□ 55298		LITTLE BOY SAD/I GO DOWN TO THE RIVER (17)	1.00	2.50
□ 55318		BIG BIG WORLD/BALLAD OF THE ONE-EYED JACKS (58)	1.25	2.50
□ 55345		GIRLS/I'VE GOT A LOT OF THINGS TO DO	1.50	2.50
□ 55379		GOD, COUNTRY AND MY BABY/HONESTLY I DO (18)	1.00	2.50
□ 55416		WHY AM I/CLOWN SHOES	1.50	2.50
□ 55448		THE FOOL OF THE YEAR/POOREST BOY IN TOWN	1.50	2.50
□ 55489		DAMN THE DEFIANT/LONESOME WATERS	1.50	2.50
		JOHNNY BURNETTE—EPs		
□ 1004	*LIBERTY*	DREAMIN'	6.00	10.00
□ 1011		JOHNNY BURNETTE HITS	5.00	8.00
		JOHNNY BURNETTE—ALBUMS		
□ 3179 (M)	*LIBERTY*	DREAMIN'	8.00	15.00
□ 7179 (S)		DREAMIN'	12.00	20.00
□ 3183 (M)		JOHNNY BURNETTE	7.00	12.00
□ 7183 (S)		JOHNNY BURNETTE	8.00	15.00
□ 3190 (M)		JOHNNY BURNETTE SINGS	7.00	12.00
□ 7190 (S)		JOHNNY BURNETTE SINGS	8.00	15.00
□ 3206 (M)		HITS AND OTHER FAVORITES	6.00	10.00
□ 7206 (S)		HITS AND OTHER FAVORITES	7.00	12.00
		JOHNNY BURNETTE TRIO		
□ 61651	*CORAL*	TEAR IT UP/YOU'RE UNDECIDED	12.00	20.00
□ 61675		MIDNIGHT TRAIN/OH BABY BABE	8.00	15.00
□ 61719		THE TRAIN KEPT A ROLLIN'/HONEY HUSH	10.00	18.00
□ 61758		LONESOME TRAIN/I JUST FOUND OUT	8.00	15.00
□ 61829		EAGER BEAVER BABY/IF YOU WANT IT ENOUGH	8.00	15.00
□ 61918		DRINKIN' WINE SPO-DEE-O-DEE/ROCK BILLY BOOGIE	8.00	15.00
		JOHNNY BURNETTE TRIO—ALBUM		
□ 57080 (M)	*CORAL*	JOHNNY BURNETTE AND THE ROCK 'N ROLL TRIO	60.00	100.00
		JERRY BUTLER		
		SEE: IMPRESSIONS		
□ 1024	*ABNER*	ONE BY ONE/LOST	1.75	3.00
□ 1028		HOLD ME MY DARLING/RAINBOW VALLEY	1.75	3.00
□ 1030		I WAS WRONG/COULDN'T GO TO SLEEP	1.75	3.00
□ 1035		A LONELY SOLDIER/I FOUND A LOVE	1.75	3.00
□ 354	*VEE JAY*	HE WILL BREAK YOUR HEART/THANKS TO YOU (7)	1.00	2.50
□ 371		O HOLY NIGHT/SILENT NIGHT	1.75	3.00
□ 375		FIND ANOTHER GIRL/WHEN TROUBLE CALLS (27)	1.00	2.00
□ 390		I'M A TELLING YOU/I SEE A FOOL (25)	1.00	2.00
□ 396		FOR YOUR PRECIOUS LOVE/SWEET WAS THE WINE	1.25	2.00
□ 405		MOON RIVER/AWARE OF LOVE (11)	.75	2.00

LATER VEE JAY SINGLES ARE WORTH UP TO $1.50 MINT

ISSUE #	LABEL	ARTIST/TITLE	VG	MINT

JERRY BUTLER—ALBUMS

ISSUE #	LABEL	ARTIST/TITLE	VG	MINT
☐ 2001 (M)	ABNER	JERRY BUTLER, ESQUIRE	7.00	12.00
☐ 1027 (M)	VEE JAY	JERRY BUTLER, ESQUIRE	6.00	10.00
☐ 1029 (M)		HE WILL BREAK YOUR HEART	5.00	8.00

EDWARD "KOOKIE" BYRNES

☐ 5047	WARNER BROTHERS	KOOKIE, KOOKIE (LEND ME YOUR COMB)/ YOU'RE THE TOP (4)	1.00	2.00
☐ 5087		LIKE I LOVE YOU/KOOKIE'S MAD PAD (42)	1.25	2.00
☐ 5114		KOOKIE'S LOVE SONG (PT. 1)/(PT. 11)	1.25	2.00
☐ 5121		YULESVILLE/LONELY CHRISTMAS	1.25	2.00

EDWARD "KOOKIE" BYRNES—EP

☐ 1309	WARNER BROTHERS	EDD "KOOKIE" BYRNES	2.50	4.00
☐ 1309 (M)	WARNER BROTHERS	KOOKIE	5.00	9.00
☐ 1309 (S)		KOOKIE	7.00	12.00

CADETS (FLARES)

☐ 985	MODERN	CHURCH BELLS MAY RING/HEARTBREAK HOTEL	3.50	6.00
☐ 996		STRANDED IN THE JUNGLE/I WANT YOU (18)	2.00	4.00

CADILLACS

☐ 765	JOSIE	GLORIA/I WONDER WHY	35.00	65.00
☐ 785		SPEEDOO/LET ME EXPLAIN (30)	3.50	6.00
☐ 792		ZOOM/YOU ARE	4.00	7.00
☐ 846		PEEK-A-BOO/ OH OH LOLITA (28)	1.50	3.00

CAESAR AND CLEO (SONNY AND CHER)

☐ 916	VAULT	THE LETTER/SPRING FEVER	1.75	3.00
☐ 0308	REPRISE	LOVE IS STRANGE/DO YOU WANT TO DANCE?	2.00	3.50
☐ 0419		LOVE IS STRANGE/LET THE GOOD TIMES ROLL	2.00	3.50

CALIFORNIA MUSIC
FEATURED: BRIAN WILSON, BRUCE JOHNSTON, TERRY MELCHER

☐ 10120	EQUINOX	DON'T WORRY BABY/TEN YEARS HARMONY	2.50	4.00
☐ 10363		DON'T WORRY BABY/WHY DO FOOLS FALL IN LOVE	2.00	3.50
☐ 10572		CALIFORNIA MUSIC/JAMAICA FAREWELL	1.75	3.00

CAMEOS

☐ 123	CAMEO	MERRY CHRISTMAS/NEW YEAR'S EVE	12.00	20.00
☐ 504	DEAN	WAIT UP/LOST LOVER	12.00	20.00

CAMERONS

☐ 1003	COUSINS	GUARDIAN ANGEL/THE GIRL I MARRY	8.00	15.00

GLEN CAMPBELL

☐ 1324	CENECO	DREAMS FOR SALE/I'VE GOT TO WIN	3.00	5.00
☐ 1087	CREST	TURN AROUND, LOOK AT ME/BRENDA (62)	2.00	3.50
☐ 1096		MIRACLE OF LOVE/ONCE MORE	2.50	4.00

ISSUE #	LABEL	ARTIST/TITLE	VG	MINT
□5360	**CAPITOL**	TOMORROW NEVER COMES/WOMAN'S WORLD	1.50	2.50
□5441		GUESS I'M DUMB/THAT'S ALL RIGHT	8.00	15.00
(BRIAN WILSON PRODUCTION ON CAPITOL 5441)				
		JO-ANN CAMPBELL		
□504	**ELDORADO**	COME ON BABY/FOREVER YOUNG	3.00	5.00
□509		FUNNY THING/I CAN'T GIVE YOU ANYTHING BUT LOVE	3.00	5.00
□4	**POINT**	WHEREVER YOU GO/I'M COMING HOME LATE TONIGHT	2.50	4.00
□5014	**GONE**	WAIT A MINUTE/I'M IN LOVE WITH YOU	2.50	4.00
□5021		ROCK AND ROLL LOVE/YOU'RE DRIVING ME MAD	2.50	4.00
□5027		WASSA MATTER WITH YOU?/YOU-OO	2.50	4.00
□5037		I'M NOBODY'S BABY NOW/ I REALLY REALLY LOVE YOU	2.50	4.00
□5049		TALL BOY/HAPPY NEW YEAR BABY	2.50	4.00
□5055		MAMA (CAN I GO OUT TONITE)/NERVOUS	2.50	4.00
□5068		I AIN'T GOT NO STEADY DATE/BEACHCOMBER	2.50	4.00
□10134	**ABC-PARAMOUNT**	A KOOKIE LITTLE PARADISE/ BOBBY BOBBY BOBBY (61)	1.75	3.00
□10172		CRAZY DAISY/BUT MAYBE THIS YEAR	1.50	2.50
□10200		MOTORCYCLE MICHAEL/PUKA PUKA PANTS	1.50	2.50
□10224		EDDIE MY LOVE/IT WASN'T RIGHT	1.50	2.50
□10258		MAMA DON'T WANT/DUANE	1.50	2.50
□10300		YOU MADE ME LOVE YOU/I CHANGED MY MIND	1.50	2.50
□10335		I WISH IT WOULD RAIN ALL SUMMER/ AMATEUR NIGHT	1.50	2.50
□223	**CAMEO**	(I'M THE GIRL ON) WOLVERTON MOUNTAIN/ SLOPPY JOE (38)	1.00	2.00
□237		MR. FIX-IT MAN/LET ME DO IT MY WAY	1.50	2.50
□249		MOTHER, PLEASE/WAITIN' FOR LOVE	1.50	2.50
		JO-ANN CAMPBELL—ALBUMS		
□393 (M)	**ABC-PARAMOUNT**	TWISTIN' AND LISTENIN'	8.00	15.00
□306	**END**	I'M NOBODY'S BABY	7.00	12.00
□1206 (M)	**CAMEO**	ALL THE HITS BY JO-ANN CAMPBELL	6.00	10.00

FREDDY CANNON

Freddy Cannon (real name Picariello) was born on December 4, 1940, in Revere, Massachusetts, and attended school in nearby Lynn. During that time Freddy was invited to play with a singing group of pals who called themselves the G-Clefs. Their 1956 single of "Ka-Ding Dong" featured Freddy Cannon—at fifteen—on guitar. After high school graduation Cannon drifted from job to job, toiling at being a soda jerk, truck driver and car-wash laborer.

He later formed his own group and began playing around Boston. A local disc jockey liked Cannon's aggressive style, especially on a song called "Tallahassee Lassie" (co-written by Freddy's mother). A tape was sent to Philadelphia's Swan Records and the production team of Slay and Crewe sent for Cannon at once.

"Tallahassee Lassie" was recorded 57 times before it was thought to be good enough for commercial release. But the effort paid off; the song clicked at the No. 6 chart spot. Dick Clark then summoned Freddy to "American Bandstand." Cannon was so broke at the time that he had to borrow five dollars to buy a Hawaiian shirt for his first TV appearance.

Today he lives in Tarzana, California, and is in constant demand at many oldies concerts.

ISSUE #	LABEL	ARTIST/TITLE	VG	MINT
		FREDDY CANNON		
☐ 4031	**SWAN**	TALLAHASSEE LASSIE/YOU KNOW (6)	1.25	3.00
☐ 4038		OKEFENOKEE/KOOKIE HAT (43)	1.50	3.50
☐ 4043		WAY DOWN YONDER IN NEW ORLEANS/ FRACTURED (3)	1.25	3.00
☐ 4050		CHATTANOOGA SHOE SHINE BOY/BOSTON (34)	1.00	2.50
☐ 4053		THE URGE/JUMP OVER (28)	1.00	2.50
☐ 4057		HAPPY SHADES OF BLUE/ CUERNAVACA CHOO CHOO (83)	1.25	2.50
☐ 4061		HUMDINGER/MY BLUE HEAVEN (59)	1.25	2.50
☐ 4066		MUSKRAT RAMBLE/TWO THOUSAND-88 (54)	1.25	2.50
☐ 4071		BUZZ BUZZ A DIDDLE-IT/OPPORTUNITY (51)	1.25	2.50
☐ 4078		TRANSISTOR SISTER/WALK ON THE MOON (35)	1.00	2.50
☐ 4083		FOR ME AND MY GAL/BLUE PLATE SPECIAL (71)	1.25	2.00
☐ 4096		TEEN QUEEN OF THE WEEK/WILD GUY (92)	1.25	2.00
☐ 4106		PALISADES PARK/JUNE, JULY AND AUGUST (3)	1.00	2.00
☐ 4117		WHAT'S GONNA HAPPEN WHEN SUMMER'S OVER/ BROADWAY (45)	1.25	2.00
☐ 4122		IF YOU WERE A ROCK AND ROLL RECORD/ THE TRUTH, RUTH (67)	1.25	2.00
☐ 4132		FOUR LETTER MAN/COME ON AND LOVE ME	1.25	2.00
☐ 4139		PATTY BABY/BETTY JEAN (65)	1.25	2.00
☐ 4149		EVERYBODY MONKEY/OH GLORIA (52)	1.25	2.00
☐ 4155		DO WHAT THE HIPPIES DO/THAT'S THE WAY THE GIRLS ARE	1.25	2.00
☐ 4168		SWEET GEORGIA BROWN/WHAT A PARTY	1.25	2.00
☐ 4178		THE UPS AND DOWNS OF LOVE/IT'S BEEN NICE	1.25	2.00
☐ 5409	**WARNER BROTHERS**	ABIGAIL BEECHER/ALL AMERICAN GIRL (16)	1.00	2.00
☐ 5434		OK WHEELER THE USED CAR DEALER/ODIE COLOGNE	1.25	2.00
☐ 5448		SUMMERTIME U.S.A./GOTTA GOOD THING GOIN'	1.25	2.00
☐ 5487		TOO MUCH MONKEY BUSINESS/ LITTLE AUTOGRAPH SEEKER	1.50	2.50
☐ 5615		LITTLE MISS A-GO-GO/IN THE NIGHT	1.25	2.00
☐ 5645		ACTION/BEACHWOOD CITY (13)	1.00	2.50
☐ 5666		LET ME SHOW YOU WHERE IT'S AT/THE OLD RAG MAN	1.25	2.00
☐ 5673		SHE'S SOMETHIN' ELSE/LITTLE BITTY CORRINE	1.25	2.00
☐ 5693		THE DEDICATION SONE/COME ON, COME ON (41)	1.00	2.00
☐ 5810		THE GREATEST SHOW ON EARTH/HOKIE POKE GAL	1.25	2.00
☐ 5832		NATALIE/THE LAUGHING SONG	1.25	2.00
☐ 5859		RUN FOR THE SUN/USE YOU IMAGINATION	1.25	2.00
☐ 5876		IN MY WILDEST DREAM/A HAPPY CLOWN	1.25	2.00
☐ 7019		MAVERICK'S FLATS/RUN TO THE POET MAN	1.25	2.00
☐ 7075		20TH CENTURY FOX/CINCINNATI WOMAN	1.50	2.50
		FREDDY CANNON—ALBUMS		
☐ 502 (M)	**SWAN**	THE EXPLOSIVE FREDDY CANNON	12.00	20.00
☐ 504 (M)		HAPPY SHADES OF BLUE	8.00	15.00
☐ 505 (M)		SOLID GOLD HITS	8.00	15.00
☐ 507 (M)		PALISADES PARK	7.00	12.00
☐ 511 (M)		FREDDY CANNON STEPS OUT	7.00	12.00
☐ 511 (S)		FREDDY CANNON STEPS OUT	8.00	15.00
☐ 1544 (S)	**WARNER BROTHERS**	FREDDY CANNON	6.00	10.00
☐ 1612 (S)		ACTION	6.00	10.00
☐ 1628 (S)		GREATEST HITS	4.50	8.00

ISSUE #	LABEL	ARTIST/TITLE	VG	MINT
		JERRY CAPEHART		
		GUITAR: EDDIE COCHRAN		
☐1021	*CASH*	WALKIN' STICK BOOGIE/ROLLIN'	4.00	7.00
☐1101	*CREST*	SONG OF NEW ORLEANS/THE YOUNG AND BLUE	3.00	5.00
		CAPITOLS		
☐721	*GATEWAY*	DAY BY DAY/LITTLE THINGS	18.00	30.00
☐807	*PET*	ANGEL OF LOVE/'CAUSE I LOVE YOU	12.00	20.00
☐3002	*CINDY*	ROSEMARY/MILLIE	12.00	20.00
		CAPRIS		
☐1010	*PLANET*	THERE'S A MOON OUT TONIGHT/INDIAN GIRL	30.00	50.00
☐101	*TROMMERS*	THERE'S A MOON OUT TONIGHT/INDIAN GIRL	2.50	4.00
☐101	*LOST NIGHT*	THERE'S A MOON OUT TONIGHT/INDIAN GIRL (pink label)	7.00	12.00
☐1094	*OLD TOWN*	THERE'S A MOON OUT TONIGHT/INDIAN GIRL (3)	1.50	3.00
☐1099		WHERE I FELL IN LOVE/SOME PEOPLE THINK (74)	2.50	4.00
☐1103		TEARS IN MY EYES/WHY DO I CRY	3.00	5.00
☐1107		GIRL IN MY DREAMS/MY ISLAND IN THE SUN (92)	2.50	4.00
☐118	*MR. PEEKE*	LIMBO/FROM THE VINE CAME THE GRAPE (99)	2.50	4.00
		CAROUSELS		
☐5118	*GONE*	IF YOU WANT TO YOU CAN COME/ PRETTY LITTLE THING	3.00	5.00
☐5131		NEVER LET HIM GO/DIRTY TRICKS	2.50	4.00
		VIKKI CARR		
☐55493	*LIBERTY*	HE'S A REBEL/BE MY LOVE	1.75	3.00
		RIC CARTY		
☐6751	*RCA*	YOUNG LOVE/OOOH-EEE	3.00	5.00
		ORIGINAL VERSION OF TAB HUNTER HIT		
		CASCADES		
☐6021	*VALIANT*	SECOND CHANCE/THERE'S A REASON	1.75	3.00
☐6026		RHYTHM OF THE RAIN/LET ME BE (3)	1.00	2.50
☐6028		THE LAST LEAF/SHY GIRL (60)	1.25	2.00
☐6032		MY FIRST DAY ALONE/I WANNA BE YOUR LOVER	1.25	2.00
☐8206	*RCA*	A LITTLE LIKE LOVIN'/CINDERELLA	1.50	2.50
☐8268		FOR YOUR SWEET LOVE/JEANNIE (86)	1.25	2.00
☐8321		LITTLE BITTY FALLING STAR/ THOSE WERE THE GOOD OLD DAYS	1.25	2.00
☐132	*ARWIN*	CHERYL'S GOIN' HOME/TRULY JULIE'S BLUES	1.50	2.50
☐134		ALL'S FAIR IN LOVE AND WAR/MIDNIGHT LACE	1.50	2.50
☐2083	*SMASH*	HEY LITTLE GIRL OF MINE/BLUE HOURS	1.25	2.00
☐2101		FLYING ON THE GROUND/MAIN STREET	1.50	2.50
☐55152	*UNI*	MAYBE THE RAIN WILL FALL/NAGGIN' CRIES (61)	1.25	2.00
☐55169		BIG CITY COUNTRY BOY/INDIAN RIVER	1.25	2.00
☐55200		BUT FOR LOVE/HAZEL AUTUMN COCOA BROWN	1.25	2.00
☐55231		APRIL, MAY, JUNE AND JULY/BIG UGLY SKY	1.25	2.00
		CASCADES—ALBUMS		
☐405 (M)	*VALIANT*	RHYTHM OF THE RAIN	6.00	10.00
☐273069 (S)	*UNI*	MAYBE THE RAIN WILL FALL	5.00	8.00
		AL CASEY		
☐1004	*MCI*	PINK PANTHER/IF I TOLD YOU	2.50	4.00
☐1004	*HIGHLAND*	STINGER/NIGHT BEAT	2.50	4.00
☐158	*UNITED ARTISTS*	STINGER/KEEP TALKING	1.75	3.00
		SINGLES ON STACY ARE WORTH UP TO $2.00 MINT		

JOHNNY CASH

Johnny Cash is a true country-music legend of this century. He first saw life on February 26, 1932, in Kingsland, Arkansas. Johnny picked cotton on his parents' farm and wrote songs and poems. During high school he sang on a local radio station. He later graduated and joined the air force.

Following his military obligation, Cash went to work door-to-door in Memphis as an appliance salesman. Cash said he often greeted people with, "You don't want to buy anything, do you?" He also attended a disc-jockey training school. In the meantime Johnny formed a backup team, the Tennessee Two, with Luther Perkins (Carl's brother) and Marshall Grant. After two rejections Sam Phillips signed Cash and his duo to Sun Records. Johnny Cash soon became a local favorite. In 1955 he toured the South with a hot young local named Elvis Presley, then also a Sun artist.

Cash's first major hit was "I Walk the Line" and it has been smooth sailing ever since for Johnny in terms of recording success. Drug problems plagued him during the early 1960s, though. He was salvaged in part by his present wife, June Carter Cash, who encouraged Johnny to enroll at a health clinic.

Today the Cash family lives in a $2,000,000 mansion overlooking a lake near Nashville.

ISSUE #	LABEL	ARTIST/TITLE	VG	MINT
		JOHNNY CASH		
		SEE: SUN DISCOGRAPHY		
		JOHNNY CASH—EPs		
□111	***SUN***	JOHNNY CASH SINGS HANK WILLIAMS	4.00	7.50
□112		JOHNNY CASH	4.00	7.50
□113		JOHNNY CASH	4.00	7.50
□114		JOHNNY CASH: HIS TOP HITS	4.00	7.50
□116		JOHNNY CASH	4.00	7.50
□117		JOHNNY CASH	4.00	7.50
		JOHNNY CASH—ALBUMS		
□1220	***SUN***	JOHNNY CASH WITH HIS HOT AND BLUE GUITAR	6.00	10.00
□1235		JOHNNY CASH SINGS THE SONGS THAT MADE HIM FAMOUS	6.00	10.00
□1240		JOHNNY CASH - GREATEST	6.00	10.00
□1245		JOHNNY CASH SINGS HANK WILLIAMS	6.00	10.00
□1255		NOW HERE'S JOHNNY CASH	6.00	10.00
□1270		ALL ABOARD THE BLUE TRAIN	6.00	10.00
□1275		THE ORIGINAL SUN SOUND OF JOHNNY CASH	6.00	10.00
		CASHMERES		
□3078	***LAURIE***	A VERY SPECIAL BIRTHDAY/I BELIEVE IN ST. NICK	6.00	10.00
		CASTALEERS		
□44	***PLANET***	THAT'S WHY I CRY/MY BABY'S ALL RIGHT	3.50	6.50
□1349	***DONNA***	THAT'S WHY I CRY/MY BABY'S ALL RIGHT	2.00	3.50
		CASTELLS		
□3038	***ERA***	LITTLE SAD EYES/ROMEO	1.75	3.00
□3048		SACRED/I GET DREAMY (20)	1.00	2.50
□3057		MAKE BELIEVE WEDDING/MY MIRACLE (98)	1.25	2.50
□3064		THE VISION OF YOU/STIKI DE BOOM BOOM	1.50	2.50
□3073		SO THIS IS LOVE/ON THE STREET OF TEARS (21)	1.00	2.50
□3083		OH! WHAT IT SEEMED TO BE/ STAND THERE MOUNTAIN (91)	1.25	2.50
□3089		ECHOES IN THE NIGHT/ONLY ONE	1.25	2.00
□3098		ETERNAL LOVE, ETERNAL SPRING/CLOWN PRINCE	1.25	2.00
□3102		INITIALS/LITTLE SAD EYES	1.25	2.00
□3107		SOME ENCHANTED EVENING/ WHAT DO LITTLE GIRLS DREAM OF?	1.25	2.00
□5421	***WARNER BROTHERS***	I DO/TEARDROPS	4.50	8.00
		(BRIAN WILSON PRODUCTION ON WARNER BROTHERS 5421)		
□5445		COULD THIS BE YOU/SHINNY UP YOUR OWN SIDE	1.25	2.00
□5486		LOVE FINDS A WAY/TELL HER IF I COULD	1.25	2.00
		CASTELLS—ALBUM		
□109 (M)	***ERA***	SO THIS IS LOVE	6.00	10.00
□109 (S)		SO THIS IS LOVE	8.00	15.00
		VINCE CASTRO		
□102	***DOE***	YOU'RE MY GIRL/BONG BONG	4.50	8.00
□25007	***APT***	YOU'RE MY GIRL/BONGO TWIST	2.50	4.00
		CASUALS (ORIGINAL CASUALS)		
□503	***BACK BEAT***	SO TOUGH/MY DARLING (42)	2.00	3.50
□15557		MY LOVE SONG FOR YOU/SOMEBODY HELP ME	1.75	3.00
□15671		TILL YOU COME BACK TO ME/HELLO LOVE	1.75	3.00

ISSUE #	LABEL	ARTIST/TITLE	VG	MINT
		CASUALS (ORIGINAL CASUALS)—EP		
☐ 40	*BACK BEAT*	THE ORIGINAL CASUALS	4.50	8.00
		CENTURIES (BUCKINGHAMS)		
☐ 641	*SPECTRA-SOUND*	IT'S ALRIGHT/I LOVE YOU NO MORE	3.50	6.00
		CHALLENGERS		
☐ 900	*VAULT*	TORQUAY/BULLDOG	1.75	3.00
☐ 902		MOONDOG/TIDAL WAVE	1.75	3.00
☐ 904		FOOT TAPPER/ON THE MOVE	1.75	3.00
☐ 910		HOT ROD HOOTENANNY/MAYBELLENE	1.75	3.00
☐ 913		HOT ROD SHOW (PT. 1)/HOT ROD SHOW (PT. 11)	1.75	3.00
☐ 918		CHANNEL NINE/CAN'T SEEM TO GET OVER YOU	1.75	3.00
☐ 53	*PRINCESS*	MR. MOTO '65/CHIEFLADO	1.75	3.00
☐ 376	*GNP-CRESCENDO*	WIPEOUT/NORTH BEACH	1.75	2.50
☐ 400		COLOR ME IN/BEFORE YOU	1.50	2.50
		CHALLENGERS—ALBUMS		
☐ 101 (M)	*VAULT*	SURFBEAT	4.00	7.00
☐ 101-A (M)		SURFING WITH THE CHALLENGERS	4.50	8.00
☐ 102 (M)		THE CHALLENGERS ON THE MOVE	4.00	7.00
☐ 107 (M)		K-39	4.00	7.00
☐ 109 (M)		SURF'S UP	3.50	6.00
☐ 110 (M)		THE CHALLENGERS A-GO GO	3.50	6.00
☐ 2010 (M)	*GNP-CRESCENDO*	THE CHALLENGERS AT THE TEENAGE FAIR	3.50	6.00
☐ 2018 (M)		THE MAN FROM U.N.C.L.E.	3.50	6.00
☐ 2025 (M)		CALIFORNIA KICKS	3.50	6.00
☐ 2031 (M)		WIPEOUT	4.00	7.00
☐ 2045 (M)		LIGHT MY FIRE	3.50	6.00
☐ 2056 (M)		VANILLA FUNK	3.50	6.00
☐ 100 (M)	*TRIUMPH*	THE CHALLENGERS GO SIDEWALK SURFING	8.00	15.00
		CHAMPS		
☐ 1016	*CHALLENGE*	TEQUILLA/TRAIN TO NOWHERE (1)	1.25	3.00
☐ 59007		EL RANCHO ROCK/MIDNIGHTER (30)	1.00	2.50
☐ 59018		CHARIOT ROCK/SUBWAY (59)	1.25	2.00
☐ 59026		ROCKIN' MARY/TURNPIKE	1.25	2.00
☐ 59035		GONE TRAIN/BEATNIK	1.25	2.00
☐ 59043		CARAMBA!/MOONLIGHT BAY	1.25	2.00
☐ 59049		NIGHT TRAIN/THE RATTLER	1.25	2.00
☐ 59053		DOUBLE EAGLE ROCK/SKY HIGH	1.25	2.00
☐ 59063		TOO MUCH TEQUILA/ TWENTY THOUSAND LEAGUES (30)	1.00	2.00
		LATER CHALLENGE SINGLES WORTH UP TO $1.50 MINT		
		CHAMPS—EPs		
☐ 7100	*CHALLENGE*	TEQUILA	4.50	8.00
☐ 7101		CARANBA!	4.00	7.00
		CHAMPS—ALBUMS		
☐ 601 (M)	*CHALLENGE*	GO CHAMPS GO	7.00	12.00
☐ 605 (M)		EVERYBODY'S ROCKIN' WITH THE CHAMPS	5.00	9.00
☐ 605 (S)		EVERYBODY'S ROCKIN' WITH THE CHAMPS	7.00	12.00
☐ 613 (M)		GREAT DANCE HITS	4.00	7.00
☐ 613 (S)		GREAT DANCE HITS	6.00	10.00

ISSUE #	LABEL	ARTIST/TITLE	VG	MINT
□614 (M)		ALL AMERICAN MUSIC FROM THE CHAMPS	4.00	7.00
□614 (S)		ALL AMERICAN MUSIC FROM THE CHAMPS	6.00	10.00
		CHANDELIERS		
□521	*ANGEL TONE*	ONE MORE STEP/BLUEBERRY SWEET	5.00	9.00
		BRUCE CHANNEL		
□601	*TEEN AGER*	RUN ROMANCE RUN/DON'T LEAVE ME	3.00	5.00
□1035	*MANCO*	RUN ROMANCE RUN/DON'T LEAVE ME	2.50	4.50
□953	*LE CAM*	HEY! BABY/DREAM GIRL	5.00	8.00
□122		GOING BACK TO LOUISIANA/FORGET ME NOT (89)	1.25	2.00
□125		BLUE MONDAY/MY BABY	1.25	2.00
□1731	*SMASH*	HEY! BABY/DREAM GIRL (1)	.75	2.00
□1752		NUMBER ONE MAN/IF ONLY I HAD KNOWN (52)	1.00	2.00
□1769		COME ON BABY/MINE EXCLUSIVELY (98)	1.00	2.00
□1780		SOMEWHERE IN THIS TOWN/STAND TOUGH	1.25	2.00
□1792		LET'S HURT TOGETHER/OH BABY	1.25	2.00
□1826		NIGHT PEOPLE/NO OTHER BABY	1.25	2.00
□1838		SEND HER HOME/DIPSY DOODLE	1.25	2.00
		BRUCE CHANNEL—ALBUM		
□27008 (M)	*SMASH*	HEY! BABY	3.50	6.00
□67008 (S)		HEY! BABY	5.00	9.00
		CHANTAYS		
□104	*DOWNEY*	PIPELINE/MOVE IT	2.50	4.00
□108		MONSOON/SCOTCH HIGH'S	2.00	3.50
□116		SPACE PROBE/CONTINENTAL MISSLE	2.00	3.50
□120		BEYOND/I'LL BE BACK SOMEDAY	2.00	3.50
□16440	*DOT*	PIPELINE/MOVE IT (4)	.75	2.00
□16492		MONSOON/SCOTCH HIGH'S	1.25	2.00
		CHANTAYS—ALBUMS		
□1002 (M)	*DOWNEY*	PIPELINE	30.00	50.00
□1002 (S)		PIPELINE	40.00	70.00
□3516 (M)	*DOT*	PIPELINE	7.00	12.00
□25516 (S)		PIPELINE	8.00	15.00
□3771 (M)		TWO SIDES OF THE CHANTAYS	4.50	8.00
□25771 (S)		TWO SIDES OF THE CHANTAYS	6.00	10.00
		CHANTELS		
□1001	*END*	HE'S GONE/THE PLEA (71)	2.50	4.00
□1005		MAYBE/COME MY LITTLE BABY (15)	2.00	3.50
□1015		EVERY NIGHT (I PRAY)/WHOEVER YOU ARE (40)	1.75	3.00
□1020		I LOVE YOU SO/HOW COULD YOU CALL IT OFF (42)	1.75	3.00
□1026		SURE OF LOVE/PRAYE	1.50	2.50
□1030		CONGRATULATIONS/IF YOU TRY	1.50	2.50
□1037		I CAN'T TAKE IT/NEVER LET YOU GO	1.50	2.50
□1048		GOODBYE TO LOVE/I'M CONFESSIN'	1.50	2.50
□555	*CARLTON*	LOOK IN MY EYES/GLAD TO BE BACK (14)	1.50	3.50
□564		WELL I TOLD YOU/I STILL (29)	1.75	3.00
□569		HERE IT COMES AGAIN/SUMMERTIME	1.50	2.50
		CHAPERONES		
□880	*JOSIE*	DANCE WITH ME/CRUISE TO THE MOON	3.50	6.00
□885		SHINING STAR/MY SHADOW AND ME	3.00	5.00
□891		THE MAN FROM THE MOON/BLUEBERRY SWEET	3.00	5.00

ISSUE #	LABEL	ARTIST/TITLE	VG	MINT
		PAUL CHAPLAIN		
☐ 100	***HARPER***	SHORTNIN' BREAD/NICOTINE (82)	1.75	3.00
		RAY CHARLES		
☐ 1050	***ATLANTIC***	I'VE GOT A WOMAN/COME BACK	3.00	5.00
☐ 1063		THIS LITTLE GIRL OF MINE/A FOOL FOR YOU	3.00	5.00
☐ 1076		GREENBACKS/BLACKJACK	2.50	4.00
☐ 1085		DROWN IN MY OWN TEARS/MARY ANN	1.75	3.50
☐ 1096		HALLELUJAH, I LOVE HER SO/ WHAT WOULD I DO WITHOUT YOU	1.75	3.50
☐ 1154		SWANEE RIVER ROCK/I WANT A LITTLE GIRL (42)	1.50	3.00
☐ 2006		ROCKHOUSE (PT. 1)/(PT. 11) (79)	1.75	3.50
☐ 2010		THE RIGHT TIME/TELL ALL THE WORLD ABOUT YOU (95)	1.50	3.00
☐ 2031		WHAT'D I SAY (PT. 1)/(PT. 11) (6)	1.00	2.50
		ALLEN CHASE		
☐ 41538	***COLUMBIA***	FAME AND FORTUNE/ALL I WANT IS YOU	2.50	4.00
☐ 108	***CINEMA***	I'M IN LOVE WITH MISS CONNIE FRANCIS/ LONELY HEART	2.00	3.50
		CHATEAUS		
☐ 5023	***WARNER BROTHERS***	BROWN EYES/SATISFIED	3.50	6.00
☐ 5043		THE MASQUERADE IS OVER/IF I DIDN'T CARE	4.50	8.00
☐ 5071		THE LADDER OF LOVE/YOU'LL REAP WHAT YOU SOW	3.00	5.00

CHUBBY CHECKER

During the 1950s he was known to his friends as Ernest Evans. He was a young (born October 3, 1941) unknown then, undistinguished from many other South Philadelphia kids. Ernie worked after school plucking chickens at a local market. To while away the time, Evans amused himself by loudly belting out the latest rock-and-roll hits. The market's owner was a friend of Kal Mann, who worked at nearby Parkway Records. Mann liked Ernest and signed him.

Dick Clark's wife later came up with the novely name of Chubby Checker after Chubby's idol, Fats Domino. His first Parkway disc in 1959 was called "The Class", a novelty on which Chubby—then eighteen—imitated several other singers. Three singles later Checker mimicked Hank Ballard's "The Twist" which squirmed up the charts to No. 1, and Chubby Checker, former chicken-plucker, was on his way to a long string of dance hits.

In 1963 he married Catharina Lodders, a former Miss World. He and his family still live in Philadelphia, and Chubby tours as a headliner at rock shows around the world.

ISSUE #	LABEL	ARTIST/TITLE	VG	MINT
		CHUBBY CHECKER		
□804	PARKWAY	THE CLASS/SCHOOLDAYS, OH, SCHOOLDAYS (38)	2.50	4.00
□808		SAMSON AND DELILAH/WHOLE LOTTA LAUGHIN'	5.00	8.00
□810		DANCING DINOSAUR/THOSE PRIVATE EYES	5.00	8.00
□811		THE TWIST/TOOT (1) (1960 release)	1.00	2.50
□811		THE TWIST/TWISTIN' U.S.A. (1) (1961 release)	.75	2.00
□813		THE HUCKLEBUCK/WHOLE LOTTA SHAKING GOIN' ON (13)	1.00	2.50
□818		PONY TIME/OH, SUSANNAH (1)	.75	2.00
□822		DANCE THE MESS AROUND/GOOD, GOOD LOVIN' (24)	1.00	2.00
□824		LET'S TWIST AGAIN/ EVERYTHING'S GONNA BE ALL RIGHT (8)	.75	2.00
□830		THE FLY/THAT'S THE WAY IT GOES (7)	.75	2.00
□835		SLOW TWISTIN'/LA PALOMA TWIST (3)	.75	2.00
□842		DANCIN' PARTY/GOTTA GET MYSELF TOGETHER (12)	.75	2.00
□849		LIMBO ROCK/POPEYE (THE HITCH-HIKER) (2)	.75	2.00
□862		TWENTY MILES/LET'S LIMBO SOME MORE (15)	.75	2.00
□873		BIRDLAND/BLACK CLOUD (12)	.75	1.50
□879		TWIST IT UP/SURF PARTY (25)	.75	1.50
□890		LODDY LO/HOOKA TOOKA (12)	.75	1.50
□907		HEY BOBBA NEEDLE/SPREAD JOY (23)	.75	1.50
□920		LAZY ELSIE MOLLY/ROSIE (40)	1.00	1.50
□922		SHE WANT T'SWIM/ YOU BETTER BELIEVE IT, BABY (50)	1.00	1.50
□936		LOVELY, LOVELY/THE WEEKEND'S HERE (70)	1.00	1.50
□949		LET'S DO THE FREDDIE/(AT THE) DISCOTEQUE (40)	1.00	1.50
		LATER PARKWAY SINGLES ARE WORTH UP TO $1.50 MINT		
		CHUBBY CHECKER—ALBUMS		
□5001 (M)	PARKWAY	CHUBBY CHECKER	4.50	8.00
□7001 (M)		TWIST WITH CHUBBY CHECKER	4.00	7.00
□7002 (M)		FOR TWISTERS ONLY	3.50	6.00
□7003 (M)		IT'S PONY TIME	3.50	6.00
□7004 (M)		LET'S TWIST AGAIN	3.50	6.00
□7007 (M)		YOUR TWIST PARTY	4.00	7.00
□7008 (M)		TWISTIN' ROUND THE WORLD	4.00	7.00
□7009 (M)		FOR TEEN TWISTERS ONLY	4.00	7.00
		CHERILYN (CHER)		
□66081	IMPERIAL	DREAM BABY/STAN QUENTZAL	3.00	5.00
		ARTIE CHICAGO (ERNIE MARESCA)		
□3424	LAURIE	THE WANDERER/PLEASE DON'T PLAY ME A-7	2.50	4.00
		CHIFFONS		
		SEE: FOUR PENNIES		
□6003	BIG DEAL	TONIGHT'S THE NIGHT/DO YOU KNOW (76)	3.50	6.00
□20103	REPRISE	AFTER LAST NIGHT/DOCTOR OF HEARTS	2.50	4.00
□3152	LAURIE	HE'S SO FINE/OH MY LOVER (1)	.75	2.00
□3166		WHY AM I SO SHY/LUCKY ME	1.75	3.00
□3179		ONE FINE DAY/WHY AM I SO SHY (5)	.75	2.00
□3195		A LOVE SO FINE/ONLY MY FRIEND (40)	1.00	2.00
□3212		I HAVE A BOYFRIEND/I'M GONNA DRY MY EYES (36)	1.00	2.00
□3224		TONIGHT I MET AN ANGEL/EASY TO LOVE	1.50	2.50
□3262		SAILOR BOY/WHEN SUMMER IS THROUGH (81)	1.00	2.00

ISSUE #	LABEL	ARTIST/TITLE	VG	MINT
□3275		WHAT AM I GONNA DO WITH YOU, BABY/ STRANGE, STRANGE FEELING	1.25	2.00
□3301		NOBODY KNOWS WHAT'S GOIN' ON/ THE REAL THING (49)	1.00	2.00
□3318		TONIGHT I'M GONNA DREAM/HEAVENLY PLACE	1.25	2.00
□3340		SWEET TALKIN' GUY/DID YOU EVER GO STEADY (10)	.75	2.00
		LATER LAURIE SINGLES ARE WORTH UP TO $2.00 MINT		
		CHIFFONS—ALBUMS		
□2018 (M)	*LAURIE*	HE'S SO FINE	5.00	8.50
□2020 (M)		ONE FINE DAY	5.00	8.00
□2036 (M)		SWEET TALKIN' GUY	3.50	6.00
□2036 (S)		SWEET TALKIN' GUY	4.00	7.00
		CHIMES		
□444	*TAG*	ONCE IN A WHILE/SUMMER NIGHT (11)	1.00	2.50
□445		I'M IN THE MOOD FOR LOVE/ONLY LOVE (38)	1.25	2.50
□447		LET'S FALL IN LOVE/DREAM GIRL	1.50	2.50
□450		PARADISE/MY LOVE	1.50	2.50
		CHOCOLATE WATCH BAND		
□740	*UPTOWN*	BABY BLUE/SWEET YOUNG THING	3.00	5.00
□749		MISTY LANE/SHE WEAVES A TENDER TRAP	3.00	5.00
□373	*TOWER*	NO WAY OUT/ARE YOU GONNA BE THERE?	2.50	4.00
		CHOCOLATE WATCH BAND—ALBUMS		
□5096 (M)	*TOWER*	NO WAY OUT	5.00	8.00
□5096 (S)		NO WAY OUT	6.00	10.00
□5106 (M)		THE INNER MYSTIQUE	5.00	8.00
□5106 (S)		THE INNER MYSTIQUE	6.00	10.00
		CHOIR (RASPBERRIES)		
□203	*CANADIAN-AMERICAN*	IT'S COLD OUTSIDE/I'M GOING HOME	8.00	15.00
□4738	*ROULETTE*	IT'S COLD OUTSIDE/I'M GOING HOME (68)	2.00	3.50
□4760		NO ONE HERE TO PLAY WITH/DON'T YOU FEEL A LITTLE SORRY FOR ME	2.50	4.00
□7005		CHANGIN' MY MIND/WHEN YOU WERE WITH ME	2.50	4.00
		CHORDS		
□104	*CAT*	SH-BOOM/CROSS OVER THE BRIDGE	6.00	10.00
□104		SH-BOOM/LITTLE MAIDEN (9)	3.00	5.00
□109		ZIPPITY ZUM/BLESS YOU	2.50	4.00
		ROGER CHRISTIAN		
□100	*NBI*	BIG BAD HO-DAD/LAST DRAG	2.50	4.00
		LOU CHRISTIE		
		SEE: LUGEE AND THE LIONS		
□006	*AMERICAN MUSIC MAKER*	THE JURY/LITTLE DID I KNOW	5.00	8.00
□508	*STARR*	THE JURY/LITTLE DID I KNOW	4.00	7.00
□1002	*WORLD*	THE JURY/LITTLE DID I KNOW	4.00	7.00
□102	*CO & CE*	THE GYPSY CRIED/RED SAILS IN THE SUNSET	7.00	12.00
□235		OUTSIDE THE GATES OF HEAVEN/ ALL THAT GLITTERS ISN'T GOLD (45)	1.25	2.50
□4457	*ROULETTE*	THE GYPSY CRIED/RED SAILS IN THE SUNSET (24)	1.25	3.00
□4481		TWO FACES HAVE I/ALL THAT GLITTER ISN'T GOLD (6)	.75	2.50

ISSUE #	LABEL	ARTIST/TITLE	VG	MINT
☐ 4504		HOW MANY TEARDROPS?/YOU AND I (46)	1.00	2.50
☐ 4527		SHY BOY/IT CAN HAPPEN	1.75	3.00
☐ 4545		STAY/THERE THEY GO	1.75	3.00
☐ 4554		WHEN YOU DANCE/MAYBE YOU'LL BE THERE	1.75	3.00
☐ 13412	MGM	LIGHTNIN' STRIKES/CRYIN' IN THE STREETS (1) ..	.75	2.00
☐ 13473		RHAPSODY IN THE RAIN/TRAPEZE (16)	1.00	2.50
☐ 13533		PAINTER/DU RONDA (81)	1.25	2.50
☐ 13576		IF MY CAR COULD ONLY TALK/SONG OF LITA	1.50	2.50
☐ 13623		SINCE I DON'T HAVE YOU/WILD LIFE'S IN SEASON ...	1.75	3.00
☐ 735	COLPIX	MERRY GO ROUND/GUITARS AND BONGOS	1.50	2.50
☐ 753		HAVE I SINNED?/POT OF GOLD	1.50	2.50
☐ 770		MAKE SUMMER LAST FOREVER/		
		WHY DID YOU DO IT, BABY?..................	1.50	2.50
☐ 778		A TEENAGER IN LOVE/BACKTRACK.............	1.75	3.00
☐ 799		BIG TIME/CRYIN' ON MY KNEES (95)	1.25	2.50
		LOU CHRISTIE—ALBUMS		
☐ 25208 (M)	ROULETTE	LOU CHRISTIE	5.00	8.00
☐ 25208 (S)		LOU CHRISTIE	6.00	10.00
☐ 25332 (M)		LOU CHRISTIE STRIKES AGAIN	4.00	7.00
☐ 25332 (S)		LOU CHRISTIE STRIKES AGAIN	4.50	9.00
☐ 1231 (M)	CO & CE	LOU CHRISTIE STRIKES BACK	3.50	6.00
☐ 1231 (S)		LOU CHRISTIE STRIKES BACK	4.50	8.00
☐ 4360 (M)	MGM	LIGHTNING STRIKES	3.00	5.00
☐ 4360 (S)		LIGHTNING STRIKES	3.50	7.00
☐ 4394 (M)		PAINTER OF HITS........................	3.00	5.00
☐ 4394 (S)		PAINTER OF HITS........................	3.50	7.00
☐ 4001 (M)	COLPIX	STRIKES AGAIN	3.50	6.00
☐ 4001 (S)		STRIKES AGAIN	4.50	8.00

CHIC CHRISTY
FEATURED: LOU CHRISTY

☐ 103	HAC	WITH THIS KISS/MY BILLET-DOUX TO YOU	2.50	4.00

DON CHRISTY (SONNY BONO)

☐ 672	SPECIALTY	ONE LITTLE ANSWER/WEARING BLACK	2.50	4.00

CHURCH STREET FIVE

☐ 1004	LEGRAND	A NIGHT WITH DADDY G (PT. 1)/(PT. 11)	1.75	3.00
☐ 1010		EVERYBODY'S HAPPY/FALLEN ARCHES..........	1.50	2.50
☐ 1014		CHURCH STREET WALK/I'M GONNA SUE	1.50	2.50
☐ 1021		DADDY G RIDES AGAIN/HEY NOW	1.75	3.00

CITY
FEATURED: CAROL KING

☐ 113	ODE	PARADISE ALLEY/SNOW QUEEN	2.00	3.50
☐ 119		THAT OLD SWEET ROLL/WHY ARE YOU LEAVING? ..	2.00	3.50
		CITY—ALBUM		
☐ 244012 (S)	ODE	NOW THAT EVERYTHING'S BEEN SAID	7.00	12.00

C. L. AND THE PICTURES
FEATURED: CURTIS LEE

☐ 2010	DUNES	LET'S TAKE A RIDE/I'M ASKING FORGIVENESS	1.75	3.00
☐ 2017		AFRAID/MARY GO ROUND	1.75	3.00
☐ 2023		I'M SORRY/THAT'S WHAT'S HAPPENING........	1.75	3.00

JIMMY CLANTON

Jimmy Clanton was born on September 2, 1940. His birthplace was Baton Rouge, Louisiana. During his early adolescence the rock-and-roll culture burst onto the scene, and Clanton caught the fever post haste. He soon formed his own band, which he dubbed Jimmy Clanton and the Rockets. Clanton played local gigs only, but was constantly in demand due to his fine voice, outgoing personality and engaging smile. After high school Jimmy moved on to dance clubs and a local radio show called "The Teen Town Rally". Clanton later took his band south to New Orleans.

He was introduced to the president of Ace Records, who auditioned young Clanton and was so impressed with him and his singing that he produced a contract on the spot. Clanton's first Ace single ("I Trusted You") was a bomb, but he struck gold with "Just a Dream", his second Ace product. Following "American Bandstand" appearances, Jimmy Clanton developed a large following.

Altogether he cut a trio of Top 10 singles for Ace, Clanton now works as a program director at a Pennsylvania radio station.

ISSUE #	LABEL	ARTIST/TITLE	VG	MINT
		JIMMY CLANTON		
		SEE: JIMMY DALE		
□537	***ACE***	I TRUSTED YOU/THAT'S YOU BABY	2.50	4.00
□546		JUST A DREAM/YOU AIM TO PLEASE (4)	1.50	3.00
□551		A LETTER TO AN ANGEL/A PART OF ME (25)	1.25	2.50
□560		A SHIP ON A STORMY SEA/MY LOVE IS STRONG	1.50	2.50
□567		MY OWN TRUE LOVE/LITTLE BOY IN LOVE (33)	1.25	2.50
□575		GO JIMMY GO/I TRUSTED YOU (5)	.75	2.00
□585		ANOTHER SLEEPLESS NIGHT/I'M GONNA TRY (22)	1.00	2.50
□600		COME BACK/WAIT (63)	1.25	2.50
□607		WHAT AM I GONNA DO/IF I (50)	1.25	2.50
□616		DOWN THE AISLE/NO LONGER BLUE (with Mary Ann Mobley)	1.50	2.50
□622		I JUST WANNA MAKE LOVE/DON'T LOOK AT ME	1.50	2.50
□634		LUCKY IN LOVE WITH YOU/NOT LIKE A BROTHER	1.50	2.50
□641		TWIST ON LITTLE GIRL/WAYWARD LOVE	1.50	2.50
□655		JUST A MOMENT/BECAUSE I DO	1.50	2.50
□664		VENUS IN BLUE JEANS/HIGHWAY BOUND	2.50	4.00
□668		HEART HOTEL/MANY DREAMS	1.50	2.50
□8001		VENUS IN BLUE JEANS/HIGHWAY BOUND (7)	.75	2.00
□8005		DARKEST STREET IN TOWN/DREAMS OF A FOOL (77)	1.25	2.00
□8006		ENDLESS NIGHT/ANOTHER DAY, ANOTHER HEARTACHE	1.25	2.00
□8007		CINDY/I CARE ENOUGH	1.25	2.00
		JIMMY CLANTON—EPs		
□101	***ACE***	THINKING OF YOU	5.00	8.00
□102		THINKING OF YOU	5.00	8.00
□103		I'M ALWAYS CHASING RAINBOWS	5.00	8.00
		JIMMY CLANTON—ALBUMS		
□1001 (M)	***ACE***	JUST A DREAM	8.00	15.00
□1007 (M)		JIMMY'S HAPPY	7.00	12.00
□1008 (M)		JIMMY'S BLUE	7.00	12.00
□1011 (M)		MY BEST TO YOU	7.00	12.00
□1014 (M)		TEENAGE MILLIONAIRE	8.00	15.00
□1026 (M)		VENUS IN BLUE JEANS	6.00	10.00
		CLAUDINE CLARK		
□521	***HERALD***	ANGEL OF HAPPINESS/TEENAGE BLUES	3.00	5.00
□1113	***CHANCELLOR***	PARTY LIGHTS/DISAPPOINTED (5)	.75	2.00
□1124		TELEPHONE GAME/WALKIN' THROUGH A CEMETERY	1.25	2.00
□1130		WALK ME HOME/WHO WILL YOU HURT	1.25	2.00
		CLAUDINE CLARK—ALBUM		
□5209 (M)	***CHANCELLOR***	PARTY LIGHTS	6.00	10.00

DAVE CLARK FIVE

They originally began as a group of British school pals who often played sports in the gymnasium after regular school hours. Clark and his associates decided to form a band in order to raise money for the school's soccer club. Seeing success on the local level, the Dave Clark Five later raised their sights when the Beatles struck 1964 gold in America.

Never pretending to be in the music business for anything but the money, the DC-5 ran up an impressive string of Epic hits (eight made the American Top 10) while earning the plaudits of such influential straights as Ed Sullivan. While openly disdaining the Beatles (although he did sign them to draw high ratings), Sullivan featured the Dave Clark Five on his popular show 32 times.

Dave Clark was the quintet's mediocre drummer who did little singing. Rather, those chores were left to Mike Smith, a handsome lad with an aggressive, grating voice that many at first interpreted as belonging to a black singer.

After the hits ended late in 1967, the Dave Clark Five disbanded, but not after first ringing up over $250,000,000 in worldwide record sales.

ISSUE #	LABEL	ARTIST/TITLE	VG	MINT
		DAVE CLARK FIVE		
□212	*CONGRESS*	I KNEW IT ALL THE TIME/THAT'S WHAT I SAID (53)	2.50	4.00
□5078	*RUST*	I WALK THE LINE/FIRST LOVE	3.50	6.00
□3188	*LAURIE*	I WALK THE LINE/FIRST LOVE	3.50	6.00
□5476	*JUBILEE*	CHAQUITA/IN YOUR HEART	3.00	5.00
□9656	*EPIC*	GLAD ALL OVER/I KNOW YOU (6)	1.00	2.50
□9671		BITS AND PIECES/ALL OF THE TIME (4)	1.00	2.50
□9678		DO YOU LOVE ME/CHAQUITA (11)	1.00	2.00
□9692		CAN'T YOU SEE THAT SHE'S MINE/ NO TIME TO LOSE (4)	1.00	2.00
□9704		BECAUSE/THEME WITHOUT A NAME (3)	1.00	2.00
□9722		EVERYBODY KNOWS/OL' SOL (15)	1.00	2.00
□9739		ANY WAY YOU WANT IT/CRYING OVER YOU (14)	1.00	2.00
□9763		COME HOME/YOUR TURN TO CRY (14)	1.00	2.00
□9786		REELIN' AND ROCKIN'/I'M THINKING (23)	1.00	2.00
□9811		I LIKE IT LIKE THAT/HURTIN' INSIDE (7)	.75	2.00
□9833		CATCH US IF YOU CAN/ON THE MOVE (4)	.75	2.00
□9863		OVER AND OVER/I'LL BE YOURS (MY LOVE) (1)	.75	2.00
□9882		AT THE SCENE/I MISS YOU (18)	.75	2.00
□10004		TRY TOO HARD/ALL NIGHT LONG (12)	.75	2.00
□10031		PLEASE TELL ME WHY/LOOK BEFORE YOU LEAP (28)	1.00	2.00
□10053		SATISFIED WITH YOU/DON'T LET ME DOWN (50)	1.00	2.00
□10076		NINETEEN DAYS/SITTING HERE BABY (48)	1.00	2.00
□10114		I'VE GOT TO HAVE A REASON/GOOD TIME BABY (44)	1.00	2.00
□10144		YOU GOT WHAT IT TAKES/DOCTOR RYTHYM (7)	.75	2.00
		LATER EPIC SINGLES ARE WORTH UP TO $2.00 MINT		
		DAVE CLARK FIVE—ALBUMS		
□24093 (M)		GLAD ALL OVER	5.00	8.00
□24104 (M)		THE DAVE CLARK FIVE RETURN	4.00	7.00
□24117 (M)		AMERICAN TOUR	4.00	7.00
□24128 (M)		COAST TO COAST	4.00	7.00
□24139 (M)		WEEKEND IN LONDON	4.00	7.00
□24162 (M)		HAVING A WILD WEEKEND	4.00	7.00
□24178 (M)		I LIKE IT LIKE THAT	4.00	7.00
□24185 (M)		DAVE CLARK FIVE'S GREATEST HITS	3.50	6.00
		(STEREO VERSIONS OF THE ABOVE HAVE THE SAME VALUE)		
		SANFORD CLARK		
□1003	*MCI*	THE FOOL/LONESOME FOR A LETTER	12.00	20.00
□15481	*DOT*	THE FOOL/LONESOME FOR A LETTER (9)	1.75	3.50
□15516		A CHEAT/USTA BE MY BABY (74)	1.75	3.00
□15534		9 LB. HAMMER/OOO BABY	1.50	2.50
□15556		THE GLORY OF LOVE/DARLING DEAR	1.50	2.50
□15585		LOVE CHARMS/LOU BE DOO	1.50	2.50
		CLASSICS		
□1015	*DART*	CINDERELLA/SO IN LOVE	3.50	6.00
□1032		ANGEL ANGELA/EENIE, MEENIE, MINIE AND MO	5.00	8.00
□1038		LIFE IS BUT A DREAM/THAT'S THE WAY	5.00	8.00
□71829	*MERCURY*	LIFE IS BUT A DREAM/THAT'S THE WAY	2.50	4.00
□1114	*MUSICTONE*	CINDERLLA/SO IN LOVE	3.00	5.00
□1116	*MUSICNOTE*	TILL THEN/EENIE, MEENIE, MINIE AND MO (20)	1.25	2.50
□1118		P.S. I LOVE YOU/WRAP YOUR TROUBLES IN DREAMS	1.50	2.50

ISSUE #	LABEL	ARTIST/TITLE	VG	MINT
		CLEFTONES		
□ 1000	***GEE***	YOU BABY YOU/I WAS DREAMING (78)	4.00	7.00
□ 1011		LITTLE GIRL OF MINE/ YOU'RE DRIVING ME MAD (57)	3.00	5.00
□ 1064		HEART AND SOUL/HOW DO YOU FEEL (18)	1.25	2.50
□ 1067		FOR SENTIMENTAL REASONS/DEED I DO (60)	1.50	2.50
□ 1074		EARTH ANGEL/BLUES IN THE NIGHT	1.75	3.00
		BUZZ CLIFFORD		
□ 41774	***COLUMBIA***	HELLO MR. MOONLIGHT/BLUE LAGOON	1.75	3.50
□ 41876		BABY SITTER BOOGIE/DRIFTWOOD	3.50	6.00
□ 41876		BABY SITTIN' BOOGIE/DRIFTWOOD (6)	.75	2.00
□ 41979		SIMPLY BECAUSE/THREE LITTLE FISHES	1.50	2.50
□ 42019		I'LL NEVER FORGET/THE AWAKENING	1.25	2.00
□ 42177		LONELINESS/MOVING DAY	1.25	2.00
		BUZZ CLIFFORD—ALBUM		
□ 1616 (M)	***COLUMBIA***	BABY SITTIN' WITH BUZZ	5.00	8.00
□ 8416 (S)		BABY SITTIN' WITH BUZZ	6.00	10.00
		CLOVERS		
□ 963	***ATLANTIC***	ONE MINT JULEP/MIDDLE OF THE NIGHT	12.00	20.00
□ 1000		GOOD LOVIN'/HERE GOES A FOOL	7.00	12.00
□ 1022		LOVEY DOVEY/LITTLE MAMA	7.00	12.00
□ 1052		BLUE VELVET/IF YOU LOVE ME	6.00	10.00
□ 1083		DEVIL OR ANGEL/HEY DOLL BABY	6.00	10.00
□ 1094		YOUR TENDER LIPS/LOVE, LOVE, LOVE (30)	1.75	3.00
□ 1107		FROM THE BOTTOM OF MY HEART/BRING ME LOVE	2.50	4.00

COASTERS

During the early 1950s Jerry Leiber and Mike Stoller were struggling but energetic young songwriters. In Los Angeles they formed a small record label called Spark. On it they signed a rhythm-and-blues group called the Robins, who had previously recorded for seven other labels and had seen a smattering of r & b success. On Spark Records the Robins cut such classic singles as "Riot In Cell Block #9" and "Framed" but found their greatest success with the Leiber-Stoller creation, "Smokey Joe's Cafe". (The master was also issued on the larger Atco label.)

The group then split into two factions after some contractural differences. Those who stayed on as the Robins slid into obscurity on the Whippet and Knight labels; those who signed with Atco as the Coasters (they all hailed from the West Coast) saw immediate success with "Down In Mexico". But it was only the beginning. The Coasters became the best-selling novelty group of the 1950s, thanks in no small part to the Leiber-Stoller writing team.

Their first million-seller—"Searchin' "/"Young Blood"—became Atco's biggest hit ever to that date.

ISSUE #	LABEL	ARTIST/TITLE	VG	MINT
		COASTERS		
		SEE: ROBINS		
☐6064	*ATCO*	DOWN IN MEXICO/TURTLE DOVIN' (maroon label)	3.50	6.00
☐6073		ONE KISS LED TO ANOTHER/ BRAZIL (maroon label) (73)	3.00	5.00
☐6087		SEARCHIN'/YOUNG BLOOD (5)	1.50	3.00
☐6098		IDOL WITH THE GOLDEN HEAD/ MY BABY COMES TO ME (64)	2.00	3.50
☐6104		SWEET GEORGIA BROWN/ WHAT'S THE SECRET OF YOUR SUCCESS	2.00	3.50
☐6111		GEE GOLLY/DANCE	2.00	3.50
☐6116		YAKETY YAK/ZING! WENT THE STRINGS OF MY HEART (1)	1.00	2.50
☐6126		THE SHADOW KNOWS/SORRY BUT I'M GONNA HAVE TO PASS	1.75	3.00
☐6132		CHARLIE BROWN/THREE COOL CATS (2)	1.00	2.50
☐6141		ALONG CAME JONES/THAT IS ROCK 'N' ROLL (9)	1.00	2.50
☐6146		POISON IVY/I'M A HOG FOR YOU (7)	1.00	2.50
☐6153		RUN RED RUN/WHAT ABOUT US (36)	1.25	2.50
☐6163		BESAME MUCHO (PT. 1)/(PT. 11) (70)	1.50	2.50
☐6168		WAKE ME, SHAKE ME/STEWBALL (51)	1.50	2.50
☐6178		SHOPPIN' FOR CLOTHES/ SNAKE AND THE BOOKWORM (83)	1.50	2.50
☐6186		WAIT A MINUTE/THUMBIN' A RIDE (37)	1.25	2.50
☐6192		LITTLE EGYPT/KEEP ON ROLLING (23)	1.00	2.00
		LATER ATCO SINGLES ARE WORTH UP TO $2.00 MINT		
		COASTERS—EPs		
☐4501	*ATCO*	ROCK AND ROLL WITH THE COASTERS	4.00	7.00
☐4502		KEEP ROCKIN' WITH THE COASTERS	4.00	7.00
☐4506		THE COASTERS	4.00	7.00
☐4507		TOP HITS	4.00	7.00
		COASTERS—ALBUMS		
☐101 (M)	*ATCO*	THE COASTERS	12.00	20.00
☐111 (M)		THE COASTERS' GREATEST HITS	7.00	12.00

EDDIE COCHRAN

Eddie Cochran was the youngest of five children and was born in Albert Lea, Minnesota, on October 3, 1938. He became a radio fanatic and spent hours listening to the r & b and country hits of the day. At twelve Eddie bought his first guitar and learned basic chords from an older brother.

The family moved to Bell Gardens, California. At sixteen Cochran dropped out of high school to form his own three-piece band. With Hank Cochran (no relation) Eddie cut three singles as one of the Cochran Brothers. When Hank moved to Tennessee, Eddie signed with Hollywood's Crest Records. His solitary single there was the unsuccessful "Skinny Jim".

Liberty Records later became Eddie's recording home, and his first single of "Sittin' In the Balcony" proved a winner. Six singles later Eddie Cochran saw his greatest success (and only Top 10 hit) with the immortal "Summertime Blues".

An instant success in England, Cochran later went on tour there with fellow rocker Gene Vincent. On April 17, 1960, Cochran died in a British taxi accident.

ISSUE #	LABEL	ARTIST/TITLE	VG	MINT
		EDDIE COCHRAN		
☐1026	*CREST*	SKINNY JIM/HALF LOVED	30.00	50.00
☐55056	*LIBERTY*	SITTIN' IN THE BALCONY/ DARK LONELY STREET (18)	2.50	4.00
☐55070		MEAN WHEN I'M MAD/ONE KISS	3.50	6.00
☐55087		DRIVE-IN SHOW/AM I BLUE (82)	3.00	5.00
☐55112		TWENTY FLIGHT ROCK/CRADLE BABY	3.50	6.00
☐55123		JEANNIE JEANNIE JEANNIE/ POCKETFUL OF HEARTACHES (94)	3.00	5.00
☐55138		PRETTY GIRL/THERESA	3.50	6.00
☐55144		SUMMERTIME BLUES/LOVE AGAIN (8)	1.50	3.00
☐55166		C'MON EVERYBODY/DON'T EVER LET ME GO (35)	1.75	3.50
☐55177		TEENAGE HEAVEN/I REMEMBER (99)	2.50	4.00
☐55203		SOMETHIN' ELSE/BOLL WEEVIL SONG (58)	2.50	4.00
☐55217		HALLELUJAH, I LOVE HER SO/LITTLE ANGEL	3.00	4.50
☐55242		FIVE STEPS TO HEAVEN/CUT ACROSS SHORTY	3.00	4.50
☐55278		SWEETIE PIE/LONELY	2.50	4.00
☐55389		WEEKEND/LONELY	2.50	4.00
		EDDIE COCHRAN—EPs		
☐3061	*LIBERTY*	SINGIN' TO MY BABY, PART 1	8.00	15.00
☐3061		SINGIN' TO MY BABY, PART 2	8.00	15.00
☐3061		SINGIN' TO MY BABY, PART 3	8.00	15.00
		EDDIE COCHRAN—ABLUMS		
☐3061 (M)	*LIBERTY*	SINGIN' TO MY BABY	30.00	50.00
☐3172 (M)		EDDIE COCHRAN	25.00	40.00
☐3220 (M)		NEVER TO BE FORGOTTEN	18.00	30.00
		COCHRAN BROTHERS		
		FEATURED: EDDIE COCHRAN		
☐1003	*EKKO*	MR. FIDDLE/TWO BLUE SINGING STARS	25.00	40.00
☐1005		GUILTY CONSCIENCE/ YOUR TOMORROWS NEVER COME	25.00	40.00
☐3001		TIRED AND SLEEPY/FOOL'S PARADISE	35.00	60.00
		JOE COCKER		
☐40255	*PHILLIPS*	I'LL CRY INSTEAD/PRECIOUS WORDS	2.50	4.00
		COMPANIONS		
☐852	*AMY*	NO FOOL AM I/HOW COULD YOU	3.00	5.00
		CAROL CONNORS		
		SEE: SURFETTES		
☐3084	*ERA*	BIG BIG LOVE/TWO RIVERS	3.50	6.00
☐3096		TOMMY, GO AWAY/I WANNA KNOW	3.50	6.00
☐5152	*CAPITOL*	NEVER/ANGEL, MY ANGEL	3.00	5.00
☐41976	*COLUMBIA*	MY DIARY/YOU ARE MY ANSWER	3.00	5.00
☐42155		MY SPECIAL BOY/LISTEN TO THE BEAT	3.00	5.00
☐42337		WHAT DO YOU SEE IN HIM?/THAT'S ALL IT TAKES	3.00	5.00
☐2005	*DUNES*	DEAR ONE/JOHNNY OH JOHNNY (Carol Collins)	2.50	4.00
		CONSORTS		
☐1004	*COUSINS*	PLEASE BE MINE/TIME AFTER TIME	15.00	25.00
☐25066	*APT*	PLEASE BE MINE/TIME AFTER TIME	2.50	4.00
		CONTOURS		
☐1008	*MOTOWN*	WHOLE LOTTA WOMAN/COME ON AND BE MINE	3.50	6.00
☐1012		THE STRETCH/FUNNY	3.00	5.00

ISSUE #	LABEL	ARTIST/TITLE	VG	MINT
□7005	**GORDY**	DO YOU LOVE ME/MOVE ME, MAN (3)	1.00	2.00
□7012		SHAKE SHERRY/YOU BETTER GET IN LINE (43)	1.25	2.00
		LATER GORDY SINGLES ARE WORTH UP TO $1.50 MINT		
		CONTOURS—ALBUM		
□901 (M)	**GORDY**	DO YOU LOVE ME	6.00	10.00

SAM COOKE

Sam Cooke was a Chicago native (born January 22, 1935) and one of eight children. As a child he sang gospels and spirituals in his father's church. While still a high school student, Sam Cooke and one of his brothers joined a gospel group called the Highway Q. C.'s. Sam later drifted into another gospel outfit, the Soul Stirrers. The group eventually signed a contract with Specialty Records, made numerous records and found success as a hit gospel outfit.

Cooke soon came to prefer pop music and approached Specialty's owner Art Rupe about doing some ballads. Rupe reluctantly agreed but admonished Cooke that gospel was his main forte. Dissatisfied later with Specialty's promotion, Sam then signed with Bob Keane's newly formed Keen label. Cooke recorded two singles before seeing success with his third effort, "You Send Me". It peaked at No. 1 on both the soul and rock charts. After moderate success with later Keen 45s, Sam left to go with RCA Records, where twelve of his songs reached the Top 20.

Sam Cooke's career was cut tragically short at age 29 when he was shot to death on December 11, 1964, in a Los Angeles motel.

ISSUE #	LABEL	ARTIST/TITLE	VG	MINT
		SAM COOKE		
□596	SPECIALTY	LOVEABLE/FOREVER (Dale Cooke)	2.50	4.00
□619		I'LL COME RUNNING BACK TO YOU/FOREVER (22)	1.50	4.00
□627		THAT'S ALL I NEED TO KNOW/I DON'T WANT TO CRY	1.75	3.00
□667		HAPPY IN LOVE/ I NEED YOU NOW	1.75	3.00
□4002	KEEN	FOR SENTIMENTAL REASONS/DESIRE ME (43)	2.00	3.50
□4009		LONELY ISLAND/YOU WERE MADE FOR ME (39)	1.75	3.00
□4013		YOU SEND ME/SUMMERTIME (1)	2.00	4.00
□2003		FOR SENTIMENTAL REASONS/DESIRE ME	1.00	2.00
□2005		ALL OF MY LIFE/STEALING KISSES	1.50	3.00
□2006		WIN YOUR LOVE FOR ME/ LOVE SONG FROM "HOUSEBOAT" (33)	1.25	2.50
□2008		LOVE YOU MOST OF ALL/BLUE MOON (26)	1.25	2.50
□2018		EVERYBODY LIKES TO CHA-CHA-CHA/ LITTLE THINGS YOU DO (31)	1.25	2.50
□2022		ONLY SIXTEEN/LET'S GO STEADY AGAIN (28)	1.25	2.50
□2101		SUMMERTIME (PT. 1)/(PT. 11)	1.25	2.50
□2105		THERE, I'VE SAID IT AGAIN/ONE HOUR AHEAD OF THE POSSE (81)	1.50	2.50
□2111		NO ONE/IT AIN'T NOBODY'S BIZNESS	1.50	3.00
□2112		WONDERFUL WORLD/ALONG THE NAVAJO TRAIL (12)	1.00	2.50
□2117		WITH YOU/I THANK GOD	1.50	3.00
□2118		STEAL AWAY/SO GLAMOROUS	1.50	3.00
□2122		MARY, MARY LOU/EE-YI-EE-YI-OH	1.50	3.00
□7701	RCA	TEENAGE SONATA/IF YOU WERE THE ONLY GIRL (50)	1.50	3.00
□7730		YOU UNDERSTAND ME/I BELONG TO YOUR HEART	1.50	3.00
□7783		CHAIN GANG/I FALL IN LOVE EVERY DAY (2)	1.00	2.50
□7816		SAD MOOD/LOVE ME (29)	1.25	2.50
□7853		THAT'S IT, I QUIT, I'M MOVIN' ON/ DO WHAT YOU SAY (31)	1.25	2.50
□7883		CUPID/FAREWELL, MY DARLING (17)	1.00	2.50
□7927		FEEL IT/IT'S ALL RIGHT (56)	1.50	2.50
□7983		TWISTIN' THE NIGHT AWAY/ONE MORE TIME (9)	1.00	2.50
□8036		BRING IT ON HOME TO ME/HAVING A PARTY (13)	1.00	2.50
□8088		NOTHING CAN CHANGE THIS LOVE/ SOMEBODY HAVE MERCY (12)	1.00	2.50
□8129		SEND ME SOME LOVIN'/BABY, BABY, BABY (13)	1.00	2.50

ISSUE #		LABEL	ARTIST/TITLE	VG	MINT
☐8164			ANOTHER SATURDAY NIGHT/ LOVE WILL FIND A WAY (10)	1.00	2.50
☐8215			FRANKIE AND JOHNNY/COOL TRAIN (14)	1.00	2.50
☐8247			LITTLE RED ROOSTER/YOU'VE GOTTA MOVE (11)	1.00	2.50
☐8299			GOOD NEWS/BASIN STREET BLUES (11)	1.00	2.50
☐8368			GOOD TIMES/TENNESSEE WALTZ (11)	1.00	2.50
☐8426			COUSIN OF MINE/THAT'S WHERE IT'S AT (31)	1.25	2.50
☐8486			SHAKE/A CHANGE IS GONNA COME (7)	1.00	2.00

LATER RCA SINGLES ARE WORTH UP TO $2.00 MINT

SAM COOKE—EPs

ISSUE #		LABEL	ARTIST/TITLE	VG	MINT
☐2001		***KEEN***	SAM COOKE	2.50	4.00
☐2002			SAM COOKE	2.50	4.00
☐2003			SAM COOKE	2.50	4.00
☐2006			ENCORE, VOL. 1	2.00	4.00
☐2007			ENCORE, VOL. 2	2.00	4.00
☐2008			ENCORE, VOL. 3	2.00	4.00
☐4372		***RCA***	ANOTHER SATURDAY NIGHT	3.00	5.00

SAM COOKE—ALBUMS

ISSUE #		LABEL	ARTIST/TITLE	VG	MINT
☐2001	(M)	***KEEN***	SAM COOKE	7.00	12.00
☐2003	(M)		ENCORE	6.00	10.00
☐2004	(M)		TRIBUTE TO THE LADY	5.00	8.00
☐2221	(M)	***RCA***	COOKE'S TOUR	4.00	7.00
☐2236	(M)		HITS OF THE 50'S	4.50	8.00
☐2293	(M)		SWING LOW	4.00	7.00
☐2392	(M)		MY KIND OF BLUES	4.00	7.00
☐2555	(M)		TWISTIN' THE NIGHT AWAY	4.00	7.00
☐2625	(M)		THE BEST OF SAM COOKE	3.50	6.00

COOKIES

ISSUE #	LABEL	ARTIST/TITLE	VG	MINT
☐1002	***DIMENSION***	CHAINS/STRANGER IN MY ARMS (17)	1.25	2.50
☐1008		DON'T SAY NOTHIN' BAD/SOFTLY IN THE NIGHT (7)	1.00	2.50
☐1012		WILL POWER/I WANT A BOY FOR MY BIRTHDAY (72)	1.50	2.50
☐1020		GIRLS GROW UP FASTER THAN BOYS/ ONLY TO OTHER PEOPLE (33)	1.25	2.50
☐1032		I NEVER DREAMED/THE OLD CROWD	1.50	2.50

EDDIE COOLEY AND THE DIMPLES

ISSUE #	LABEL	ARTIST/TITLE	VG	MINT
☐621	***ROYAL ROOST***	PRISCILLA/GOT A LITTLE WOMAN (26)	1.50	3.00
☐626		A SPARK MET A FLAME/DRIFTWOOD	1.50	2.50
☐628		HEY YOU/PULL, PULL	1.25	2.00

KEN COPELAND

ISSUE #	LABEL	ARTIST/TITLE	VG	MINT
☐5008	***LIN***	PLEDGE OF LOVE/NIGHT AIR (Mints)	3.50	6.00
☐5432	***IMPERIAL***	PLEDGE OF LOVE/NIGHT AIR (Mints) (17)	1.25	3.00

CORDELLS

ISSUE #	LABEL	ARTIST/TITLE	VG	MINT
☐1017	***BULLSEYE***	PLEASE DON'T GO/BELIEVE IN ME	7.00	12.00

CORDIALS

ISSUE #	LABEL	ARTIST/TITLE	VG	MINT
☐276	***WHIP***	LISTEN MY HEART/MY HEART'S DESIRE	12.00	20.00
☐106	***REVEILLE***	ETERNAL LOVE/THE INTERNATIONAL TWIST	8.00	15.00

CORNELLS

ISSUE #	LABEL	ARTIST/TITLE	VG	MINT
☐102	***GAREX***	MALIBU SURF/AGUA CALIENTE	2.00	3.50
☐201		BEACH BOUND/LONE STAR STOMP	1.75	3.00
☐206		SURF FEVER/DO THE SLAUSON	1.75	3.00

ISSUE #	LABEL	ARTIST/TITLE	VG	MINT
		CORNELLS—ALBUM		
□ 100 (M)		BEACH BOUND	5.00	8.00
		DAVE "BABY" CORTEZ		
□ 213	*WINLEY*	SATURDAY NIGHT ROCK/SOFT LIGHTS	2.50	4.00
□ 259		JAMIN' (PT. 1)/(PT. 11)	2.50	4.00
□ 262		SKINS AND SOUNDS/LITTLE PARIS MELODY	2.50	4.00
□ 267		SCOTTY (PT. 1)/(PT. 11)	2.50	4.00
		LATER SINGLES ON CLOCK AND CHESS ARE WORTH UP TO $2.00 MINT		
		COUNT FIVE		
□ 104	*DOUBLE SHOT*	PSYCHOTIC REACTION/ THEY'RE GONNA GET YOU (5)	.75	2.00
□ 106		PEACE OF MIND/THE MORNING AFTER	1.25	2.00
□ 110		YOU MUST BELIEVE ME/ TEENY BOPPER, TEENY BOPPER	1.25	2.00
□ 115		CONTRAST/MERRY-GO-ROUND	1.25	2.00
		COUNT FIVE—ALBUM		
□ 1001 (M)	*DOUBLE SHOT*	PSYCHOTIC REACTION	5.00	8.00
□ 5001 (S)		PSYCHOTIC REACTION	6.00	10.00
		COUNTS		
□ 100	*NAT*	YOU'LL FEEL IT TOO/COUNTED OUT	2.50	4.00
□ 101		STORMY WEATHER/TRUE LOVE GONE	2.50	4.00
		CRAFTSMEN (JOHNNY AND THE HURRICANES)		
□ 538	*WARWICK*	GOOFUS/ROCK ALONG	2.50	4.00
□ 586		TWEEDLE DEE/WALKIN' WITH MR. LEE	2.50	4.00
		JOHNNY CRAWFORD		
□ 124	*WYNNE*	DANCE WITH THE DOLLY/ASK	2.50	4.00
□ 4162	*DEL-FI*	DAYDREAMS/SO GOES THE STORY (70)	1.75	3.00
□ 4165		YOU LOVE IS GROWING COLD/TREASURE	2.00	3.50
□ 4172		PATTI ANN/DONNA (43)	1.25	2.50
□ 4178		CINDY'S BIRTHDAY/SOMETHING SPECIAL (8)	1.00	2.50
□ 4181		YOUR NOSE IS GONNA GROW/MR. BLUE (14)	1.00	2.50
□ 4188		RUMORS/NO ONE REALLY LOVES A CLOWN (12)	1.00	2.50
□ 4193		PROUD/LONESOME TOWN (29)	1.00	2.00
□ 4203		WHEN I FALL IN LOVE/CRY ON MY SHOULDER	1.25	2.00
□ 4215		WHAT HAPPENED TO JANIE?/PETITE CHANSON	1.25	2.00
□ 4221		CINDY'S GONNA CRY/DEBBIE (72)	1.25	2.00
□ 4229		SANDY/OL' SHORTY	1.25	2.00
□ 4231		JUDY LOVE ME/LIVING IN THE PAST (95)	1.75	3.00
		PRODUCER: JAN BERRY (DEL-FI 4231)		
□ 4242		THE GIRL NEXT DOOR/SITTIN' AND A WATCHIN'	1.25	2.00
		JOHNNY CRAWFORD—ALBUMS		
□ 1220 (M)	*DEL-FI*	THE CAPTIVATING JOHNNY CRAWFORD	6.00	10.00
□ 1223 (M)		A YOUNG MAN'S FANCY	3.50	6.00
□ 1223 (S)		A YOUNG MAN'S FANCY	4.50	8.00
□ 1224 (M)		RUMORS	3.50	6.00
□ 1224 (S)		RUMORS	4.50	8.00
□ 1229 (M)		HIS GREATEST HITS	4.00	7.00
□ 1229 (S)		HIS GREATEST HITS	5.00	9.00

ISSUE #	LABEL	ARTIST/TITLE	VG	MINT
		CREEDENCE CLEARWATER REVIVAL		
		SEE: TOMMY FOGERTY AND THE BLUE VELVETS, GOLLIWOGS		
☐412	***SCORPIO***	PORTERVILLE/CALL IT PRETENDING	6.00	10.00
		LATER FANTASY SINGLES ARE WORTH UP TO $1.50 MINT		
		CRESCENDOS		
☐831	***MUSIC CITY***	MY HEART'S DESIRE/TAKE MY HEART	5.00	8.00
☐4007	***SCARLET***	STRANGE LOVE/LET'S TAKE A WALK	3.50	6.00
☐7027	***TAP***	OH JULIE/MY LITTLE GIRL	6.00	10.00
☐6005	***NASCO***	OH JULIE/MY LITTLE GIRL (5)	1.25	3.00
☐6009		SCHOOLGIRL/CRAZY HOP	1.75	3.00
☐6021		YOUNG AND IN LOVE/RAINY SUNDAY	1.75	3.00
		CRESCENDOS—ALBUM		
☐1453	(M)***GUEST STAR***	OH JULIE	7.00	12.00
		CRESCENTS		
☐4	***BREAK OUT***	DEVIL SURF/PINK DOMINOS	2.50	4.00

CRESTS

The Crests first formed in 1957. At the time they were all high school students and neighborhood friends. Leader Johnny Mastrangelo (later to record as Johnny Maestro) organized the group, rehearsed them whenever and wherever he could, and finally landed an audition for them at Joyce Records. Their first outing was a sweet r & b number called "Sweetest One". A local success, nationally the song barely dented the Top 100. A second Joyce 45 didn't make the sales charts at all.

The Crests then went with Coed Records, who promised better promotion and distribution. But the quartet's first Coed recording—"Pretty Little Angel"—did nothing. And, for a while, neither did their second disc of "Sixteen Candles". Then Dick Clark began playing the single on his popular afternoon "American Bandstand" show. "Sixteen Candles" then shot into the Top 5 and sold over a million copies. It became the Crests' biggest seller and best-known single, although the group did eventually manage four more Top 30 Coed singles before disbanding. Maestro briefly reappeared in 1968 as leader of the Brooklyn Bridge with the hit of "Worst That Could Happen".

ISSUE #	LABEL	ARTIST/TITLE	VG	MINT
		CRESTS		
		SEE: JOHNNY MAESTRO		
☐103	***JOYCE***	SWEETEST ONE/MY JUANITA (86)	12.00	20.00
☐105		NO ONE TO LOVE/WISH SHE WAS MINE	15.00	25.00
☐501	***COED***	LITTLE ANGEL/I THANK THE MOON	6.00	10.00
☐506		SIXTEEN CANDLES/BESIDE YOU (2)	1.25	3.00
☐509		SIX NIGHTS A WEEK/I DO (28)	1.50	2.50
☐511		FLOWER OF LOVE/MOLLY MAE (79)	1.75	3.00
☐515		THE ANGELS LISTENED IN/I THANK THE MOON (22)	1.25	2.50
☐521		A YEAR AGO TONIGHT/PAPER CROWN (42)	1.50	2.50
☐525		STEP BY STEP/GEE (14)	1.25	2.50
☐531		TROUBLE IN PARADISE/ALWAYS YOU (20)	1.25	2.50
☐535		JOURNEY OF LOVE/IF MY HEART COULD WRITE A LETTER (81)	1.50	2.50
☐537		ISN'T IT AMAZING/MOLLY ME (100)	1.50	2.50
☐543		IN THE STILL OF THE NIGHT/ GOOD GOLLY MISS MOLLY	1.75	3.00
☐561		LITTLE MIRACLES/BABY I GOTTA KNOW	1.50	2.50
☐696	***TRANS ATLAS***	THE ACTOR/THREE TEARS IN A BUCKET	1.75	3.00
☐311	***SELMA***	GUILTY/NUMBER ONE WITH ME	1.75	3.00
☐400		TEARS WILL FALL/DID I REMEMBER	1.75	3.00
		CRESTS—EP		
☐101	***COED***	THE ANGELS LISTENED IN	9.00	16.00
		CRESTS—ALBUMS		
☐901 (M)	***COED***	THE CRESTS SING ALL BIGGIES	15.00	25.00
☐904 (M)		THE BEST OF THE CRESTS	12.00	20.00
		CREW CUTS		
☐70341	***MERCURY***	CRAZY 'BOUT YA, BABY/ANGELA MIA (8)	1.25	3.00
☐70404		SH-BOOM/I SPOKE TOO SOON (1)	1.25	3.00
☐70443		OOP SHOOP/DO ME GOOD, BABY (18)	1.00	2.50
☐70529		EARTH ANGEL/KO KO MO (10)	1.00	2.50
☐70597		DON'T BE ANGRY/CHOP CHOP BOOM (14)	1.00	2.00
☐70634		A STORY UNTOLD/CARMEN'S BOOGIE	1.00	2.00
☐70668		GUM DROP/SONG OF THE FOOL (10)	1.00	2.00
☐70741		ANGELS IN THE SKY/MOSTLY MARTHA (13)	1.00	2.00

CRICKETS

The Crickets were formed by Buddy Holly in 1957. Following an unsuccessful recording session for Decca Records in Nashville, Buddy recruited three fellow Lubbock, Texas, musicians. (One—Niki Sullivan—left a few months later.) When it came time to choose a group name, someone suggested Buddy Holly and the Beetles. The name was rejected, though, in favor of the Crickets, the only insect to produce a singing sound.

The Crickets motored to Clovis, New Mexico, and cut their first records at the Norman Petty Studio. Contrary to popular belief, the Crickets didn't sing; rather, two studio backup groups—the Picks and the Roses—were used alternately.

Roulette Records passed on Petty's offer of a Crickets contract, so Norman approached Brunswick Records. They signed the rocking Texans and released "That'll Be the Day" during the summer of 1957.

Buddy Holly left the group a year later, as he was headed in a different musical direction. After Buddy's death early in 1959, the Crickets continued recording but without commercial success.

ISSUE #	LABEL	ARTIST/TITLE	VG	MINT
		CRICKETS		
		FEATURED: BUDDY HOLLY		
☐55009	***BRUNSWICK***	THAT'LL BE THE DAY/I'M LOOKING FOR SOMEONE TO LOVE (3)	2.00	3.50
☐55035		OH BOY!/NOT FADE AWAY (10)	2.00	3.50
☐55053		MAYBE BABY/TELL ME HOW (18)	2.00	3.50
☐55072		THINK IT OVER/FOOL'S PARADISE (27)	2.50	4.00
☐55094		IT'S SO EASY/LONESOME TEARS	3.00	5.00
		CRICKETS—EPs		
☐71036	***BRUNSWICK***	THE "CHIRPING" CRICKETS	12.00	20.00
☐71038		THE SOUND OF THE CRICKETS	15.00	22.00
		CRICKETS—ALBUM		
☐54038	***BRUNSWICK***	THE "CHIRPING" CRICKETS	30.00	50.00
		CRICKETS		
☐55124	***BRUNSWICK***	LOVE'S MADE A FOOL OF YOU/SOMEONE, SOMEONE	2.00	3.50
☐55153		WHEN YOU ASK ABOUT LOVE/DEBORAH	2.50	4.00
☐62198	***CORAL***	MORE THAN I CAN SAY/BABY MY HEART	3.00	5.00
☐62238		PEGGY SUE GOT MARRIED/DON'T CHA KNOW	5.00	8.00
☐55392	***LIBERTY***	I'M FEELING BETTER/ HE'S OLD ENOUGH TO KNOW BETTER	1.75	3.00
☐55441		DON'T EVER CHANGE/I'M NOT A BAD GUY	1.75	3.00
☐55495		LITTLE HOLLYWOOD GIRL/PARISIAN GIRL	1.50	2.50
☐55540		TEARDROPS FALL LIKE RAIN/MY LITTLE GIRL	1.50	2.50
☐55668		PLEASE PLEASE ME/FROM ME TO YOU	2.00	3.50
☐55767		EVERYBODY'S GOT A LITTLE PROBLEM/ NOW HEAR THIS	1.50	2.50
		CRICKETS—ALBUMS		
☐3272 (M)	***LIBERTY***	SOMETHING OLD, SOMETHING NEW, SOMETHING BLUE, SOMETHIN' ELSE!	7.00	12.00
☐7272 (S)		SOMETHING OLD, SOMETHING NEW, SOMETHING BLUE, SOMETHIN' ELSE!	8.00	15.00
☐3351 (M)		CALIFORNIA SUN	5.00	8.00
☐7351 (S)		CALIFORNIA SUN	6.00	10.00
		CROSSFIRES (TURTLES)		
☐104	***CAPCO***	FIBERGLASS JUNGLE/DR. JEKYLL AND MR. HYDE	3.00	5.00
☐112	***LUCKY TOKEN***	THAT'LL BE THE DAY/ONE POTATO, TWO POTATO	2.50	4.00
		CROSSFIRES (TURTLES)—ALBUM		
☐1083 (M)	***STRAND***	LIMBO ROCK	5.00	8.00
		CROWS		
☐5	***RAMA***	GEE/I LOVE YOU SO (17)	5.00	10.00
☐5		GEE/I LOVE YOU SO (colored wax)	25.00	50.00
		CYRSTALS		
☐114	***INDIGO***	DREAMS AND WISHES/MR BRUSH	6.00	10.00
☐100	***PHILLIES***	THERE NO OTHER/OH YEAH, MAYBE BABE (20)	2.00	4.00
☐102		UPTOWN/WHAT A NICE WAY TO TURN SEVENTEEN (20)	1.75	3.50
☐105		HE HIT ME (AND IT FELT LIKE A KISS)/ NO ONE EVER TELLS YOU	3.50	6.00
☐106		HE'S A REBEL/I LOVE YOU EDDIE (1)	1.50	3.00
☐109		HE'S SURE THE BOY I LOVE/WALKIN' ALONG (11)	1.50	3.00
☐111		DO THE SCREW (PT. 1)/(PT. 11)(dj copies only)	125.00	200.00
☐112		DA DOO RON RON/GIT IT (3)	1.50	3.00

ISSUE #	LABEL	ARTIST/TITLE	VG	MINT
□115		THEN HE KISS ME/BROTHER JULIUS (6)	1.50	3.00
□119		LITTLE BOY/HARRY AND MILT (92)	2.50	4.00
□122		ALL GROWN UP/IRVING (92)	2.50	4.00
□927	*UNITED ARTISTS*	MY PLACE/YOU CAN'T TIE A GOOD GIRL DOWN	2.50	4.00
□994		I GOT A MAN/ARE YOU TRYING TO GET RID OF ME, BABY?	2.50	4.00

CRYSTALS—ALBUMS

□4000 (M)	*PHILLIES*	TWIST UPTOWN	18.00	30.00
□4001 (M)		HE'S A REBEL	15.00	25.00
□4003 (M)		THE CRYSTALS SING THE GREATEST HITS, VOL. 1	12.00	20.00

JOHNNY CYMBAL

□12935	*MGM*	IT'LL BE ME/ALWAYS	2.00	3.50
□503	*KAPP*	MR. BASS MAN/SACRED LOVER'S VOW (16)	1.00	2.50
□524		TEENAGE HEAVEN/CINDERELLA BABY (58)	2.00	3.50
□539		DUM DUM DEE DUM/TIJUANA (77)	1.25	2.50
□556		HURDY GURDY MAN/MARSHMALLOW	1.50	2.50
□576		THERE'S GOES A BAD GIRL/REFRESHMENT TIME	1.50	2.50
□614		LITTLE MISS LONELY/CONNIE	1.75	3.00

JOHNNY CRYSTAL—ALBUM

□1324 (M)	*KAPP*	MR. BASS MAN	5.00	8.00
□3324 (S)		MR. BASS MAN	6.00	10.00

CYRUS ERIE

FEATURED: ERIC CARMEN

□10451	*EPIC*	SPARROW/GET THE MESSAGE	3.00	5.00

D

ISSUE #	LABEL	ARTIST/TITLE	VG	MINT

BERTELL DACHE (TONY ORLANDO)

FEATURED: CAROLE KING

□290	*UNITED ARTISTS*	LOVE EYES/NOT JUST TOMORROW BUT ALWAYS	6.00	10.00

DALE AND GRACE

□921	*MICHELLE*	I'M LEAVING IT UP TO YOU/ THAT'S WHAT I LIKE ABOUT YOU	3.00	5.00
□922		STOP AND THINK IT OVER/BAD LUCK	3.00	5.00
□928		THE LONELIEST NIGHT/I'M NOT FREE	2.50	4.00

MONTEL SINGLES ARE WORTH UP TO $1.50 MINT

DICK DALE

FEATURED: THE DEL-TONES

□5012	*DELTONE*	OH WHEE MARIE/BREAKING HEART	5.00	8.00
□5013		STOP TEASIN'/WITHOUT YOUR LOVE	5.00	8.00
□5014		JESSIE PEARL/ST. LOUIS BLUES	8.00	15.00
□5017		LET'S GO TRIPPIN'/DEL-TONES ROCK (60)	2.00	3.50
□5018		SHAKE 'N' STOMP/JUNGLE FEVER	2.50	4.00
□5019		MISERLOU/EIGHT TILL MIDNIGHT	2.50	4.00
□5020		SURF BEAT/PEPPERMINT MAN	2.50	4.00
□5028		LOVIN' ON MY BRAIN/RUN FOR YOUR LIFE	7.00	12.00

ISSUE #	LABEL	ARTIST/TITLE	VG	MINT
□ 106	*CUPID*	WE'LL NEVER HEAR THE END OF IT/		
		FAIREST OF THEM ALL......................	3.50	6.00
□ 371	*CONCERT ROOM*	WE'LL NEVER HEAR THE END OF IT/		
		FAIREST OF THEM ALL......................	2.50	4.00
□ 401	*SATURN*	WE'LL NEVER HEAR THE END OF IT/		
		FAIREST OF THEM ALL......................	2.50	4.00
□ 7014	*YES*	WE'LL NEVER HEAR THE END OF IT/		
		FAIREST OF THEM ALL......................	1.75	3.00
□ 4939	*CAPITOL*	MISERLOU/EIGHT TILL MIDNIGHT	1.75	3.00
□ 4940		SURF BEAT/PEPPERMINT MAN................	1.75	3.00
□ 4963		KING OF THE SURF GUITAR/HAVA NAGILA........	1.75	3.00
□ 5010		SECRET SURFIN' SPOT/SURFIN' AND A SWINGIN' .	1.75	3.00
□ 5048		THE SCAVENGER/WILD IDEAS (98)..............	1.75	3.00
□ 5098		THE WEDGE/NIGHT RIDER....................	1.75	3.00
□ 5140		MR. ELIMINATOR/THE VICTOR	1.75	3.00
□ 5187		GRUDGE RUN/WILD, WILD MUSTANG............	1.75	3.00
□ 5225		GLORY WAY/NEVER ON SUNDAY	1.75	3.00
□ 5290		WHO CAN HE BE/OH MARIE	1.50	2.50
□ 5389		LET'S GO TRIPPIN' '65/WATUSI JOE	1.75	3.00
		DICK DALE—ALBUMS		
□ 1001 (M)	*DELTONE*	SURFER'S CHOICE...........................	8.00	15.00
□ 1930 (M)	*CAPITOL*	KING OF THE SURF GUITAR...................	6.00	10.00
□ 1930 (S)		KING OF THE SURF GUITAR...................	7.00	12.00
□ 2002 (M)		CHECKERED FLAG	5.00	8.00
□ 2002 (S)		CHECKERED FLAG	6.00	10.00
□ 2052 (M)		MR. ELIMINATOR..........................	5.00	8.00
□ 2053 (S)		MR. ELIMINATOR..........................	6.00	10.00
□ 2111 (M)		SUMMER SURF	5.00	8.00
□ 2111 (S)		SUMMER SURF	7.00	12.00
□ 2200 (M)		LIVE AT CIRO'S	6.00	10.00
□ 2292 (S)		LIVE AT CIRO'S	7.00	12.00
		JIMMY DALE (JIMMY CLANTON)		
□ 1003	*DREW-BLAN*	EMMA LEE/MY PRIDE AND JOY.................	3.50	6.00
		DANLEERS		
□ 3	*AMP*	ONE SUMMER NIGHT/WHEELIN' AND A DEALIN'	6.00	10.00
□ 71322	*MERCURY*	ONE SUMMER NIGHT/WHEELIN' AND A DEALIN' (16) .	1.25	3.00

DANNY AND THE JUNIORS

The Juvenairs got together in Philadelphia in 1957. After practicing several current hit songs, the group tried out for—and signed with—the Singular label in Philadelphia. It was then that a name change was suggested. As they were led by a lad named Danny (Rapp) and were all juniors in high school, they took on the name of Danny and the Juniors.

They recorded a song that group member David White had co-written called "Do the Bop," named after a popular 1950s dance. Dick Clark heard the song and suggested the title be changed to "At the Hop". Singular then released the single. When it began getting East Coast airplay, ABC-Paramount Records offered to lease the master and release it on their label. Singular agreed. With better promotion and distribution, ABC-Paramount's release of "At the Hop" went all the way to the top.

Danny and the Juniors' follow-up was the Top 20 hit of "Rock and Roll Is Here To Stay." After "Dottie" (a mild success) Danny and the Juniors never again made the charts for ABC-Paramount. A switch to Swan Records resulted in a Top 30 single, but after that the group faded into oblivion.

ISSUE #	LABEL	ARTIST/TITLE	VG	MINT
		DANNY AND THE JUNIORS		
□711	*SINGULAR*	AT THE HOP/SOMETIMES	15.00	25.00
□9871	*ABC-PARAMOUNT*	AT THE HOP/SOMETIMES (1)	1.50	3.00
□9888		ROCK AND ROLL IS HERE TO STAY/ SCHOOL BOY ROMANCE (19)	1.50	3.00
□9926		DOTTIE/IN THE MEANTIME (41)	1.50	2.50
□9953		CRAZY CAFE/A THIEF	1.75	3.00
□9978		I FEEL SO LONELY/SASSY FRAN	1.75	3.00
□10004		DO YOU LOVE ME?/SOMEHOW I CAN'T FORGET	1.75	3.00
□10052		PLAYING HARD TO GET/OF LOVE	1.75	3.00
□4060	*SWAN*	TWISTIN' U.S.A./A THOUSAND MILES AWAY (27)	1.25	2.50
□4064		O HOLY NIGHT/CANDY CANE, SUGARY PLUM	1.75	3.00
□4068		PONY EXPRESS/DAY DREAMER (60)	1.50	2.50
□4072		CHA CHA GO-GO/MR. WHISPER	1.50	2.50
□4082		BACK TO THE HOP/CHARLESTON FISH (80)	1.50	2.50
□4092		TWISTIN' ALL NIGHT LONG/SOME KIND OF NUT (68)	1.50	2.50
□4100		DOIN' THE CONTINENTAL WALK/ DO THE MASHED POTATO (93)	1.50	2.50
□4113		WE GOT SOUL/FUNNY	1.50	2.50
□2076	*GUYDEN*	OO-LA-LA-LIMBO/NOW AND THEN (99)	1.75	3.00
		DANNY AND THE JUNIORS—EP		
□11	*ABC-PARAMOUNT*	AT THE HOP	8.00	15.00
		DANTE AND THE EVERGREENS		
		PRODUCERS: JAN AND DEAN		
□130	*MADISON*	ALLEY-OOP/THE RIGHT TIME (15)	1.50	3.00
□135		TIME MACHINE/DREAM LAND (73)	1.75	3.00
□143		WHAT ARE YOU DOING NEW YEAR'S EVE/YEAH BABY	2.00	3.50
□154		THINK SWEET THOUGHTS/DA DOO	2.00	3.50
		DANTE AND THE EVERGREENS—ALBUM		
□1002 (M)	*MADISON*	DANTE AND THE EVERGREENS	12.00	20.00

BOBBY DARIN

He was born Walden Robert Cassotto in the Bronx on May 14, 1936. The Cassottos were so destitute that Bobby slept in a dresser drawer when he was first born. (Mr. Cassotto had died, and the surviving family existed on welfare.) As a youngster Bobby suffered from scarlet fever. Knowing that his lifespan could be decidedly shorter than that of the average person (he had suffered severe heart damage) perhaps drove Bobby Darin to accomplish as much as possible in the time he had. This attitude was often deciphered as conceited aggresiveness.

As an adolescent Darin (the name was taken from a New York phone book) mastered the piano, guitar and drums. After a brief stint as a Hunter College drama major, Bobby entered the recording world. In 1956 he signed with Decca Records and recorded five singles. None was a hit. A year later he went with Atco.

Bobby Darin's third Atco single was "Splish Splash", a song penned in only ten minutes. His later accomplishments included such classics as "Dream Lover" and 1959's best-seller, "Mack the Knife". In 1962 Darin signed with Capitol Records but was never able to match his heydays at Atco. He died at age 37 on December 20, 1973, while undergoing open-heart surgery in Los Angeles.

BOBBY DARIN

ISSUE #	LABEL	ARTIST/TITLE	VG	MINT
□ 29883	***DECCA***	ROCK ISLAND LINE/TIMBER	7.00	12.00
□ 29922		SILLY WILLIE/BLUE EYED MERMAID	6.00	10.00
□ 30031		HEAR THEM BELLS/THE GREATEST BUILDER	6.00	10.00
□ 30225		DEALER IN DREAMS/HELP ME	6.00	10.00
□ 30737		SILLY WILLIE/DEALER IN DREAMS	4.00	7.00
□ 6092	***ATCO***	I FOUND A MILLION DOLLAR BABY/TALK TO ME	2.00	3.50
□ 6103		PRETTY BABY/DON'T CALL MY NAME	2.00	3.50
□ 6109		JUST IN CASE YOU CHANGE YOUR MIND/SO MEAN	1.75	3.00
□ 6117		SPLISH SPLASH/JUDY, DON'T BE MOODY (3)	1.25	3.00
□ 6127		QUEEN OF THE HOP/LOST LOVE (9)	1.25	3.00
□ 6133		PLAIN JANE/WHILE I'M GONE (38)	1.50	3.00
□ 6140		DREAM LOVER/BULL MOOSE (2)	1.25	3.00
□ 6147		MACK THE KNIFE/WAS THERE A CALL FOR ME (1)	1.25	3.00
□ 6158		BEYOND THE SEA/THAT'S THE WAY LOVE IS (6)	1.25	2.50
□ 6161		CLEMENTINE/TALL STORY (21)	1.50	2.50
□ 6167		WON'T YOU COME HOME BILL BAILEY/ I'LL BE THERE (19)	1.50	2.50
□ 6173		BEACHCOMBER/AUTUMN BLUES (100)	1.75	2.50
□ 6179		ARTIFICIAL FLOWERS/SOMEBODY TO LOVE (20)	1.50	2.50
□ 6183		CHRISTMAS AULD LANG SYNE/CHILD OF GOD (51)	1.50	2.50
□ 6188		LAZY RIVER/OO-EE-TRAIN (14)	1.25	2.50
□ 6196		NATURE BOY/LOOK FOR MY TRUE LOVE (40)	1.50	2.50
□ 6200		COME SEPTEMBER/WALK BACK WITH ME	1.75	3.00
□ 6206		YOU MUST HAVE BEEN A BEAUTIFUL BABY/ SORROW TOMORROW (5)	1.25	2.50
□ 6211		AVE MARIA/O COME, ALL YE FAITHFUL	1.50	2.50
□ 6214		IRRESISTABLE YOU/MULTIPLICATION (15)	1.00	2.50
□ 6221		WHAT'D I SAY (PT. 1)/(PT. 11) (24)	1.25	2.50
□ 6229		THINGS/JAILER, BRING ME WATER (3)	1.00	2.00
□ 6236		BABY FACE/YOU KNOW HOW (42)	1.25	2.00
□ 6244		I FOUND A NEW BABY/KEEP A WALKIN' (90)	1.25	2.00
□ 6297		MILORD/GOLDEN EARRINGS (45)	1.25	2.00
□ 6316		SWING LOW, SWEET CHARIOT/SIMILAU	1.25	2.00
□ 6334		HARD HEARTED HANNAH/MINNIE THE MOOCHER	1.25	2.00
□ 4837	***CAPITOL***	IF A MAN ANSWERS/TRUE TRUE LOVE (32)	1.00	2.50
□ 4897		YOU'RE THE REASON I'M LIVING/ NOW YOU'RE GONE (3)	.75	2.00
□ 4970		EIGHTEEN YELLOW ROSES/NOT FOR ME (10)	.75	2.00
□ 5019		TREAT MY BABY GOOD/DOWN SO LONG (43)	1.00	2.00
□ 5079		BE MAD LITTLE GIRL/SINCE YOU'VE BEEN GONE (64)	1.00	2.00
□ 5126		I WONDER WHO'S KISSING HER NOW/ AS LONG AS I'M SINGING (93)	1.00	2.00
□ 5257		THE THINGS IN THIS HOUSE/WAIT BY THE WATER (86)	1.00	2.00
□ 5359		HELLO, DOLLY!/GOLDEN EARRINGS (79)	1.00	2.00
□ 5399		A WORLD WITHOUT YOU/VENICE	1.25	2.00
□ 5443		WHEN I GET HOME/LONELY ROAD	1.25	2.00
□ 5481		THAT FUNNY FEELING/GYP THE CAT	1.25	2.00

BOBBY DARIN—EPs

ISSUE #	LABEL	ARTIST/TITLE	VG	MINT
□ 2676	***DECCA***	BOBBY DARIN	8.00	15.00
□ 4502	***ATCO***	BOBBY DARIN	4.00	7.00
□ 4504		THAT'S ALL	3.50	6.00
□ 4505		BOBBY DARIN	3.50	6.00
□ 4508		THIS IS DARIN	3.00	5.00

ISSUE #	LABEL	ARTIST/TITLE	VG	MINT
		BOBBY DARIN—ALBUMS		
□ 102 (M)	*ATCO*	BOBBY DARIN	8.00	15.00
□ 104 (M)		THAT'S ALL	7.00	12.00
□ 104 (S)		THAT'S ALL	8.00	15.00
□ 115 (M)		THIS IS DARIN	6.00	10.00
□ 115 (S)		THIS IS DARIN	7.00	12.00
□ 131 (M)		THE BOBBY DARIN STORY (greatest hits)	6.00	10.00
□ 131 (S)		THE BOBBY DARIN STORY (greatest hits)	7.00	12.00
□ 1826 (M)	*CAPITOL*	EARTHY	3.50	6.00
□ 1826 (S)		EARTHY	4.50	8.00
□ 1866 (M)		YOU'RE THE REASON I'M LIVING	3.50	6.00
□ 1866 (S)		YOU'RE THE REASON I'M LIVING	4.50	8.00
□ 1942 (M)		18 YELLOW ROSES	3.50	6.00
□ 1942 (S)		18 YELLOW ROSES	4.50	8.00
		DARREL AND THE OXFORDS (TOKENS)		
□ 4174	*ROULETTE*	PICTURE IN MY WALLET/ROSES ARE RED	5.00	8.00
□ 4230		CAN'T YOU TELL?/YOUR MOTHER SAID NO	5.00	8.00
		JAMES DARREN		
□ 102	*COLPIX*	THERE'S NO SUCH THING/ MIGHTY PRETTY TERRITORY	2.00	3.50
□ 113		GIDGET/YOU (41)	1.50	3.00
□ 119		ANGEL FACE/I DON'T WANNA LOSE YA (47)	1.75	3.00
□ 130		TEENAGE TEARS/LET THERE BE LOVE	1.50	2.50
□ 142		BECAUSE THEY'RE YOUNG/TEARS IN MY EYES	1.50	2.50
□ 609		GOODBYE CRUEL WORLD/VALERIE (3)	1.00	2.00
□ 622		HER ROYAL MAJESTY/ IF I COULD ONLY TELL YOU (6)	1.00	2.00
□ 630		CONSCIENCE/DREAM BIG (11)	1.25	2.00
□ 644		MARY'S LITTLE LAMB/ THE LIFE OF THE PARTY (39)	1.25	2.00
□ 655		HAIL TO THE CONQUERING HERO/ TOO YOUNG TO GO STEADY (97)	1.25	2.00
		LATER COLPIX SINGLES ARE WORTH UP TO $1.50 MINT		
		JAMES DARREN—ALBUM		
□ 406 (M)	*COLPIX*	ALBUM NO. 1	6.00	10.00
		DARTELLS		
□ 509	*ARLEN*	HOT PASTRAMI/DARTELL STOMP	3.00	5.00
□ 513		DANCE, EVERYBODY, DANCE/THE SCOOBIE SONG	2.50	4.00
□ 16453	*DOT*	HOT PASTRAMI/DARTELL STOMP (11)	.75	2.00
□ 16502		DANCE, EVERYONE, DANCE/ THE SCOOBIE SONG (99)	1.25	2.00
		DARTELLS—ALBUM		
□ 3522 (M)	*DOT*	HOT PASTRAMI	4.50	8.00
□ 25522 (S)		HOT PASTRAMI	5.50	10.00
		DAVE DAVIES		
		SEE: KINKS		
□ 0614	*REPRISE*	DEATH OF A CLOWN/ LOVE ME TILL THE SUN SHINES	2.50	4.00
□ 0660		SUSANNAH'S STILL ALIVE/FUNNY FACE	2.50	4.00

ISSUE #	LABEL	ARTIST/TITLE	VG	MINT
		TERRY DAY (TERRY MELCHER)		
		SEE: BRUCE AND TERRY		
☐42427	*COLUMBIA*	THAT'S ALL I WANT/I WAITED TOO LONG	2.50	4.00
☐42678		BE A SOLDIER/I LOVE YOU BETTY	3.00	5.00
		DEAN AND JEAN		
☐1048	EMBER	TOO YOUNG TO KNOW/ WE'RE GONNA GET MARRIED	2.00	3.50
☐1054		TURN IF OFF/NEVER LET YOUR LOVE FADE AWAY	2.00	3.50
☐1086		CROSS MY HEART/THAT'S THE WAY IT GOES	2.00	3.50
☐5044	*RUST*	COME TAKE A WALK WITH ME/ DANCE THE ROACH	1.75	3.00
☐5046		YOU CAN'T BE HAPPY BY YOURSELF/ MACK THE KNIFE	1.75	3.00
☐5067		TRA LA LA SUZY/ I LOVE THE SUMMERTIME (35)	1.00	2.00
☐5075		HEY JEAN, HEY DEAN/ PLEASE DON'T TELL ME NOW (32)	1.00	2.00
☐5081		I WANNA BE LOVED/THREAD YOUR NEEDLE (91)	1.25	2.00
☐5085		THE GODDESS OF LOVE/THE MAN WHO	1.25	2.00
☐5089		STICKS AND STONES/IN MY WAY	1.25	2.00
☐5100		THE GODDESS OF LOVE/LOVINGLY YOURS	.75	1.00
		JANET DEANE		
		FEATURED: SKYLINGERS		
☐719	*GATEWAY*	ANOTHER NIGHT ALONE/I'M GLAD I WAITED	2.50	4.00
		JACKIE DEE (JACKIE DeSHANNON)		
☐55148	*LIBERTY*	BUDDY/STROLYPSO DANCE	3.00	4.00
		JOEY DEE		
☐7009	*BONUS*	LORRAINE/THE GIRL I WALK TO SCHOOL	2.50	4.00
☐1210	*SCEPTER*	THE FACE OF AN ANGEL/SHIMMY BABY	2.00	3.50
		JOEY DEE AND THE STARLITERS		
☐5539	*JUBILEE*	DANCIN' ON THE BEACH/GOOD LITTLE YOU	2.50	4.00
☐5554		SHE'S SO EXCEPTIONAL/IT'S GOT YOU	2.50	4.00
☐5566		YOU CAN'T SIT DOWN/PUT YOUR HEART IN IT	2.50	4.00
☐4401	*ROULETTE*	PEPPERMINT TWIST (PT. 1)/(PT. 11) (11)	.75	2.00
☐4408		HEY, LET'S TWIST/ROLY POLY (20)	1.00	2.00
☐4416		HOUT (PT. 1)/(PT. 11) (6)	.75	2.00
☐4431		EVERYTIME (PT. 1)/(PT. 11)	1.50	2.50
☐4438		WHAT KIND OF LOVE IS THIS?/WING DING (18)	1.00	2.00
☐4456		I LOST MY BABY/KEEP YOUR MIND ON WHAT YOU'RE DOIN' (61)	1.25	2.00
☐4467		BABY, YOU'RE DRIVING ME CRAZY/ HELP ME PICK UP THE PIECES (100)	1.25	2.00
☐4488		HOT PASTRAMI WITH MASHED POTATOES (PT. 1)/(PT. 11) (36)	1.00	2.00
☐4503		DANCE, DANCE, DANCE/LET'S HAVE A PARTY (89)	1.25	2.00
☐4525		FANNIE MAE/YA YA	1.25	2.00
☐4539		DOWN BY THE RIVERSIDE/GETTING NEARER	1.25	2.00
		JOEY DEE AND THE STARLITERS—ALBUMS		
☐503 (M)	*SCEPTER*	PEPPERMINT TWISTERS	6.00	10.00
☐25166 (M)	*ROULETTE*	DOIN' THE TWIST AT THE PEPPERMINT LOUNGE	3.50	6.00
☐25166 (S)		DOIN' THE TWIST AT THE PEPPERMINT LOUNGE	4.50	8.00

ISSUE #		LABEL	ARTIST/TITLE	VG	MINT
☐ 25168	(M)		HEY, LET'S TWIST	3.50	6.00
☐ 25168	(S)		HEY, LET'S TWIST	4.50	8.00
☐ 25171	(M)		ALL THE WORLD IS TWISTIN'	3.00	5.00
☐ 25171	(S)		ALL THE WORLD IS TWISTIN'	4.00	7.00

JOHNNY DEE (JOHN D. LOUDERMILK)

☐ 430		COLONIAL	SITTIN' IN THE BALCONY/A-PLUS IN LOVE) (38)	1.50	3.00
☐ 433			TEENAGE QUEEN/IT'S GOTTA BE YOU	2.00	3.50

TOMMY DEE

☐ 1057		CREST	THREE STARS/I'LL NEVER CHANGE (11)	2.00	3.50
☐ 1067			ANGEL OF LOVE/MERRY CHRISTMAS, MARY	1.75	3.00
☐ 5905		PIKE	LOOK HOMEWARD DEAR ANGEL/		
			A LITTLE DOG CRIED	1.75	3.00
☐ 59087		CHALLENGE	BALLAD OF A DRAG RACE/THE STORY OF SUSIE	1.50	2.50

DELL-VIKINGS

☐ 106		LUNIVERSE	OVER THE RAINBOW/HEY SENORITA	7.00	12.00
☐ 205		FEE BEE	COME GO WITH ME/HOW CAN I FIND TRUE LOVE	20.00	30.00
☐ 210			TRUE LOVE/UH UH BABY	3.50	6.00
☐ 214			WHISPERING BELLS/DON'T BE A FOOL	12.00	20.00
☐ 15538		DOT	COME GO WITH ME/HOW CAN I FIND TRUE LOVE (5)	2.00	3.50
☐ 15571			WHAT MADE MAGGIE RUN/LITTLE BILLY BOY	2.50	4.00
☐ 15592			WHISPERING BELLS/DON'T BE A FOOL (9)	2.00	3.50
☐ 15636			I'M SPINNING/WHEN I COME HOME	1.75	3.00
☐ 71132		MERCURY	COOL SHAKE/JITTERBUG MARY (46)	1.25	2.50
☐ 71880			COME ALONG WITH ME/WHAT 'CHA GOTTA LOSE	1.75	3.00
☐ 71241			YOUR BOOK OF LIVE/SNOWBOUND	1.50	2.50
☐ 71266			THE VOODOO MAN/CAN'T WAIT	1.50	2.50

DELL-VIKINGS—EPs

☐ 1058		DOT	COME GO WITH US	6.00	10.00
☐ 3362		MERCURY	THEY SING - THEY SWING	6.00	10.00

DELL-VIKINGS—ALBUMS

☐ 1000	(M)	LUNIVERSE	COME GO WITH THE DELL-VIKINGS	35.00	60.00
☐ 1003	(M)	DOT	BEST OF THE DELL-VIKINGS	25.00	40.00
☐ 20314	(M)	MERCURY	THEY SING - THEY SWING	40.00	70.00

DEMENSIONS

☐ 116		MOHAWK	OVER THE RAINBOW/		
			NURSERY RHYME ROCK (16)	1.75	3.50
☐ 120			ZING! WENT THE STRINGS OF MY HEART	1.75	3.00
☐ 121			AVE MARIA/GOD'S CHRISTMAS	1.75	3.00
☐ 123			A TEAR FELL/THERESA	1.75	3.00

LEE DENSON
GUITAR: EDDIE COCHRAN

☐ 0281		VIK	NEW SHOES/CLIMB LOVE MOUNTAIN	3.50	6.00

JACKIE DeSHANNON

☐ 416		EDISON			
		INTERNATIONAL	I WANNA GO HOME/SO WARM	2.50	4.00
☐ 418			PUT MY BABY DOWN/THE FOOLISH ONE	2.50	4.00
☐ 55288		LIBERTY	LONELY GIRL/TEACH ME	2.00	3.50
☐ 55342			THINK ABOUT YOU/HEAVEN IS BEING WITH YOU	2.00	3.50
☐ 55358			WISH I COULD FIND A BOY/		
			I WON'T TURN YOU DOWN	2.00	3.50

ISSUE #	LABEL	ARTIST/TITLE	VG	MINT
☐ 55387		BABY (WHEN YA KISS ME)/AIN'T THAT LOVE	2.00	3.50
☐ 55425		THE PRINCE/I'LL DROWN IN MY OWN TEARS	2.00	3.50
☐ 55425		THE PRINCE/THAT'S WHAT BOYS ARE MADE OF	2.00	3.00
☐ 55484		JUST LIKE IN THE MOVIES/ GUESS WHO	2.00	3.00
☐ 55497		YOU WON'T FORGET ME/ I DON'T THINK SO MUCH OF MYSELF	2.00	3.50
☐ 55526		FADED LOVE/DANCING SILHOUETTES (97)........	1.75	3.00
☐ 55563		NEEDLES AND PINS/DID HE CALL TODAY, MAMA? (84)	1.75	3.00
☐ 55602		LITTLE YELLOW ROSES/OH SWEET CHARIOT	1.75	3.00
☐ 55602		LITTLE YELLOW ROSES/500 MILES	1.75	3.00
☐ 55645		WHEN YOU WALK IN THE ROOM/ TILL YOU SAY YOU'RE MINE (99	1.75	3.00
☐ 55678		OH BOY!/I'M LOOKIN' FOR SOMEONE TO LOVE	2.00	3.50
☐ 55705		SHE DON'T UNDERSTAND HIM LIKE I DO/HOLD YOUR HEAD HIGH.................	1.75	3.00
☐ 55730		HE'S GOT THE WHOLE WORLD IN IN HIS HANDS/IT'S LOVE BABY..............	1.75	3.00
☐ 55735		OVER YOU/WHEN YOU WALK IN THE ROOM	1.50	2.50
☐ 56187		IT'S SO NICE/MEDITERRANEAN SKY	1.75	3.00
		SINGLES ON IMPERIAL ARE WORTH UP TO $2.00 MINT		
		JACKIE DeSHANNON—ALBUMS		
☐ 3320 (M)	*LIBERTY*	JACKIE DeSHANNON	3.50	6.00
☐ 7320 (S)		JACKIE DeSHANNON	4.50	8.00
☐ 3390 (M)		BREAKIN' IT UP ON THE BEATLES TOUR	5.00	8.00
☐ 7390 (S)		BREAKIN' IT UP ON THE BEATLES TOUR	6.00	10.00
☐ 3430 (M)		C'MON, LET'S LIVE A LITTLE (soundtrack)	3.50	6.00
☐ 7430 (S)		C'MON, LET'S LIVE A LITTLE (soundtrack)	4.50	8.50
		DESIRES (REGENTS)		
☐ 118	*SEVILLE*	STORY OF LOVE/I ASK YOU..................	3.00	5.00
		DETERGENTS		
☐ 4590		LEADER OF THE LAUNDROMAT/ULCERS (19)75	2.00
☐ 4603		DOUBLE-O-SEVEN/THE BLUE KANGAROO (89)	1.00	2.00
☐ 4616		LITTLE DUM-DUM/SOLDIER GIRL	1.25	2.00
		DETERGENTS—ALBUM		
☐ 25308 (M)	*ROULETTE*	THE MANY FACES OF THE DETERGENTS	3.50	6.00
☐ 25308 (S)		THE MANY FACES OF THE DETERGENTS	4.50	8.00
		BARRY DeVORZON		
☐ 7124	*RCA*	BABY DOLL/BARBARA JEAN	1.75	3.00
☐ 7510		CORA LEE/ BLUE, GREEN AND GOLD............	1.75	3.00
☐ 41612	*COLUMBIA*	HEY LITTLE DARLIN'/ROSEMARY	1.75	3.00
		DEVOTIONS		
☐ 1001	*DELTA*	RIP VAN WINKLE/I LOVE YOU FOR SENTIMENTAL REASONS	8.00	15.00
		DIALTONES (RANDY AND THE RAINBOWS)		
☐ 3005	*GOLDISC*	TILL I HEARD IT FROM YOU/JOHNNY	3.00	5.00
☐ 3020		TILL I HEARD IT FROM YOU/JOHNNY	2.50	4.00

NEIL DIAMOND

Neil Diamond was, as he once said in a hit song, "New York City born and raised". (His birthdate: January 21, 1939.) But when Neil was four his soldier father moved the family to Cheyenne, Wyoming. Later the family returned to Brooklyn, where Neil attended nine schools before he reached the age of sixteen. A lonely, withdrawn and mostly friendless child, Diamond had two main interests during high school: singing in the school choir and fencing. His latter talents won him a scholarship to New York University, where he enrolled as a pre-med major following graduation from high school in 1957.

Eight credits short of graduating, Neil Diamond quit NYU to pursue a songwriting career. He cut one unsuccessful single for Columbia. Diamond later earned fifty dollars a week, rented a cheap flat and lived on 33¢ a day—23¢ for a budget sandwich, 10¢ for a Coke. At one time Neil wrote songs for Don Kirshner.

Reluctantly Diamond asked Bang records for an audition. Still smarting from his three-year-old failure at Columbia, Neil was unsure if his singing was good enough. As it turned out, he racked up half-a-dozen Top 30 hits for Bang before moving on to Uni. Today he records for Columbia—his first label—and stands as one of the highest-paid performers in popular music.

ISSUE #	LABEL	ARTIST/TITLE	VG	MINT
		NEIL DIAMOND		
□42809	***COLUMBIA***	CLOWN TOWN/AT NIGHT........................	7.00	12.00
		SINGLES ON BANG ARE WORTH UP TO $1.50 MIND		

DIAMONDS

The Diamonds came from Ontario, Canada. Their first gigs were at local clubs and churches. Later a Cleveland, Ohio, disc jockey saw the Diamonds perform and suggested they go on record. With the disc jockey's assistance the quartet signed a contract with Mercury Records a few days later.

Their hits were chiefly "cover" versions of r & b hits, usually proving to be inferior to the originals (as were most "covers"). They sang such black hits as "Why Do Fools Fall In Love", "Church Bells May Ring" and "Ka-Ding Dong" before cutting one of the 1957's best-selling singles.

"Little Darlin' " had been originally done by the Gladiolas, a Southern group led by Maurice Williams. (The group would resurface in 1960 as Maurice Williams and the Zodiacs.) The Diamonds' manager insisted that the group sing the Gladiolas' song. Legend has it that the Diamonds, tired of the song after practicing it all night in a hotel room, intended their version of "Little Darlin' " to be a satire, with the falsetto and bass parts highly exaggerated in comparison with the original. The result was a single that sold 4,000,000 copies, with the buying public unaware of the joke.

ISSUE #	LABEL	ARTIST/TITLE	VG	MINT
		DIAMONDS		
☐61502	***CORAL***	BLACK DENIM TROUSERS AND MOTORCYCLE BOOTS/NIP SIP	2.50	4.00
☐61577		BE MY LOVIN' BABY/SMOOCH ME	2.50	4.00
☐70790	***MERCURY***	WHY DO FOOLS FALL IN LOVE/YOU BABY YOU (16)	1.50	3.00
☐70835		THE CHURCH BELLS MAY RING/ LITTLE GIRL OF MINE (20)	1.50	3.00
☐70889		LOVE, LOVE, LOVE/EV'RY NIGHT ABOUT THIS TIME (30)	1.75	3.00
☐70934		SOFT SUMMER BREEZE/KA-DING-DONG (34)	1.25	2.50
☐71021		A THOUSAND MILES AWAY/ EV'RY MINUTE OF THE DAY	1.75	3.00
☐71060		LITTLE DARLIN'/FAITHFUL AND TRUE (2)	1.25	2.50
☐71128		WORDS OF LOVE/DON'T SAY GOODBYE (76)	1.75	3.00
☐71165		ZIP ZIP/OH, HOW I WISH (45)	1.50	2.50
☐71197		SILHOUETTES/DADDY COOL (60)	1.50	2.50
☐71242		THE STROLL/LAND OF BEAUTY (5)	1.25	2.50
☐71291		HIGH SIGN/CHICK-LETS (DON'T LET ME DOWN) (38)	1.50	2.50
☐71330		KATHY-O/HAPPY YEARS (45)	1.50	2.50
☐71366		WALKING ALONG/ETERNAL LOVERS (29)	1.25	2.50
☐71404		SHE SAY (OOM DOOBY DOOM)/ FROM THE BOTTOM OF MY HEART (18)	1.25	2.50
☐71831		ONE SUMMER NIGHT/IT'S A DOGGONE SHAME (22)	1.25	2.50
		DIAMONDS—EPs		
☐3356	***MERCURY***	THE DIAMONDS	3.00	5.00
☐3357		THE DIAMONDS	3.00	5.00
☐3358		THE DIAMONDS	3.00	5.00
☐3367		THE DIAMONDS	2.50	4.00
☐3390		THE STROLL	2.50	4.00
		DIAMONDS—ALBUM		
☐20309	(M) ***MERCURY***	THE DIAMONDS	8.00	15.00
		DICK AND DEEDEE		
☐7778	***LAMA***	THE MOUNTAIN'S HIGH/I WANT SOMEONE	5.00	8.00
☐7780		GOODBYE TO LOVE/SWING LOW	3.00	5.00
☐7783		TELL ME/WILL YOU ALWAYS LOVE ME?	4.00	6.00
☐55350	***LIBERTY***	THE MOUNTAIN'S HIGH/I WANT SOMEONE (2)	1.00	2.50
☐55382		GOODBYE TO LOVE/SWING LOW	1.50	2.50
☐55412		TELL ME/WILL YOU ALWAYS LOVE ME? (22)	1.25	2.50
☐55478		ALL I WANT/LIFE'S JUST A PLAY	1.50	2.50
☐5320	***WARNER BROTHERS***	THE RIVER TOOK MY BABY/MY LONELY SELF	1.50	2.50
☐5342		YOUNG AND IN LOVE/SAY TO ME (17)	1.25	2.50
☐5364		LOVE IS A ONCE IN A LIFETIME THING/ CHUG-A-CHUG-A-CHOO-CHOO	1.50	2.50
☐5383		WHERE DID THE GOOD TIMES GO/ GUESS OUT LOVE MUST SHOW (93)	1.50	2.50
☐5396		TURN AROUND/DON'T LEAVE ME (27)	1.25	2.50
☐5411		ALL MY TRIALS/DON'T THINK TWICE, IT'S ALL RIGHT (89)	1.50	2.50
☐5426		THE GIFT/NOT FADE AWAY	1.50	2.50
☐5451		YOU WERE MINE/REMEMBER THEN	1.50	2.50
☐5470		WITHOUT YOUR LOVE/THE RIDDLE SONG	1.50	2.50

ISSUE #		LABEL	ARTIST/TITLE	VG	MINT
□5482			THOU SHALT NOT STEAL/ JUST 'ROUND THE RIVER BEND (13)	1.00	2.50
□5608			BE MY BABY/ROOM 404 (87)	1.50	2.50

LATER WARNER BROTHERS SINGLES ARE WORTH UP TO $2.00 MINT

DICK AND DEEDEE—ALBUMS

ISSUE #		LABEL	ARTIST/TITLE	VG	MINT
□3236	(M)	***LIBERTY***	TELL ME	4.00	7.00
□7236	(S)		TELL ME	5.00	9.00
□1500	(M)	***WARNER BROTHERS***	YOUNG AND IN LOVE	3.50	6.00
□1500	(S)		YOUNG AND IN LOVE	4.50	8.00
□1538	(M)		TURN AROUND	3.50	6.00
□1538	(S)		TURN AROUND	4.50	8.00

BO DIDDLEY

Bo Diddley began life as Ellis McDaniels on December 30, 1928, in the Mississippi farming village of McComb. The McDaniels family soon moved to Chicago, and during his early school years Ellis took on the nickname of "Bo Diddley." (He would later use the name during a brief stint at boxing.) On Christmas of 1938—just before his tenth birthday—Bo was given a guitar. He soon mastered the instrument, listening to Chicago blues artists all the while.

During the early 1950s he took a club job in Chicago. After a few years he tried out for Chess Records as a recording artist. Bo used an original song called "Uncle John" for his audition. Leonard Chess liked what he heard, but suggested a title change to that of "Bo Diddley." A total of 35 "takes" was required to get the right sound, but the efforts paid off. "Bo Diddley," the first hit r & b disc to use Spanish maracas, became a major r & b single.

Bo influenced everyone from Elvis Presley to a host of British blues guitarists. Today he lives on a New Mexico ranch but is often on the road appearing in a variety of traveling oldies shows.

ISSUE #	LABEL	ARTIST/TITLE	VG	MINT
		BO DIDDLEY		
□814	*CHECKER*	BO DIDDLEY/I'M A MAN	3.50	6.00
□819		DIDDLEY DADDY/SHE'S FINE, SHE'S MINE	3.00	5.00
□827		PRETTY THING/BRING IT TO JEROME	3.00	5.00
□842		WHO DO YOU LOVE/I'M BAD	3.00	5.00
□850		DOWN HOME TRAIN/COPS AND ROBBERS	3.00	5.00
□860		HEY BO DIDDLEY/MONA	3.50	6.00
□907		WILLIE AND LITTLE/BO MEETS THE MONSTER	3.00	5.00
		DING DONGS (RINKY-DINKS)		
		FEATURED: BOBBY DARIN		
□55073	*BRUNSWICK*	EARLY IN THE MORNING/NOW WE'RE ONE	12.00	20.00
		MARK DINNING		
□12775	*MGM*	CUTIE CUTIE/LIFE OF LOVE	1.75	3.50
□12845		TEEN ANGEL/BYE NOW BABY (1)	1.25	3.00
□12888		A STAR IS BORN/YOU WIN AGAIN (68)	1.25	2.50
□12929		THE LOVIN' TOUCH/COME BACK TO ME (84)	1.25	2.50
□12958		SHE CRIED ON MY SHOULDER/ THE WORLD IS GETTING SMALLER	1.50	2.50
□12980		TOP FORTY NEWS, WEATHER AND SPORTS/SUDDENLY (81)	1.25	2.50
□13007		ANOTHER LONELY GIRL/CAN'T FORGET	1.50	2.50
□13024		LONELY ISLAND/TURN ME ON	1.50	2.50
□13061		ALL OF THIS FOR SALLY/THE PICKUP	1.50	2.50
		MARK DINNING—ALBUM		
□3828 (M)	*MGM*	TEEN ANGEL	6.00	10.00
□3828 (S)		TEEN ANGEL	7.00	12.00

DION

Dion DiMucci, born on July 18, 1939, was a child of the Bronx streets. He was an average student at a Catholic high school, but had more interest in street harmony with some local buddies. Dion soon teamed with a vocal group called the Timberlanes. After one single (released on two different labels) Dion left the group and took up with some other pals from his neighborhood. Alternating street-fighting with singing, the boys later took on the name Dion and the Belmonts, after Belmont Avenue in the Bronx.

The quartet saw instant success with their first Laurie single. Then, to the record-buying public's great surprise, Dion went solo at the peak of the group's popularity. He was wise in doing this, though; as a solo artist Dion saw even greater success than ever.

After several hit singles on Laurie, Dion switched to Columbia, where more chart winners followed. Then Dion walked away from Columbia, complaining of restrictive formula material being pushed at him but, even more, departing to combat an all-consuming drug problem.

After a five-year absence from the charts, Dion returned in 1968 with "Abraham, Martin and John." Now off all drugs and living with his family in Miami, Florida, Dion plays small theaters and clubs.

DION

ISSUE #	LABEL	ARTIST/TITLE	VG	MINT
□3070	*LAURIE*	LONELY TEENAGER/LITTLE MISS BLUE (12)	1.00	2.50
□3081		HAVIN' FUN/NORTHEAST END OF THE CORNER (42)	1.25	2.50
□3090		KISSIN' GAME/HEAVEN HELP ME (82)	1.50	2.50
□3101		SOMEBODY NOBODY WANTS/COULD SOMEBODY TAKE MY PLACE TONIGHT?	1.75	3.00
□3110		RUNAROUND SUE/RUNAWAY GIRL (1)	1.00	2.00
□3115		THE WANDERER/THE MAJESTIC (2)	1.00	2.00
□3123		LOVERS WHO WANDER/(I WAS) BORN TO CRY (3)	1.00	2.00
□3134		LITTLE DIANE/LOST FOR SURE (8)	1.00	2.00
□3145		LOVE CAME TO ME/LITTLE GIRL (10)	1.00	2.00
□3153		SANDY/FAITH (21)	1.25	2.50
□3171		COME GO WITH ME/KING WITHOUT A QUEEN (48)	1.50	2.50
□3187		LONELY WORLD/TAG ALONG	1.75	3.00
□3225		THEN I'LL BE TIRED OF YOU/AFTER THE DANCE	1.75	3.00
□3240		SHOUT/LITTLE GIRL	1.75	3.00
□3303		I GOT THE BLUES/(I WAS) BORN TO CRY	1.50	2.50
□3464		ABRAHAM, MARTIN AND JOHN/DADDY ROLLIN' (4)	.75	2.00
□3478		PURPLE HAZE/THE DOLPHINS (63)	1.25	2.50
□3495		BOTH SIDES NOW/SUN FUN SONG (91)	1.75	3.00
□3504		LOVING YOU IS SWEETER THAN EVER/ HE LOOKS A LOT LIKE ME	1.75	3.00
□42662	*COLUMBIA*	RUBY BABY/HE'LL ONLY HURT YOU (2)	1.00	2.50
□42776		THIS LITTLE GIRL/THE LONELIEST MAN IN THE WORLD (21)	1.25	2.50
□42810		BE CAREFUL OF STONES THAT YOU THROW/ I CAN'T BELIEVE (31)	1.25	2.50
□42852		DONNA THE PRIMA DONNA/YOU'RE MINE (6)	1.00	2.00
□42917		DRIP DROP/NO ONE'S WAITING FOR ME (6)	1.00	2.00
□42977		I'M YOU HOOCHIE COOCHI MAN/ THE ROAD I'M ON	1.50	2.50
□43096		JOHNNY B. GOODE/CHICAGO BLUES (71)	1.25	2.50
□43213		UNLOVED, UNWANTED ME/SWEET SWEET BABY	1.50	2.50
□43293		SPOONFUL/KICKIN' CHILD	1.50	2.50
□43423		TOMORROW WON'T BRING THE RAIN/ YOU MOVE ME BABE	1.75	3.00
□43483		TIME IN MY HEART FOR YOU/WAKE UP BABY	1.50	2.50
□43692		TWO TON FEATHER/SO MUCH YOUNGER	1.50	2.50
□44719		SOUTHERN TRAIN/I CAN'T HELP BUT WONDER WHERE I'M BOUND	1.50	2.50

DION—ALBUMS

ISSUE #	LABEL	ARTIST/TITLE	VG	MINT
□2004 (M)	*LAURIE*	ALONE WITH DION	6.00	10.00
□2009 (M)		RUNAROUND SUE	5.00	8.00
□2012 (M)		LOVERS WHO WANDER	4.00	7.00
□2013 (M)		DION SINGS HIS GREATEST HITS	5.00	8.00
□2015 (M)		LOVE CAME TO ME	4.00	7.00
□2017 (M)		DION SINGS TO SANDY	4.00	7.00
□2019 (M)		DION SINGS THE 15 MILLION SELLERS	5.00	8.00
□2022 (M)		MORE OF DION'S GREATEST HITS	5.00	8.00
□2047 (S)		DION	4.00	7.00
□2010 (M)	*COLUMBIA*	RUBY BABY	4.00	7.00
□8810 (S)		RUBY BABY	5.00	9.00
□2107 (M)		DONNA THE PRIMA DONNA	4.00	7.00
□8907 (S)		DONNA THE PRIMA DONNA	5.00	9.00
□9773 (S)		WONDER WHERE I'M BOUND	4.50	8.00

DION AND THE BELMONTS

Dion and the Belmonts emerged from the same New York City area that produced Bobby Darin and the Regents. The quartet got together early in 1958, rehearsed their distinctive "do-wop" sound and landed a contract with New York's small Mohawk label. A pair of singles found no widespread success. Then Dion and the Belmonts heard of the formation of a new label, Laurie Records. The lads became the first group to sign with that company.

Their first single ("I Wonder Why") became a Top 30 hit, and Dion and the Belmonts were on their way. A pair of hit singles followed "I Wonder Why", and the group went on the road with the fated Buddy Holly tour early in 1959. That spring the quartet earned its first gold record with the million-selling "A Teenager In Love". Then came a second gold disc with Dion and the Belmonts' interpretation of the standard "Where Or When". It was backed up by another classic, "That's My Desire".

Late in 1960 Dion left the group. As the Belmonts sans Dion, they managed to record a pair of Top 30 hits with "Tell Me Why" and "Come On Little Angel" before their career declined.

ISSUE #	LABEL	ARTIST/TITLE	VG	MINT
		DION AND THE BELMONTS		
		SEE: DION, BELMONTS		
☐ 106	*MOHAWK*	TEENAGE CLEMENTINE/SANTA MARGARITA	12.00	20.00
☐ 107		WE WENT AWAY/TAG ALONG	12.00	20.00
☐ 3013	*LAURIE*	I WONDER WHY/TEEN ANGEL (22)	2.50	4.00
☐ 3015		NO ONE KNOWS/I CAN'T GO ON (ROSALIE) (24)	2.00	3.50
☐ 3021		DON'T PITY ME/JUST YOU (40)	2.00	3.50
☐ 3027		A TEENAGER IN LOVE/I'VE CRIED BEFORE (5)	1.00	2.50
☐ 3035		EVERY LITTLE THING I DO/A LOVER'S PRAYER (48)	1.50	3.00
☐ 3044		WHERE AND WHEN/THAT'S MY DESIRE (3)	1.00	2.50
☐ 3052		WHEN YOU WISH UPON A STAR/WONDERFUL GIRL (30)	1.25	3.00
☐ 3059		IN THE STILL OF THE NIGHT/A FUNNY FEELING (38)	1.25	3.00
☐ 10868	*ABC*	MY GIRL, THE MONTH OF MAY/BERIMBAU	2.00	3.50
☐ 10896		MOVIN' MAN/FOR BOBBY	2.00	3.50
		DION AND THE BELMONTS—EPs		
☐ 301	*LAURIE*	THEIR HITS	5.00	8.00
☐ 302		WHERE OR WHEN	5.00	8.00
		DION AND THE BELMONTS—ALBUMS		
☐ 2002 (M)	*LAURIE*	PRESENTING DION AND THE BELMONTS	7.00	12.00
☐ 2006 (M)		WISH UPON A STAR	6.00	10.00
☐ 2016 (M)		BY SPECIAL REQUEST	6.00	10.00
☐ 599 (M)	*ABC*	TOGETHER AGAIN	3.50	6.00
☐ 599 (S)		TOGETHER AGAIN	4.50	8.00
		DION AND THE TIMBERLANES (BEFORE BELMONTS)		
☐ 5294	*JUBILEE*	THE CHOSEN FEW/OUT IN COLORADO	12.00	20.00
☐ 105	*MOHAWK*	THE CHOSEN FEW/OUT IN COLORADO	12.00	20.00
		DIXIE CUPS		
☐ 10-001	*RED BIRD*	CHAPEL OF LOVE/AIN'T THAT NICE (1)	1.00	2.50
☐ 10-006		PEOPLE SAY/GIRLS CAN TELL (12)	1.25	2.50
☐ 10-012		YOU SHOULD HAVE SEEN THE WAY HE LOOKED AT ME/NO TRUE LOVE (39)	1.25	2.50
☐ 10-017		LITTLE BELL/ANOTHER BOY LIKE MINE (51)	1.50	2.50
☐ 10-024		IKO IKO/GEE BABY GEE (20)	1.25	2.50
☐ 10-032		GEE THE MOON IS SHINING BRIGHT/ I'M GONNA GET YOU YET	1.75	3.00
		DIXIE CUPS—ALBUMS		
☐ 100 (M)	*RED BIRD*	CHAPEL OF LOVE	6.00	10.00
☐ 100 (S)		CHAPEL OF LOVE	7.00	12.00
☐ 103 (M)		IKO IKO	3.50	6.00
☐ 103 (S)		IKO IKO	4.50	8.00

CARL DOBKINS, JR.

Carl Dobkins, Jr., was born in Cincinnati, Ohio, in January of 1941. He was a junior high student when rock-and-roll emerged during the 1950s. Carl soon became caught up in the early success of such pioneers as Elvis Presley, Little Richard, Chuck Berry and Fats Domino. However, Dobkins showed an inclination towards ballads and pursued those when he began his musical career in earnest.

As a high school student Carl began singing part-time on a Cincinnati television show called "The Sunday Swing Dance Club At Castle Farm." One night he was seen singing on the show by a talent scout from Decca Records. Dobkins was later offered a contract with Decca, where he recorded his first single, "My Heart Is An Open Book." The song took off during the spring of 1959 and Carl, then a high school senior, saw the song become his only million-seller.

Two singles later Dobkins hit the Top 30 with his "Lucky Devil". Today he is chiefly remembered for his one major hit. After a third minor chart single—"Exclusively Yours"—Carl Dobkins never again experienced recording success.

ISSUE #	LABEL	ARTIST/TITLE	VG	MINT
		CARL DOBKINS, JR.		
□30803	***DECCA***	MY HEART IS AN OPEN BOOK/MY PLEDGE TO YOU (3) .	1.25	3.00
□30856		IF YOU DON'T WANT MY LOVIN'/ LOVE IS EVERYTHING (67)	1.25	2.50
□31020		LUCKY DEVIL/IN MY HEART (25)	1.00	2.50
□31088		EXCLUSIVELY YOURS/ONE LITTLE GIRL (62)	1.25	2.50
□31301		SAWDUST DOLLY/A CHANCE TO BELONG	1.25	2.00
		CARL DOBKINS, JR.—EP		
□2664	***DECCA***	MY HEART IS AN OPEN BOOK	5.00	8.00
		CARL DOBKINS, JR.—ALBUM		
□8938 (M)	***DECCA***	CARL DOBKINS, JR.	7.00	12.00
□8938 (S)		CARL DOBKINS, JR.	8.00	15.00
		MICKEY DOLENZ		
		SEE: MONKEES		
□59353	***CHALLENGE***	DON'T DO IT/PLASTIC SYMPHONY III (75)	1.25	2.50
□59372		HUFF PUFF/(THE OBVIOUS) FATE	1.50	3.00
□14309	***MGM***	EASY ON YOU/OH, SOMEONE	1.50	2.50
□14395		A LOVER'S PRAYER/UNATTENDED IN THE DUNGEON	1.50	2.50

FATS DOMINO

Antoine "Fats" Domino came from New Orleans, Louisiana, where he was born on February 26, 1928. One of nine children, Fats showed an early interest in the piano and played it daily after school. He departed the halls of learning at fifteen, first to drive an ice cream truck, then to toil in a bedspring factory to support his family. One day at the factory a heavy bedspring fell across Fats' hands. Doctors at first told the burly teenager that he would never again be able to write or play the piano. Fats didn't listen and, through determination and constant exercise, he eventually regained the use of his hands.

By the end of the 1940s Fats was playing regularly at New Orleans clubs. He signed a contract with Imperial Records and began a working partnership with the sax player Dave Bartholomew. Domino's first single was "The Fat Man". An instant r & b hit, it was followed by two dozen more winners. Fats finally "crossed over" to the rock charts in 1955 with the rocking "Ain't That A Shame".

During his recording career he earned nineteen gold records, including one for his biggest hit, "Blueberry Hill". Today Domino—still a New Orleans resident—appears in Las Vegas showrooms and headlines various oldies shows.

ISSUE #	LABEL	ARTIST/TITLE	VG	MINT
		FATS DOMINO		
□5058	*IMPERIAL*	THE FAT MAN/DETROIT CITY BLUES	15.00	25.00
□5065		BOOGIE WOOGIE BABY/LITTLE BEE	15.00	25.00
□5077		SHE'S MY BABY/HIDEAWAY BLUES	15.00	25.00
□5085		HE LA BAS BOOGIE/BRAND NEW BABY	15.00	25.00
		(THE FIRST FOUR RELEASES WERE ISSUED ONLY ON 78 RPM. THE FOLLOWING REFLECT PRICES FOR 45 RPM DISCS.)		
□5099		KOREA BLUES/EVERY NIGHT ABOUT THIS TIME	20.00	30.00
□5114		TIRED OF CRYING/WHAT'S THE MATTER, BABY?	15.00	25.00
□5123		DON'T YOU LIE TO ME/SOMETIMES I WONDER	15.00	25.00
□5138		NO, NO BABY/RIGHT FROM WRONG	12.00	22.00
□5145		ROCKIN' CHAIR/CARELESS LOVE	12.00	20.00
□5167		YOU KNOW I MISS YOU/I'LL BE GONE	10.00	18.00
□5180		GOIN' HOME/REELING AND ROCKING	12.00	20.00
□5197		POOR POOR ME/TRUST IN ME	10.00	18.00
□5209		HOW LONG?/DREAMING	8.00	15.00
□5220		NOBODY LOVES ME/CHEATIN'	7.00	12.00
□5231		GOING TO THE RIVER/MARDI GRAS IN NEW ORLEANS	7.00	12.00
□5240		PLEASE DON'T LEAVE ME/THE GIRL I LOVE	6.00	10.00
□5251		ROSE MARY/YOU SAID YOU LOVED ME	6.00	10.00
□5262		DON'T LEAVE ME THIS WAY/SOMETHING'S WRONG	6.00	10.00
□5272		LITTLE SCHOOL GIRL/YOU DONE ME WRONG	6.00	10.00
□5283		BABY, PLEASE/WHERE DID YOU STAY?	6.00	10.00
□5301		YOU CAN PACK YOUR SUITCASE/I LIVED MY LIFE	6.00	10.00
□5313		DON'T YOU HEAR ME CALLING YOU/LOVE ME	5.00	8.00
□5323		I KNOW/THINKING OF YOU	4.00	7.00
□5340		DON'T YOU KNOW/HELPING HAND	3.50	6.00
□5348		AIN'T IT A SHAME/LA LA (16)	3.00	5.00
□5357		ALL BY MYSELF/TROUBLES OF MY OWN	3.50	6.00
□5369		POOR ME/I CAN'T GO ON	3.00	5.00
□5375		BO WEEVIL/DON'T BLAME IT ON ME (35)	2.50	4.00
□5386		I'M IN LOVE AGAIN/MY BLUE HEAVEN (5)	2.00	4.00
□5396		WHEN MY DREAMBOAT COMES HOME/SO-LONG (22)	2.50	4.00
□5407		BLUEBERRY HILL/HONEY CHILE (4)	2.00	3.50
□5417		BLUE MONDAY/WHAT'S THE REASON I'M NOT PLEASING YOU (9)	2.00	3.50
□5428		I'M WALKIN'/I'M IN THE MOOD FOR LOVE (5)	2.00	3.50
□5442		VALLEY OF TEAR/IT'S YOU I LOVE (13)	1.50	3.00
□5454		WHEN I SEE YOU/WHAT WILL I TELL MY HEART (36)	1.75	3.00
□5467		WAIT AND SEE/I STILL LOVE YOU (27)	1.50	3.00
□5477		THE BIG BEAT/I WANT YOU TO KNOW (36)	1.50	2.50
□5492		YES, MY DARLING/DON'T YOU KNOW I LOVE YOU (55)	1.50	2.50
□5515		SICK AND TIRED/NO, NO (30)	1.25	2.50
□5526		LITTLE MARY/PRISONER'S SONG (49)	1.50	2.50
□5537		YOUNG SCHOOL GIRL/IT MUST BE LOVE (92)	1.50	2.50
□5553		WHOLE LOTTA LOVING/COQUETTE (6)	1.25	2.50
□5569		WHEN THE SAINTS GO MARCHING IN/ TELLING LIES (50)	1.50	2.50
□5585		I'M READY/MARGIE (16)	1.25	2.50
□5606		I WANT TO WALK YOU HOME/ I'M GONNA BE A WHEEL SOMEDAY (8)	1.25	2.50
□5629		BE MY GUEST/I'VE BEEN AROUND (8)	1.25	2.50
□5645		COUNTRY BOY/IF YOU NEED ME (25)	1.00	2.50

ISSUE #	LABEL	ARTIST/TITLE	VG	MINT
□5660		TELL ME THAT YOU LOVE ME/ BEFORE I GROW TOO OLD (51)	1.25	2.50
□5675		WALKING TO NEW ORLEANS/ DON'T COME KNOCKING (6)	1.00	2.50
□5687		THREE NIGHTS A WEEK/PUT YOUR ARMS AROUND ME HONEY (15)	1.00	2.50
□5704		MY GIRL JOSEPHINE/NATURAL BORN LOVER (14)	1.00	2.50
□5723		WHAT A PRICE/AIN'T THAT JUST LIKE A WOMAN (22)	1.00	2.00
□5734		SHU RAH/FELL IN LOVE ON MONDAY (32)	1.00	2.00
□5753		IT KEEPS RAININ'/I JUST CRY (23)	1.00	2.00
□5764		LET THE FOUR WINDS BLOW/GOOD HEARTED MAN (15)	1.00	2.00
□5779		WHAT A PARTY/ROCKIN' BICYCLE (22)	1.00	2.00
□5796		JAMBALAYA (ON THE BAYOU)/ I HEAR YOU KNOCKING (30)	1.00	2.00
□5816		YOU WIN AGAIN/IDA JANE (22)	1.00	2.00
□5833		MY REAL NAME/MY HEART IS BLEEDING (59)	1.25	2.00
□5863		NOTHING NEW (SAME OLD THING)/ DANCE WITH MR. DOMINO (77)	1.25	2.00
□5875		DID YOU EVER SEE A DREAM WALKING?/ STOP THE CLOCK (79)	1.25	2.00

LATER IMPERIAL SINGLES ARE WORTH UP TO $1.50 MINT

ISSUE #	LABEL	ARTIST/TITLE	VG	MINT
□127	***IMPERIAL***	FATS DOMINO	8.00	15.00
□139		ROCK AND ROLLIN' WITH FATS DOMINO	7.00	12.00
□141		FATS DOMINO: ROCK AND ROLLIN'	6.00	10.00
□142		FATS DOMINO: ROCK AND ROLLIN'	6.00	10.00
□143		FATS DOMINO: ROCK AND ROLLIN'	6.00	10.00
□146		THIS IS FATS DOMINO	6.00	10.00
□147		HERE COMES FATS	6.00	10.00
□148		HERE STANDS FATS DOMINO	5.00	8.00
□149		HERE STANDS FATS DOMINO	5.00	8.00
□150		HERE STANDS FATS DOMINO	5.00	8.00
□151		COOKIN' WITH FATS	5.00	8.00
□152		ROCKIN' WITH FATS	5.00	8.00

(PRICES SHOWN ARE FOR BLOCK-LETTER LABELS; EPs WITH SCRIPT LETTERING WOULD BE WORTH TWICE THE AMOUNT SHOWN)

FATS DOMINO—ALBUMS

ISSUE #	LABEL	ARTIST/TITLE	VG	MINT
□9004 (M)	***IMPERIAL***	ROCK AND ROLLIN' WITH FATS DOMINO	15.00	25.00
□9009 (M)		ROCK AND ROLLIN'	12.00	20.00
□9028 (M)		THIS IS FATS DOMINO	12.00	20.00
□9038 (M)		HERE STANDS FATS DOMINO	12.00	20.00
□9040 (M)		THIS IS FATS	10.00	18.00
□9055 (M)		THE FABULOUS MR. D.	8.00	15.00
□9062 (M)		FATS DOMINO SWINGS	7.00	12.00
□9065 (M)		LET'S PLAY	7.00	12.00
□9103 (M)		FATS DOMINO SINGS	6.00	10.00
□9138 (M)		A LOT OF DOMINOS	6.00	10.00
□9153 (M)		LET THE FOUR WINDS BLOW	6.00	10.00
□9164 (M)		WHAT A PARTY	6.00	10.00
□9170 (M)		TWISTIN' THE STOMP	6.00	10.00
□9195 (M)		MILLION SELLERS	6.00	10.00

DON AND DEWEY

ISSUE #	LABEL	ARTIST/TITLE	VG	MINT
□599	***SPECIALTY***	JUNGLE HOP/A LITTLE LOVE	2.50	4.00
□610		LEAVIN' IT ALL UP TO YOU/JELLY BEAN	2.00	3.50

ISSUE #	LABEL	ARTIST/TITLE	VG	MINT
□631		JUSTINE/BIM BAM	2.00	3.50
□639		THE LETTER/KOKO JOE	2.00	3.50
□659		BIG BOY PETE/FARMER JOHN	2.00	3.50

RAL DONNER

Ral Donner hails from Chicago, Illinois. He was born there in 1943 on February 10th. By the age of ten Ral was singing in a church choir. He gained confidence and, by the time he entered his teens, had formed his own band. Every time a talent contest was announced, Donner would rush to sign up. He never lost.

By the age of fifteen Ral Donner had gained experience at the Apollo Theater in New York and at Chicago's Chez Paree club. He finished high school in June of 1961. An earlier disc on the Scottie label had failed, but with Donner's later signing to the Gone label, Ral was soon to become the most talked-about recording star of his day.

People refused to believe that Donner's "Girl Of My Best Friend" was not Elvis singing under another name. Gradually, even though he never lost his "Presley sound", Ral Donner began developing his own style. By then, unfortunately, his career was fading fast. Recordings on other labels produced no hits, and the name and impact of Ral Donner soon slipped into obscurity.

ISSUE #	LABEL	ARTIST/TITLE	VG	MINT
		RAL DONNER		
☐1310	***SCOTTIE***	TELL ME WHY/THAT'S ALL RIGHT WITH ME	6.00	10.00
☐5102	***GONE***	GIRL OF MY BEST FRIEND/ IT'S BEEN A LONG LONG TIME	5.00	8.00
		(THE ABOVE PRICE IS FOR THE BLACK-LABEL VERSION)		
☐5102		GIRL OF MY BEST FRIEND/ IT'S BEEN A LONG LONG TIME (19)	1.25	2.50
☐5108		YOU DON'T KNOW WHAT YOU'VE GOT/ SO CLOSE TO HEAVEN (4)	1.25	2.50
☐5114		PLEASE DON'T GO/I DIDN'T FIGURE ON HIM TO COME BACK (39)	1.50	2.50
☐5119		SCHOOL OF HEARTBREAKERS/BECAUSE WE'RE YOUNG	5.00	8.00
☐5121		SHE'S EVERYTHING/WILL YOU LOVE ME IN HEAVEN	3.00	5.00
☐5121		SHE'S EVERYTHING/BECAUSE WE'RE YOUNG (18)	1.25	2.50
☐5125		TO LOVE SOMEONE/WILL YOU LOVE ME IN HEAVEN (74)	1.50	2.50
☐5129		LOVELESS LIFE/BELLS OF LOVE	2.50	4.00
☐5133		TO LOVE/SWEETHEART	2.50	4.00
☐105	***TAU***	LONELINESS OF A STAR/AND THEN	2.50	4.00
☐20135	***REPRISE***	SECOND MIRACLE/CHRISTMAS DAY	3.00	6.00
☐20141		I GOT BURNED/A TEAR IN MY EYE	3.00	5.00
☐20176		I WISH THIS NIGHT WOULD NEVER END/ DON'T PUT YOUR HEART IN HIS HAND	3.00	5.00
☐20192		RUN LITTLE LINDA/BEYOND THE HEARTBREAK	3.00	5.00
☐1502	***FONTANA***	POISON IVY LEAGUE/YOU FINALLY SAID SOMETHING GOOD	3.50	6.00
☐1502		POISON IVY LEAGUE/TEAR IN MY EYE	3.00	5.00
☐1515		GOOD LOVIN'/OTHER SIDE OF ME	3.00	5.00
☐10-051	***RED BIRD***	LOVE ISN'T LIKE THAT/IT WILL ONLY MAKE YOU LOVE ME MORE	3.00	5.00
☐10-057		LOVE ISN'T LIKE THAT/IT WILL ONLY MAKE YOU LOVE ME MORE	2.50	4.00
		RAL DONNER—ALBUM		
☐5012 (M)	***GONE***	TAKIN' CARE OF BUSINESS	15.00	25.00
		DONNIE AND THE DEL-CHORDS		
☐352	***TAURUS***	WHEN YOU'RE ALONE/SO LONELY	3.50	6.00
☐357		I DON'T CARE/I'LL BE WITH YOU IN APPLE BLOSSOM TIME	3.00	5.00
☐361		THAT OLD FEELING/TRANSYLVANIA MIST	3.00	5.00
☐363		I FOUND HEAVEN/BE WITH YOU	5.00	8.00
☐364		I'M IN THE MOOD FOR LOVE/I'VE GOT A WOMAN	2.50	4.00
		DONNIE AND THE DREAMERS		
☐500	***WHALE***	COUNT EVERY STAR/DOROTHY (35)	2.00	3.50
☐505		MY MEMORIES OF YOU/TEENAGE LOVE (79)	2.50	4.00
		DICKEY DOO AND THE DON'TS *FEATURED: GERRY GRANAHAN*		
☐4001	***SWAN***	CLICK CLACK/DID YOU CRY? (28)	1.75	3.00
☐4006		NEE NEE NA NA NA NA NU NU/FLIP TOP BOX (40)	2.50	4.00
☐4014		LEAVE ME ALONE (LET ME CRY)/WILD PARTY (44)	1.75	3.00
☐4025		TEARDROPS WILL FALL/COME WITH US (61)	1.75	3.00
☐4033		DEAR HEART, DON'T CRY/BALLAD OF A TRAIN	2.00	3.50
☐4046		WABASH CANNONBALL/ THE DRUMS OF RICHARD-A-DOO	2.00	3.50

ISSUE #	LABEL	ARTIST/TITLE	VG	MINT
□238	**UNITED ARTISTS**	TEEN SCENE/PITY, PITY	1.75	3.00
□362		THE JUDGE/A LITTLE DOG CRIED	1.75	3.00
		DICKEY DOO AND THE DON'TS—ALBUMS		
□3094 (M)	**UNITED ARTISTS**	MADISON	7.00	12.00
□6094 (S)		MADISON	8.00	15.00
□3097 (M)		TEEN SCENE	6.00	10.00
□6097 (S)		TEEN SCENE	7.00	12.00

DOORS

Jim Morrison was the Doors. Born in Melbourne, Florida, to a naval submarine commander and his wife, Morrison became a handsome, withdrawn and brilliant high school student. After graduation in 1961, Jim headed west to UCLA, where he had won a scholarship in the film arts department.

While at UCLA Morrison fell in with a trio of UCLA musicians. They invited Jim to become the lead singer of a group they were forming. A name was needed. Morrison, long an expert on English poetry, came up with the title Doors, based on a William Blake poem.

The Doors quit UCLA and soon developed an L. A. cult following. A contract was signed with Elektra Records. After an initial single bombed, the Doors saw instant success with a second offering, "Light My Fire". The Doors became a national phenomenon and scored five Top 10 hits during the late 1960s.

Jim Morrison died in Paris, France, on July 3, 1971, shortly after the Doors had earned a sixth major hit with "Love Her Madly". No autopsy was performed, and Morrison's death was attributed to a heart attack. Though she denied Jim's drug usage, Morrison's wife died one year later of a heroin overdose.

ISSUE #	LABEL	ARTIST/TITLE	VG	MINT
		DOORS		
		FEATURED: JIM MORRISON		
□45611	*ELEKTRA*	BREAK ON THROUGH/END OF THE NIGHT	3.00	5.00
□45615		LIGHT MY FIRE/CRYSTAL SHIP (1)	1.00	2.00
□45621		PEOPLE ARE STRANGE/UNHAPPY GIRL (12)	1.00	2.00
□45624		LOVE ME TWO TIMES/STARLIGHT DRIVE (25)	1.00	2.00
□45628		UNKNOWN SOLDIER/WE COULD BE SO GOOD TOGETHER (39)	1.25	2.00
□45635		HELLO, I LOVE YOU/LOVE STREET (1)	.75	2.00
□45646		TOUCH ME/WILD CHILD (3)	.75	2.00
□45656		WISHFUL, SINFUL/WHO SCARED YOU (44)	1.25	2.00
□45663		TELL ALL THE PEOPLE/EASY RIDE (57)	1.25	2.00
□45675		RUNNIN' BLUE/DO IT (64)	1.25	2.00
□45685		YOU MAKE ME REAL/ROADHOUSE BLUES (50)	1.25	2.00
□45726		LOVE HER MADLY/DON'T GO NO FURTHER (11)	.75	1.50
□45738		RIDERS ON THE STORM/CHANGELING (14)	.75	1.50
		HAROLD DORMAN		
		SEE: SUN DISCOGRAPHY		
□1003	*RITA*	MOUNTAIN OF LOVE/TO BE WITH YOU (21)	1.25	2.50
□1008		RIVER OF TEARS/I'LL COME RUNNING	1.50	2.50
□1012		MOVED TO KANSAS CITY/TAKE A CHANCE ON ME	1.50	2.50
□2092	*TOP RANK*	MOVED TO KANSAS CITY/TAKE A CHANCE ON ME	1.50	2.50
□1002	*TINCE*	RIVER OF TEARS/I'LL COME RUNNING	1.50	2.50
		LEE DORSEY		
□1053	*FURY*	YA YA/GIVE ME YOU (7)	1.00	2.50
□1056		DO-RE-MI/PEOPLE ARE GONNA TALK (27)	1.25	2.50
□1061		EENIE MEENIE MINY MOE/BEHIND THE EIGHT BALL	1.25	2.00
		LEE DORSEY—ALBUM		
□1002 (M)	*FURY*	YA YA	6.00	10.00
		STEVE DOUGLAS		
□104	*PHILLES*	YES SIR, THAT'S MY BABY/ COLONEL BOGEY'S PARADE	3.50	6.00
		DOVELLS		
		FEATURED: LEN BARRY		
□819	*PARKWAY*	NO NO NO/LETTERS OF LOVE	2.50	4.00
□827		BRISTOL STOMP/OUT IN THE COLD AGAIN	2.00	3.50
□827		BRISTOL STOMP/LETTERS OF LOVE (2)	.75	2.00
□833		DOIN' THE NEW CONTINENTAL/ MOPE-ITTY MOPE STOMP (37)	1.00	2.00
□838		BRISTOL TWISTIN' ANNIE/THE ACTOR (27)	1.00	2.00
□845		HULLY GULLY BABY/YOUR LAST CHANCE (25)	1.00	2.00
□855		THE JITTERBUG/KISSIN' IN THE KITCHEN (82)	1.25	2.00
□861		YOU CAN'T RUN AWAY FROM YOURSELF/HELP ME BABY	1.25	2.00
□867		YOU CAN'T SIT DOWN/STOMPIN' EVERYWHERE	1.75	3.00
□867		YOU CAN'T SIT DOWN/WILDWOOD DAYS (3)	.75	2.00
□882		BETTY IN BERMUDAS/DANCE THE FROOG (50)	1.00	2.00
□889		STOP MONKEYIN' AROUN'/NO NO NO (94)	1.25	2.00
□901		BE MY GIRL/DRAGSTER ON THE PROWL	1.25	2.00
□911		HAPPY BIRTHDAY JUST THE SAME/ ONE POTATO, TWO POTATO	1.25	2.00
□925		WATUSI WITH LUCY/WHAT IN THE WORLD'S COME OVER YOU?	1.25	2.00
□4231	*SWAN*	(HEY HEY HEY) ALRIGHT/HAPPY	1.50	2.50

ISSUE #	LABEL	ARTIST/TITLE	VG	MINT
		DOVELLS—ALBUMS		
□7006 (M)	***PARKWAY***	BRISTOL STOMP	5.00	8.00
□7021 (M)		FOR YOUR HULLY GULLY PARTY	4.00	7.00
□7025 (M)		YOU CAN'T SIT DOWN	4.00	7.00
		DREAMERS		
□1005	***COUSINS***	BECAUSE OF YOU/LITTLE GIRL	7.00	12.00
□133	***MAY***	BECAUSE OF YOU/LITTLE GIRL	2.50	4.00
□3015	***GOLDISC***	NATALIE/TEENAGE VOWS OF LOVE	2.50	4.00
		DREAMLOVERS		
□102	***HERITAGE***	WHEN WE GET MARRIED/JUST BECAUSE (10)	1.25	3.00
□104		WELCOME HOME/LET THEM LOVE	1.50	2.50
□107		ZOOM ZOOM ZOOM/WHILE WE WERE DANCING	1.50	2.50

DRIFTERS

In 1953 Clyde McPhatter, a former lead singer with the Dominoes, joined forces with three gospel singers. As they drifted from group to group, the quartet settled on the name Drifters. They signed with Atlantic Records and began a string of r & b winners. In 1954 Clyde joined the army. Later Drifters lead vocalists included David Baughan and Bobby Hendricks, who had a solo hit with "Itchy Twitchy Feeling". By the summer of 1958, the original Drifters had disbanded.

That fall the Drifters' manager recruited a rhythm-and-blues group called the Five Crowns to become the new Drifters. They were fronted by Benney Nelson, later to be known as Ben E. King. (He is shown at the far left in the above picture.)

The new group's first single was "There Goes My Baby", the first rock record to utilize a full symphony orchestra. The record became a 1959 smash, sold over a million copies and established the (new) Drifters as a major force in popular music.

Ben E. King went solo in 1960 and had hits of his own with "Spanish Harlem" and "Stand By Me". He was replaced by Rudy Lewis, who sang lead on most Drifters' records until his death in 1963. During their peak years the Drifters recorded nearly a dozen Top 20 hits.

ISSUE #	LABEL	ARTIST/TITLE	VG	MINT
		DRIFTERS		
□1006	***ATLANTIC***	MONEY HONEY/THE WAY I FEEL	8.00	15.00
□1019		SUCH A NIGHT/LUCILLE	7.00	12.00
□1029		HONEY LOVE/WARM YOUR HEART	6.00	10.00
□1043		BIP BAM/ SOMEDAY YOU'LL WANT ME TO WANT YOU	5.00	8.00
□1048		WHITE CHRISTMAS/THE BELLS OF ST. MARY'S (80)	3.50	6.00
□1055		GONE/WHAT 'CHA GONNA DO?	4.00	7.00
		(FEATURED ABOVE: CLYDE McPHATTER)		
□1078		ADORABLE/STEAMBOAT	4.00	7.00
□1089		RUBY BABY/YOUR PROMISE TO BE MINE	3.50	6.00
□1101		SOLDIER OF FORTUNE/ I GOTTA GET MYSELF A WOMAN	3.50	6.00
□1123		FOOLS FALL IN LOVE/IT WAS A TEAR (69)	2.50	4.00
□1141		HYPNOTIZED/DRIFTING AWAY FROM YOU (79)	2.50	4.00
□1161		I KNOW/YODEE YAKEE	2.50	4.00
□1187		DRIP DROP/MOONLIGHT BAY (58)	1.50	3.00
□2025		THERE GOES MY BABY/OH MY LOVE (2)	1.25	2.50
□2038		THERE YOU GO/YOU WENT BACK ON YOUR WORD	1.75	3.00
□2040		DANCE WITH ME/TRUE LOVE, TRUE LOVE (15)	1.25	2.50
□2050		THIS MAGIC MOMENT/BALTIMORE (16)	1.25	2.50
□2062		LONELY WINDS/HEY SENORITA (54)	1.50	3.00
□2071		SAVE THE LAST DANCE FOR ME/ NOBODY BUT ME (1)	1.00	2.50
□2087		I COUNT THE TEARS/ SUDDENLY THERE'S A VALLEY (17)	1.25	2.50
□2096		SOME KIND OF WONDERFUL/HONEY BEE (32)	1.25	2.50
□2105		PLEASE STAY/NO SWEET LOVIN' (14)	1.25	2.50
□2117		SWEETS FOR MY SWEET/ LONELINESS OR HAPPINESS (16)	1.25	2.50
□2127		ROOM FULL OF TEARS/SOMEBODY NEW DANCIN' WITH YOU (72)	1.50	2.50
□2134		WHEN MY LITTLE GIRL IS SMILING/ MEXICAN DIVORCE (28)	1.25	2.50
□2143		STRANGER ON THE SHORE/WHAT TO DO (73)	1.25	2.00
□2151		SOMETIMES I WONDER/JACKPOT	1.50	2.50
□2162		UP ON THE ROOF/ ANOTHER NIGHT WITH THE BOYS (5)	.75	2.00
□2182		ON BROADWAY/LET THE MUSIC PLAY (9)	.75	2.00
□2191		RAT RACE/IF YOU DON'T COME BACK (71)	1.25	2.00
□2201		I'LL TAKE YOU HOME/I FEEL GOOD ALL OVER (25)	1.00	2.00
□2216		VAYA CON DIOS/IN THE LAND OF MAKE BELIEVE (43)	1.00	2.00

ISSUE #	LABEL	ARTIST/TITLE	VG	MINT
☐ 2225		ONE WAY LOVE/DIDN'T IT (56)	1.00	2.00
☐ 2237		UNDER THE BROADWALK/I DON'T WANT		
		TO GO ON WITHOUT YOU (4)75	2.00
☐ 2253		I'VE GOT SAND IN MY SHOES/		
		HE'S JUST A PLAYBOY (33)	1.00	2.00
☐ 2260		SATURDAY NIGHT AT THE MOVIES/		
		SPANISH LACE (18)75	2.00

LATER ATLANTIC SINGLES ARE WORTH UP TO $1.50 MINT

DRIFTERS—EP

☐ 534	ATLANTIC	THE DRIFTERS FEATURING CLYDE McPHATTER	6.00	10.00

DRIFTERS—ALBUMS

☐ 8003 (M)		CLYDE McPHATTER AND THE DRIFTERS	12.00	20.00
☐ 8022 (M)		ROCKIN' AND DRIFTIN'	8.00	15.00
☐ 8041 (M)		GREATEST HITS	8.00	15.00
☐ 8059 (M)		SAVE THE LAST DANCE FOR ME	5.00	8.00
☐ 8059 (S)		SAVE THE LAST DANCE FOR ME	6.00	10.00
☐ 8073 (M)		UP ON THE ROOF	5.00	8.00
☐ 8073 (S)		UP ON THE ROOF	6.00	10.00
☐ 8093 (M)		OUR BIGGEST HITS	5.00	8.00
☐ 8093 (S)		OUR BIGGEST HITS	6.00	10.00
☐ 8099 (M)		UNDER THE BOARDWALK	5.00	8.00
☐ 8099 (S)		UNDER THE BOARDWALK	6.00	10.00

DUALS

☐ 1031	STAR REVUE	STICK SHIFT/CRUISIN'	3.00	5.00
☐ 745	SUE	STICK SHIFT/CRUISIN' (25)	1.00	2.00

DUALS—ALBUM

☐ 2002 (M)		STICK SHIFT	5.00	8.00

DUBS

☐ 5002	GONE	DON'T ASK ME (TO BE LONELY)/DARLING (72)	5.00	8.00
☐ 5011		COULD THIS BE MAGIC?/SUCH LOVIN' (24)	3.50	6.00
☐ 5046		CHAPEL OF DREAMS/IS THERE A LOVE FOR ME? ...	4.00	7.00
☐ 5069		CHAPEL OF DREAMS/		
		IS THERE A LOVE FOR ME? (74)	3.50	6.00

FIRST-PRESS SINGLES WERE ON THE BLACK GONE LABEL

DUPREES

☐ 569	COED	YOU BELONG TO ME/TAKE ME AS I AM (7)	1.00	2.50
☐ 571		MY OWN TRUE LOVE/GINNY (13)	1.00	2.50
☐ 574		I'D RATHER BE HERE IN YOU ARMS/		
		I WISH I COULD BELIEVE YOU (91)	1.50	2.50
☐ 576		GONE WITH THE WIND/		
		LET'S MAKE LOVE AGAIN (89)	1.50	2.50
☐ 580		I GOTTA TELL HER NOW/TAKE ME AS I AM	1.50	2.50
☐ 584		WHY DON'T YOU BELIEVE ME/THE THINGS I LOVE .	1.75	3.00
☐ 584		WHY DON'T YOU BELIEVE ME/		
		MY DEAREST ONE (37)	1.25	2.50
☐ 585		HAVE YOU HEARD?/LOVE EYES (18)	1.00	2.50
☐ 587		(IT'S NO) SIN/THE SAND AND THE SEA (74)	1.50	2.50
☐ 591		WHERE ARE YOU/PLEASE LET HER KNOW	1.50	2.50
☐ 593		SO MANY HAVE TOLD YOU/UNBELIEVABLE	1.50	2.50
☐ 595		IT ISN'T FAIR/SO LITTLE TIME	1.50	2.50
☐ 596		I'M YOURS/WISHING RING	1.50	2.50

DUPREES—ALBUMS

☐ 905 (M)	COED	YOU BELONG TO ME........................	8.00	15.00
☐ 906 (M)		HAVE YOU HEARD?	8.00	15.00

ISSUE #	LABEL	ARTIST/TITLE	VG	MINT
		BOB DYLAN		
☐42656	*COLUMBIA*	MIXED UP CONFUSION/CORRINA CORRINA	60.00	100.00
☐42856		BLOWIN' IN THE WIND/ DON'T THINK TWICE, IT'S ALL RIGHT	35.00	60.00
☐43242		SUBTERRANEAN HOMESICK BLUES/ SHE BELONGS TO ME (39)	2.00	3.50
☐43346		LIKE A ROLLING STONE/GATES OF EDEN (2)	1.00	2.50
☐43389		POSITIVELY 4TH STREET/FROM A BUICK 6 (7)	1.00	2.50
☐43477		CAN YOU PLEASE CRAWL OUT YOUR WINDOW?/ HIGHWAY 61 REVISITED (58)	2.00	3.50
☐43541		QUEEN JANE APPROXIMATELY/ONE OF US MUST NOW	3.00	5.00
☐43592		RAINY DAY WOMAN #12 AND 35/ PLEDGING MY TIME (2)	.75	2.00
☐43683		I WANT YOU/JUST LIKE TOM THUMB'S BLUES (20)	1.00	2.00
☐43792		JUST LIKE A WOMAN/OBVIOUSLY 5 BELIEVERS (33)	1.25	2.00
☐44069		LEOPARD SKIN PILL-BOX HAT/MOST LIKELY YOU'LL GO YOUR WAY AND I'LL GO MINE (81)	2.00	3.50
		LATER COLUMBIA SINGLES ARE WORTH UP TO $1.50 MINT		
		BOB DYLAN—ALBUMS		
☐1779 (M)	*COLUMBIA*	BOB DYLAN	5.00	8.00
☐8579 (S)		BOB DYLAN	6.00	10.00
☐1986 (M)		FREEWHEELIN'	5.00	8.00
☐8786 (S)		FREEWHEELIN'	6.00	10.00
☐2105 (M)		THE TIMES ARE A-CHANGIN'	4.00	7.00
☐8905 (S)		THE TIMES ARE A-CHANGIN'	4.00	7.00
☐2193 (M)		ANOTHER SIDE OF BOB DYLAN	4.00	7.00
☐8993 (S)		ANOTHER SIDE OF BOB DYLAN	4.00	7.00
☐2328 (M)		BRINGING IT ALL BACK HOME	3.50	6.00
☐9128 (S)		BRINGING IT ALL BACK HOME	3.50	6.00
☐2389 (M)		HIGHWAY 61 REVISITED	3.50	6.00
☐9189 (S)		HIGHWAY 61 REVISITED	3.50	6.00
☐2517 (M)		BLONDE ON BLONDE	5.00	8.00
☐9517 (S)		BLONDE ON BLONDE	3.50	6.00

E

ISSUE #	LABEL	ARTIST/TITLE	VG	MINT
		EARLS		
☐101	*ROME*	LIFE IS BUT A DREAM/IT'S YOU	3.00	5.00
☐101		LIFE IS BUT A DREAM/WITHOUT YOU	3.00	5.00
☐102		LOOKIN' FOR MY BABY/CROSS MY HEART	3.00	5.00
☐111		STORMY WEATHER/ COULD THIS BE MAGIC (Pretenders)	2.50	4.00
☐112		LITTLE BOY AND GIRL/LOST LOVE	2.50	4.00
☐113		WHOEVER YOU ARE/LOST LOVE	2.50	4.00
☐114		ALL THROUGH OUR TEENS/WHOEVER YOU ARE	2.50	4.00
☐114		ALL THROUGH OUR TEENS/WHOEVER YOU ARE (colored wax)	5.00	8.00
☐1130	*OLD TOWN*	REMEMBER THEN/LET'S WADDLE (24)	1.50	3.00
☐1133		NEVER/KEEP A-TELLIN' YOU	2.50	4.00

ISSUE #	LABEL	ARTIST/TITLE	VG	MINT
□1141		LOOK MY WAY/EYES	2.50	4.00
□1145		CRY, CRY, CRY/KISSIN'	2.50	4.00
□1149		I BELIEVE/DON'T FORGET	3.00	5.00
□1169		ASK ANYBODY/OH WHAT A TIME	2.50	4.00
□1182		REMEMBER ME, BABY/AMOR	2.50	4.00
		EARLS—ALBUM		
□104 (M)	*OLD TOWN*	REMEMBER ME, BABY	12.0	20.00
		ECHOES		
□101	*SRG*	BABY BLUE/BOOMERANG	5.00	8.00
□102	*SEG-WAY*	ANGEL OF MY HEART/GEE OH GEE	2.50	4.00
□103		BABY BLUE/BOOMERANG (12)	1.50	3.00
□106		SAD EYES/IT'S RAININ' (88)	1.75	3.00

DUANE EDDY

In 1943 Duane Eddy, age five (birthdate: April 26, 1938), first picked up a guitar and began strumming its strings. That was all it took. Eddy, then a pre-schooler, became hooked on the instrument.

By the time he entered high school, Duane Eddy had become one of the hottest guitarists in his Arizona hometown of Phoenix. Most of his gigs (he had formed a small band by then) came from dances in the area. At nineteen Duane met a local disc jockey named Lee Hazelwood, who was favorably impressed with the handsome young guitarist. Hazelwood became Duane Eddy's producer. Eddy was later to meet master guitarist Al Casey. Duane then formed a group called the Rebels, and Casey joined as a backup member.

One single on the local Ford label proved to be less than a winner, so Duane Eddy and the Rebels signed with the larger Jamie outfit. "Movin' 'n' Groovin' ", Eddy's maiden Jamie outing, was a minor chart single. But his second release, "Rebel Rouser", was a solid smash across the country, and Eddy enjoyed the first of many hits for Jamie. A later signing with RCA produced a trio of Top 30 singles.

ISSUE #	LABEL	ARTIST/TITLE	VG	MINT
		DUANE EDDY		
□500	FORD	RAMROD/CARAVAN	7.00	12.00
□1101	JAMIE	MOVIN' 'N' GROOVIN'/UP AND DOWN (72)	2.00	3.50
□1104		REBEL-ROUSER/STALKIN' (6)	1.25	2.50
□1109		RAMROD/THE WALKER (28)	1.25	2.50
□1111		CANNONBALL/MASON DIXON LINE (15)	1.00	2.50
□1117		THE LONELY ONE/DETOUR (23)	1.25	2.50
□1122		YEP!/DETOUR (30)	1.25	2.50
□1126		FORTY MILES OF BAD ROAD/THE QUIET THREE (9)	1.00	2.50
□1130		SOME KIND-A EARTHQUAKE/ FIRST LOVE, FIRST TEARS (37)	1.25	2.50
□1144		BONNIE CAME BACK/LOST ISLAND (26)	1.25	2.50
□1151		SHAZAM!/THE SECRET SEVEN (45)	1.25	2.50
□1156		BECAUSE THEY'RE YOUNG/REBEL WALK (4)	1.00	2.00
□1158		THE GIRL ON DEATH ROW/WORDS MEAN NOTHING	1.50	2.50
□1163		KOMOTION/THESE FOR MOON CHILDREN (78)	1.25	2.00
□1168		PETER GUNN/ALONG THE NAVAJO TRAIL (27)	1.00	2.00
□1175		PEPE/LOST FRIEND (18)	1.00	2.00
□1183		THEME FROM DIXIE/GIDGET GOES HAWAIIAN (39)	1.25	2.00
□1187		RING OF FIRE/BOBBIE (84)	1.25	2.00
□1195		DRIVIN' HOME/TAMMY (87)	1.25	2.00
□1200		MY BLUE HEAVEN/ALONG CAME LINDA (50)	1.25	2.00
□1206		THE AVENGER/LONDONBERRY AIR	1.25	2.00
□1209		THE BATTLE/TROMBONE	1.25	2.00
□1224		RUNAWAY PONY/JUST BECAUSE	1.00	1.50
□7999	RCA	DEEP IN THE HEART OF TEXAS/ SAINTS AND SINNERS (78)	1.25	2.00
□8047		THE BALLAD OF PALADIN/ THE WILD WESTERNERS (33)	1.00	2.00
□8087		(DANCE WITH THE) GUITAR MAN/ STRETCHIN' OUT (12)	.75	2.00
□8131		BOSS GUITAR/THE DESERT RAT (28)	1.00	2.00
□8180		LONELY BOY, LONELY GUITAR/JOSHIN' (82)	1.25	2.00
□8214		YOUR BABY'S GONE SURFIN'/SHUCKIN' (93)	1.25	2.00
□8276		THE SON OF REBEL ROUSER/ THE STORY OF THREE LOVES (97)	1.25	2.00
□8335		GUITAR CHILD/JERKY JALOPY	1.00	1.50

ISSUE #	LABEL	ARTIST/TITLE	VG	MINT
☐ 8376		THEME FROM A SUMMER PLACE/WATER SKIING ..	1.00	1.50
☐ 8442		GUITAR STAR/THE IGUANA....................	1.00	1.50
☐ 8507		MOONSHOT/ROUGHNECK.....................	1.00	1.50
		DUANE EDDY—EPs		
☐ 100	*JAMIE*	DUANE EDDY	3.00	5.00
☐ 301		DETOUR	2.50	4.00
☐ 302		YEP!....................................	2.50	4.00
☐ 303		SHAZAM!.................................	2.50	4.00
☐ 304		BECAUSE THEY'RE YOUNG	2.50	4.00
		DUANE EDDY—ALBUMS		
☐ 3000 (M)	*JAMIE*	HAVE TWANGY GUITAR, WILL TRAVEL	7.00	12.00
☐ 3000 (S)		HAVE TWANGY GUITAR, WILL TRAVEL	8.00	15.00
☐ 3006 (M)		ESPECIALLY FOR YOU	5.00	8.00
☐ 3006 (S)		ESPECIALLY FOR YOU	6.00	10.00
☐ 3009 (M)		THE TWANG'S THE THING	5.00	8.00
☐ 3009 (S)		THE TWANG'S THE THING	6.00	10.00
☐ 3011 (M)		SONGS OF OUR HERITAGE	5.00	8.00
☐ 3011 (S)		SONGS OF OUR HERITAGE	6.00	10.00
☐ 3014 (M)		$1,000,000 WORTH OF TWANG	5.00	8.00
☐ 4014 (S)		$1,000,000 WORTH OF TWANG	6.00	10.00
☐ 2525 (M)	*RCA*	TWISTIN' AND TWANGIN'	3.50	6.00
☐ 2525 (S)		TWISTIN' AND TWANGIN'	4.50	8.00
☐ 2576 (M)		TWANGY GUITAR, SILKY STRINGS	3.50	6.00
☐ 2576 (S)		TWANGY GUITAR, SILKY STRINGS	4.50	8.00
☐ 2648 (M)		DANCE WITH THE GUITAR MAN	3.50	6.00
☐ 2648 (S)		DANCE WITH THE GUITAR MAN	4.50	8.00

EDSELS

☐ 2843	*DUB*	LAMA RAMA DING DONG/BELLS (original title)	6.00	10.00
☐ 2843		RAMA LAMA DING DONG/BELLS (revised title)	3.50	6.00
☐ 700	*TWIN*	RAMA LAMA DING DONG/BELLS (21)	1.50	3.00

EL DORADOS

☐ 147	*VEE JAY*	AT MY FRONT DOOR/		
		WHAT'S BUGGIN' YOU BABY (21)	3.50	6.00
☐ 165		I'LL BE FOREVER LOVING YOU/I BEGAN TO REALIZE ..	4.00	7.00

ELEGANTS

Whenever a singing group forms, a name must be chosen if the group ever hopes to go on record. So it was that in 1957 a group of Staten Island, New York, teenagers got together and decided they would become singers. Casting about for a name, somebody noticed the word "Elegance" on a bottle of Schenley's whiskey. The boys adopted the name after altering the spelling to fit the quintet.

The Elegants sang at schools and dances around Staten Island. A year later they took an original song called "Little Star" (based on the nursery rhyme "Twinkle, Twinkle Little Star") to Hull Records. Hull wasn't interested, so the Elegants approached ABC-Paramount, who liked the song and had the boys record it. Released on the ABC-Paramount Subsidiary of Apt, "Little Star" shot to No. 1 nationally.

Later Apt singles, although excellent, never made the charts. The Elegants returned to Hull Records but had no luck commercially. Recordings made for United Artists and Laurie also brought them no success. Although masters of New York street "do-wop," the Elegants became a one-hit group.

ISSUE #	LABEL	ARTIST/TITLE	VG	MINT
		ELEGANTS		
□25005	*APT*	LITTLE STAR/GETTING DIZZY (black label)	5.00	8.00
□25005		LITTLE STAR/GETTING DIZZY (1) (colored label)	1.50	3.00
□25017		PLEASE BELIEVE ME/GOODNIGHT	2.50	4.00
□25029		TRUE LOVE AFFAIR/PAYDAY	2.50	4.00
□732	*HULL*	LITTLE BOY BLUE/GET WELL SOON	8.00	15.00
□230	*UNITED ARTISTS*	LET MY PRAYERS BE WITH YOU/SPEAK LOW	3.00	5.00
□295		HAPPINESS/SPIRAL HAPPINESS	3.00	5.00
□3283	*LAURIE*	BARBARA, BEWARE/A LETTER FROM VIETNAM	2.50	4.00
□3298		BRING BACK WENDY/WAKE UP	3.00	5.00
□3324		BELINDA/LAZY LOVE	2.50	4.00

ISSUE #	LABEL	ARTIST/TITLE	VG	MINT
		EMPIRES		
		FEATURED: JAY BLACK		
□9526	*EPIC*	A TIME AND A PLACE/PUNCH YOUR NOSE	2.50	4.00
		ENEMYS		
		FEATURED: COREY WELLS OF THREE DOG NIGHT		
□714	*VALIANT*	SAY GOODBYE TO DONNA/SINNER MAN	2.00	3.50
□13485	*MGM*	TOO MUCH MONKEY BUSINESS/GLITTER AND GOLD	1.75	3.00
□13525		HEY JOE/MY DUES HAVE BEEN PAID	1.75	3.00
□13573		MOJO WOMAN/MY DUES HAVE BEEN PAID	1.50	2.50
		SCOTT ENGLISH		
□16099	*DOT*	THE WHITE CLIFFS OF DOVER/4,000 MILES AWAY	1.75	3.00
□4003	*SULTAN*	HIGH ON A HILL/WHEN	3.50	6.00
□5500		RAGS TO RICHES/WHERE CAN I GO?	1.75	3.00
□4003	*SPOKANE*	HIGH ON A HILL/WHEN (77)	1.50	2.50
□4007		HERE COMES THE PAIN/ALL I WANT IS YOU	1.25	2.00
		ESSEX		
□4494	*ROULETTE*	EASIER SAID THAN DONE/ ARE YOU GOING MY WAY? (1)	.75	2.00
□4515		A WALKIN' MIRACLE/WHAT I DON'T KNOW WON'T HURT ME (12)	.75	2.00
□4530		SHE'S GOT EVERYTHING/OUT OF SIGHT, OUT OF MIND (56)	1.00	2.00
□4542		WHAT DID I DO?/CURFEW LOVER	1.25	2.00
		ESSEX—ALBUMS		
□25234 (M)	*ROULETTE*	EASIER SAID THAN DONE	3.50	6.00
□25234 (S)		EASIER SAID THAN DONE	4.50	8.00
□25235 (M)		A WALKIN' MIRACLE	3.00	5.00
□25235 (S)		A WALKIN' MIRACLE	3.50	7.00
		DAVID ESSEX		
□55020	*UNI*	SHE'S LEAVING HOME/HE'S A BETTER MAN THAN ME	2.50	4.00
		BOB EUBANKS		
□6101	*TRACY*	HEAVEN OF THE STARS/HEAVEN OF THE STARS	2.00	3.50
□1354	*GOLIATH*	KEEP IT BURNIN'/SMOKE, SMOKE, SMOKE THAT CIGARETTE	1.50	2.50
		PAUL EVANS		
□6906	*RCA*	WHAT DO YOU KNOW/DOROTHY	2.50	4.00
□6992		CAUGHT/POOR BROKEN HEART	2.50	4.00
□6138	*ATCO*	AT MY PARTY/BEAT GENERATION	1.75	3.00
□6170		LONG GONE/MICKEY, MY LOVE	1.75	3.00
□200	*GUARANTEED*	SEVEN LITTLE GIRLS SITTING IN THE BACK SEAT/WORSHIPPING AN IDOL (9)	1.00	2.50
□205		MIDNIGHT SPECIAL/SINCE I MET YOU BABY (16)	1.25	2.50
□208		HAPPY-GO-LUCKY-ME/FISH IN THE OCEAN (10)	1.25	2.50
□210		THE BRIGADE OF BROKEN HEARTS/TWINS (81)	1.50	2.50
□213		HUSHABYE LITTLE GUITAR/BLIND BOY	1.50	2.50
		PAUL EVANS—ALBUM		
□1000 (M)	*GUARANTEED*	FABULOUS TEENS	6.00	10.00
□1000 (S)		FABULOUS TEENS	7.00	12.00

ISSUE #	LABEL	ARTIST/TITLE	VG	MINT
		VINCE EVERETT		
☐1964	***TOWN***	BUTTERCUP/LAND OF NO RETURN	5.00	8.00
☐10313	***ABC-PARAMOUNT***	SUCH A NIGHT/DON'T GO	5.00	8.00
☐10360		I AIN'T GONNA BE YOU LOW DOWN DOG NO MORE/SUGAR BEE	5.00	8.00
☐10472		BABY LET'S PLAY HOUSE/LIVIN' HIGH	6.00	10.00
☐10624		TO HAVE, TO HOLD, AND LET GO/BIG BROTHER	3.50	6.00

EVERLY BROTHERS

Ike and Margaret Everly were well-known country artists who went into semi-retirement when it came time to raise a family. Their two children were Don (born February 1, 1937) and Phil (born January 19, 1939). The Everly Brothers first sang together on an Iowa radio station when they were eight and six.

After both finished high school they headed for country music's capitol, Nashville, Tennessee. (An earlier single on Columbia had bombed.) Chet Atkins helped get the youngsters signed to Cadence Records. Their first single for them was "Bye Bye Love", an instant winner. The Everlys also earned a large English and European following. (The Beatles at one time called themselves the Four Everlys.)

After eight Cadence hits the Everlys signed with Warner Brothers. Their first single for them was "Cathy's Clown", the duo's best-selling single ever. Everly Brothers hits continued through the early 1960s. The most popular twosome of the 1950s, the Everlys ended a brilliant, productive career in 1973 when they sought solo artistic pathways.

ISSUE #	LABEL	ARTIST/TITLE	VG	MINT
		EVERLY BROTHERS		
☐21496	COLUMBIA	KEEP A-LOVING ME/THE SUN KEEPS SHINING	20.00	30.00
☐1315	CADENCE	BYE BYE LOVE/I WONDER IF I CARE AS MUCH (2)	1.25	3.00
☐1337		WAKE UP LITTLE SUZIE/MAYBE TOMORROW (2)	1.25	3.00
☐1342		THIS LITTLE GIRL OF MINE/ SHOULD WE TELL HIM? (28)	1.50	3.00
☐1348		ALL I HAVE TO DO IS DREAM/CLAUDETTE (1)	1.25	3.00
☐1350		BIRD DOG/DEVOTED TO YOU (2)	1.25	3.00
☐1355		PROBLEMS/LOVE OF MY LIFE (2)	1.25	3.00
☐1364		TAKE A MESSAGE TO MARY/POOR JENNY (16)	1.50	3.00
☐1369		('TIL) I KISSED YOU/OH, WHAT A FEELING (4)	1.00	2.50
☐1376		LET IT BE ME/SINCE YOU BROKE MY HEART (7)	1.00	2.50
☐1380		WHEN WILL I BE LOVED?/BE BOP A LULA (8)	1.00	2.50
☐1388		LIKE STRANGERS/A BRAND NEW HEARTACHE (22)	1.25	2.50
☐1429		I'M HERE TO GET MY BABY OUT OF JAIL/ LIGHTNING EXPRESS (76)	1.75	3.00
☐5151	WARNER BROTHERS	CATHY'S CLOWN/ALWAYS IT'S YOU (1)	1.00	2.50
☐5163		SO SAD/ LUCILLE (7)	1.00	2.50
☐5199		EBONY EYES/WALK RIGHT BACK (7)	1.00	2.50
☐5220		TEMPTATION/STICK WITH ME BABY (27)	1.25	2.50
☐5250		CRYING IN THE RAIN/I'M NOT ANGRY (6)	1.00	2.50
☐5273		THAT'S OLD FASHIONED/HOW CAN I MEET HER? (9)	1.00	2.50
☐5297		DON'T ASK ME TO BE FRIENDS/NO ONE CAN MAKE MY SUNSHINE SMILE (48)	1.25	2.50
☐5346		NANCY'S MINUET/SO IT ALWAYS WILL BE	1.25	2.00
☐5362		IT'S BEEN NICE/I'M AFRAID	1.25	2.00
☐5389		THE GIRL SANG THE BLUES/LOVE HER	1.25	2.00
☐5422		HELLO AMY/AIN'T THAT LOVING YOU BABY	1.25	2.00
☐5441		THE FERRIS WHEEL/DON'T FORGET TO CRY (72)	1.00	2.00
☐5466		YOU'RE THE ONE I LOVE/RING AROUND MY ROSIE	1.25	2.00
☐5478		GONE, GONE, GONE/TORTURE (31)	1.00	2.00
		LATER WARNER BROTHERS SINGLES ARE WORTH UP TO $2.00 MINT		
		EVERLY BROTHERS—EPs		
☐104	CADENCE	THE EVERLY BROTHERS	5.00	8.00
☐105		THE EVERLY BROTHERS	5.00	8.00
☐107		THE EVERLY BROTHERS	5.00	8.00
☐108		SONGS OUR DADDY TAUGHT US	4.00	7.00
☐109		SONGS OUR DADDY TAUGHT US	4.00	7.00

ISSUE #	LABEL	ARTIST/TITLE	VG	MINT
□ 110		SONGS OUR DADDY TAUGHT US	4.00	7.00
□ 111		THE EVERLY BROTHERS	4.00	7.00
□ 118		THE EVERLY BROTHERS	4.00	7.00
□ 121		THE VERY BEST OF THE EVERLY BROTHERS	4.00	7.00
□ EA-1381	*WARNER BROTHERS*	FOREVERLY YOURS	3.00	5.00
□ EB-1381		ESPECIALLY FOR YOU	3.00	5.00
□ 5501		THE EVERLY BROTHERS + TWO OLDIES (20)	1.50	3.00
		EVERLY BROTHERS—ALBUMS		
□ 3003 (M)	*CADENCE*	THE EVERLY BROTHERS	15.00	25.00
□ 3016 (M)		SONGS OUR DADDY TAUGHT US	12.00	20.00
□ 3025 (M)		THE EVERLY BROTHERS' BEST	8.00	15.00
□ 3040 (M)		THE FABULOUS STYLE OF THE EVERLY BROTHERS	8.00	15.00
□ 3059 (M)		FOLK SONGS	6.00	10.00
□ 25029 (S)		FOLK SONGS	7.00	12.00
□ 3062 (M)		15 EVERLY HITS	6.00	10.00
□ 25062 (S)		15 EVERLY HITS	7.00	12.00
□ 1381 (M)	*WARNER BROTHERS*	IT'S EVERLY TIME	3.50	6.00
□ 1381 (S)		IT'S EVERLY TIME	4.50	8.00
□ 1395 (M)		A DATE WITH THE EVERLY BROTHERS	3.50	6.00
□ 1395 (S)		A DATE WITH THE EVERLY BROTHERS	4.50	8.00
□ 1418 (M)		THE EVERLY BROTHERS	3.50	6.00
□ 1418 (S)		THE EVERLY BROTHERS	4.50	8.00
□ 1471 (M)		GOLDEN HITS OF THE EVERLY BROTHERS	3.50	6.00
□ 1471 (S)		GOLDEN HITS OF THE EVERLY BROTHERS	4.50	8.00

EXILES

FEATURED: DICK DALE

ISSUE #	LABEL	ARTIST/TITLE	VG	MINT
□ 1111	*CAMPUS*	TAKE IT OFF/TEN LITTLE INDIANS	7.00	12.00

F

ISSUE #	LABEL	ARTIST/TITLE	VG	MINT
		SHELLEY FABRES		
□ 621	*COLPIX*	JOHNNY ANGEL/ WHERE'S IT GONNA GET ME? (1)	1.00	2.00
□ 636		JOHNNY LOVES ME/I'M GROWING UP (21)	1.25	2.50
□ 654		THE THINGS WE DID LAST SUMMER/ BREAKING UP IS HARD TO DO (46)	1.50	2.50
□ 667		BIG STAR/TELEPHONE (WON'T YOU RING)	1.50	2.50
□ 682		RONNIE, CALL ME WHEN YOU GET A CHANCE/ I LEFT A NOTE TO SAY GOODBYE (72)	1.50	2.50
□ 705		WELCOME HOME/BILLY BOY	1.50	2.50
□ 721		FOOTBALL SEASON'S OVER/HE DON'T LOVE ME	1.50	2.50
		SHELLEY FABRES—ALBUMS		
□ 426 (M)	*COLPIX*	SHELLEY	5.00	8.00
□ 431 (M)		THE THINGS WE DID LAST SUMMER	4.00	7.00

FABIAN

Frankie Avalon's manager was seeking another Avalon—handsome, young and ready for "American Bandstand". Avalon spoke highly of Fabian Forte, a fellow student at Southern High in Philadelphia, Pennsylvania. Fabian, it seemed, was fifteen, sophomore class president, and thought to be the best-looking lad on campus. Avalon's manager was interested.

He found Fabian sitting on the doorstep of his home. The boy was upset as his father, a Philadelphia detective, had just had a heart attack and had been rushed away by ambulance. Fabian was in no mood to talk and dismissed the possibility of his becoming a singer.

He later changed his mind, although three voice teachers ended up walking out of Chancellor Records' office, saying that Fabian couldn't carry a tune in a bucket. No matter. A loud backup group drowned out most of Fabian's growls. Fabian was also given good material to sing and made frequent "Bandstand" appearances.

He scored three 1959 Top 10 singles and became that year's hottest teen idol. Fabian turned to movies after his recording career declined and starred in a few low-budget teen films.

ISSUE #	LABEL	ARTIST/TITLE	VG	MINT
		FABIAN		
☐1020	*CHANCELLOR*	SHIVERS/I'M IN LOVE	3.00	5.00
☐1024		LILLY LOU/BE MY STEADY DATE	3.00	5.00
☐1029		I'M A MAN/HYPNOTIZED (31)	1.50	3.00
☐1033		TURN ME LOOSE/STOP THIEF (9)	1.00	2.50
☐1037		TIGER/MIGHTY COLD (TO A WARM, WARM HEART) (3)	1.00	2.50
☐1041		COME ON AND GET ME/GOT THE FEELING)29)	1.25	2.50
☐1044		HOUND DOG MAN/THIS FRIENDLY WORLD (9)	1.00	2.50
☐1047		ABOUT THIS THING CALLED LOVE/STRING ALONG (31)	1.25	2.50
☐1051		STROLLIN' IN THE SUMMERTIME/I'M GONNA SIT RIGHT DOWN AND WRITE MYSELF A LETTER	1.50	2.50
☐1055		TOMORROW/KING OF LOVE	1.75	3.00
☐1061		KISSIN' AND TWISTIN'/LONG BEFORE (91)	1.50	2.50
☐1067		YOU KNOW YOU BELONG TO SOMEBODY ELSE/HOLD ON	1.50	2.50
☐1072		GRAPEVINE/DAVID AND GOLIATH	1.50	2.50
☐1079		THE LOVE THAT I'M GIVING TO YOU/ YOU'RE ONLY YOUNG ONCE	1.50	2.50
☐1084		A GIRL LIKE YOU/DREAM FACTORY	1.50	2.50
☐1086		KANSAS CITY/TONGUE-TIED	1.50	2.50
☐1092		WILD PARTY/THE GOSPEL TRUTH	1.50	2.50
☐1092		WILD PARTY/MADE YOU	1.50	2.50
		FABIAN—EPs		
☐5003	*CHANCELLOR*	HOLD THAT TIGER	4.00	7.00
☐A-5005		THE FABULOUS FABIAN	3.50	6.00
☐B-5005		THE FABULOUS FABIAN	3.50	6.00
☐C-5005		THE FABULOUS FABIAN	3.50	6.00
☐301		HOUND DOG MAN	3.00	5.00
		FABIAN—ALBUMS		
☐5003 (M)	*CHANCELLOR*	HOLD THAT TIGER	7.00	12.00
☐5005 (M)		THE FABULOUS FABIAN	6.00	10.00
☐5012 (M)		THE GOOD OLD SUMMERTIME	6.00	10.00
☐5019 (M)		ROCKIN' HOT	7.00	12.00
☐5024 (M)		FABIAN'S 16 FABULOUS HITS	6.00	10.00
		ADAM FAITH		
☐9061	*CUB*	WHAT DO YOU WANT?/FROM NOW UNTIL FOREVER	1.50	2.50
☐9068		POOR ME/THE REASON	1.50	2.50
☐9074		I DID WHAT YOU TOLD ME/ JOHNNY COMES MARCHING HOME	1.50	2.50
☐16405	*DOT*	DON'T THAT BEAT ALL/MIX ME A PERSON	1.50	2.50
☐895	*AMY*	SO LONG BABY/THE FIRST TIME	1.75	3.00
☐899		WE ARE IN LOVE/WHAT NOW?	1.50	2.50
☐913		IT'S ALRIGHT/I JUST DON'T KNOW (31)	1.25	2.50
☐922		TALK ABOUT LOVE/STOP FEELING SORRY FOR YOURSELF (97)	1.50	2.50
		ADAM FAITH—ALBUMS		
☐3951 (M)	*MGM*	ENGLAND'S TOP SINGER	6.00	10.00
☐8005 (M)	*AMY*	ADAM FAITH	5.00	8.00
		MARIANNE FAITHFULL		
☐9697	*LONDON*	AS TEARS GO BY/GLEENSLEEVES (22)	1.25	2.50
☐9731		COME AND STAY WITH ME/ WHAT HAVE I DONE WRONG? (26)	1.25	2.50

ISSUE #	LABEL	ARTIST/TITLE	VG	MINT
□ 9759		THIS LITTLE BIRD/MORNING SUN (32)	1.25	2.50
□ 9780		SUMMER NIGHTS/THE SHA-LA-LA SONG (24)	1.25	2.50
□ 9802		GO AWAY FROM MY WORLD/ OH, LOOK AROUND YOU (89)	1.50	2.50
□ 1022		SISTER MORPHINE/SOMETHING BETTER	2.50	4.00

MARIANNE FAITHFULL—ALBUMS

ISSUE #	LABEL	ARTIST/TITLE	VG	MINT
□ 3423 (M)	*LONDON*	MARIANNE FAITHFUL	3.50	6.00
□ 423 (S)		MARIANNE FAITHFUL	4.50	8.00
□ 3452 (M)		GO AWAY FROM MY WORLD	3.50	6.00
□ 452 (S)		GO AWAY FROM MY WORLD	4.50	8.00
□ 3482 (M)		FAITHFULL FOREVER	3.50	6.00
□ 482 (S)		FAITHFULL FOREVER	4.50	8.00
□ 3547 (M)		GREATEST HITS	3.00	5.00
□ 547 (S)		GREATEST HITS	4.00	7.00

FALLING PEBBLES (BUCKINGHAMS)

ISSUE #	LABEL	ARTIST/TITLE	VG	MINT
□ 201	*ALLEY CAT*	LAWDY MISS CLAWDY/VIRGINIA WOLF	5.00	8.00

FANTASTIC BAGGIES

FEATURED: STEVE BARRI

ISSUE #	LABEL	ARTIST/TITLE	VG	MINT
□ 66047	*IMPERIAL*	TELL 'EM I'M SURFIN'/SURFER BOY'S DREAM	3.00	5.00
□ 66072		ANYWHERE THE GIRLS ARE/DEBBIE BE TRUE	3.50	6.00
□ 66092		ALONE ON THE BEACH/IT WAS I	4.00	7.00

FANTASTIC BAGGIES—ALBUM

ISSUE #	LABEL	ARTIST/TITLE	VG	MINT
□ 9270 (M)	*IMPERIAL*	TELL 'EM I'M SURFIN'	7.00	12.00
□ 12270 (S)		TELL 'EM I'M SURFIN'	8.00	15.00

FELIX AND THE ESCORTS (YOUNG RASCALS)

ISSUE #	LABEL	ARTIST/TITLE	VG	MINT
□ 685	*JAG*	THE SYRACUSE/SAVE	6.00	10.00

NARVEL FELTS

ISSUE #	LABEL	ARTIST/TITLE	VG	MINT
□ 71140	*MERCURY*	KISS-A-ME BABY/FOOLISH THOUGHTS	3.50	6.00
□ 71190		CRY BABY CRY/LONESOME FEELING	3.00	5.00
□ 71249		DREAM WORLD/ROCKET RIDE	3.00	5.00

FENDER IV

ISSUE #	LABEL	ARTIST/TITLE	VG	MINT
□ 66061	*IMPERIAL*	MAY GAYA/YOU BETTER TELL ME HOW	2.50	4.00
□ 66098		MALIBU RUN/EVERYBODY UP	2.00	3.50

FENDERMEN

ISSUE #	LABEL	ARTIST/TITLE	VG	MINT
□ 1137	*SOMA*	MULE SKINNER BLUES/TORTURE (5)	1.25	3.00
□ 1142		DON'T YOU JUST KNOW IT/BEACH PARTY	1.50	2.50
□ 1152		HEARTBREAKIN' SPECIAL/CAN'T YOU WAIT?	1.50	2.50

FENDERMEN—ALBUM

ISSUE #	LABEL	ARTIST/TITLE	VG	MINT
□ 1240 (M)	*SOMA*	MULE SKINNER BLUES	25.00	40.00

LARRY FINNEGAN

ISSUE #	LABEL	ARTIST/TITLE	VG	MINT
□ 62313	*CORAL*	THERE AIN'T NOTHIN' IN THIS WORLD/ I'LL BE BACK, JACK	1.75	3.00
□ 1113	*OLD TOWN*	DEAR ONE/CANDY LIPS (11)	1.00	2.50
□ 1120		PRETTY SUZIE SUNSHINE/ THE WALKIN', TALKIN' BLUES	1.25	2.00
□ 146	*RIC*	A TRIBUTE TO RINGO STARR/ WHEN MY LOVE PASSES BY	1.75	3.00

FIREBALLS

Norman Petty's greatest "find" was Buddy Holly and the Crickets, who appeared one day at Petty's recording studio in the parched New Mexico town of Clovis. That was in 1957. Two years later another group walked through Petty's door. Like the Crickets, they sought a recording home in Clovis. All but one of the Fireballs had come from Raton, New Mexico. (The lone exception was a LaGrange, Illinois, pianist named Jimmy Gilmer.) Petty liked the group, recorded them, and negotiated a contract with Top Rank Records. In the fall of 1959 "Torquay" became the Fireballs' first hit. A Top 40 winner, "Torquay" was followed by the even bigger single of "Bulldog."

The Fireballs later drifted to other labels and managed to score another hit with "Quite A Party" on Warwick. Dot singles as the Fireballs produced no hits; however, when the group changed personnel and became Jimmy Gilmer and the Fireballs, their first Dot disc under the new name resulted in "Sugar Shack", a song that not only became No. 1 but ended up being the best-selling single of 1963.

ISSUE #	LABEL	ARTIST/TITLE	VG	MINT
		FIREBALLS		
		FEATURED: JIMMY GILMER		
☐2008	*TOP RANK*	TORQUAY/CRY BABY (39)	1.50	3.00
☐2026		BULLDOG/NEARLY SUNRISE (24)	1.50	3.00
☐2038		FOOT PATTER/KISSIN'	1.75	3.00
☐2054		VAQUERO/CHIEF WHOOPEN KOFF (99)	1.75	3.00
☐2081		ALMOST PARADISE/SWEET TALK	1.50	2.50
☐3003		RIK-A-TIK/YACKY DOO	1.75	3.00
☐248	*KAPP*	FIREBALL/I DON'T KNOW	1.50	2.50
☐630	*WARWICK*	RIK-A-TIK/YACKY DOO	1.50	2.50
☐644		QUITE A PARTY/GUNSHOT (27)	1.00	2.00
☐16493	*DOT*	TORQUAY TWO/PEG LEG	1.50	2.50
☐16661		DUMBO/MR. REED	1.25	2.00
☐16715		MORE THAN I CAN SEE/THE BEATING OF MY HEART	1.50	2.50
☐16745		CAMPUSOLOGY/AHHH, SOUL	1.50	2.50
☐16992		SHY GIRL/I THINK I'LL CATCH A BUG	1.25	2.00
		FIREBALLS—EP		
☐1000	*TOP RANK*	THE FIREBALLS	7.00	12.00
		FIREBALLS—ALBUMS		
☐324 (M)	*TOP RANK*	THE FIREBALLS	12.00	20.00
☐343 (M)		VAQUERO	8.00	15.00
☐2042 (M)	*WARWICK*	HERE ARE THE FIREBALLS	7.00	12.00
☐3512 (M)	*DOT*	TORQUAY	5.00	8.00
☐25512 (S)		TORQUAY	6.00	10.00
☐3709 (M)		CAMPUSOLOGY	5.00	8.00
☐25709 (S)		CAMPUSOLOGY	6.00	10.00
		FIREFLIES		
☐6901	*RIBBON*	YOU WERE MINE/STELLA'S GOT A FELLA (21)	1.25	3.00
☐6904		I CAN'T SAY GOODBYE/WHAT DID I DO WRONG? (90)	1.75	3.00
☐6906		MY GIRL/BECAUSE OF MY PRIDE	1.75	3.00
☐117	*CANADIAN-AMERICAN*	MARIANNE/GIVE ALL YOUR LOVE TO ME	1.75	3.00
☐355	*TAURUS*	YOU WERE MINE FOR AWHILE/ONE O'CLOCK TWIST	1.75	3.00
		FIREFLIES—ALBUM		
☐1002 (S)	*TAURUS*	YOU WERE MINE	12.00	20.00
		FIVE BLOBS		
☐41250	*COLUMBIA*	THE BLOB/SATURDAY NIGHT IN TIJUANA (33)	2.00	4.00
		FIVE DISCS		
☐607	*DWAIN*	MY CHINESE GIRL/ROSES	12.00	20.00
☐803		MY CHINESE GIRL/ROSES	8.00	15.00
☐1002	*MELLO MOOD*	MY CHINESE GIRL/ROSES	8.00	15.00
☐1004	*EMGE*	I REMEMBER/THE WORLD IS A BEAUTIFUL PLACE	7.00	12.00
☐0327	*VIK*	I REMEMBER/THE WORLD IS A BEAUTIFUL PLACE	5.00	12.00
☐5027	*RUST*	I REMEMBER/THE WORLD IS A BEAUTIFUL PLACE	2.50	4.00
☐240	*YALE*	WHEN LOVE COMES KNOCKING/GO-GO	5.00	8.00
☐243		COME ON BABY/I DON'T KNOW WHAT I'LL DO	8.00	15.00
		FIVE KEYS		
☐2945	*CAPITOL*	LING, TING, TONG/I'M ALONE (28)	2.50	5.00
☐3032		CLOSE YOUR EYES/DOGGONE IT, YOU DID IT	3.00	5.00
☐3267		GEE WHITTAKERS!/'CAUSE YOU'RE MY LOVER	3.00	5.00
☐3502		OUT OF SIGHT, OUT OF MIND (27)	2.50	5.00
☐3597		WISDOM OF A FOOL/NOW DON'T THAT PROVE I LOVE YOU (35)	2.50	5.00

ISSUE #	LABEL	ARTIST/TITLE	VG	MINT
		FIVE PENNIES		
□1182	*SAVOY*	MR. MOON/LET IT RAIN	3.00	5.00
□1190		MY HEART TREMBLES/MONEY	3.00	5.00

FIVE SATINS

In 1954 a New Haven, Connecticut, lad named Fred Parris formed a singing quintet called the Scarletts. However, Fred had to disband the group when he joined the army shortly thereafter. One night as he was walking monotonous guard duty, Private Parris hit upon a song idea. As it was a quiet and lonely 3:00 A.M., Fred began forming a song in his mind. The title: "In the Still of the Night".

After Parris' military career ended in 1956, he reorganized the group under a new name, the Five Satins. They rehearsed "In the Still of the Night". then approached the small Standord label in Connecticut. Standord agreed to record the song, which they did, and leased it to the larger Ember label in hopes of getting a national hit. Ember agreed to take the master, but they wanted to promote the flip side of "The Jones Girl" as the hit. As history has proven, though, "In the Still of the Night" became the winner and a true 1950s classic.

The Five Satins had only one other hit—"To the Aisle"—a year later.

ISSUE #	LABEL	ARTIST/TITLE	VG	MINT
		FIVE SATINS		
□106	*STANDORD*	IN THE STILL OF THE NIGHT/THE JONES GIRL	50.00	80.00
□1005	*EMBER*	IN THE STILL OF THE NIGHT/THE JONES GIRL (29) .	4.00	8.00
□1019		TO THE AISLE/WISH I HAD MY BABY (25)	3.00	6.00
		FLAMINGOS		
□1035	*END*	LOVERS NEVER SAY GOODBYE/ THAT LOVE IS YOU (52)	2.50	4.00
□1044		LOVE WALKED IN/AT THE PROM	2.00	3.50
□1046		I ONLY HAVE EYES FOR YOU/ GOONIGHT SWEETHEART (11)	1.50	3.00
□1055		LOVE WALKED IN/YOURS (88)	1.75	3.00
□1062		I WAS SUCH A FOOL/HEAVENLY ANGEL (71)	1.75	3.00
□1068		NOBODY LOVES ME LIKE YOU/BESAME MUCHO (30) ..	1.25	2.50
		FLARES (CADETS)		
□8624	*FELSTED*	FOOT STOMPIN' (vocal)/ FOOT STOMPIN' (instrumental) (25)............	1.25	2.50
		FLEETWOOD MAC		
□10386	*EPIC*	STOP MESSIN' 'ROUND/NEED YOUR LOVE SO BAD ...	2.50	4.00
□10436		ALBATROSS/JIGSAW PUZZLE BLUES	2.50	4.00
□11029		ALBATROSS/BLACK MAGIC WOMAN	1.75	3.00
□0860	*REPRISE*	COMING YOUR WAY/RATTLESNAKE SHAKE	2.00	3.50
□0883		OH WELL (PT. 1)/(PT. 11) (55)	1.75	3.00
□0925		WORLD IN HARMONY/GREEN MANALISHI	1.75	3.00
□0984		JEWEL EYED JUDY/STATION MAN	1.75	3.00
□1057		SANDS OF TIME/LAY IT ALL DOWN.............	1.75	3.00
□1079		OH WELL/GREEN MANALISHI	1.50	2.50
□1093		SENTIMENTAL LADY/SUNNY SIDE OF HEAVEN	2.50	4.00
□1172		DID YOU EVER LOVE ME?/REVELATION	1.75	4.00

FLEETWOODS

Two Girls And a Guy?

That was the original name of the Fleetwoods. They were classmates at Olympia High in Olympia, Washington. At first the two girls (Barbara Ellis and Gretchen Christopher) sang as a nameless duo. Then they asked school pal Gary Troxel to join them—as a trumpet player. However, the girls soon discovered that Troxel's singing talents outdistanced his trumpeting.

They finished high school in June of 1958 and signed with the Liberty Records subsidiary of Dolton. The manager of Two Girls And a Guy thought the youngsters should choose a more commercial name. They decided on their Olympia telephone prefix, FLeetwood. (Prefixes were used long before all-digit phone numbers.)

The Fleetwoods' first release was a song they had written a year earlier called "Come Softly To Me". It shot to No. 1, as did another 1959 single, "Mr. Blue". After "covering" Thomas Wayne's hit of "Tragedy" the Fleetwoods' last chart hit came in 1963 with another "cover"—a 1950s r & b hit called "Goodnight My Love", originally done by Jesse Belvin.

ISSUE #	LABEL	ARTIST/TITLE	VG	MINT
		FLEETWOODS		
□55188	*LIBERTY*	COME SOFTLY TO ME/I CARE SO MUCH	2.50	4.00
□1	*DOLPHIN*	COME SOFTLY TO ME/I CARE SO MUCH (1)	1.00	2.50
□3	*DOLTON*	GRADUATION'S HERE/OH LORD, LET IT BE (39)	1.25	2.50
□5		MR. BLUE/YOU MEAN EVERYTHING TO ME (1)	1.00	2.50
□15		OUTSIDE MY WINDOW/MAGIC STAR (28)	1.25	2.50
□22		RUNAROUND/TRULY DO (23)	1.25	2.50
□27		THE LAST ONE TO KNOW/DORMILONA (96)	1.50	2.50
□30		CONFIDENTIAL/I LOVE YOU SO	1.75	3.00
□40		TRAGEDY/LITTLE MISS SAD ONE (10)	1.00	2.50
□45		(HE'S) THE GREAT IMPOSTER/ POOR LITTLE GIRL (30)	1.25	2.50
□49		BILLY OLD BUDDY/TROUBLE	1.50	2.50
□62		LOVERS BY NIGHT, STRANGERS BY DAY/ THEY TELL ME IT'S SUMMER (36)	1.25	2.00
□74		YOU SHOULD HAVE BEEN THERE/ SURE IS LONESOME DOWNTOWN	1.25	2.00
□75		GOODNIGHT MY LOVE/JIMMY BEWARE (32)	1.00	1.50
		LATER DOLTON SINGLES ARE WORTH UP TO $1.50 MINT		
		FLEETWOODS—EP		
□502	*DOLTON*	RUNAROUND	3.00	5.00
		FLEETWOODS—ALBUMS		
□2001 (M)	*DOLTON*	MR. BLUE	3.50	6.00
□8001 (S)		MR. BLUE	4.50	8.00
□2002 (M)		FLEETWOODS	3.50	6.00
□8002 (S)		FLEETWOODS	4.50	8.00
□2005 (M)		SOFTLY	3.00	5.00
□8005 (S)		SOFTLY	4.00	7.00
□2007 (M)		DEEP IN A DREAM	3.00	5.00
□8007 (S)		DEEP IN A DREAM	4.00	7.00
□2011 (M)		THE FLEETWOODS SING THE BEST OF THE OLDIES	3.00	5.00
□8011 (S)		THE FLEETWOODS SING THE BEST OF THE OLDIES	4.00	7.00
□2018 (M)		THE FLEETWOODS' GREATEST HITS	3.00	5.00
□8018 (S)		THE FLEETWOODS' GREATEST HITS	4.00	7.00
		FLOURESCENTS		
□4520	*HANOVER*	THE FACTS OF LOVE/SHOOPY POP-A-DOO	15.00	25.00
		TOMMY FOGERTY AND THE BLUE VELVETS		
		SEE: CREEDENCE CLEARWATER REVIVAL		
□1010	*ORCHESTRA*	HAVE YOU EVEN BEEN LONELY?/BONITA	7.00	12.00
		WAYNE FONTANA AND THE MINDBENDERS		
□1503	*FONTANA*	THE GAME OF LOVE/SINCE YOU'VE BEEN GONE	1.50	2.50
□1509		THE GAME OF LOVE/ONE MORE TIME (1)	.75	2.00
□1514		IT'S JUST A LITTLE BIT TOO LATE/ A LONG TIME COMIN' (45)	1.00	2.00
□1524		SHE NEEDS LOVE/LIKE I DID	1.25	2.00
		WAYNE FONTANA AND THE MINDBENDERS—ALBUM		
□27542 (M)	*FONTANA*	THE GAME OF LOVE	3.00	5.00
□67542 (S)		THE GAME OF LOVE	4.00	7.00
		FONTANE SISTERS		
□15265	*DOT*	HEARTS OF STONE/BLESS YOUR HEART (1)	1.50	3.00
□15333		ROCK LOVE/YOU'RE MINE (19)	1.50	3.00

ISSUE #	LABEL	ARTIST/TITLE	VG	MINT
☐15352		MOST OF ALL/PUT ME IN THE MOOD	1.50	2.50
☐15370		ROLLIN' STONE/PLAYMATES	1.50	2.50
☐15386		SEVENTEEN/IF I COULD BE WITH YOU (6)	1.50	3.00
☐15428		DADDY-O/ADORABLE (11)	1.50	3.00
☐15450		EDDIE MY LOVE/YUM YUM (12)	1.50	2.50
☐15462		I'M IN LOVE AGAIN/YOU ALWAYS HURT THE ONE YOU LOVE (38)	1.50	2.50
☐15555		I'M STICKIN' WITH YOU/ LET THE REST OF THE WORLD (72)	1.50	2.50
		FONTANE SISTERS—EPs		
☐1019	*DOT*	THE FONTANE SISTERS	2.50	4.00
☐1020		THE FONTANE SISTERS	2.50	4.50
		FONTANE SISTERS—ALBUMS		
☐3004 (M)	*DOT*	THE FONTANE SISTERS	4.00	7.00
☐3042 (M)		THE FONTANES SING	3.50	6.00

FRANKIE FORD

Frankie Ford came from the Louisiana town of Fretna. At an early age he became interested in music and enjoyed singing along with hits of the day that blasted from his bedroom radio. While a student at Holy Name of Mary High School, Ford applied for a music scholarship. He won and enrolled at Southeastern College in Hammond, Louisiana.

Frankie left college late in 1958 and auditioned at Southern-based Ace Records. Ace then offered a contract. Frankie Ford's maiden single was "Cheatin' Woman", which went nowhere. He fared better with his second release, "Sea Cruise", It was a song written by Huey "Piano" Smith, whose band (the Clowns) provided the background on "Sea Cruise", one of the best rockers of 1959.

After "Sea Cruise" went to the Top 20, Ford then recorded "Alimony". It barely made the hit charts. A third chart disc—peaking at No. 75—was "Time After Time", an upbeat standard. Frankie Ford later opened his own night club in New Orleans.

ISSUE #	LABEL	ARTIST/TITLE	VG	MINT
		FRANKIE FORD		
☐549	*ACE*	CHEATIN' WOMAN/THE LAST ONE TO CRY	2.50	4.00
☐554		SEA CRUISE/ROBERTA (14)	1.50	3.00
☐566		ALIMONY/CAN'T TELL MY HEART (WHAT TO DO) (97)	1.50	2.50
☐580		TIME AFTER TIME/I WANT TO BE YOUR MAN (75)	1.50	2.50
☐592		CHINATOWN/WHAT'S GOIN' ON?	1.50	2.50
☐8009		OCEAN FULL OF TEARS/HOURS OF NEED	1.25	2.00
		FRANKIE FORD—EP		
☐105	*ACE*	THE BEST OF FRANKIE FORD	4.00	7.00
		FRANKIE FORD—ALBUM		
☐1005 (M)	*ACE*	ON A SEA CRUISE WITH FRANKIE FORD	7.00	12.00
		4 AFTER 5's (RIVINGTONS)		
☐9076	*ALL TIME*	HELLO, SCHOOLTEACHER/ I GOTTA HAVE SOMEBODY	4.00	7.00
		FOUR CAL-QUETTES		
☐4534	*CAPITOL*	SPARKLE AND SHINE/ IN THIS WORLD (Couquettes)	2.00	3.50
☐4574		STARBRIGHT/BILLY MY BILLY	1.75	3.00
☐4657		MOST OF ALL/I'M GONNA LOVE HIM ANYWAY	1.75	3.00
☐4725		I'LL NEVER COME BACK/AGAIN	1.75	3.00
		FOUR DOTS (WITH JEWEL AKENS)		
		GUITAR: EDDIE COCHRAN		
☐44005	*FREEDOM*	DON'T WAKE UP THE KIDS/PLEADING FOR LOVE	3.50	6.00
		FOUR GRADUATES (HAPPENINGS)		
☐5062	*RUST*	A LOVELY WAY TO SPEND AN EVENING/ PICTURE OF AN ANGEL	3.00	5.00
☐5084		CANDY QUEEN/A BOY IN LOVE	2.50	4.00
		FOUR J'S		
☐528	*HERALD*	DREAMS ARE A DIME A DOZEN/ KISSIN' AT THE DRIVE-IN	3.00	5.00
☐125	*UNITED ARTISTS*	ROCK AND ROLL AGE/BE NICE, DON'T FIGHT	2.50	4.00
		FOUR JOKERS		
		FEATURED: NERVOUS NORVUS		
☐3004	*DIAMOND*	TRANSFUSION/YOU DID	7.00	12.00
		THIS WAS THE ORIGINAL VERSION OF THE NERVOUS NORVUS HIT		
		FOUR LOVERS (FOUR SEASONS)		
☐6518	*RCA*	YOU'RE THE APPLE OF MY EYE/ THE GIRL IN MY DREAMS (62)	6.00	10.00

ISSUE #		LABEL	ARTIST/TITLE	VG	MINT
□6519			HONEY LOVE/PLEASE DON'T LEAVE ME	7.00	12.00
□6646			JAMBALAYA/BE LOVEY DOVEY	7.00	12.00
□6768			NEVER NEVER/HAPPY AM I	8.00	15.00
□6812			SHAKE A HAND/THE STRANGER	8.00	15.00
			FOUR LOVERS (FOUR SEASONS)—EP		
□871		*RCA*	JOYRIDE	30.00	50.00
			FOUR LOVERS (FOUR SEASONS)—ALBUM		
□1317	(M)	*RCA*	JOYRIDE	60.00	100.00
			FOURMOST		
□6280		*ATCO*	HELLO, LITTLE GIRL/JUST IN CASE	3.00	5.00
□6285			RESPECTABLE/I'M IN LOVE	3.00	5.00
□6307			IF YOU CRY/A LITTLE BIT OF LOVING	2.50	4.00
□6317			HOW CAN I TELL HER?/YOU GOT THAT WAY	2.50	4.00
□5591		*CAPITOL*	WHY DO FOOLS FALL IN LOVE/ GIRLS, GIRLS, GIRLS	2.00	3.50
□5738			HERE, THERE AND EVERYWHERE/YOU'VE CHANGED	2.00	3.50
			FOUR PALS		
□610		*ROYAL ROOST*	IF I CAN'T HAVE THE ONE I LOVE/I FLIPPED	4.00	7.00
□616			NO ONE EVER LOVE ME/ CAN'T STAND IT ANY LONGER	3.50	6.00
			FOUR PENNIES (CHIFFONS)		
□5070		*RUST*	WHEN THE BOY'S HAPPY/HOCKADAY, PART 1 (95)	2.50	4.00
□5071			MY BLOCK/DRY YOUR EYES (67)	2.00	3.50

FOUR SEASONS

They originally were a New York City quartet called the Four Lovers. Under that name they scored on the East Coast with a 1956 RCA single called "The Apple of My Eye". Nationally the song failed to do well, and the Four Lovers later slipped into a half-dozen years of obscurity.

By 1962 they had added one new member, Bob Gaudio, who had recently left the Royal Teens ("Short Shorts", "Believe Me"). They had also changed their name by 1962. While working as a bowling alley lounge act at a place called the Four Seasons, the group decided to adopt the name of their place of employment.

A Gone Records single went nowhere, but the Four Sesons' first Vee Jay 45 ("Sherry") was a million-selling monster. Thanks to Frankie Valli's wailing falsetto, the Four Seasons established a distinctive sound and name for themselves. After a successful career on Vee Jay, the Four Seasons went to the Phillips label, where their hit streak continued.

In 1978 Valli left the group to concentrate on solo efforts ("Grease," etc.). Without the Valli trademark the Four Seasons eventually fell apart.

ISSUE #	LABEL	ARTIST/TITLE	VG	MINT
		FOUR SEASONS		
		FEATURED: FRANKIE VALLI		
☐5122	*GONE*	BERMUDA/SPANISH LACE	8.00	15.00
☐456	*VEE JAY*	SHERRY/I'VE CRIED BEFORE (1)	1.00	2.50
☐465		BIG GIRLS DON'T CRY/CONNIE-O (1)	1.00	2.50
☐478		SANTA CLAUS IS COMING TO TOWN/ CHRISTMAS TEARS (23)	1.25	3.00
☐485		WALK LIKE A MAN/LUCKY LADYBUG (1)	1.00	2.50
☐512		AIN'T THAT A SHAME/SOON (22)	1.25	2.50
☐539		CANDY GIRL/MARLENA (3)	1.00	2.50
☐562		NEW MEXICAN ROSE/THAT'S THE ONLY WAY (36)	1.25	2.50
☐576		PEANUTS/STAY	1.75	3.00
☐582		STAY/GOODNIGHT MY LOVE (16)	1.00	2.50
☐597		ALONE/LONG LONELY NIGHTS (28)	1.25	2.50
☐608		SINCERELY/ONE SONG (75)	1.50	2.50
☐618		HAPPY, HAPPY BIRTHDAY BABY/ YOU'RE THE APPLE OF MY EYE	1.75	3.00
☐620		I SAW MOMMY KISSING SANTA CLAUS/ CHRISTMAS TEARS	1.75	3.00
☐639		NEVER ON SUNDAY/CONNIE-O	1.75	3.00
☐664		SINCE I DON'T HAVE YOU/TONITE, TONITE	2.50	4.00
☐713		LITTLE BOY (IN GROWN-UP CLOTHES)/ SILVER WINGS (60)	1.50	2.50
☐719		MY MOTHER'S EYES/STAY	1.75	3.00
☐40166	*PHILIPS*	DAWN/NO SURFIN' TODAY (3)	.75	2.00
☐40185		RONNIE/BORN TO WANDER (6)	.75	2.00
☐40211		RAG DOLL/SILENCE IS GOLDEN (1)	.75	2.00
☐40225		SAVE IT FOR ME/FUNNY FACE (10)	.75	2.00
☐40238		BIG MAN IN TOWN/LITTLE ANGEL (20)	1.00	2.00
☐40260		BYE, BYE, BABY/SEARCHING WIND (12)	.75	2.00
☐40278		TOY SOLDIER/BETRAYED (64)	1.25	2.00
☐40305		GIRL COME RUNNING/CRY MYSELF TO SLEEP (30)	1.00	2.00
☐40317		LET'S HANG ON/ON BROADWAY TONIGHT (3)	.75	1.50
☐40350		WORKING MY WAY BACK TO YOU/ TOO MANY MEMORIES (9)	.75	1.50
☐40370		OPUS 17/BEGGAR'S PARADISE (13)	.75	1.50
☐40393		I'VE GOT YOU UNDER MY SKIN/ HUGGIN' MY PILLOW (9)	.75	1.50
☐40412		TELL IT TO THE RAIN/SNOW GIRL (10)	.75	1.50
☐40433		BEGGIN'/DODY (16)	.75	1.50
☐40460		C'MON MARIANNE/LET'S RIDE AGAIN (9)	.75	1.50
☐40490		WATCH THE FLOWERS GROW/RAVEN (30)	1.00	1.50
		LATER PHILIPS SINGLES ARE WORTH UP TO $1.50 MINT		
		FOUR SEASONS—EPs		
☐1901	*VEE JAY*	THE FOUR SEASONS SING	3.00	5.00
☐1902		THE FOUR SEASONS SING	3.00	5.00
		FOUR SEASONS—ALBUMS		
☐1053 (M)	*VEE JAY*	SHERRY AND 11 OTHERS	3.50	6.00
☐1053 (S)		SHERRY AND 11 OTHERS	4.50	8.00
☐1055 (M)		FOUR SEASONS' GREETINGS	3.50	6.00
☐1055 (S)		FOUR SEASONS' GREETINGS	4.50	8.00
☐1056 (M)		BIG GIRLS DON'T CRY	3.50	6.00
☐1056 (S)		BIG GIRLS DON'T CRY	4.50	8.00

ISSUE #	LABEL	ARTIST/TITLE	VG	MINT
□ 1059 (M)		AIN'T THAT A SHAME	3.50	6.00
□ 1059 (S)		AIN'T THAT A SHAME	4.50	8.00
□ 1065 (M)		GOLDEN HITS OF THE FOUR SEASONS	3.50	6.00
□ 1065 (S)		GOLDEN HITS OF THE FOUR SEASONS	4.50	8.00
□ 200124 (M)	***PHILIPS***	DAWN	3.00	5.00
□ 600124 (S)		DAWN	4.00	7.00
□ 200129 (M)		BORN TO WANDER	3.00	5.00
□ 600129 (S)		BORN TO WANDER	4.00	7.00
□ 200146 (M)		RAG DOLL	3.00	5.00
□ 600146 (S)		RAG DOLL	4.00	7.00
□ 200150 (M)		ALL THE SONG HITS OF THE FOUR SEASONS	3.00	5.00
□ 600150 (S)		ALL THE SONG HITS OF THE FOUR SEASONS	4.00	7.00

FOUR SPEEDS

FEATURED: DENNIS WILSON, GARY USHER

□ 9187	***CHALLENGE***	R.P.M./MY STING RAY	3.00	5.00
□ 9202		FOUR ON THE FLOOR/CHEATER SLICKS	5.00	8.00

FOUR TOPS

□ 1623	***CHESS***	COULD IT BE YOU?/KISS ME BABY	8.00	15.00
□ 4534	***RIVERSIDE***	PENNIES FROM HEAVEN/WHERE ARE YOU?	7.00	15.00
□ 41755	***COLUMBIA***	AIN'T THAT LOVE/LONELY SUMMER	5.00	8.00
□ 43356		AIN'T THAT LOVE/LONELY NIGHTS	4.00	7.00

FOUR TUNES

□ 5128	***JUBILEE***	MARIE/I GAMBLED WITH LOVE (18)	2.00	3.50
□ 5132		I UNDERSTAND JUST HOW YOU FEEL/SUGAR LUMP (8)	1.75	3.00
□ 5174		I SOLD MY HEART TO THE JUNKMAN/ LET ME GO, LOVER	2.00	3.50

FOUR WINDS (TOKENS)

□ 102	***CRYSTAL BALL***	COME SOFTLY TO ME/DEAR JUDY	3.50	6.00
□ 100	***SWING***	REMEMBER LAST SUMMER/STRANGE FEELINGS	3.00	5.00
□ 555	***B. T. PUPPY***	LET IT RIDE/ONE FACE IN THE CROWD	2.50	4.00

KIM FOWLEY

□ 216	***CORBY***	BIG SUR/THE TRIP	3.00	5.00
□ 209	***MIRA***	AMERICAN DREAM/THE STATUE	3.00	5.00
□ 721	***LIVING LEGEND***	MR. RESPONSIBILITY/MY FOOLISH HEART	3.00	5.00
□ 725		UNDERGROUND LADY/POP ART '66	3.50	6.00
□ 0569	***REPRISE***	DON'T BE CRUEL/STRANGERS FROM THE SKY	3.00	5.00
□ 342	***TOWER***	LOVE IS ALIVE AND WELL/REINCARNATION	2.50	4.00
□ 66326	***IMPERIAL***	BORN TO BE WILD/SPACE ODYSSEY	3.00	5.00

KIM FOWLEY—ALBUMS

□ 5080 (M)	***TOWER***	LOVE IS ALIVE AND WELL	6.00	10.00
□ 12413 (M)	***IMPERIAL***	BORN TO BE WILD	5.00	8.00
□ 12423 (M)		OUTRAGEOUS	5.00	8.00
□ 12443 (M)		GOOD CLEAN FUN	4.00	7.00

NORMAN FOX AND THE ROB-ROYS

□ 501	***BACK BEAT***	TELL MY WHY/AUDREY	2.50	4.00
□ 508		MY DEAREST ONE/DANCE, GIRL, DANCE	3.00	5.00
□ 4128	***CAPITOL***	DREAM GIRL/PIZZA PIE	15.00	25.00

ISSUE #	LABEL	ARTIST/TITLE	VG	MINT
		PETER FRAMPTON		
		SEE: HERD		
□1379	**A & M**	JUMPING JACK FLASH/OH, FOR ANOTHER DAY	1.75	3.00
□1506		I WANNA GO TO THE SUN/ SOMETHING'S HAPPENING	1.50	2.50
□1693		SHOW ME THE WAY/CRYING CLOWN	1.75	3.00
□1738		BABY, I LOVE YOUR WAY/MONEY	1.75	3.00

CONNIE FRANCIS

Constance Franconero first saw the light of day on December 12, 1938. Belleville, New Jersey, was her birthplace. Young Connie took up the accordian when she was four. Becoming highly adept at the instrument, she made her first professional appearance at the age of eleven. She also sang at that appearance. After a fine reaction to her singing, Connie then knew that she was destined to become a singer rather than an accordian player.

A year later—before she entered her teens—she began singing on NBC Radio. Connie auditioned for "Arthur Godfrey's Talent Scouts" and earned a chance to sing on the show. It was Godfrey who suggested Connie change her name to something simpler and easier to remember.

In 1955 Connie Francis signed on with MGM Records as a sixteen-year-old vocalist. Single after single went nowhere. Connie finally hit pay dirt with her eleventh release, "Who's Sorry Now", in 1958. And that million-seller was just the beginning. During her recording career Ms. Francis scored nineteen Top 20 singles, including three that reached the No. 1 spot.

ISSUE #	LABEL	ARTIST/TITLE	VG	MINT
		CONNIE FRANCIS		
□ 12015	***MGM***	FREDDY/DIDN'T I LOVE YOU ENOUGH?	2.50	4.00
□ 12056		MAKE HIM JEALOUS/GOODY GOODBYE	2.50	4.00
□ 12122		ARE YOU SATIFIED?/MY TREASURE	2.50	4.00
□ 12191		MY FIRST REAL LOVE/BELIEVE IN ME	2.50	4.00
□ 12251		SEND FOR MY BABY/FORGETTING	2.50	4.00
□ 12335		MY SAILOR BOY/EVERYONE NEEDS SOMEONE	2.00	3.50
□ 12375		I NEVER HAD A SWEETHEART/LITTLE BLUE WREN	2.00	3.50
□ 12440		NO OTHER ONE/I LEANED ON A MAN	2.00	3.50
□ 12490		EIGHTEEN/FADED ORCHID	2.00	3.50
□ 12555		YOU, MY DARLIN', YOU/THE MAJESTY OF LOVE	2.00	3.50
□ 12588		WHO'S SORRY NOW/YOU WERE ONLY FOOLING (4)	1.25	3.00
□ 12647		I'M SORRY I MADE YOU CRY/ LOCK UP YOUR HEART (36)	1.50	3.50
□ 12683		STUPID CUPID/CAROLINA MOON (17)	1.25	3.00
□ 12713		FALLIN'/HAPPY DAYS AND LONELY NIGHTS (30)	1.50	3.00
□ 12738		MY HAPPINESS/NEVER BEFORE (2)	1.25	3.00
□ 12769		IF I DIDN'T CARE/TOWARD THE END OF THE DAY (22)	1.50	3.00
□ 12793		LIPSTICK ON YOUR COLLAR/FRANKIE (5)	1.25	3.00
□ 12824		YOU'RE GONNA MISS ME/PLENTY GOOD LOVIN' (34)	1.25	2.50
□ 12841		AMONG MY SOUVENIRS/GOD BLESS AMERICA (7)	1.00	2.50
□ 12878		MAMA/TEDDY (8)	1.00	2.50
□ 12899		EVERYBODY'S SOMEBODY'S FOOL/ JEALOUS OF YOU (1)	1.00	2.50
□ 12923		MY HEART HAS A MIND OF IT OWN/MALAGUENA (1)	1.00	2.50
□ 12964		MANY TEARS AGO/SENZA MAMA (7)	1.00	2.50
□ 12971		WHERE THE BOYS ARE/NO ONE (4)	1.00	2.50
□ 12995		BREAKIN' IN A BRAND NEW BROKEN HEART/ SOMEONE ELSE'S BOY (7)	.75	2.00
□ 13005		SWANEE/ATASHI NO	1.50	2.50
□ 13019		TOGETHER/TOO MANY RULES (6)	.75	2.00
□ 13039		(HE'S MY) DREAMBOAT/HOLLYWOOD (14)	1.00	2.00
□ 13051		WHEN THE BOY IN YOUR ARMS/ BABY'S FIRST CHRISTMAS (10)	.75	2.00
□ 13059		DON'T BREAK THE HEART THAT LOVES YOU/ DROP IT, JOE (1)	.75	2.00
□ 13074		SECOND HAND LOVE/GONNA GIT THAT MAN (7)	.75	2.00
□ 13087		VACATION/THE BIGGEST SIN OF ALL (9)	.75	2.00

LATER MGM SINGLES ARE WORTH UP TO $1.50 MINT

ISSUE #	LABEL	ARTIST/TITLE	VG	MINT
		CONNIE FRANCIS—EPs		
☐1599	*MGM*	CONNIE FRANCIS	2.50	5.00
☐1603		WHO'S SORRY NOW	2.00	4.00
☐1604		WHO'S SORRY NOW	2.00	4.00
☐1605		WHO'S SORRY NOW	2.00	4.00
☐1655		MY HAPPINESS	2.00	4.00
☐1662		IF I DIDN'T CARE	2.00	4.00
		CONNIE FRANCIS—ALBUMS		
☐3686 (M)	*MGM*	WHO'S SORRY NOW	4.50	8.00
☐3761 (M)		EXCITING CONNIE FRANCIS	2.50	5.00
☐3761 (S)		EXCITING CONNIE FRANCIS	3.50	7.00
☐3791 (M)		ITALIAN FAVORITES	2.50	5.00
☐3791 (S)		ITALIAN FAVORITES	3.50	7.00
☐3792 (M)		CONNIE'S GREATEST HITS	2.50	5.00
☐3792 (S)		CONNIE'S GREATEST HITS	3.50	7.00
		JOHN FRED AND HIS PLAYBOY BAND		
☐904	*MONTEL*	DOWN IN NEW ORLEANS/I LOVE YOU	2.50	4.00
☐1002		SHIRLEY/MY LOVE FOR YOU (83)	2.00	3.50
☐1007		GOOD LOVIN'/YOU KNOW YOU MADE ME CRY	1.75	3.00
☐2001		MIRROR MIRROR/TO HAVE AND TO HOLD	1.75	3.00
☐730	*JEWEL*	THERE GOES THAT TRAIN/DIAL 101	1.50	2.50
☐736		YOU'RE MAD AT ME/LENNIE	1.50	2.50
☐737		MY FIRST LOVE/BOOGIE CHILDREN	1.50	2.50
☐743		WRONG TO ME/HOW CAN I PROVE IT?	1.50	2.50
		SINGLES ON PAULA ARE WORTH UP TO $1.50 MINT		
		FREDDIE AND THE DREAMERS		
☐5053	*CAPITOL*	I'M TELLIN YOU NOW/ WHAT HAVE I DONE TO YOU?	3.00	5.00
☐5137		YOU WERE MADE FOR ME/SEND A LETTER TO ME	2.50	4.00
☐125	*TOWER*	I'M TELLING YOU NOW/ WHAT HAVE I DONE TO YOU? (1)	1.00	2.00
☐127		YOU WERE MADE FOR ME/SO FINE (21)	1.25	2.00
☐72327	*MERCURY*	DON'T DO THAT TO ME/JUST FOR YOU	1.75	3.00
☐72377		I UNDERSTAND/I WILL (36)	1.25	2.50
☐72428		DO THE FREDDIE/TELL MY WHEN (18)	1.25	2.00
☐72462		A LITTLE YOU/THINGS I'D LIKE TO SAY (48)	1.25	2.50
☐72487		I DON'T KNOW/WINDMILL IN OLD AMSTERDAM	1.50	2.50
		FREDDIE AND THE DREAMERS—ALBUMS		
☐21017 (M)	*MERCURY*	FREDDIE AND THE DREAMERS	3.50	6.00
☐61017 (S)		FREDDIE AND THE DREAMERS	4.50	8.00
☐21026 (M)		DO THE FREDDIE	3.50	6.00
☐61026 (S)		DO THE FREDDIE	4.50	8.00
☐21031 (M)		SEASIDE SWINGERS	3.50	6.00
☐61031 (S)		SEASIDE SWINGERS	4.50	8.00
		BOBBY FREEMAN		
☐835	*JOSIE*	DO YOU WANT TO DANCE?/BIG FAT WOMAN (5)	1.25	3.00
☐841		BETTY LOU GOT A NEW PAIR OF SHOES/ STARLIGHT (37)	1.50	3.00
☐844		NEED YOUR LOVE/ SHAME ON YOU, MISS JOHNSON (54)	1.50	2.50
☐855		WHEN YOU'RE SMILING/ A LOVE TO LAST A LIFETIME	1.50	2.50

ISSUE #	LABEL	ARTIST/TITLE	VG	MINT
□863		MARY ANN THOMAS/LOVE ME (90)	1.25	2.50
□867		MY GUARDIAN ANGEL/WHERE DID MY BABY GO?	1.50	2.50
□872		EBB TIDE/SINBAD (93)	1.25	2.50
□886		BABY, WHAT WOULD YOU DO?/I MISS YOU SO	1.25	2.00
□887		MESS AROUND/SO MUCH TO DO (89)	1.00	2.00
□896		LITTLE GIRL DON'T UNDERSTAND/LOVE ME	1.25	2.00
□5373	*KING*	(I DO THE) SHIMMY SHIMMY/ YOU DON'T UNDERSTAND ME (37)	1.25	2.50
□1	*AUTUMN*	LET'S SURF AGAIN/COME TO ME	1.50	2.50
□2		C'MON AND SWIM (PT. 1)/(PT. 11) (5)	.75	2.00
□5		S-W-I-M/THAT LITTLE OLD HEARTBREAKER ME (56)	1.25	2.00
□9		I'LL NEVER FALL IN LOVE AGAIN/FRIENDS	1.25	2.00
		BOBBY FREEMAN—ALBUMS		
□1086 (M)	*JUBILEE*	DO YOU WANNA DANCE?	9.00	16.00
□1086 (S)		DO YOU WANNA DANCE?	12.00	20.00
□930	*KING*	THE LOVEABLE SIDE OF BOBBY FREEMAN	7.00	12.00
□4007 (M)	*JOSIE*	GET IN THE SWIM WITH BOBBY FREEMAN	5.00	8.00
□4007 (S)		GET IN THE SWIM WITH BOBBY FREEMAN	6.00	10.00
□102 (M)	*AUTUMN*	C'MON AND SWIM	3.50	6.00
		DON FRENCH		
□104	*LANCER*	LONELY SATURDAY NIGHT/GOLDILOCKS (72)	2.50	4.00
		FROGMEN		
□101	*SCOTT*	SEAHORSE FLATS/TIOGA	2.50	4.00
□102		BEWARE BELOW/TIOGA	2.50	4.00
□314	*CANDIX*	UNDERWATER/THE MAD RUSH (44)	1.50	3.00
□326		BEWARE BELOW/TIOGA	2.00	3.50
□131	*TEE JAY*	SEA HUNT/DIAMOND BACK	1.75	3.00
		BOBBY FULLER FOUR		
□1090	*TODD*	STINGER/SATURDAY NIGHT	4.00	7.00
□345	*EASTWOOD*	NOT FADE AWAY/NERVOUS BREAKDOWN	4.00	7.00
□141	*YUCCA*	YOU'RE IN LOVE/GUESS WE'LL FALL IN LOVE	3.50	6.00
□144		MY HEART JUMPED/GENTLY, MY LOVE	3.50	6.00
□1403	*DONNA*	THOSE MEMORIES OF YOU/ OUR FAVORITE MARTIAN	3.50	6.00
□122	*EXETER*	KING OF THE BEACH/WINE, WINE, WINE	3.50	6.00
□3003	*MUSTANG*	WOLFMAN/THUNDER REEF (Shindigs)	2.50	4.00
□3004		SHE'S MY GIRL/TAKE MY WORD	2.50	4.00
□3006		LET HER DANCE/ANOTHER SAD AND LONELY NIGHT	2.00	3.50
□3011		NEVER TO BE FORGOTTEN/YOU KISS ME	2.00	3.50
□3012		LET HER DANCE/ANOTHER SAD AND LONELY NIGHT	1.75	3.00
□3014		I FOUGHT THE LAW/LITTLE ANNIE LOU (9)	1.00	2.50
□3016		LOVE'S MADE A FOOL OF YOU/ DON'T EVER LEAVE ME (26)	1.25	2.50
□3018		THE MAGIC TOUCH/MY TRUE LOVE	1.50	2.50
		BOBBY FULLER FOUR—ALBUMS		
□900 (M)	*MUSTANG*	KRLA KING OF THE WHEELS	6.00	10.00
□901 (M)		I FOUGHT THE LAW	5.00	8.00
		JERRY FULLER		
□5011	*LIN*	I'VE FOUND A NEW LOVE/BLUE MEMORIES	3.50	6.00
□5012		TEENAGE LOVE/DO YOU LOVE ME?	3.50	6.00
□5019		LIPSTICK AND ROUGE/ MOTHER GOOSE AT THE BANDSTAND	3.00	5.00

ISSUE #	LABEL	ARTIST/TITLE	VG	MINT
☐ 59052	*CHALLENGE*	BETTY MY ANGEL/MEMORIES OF YOU (90)	1.50	2.50
☐ 59057		TENNESSEE WALTZ/CHARLENE (63)	1.25	2.50
☐ 59068		TWO LOVES HAVE I/I DREAMED ABOUT MY LOVER ...	1.25	2.00
☐ 59085		ANNA FROM LOUISIANA/GONE FOR THE SUMMER ...	1.25	2.00
☐ 59104		SHY AWAY/HEAVENLY (71)	1.00	2.00
☐ 9114		GUILTY OF LOVING YOU/		
		FIRST LOVE NEVER DIES (94)	1.00	2.00

LATER CHALLENGE SINGLES ARE WORTH UP TO $1.50 MINT

JERRY FULLER—ALBUM

☐ 100 (M)	*LIN*	TEENAGE LOVE	8.00	15.00

BILLY FURY

☐ 1857	*LONDON*	MAYBE TOMORROW/GONNA TYPE A LETTER	1.75	3.00
☐ 1925		BABY, HOW I CRIED/COLETTE.................	1.75	3.00
☐ 9740		GO AHEAD AND ASK HER/I'M LOST WITHOUT YOU ...	1.50	2.50
☐ 9682	*PARROT*	IT'S ONLY MAKE BELIEVE/		
		BABY, WHAT DO YOU WANT ME TO DO?	1.75	3.00

FURYS

☐ 112	*MACK IV*	ZING! WENT THE STRINGS OF MY HEART/		
		NEVER MORE (92)	1.25	2.50
☐ 115		I REALLY FEEL GOOD/THE OLD DAYS	1.50	2.50

ISSUE #	LABEL	ARTIST/TITLE	VG	MINT

GALAXIES
GUITAR: EDDIE COCHRAN

☐ 216	*GUARANTEED*	MY TATTLE TALE/LOVE HAS ITS WAY	3.50	6.00

BILLY GALLANT

☐ 501	*DEE DEE*	THINKING, HOPING, WISHING/		
		SCRIBBLING ON THE WALL	3.50	6.00
☐ 1012	*GOLD DISC*	THINKING, HOPING, WISHING/		
		SCRIBBLING ON THE WALL	2.00	3.50

GAMBLERS

☐ 815	*WORLD PACIFIC*	MOON DAWG/LSD-25	2.50	4.00

FRANK GARI

☐ 6903	*RIBBON*	YOUR ONLY LOVE/LIL' GIRL	2.00	3.50
☐ 1020	*CRUSADE*	UTOPIA/I AIN'T GOT A GIRL (27)..............	1.25	3.00
☐ 1021		LULLABY OF LOVE/TONIGHT IS OUR LAST NIGHT (23).	1.25	3.00
☐ 1022		PRINCESS/THE LAST BUS LEFT AT MIDNIGHT (30) ...	1.25	3.00

ARTIE GARR (ART GARFUNKEL)

☐ 515	*WARWICK*	DREAM ALONE/BEAT LOVE	4.00	7.00
☐ 8002	*OCTAVIA*	PRIVATE WORLD/FORGIVE ME	4.00	7.00

SCOTT GARRETT

☐ 7104	*OKEH*	THE DAY I DIED/IN MY HEART................	2.00	3.50
☐ 3023	*LAURIE*	A HOUSE OF LOVE/SO FAR SO GOOD (92)	1.50	2.50
☐ 3029		LOVE STORY/GRADUATION SOUVENIRS	1.50	2.50
☐ 3034		WHERE ARE YOU/JUMPIN' BLUE BLAZES	1.50	2.50

ISSUE #	LABEL	ARTIST/TITLE	VG	MINT
		GARY AND CLYDE (SKIP AND FLIP)		
☐3523	*REV*	WHY NOT CONFESS/JOHNNY RISK	3.50	6.00
		GARY AND THE NITE LITES (AMERICAN BREED)		
☐3016	*SEEBURG JUKE BOX*	SWEET LITTLE SIXTEEN/TAKE ME BACK	3.00	5.00
☐3017		BONY MARONIE/GLAD YOU'RE MINE	3.00	5.00
☐833	*U.S.A.*	I DON'T NEED YOUR HELP/BIG BAD WOLF	2.50	4.00
		DAVID GATES		
☐1008	*ROBBINS*	LOVIN' AT NIGHT/JO BABY	6.00	10.00
☐123	*EAST WEST*	SWINGIN' BABY DOLL/WALKIN' AND TALKIN'	4.00	7.00
☐413	*MALA*	YOU'LL BE MY BABY/WHAT'S THIS I HEAR	3.50	6.00
☐418		THE HAPPIEST MAN ALIVE/THE ROAD LEADS TO LOVE	3.50	6.00
☐427		TEARDROPS IN MY HEART/JO BABY	3.00	5.00
☐4206	*DEL-FI*	NO ONE REALLY LOVES A CLOWN/ YOU HAVE IT COMIN' TO YOU	3.00	5.00
☐108	*PLANETARY*	ONCE UPON A TIME/LET YOU GO	3.00	5.00
		MARVIN GAYE		
☐54041	*TAMLA*	LET YOUR CONSCIENCE BE YOUR GUIDE/ NEVER LET YOU GO	2.50	4.00
☐54055		I'M YOURS, YOU'RE MINE/SANDMAN	2.00	3.50
☐54063		SOLDIER'S PLEA/TAKING MY TIME	1.75	3.00
☐54069		STUBBORN KIND OF FELLOW/IT HURTS ME TOO (46)	1.50	2.50
☐54075		HITCH HIKE/HELLO THERE ANGEL (30)	1.25	2.50
☐54079		PRIDE AND JOY/ONE OF THESE DAYS (10)	1.00	2.00
☐54087		CAN I GET A WITNESS/ I'M CRAZY 'BOUT MY BABY (22)	1.25	2.00
☐54093		YOU'RE A WONDERFUL ONE/ WHEN I'M ALONE I CRY (15)	1.00	2.00
☐54095		TRY IT BABY/IF MY HEART COULD SING (15)	1.00	2.00
☐54101		BABY DON'T YOU DO IT/WALK ON THE WILD SIDE (27)	1.25	2.00
☐54107		HOW SWEET IT IS (TO BE LOVED BY YOU)/FOREVER (6)	.75	1.00
		LATER TAMLA SINGLES ARE WORTH UP TO $1.50 MINT		
		MARVIN GAYE—ALBUMS		
☐221 (M)	*TAMLA*	SOULFUL MOODS OF MARVIN GAYE	3.50	7.00
☐239 (M)		THAT STUBBORN KINDA FELLA	3.00	6.00
		GENE AND EUNICE		
☐64	*COMBO*	KO KO MO/YOU AND ME	3.00	5.00
☐3276	*ALADDIN*	KO KO MO/YOU AND ME	2.00	3.50
☐3282		THIS IS MY STORY/MOVE IT OVER BABY	2.50	4.00
☐3351		BOM BOM LULU/HI DIDDLE DIDDLE	2.00	3.50
☐3374		STRANGE WORLD/THE VOW	2.00	3.50
		G-CLEFS		
☐715	*PILGRIM*	KA-DING DONG/DARLA MY DARLIN' (53)	2.50	4.00
		(GUITAR ON PILGRIM 715: FREDDIE CANNON [AGE 15])		
☐720		'CAUSE YOU'RE MINE/ PLEASE WRITE WHILE I'M AWAY	2.50	4.00
☐502	*PARIS*	SYMBOL OF LOVE/LOVE HER IN THE MORNIN'	2.00	3.50
☐506		IS THIS THE WAY/ZING ZANG ZOO	2.00	3.50
☐7500	*TERRACE*	I UNDERSTAND (JUST HOW YOU FEEL)/ LITTLE GIRL, I LOVE YOU (9)	.75	2.00
☐7503		A GIRL HAS TO KNOW/LAD (81)	1.25	2.00

ISSUE #	LABEL	ARTIST/TITLE	VG	MINT
□ 7507		MAKE UP YOUR MIND/THEY'LL CALL ME AWAY	1.25	2.00
□ 7510		LOVER'S PRAYER/SITTING IN THE MOONLIGHT	1.50	2.50
□ 7514		ALL MY TRIALS/THE BIG RAIN	1.25	2.00

GEE CEES

FEATURED: EDDIE COCHRAN (GUITAR), GLEN CAMPBELL (VOCALS)

□ 1088	*CREST*	ANNIE HAD A PARTY/BUZZSAW	5.00	8.00

GENTRYS

□ 600	*YOUNGSTOWN*	LITTLE DROPS OF WATER/SOMETIMES	2.50	4.00
□ 601		KEEP ON DANCING/MAKE UP YOUR MIND	5.00	8.00
□ 13379	*MGM*	KEEP ON DANCING/MAKE UP YOUR MIND (4)	.75	2.00
□ 13432		SPREAD IT ON THICK/BROWN PAPER SACK (50)	1.00	2.00
□ 13495		EVERY DAY I HAVE TO CRY/DON'T LET IT BE (77)	1.25	2.00
□ 13561		WOMAN OF THE WORLD/ THERE ARE TWO SIDES TO EVERY STORY	1.25	2.00

GENTRYS—ALBUM

□ 4336 (M)	*MGM*	KEEP ON DANCING	3.50	6.00
□ 4336 (S)		KEEP ON DANCING	4.50	8.00

GERMZ

FEATURED: CAROLE KING

□ 8001	*VERTIGO*	BOY-GIRL LOVE/NO EASY WAY DOWN	3.50	6.00

GERRY AND THE PACEMAKERS

□ 3162	*LAURIE*	HOW DO YOU DO IT/AWAY FROM YOU	2.00	3.50
□ 3196		I LIKE IT/IT HAPPENED TO ME	2.00	3.50
□ 3218		IT'S ALL RIGHT/YOU'LL NEVER WALK ALONE	1.75	3.00
□ 3233		I'M THE ONE/YOU'VE GOT WHAT I LIKE (82)	1.50	2.50
□ 3251		DON'T LET THE SUN CATCH YOU CRYING/ I'M THE ONE	1.50	2.50
□ 3251		DON'T LET THE SUN CATCH YOU CRYING/ AWAY FROM YOU (4)	1.00	2.00
□ 3261		HOW DO YOU DO IT/YOU'LL NEVER WALK ALONE (9)	1.00	2.00
□ 3271		I LIKE IT/JAMBALAYA (17)	1.25	2.00
□ 3279		I'LL BE THERE/YOU, YOU, YOU (14)	1.25	2.00
□ 3284		FERRY ACROSS THE MERSEY/PRETEND (6)	.75	2.00
□ 3293		IT'S GONNA BE ALRIGHT/SKINNY MINNIE (23)	1.25	2.00
□ 3302		YOU'LL NEVER WALK ALONE/AWAY FROM YOU (48)	1.00	2.00
□ 3313		GIVE ALL YOU LOVE TO ME/YOU'RE THE REASON	1.25	2.00
□ 3323		WALK HAND IN HAND/DREAMS	1.25	2.00
□ 3337		LA LA LA/WITHOUT YOU (90)	1.25	2.00
□ 3354		GIRL ON A SWING/THE WAY YOU LOOK TONIGHT (28)	1.00	2.00
□ 3370		LOOKING FOR MY LIFE/ THE BIG BRIGHT GREEN PLEASURE MACHINE	1.25	2.00

GERRY AND THE PACEMAKERS—ALBUMS

□ 2024 (M)	*LAURIE*	DON'T LET THE SUN CATCH YOU CRYING	3.50	6.00
□ 2024 (S)		DON'T LET THE SUN CATCH YOU CRYING	4.50	8.00
□ 2027 (M)		SECOND ALBUM	3.50	6.00
□ 2027 (S)		SECOND ALBUM	4.50	8.00
□ 2030 (M)		I'LL BE THERE	3.50	6.00
□ 2030 (S)		I'LL BE THERE	4.50	8.00
□ 2031 (M)		GREATEST HITS	3.00	5.00
□ 2031 (S)		GREATEST HITS	4.00	7.00

ISSUE #	LABEL	ARTIST/TITLE	VG	MINT
		GESTICS		
□106	***SURFER***	LET'S GO TRIPPIN'/KAHUNA	2.50	4.00
□114		ROCKIN' FURY/INVASION	2.50	4.00
		GEORGIA GIBBS		
□70517	***MERCURY***	TWEEDLE DEE/YOU'RE WRONG, ALL WRONG (3)	1.00	2.50
□70572		DANCE WITH ME HENRY/BALLIN' THE JACK (2)	1.00	2.50
□70998		TRA LA LA/MORNING, NOON AND NIGHT (39)	1.25	2.50
		JILL GIBSON		
		PRODUCER: JAN BERRY		
□66068	***IMPERIAL***	IT'S AS EASY AS 1,2,3/JILLY'S FLIP SIDE	2.50	4.00
		STEVE GIBSON AND THE RED CAPS		
□796	***JAY DEE***	IT HURTS ME BUT I LIKE IT/OUCH!	4.00	7.00
□9702	***ABC-PARAMOUNT***	ROCK AND ROLL STOMP/LOVE ME TENDERLY	2.00	3.50
□9856		SILHOUETTES/FLAMINGO (63)	1.50	3.00
□326	***HUNT***	BLESS YOU/CHERL LEE	1.75	3.00
□330		WHERE ARE YOU?/SAN ANTONIO ROSE	1.75	3.00
		GIGOLOS		
		GUITAR: DUANE EDDY		
□1	***DAYNITE***	SWINGIN' SAINTS/NIGHT CRAWLERS	4.00	7.00
		JIMMY GILMER AND THE FIREBALLS		
		SEE: FIREBALLS		
□30942	***DECCA***	LOOK ALIVE/BECAUSE I NEED YOU	2.00	3.50
□547	***WARWICK***	TRUE LOVE WAYS/WISHING	1.75	3.00
□592		GOOD, GOOD LOVIN'/DO YOU THINK	1.50	2.50
□50037	***HAMILTON***	I'M GONNA GO WALKING/WON'T BE LONG	1.50	2.50
□16487	***DOT***	SUGAR SHACK/MY HEART IS FREE (1)	.75	2.00
□16539		DAISY PETAL PICKIN'/ WHEN MY TEARS HAVE DRIED (15)	1.00	2.00
□16583		AIN'T GONNA TELL ANYBODY/YOU AM I (53)	1.25	2.00
□16666		CRY BABY/THUNDER AND LIGHTNIN'	1.50	2.50
□16714		LONESOME TEARS/BORN TO BE WITH YOU	1.50	2.50
□16743		THE FOOL/SOMEBODY STOLE MY WATERMELON	1.25	2.00
		JIMMY GILMER AND THE FIREBALLS—ALBUM		
□3577 (M)	***DOT***	BUDDY'S BUDDY	5.00	8.00
□25577 (S)		BUDDY'S BUDDY	6.00	10.00
		LOU GIORDANO		
		GUITAR: BUDDY HOLLY		
□55115	***BRUNSWICK***	STAY CLOSE TO ME/DON'T CHA KNOW	80.00	150.00
		CLIFF GLEAVES		
□55263	***LIBERTY***	LONG BLACK HEARSE/YOU AND YOUR KIND	1.75	3.00
		GOLLIWOGS		
		SEE: CREEDENCE CLEARWATER REVIVAL		
□404	***SCORPIO***	BROWN EYED GIRL/YOU BETTER BE CAREFUL	3.50	6.00
□405		FIGHT FIRE/FRAGILE GIRL	3.50	6.00
□408		WALKING ON THE WATER/YOU BETTER GET IT	4.00	7.00
□412		PORTERVILLE/CALL IT PRETENDING	3.50	6.00
□590	***FANTASY***	DON'T TELL ME NO LIES/ LITTLE GIRL, DOES YOU MAMA KNOW?	5.00	8.00
□597		YOU CAME WALKING/WHERE YOU BEEN?	4.00	7.00
□599		YOU GOT NOTHIN' ON ME/YOU CAN'T BE TRUE	4.00	7.00

LESLEY GORE

ISSUE #	LABEL	ARTIST/TITLE	VG	MINT
☐72119	*MERCURY*	IT'S MY PARTY/DANNY (1)	1.00	2.00
☐72143		JUDY'S TURN TO CRY/JUST LET ME CRY (5)	1.00	2.00
☐72180		SHE'S A FOOL/THE OLD CROWD (5)	1.00	2.00
☐72206		YOU DON'T OWN ME/RUN, BOBBY, RUN (2)	1.00	2.00
☐72259		THAT'S THE WAY BOYS ARE/ THAT'S THE WAY THE BALL BOUNCES (12)	1.00	2.00
☐72270		I DON'T WANNA BE A LOSER/IT'S GOTTA BE YOU (37)	1.25	2.00
☐72309		MAYBE I KNOW/WONDER BOY (14)	1.25	2.00
☐72352		SOMETIMES I WISH I WERE A BOY/HEY NOW (86)	1.50	2.50
☐72372		THE LOOK OF LOVE/LITTLE GIRL, GO HOME (27)	1.25	2.00
☐72412		ALL OF MY LIFE/I CANNOT HOPE FOR ANYONE (71)	1.50	2.50
☐72433		SUNSHINE, LOLLIPOPS AND ROSES/ YOU'VE COME BACK (13)	1.00	2.00
☐72475		MY TOWN, MY GUY AND ME/A GIRL IN LOVE (32)	1.00	2.00
☐72513		I WON'T LOVE YOU ANYMORE (SORRY)/ NO MATTER WHAT YOU DID (80)	1.25	2.00
☐72530		WE KNOW WE'RE IN LOVE/THAT'S WHAT I'LL DO (76)	1.25	2.00
☐72553		YOUNG LOVE/I JUST DON'T KNOW IF I CAN (50)	1.25	2.00
☐72580		OFF AND RUNNING/I DON'T CARE	1.25	2.00
☐72611		TREAT ME LIKE A LADY/MAYBE NOW	1.25	2.00
☐72649		CALIFORNIA NIGHTS/I'M GOING OUT (16)	.75	2.00
☐72683		SUMMER AND SANDY/I'M FALLIN' DOWN (65)	1.25	2.00
☐72726		BRINK OF DISASTER/ON A DAY LIKE THIS (82)	1.25	2.00

LATER MERCURY SINGLES ARE WORTH UP TO $1.50 MINT

LESLEY GORE—ALBUMS

ISSUE #	LABEL	ARTIST/TITLE	VG	MINT
☐20805 (M)	*MERCURY*	I'LL CRY IF I WANT TO	5.00	8.00
☐60805 (S)		I'LL CRY IF I WANT TO	6.00	10.00
☐20849 (M)		LESLEY GORE SINGS OF MIXED UP HEARTS	3.50	6.00
☐60849 (S)		LESLEY GORE SINGS OF MIXED UP HEARTS	4.50	8.00
☐20901 (M)		BOYS, BOYS, BOYS	3.50	6.00
☐60901 (S)		BOYS, BOYS, BOYS	4.50	8.00
☐20943 (M)		GIRL TALK	3.50	6.00
☐60943 (S)		GIRL TALK	4.50	8.00
☐21024 (M)		GOLDEN HITS OF LESLEY GORE	3.50	6.00
☐61024 (S)		GOLDEN HITS OF LESLEY GORE	4.50	8.00

CHARLIE GRACIE

Philadelphia, Pennsylvania, has been the birthplace of a host of 1950s rock-and-roll stars. One of the first was Charlie Gracie, who was born there on January 12, 1936. Sam Gracie, Charlie's father, noticed his young son's interest in music. Sam then bought Charlie a guitar and taught him how to play it.

Gracie attended South Philadelphia High, from which Frankie Avalon and Fabian would later emerge. Charlie graduated in 1954 and passed up music scholarship offers from Temple University and the University of Pennsylvania.

Charlie Gracie began playing and singing at local clubs and later had his own Pittsburgh television show. Near the end of 1956 he signed with a new Philadelphia company called Cameo. Gracie's single of "Butterfly" became Cameo's fifth release and its first to make the hit lists. "Butterfly" became a Top 10 sensation, but Charlie's sales were hurt by balladeer Andy Williams, whose own version of "Butterfly" went all the way to the top chart position.

ISSUE #	LABEL	ARTIST/TITLE	VG	MINT
		CHARLIE GRACIE		
☐ 105	*CAMEO*	BUTTERFLY/NINETY-NINE WAYS (7)	1.50	3.00
☐ 107		FABULOUS/JUST LOOKIN' (26)	1.75	3.00
☐ 111		I LOVE YOU SO MUCH IT HURTS/ WANDERIN' EYES (71)	1.50	2.50
☐ 118		COOL BABY/YOU'VE GOT A HEART LIKE A ROCK	1.50	2.50
☐ 127		DRESSIN' UP/CRAZY GIRL	1.50	2.50
☐ 141		LOVE BIRD/TRYING	1.50	2.50

ISSUE #	LABEL	ARTIST/TITLE	VG	MINT
		BILLY GRAMMER		
☐400	*MONUMENT*	GOTTA TRAVEL ON/CHASING A DREAM (4)	1.00	2.50
☐403		BONAPARTE'S RETREAT/THE KISSING TREE (50)	1.25	2.50
☐407		IT TAKES YOU/WILLY, QUIT YOUR PLAYING	1.50	2.50
☐413		ON THE JOB TOO LONG/LOVELAND	1.50	2.50
		BILLY GRAMMER—ALBUM		
☐4000 (M)	*MONUMENT*	TRAVELIN' ON	6.00	10.00
		GERRY GRANAHAN		
		SEE: DICKEY DOO AND THE DON'TS		
☐102	*SUNBEAM*	NO CHEMISE, PLEASE/GIRL OF MY DREAMS (23)	1.00	2.50
☐108		BABY, WAIT/COMPLETELY	1.50	2.50
☐112		AS READY AS I'LL EVER BE/ NOBODY CAN HANDLE THIS JOB	1.50	2.50
☐122		KING SIZE/I'M AFRAID YOU'LL NEVER KNOW	1.50	2.50
☐127		A RING, A BRACELET, A HEART/ "A" YOU'RE ADORABLE	1.50	2.00
		JANIE GRANT		
☐104	*CAPRICE*	TRIANGLE/SHE'S GOING STEADY WITH YOU (29)	1.25	2.50
☐109		ROMEO/ROLLER COASTER (75)	1.50	2.50
☐111		UNHAPPY/I WONDER WHO'S KISSING HER NOW	1.50	2.50
☐113		OH JOHNNY/OH, MY LOVE	1.50	2.50
☐115		THAT GREASY KID STUFF/ TRYING TO FORGET (74)	1.50	2.50
☐119		PEGGY GOT ENGAGED/ TWO'S COMPANY, THREE'S A CROWD	1.50	2.50
		GREAT SOCIETY		
		FEATURED: GRACE SLICK		
		SEE: JEFFERSON AIRPLANE		
☐1001	*NORTH BEACH*	SOMEONE TO LOVE/FREE ADVICE	12.00	20.00
☐44583	*COLUMBIA*	SALLY GO 'ROUND THE ROSES/DIDN'T THINK SO	2.50	4.00
		GREAT SOCIETY—ALBUMS		
☐9624 (S)	*COLUMBIA*	CONSPICUOUS ONLY IN ITS ABSENCE	3.50	6.00
☐9702 (S)		HOW IT WAS	3.50	6.00
		GUESS WHO		
☐1295	*SCEPTER*	SHAKIN' ALL OVER/TILL WE KISSED (22)	1.25	2.50
☐12108		GOODNIGHT, GOODNIGHT/ HEY, HO, WHAT YOU DID TO ME	1.50	2.50
☐12188		HURTING EACH OTHER/BABY'S BIRTHDAY	1.50	2.50
☐12131		BABY FEELIN'/BELIEVE ME	1.50	2.50
☐12144		CLOCK ON THE WALL/ONE DAY	1.50	2.50
		GUESS WHO—ALBUM		
☐533 (M)	*SCEPTER*	SHAKIN' ALL OVER	4.00	7.00
☐533 (S)		SHAKIN' ALL OVER	5.00	9.00
		BOB GUY (FRANK ZAPPA)		
☐1380	*DONNA*	LETTER FROM JEEPERS/DEAR JEEPERS	6.00	10.00

H

BILL HALEY AND THE COMETS

William John Clifton Hayley, Jr., was born in Highland Park, Michigan, in March of 1927. At age thirteen he was earning $1.00 a night playing and singing at auctions. Two years later a restless Haley left school to go on the road as a guitarist with a country band called the Down Homers. He later formed his own group, Bill Haley's Saddlemen. They cut a few country singles, none successful.

In 1952 Haley renamed his band Bill Haley and the Comets, changing the name to suggest lightning-fast speed. (At the time Bill was one of the hottest guitarists around.) By the spring of 1953 Haley and his group had recorded what many consider to be the first real rock-and-roll record, "Crazy Man Crazy".

Bill Haley and the Comets signed with Decca and cut "Rock Around the Clock". It flopped, so the band recorded a "cover" version of Joe Turner's "Shake, Rattle and Roll". Haley's version—with laundered lyrics—became a best-seller.

In 1955 "Rock Around the Clock", by then a forgotten bomb, became the theme song for the movie "Blackboard Jungle". Decca then reissued the single. Today it holds the distinction of being the world's best-selling rock song in history.

ISSUE #	LABEL	ARTIST/TITLE	VG	MINT
		BILL HALEY AND THE COMETS		
□303	*ESSEX*	ROCK THE JOINT/ICY HEART	12.00	20.00
□305		DANCE WITH THE DOLLY/ ROCKING CHAIR ON THE MOON	12.00	20.00
□310		REAL ROCK DRIVE/STOP BEATIN' 'ROUND THE MULBERRY BUSH	8.00	15.00
□321		CRAZY MAN CRAZY/WHATCHA GONNA DO (15)	6.00	10.00
□327		FRACTURED/PAT-A-CAKE	7.00	12.00
□332		LIVE IT UP/FAREWELL, SO LONG, GOODBYE	6.00	10.00
□340		I'LL BE TRUE/TEN LITTLE INDIANS	5.00	8.00
□348		STRAIGHT JACKET/CHATTANOOGA CHOO-CHOO	5.00	8.00
□374		SUNDOWN BOOGIE/JUKEBOX CANNONBALL	6.00	10.00
□381		ROCKET 88/GREEN TREE BOOGIE	6.00	10.00
□399		ROCK THE JOINT/FAREWELL, SO LONG, GOODBYE	5.00	7.00
□718	*TRANS WORLD*	REAL ROCK DRIVE/YES INDEED	5.00	8.00
□29124	*DECCA*	ROCK AROUND THE CLOCK/THIRTEEN WOMEN (1)	2.00	4.00
□29204		SHAKE, RATTLE AND ROLL/A.B.C. BOOGIE (7)	2.00	3.50
□29317		DIM, DIM THE LIGHTS/HAPPY BABY (11)	1.50	3.00
□29418		MAMBO ROCK/BIRTH OF THE BOOGIE (18)	1.50	3.00
□29552		RAZZLE-DAZZLE/TWO HOUND DOGS (15)	1.50	3.00
□29713		BURN THAT CANDLE/ROCK-A-BEATIN' BOOGIE (20)	1.50	3.00
□29791		SEE YOU LATER ALLIGATOR/THE PAPER BOY (6)	1.50	3.00
□29870		R-O-C-K/THE SAINTS ROCK 'N' ROLL (29)	1.25	2.50
□29948		HOT DOG BUDDY BUDDY/ ROCKIN' THROUGH THE RYE (60)	1.50	2.50
□30028		RIP IT UP/TEENAGER'S MOTHER (30)	1.25	2.50
□30085		RUDY'S ROCK/BLUE COMET BLUES (34)	1.25	2.50
□30148		DON'T KNOCK THE ROCK/CHO CHO CH'BOOGIE	1.50	2.50
□30214		FORTY CUPS OF COFFEE/ HOOK, LINE AND SINKER (70)	1.25	2.00
□30314		BILLY GOAT/ROCKIN' ROLLIN' ROVER (60)	1.25	2.00
□30394		THE DIPSY DOODLE/MISS YOU	1.25	2.00
□30461		ROCK THE JOINT/HOW MANY	1.25	2.00
□30530		MARY, MARY LOU/IT'S A SIN	1.25	2.00
□30592		SKINNY MINNIE/SWAY WITH ME (22)	1.25	2.50
□30681		LEAN JEAN/DON'T NOBODY MOVE (67)	1.25	2.00
		LATER DECCA SINGLES ARE WORTH UP TO $2.00 MINT		
		BILL HALEY AND THE COMETS—EPs		
□102	*ESSEX*	DANCE PARTY	15.00	25.00
□117		ROCK WITH BILL HALEY AND THE COMETS	12.00	20.00
□118		ROCK WITH BILL HALEY AND THE COMETS	12.00	20.00
□2168	*DECCA*	SHAKE, RATTLE AND ROLL	6.00	10.00
□2209		DIM, DIM THE LIGHTS	5.00	9.00
□2322		ROCK AND ROLL	4.50	8.00
□2398		HE DIGS ROCK AND ROLL	4.50	8.00
□2399		HE DIGS ROCK AND ROLL	4.50	8.00
□2400		HE DIGS ROCK AND ROLL	4.50	8.00
□2416		ROCK AND ROLL STAGE SHOW	3.50	6.00
□2417		ROCK AND ROLL STAGE SHOW	3.50	6.00
□2418		ROCK AND ROLL STAGE SHOW	3.50	6.00

ISSUE #	LABEL	ARTIST/TITLE	VG	MINT
		BILL HALEY AND THE COMETS—ALBUMS		
□202 (M)	*ESSEX*	ROCK WITH BILL HALEY AND HIS COMETS	35.00	60.00
□202 (M)	*TRANS WORLD*	ROCK WITH BILL HALEY AND HIS COMETS	15.00	25.00
□5560 (M)	*DECCA*	SHAKE RATTLE AND ROLL (10" LP)	25.00	40.00
□8225 (M)		ROCK AROUND THE CLOCK	7.00	12.00
□8315 (M)		HE DIGS ROCK AND ROLL	6.00	10.00
□8345 (M)		ROCK AND ROLL STAGE SHOW	6.00	10.00
		LARRY HALL		
□1	*HOT*	SANDY/LOVIN' TREE	4.00	7.00
□25007	*STRAND*	SANDY/LOVIN' TREE (15)	1.25	2.50
□25013		ROSEMARY/A GIRL LIKE YOU	1.50	2.50
□25016		FOR EVERY BOY/I'LL STAY SINGLE	1.25	2.00
□25025		KOOL LUV/THE GIRL I LEFT BEHIND	1.25	2.00
□25029		SWEET LIPS/REBEL HEART	1.25	2.00
		LARRY HALL—ALBUM		
□1005 (M)	*STRAND*	SANDY AND OTHER LARRY HALL HITS	8.00	15.00
		JOHNNY HALLYDAY		
□40024	*PHILIPS*	BE BOP A LULA/I GOT A WOMAN	1.75	3.00
□40043		HEY LITTLE GIRL/CARAVAN OF LONELY MEN	1.50	2.50
		JOHNNY HALLYDAY—ALBUM		
□200019 (M)	*PHILIPS*	AMERICA'S ROCKIN' HITS	5.00	8.00
□600019 (S)		AMERICA'S ROCKIN' HITS	6.00	10.00
		GEORGE HAMILTON IV		
□420	*COLONIAL*	A ROSE AND A BABY RUTH/ IF YOU DON'T KNOW	8.00	15.00
□9765	*ABC-PARAMOUNT*	A ROSE AND A BABY RUTH/ IF YOU DON'T KNOW (6)	2.00	3.50
□9782		ONLY ONE LOVE/ IF I POSSESSED A PRINTING PRESS (33)	1.50	3.00
□9838		HIGH SCHOOL DANCE/EVERYBODY'S BODY (80)	3.50	6.00
□9862		WHY DON'T THEY UNDERSTAND/EVEN THO (17)	1.25	2.50
□9898		NOW AND FOR ALWAYS/ONE HEART (37)	1.25	2.50
□9924		I KNOW WHERE I'M GOIN'/ WHO'S TAKING YOU TO THE PROM? (43)	1.25	2.50
□9966		THE TWO OF US/LUCY, LUCY	1.25	2.00
□10009		STEADY GAME/CAN YOU BLAME US?	1.25	2.00
□10028		GEE, I KNOW/YOUR SWEETHEART (73)	1.25	2.00
		GEORGE HAMILTON IV—ALBUM		
□461 (M)	*ABC-PARAMOUNT*	BIG 15	6.00	10.00
□461 (S)		BIG 15	7.00	12.00
		HAPPENINGS		
		SEE: FOUR GRADUATES, HONOR SOCIETY		
□517	*B.T.PUPPY*	GIRLS ON THE GO/GO-GO	2.00	3.50
□520		SEE YOU IN SEPTEMBER/ HE THINKS HE'S A HERO (3)	1.00	2.00

ISSUE #	LABEL	ARTIST/TITLE	VG	MINT
☐522		GO AWAY LITTLE GIRL/TEA TIME (12)	1.00	2.00
☐523		GOODNIGHT MY LOVE/LILIES MY MONET (51)	1.25	2.00
☐527		I GOT RHYTHM/YOU'RE IN A BAD WAY (3)	1.00	2.00
☐530		MY MAMMY/I BELIEVE IN NOTHING (13)	1.00	2.00
☐532		WHY DO FOOLS FALL IN LOVE/ WHEN SUMMER IS THROUGH (41)	1.25	2.00
☐538		MUSIC MUSIC MUSIC/WHEN I LOCK MY DOOR (96)	1.25	2.00
☐540		RANDY/LOVE SONG OF MOM AND DAD	1.25	2.00
☐542		SEALED WITH A KISS/ANYWAY	1.25	2.00
☐543		BREAKING UP IS HARD TO DO/ANYWAY (67)	1.25	2.00
☐544		GIRL ON A SWING/WHEN I LOCK MY DOOR (67)	1.25	2.00
☐545		CRAZY RHYTHM/LOVE SONG OF MOM AND DAD	1.25	2.00
☐549		THAT'S ALL I WANT FROM YOU/ HE THINKS HE'S A HERO	1.25	2.00
		HAPPENINGS—ALBUMS		
☐1001 (M)	***B.T.PUPPY***	THE HAPPENINGS	3.50	7.00
☐1004 (M)		THE HAPPENINGS' GREATEST HITS	3.50	7.00

HARBOR LIGHTS (JAY AND THE AMERICANS)

ISSUE #	LABEL	ARTIST/TITLE	VG	MINT
☐422	***MALA***	ANGEL OF LOVE/TICK-A-TICK-A-TOCK	4.00	7.00
☐77020	***JARO***	WHAT WOULD I DO WITHOUT YOU?/ IS THAT TOO MUCH TO ASK?	3.00	5.00

WILBERT HARRISON

ISSUE #	LABEL	ARTIST/TITLE	VG	MINT
☐1023	***FURY***	KANSAS CITY/LISTEN MY DARLING (1)	1.25	3.00
☐1027		DON'T WRECK MY LIFE/CHEATING BABY	1.50	2.50
☐1028		GOODBYE KANSAS CITY/1960	1.75	3.00

BOBBY HART

ISSUE #	LABEL	ARTIST/TITLE	VG	MINT
☐3039	***ERA***	GIRL IN THE WINDOW/JOURNEY OF LOVE	1.75	3.00
☐017	***INFINITY***	TOO MANY TEARDROPS/THE PEOPLE NEXT DOOR	1.50	2.50

ROCKY HART

ISSUE #	LABEL	ARTIST/TITLE	VG	MINT
☐9052	***CUB***	EVERYDAY/COME WITH ME	2.50	4.00

PHIL HARVEY (SPECTOR)

ISSUE #	LABEL	ARTIST/TITLE	VG	MINT
☐5583	***IMPERIAL***	BUMBERSHOOT/WILLY BOY	4.00	7.00

ALI HASSAN

ISSUE #	LABEL	ARTIST/TITLE	VG	MINT
☐103	***PHILLES***	MALAGUANE/CHOP STICKS	3.00	5.00

THE HAWK (JERRY LEE LEWIS)

ISSUE #	LABEL	ARTIST/TITLE	VG	MINT
☐3559	***PHILLIPS INTERNATIONAL***	IN THE MOOD/I GET THE BLUES WHEN IT RAINS	5.00	9.00

DALE HAWKINS

His real name is Delmar Allen Hawkins. He was born in Goldmine, Louisiana, on August 30, 1938. Young Hawkins grew up listening to the Southern blues of Howlin' Wolf and Lonnie Johnson.

Dale earned his first guitar at eleven by selling newspapers. Four years later Hawkins left high school and joined the navy. After his military obligation he moved to Shreveport, Louisiana, and went to work in a record store.

Dale sang some songs he had written into a home tape recorder. They were given airplay by a local radio station and were heard by a local talent scout. The tape later ended up on the desk of Leonard Chess of Chicago's Chess records. Chess released Hawkins' "See You Soon Baboon" on the Checker subsidiary. The single wasn't a hit.

Dale Hawkins' second release was the legendary "Susie Q", an overnight hit and the song that first gave Creedence Clearwater Revival mass radio exposure in 1968.

Hawkins recorded many more Checker singles and recorded one LP, now an extremely rare collection item.

ISSUE #	LABEL	ARTIST/TITLE	VG	MINT
		DALE HAWKINS		
☐843	*CHECKER*	SEE YOU SOON, BABOON/FOUR LETTER WORD	2.50	4.00
☐863		SUSIE-Q/DON'T TREAT ME THIS WAY (29)	2.00	3.50
☐876		BABY, BABY/MRS. MERGUITORY'S DAUGHTER	1.75	3.00
☐892		LITTLE PIG/TORNADO	1.75	3.00
☐900		LA-DO-DADA/CROSS TIES (32)	1.50	3.00
☐906		A HOUSE, A CAR, AND A WEDDING RING/ MY BABE (88)	1.75	3.00
☐913		TAKE MY HEART/SOMEDAY, ONE DAY	1.75	3.00
☐916		CLASS CUTTER (YEAH, YEAH)/LONELY NIGHTS (52)	1.50	3.00
☐923		AIN'T THAT LOVIN' YOU BABY/MY DREAM	1.75	3.00
☐929		OUR TURN/LIFEGUARD MAN	1.75	3.00
☐934		LIZA JANE/BACK TO SCHOOL BLUES	1.75	3.00
☐940		HOT DOG/DON'T BREAK YOUR PROMISE TO ME	1.75	3.00
☐944		EVERY LITTLE GIRL/POOR LITTLE RHODE ISLAND	1.75	3.00
☐962		LINDA/WHO	1.75	3.00
☐970		GRANDMA'S HOUSE/I WANT TO LOVE YOU	1.75	3.00
		DALE HAWKINS—ALBUM		
☐1429 (M)	*CHESS*	OH! SUZY-Q	30.00	50.00
		RONNIE HAWKINS		
		FEATURED: HAWKS (THE BAND)		
☐6128	*QUALITY*	HEY BO DIDDLEY/LOVE ME LIKE YOU CAN	5.00	8.00
☐4154	*ROULETTE*	FORTY DAYS/ONE OF THESE DAYS (45)	2.00	3.50
☐4177		MARY LOU/NEED YOUR LOVIN' (26)	1.50	3.00
☐4209		SOUTHERN LOVE/LOVE ME LIKE YOU CAN	1.50	2.50
☐4228		LONELY HOURS/CLARA	1.50	2.50
☐4231		THE BALLAD OF CARYL CHESSMAN/ DEATH OF FLOYD COLLINS	2.50	4.00
☐4249		RUBY BABY/HAYRIDE	1.75	3.00
☐4267		SUMMERTIME/MISTER AND MISSISSIPPI	1.50	2.50
☐4311		COLD, COLD HEART/NOBODY'S LONESOME FOR ME	1.50	2.50
☐4400		COME, LOVE/I FEEL GOOD	1.50	2.50
☐4483		BO DIDDLEY/WHO DO YOU LOVE	1.75	3.00
☐4503		HIGH BLOOD PRESSURE/THERE'S A SCREW LOOSE	1.75	3.00
		RONNIE HAWKINS—ALBUMS		
☐25078 (M)	*ROULETTE*	RONNIE HAWKINS	8.00	15.00
☐25078 (S)		RONNIE HAWKINS	12.00	20.00
☐25102 (M)		MR. DYNAMO	8.00	15.00
☐25102 (S)		MR. DYNAMO	12.00	20.00
		MICKEY HAWKS		
☐4002	*PROFILE*	BIP BOB BOOM/ROCK AND ROLL RYTHYM	8.00	15.00
		DEANE HAWLEY		
☐554	*DORE*	LOOK FOR A STAR/BOSSMAN (29)	1.50	2.50
☐569		LIKE A FOOL/STAY AT HOME BLUES	1.50	2.50
☐577		RAINBOW/HEY THERE	1.50	2.50
☐55359	*LIBERTY*	POCKETFUL OF RAINBOWS/ THAT DREAM COULD (93)	1.50	2.50
☐55446		QUEEN OF THE ANGELS/YOU CONQUERED ME	1.50	2.50

ISSUE #	LABEL	ARTIST/TITLE	VG	MINT

ROY HEAD

☐194	*TNT*	ONE MORE TIME/DON'T BE BLUE	2.50	4.00
☐12116	*SCEPTER*	JUST A LITTLE BIT/TREAT ME RIGHT (39)	1.25	2.50
☐12124		GET BACK (PT. 1)/(PT. 11) (88)	1.50	2.50
☐543	*BACK BEAT*	TEENAGE LETTER/PAIN	1.75	3.00
☐546		TREAT HER RIGHT/SO LONG, MY LOVE (2)	1.00	2.00
☐555		APPLE OF MY EYE/I PASS THE DAY (32)	1.25	2.00
☐560		MY BABE/PAIN (99)	1.25	2.00
☐563		DRIVING WHEEL/WIGGLIN' AND GIGGLIN'	1.25	2.00
☐571		TO MAKE A BIG MAN CRY/DON'T CRY NO MORE (95)	1.25	2.00
☐576		YOU'RE (ALMOST) TUFF/TUSH HOG	1.25	2.00
☐582		NOBODY BUT ME/A GOOD MAN IS HARD TO FIND	1.25	2.00

ROY HEAD—ALBUMS

☐101 (M)	*TNT*	ROY HEAD AND THE TRAITS	12.00	20.00
☐532 (M)	*SCEPTER*	TREAT ME RIGHT	5.00	8.00
☐532 (S)		TREAT ME RIGHT	6.00	10.00

HEARTBEATS (SHEP AND THE LIMELITES)

☐720	*HULL*	A THOUSAND MILES AWAY/OH BABY DON'T	20.00	35.00
☐216	*RAMA*	A THOUSAND MILES AWAY/OH BABY DON'T (53)	3.50	6.00
☐231		EVERYBODY'S SOMEBODY'S FOOL/ I WANT TO KNOW (78)	3.00	5.00
☐4054	*ROULETTE*	DOWN ON MY KNEES/I FOUND A JOB	2.50	4.00
☐4091		ONE DAY NEXT YEAR/SOMETIMES I WONDER	2.50	4.00
☐4194		DOWN ON MY KNEES/CRAZY FOR YOU	2.00	3.50

HEARTBEATS (SHEP AND THE LIMELITES)—ALBUM

☐25107 (M)	*ROULETTE*	A THOUSAND MILES AWAY	12.00	20.00
☐25107 (S)		A THOUSAND MILES AWAY	15.00	25.00

HEARTBREAKERS

☐261	*VIK*	1, 2, I LOVE YOU/WITHOUT A CAUSE	8.00	15.00

HEARTS AND FLOWERS

☐5829	*CAPITOL*	ROCK AND ROLL GYPSIES/ROAD TO NOWHERE	1.75	3.00
☐5897		PLEASE/THE VIEW FROM WARD 3	1.50	2.50
☐2127		TIN ANGEL/SHE SANG HYMNS OUT OF TUNE	1.50	2.50

HEARTS AND FLOWERS—ALBUM

☐2762 (S)	*CAPITOL*	NOW IS THE TIME FOR HEARTS AND FLOWERS	4.00	7.00

BOBBY HELMS

☐29947	*DECCA*	TENNESSEE ROCK AND ROLL/ I DON'T OWE YOU NOTHING	8.00	15.00
☐30194		FRAULEIN/HEARTSICK FEELING (36)	1.25	2.50
☐30423		MY SPECIAL ANGEL/STANDING AT THE END OF THE WORLD (7)	1.00	2.50
☐30513		JINGLE BELL ROCK/CAPTAIN SANTA CLAUS (6)	1.00	2.50

BOBBY HELMS—EP

☐2555	*DECCA*	SINGS TO MY SPECIAL ANGEL	2.00	4.00

BOBBY HELMS—ALBUM

☐8638 (M)	*DECCA*	SINGS TO MY SPECIAL ANGEL	4.00	8.00

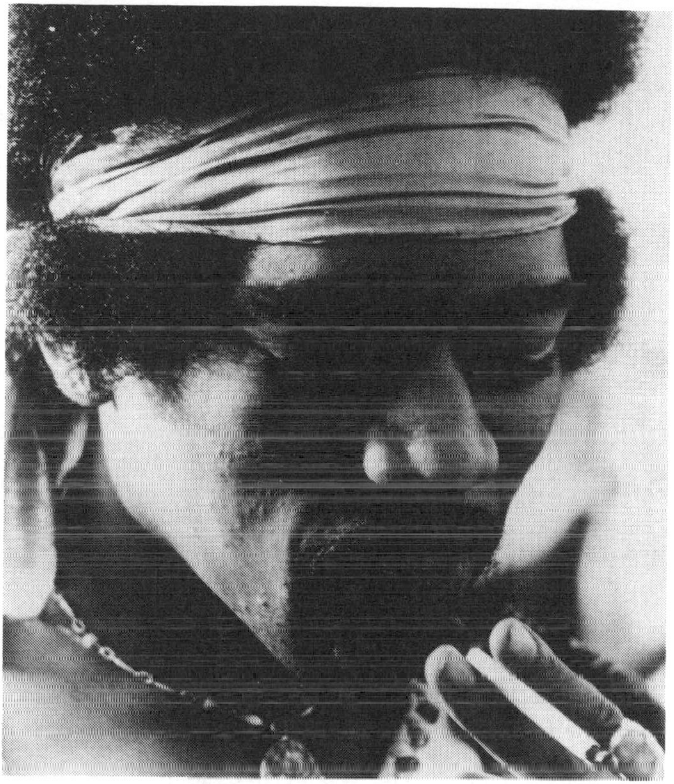

JIMI HENDRIX

He was born James Marshall Hendrix in Seattle, Washington, on November 27, 1942. Jimi grew up listening to the blues masters—Elmore James, Muddy Waters, B. B. King. Hendrix "played" a broomstick as a guitar until he bought an old electric one for $5.00 from a friend. Hendrix was left-handed and had to re-string the instrument. Jimi's first "gig" was playing intermission music at a National Guard Armory dance. His pay that night was 35¢.

Jimi quit school to work for his father but soon joined the paratroopers. On his 26th jump he broke his ankle and was discharged. Hendrix then set out on the road, playing for such diverse talents as Little Richard, Joey Dee and the Starliters, and the Isley Brothers. In 1965 he began his own group, Jimmy James and the Flames. After a year he was earning only $3.00 a night playing New York City clubs.

He went to London, formed a trio, and became the hottest guitarist around. Then he returned solo to America, where he toured with the Monkees (!) as an opening act. It was a ploy to gain attention—and it worked. Soon Hendrix's name spread everywhere.

On September 18, 1970, Jimi Hendrix, the world's greatest rock guitarist, died by choking on his own vomit in a London apartment. An autopsy revealed alcohol and narcotics in his bloodstream.

ISSUE #	LABEL	ARTIST/TITLE	VG	MINT
		JIMMY HENDRIX		
☐ 167	***AUDIO FIDELITY***	NO SUCH ANIMAL (PT. 1)/(PT. 11)	3.00	5.00
☐ 0572	***REPRISE***	HEY JOE/51ST ANNIVERSARY	2.40	4.00
☐ 0597		PURPLE HAZE/THE WIND CRIES MARY (65)	1.75	3.00
☐ 0641		FOXEY LADY/HEY JOE (67)	1.75	3.00
☐ 0665		UP FROM THE SKIES/ONE RAINY WISH (82)	1.75	3.00
☐ 0767		ALL ALONG THE WATCHTOWER/ BURNING OF THE MIDNIGHT LAMP (20)	1.00	2.00
☐ 0792		CROSSTOWN TRAFFIC/GYPSY EYES (52)	1.50	2.50
☐ 0853		IF 6 WAS 9/STONE FREE	1.75	3.00
☐ 1000		FREEDOM/ANGEL (59)	1.50	2.50
☐ 1044		STAR-SPANGLED BANNER/DOLLY DAGGER (74)	1.50	2.50
☐ 1082		JOHNNY B. GOODE/LOVER MAN	1.75	3.00
		HERD		
		FEATURED: PETER FRAMPTON		
☐ 1588	***FONTANA***	I CAN FLY/UNDERSTAND ME	2.50	4.00
☐ 1602		FROM THE UNDERGROUND/SWEET WILLIAM	2.50	4.00
☐ 1610		COME ON, BELIEVE ME/PARADISE LOST	2.50	4.00
☐ 1618		I DON'T WANT OUR LOVING TO DIE/OUR FAIRY TALE	2.50	4.00
		HERD—ALBUM		
☐ 67579 (S)	***FONTANA***	LOOKIN' THROUGH YOU	7.00	12.00
		HERMAN'S HERMITS		
☐ 13280	***MGM***	I'M INTO SOMETHING GOOD/ YOUR HAND IN MINE (13)	1.00	2.00
☐ 13310		CAN'T YOU HEAR MY HEARTBEAT/I KNOW WHY (2)	.75	1.50
☐ 13332		SILHOUETTES/WALKIN' WITH MY ANGEL (5)	.75	1.50
☐ 13341		MRS. BROWN, YOU'VE GOT A LOVELY DAUGHTER/ I GOTTA DREAM ON (1)	.75	1.50
☐ 13354		WONDERFUL WORLD/TRAVELING LIGHT (4)	.75	1.50
☐ 13367		I'M HENRY VII I AM/THE END OF THE WORLD (1)	.75	1.50
☐ 13398		JUST A LITTLE BIT BETTER/SEA CRUISE (7)	.75	1.50
☐ 13437		A MUST TO AVOID/THE MAN WITH THE CIGAR (8)	.75	1.50
☐ 13462		LISTEN PEOPLE/GOT A FEELING (3)	.75	1.50
☐ 13500		LEANING ON THE LAMP POST/HOLD ON (9)	.75	1.50
☐ 13548		THIS DOOR SWINGS BOTH WAYS/FOR LOVE (12)	1.00	1.50
☐ 13603		DANDY/MY RESERVATIONS HAVE BEEN CONFIRMED (5)	.75	1.50
☐ 13639		EAST WEST/WHAT IS WRONG, WHAT IS RIGHT (27)	1.00	1.50
☐ 13681		THERE'S A KIND OF HUSH/NO MILK TODAY (4)	.75	1.50
		LATER MGM SINGLES ARE WORTH UP TO $1.50 MINT		
		HERMAN'S HERMITS—ALBUMS		
☐ 4282 (M)		INTRODUCING HERMAN'S HERMITS	3.50	6.00
☐ 4292 (S)		INTRODUCING HERMAN'S HERMITS	4.50	8.00
☐ 4295 (M)		ON TOUR	3.00	5.00
☐ 4295 (S)		ON TOUR	4.00	7.00
☐ 4315 (M)		THE BEST OF HERMAN'S HERMITS	3.00	5.00
☐ 4315 (S)		THE BEST OF HERMAN'S HERMITS	4.00	7.00

ERSEL HICKEY

Ersel Hickey was born in the South during the late 1930s. As did many boys in that area and during that time, he grew into adolescence listening to the black r & b sound as well as country music. He also learned to play the guitar—first a Spanish six-string, then an electric.

He worked after school as a locksmith and planned on entering that profession. But Hickey became restless and quit school during his sophomore year. Only fifteen, Ersel Hickey left home to tour and sing with a carnival. He felt he had musical talent, as he had earlier won $500 imitating crooner Johnny Ray in a talent contest.

Ersel wrote "Bluebirds Over the Mountain" and approached Epic Records with it early in 1958. Singing in a style much like Elvis Presley and Gene Vincent, "Bluebirds Over the Mountain" by Ersel Hickey proved most impressive to Epic. The song, one of the shortest records in rock history, was only a minor chart single. Later songs—including the great "Goin' Down the Road"—failed to establish Hickey's name as anything other than a "one-shot" artist.

ISSUE #	LABEL	ARTIST/TITLE	VG	MINT
		ERSEL HICKEY		
☐9263	*EPIC*	BLUEBIRDS OVER THE MOUNTAIN/ HANGIN' AROUND (75)	1.75	3.00
☐9278		LOVER'S LAND/GOIN' DOWN THAT ROAD	3.00	5.00
☐9298		YOU NEVER CAN TELL/WEDDING DAY	1.75	3.00
☐9309		DON'T BE AFRAID OF LOVE/YOU THREW A DART	1.50	2.50
☐9357		WHAT DO YOU WANT?/LOVE IN BLOOM	1.50	2.50
☐602	*TOOT*	TRYIN' TO GET TO YOU/BLUE SKIES	1.50	2.50
		HI-FIVES		
☐30576	*DECCA*	MY FRIEND/HOW CAN I WIN?	6.00	10.00
☐30657		DOROTHY/JUST A SHOULDER TO CRY ON	4.00	7.00
☐30744		WHAT'S NEW, WHAT'S NEW/LONELY	3.00	5.00
		HIGH AND MIGHTY (REFLECTIONS)		
☐10821	*ABC*	TRYIN' TO STOP CRYIN'/ESCAPE FROM CUBA	1.75	3.00
		HIGH NUMBERS (WHO)		
☐480	*FONTANA*	ZOOT SUIT/I'M THE FACE (British Release)	125.00	200.00
		HIGH SEAS		
☐4000	*D-M-G*	A SUNDAY KIND OF LOVE/WE GO TOGETHER	5.00	8.00
		JOEL HILL		
☐519	*TRANS-AMERICAN*	LITTLE LOVER/I THOUGHT IT OVER	8.00	15.00
		RON HOLDER		
		PRODUCER: BRUCE JOHNSON		
☐1315	*DONNA*	LOVE YOU SO/MY BABE (7)	1.25	3.00
☐1324		GEE BUT I'M LONESOME/SUSIE JANE	1.75	3.00
☐1328		TRUE LOVE CAN BE/ EVERYTHING'S GONNA BE ALRIGHT	1.75	3.00
☐1331		YOUR LINE IS BUSY/WHO SAYS THERE AIN'T NO SANTA CLAUS	1.50	2.50
☐1335		LET NO ONE TELL YOU/THE BIG SHOE	1.50	2.50
		RON HOLDEN—ALBUM		
☐2111 (M)	*DONNA*	LOVE YOU SO	8.00	15.00
		EDDIE HOLLAND		
☐102	*TAMLA*	MERRY-GO-ROUND/IT MOVES ME	20.00	30.00
☐172	*UNITED ARTISTS*	MERRY-GO-ROUND/IT MOVES ME	2.50	4.00
☐1021	*MOTOWN*	JAMIE/TAKE A CHANCE ON ME (30)	1.00	2.00
		LATER MOTOWN SINGLES ARE WORTH UP TO $1.50 MINT		
		EDDIE HOLLAND—ALBUM		
☐604 (M)	*MOTOWN*	EDDIE HOLLAND	5.00	8.00

HOLLIES

The Hollies were England's Buffalo Springfield. Considered the "group's group", the clean-cut quintet racked up fifteen straight Top 10 hits in England before riding the coattails of the Beatles into America in mid-1964. (A single on Liberty had died earlier that year.)

The Hollies first toured with Herman's Hermits, paying their road dues and drawing audiences on the strength of their early Imperial singles. Their first American hit to sell a million came in 1966 with "Bus Stop". "Stop Stop Stop" also made the American Top 10, and "On A Carousel" came close.

Just before the 1960s came to a close, the Hollies switched to Epic Records and lead singer Graham Nash. Seeking greener artistic pastures, Nash had joined forces with Stephen Stills (late of Buffalo Springfield) and David Crosby (a former Byrd) to form the highly respected Crosby, Stills and Nash trio.

A Nashless Hollies group earned four Top 10 singles on Epic during the early 1970s, but they had lost their freshness and momentum from earlier days.

ISSUE #	LABEL	ARTIST/TITLE	VG	MINT
		HOLLIES		
☐55674	***LIBERTY***	STAY/NOW'S THE TIME	5.00	8.00
☐66026	***IMPERIAL***	JUST ONE LOOK/KEEP OFF THAT FRIEND OF MINE (98)	1.50	3.00
☐66044		HERE I GO AGAIN/LUCILLE	1.75	3.00
☐66070		COME ON BACK/WE'RE THROUGH	1.75	3.00
☐6099		NOBODY/YES I WILL	1.75	3.00
☐66119		I'M ALIVE/YOU KNOW HE DID	1.75	3.00
☐66134		LOOK THROUGH ANY WINDOW/SO LONELY (32)	1.25	2.50
☐66158		I CAN'T LET GO/I'VE GOT A WAY OF MY OWN (42)	1.25	2.50
☐66186		BUS STOP/DON'T RUN AND HIDE (5)	1.00	2.50
☐66214		STOP STOP STOP/IT'S YOU (7)	1.00	2.50
☐66231		ON A CAROUSEL/ALL THE WORLD IS LOVE (11)	1.00	2.50
☐66240		PAY YOU BACK WITH INTEREST/ WHATCHA GONNA DO 'BOUT IT (28)	1.25	2.50
☐66258		JUST ONE LOOK/ RUNNING THROUGH THE NIGHT (44)	1.25	2.00
☐66271		IF I NEED SOMEONE/I'LL BE TRUE TO YOU	1.50	2.50
☐50079	***UNITED ARTISTS***	AFTER THE FOX/THE FOX TROT (with Peter Sellers)	4.00	7.00
		SINGLES ON EPIC ARE WORTH UP TO $1.50 MINT		
		HOLLIES—ALBUMS		
☐9265 (M)	***IMPERIAL***	HERE I GO AGAIN	5.00	8.00
☐12265 (S)		HERE I GO AGAIN	6.00	10.00
☐9299 (M)		HEAR! HEAR!	3.50	6.00
☐12299 (S)		HEAR! HEAR	4.50	8.00
☐9312 (M)		THE HOLLIES	3.50	6.00
☐12312 (S)		THE HOLLIES	4.50	8.00
☐9330 (M)		BUS STOP	3.50	6.00
☐12330 (S)		BUS STOP	4.50	8.00
☐9339 (M)		STOP! STOP! STOP!	3.50	6.00
☐12339 (S)		STOP! STOP! STOP!	4.50	8.00
☐9350 (M)		GREATEST HITS	3.50	6.00
☐12350 (S)		GREATEST HITS	4.50	8.00

BUDDY HOLLY

Born in Lubbock, Texas, on September 7, 1936, Charles Hardin ("Buddy") Holley was the youngest of four children. At age eight Buddy took up the violin but soon switched to guitar. Later Buddy and a school classmate named Bob Montgomery began singing as the Buddy and Bob duo. They even landed a regular spot on a Lubbock radio station.

When Bill Haley and the Comets played Lubbock, Buddy and Bob worked as the warmup act. A talent scout in the audience singled out Holly (the "e" was dropped on records for simplicity) and signed him to Decca Records. Five 1956 singles proved unsuccessful.

Holly then formed the Crickets. When the group came under management with Norman Petty, a separate contract was negotiated for Buddy Holly. He sang lead on the Crickets' hits but achieved great solo success on his own, especially with "Peggy Sue", co-written by Jerry Allison for his girl friend.

Late in 1958, after a two-week courtship, Holly married Maria Elena Santiago, a record-company receptionist. Buddy Holly, the first solo rocker to use strings on his later records, died in an Iowa plane crash on February 3, 1959. As Don McLean said in 1971, it was "the day the music died".

ISSUE #	LABEL	ARTIST/TITLE	VG	MINT
		BUDDY HOLLY *SEE: CRICKETS*		
□29854	*DECCA*	LOVE ME/BLUE DAYS, BLACK NIGHTS	15.00	25.00
□30166		MODERN DON JUAN/YOU ARE MY ONE DESIRE	12.00	20.00
□30534		THAT'LL BE THE DAY/ROCK AROUND WITH OLLIE VEE	15.00	25.00
□30543		LOVE ME/YOU ARE MY ONE DESIRE	8.00	15.00
□30650		GIRL ON MY MIND/TING-A-LING	12.00	20.00
□61852	*CORAL*	WORDS OF LOVE/ MAILMAN, BRING ME NO MORE BLUES	18.00	30.00
□61885		PEGGY SUE/EVERYDAY (3)	1.50	3.50
□61947		I'M GONNA LOVE YOU TOO/LISTEN TO ME	3.00	5.00
□61985		RAVE ON/TAKE YOUR TIME (37)	2.00	4.00
□62006		EARLY IN THE MORNING/NOW WE'RE ONE (32)	2.00	4.00
□62051		HEARTBEAT/WELL . . . ALL RIGHT (82)	3.00	4.50
□62074		IT DOESN'T MATTER ANYMORE/ RAINING IN MY HEART (13)	1.50	3.00
□62134		PEGGY SUE GOT MARRIED/CRYING, WAITING, HOPING	6.00	10.00
□62210		TRUE LOVE WAYS/THAT MAKES IT TOUGH	6.00	10.00
□62238		DON'T CHA KNOW/PEGGY SUE GOT MARRIED	2.50	4.00
□62283		YOU'RE SO SQUARE/VALLEY OF TEARS (Canadian Release)	7.00	12.00
□62329		REMINISCING/WAIT TILL THE SUN SHINES NELLIE	3.50	6.00
□62352		TRUE LOVE WAYS/BO DIDDLEY	3.50	6.00
□62369		BROWN EYED HANDSOME MAN/WISHING	3.50	6.00
□62390		I'M GONNA LOVE YOU TOO/ ROCK AROUND WITH OLLIE VEE	3.50	6.00
□62448		SLIPPIN' AND SLIDIN'/WHAT TO DO	6.00	10.00
□62554		RAVE ON/EARLY IN THE MORNING	5.00	8.00
□62558		LOVE IS STRANGE/YOU'RE THE ONE	3.50	6.00
		BUDDY HOLLY—EPs		
□2575	*DECCA*	THAT'LL BE THE DAY	80.00	150.00
□81169	*CORAL*	LISTEN TO ME	5.00	8.00
□81182		THE BUDDY HOLLY STORY	5.00	8.00
□81191		PEGGY SUE GOT MARRIED	5.00	8.00
□81193		BROWN EYED HANDSOME MAN	5.00	8.00
		BUDDY HOLLY—ALBUMS		
□8707 (M)	*DECCA*	THAT'LL BE THE DAY (flat black label)	75.00	125.00
□8708 (M)		THAT'LL BE THE DAY (rainbow label)	60.00	100.00
□57210 (M)	*CORAL*	BUDDY HOLLY	12.00	20.00
□57279 (M)		THE BUDDY HOLLY STORY	6.00	10.00
□57279 (S)		THE BUDDY HOLLY STORY	10.00	18.00
□57326 (M)		THE BUDDY HOLLY STORY, VOL. 2	7.00	12.00
□57326 (S)		THE BUDDY HOLLY STORY, VOL. 2	12.00	20.00
□57405 (M)		BUDDY HOLLY AND THE CRICKETS	7.00	12.00
□57405 (S)		BUDDY HOLLY AND THE CRICKETS	12.00	20.00
□57426 (M)		REMINISCING	6.00	10.00
□57426 (S)		REMINISCING	7.00	12.00
□57450 (M)		SHOWCASE	6.00	10.00
□57450 (S)		SHOWCASE	7.00	12.00
□57463 (M)		HOLLY IN THE HILLS	6.00	10.00
□57463 (S)		HOLLY IN THE HILLS	7.00	12.00
□57492 (M)		GREATEST HITS	3.50	6.00
□57492 (S)		GREATEST HITS	4.50	8.00

ISSUE #	LABEL	ARTIST/TITLE	VG	MINT
		HOLLYWOOD ARGYLES		
		FEATURED: KIM FOWLEY, GARY PAXTON		
□5905	*LUTE*	ALLEY-OOP/SHO KNOW A LOT ABOUT LOVE (1)	1.00	2.50
□5908		GUN TOTIN' CRITTER NAMED JACK/BUG EYE	1.50	2.50
□6002		HULLY GULLY/SO FINE	1.50	2.50
□752	*PAXLEY*	YOU'VE BEEN TORTURING ME/THE GRUBBLE	1.50	2.50
□691	*CHATTAHOOCHIE*	LONG HAIRED UNSQUARE DUDE NAMED JACK/ OLE'	1.50	2.50
□105	*KAMMY*	ALLEY OOP '66/DO THE FUNKY FOOT	1.75	3.00
		HOLLYWOOD ARGYLES—ALBUM		
□9001 (M)	*LUTE*	ALLEY-OOP	25.00	40.00
		HOLLYWOOD TORNADOES		
		SEE: TORNADOES		
□101	*AERTAUM*	THE GREMIE (PT. 1)/(PT. 11)	1.75	3.00
□102		MOON DAWG/THE INEBRIATED SURFER	1.75	3.00
		THE HONDELLS		
		FEATURED: GARY USHER		
□72324	*MERCURY*	LITTLE HONDA/HOT ROD HIGH (9)	1.00	2.50
□72366		MY BUDDY SEAT/ YOU'RE GONNA RIDE WITH ME (07)	1.50	2.50
□72405		LITTLE SIDEWALK SURFER GIRL/ COME ON (PACK IT ON)	1.75	3.00
□72443		SEA OF LOVE/DO AS I SAY	1.75	3.00
□72479		YOU MEET THE NICEST PEOPLE ON A HONDA/ SEA CRUISE	1.75	3.00
□72563		YOUNGER GIRL/ALL-AMERICAN GIRL (52)	1.25	2.50
		HONDELLS—ALBUMS		
□20940 (M)	*MERCURY*	GO LITTLE HONDA	6.00	10.00
□20940 (S)		GO LITTLE HONDA	7.00	12.00
□20982 (M)		THE HONDELLS	5.00	8.00
□20982 (S)		THE HONDELLS	6.00	10.00
		HONEYCOMBS		
□7707	*INTERPHON*	HAVE I THE RIGHT?/ PLEASE DON'T PRETEND AGAIN (5)	1.00	2.50
□7713		I CAN'T STOP/I'LL CRY TOMORROW (48)	1.25	2.50
□7716		THAT'S THE WAY/COLOR SLIDE	1.50	2.50
		HONEYCOMBS—ALBUM		
□88001 (M)	*INTERPHON*	HERE ARE THE HONEYCOMBS	5.00	8.00
		HONEYS		
		SEE: AMERICAN SPRING, SPRING		
		PRODUCER: BRIAN WILSON		
□4952	*CAPITOL*	SURFIN' DOWN THE SWANEE RIVER/ SHOOT THE CURL	12.00	20.00
□5034		PRAY FOR SURF/HIDE AND GO SEEK	10.00	18.00
□5093		THE ONE YOU CAN'T HAVE/ FROM JIMMY WITH TEARS	10.00	18.00
□2454		TONIGHT YOU BELONG TO ME/ GOODNIGHT MY LOVE	7.00	12.00

ISSUE #	LABEL	ARTIST/TITLE	VG	MINT
☐5430	*WARNER BROTHERS*	HE'S A DOLL/LOVE OF A BOY AND GIRL	8.00	15.00
		HONOR SOCIETY (HAPPENINGS)		
☐5703	*JUBILEE*	SWEET SEPTEMBER/CONDITION RED	2.50	4.00
		HOT-TODDYS		
☐0056	*SHAN-TODD*	ROCKIN' CRICKETS/SHAKIN' AND STOMPIN' (59)	1.50	3.00
☐25011	*STRAND*	HOEDOWN/NAN-JE-DI	1.75	3.00
		HULLABALOOS		
☐4587	*ROULETTE*	I'M GONNA LOVE YOU TOO/PARTY DOLL (56)	1.50	3.00
☐4593		DID YOU EVER/BEWARE (74)	1.25	2.50
☐4612		LEARNING THE GAME/DON'T STOP	1.50	2.50
☐4662		I WON'T TURN AWAY NOW/ MY HEART KEEPS TELLING ME	1.50	2.50
		HULLABALOOS—ALBUM		
☐25297 (M)	*ROULETTE*	ENGLAND'S NEWEST SINGING SENSATIONS	5.00	8.00
☐25297 (S)		ENGLAND'S NEWEST SINGING SENSATIONS	6.00	10.00
		HUMAN BEINZ		
☐828	*GATEWAY*	GLORIA/THE TIMES THEY ARE A-CHANGIN'	3.00	5.00
☐5990	*CAPITOL*	NOBODY BUT ME/SUENO (8)	1.00	2.00
☐2119		TURN ON YOUR LOVE LIGHT/ IT'S FUN TO BE CLEAN (80)	1.25	2.50
☐2198		EVERY TIME WOMAN/THE FACE	1.50	2.50
☐2431		THIS LITTLE GIRL OF MINE/ I'VE GOT TO KEEP ON PUSHIN'	1.50	2.50
		HUMAN BEINZ—ALBUM		
☐2906 (S)	*CAPITOL*	NOBODY BUT ME	4.00	7.00
		IVORY JOE HUNTER		
☐1111	*ATLANTIC*	SINCE I MET YOU BABY/YOU CAN'T STOP THIS ROCKING AND ROLLING (12)	2.00	3.50
☐1128		EMPTY ARMS/LOVE'S A HURTIN' GAME (43)	1.50	3.00
		TAB HUNTER		
☐15533	*DOT*	YOUNG LOVE/RED SAILS IN THE SUNSET (1)	1.25	2.50
☐15548		NINETY-NINE WAYS/DON'T GET AROUND MUCH ANYMORE (11)	1.25	2.50
☐15657		I'M ALONE BECAUSE I LOVE YOU/ DON'T GET AROUND MUCH ANYMORE	1.25	2.00
☐15767		I'M A RUNAWAY/IT'S ALL OVER TOWN	1.25	2.00
☐16264		THE WAY YOU LOOK TONIGHT/YOU CHEATED	1.50	2.00
		SINGLES ON WARNER BROTHERS ARE WORTH UP TO $2.00 MINT		
		TAB HUNTER—ALBUM		
☐3370 (M)	*DOT*	YOUNG LOVE	5.00	8.00
		DANNY HUTTON (OF THREE DOG NIGHT)		
☐213	*ALMO*	WHY DON'T YOU LOVE ME ANYMORE/ HOME IN PASADENA	1.75	3.00
☐447	*HBR*	ROSES AND RAINBOWS/MONSTER SHINDIG (73)	1.50	2.50
☐453		BIG BRIGHT EYES/MONSTER SHINDIG	1.75	2.50
☐13502	*MGM*	FUNNY HOW LOVE CAN BE/ DREAMIN' ISN'T GOOD FOR YOU	1.75	3.00

ISSUE #	LABEL	ARTIST/TITLE	VG	MINT
□ 13613		HANG ON TO A DREAM/HIT THE WALL	1.50	2.50

DANNY HUTTON—ALBUM

□ 4664 (S)	*MGM*	PRE-DOG NIGHT	3.50	6.00

BRIAN HYLAND

□ 801	*LEADER*	ROSEMARY/LIBRARY LOVE AFFAIR	3.00	5.00
□ 805		ITSY BITSY TEENIE WEENIE YELLOW POLKADOT BIKINI/DON'T DILLY DALLY, SALLY (1)	1.25	3.00
□ 342	*KAPP*	ITSY BITSY TEENIE WEENIE YELLOW POLKADOT BIKINI/DON'T DILLY DALLY, SALLY (1)	1.00	2.50
□ 352		FOUR LITTLE HEELS/THAT'S HOW MUCH (73)	1.25	2.50
□ 363		I GOTTA GO/LOP-SIDED, OVERLOADED	1.50	2.50
□ 401		LIPSTICK ON YOUR LIPS/WHEN WILL I KNOW	1.50	2.50
□ 10236	*ABC-PARAMOUNT*	LET ME BELONG TO YOU/LET IT DIE (29)	1.25	2.50
□ 10262		I'LL NEVER STOP WANTING YOU/ THE NIGHT I CRIED (83)	1.50	2.50
□ 10294		GINNY COME LATELY/ I SHOULD BE GETTING BETTER (21)	1.00	2.50
□ 10336		SEALED WITH A KISS/SUMMER JOB (3)	.75	2.00
□ 10359		WARMED OVER KISSES/WALK A LONELY MILE (25)	1.25	2.50
□ 10374		I MAY NOT LIVE TO SEE TOMORROW/ IT AIN'T THAT WAY (69)	1.50	2.50
□ 10400		IF MARY'S THERE/REMEMBER ME (88)	1.50	2.50
□ 10427		SOMEWHERE IN THE NIGHT/ I WISH TODAY WAS YESTERDAY	1.25	2.00
□ 10452		I'M AFRAID TO GO HOME/ SAVE YOUR HEART FOR ME (63)	1.25	2.00
□ 10494		NOTHING MATTERS BUT YOU/ LET US MAKE OUR OWN MISTAKES	1.25	2.00
□ 10549		OUT OF SIGHT, OUT OF MIND/ACT NATURALLY	1.50	2.50

SINGLES ON PHILIPS ARE WORTH UP TO $1.50 MINT

BRIAN HYLAND—ALBUMS

□ 1202 (M)	*KAPP*	THE BASHFUL BLONDE	5.00	8.00
□ 1202 (S)		THE BASHFUL BLONDE	6.00	10.00
□ 400 (M)	*ABC-PARAMOUNT*	LET ME BELONG TO YOU	3.50	6.00
□ 400 (S)		LET ME BELONG TO YOU	4.50	8.00
□ 431 (M)		SEALED WITH A KISS	3.50	6.00
□ 431 (S)		SEALED WITH A KISS	4.50	8.00

ISSUE #	LABEL	ARTIST/TITLE	VG	MINT

IAN AND SYLVIA

□ 35025	*VANGUARD*	YOU WERE ON MY MIND/ SOMEDAY SOON (original versions)	1.75	3.00

IDEALS

□ 1001	*STARS OF HOLLYWOOD*	PLEASE JAN/ALWAYS YOURS	6.00	10.00

ISSUE #	LABEL	ARTIST/TITLE	VG	MINT
		IDES OF MARCH		
□ 304	*PARROT*	YOU WOULDN'T LISTEN/I'LL KEEP SEARCHING (42) . .	1.50	3.00
□ 310		ROLLER COASTER/THINGS AREN'T ALWAYS WHAT THEY SEEM (92)	1.75	3.00
□ 312		YOU NEED LOVE/SHA-LA-la-LA-LEE	1.50	2.50
□ 321		MY FOOLISH PRIDE/GIVE ME YOUR MIND WINGS . .	1.50	2.50
□ 326		HOLE IN MY SOUL/GIRLS DON'T GROWN ON TREES .	1.50	2.00
		IDES OF MARCH—ALBUM		
□ 0143 (M)	*RCA*	MIDNIGHT OIL	3.50	6.00
		FRANK IFIELD		
□ 457	*VEE JAY*	I REMEMBER YOU/I LISTEN TO MY HEART (5)	1.00	2.50
□ 477		LOVESICK BLUES/ANYTIME (44)	1.25	2.50
□ 499		THE WAYWARD WIND/I'M SMILING NOW	1.25	2.00
□ 525		UNCHAINED MELODY/NOBODY'S DARLIN' BUT MINE .	1.25	2.00
□ 553		I'M CONFESSIN' (THAT I LOVE YOU)/HEART AND SOUL	1.50	2.50
		FRANK IFIELD—ALBUM		
□ 1054 (M)	*VEE JAY*	I REMEMBER YOU	3.50	6.00
□ 1054 (S)		I REMEMBER YOU	4.50	8.00

IMPALAS

At first three Brooklyn teenagers formed a nameless singing trio. With the cooperation of a neighbor, the boys set up a practice area in the back room of a neighborhood candy store. As they practiced and improved, they became determined to stick together and become successful. The trio later took on a fourth member, then cast about in search of a catchy and unique name for the quartet. The father of one of the boys had just purchased a new Chevrolet Impala. The boys liked the name and decided to dub their group the Impalas.

They worked hard at making as many contacts as they could. Finally they were signed to the small Hamilton label to do a single called "First Date". Sales were nil. Still determined, the boys soon met a businessman who knew Alan Freed. When Freed heard the boys, he was sufficiently impressed to recommend an audition with Cub records, an MGM subsidiary.

The Impalas recorded "(Sorry) I Ran All the Way Home" in 1959, and it sold a million. However, the Impalas proved to be a one-hit wonder. A follow-up 45 of "Oh, What A Fool" barely made the charts and later attempts failed altogether.

ISSUE #	LABEL	ARTIST/TITLE	VG	MINT
		IMPALAS		
☐50026	***HAMILTON***	FIRST DATE/I WAS A FOOL	3.50	6.00
☐9022	***CUB***	SORRY (I RAN ALL THE WAY HOME)/ FOOL FOOL FOOL (2)	1.25	3.00
☐9033		OH, WHAT A FOOL/SANDY WENT AWAY (86)	1.50	3.00
☐9053		PEGGY DARLING/BYE EVERYBODY	1.75	3.00
☐9066		WHEN MY HEART DOES ALL THE TALKING/ALL ALONE	2.00	3.50
		IMPALAS—EP		
☐5000	***CUB***	SORRY (I RAN ALL THE WAY HOME)	5.00	8.00
		IMPALAS—ALBUM		
☐8003 (M)	***CUB***	SORRY (I RAN ALL THE WAY HOME)	12.00	20.00
☐8003 (S)		SORRY (I RAN ALL THE WAY HOME)	15.00	25.00
		IMPRESSIONS		
		FEATURED: JERRY BUTLER		
☐2504	***BANDERA***	LISTEN TO ME/SHORTY'S GOTTA GO	3.50	6.00
☐107	***SWIRL***	DON'T LEAVE ME/I NEED YOUR LOVE	3.00	5.00
☐280	***VEE JAY***	FOR YOUR PRECIOUS LOVE/SWEET WAS THE WINE	60.00	100.00
☐424		SAY THAT YOU LOVE ME/SENORITA, I LOVE YOU	3.00	5.00
☐575		THE GIFT OF LOVE/AT THE COUNTY FAIR	2.50	4.00
☐621		SAY THAT YOU LOVE ME/SENORITA, I LOVE YOU	3.00	3.50
☐1013	***FALCON***	FOR YOUR PRECIOUS LOVE/SWEET WAS THE WINE	5.00	8.00
☐1013	***ABNER***	FOR YOUR PRECIOUS LOVE/ SWEET WAS THE WINE (11)	2.00	3.50
		SINGLES ON ABC-PARAMOUNT ARE WORTH UP TO $1.50 MINT		
		IMPRESSIONS—ALBUM		
☐1075 (M)	***VEE JAY***	FOR YOUR PRECIOUS LOVE	8.00	15.00
☐1075 (S)		FOR YOUR PRECIOUS LOVE	12.00	20.00
		INFATUATORS		
☐504	***DESTINY***	I FOUND MY LOVE/WHERE ARE YOU?	15.00	25.00
☐395	***VEE JAY***	I FOUND MY LOVE/WHERE ARE YOU?	3.00	5.00
		INITIALS		
☐1001	***DEE***	BELLS OF JOY/YOU	3.00	5.00
☐667	***SHERRY***	BELLS OF JOY/YOU	2.50	4.00
		INNOCENTS		
☐105	***INDIGO***	HONEST I DO/MY BABY HULLY GULLY'S (28)	1.25	2.50
☐111		GEE WHIZ/PLEASE MR. SUN (28)	1.25	2.50
☐116		KATHY/IN THE BEGINNING	1.50	2.50
☐124		BEWARE/BECAUSE I LOVE YOU	1.50	2.50
☐128		DONNA/YOU GOT ME GOIN'	1.50	2.50
☐141		TIME/DEE DEE DI OH	1.50	2.50
		INNOCENTS—ALBUM		
☐503 (M)	***INDIGO***	INNOCENTLY YOURS	8.00	15.00
		INSPIRATIONS		
☐1212	***JAMIE***	DRY YOUR EYES/GOODBYE	7.00	12.00
		INTERVALS (FIFTH DIMENSION)		
☐304	***CLASS***	HERE'S THAT RAINY DAY/ I WISH I COULD CHANGE MY MIND	12.00	20.00

ISLEY BROTHERS

The Isley Brothers hailed from Cincinnati, Ohio. They were raised in the church and surrounded by gospel music as children. (Ronald Isley won a spiritual-singing contest when he was three.)

They began as an r & b quartet, but Vernon—the youngest member—died in a car wreck. The three remaining Isleys then vowed to stay together no matter what. They played cheap bars and clubs around Cincinnati, then spread out through the Midwest, building a name as they went. They first recorded in 1957, singing for their first single a beautiful ballad called "The Angels Cried".

One night near the end of a 1959 stage show, one of the Isleys commanded their audience to "put up your hands and shout!" Later the request became a song and "Shout!" became an RCA hit. Their second RCA disc, "Respectable", later became a hit for the Outsiders, although it did little for the Isley Brothers.

A shift to Wand Records produced a Top 20 single of "Twist and Shout" to cash in on the dance craze at the time.

ISLEY BROTHERS

ISSUE #	LABEL	ARTIST/TITLE	VG	MINT
☐ 1004	***TEENAGE***	THE ANGELS CRIED/ THE COW JUMPED OVER THE MOON	20.00	35.00
☐ 3009	***CINDY***	DON'T BE JEALOUS/THIS IS THE END	3.00	5.00
☐ 5022	***GONE***	I WANNA KNOW/ EVERYBODY'S GONNA ROCK AND ROLL	5.00	8.00
☐ 5048		MY LOVE/THE DRAG	5.00	8.00
☐ 8000	***MARK X***	ROCKIN' MACDONALD/THE DRAG	3.50	6.00
☐ 7588	***RCA***	SHOUT (PT. 1)/(PT. 11) (47)	1.50	3.00
☐ 7657		RESPECTABLE/WITHOUT A SONG	2.00	3.50
☐ 124	***WAND***	TWIST AND SHOUT/SPANISH TWIST (17)	1.25	2.50
☐ 127		TWISTIN' WITH LINDA/YOU BETTER COME HOME (54)	1.50	2.50
☐ 501	***T NECK***	TESTIFY (PT. 1)/(PT. 11) (Jimi Hendrix on guitar)	3.00	5.00
☐ 54128	***TAMLA***	THIS OLD HEART OF MINE/ THERE'S NO LOVE LEFT (12)	1.00	2.00

ISLEY BROTHERS—ALBUMS

ISSUE #	LABEL	ARTIST/TITLE	VG	MINT
☐ 2156 (M)	***RCA***	SHOUT!	8.00	15.00
☐ 2156 (S)		SHOUT!	12.00	20.00
☐ 653 (M)	***WAND***	TWIST AND SHOUT	6.00	10.00
☐ 269 (S)	***TAMLA***	THIS OLD HEART OF MINE	5.00	8.00

IVAN (JERRY ALLISON)

GUITAR: BUDDY HOLLY

ISSUE #	LABEL	ARTIST/TITLE	VG	MINT
☐ 62017	***CORAL***	REAL WILD CHILD/OH YOU BEAUTIFUL DOLL (68)	5.00	8.00
☐ 62081		FRANKIE FRANKENSTEIN/THAT'LL BE ALRIGHT	7.00	12.00
☐ 65607		REAL WILD CHILD/THAT'LL BE ALRIGHT	3.00	5.00

I. V. LEAGUERS

ISSUE #	LABEL	ARTIST/TITLE	VG	MINT
☐ 1003	***PORTER***	RING CHIMES/THE STORY	5.00	8.00
☐ 15677	***DOT***	RING CHIMES/THE STORY	1.75	3.00

IVOLEERS

ISSUE #	LABEL	ARTIST/TITLE	VG	MINT
☐ 101	***BUZZ***	LOVER'S QUARREL/COME WITH ME	6.00	10.00

IVY THREE

ISSUE #	LABEL	ARTIST/TITLE	VG	MINT
☐ 720	***SHELL***	YOGI/WAS JUDY THERE? (8)	1.00	2.50
☐ 723		ALONE IN THE CHAPEL/HUSH LITTLE BABY	2.00	3.50
☐ 302		NINE OUT OF TEN/I'VE CRIED ENOUGH FOR TWO	1.75	3.00
☐ 306		BAGOO/SUICIDE	1.50	2.50

J

JACKSON 5

ISSUE #	LABEL	ARTIST/TITLE	VG	MINT
☐ 681	***STEELTOWN***	YOU'VE CHANGED/BIG BOY	6.00	10.00
☐ 684		YOU DON'T HAVE TO BE OVER 21 TO FALL IN LOVE/ SOME GIRLS WANT ME FOR THEIR LOVE	6.00	10.00

PYTHON LEE JACKSON (ROD STEWART)

ISSUE #	LABEL	ARTIST/TITLE	VG	MINT
☐ 449	***GNP-CRESCENDO***	IN A BROKEN DREAM/DOIN' FINE	3.00	5.00
☐ 462		CLOUD NINE/ROD'S BLUES	3.00	5.00

WANDA JACKSON

Oklahoma City, Oklahoma, was the birthplace of Wanda Jackson. Born there in 1937 on October 20th, Wanda learned how to read music and play both guitar and piano from her father, a country-music devotee.

As a teenager Wanda began singing in earnest and entered talent contests whenever she could. While still in high school in Oklahoma City, she impressed country great Hank Thompson so much that he hired Wanda to sing in his band. When Wanda finished high school in 1955, she went on the road with Thompson and another country artist, Elvis Presley.

Wanda did well with her Capitol singles from the time she began recording. Her first three efforts were great, aggressive country rockers. Her fourth single was "Let's Have A Party" (from the 1957 Elvis movie of "Loving You"). Not only a solid country hit, "Let's Have A Party" crossed over onto the rock charts and became a Top 40 smash. Her next song—"Right Or Wrong"—fared even better.

Though her name has stopped guaranteeing record hits, Wanda Jackson still sings on occasion in Oklahoma City, where she was born, raised and resides to this day.

ISSUE #	LABEL	ARTIST/TITLE	VG	MINT
		WANDA JACKSON		
□3575	*CAPITOL*	HOT DOG, THAT MADE HIM MAD!/ SILVER THREADS AND GOLDEN NEEDLES	3.50	6.00
□3941		HONEY BOP/JUST A QUEEN FOR A DAY	3.50	6.00
□4081		ROCK YOUR BABY/SINFUL HEART	3.00	5.00
□4397		LET'S HAVE A PARTY/COOL LOVE (37)	2.50	4.00
□4553		RIGHT OR WRONG/TUNNEL OF LOVE (29)	2.00	3.50
□4635		IN THE MIDDLE OF A HEARTACHE/ I'D BE ASHAMED (27)	2.00	3.50
□4681		A LITTLE BITTY TEAR/I DON'T WANTA GO (84)	1.50	3.00
		WANDA JACKSON—ALBUMS		
□1041 (M)	*CAPITOL*	WANDA JACKSON	20.00	30.00
□1384 (M)		ROCKIN' WITH WANDA	25.00	40.00
□1511 (M)		THERE'S A PARTY GOIN' ON	18.00	30.00
□1511 (S)		THERE'S A PARTY GOIN' ON	20.00	35.00
		JAMIES		
□9281	*EPIC*	SUMMERTIME, SUMMERTIME/ SEARCHING FOR YOU (26)	1.25	3.00
□9299		SNOW TRAIN/WHEN THE SUN GOES DOWN	1.50	2.50
□9565		SNOW TRAIN/WHEN THE SUN GOES DOWN	1.25	2.00

JAN AND ARNIE

Jan Berry and Arnie Ginsberg were classmates at University High in the posh L.A. suburb of Bel Air. They were also members of a car club called the Barons. One night Jan, Arnie and several other Barons took in a burlesque show in seedy downtown Los Angeles. That night they saw a stripper billed as Jennie Lee. Jan was particularly taken by the way Jennie bounced when she moved. On the way home he began a silly repetition of the words. ". . bomp-bomp-bomp-bomp-" in between verbalizing about the physical attributes of Ms. Lee.

Before long Jan and Arnie had set up a makeshift recording studio in Jan's garage. Using a two-track home recorder, Jan found that he could produce an echo effect with a second recorder. He and Arnie then made the tape of their original "Jennie Lee". Jan banged on an old piano and Arnie drummed on a wooden box with a pair of sticks.

The tape was later taken to the small Arwin Record Company in Beverly Hills. With added studio instruments, "Jennie Lee" was released and—surprise!—became a Top 10 winner.

ISSUE #	LABEL	ARTIST/TITLE	VG	MINT
		JAN AND ARNIE		
□ 108	*ARWIN*	JENNIE LEE/GOTTA GET A DATE (8)	2.00	4.00
□ 111		GAS MONEY/BONNIE LOU (81)	3.00	5.00
□ 113		I LOVE LINDA/THE BEAT THAT CAN'T BE BEAT	3.50	6.00
□ 522	*DORE*	BABY TALK/JEANETTE, GET YOU HAIR DONE (really Jan and Dean)	30.00	50.00
		JAN AND ARNIE—EP		
□ 1097	*DOT*	JAN AND ARNIE	20.00	30.00

JAN AND DEAN

After Arnie Ginsberg joined the navy, Jan Berry wanted to continue recording. He recruited another school friend, Dean Torrence. (They played together on the football team at University High in Bel Air.) The duo made their first three singles in Jan's garage—just as Jan and Arnie had done—and scored a Top 10 single (Jan's second one) with the infectious "Baby Talk".

Leaving garages behind, Jan and Dean often sang on the Beach Boys' Capitol records, and the Beach Boys returned the favor on some of Jan and Dean's Liberty sides.

After major 1963-64 success, the Jan and Dean hits began to subside under the onslaught of the Beatles. It was no problem, though, as both were college students and recording had been only a fun part-time job. Still, Jan and Dean continued recording until 1966 when Jan nearly died in a car crash. His new Corvette was shattered and Jan was left with brain damage. Jan managed to pull himself back from the brink of death and has improved. He and Dean now make infrequent appearances.

JAN AND DEAN

ISSUE #	LABEL	ARTIST/TITLE	VG	MINT
□522		BABY TALK/JEANETTE, GET YOUR HAIR DONE (10)	1.50	3.00
□531		THERE'S A GIRL/MY HEART SINGS (97)	2.50	4.00
□539		CLEMENTINE/YOU'RE ON MY MIND (65)	2.00	3.50
□548		WHITE TENNIS SNEAKERS/CINDY	2.50	4.00
□555		WE GO TOGETHER/ROSILANE (53)	2.00	3.50
□576		GEE/SUCH A GOOD NIGHT FOR DREAMING (81)	2.00	3.50
□583		BAGGY PANTS/JUDY'S AN ANGEL	2.50	4.00
□610		JULIE/DON'T FLY AWAY	3.00	5.00
□9111	***CHALLENGE***	HEART AND SOUL/THOSE WORDS	5.00	8.00
□9111		HEART AND SOUL/MIDSUMMER NIGHT'S DREAM (25)	1.25	2.50
□9120		WANTED, ONE GIRL/ SOMETHING A LITTLE BIT DIFFERENT	2.00	3.50
□55397	***LIBERTY***	A SUNDAY KIND OF LOVE/POOR LITTLE PUPPET (95)	2.00	3.50
□55454		TENNESSEE/YOUR HEART HAS CHANGED ITS MIND (69)	1.75	3.00
□55496		WHO PUT THE BOMP/MY FAVORITE DREAM	3.00	5.00
□55522		SHE'S STILL TALKING BABY TALK/ FROSTY THE SNOWMAN	6.00	10.00
□55531		LINDA/WHEN I LEARN HOW TO CRY (28)	1.25	2.50
□55580		SURF CITY/SHE'S MY SUMMER GIRL (1)	1.00	2.00
□55613		HONOLULU LULU/SOMEDAY YOU'LL GO WALKING BY (11)	1.00	2.00
□55641		DRAG CITY/SCHLOCK ROD, PT. 1 (10)	1.00	2.00
□55672		DEAD MAN'S CURVE/THE NEW GIRL IN SCHOOL (8)	1.00	2.00
□55704		THE LITTLE OLD LADY (FROM PASADENA)/ MY MIGHTY G.T.O. (3)	1.00	2.00
□55724		RIDE THE WILD SURF/THE ANAHEIM, AZUSA AND CUCAMONGA SEWING CIRCLE, BOOK REVIEW AND TIMING ASSOCIATION (16)	1.25	2.00
□55727		SIDEWALK SURFIN'/WHEN IT'S OVER (25)	1.25	2.00
□55766		FROM ALL OVER THE WORLD/FREEWAY FLYER (56)	1.25	2.50
□55792		YOU REALLY KNOW HOW TO HURT A GUY/ IT'S AS EASY AS 1, 2, 3 (27)	1.25	2.00
□55833		I FOUND A GIRL/IT'S A SHAME TO SAY GOODBYE (30)	1.25	2.00
□55849		FOLK CITY/BEGINNING TO AN END	1.75	3.00
□55860		BATMAN/BUCKET ''T'' (66)	1.50	2.50
□55886		POPSICLE/NORWEGIAN WOOD (21)	1.00	2.00
□55905		FIDDLE AROUND/A SURFER'S DREAM (93)	1.50	2.50
□55923		SCHOOL DAY/THE NEW GIRL IN SCHOOL	1.75	3.00
□10	***JAN AND DEAN***	HAWAII/TIJUANA	20.00	30.00
□11		FAN TAN/LOVE AND HATE	20.00	30.00
□001	***J & D***	SUMMERTIME, SUMMERTINE/CALIFORNIA LULLABY	12.00	20.00
□401		SUMMERTIME, SUMMERTIME/CALIFORNIA LULLABY	6.00	10.00
		LULLABY	6.00	10.00
□402		LOUISIANA MAN/LIKE A SUMMER RAIN	7.00	12.00
□401	***MAGIC LAMP***	SUMMERTIME, SUMMERTIME/CALIFORNIA LULLABY	3.00	5.00
□44036	***COLUMBIA***	YELLOW BALLOON/TASTE OF RAIN	3.00	5.00
□7151	***WARNER BROTHERS***	ONLY A BOY/LOVE AND HATE	7.00	12.00

ISSUE #	LABEL	ARTIST/TITLE	VG	MINT
☐7219		LAUREL AND HARDY/I KNOW MY MIND	7.00	12.00
☐7240		IN THE STILL OF THE NIGHT/ GIRL, YOU'RE BLOWING MY MIND	18.00	30.00
		JAN AND DEAN—ALBUMS		
☐101 (M)	*DORE*	JAN AND DEAN	25.00	40.00
☐3248 (M)	*LIBERTY*	JAN AND DEAN'S GREATEST HITS	3.50	6.00
☐3248 (S)		JAN AND DEAN'S GREATEST HITS	4.50	8.00
☐3294 (M)		JAN AND DEAN TAKE LINDA SURFING	3.50	6.00
☐3294 (S)		JAN AND DEAN TAKE LINDA SURFING	4.50	8.00
☐3314 (M)		SURF CITY	3.50	6.00
☐3314 (S)		SURF CITY	4.50	8.00
☐3339 (M)		DRAG CITY	3.00	8.00
☐3339 (S)		DRAG CITY	3.00	5.00
☐3361 (M)		DEAD MAN'S CURVE/NEW GIRL IN SCHOOL	3.50	6.00
☐3361 (S)		DEAD MAN'S CURVE/NEW GIRL IN SCHOOL	4.50	8.00
☐3388 (M)		RIDE THE WILD SURF	3.00	5.00
☐3388 (S)		RIDE THE WILD SURF	4.00	7.00
☐3377 (M)		LITTLE OLD LADY FROM PASADENA	3.50	6.00
☐3377 (S)		LITTLE OLD LADY FROM PASADENA	4.50	8.00
☐3403 (M)		COMMAND PERFORMANCE	4.00	7.00
☐3403 (S)		COMMAND PERFORMANCE	5.00	9.00
☐3414 (M)		JAN AND DEAN'S POP SYMPHONY NO. 1	6.00	10.00
☐3414 (S)		JAN AND DEAN'S POP SYMPHONY NO. 1	7.00	12.00
☐3417 (M)		JAN AND DEAN'S GOLDEN HITS, VOL. 2	3.50	6.00
☐3417 (S)		JAN AND DEAN'S GOLDEN HITS, VOL. 2	4.50	8.00
☐3431 (M)		FOLK 'N' ROLL	3.50	6.00
☐3431 (S)		FOLK 'N' ROLL	4.50	8.00
☐3441 (M)		FILET OF SOUL	3.50	6.00
☐3441 (S)		FILET OF SOUL	4.50	8.00
☐3444 (M)		JAN AND DEAN MEET BATMAN	3.50	6.00
☐3444 (S)		JAN AND DEAN MEET BATMAN	4.50	8.00
☐3458 (M)		POPSICLE	3.00	5.00
☐3458 (S)		POPSICLE	4.00	7.00
☐3460 (M)		JAN AND DEAN'S GOLDEN HITS, VOL. 3	5.00	8.00
☐3460 (S)		JAN AND DEAN'S GOLDEN HITS, VOL. 3	6.00	10.00
☐101 (M)	*J & D*	SAVE FOR A RAINY DAY	12.00	20.00
		JARMELS		
☐3085	*LAURIE*	LITTLE LONELY ONE/SHE LOVES TO DANCE	1.75	3.00
☐3098		A LITTLE BIT OF SOAP/ THE WAY YOU LOOK TONIGHT (12)	1.00	2.00
☐3116		I'LL FOLLOW YOU/GEE OH GOSH	1.50	2.50
☐3124		RED SAILS IN THE SUNSET/LONELINESS	1.50	2.50
☐3141		ONE BY ONE/LITTLE BUG	1.50	2.50
☐3174		COME ON GIRL/KEEP YOUR MIND ON ME	1.50	2.50
		CAROL JARVIS		
☐15586	*DOT*	REBEL/WHIRLPOOL OF LOVE (48)	1.50	3.00
☐15679		GOLDEN BOY/ACORN	1.50	2.50
☐3032	*ERA*	I'M BREAKING IN A BRAND NEW HEART/ DON'T THROW PEBBLES	1.50	2.50
☐3043		GIVE HIM A KISS FOR ME/MY PRIVATE DREAMS	1.50	2.50

ISSUE #	LABEL	ARTIST/TITLE	VG	MINT
		JAY AND THE AMERICANS		
		SEE: JAY BLACK, HARBOR LIGHTS, ROCKAWAYS		
□ 353	*UNITED ARTISTS*	TONIGHT/THE OTHER GIRLS (without Jay Black)	2.00	3.50
□ 415		SHE CRIED/DAWNING (5)	1.00	2.50
□ 479		THIS IS IT/IT'S MY TURN TO CRY	1.75	3.00
□ 504		TOMORROW/YES	1.75	3.00
□ 566		WHAT'S THE USE/STRANGERS TOMORROW	1.75	3.00
□ 626		ONLY IN AMERICA/MY CLAIR DE LUNE (25)	1.25	2.50
□ 669		COME DANCE WITH ME/ LOOK IN MY EYES, MARIE (76)	1.50	2.50
□ 693		TO WAIT FOR LOVE/FRIDAY	1.50	2.50
□ 759		COME A LITTLE BIT CLOSER/ GOODBYE, BOYS, GOODBYE (3)	.75	2.00
□ 805		LET'S LOCK THE DOOR/I'LL REMEMBER YOU (11)	1.00	2.00
□ 845		THINK OF THE GOOD TIMES/ IF YOU WERE MINE, GIRL (57)	1.25	2.00
□ 881		CARA MIA/WHEN IT'S ALL OVER (4)	.75	2.00
□ 919		SOME ENCHANTED EVENING/GIRL (13)	1.00	2.00
□ 948		SUNDAY AND ME/THROUGH THIS DOORWAY (18)	1.25	2.00
□ 992		WHY CAN'T YOU BRING ME HOME?/ BABY, STOP YOUR CRYIN' (63)	1.25	2.00
□ 50016		CRYING/I DON'T NEED A FRIEND (25)	1.25	2.00
□ 50046		LIVIN' ABOVE YOUR HEAD/LOOK AT ME, WHAT DO YOU SEE? (76)	1.25	2.00
□ 50086		STOP THE CLOCK/BABY, COME HOME	1.25	2.00
□ 50094		HE'S RAINING IN MY SUNSHINE/ THE REASON FOR LIVING (90)	1.25	2.00
□ 50139		NATURE BOY/YOU AIN'T AS HIP AS ALL THAT, BABY	1.25	2.00
□ 50196		GOT HUNG UP ALONG THE WAY/YELLOW FOREST	1.25	2.00
□ 50222		FRENCH PROVINCIAL/SHANGHAI NOODLE FACTORY	1.25	2.00
□ 50282		NO OTHER LOVE/NO, I DON'T KNOW HER	1.25	2.00
□ 50448		YOU AIN'T GONNA WAKE UP CRYIN'/GEMINI	1.25	2.00
□ 50475		THIS MAGIC MOMENT/SINCE I DON'T HAVE YOU (6)	.75	2.00
□ 50510		WHEN YOU DANCE/NO, I DON'T KNOW HER (70)	1.00	2.00
□ 50535		HUSHABYE/GYPSY WOMAN (62)	1.00	2.00
□ 50567		LEARNIN' HOW TO FLY/FOR THE LOVE OF A LADY	1.25	2.00
□ 50605		WALKIN' IN THE RAIN/ FOR THE LOVE OF A LADY (19)	1.00	2.00
□ 50654		CAPTURE THE MOMENT/ DO YOU EVER THINK OF ME? (57)	1.25	2.00
□ 50683		DO I LOVE YOU/TRICIA (TELL YOUR DADDY)	1.25	2.00
□ 50858		THERE GOES MY BABY/SOLITARY MAN	1.25	2.00
		JAY AND THE AMERICANS—ALBUMS		
□ 3222 (M)	*UNITED ARTISTS*	SHE CRIED	4.00	7.00
□ 6222 (S)		SHE CRIED	5.00	9.00
□ 3300 (M)		JAY AND THE AMERICANS AT THE CAFE WHA?	3.50	6.00
□ 6300 (S)		JAY AND THE AMERICANS AT THE CAFE WHA?	4.50	8.00
□ 3417 (M)		BLOCKBUSTERS	3.50	6.00
□ 6417 (S)		BLOCKBUSTERS	4.50	8.00
□ 3453 (M)		GREATEST HITS	3.00	5.00
□ 6453 (S)		GREATEST HITS	4.00	7.00
□ 3474 (M)		SUNDAY AND ME	3.50	6.00

ISSUE #	LABEL	ARTIST/TITLE	VG	MINT
☐ 6474 (S)		SUNDAY AND ME............................	4.50	8.00
☐ 3534 (M)		LIVIN' ABOVE YOUR HEAD....................	3.00	5.00
☐ 6534 (S)		LIVIN' ABOVE YOUR HEAD....................	4.00	7.00
☐ 3555 (M)		GREATEST HITS, VOL. 2	3.50	6.00
☐ 6555 (S)		GREATEST HITS, VOL. 2	4.50	8.00

JAY AND THE DEANS

☐ 5405	*WARNER BROTHERS*	BELLS ARE RINGING/SUPER HAWK	5.00	8.00

JAYHAWKS
SEE: MARATHONS, VIBRATIONS

☐ 100	*FLASH*	STRANDED IN THE JUNGLE/MY ONLY DARLING (29)	2.50	4.00

JAYNETTS

☐ 1102	*GOLDIE*	WE BELONG TO EACH OTHER/HE'S CRYING INSIDE .	1.75	3.00
☐ 369	*TUFF*	SALLY GO 'ROUND THE ROSES (PT. 1)/(PT. 11) (2) .	1.00	2.50
☐ 371		KEEP AN EYE ON HER (PT. 1)/(PT. 11)	1.50	2.50

JAYNETTS—ALBUM

☐ 13 (M)	*TUFF*	SALLY, GO 'ROUND THE ROSES	5.00	8.00

CATHY JEAN AND THE ROOMATES

☐ 007	*VALMOR*	PLEASE LOVE ME FOREVER/CANADIAN SUNSET (12) .	1.25	3.00
☐ 009		MAKE ME SMILE AGAIN/SUGAR CAKE	1.50	2.50
☐ 016		PLEASE TELL ME/SUGAR CAKE	1.50	2.50
☐ 40014	*PHILIPS*	BELIEVE ME/DOUBLE TROUBLE	2.50	4.00

CATHY JEAN AND THE ROOMATES—ALBUM

☐ 789 (M)	*VALMOR*	AT THE HOP	15.00	25.00

CATHY JEAN

☐ 40106	*PHILIPS*	MY HEART BELONGS TO ONLY YOU/ I ONLY WANT YOU	1.50	2.50
☐ 40143		BELIEVE ME/DOUBLE TROUBLE	1.50	2.50

JEANIE AND THE BOY FRIENDS

☐ 508	*WARWICK*	IT'S ME KNOCKING/BABY	2.50	4.00

JEFFERSON AIRPLANE
SEE: GREAT SOCIETY

☐ 8769	*RCA*	RUNNIN' AROUND THIS WORLD/IT'S NO SECRET ..	2.00	3.50
☐ 8848		COME UP THE YEARS/BLUES FROM AN AIRPLANE..	2.00	3.50
☐ 8967		BRINGING ME DOWN/LET ME IN	1.75	3.00
☐ 9063		MY BEST FRIEND/HOW DO YOU FEEL?	1.75	3.00
☐ 9140		SOMEBODY TO LOVE/SHE HAS FUNNY CARS (5) ...	1.25	2.00
☐ 9248		WHITE RABBIT/PLASTIC FANTASTIC LOVER (8)....	1.25	2.00
☐ 9297		BALLAD OF YOU AND ME AND POONEIL/ TWO HEADS (42)	1.50	2.50
☐ 9389		WATCH HER RIDE/MARTHA (61)...............	1.50	2.50
☐ 9496		GREASY HEART/SHARE A LITTLE JOKE (98).......	1.50	2.50
☐ 9644		CROWN OF CREATION/LATHER (64)	1.50	2.50
☐ 0245		VOLUNTEERS/WE CAN BE TOGETHER (65)	1.50	2.50
☐ 0150		THE OTHER SIDE OF THIS LIFE/ PLASTIC FANTASTIC LOVER	1.50	2.50

ISSUE #	LABEL	ARTIST/TITLE	VG	MINT
		JELLY BEANS		
□ 10-003	***RED BIRD***	I WANNA LOVE HIM SO BAD/SO LONG (9)	1.25	2.50
□ 10-011		BABY BE MINE/THE KIND OF BOY YOU CAN'T FORGET (51)	1.50	2.50
□ 001	***ESKEE***	I'M HIP TO YOU/YOU DON'T MEAN NO GOOD TO ME	1.50	2.50
		WAYLON JENNINGS		
□ 55130	***BRUNSWICK***	JOLE BLON/WHEN SIN STOPS	30.00	50.00
		(GUITAR ON BRUNSWICK 55130: BUDDY HOLLY)		
□ 121639	***BAT***	CRYING/DREAM BABY	5.00	8.00
□ 722	***A & M***	RAVE ON/LOVE DENIED	3.00	5.00
		KRIS JENSEN		
□ 1173	***HICKORY***	TORTURE/LET'S SIT DOWN (20)	1.25	2.50
□ 1195		CLAUDETTE/DON'T TAKE HER FROM ME	1.25	2.00
□ 1203		CUT ME DOWN/POOR UNLUCKY ME	1.25	2.00
		KRIS JENSEN—ALBUM		
□ 110 (M)	***HICKORY***	TORTURE	5.00	8.00
		JEWEL AND EDDIE (WITH JEWEL AKENS)		
		GUITAR: EDDIE COCHRAN		
□ 1004	***SILVER***	OPPORTUNITY/DOIN' THE HULLY GULLY	2.50	4.00
□ 1004		OPPORTUNITY/STROLLIN' GUITAR	2.50	4.00
□ 1008		SIXTEEN TONS/MY EYES ARE CRYING FOR YOU	3.00	5.00
		JILL AND RAY		
		SEE: PAUL AND PAULA		
□ 979	***LE CAM***	HEY PAULA/BOBBIE IS THE ONE	5.00	8.00
		JIVE FIVE		
□ 1006	***BELTONE***	MY TRUE STORY/WHEN I WAS SINGLE (3)	1.00	2.50
□ 1014		NEVER, NEVER/PEOPLE FROM ANOTHER WORLD (74)	1.50	2.50
□ 2019		NO, NOT AGAIN/HULLY GULLY CALLIN' TIME	1.50	2.50
□ 2024		WHAT TIME IS IT?/BEGGIN' YOU PLEASE (67)	1.50	2.50
□ 2029		THESE GOLDEN RINGS/ DO YOU HEAR WEDDING BELLS?	1.50	2.50
□ 2030		JOHNNY NEVER KNEW/LILI MARLENE	1.50	2.50
□ 2034		SHE'S MY GIRL/RAIN	1.50	2.50
		JIVE FIVE—ALBUM		
□ 3455 (M)	***UNITED ARTISTS***	JIVE FIVE	3.50	6.00
□ 6455 (S)		JIVE FIVE	4.50	8.00
		JIVETONES		
□ 25020	***ART***	DING DING DONG/GERALDINE	6.00	10.00
		JIVIN' GENE AND THE JOKERS		
□ 71485	***MERCURY***	BREAKIN' UP IS HARD TO DO/ MY NEED FOR LOVE (69)	1.50	2.50
□ 71561		YOU'RE JEALOUS/GO ON, GO ON	1.25	2.00
□ 71751		POOR ME/THAT'S WHAT IT'S LIKE	1.25	2.00

ISSUE #	LABEL	ARTIST/TITLE	VG	MINT
		MARCY JOE		
		FEATURED: LOU CHRISTIE		
□110	***ROBBEE***	RONNIE/MY FIRST MISTAKE (81)	1.50	2.50
□115		WHAT I DID THIS SUMMER/ SINCE GARY WENT IN THE NAVY	1.50	2.50
□117		JUMPING JACK/TAKE A WORD	1.50	2.50
		ELTON JOHN		
		SEE: BLUESOLOGY		
□1643	***PHILIPS***	I'VE BEEN LOVING YOU/ HERE'S TO THE NEXT TIME (British)	12.00	20.00
□70-000	***DJM***	LADY SAMANTHA/ALL ACROSS THE HEAVENS	8.00	15.00
□0017	***CONGRESS***	LADY SAMANTHA/IT'S ME THAT YOU NEED	8.00	15.00
□6022		BORDER SONG/BAD SIDE OF THE MOON	6.00	10.00
□55246	***UNI***	BORDER SONG/BAD SIDE OF THE MOON (92)	1.50	2.50
		LATER UNI SINGLES ARE WORTH UP TO $2.00 MINT		
		JOHNNIE AND JOE		
□1641	***J & S***	I'LL BE SPINNING/FEEL ALRIGHT	6.00	10.00
□1654		OVER THE MOUNTAIN, ACROSS THE SEA/ MY BABY'S GONE, ON, ON	20.00	35.00
□1641	***CHESS***	I'LL BE SPINNING/FEEL ALRIGHT	3.00	5.00
□1654		OVER THE MOUNTAIN, ACROSS THE SEA/ MY BABY'S GONE, ON, ON (8)	2.00	4.00
□1706		DARLING/MY BABY'S GONE	2.50	4.00

JOHNNY AND THE HURRICANES

Johnny and the Hurricanes were formed by Johnny Paris in 1959. Paris, like the other members of his group, was born in Toledo, Ohio, in 1941. During his junior-high years young Paris came under the spell of rock-and-roll in general and the saxophone in particular.

Johnny and the Hurricanes banded together as an instrumental group. While still in high school during the late 1950s, the band played school talent shows and dances. Later they moved to teen-oriented dance clubs in and around Toledo.

An associate helped them get a demo tape heard at Warwick Records, and Johnny and the Hurricanes were on their way. Still high-school seniors, they broke big in 1959 with "Crossfire", a Top 30 single. Their next record, released during the summer of 1959, was given heavy airplay on Dick Clark's "American Bandstand", and the group enjoyed its biggest hit ever with the million-selling "Red River Rock".

With four Warwick hits in four tries, Johnny and the Hurricanes were wooed away by Big Top Records. Warwick then released Hurricane singles under the name of the Craftsmen, but without success. On Big Top their best-seller was the oldie "Down Yonder".

ISSUE #	LABEL	ARTIST/TITLE	VG	MINT

JOHNNY AND THE HURRICANES
SEE: CRAFTSMEN

☐ 502	*WARWICK*	CROSSFIRE/LAZY (23)	1.50	3.00
☐ 509		RED RIVER ROCK/BUCKEYE (5)	1.25	2.50
☐ 513		REVILLE ROCK/TIME BOMB (25)	1.25	2.50
☐ 520		BEATNIK FLY/SAND STORM (15)	1.25	2.50
☐ 3036	*BIG TOP*	DOWN YONDER/SHEBA (48)	1.25	2.50
☐ 3051		ROCKING GOOSE/REVIVAL (60)................	1.25	2.50
☐ 3056		YOU ARE MY SUNSHINE/MOLLY-O (91)	1.50	2.50
☐ 3063		JA-DA/MR. LONELY (06)......................	1.50	2.50
☐ 3076		OLD SMOKIE/HIGH VOLTAGE	1.25	2.00
☐ 3090		TRAFFIC JAM/FAREWELL, FAREWELL	1.25	2.00
☐ 3103		MISERLOU/SALVATION.......................	1.50	2.50
☐ 3113		SAN ANTONIO ROSE/COME ON TRAIN...........	1.25	2.00
☐ 3125		SHIEK OF ARABY/MINNESOTA FATS	1.25	2.00
☐ 3132		WHATEVER HAPPENED TO BABY JANE?/		
		GREENS AND BEANS	1.25	2.00
☐ 3146		JAMES BOND THEME/HUNGRY EYES	1.25	2.00
☐ 3159		KAW-LIGA/ROUGH ROAD.....................	1.25	2.00

JOHNNY AND THE HURRICANES—EP

☐ 700	*WARWICK*	JOHNNY AND THE HURRICANES	6.00	10.00

JOHNNY AND THE HURRICANES—ALBUMS

☐ 2007 (M)	*WARWICK*	JOHNNY AND THE HURRICANES	12.00	20.00
☐ 2010 (M)		STORMSVILLE	8.00	15.00
☐ 2010 (S)		STORMSVILLE	12.00	20.00
☐ 1302 (M)	*BIG TOP*	THE BIG SOUND OF JOHNNY AND THE HURRICANES	8.00	15.00

MARV JOHNSON

☐ 101	*TAMLA*	COME TO ME/WHISPER.......................	8.00	15.00
☐ 160	*UNITED ARTISTS*	COME TO ME/WHISPER (30)	1.25	2.50
☐ 175		I'M COMING HOME/RIVER OF TEARS (82)	1.50	2.50
☐ 185		YOU GOT WHAT IT TAKES/DON'T LEAVE ME (10) ...	1.00	2.50
☐ 208		I LOVE THE WAY YOU LOVE/LET ME LOVE YOU (9)..	1.00	2.50
☐ 226		ALL THE LOVE I'VE GOT/		
		AIN'T GONNA BE THAT WAY (63)..............	1.25	2.50
☐ 241		MOVE TWO MOUNTAINS/I NEED YOU (20)	1.25	2.50
☐ 273		HAPPY DAYS/BABY, BABY (58)	1.25	2.00
☐ 294		MERRY-GO-ROUND/TELL ME THAT YOU LOVE ME (61)	1.25	2.00
☐ 322		I'VE GOT A NOTION/HOW CAN WE TELL HIM?	1.25	2.00
☐ 359		OH MARY/SHOW ME	1.25	2.00
☐ 423		MAGIC MIRROR/WITH ALL THAT'S IN ME	1.25	2.00
☐ 617		COME ON AND STOP/NOT AVAILABLE............	1.00	1.50

MARV JOHNSON—ALBUM

☐ 3081 (M)	*UNITED ARTISTS*	MARVELOUS	7.00	12.00

BRUCE JOHNSON
SEE: BRUCE AND TERRY

☐ 1003	*RONDA*	DO THE SURFER STOMP (PT. 1)/(PT. 11)	3.50	6.00
☐ 1354	*DONNA*	DO THE SURFER STOMP (PT. 1)/(PT. 11)	2.50	4.00
☐ 4202	*DEL-FI*	THE ORIGINAL SURFER STOMP/PAJAMA PARTY ...	2.50	4.00

ISSUE #	LABEL	ARTIST/TITLE	VG	MINT
		BRUCE JOHNSON—ALBUMS		
☐1228 (M)	*DEL-FI*	SURFER'S PAJAMA PARTY	7.00	12.00
☐1228 (S)		SURFER'S PAJAMA PARTY	8.00	15.00
☐2057 (M)	*COLUMBIA*	SURFIN' AROUND THE WORLD	8.00	15.00
☐8857 (S)		SURFIN' AROUND THE WORLD	12.00	20.00
		DAVY JONES		
		SEE: MONKEES		
☐764	*COLPIX*	DREAM GIRL/TAKE ME TO PARADISE	2.00	3.50
☐784		WHAT ARE WE GOING TO DO?/ THIS BOUQUET (93)	1.50	2.50
☐789		GIRL FROM CHELSEA/THEME FOR A NEW LOVE	1.75	3.00
		DAVY JONES—ALBUM		
☐493 (M)	*COLPIX*	DAVID JONES	5.00	8.00
		JIMMY JONES		
☐210	*RAMA*	PLAIN OLD LOVE/LOVER	3.00	5.00
☐9049	*CUB*	HANDY MAN/THE SEARCH IS OVER (2)	1.25	2.50
☐9067		GOOD TIMIN'/MY PRECIOUS ANGEL (3)	1.25	2.50
☐9072		THAT'S WHEN I CRIED/I JUST GO FOR YOU (83)	1.75	2.50
☐9076		ITCHIN'/EE-I-EE-OH	1.50	2.50
☐9082		FOR YOU/READY FOR LOVE	1.50	2.50
☐9085		I TOLD YOU SO/YOU GOT IT (85)	1.50	2.50
☐9093		DEAR ONE/I SAY LOVE	1.50	2.50
☐9102		MR. MUSIC MAN/HOLLER HEY	1.50	2.50
☐9110		YOU'RE MUCH TOO YOUNG/NIGHTS OF MEXICO	1.50	2.50
		JIMMY JONES—ALBUM		
☐3847 (M)	*MGM*	GOOD TIMIN'	12.00	20.00
☐3847 (S)		GOOD TIMIN'	15.00	25.00
		JOE JONES		
☐488	*HERALD*	YOU DONE ME WRONG/WHEN YOUR HAIR HAS TURNED TO SILVER	2.50	4.00
☐972	*RIC*	YOU TALK TOO MUCH/I LOVE YOU STILL	1.50	3.00
☐4304	*ROULETTE*	YOU TALK TOO MUCH/I LOVE YOU STILL (3)	1.00	2.50
☐4344		CALIFORNIA SUN/PLEASE DON'T TALK ABOUT ME (89)	1.50	2.50
☐4377		THE BIG MULE/UH UH WIFE	1.25	2.00
		JOE JONES—ALBUM		
☐25143 (M)	*ROULETTE*	YOU TALK TOO MUCH	6.00	10.00
☐25143 (S)		YOU TALK TOO MUCH	7.00	12.00
		JUMPIN' TONES		
☐8004	*RAVEN*	I HAD A DREAM/I WONDER	8.00	15.00
☐8005		THAT ANGEL IS YOU/GRANDMA'S HEARING AID	12.00	20.00
		BILL JUSTIS		
☐3519	*PHILLIPS INTERNATIONAL*	RAUNCHY/MIDNIGHT MAN (3)	1.25	3.00
☐3522		COLLEGE MAN/THE STRANGER (42)	1.50	3.00
☐3525		SCROUNGIE/WILD RICE	1.75	3.00
☐3529		SUMMER HOLIDAY/CATTYWAMPUS	1.75	3.00
☐3535		BOP TRAIN/STRING OF PEARLS	1.75	3.00
☐3544		CLOUD NINE/FLEA CIRCUS	1.75	3.00
		BILL JUSTIS—ALBUM		
☐1950 (M)	*PHILLIPS INTERNATIONAL*	CLOUD NINE	8.00	15.00

K

ISSUE #	LABEL	ARTIST/TITLE	VG	MINT
		KALIN TWINS		
☐30552	*DECCA*	JUMPIN' JACK/WALKIN' TO SCHOOL	1.75	3.00
☐30642		WHEN/THREE O'CLOCK THRILL (5)	1.25	3.00
☐30745		FORGET ME NOT/DREAM OF ME (12)	1.50	3.00
☐30807		IT'S ONLY THE BEGINNING/OH! MY GOODNESS! (42)	1.50	2.50
☐30868		WHEN I LOOK IN THE MIRROR/COOL	1.50	2.50
☐30911		SWEET SUGAR LIPS/MOODY (97)	1.50	2.50
☐30977		THE MEANING OF THE BLUES/ WHY DON'T YOU BELIEVE ME?	1.25	2.00
☐31064		LONELINESS/CHICKEN THIEF	1.25	2.00
		KALIN TWINS—EPs		
☐2623	*DECCA*	WHEN	4.00	7.00
☐2641		FORGET ME NOT	4.50	8.00
		KALIN TWINS—ALBUM		
☐8812 (M)	*DECCA*	KALIN TWINS	5.00	9.00
☐78812 (S)		KALIN TWINS	7.00	12.00
		PAUL KANE (PAUL SIMON)		
☐128	*TRIBUTE*	HE WAS MY BROTHER/CARLOS DOMINGUEZ	12.00	20.00
		ERNIE K-DOE		
☐1050	*EMBER*	TUFF-ENUFF/MY LOVE FOR YOU (Ernie Kado)	1.75	3.00
☐1075		SHIRLEY'S TUFF/MY LOVE FOR YOU (Ernie Kado)	1.75	3.00
☐623	*MINIT*	MOTHER-IN-LAW/WANTED: $10,000 REWARD (1)	1.00	2.50
☐627		TE-TA-TE-TA-TA/REAL MAN (53)	1.50	2.50
☐634		I CRIED MY LAST TEAR/A CERTAIN GIRL (69)	1.50	2.50
☐641		POPEYE JOE/COME ON HOME (90)	1.50	2.50
☐645		HEY, HEY, HEY/I LOVE YOU THE BEST	1.25	2.00
☐651		I GOT TO FIND SOMEBODY/BEATING LIKE A TOM-TOM	1.25	2.00
☐656		GET OUT OF MY HOUSE/LOVING YOU	1.25	2.00
☐661		EASIER SAID THAN DONE/BE SWEET	1.25	2.00
		ERNIE K-DOE—ALBUM		
☐0002 (M)	*MINIT*	MOTHER-IN-LAW	7.00	12.00
		KEITH		
☐72596	*MERCURY*	AIN'T GONNA LIE/IT STARTED ALL OVER AGAIN (39)	1.25	2.50
☐72639		98.6/TEENIE BOPPER SONG (7)	1.00	2.00
☐72652		TELL ME TO MY FACE/PRETTY LITTLE SHY ONE (37)	1.25	2.00
☐72695		DAYLIGHT SAVIN' TIME/ HAPPY WALKING AROUND (79)	1.25	2.00
☐72715		SUGAR MAN/EASY AS PIE	1.25	2.00
☐72746		CANDY, CANDY/I'M SO PROUD	1.25	2.00
☐72794		THE PLEASURE OF YOUR COMPANY/HURRY	1.25	2.00
		KEITH—ALBUMS		
☐21102 (M)	*MERCURY*	98.6/AIN'T GONNA LIE	3.00	5.00
☐61102 (S)		98.6/AIN'T GONNA LIE	4.00	7.00
☐21129 (M)		OUT OF CRANK	3.00	5.00
☐61129 (S)		OUT OF CRANK	4.00	7.00
		JERRY KELLER		
☐277	*KAPP*	HERE COMES SUMMER/TIME HAS A WAY (14)	1.25	2.50
☐310		THERE ARE SUCH THINGS/NOW, NOW, NOW	1.25	2.00

ISSUE #	LABEL	ARTIST/TITLE	VG	MINT
☐ 322		AMERICAN BEAUTY ROSE/LONESOME LULLABY ...	1.25	2.00
☐ 337		WHITE FOR YOU AND BLUES FOR ME/		
		MY NAME AIN'T JOE	1.25	2.00

JERRY KELLER—ALBUM

☐ 1178 (M)	*KAPP*	HERE COMES SUMMER	5.00	9.00
☐ 3178 (S)		HERE COMES SUMMER	7.00	12.00

KELLY FOUR
GUITAR: EDDIE COCHRAN

☐ 1001	*SILVER*	STROLLIN' GUITAR/GUYBO..................	2.50	4.00
☐ 1006		ANNIE HAD A PARTY/SO FINE, BE MINE	2.50	4.00

KENJOLAIRS

☐ 704	*A & M*	LITTLE WHITE LIES/THE STORY OF		
		AN EVERGREEN TREE......................	1.50	2.50
☐ 708		SUCH A GOOD NIGHT FOR DREAMING/		
		WHEN IT COMES TO LOVING YOU	1.25	2.00

CHRIS KENNER

☐ 5448	*IMPERIAL*	SICK AND TIRED/NOTHING WILL KEEP ME FROM YOU .	2.50	4.00
☐ 3229	*INSTANT*	I LIKE IT LIKE THAT (PT. 1)/(PT. 11) (2)	1.00	2.50
☐ 3234		PACKIN' UP/VERY TRUE STORY	1.25	2.00
☐ 3237		SOMETHING YOU GOT/COME SEE ABOUT ME	1.25	2.00
☐ 3252		LAND OF 1,000 DANCES/THAT'S MY GIRL (77)	1.25	2.00

KENNY AND THE CADETS (BEACH BOYS)

☐ 422	*RANDY*	BARBIE/WHAT IS A YOUNG GIRL MADE OF		
		(colored wax)	80.00	150.00
☐ 422		BARBIE/WHAT IS A YOUNG GIRL MADE OF		
		(black wax)	50.00	80.00

KENNY AND THE BEACH FIENDS

☐ 871	*POSAE*	HOUSE ON HAUNTED HILL/THE GREEN DOOR......	3.00	5.00

JOHNNY KIDD AND THE PIRATES

☐ 25040	*APT*	SHAKIN' ALL OVER/YES SIR,		
		THAT'S MY BABY	2.50	4.00
☐ 5065	*CAPITOL*	THEN I GOT EVERYTHING/I'LL NEVER GET OVER YOU .	1.75	3.00

CAROLE KING
SEE: CITY, BERTELL DACHE, GERMZ, PALISADES

☐ 9921	*ABC-*			
	PARAMOUNT	GOIN' WILD/THE RIGHT GIRL	12.00	20.00
☐ 9986		BABY SITTIN'/UNDER THE STARS	12.00	20.00
☐ 7560	*RCA*	QUEEN OF THE BEACH/SHORT MORT	8.00	15.00
☐ 57	*ALPINE*	OH NEIL!/A VERY SPECIAL BOY	15.00	25.00
☐ 2000	*COMPANION*	IT MIGHT AS WELL RAIN UNTIL SEPTEMBER/		
		NOBODY'S PERFECT......................	12.00	20.00
☐ 2000	*DIMENSION*	IT MIGHT AS WELL RAIN UNTIL SEPTEMBER/		
		NOBODY'S PERFECT (22)	1.50	3.00
☐ 1004		SCHOOL BELLS ARE RINGING/I DID'NT HAVE ANY ..	4.00	7.00
☐ 1009		HE'S A BAD BOY/WE GROW UP TOGETHER (94)	3.00	5.00
☐ 7502	*TOMORROW*	A ROAD TO NOWHERE/SOME OF YOUR LOVIN'	6.00	10.00

ISSUE #	LABEL	ARTIST/TITLE	VG	MINT
		KING CROONERS		
□2168	*EXCELLO*	NOW THAT SHE'S GONE/WON'T YOU LET ME KNOW	7.00	12.00
□2187		MEMORIES/SCHOOL DAZE	6.00	10.00
		JONATHAN KING		
□9774	*PARROT*	EVERYONE'S GONE TO THE MOON/ SUMMER'S COMING (17)	1.25	2.50
□9804		WHERE THE SUN HAS NEVER SHONE/ GREEN IS THE GRASS (97)	1.50	2.50
□3005		JUST LIKE A WOMAN/LAND OF THE GOLDEN TREE	1.75	3.00
□3008		ICICLES/IN A HUNDRED YEARS FROM NOW	1.50	2.50
□3011		ROUND ROUND/TIME AND MOTION	1.75	3.00
		JONATHAN KING—ALBUM		
□61013 (M)	*PARROT*	OR THEN AGAIN	3.00	5.00
□71013 (S)		OR THEN AGAIN	4.00	7.00
		KING LIZARD (KIM FOWLEY)		
□99	*ORIGINAL SOUND*	BIG BAD CADILLAC/MAN WITHOUT A COUNTRY	2.50	4.00
		KINGSMEN		
□108	*JALYNNE*	LADY'S CHOICE/DIG THIS	3.00	5.00
□712	*JERDEN*	LOUIE LOUIE/HAUNTED CASTLE	8.00	15.00
□143	*WAND*	LOUIE LOUIE/HAUNTED CASTLE (2)	1.00	2.00
□150		MONEY/BENT SCEPTER (16)	1.25	2.00
□157		LITTLE LATIN LUPE LU/DAVID'S MOOD (46)	1.25	2.00
□164		DEATH OF AN ANGEL/SEARCHING FOR LOVE (42)	1.25	2.00
□172		THE JOLLY GREEN GIANT/LONG GREEN (4)	.75	2.00
□183		THE CLIMB/I'M WAITING (65)	1.25	2.00
□189		ANNIE FANNY/GIVE HER LOVIN' (47)	1.25	2.00
□1107		THE GAMMA GOOCHEE/IT'S ONLY THE DOG	1.25	2.00
□1115		KILLER JOE/LITTLE GREEN THING (77)	1.25	2.00
		LATER WAND SINGLES ARE WORTH UP TO $1.50 MINT		
		KINGSMEN—ALBUMS		
□657 (M)	*WAND*	IN PERSON	4.00	7.00
□659 (M)		VOLUME 2	3.50	6.00
□662 (M)		VOLUME 3	3.50	6.00
□670 (M)		ON CAMPUS	3.00	5.00
□674 (M)		16 GREATEST HITS	3.00	5.00
		KINGSMEN		
		FEATURED: BILL HALEY'S COMETS		
□115	*EAST WEST*	WEEKEND/BETTER BELIEVE IT (84)	2.00	3.50
□120		THE CAT WALK/CONGA ROCK	1.75	3.00
		KINKS		
□308	*CAMEO*	LONG TALL SALLY/I TOOK MY BABY HOME	35.00	60.00
□345		LONG TALL SALLY/I TOOK MY BABY HOME	20.00	30.00
□0306	*REPRISE*	YOU REALLY GOT ME/IT'S ALL RIGHT (7)	1.25	2.50
□0334		ALL DAY AND ALL OF THE NIGHT/I GOTTA MOVE (7)	1.25	2.50
□0347		TIRED OF WAITING FOR YOU/COME ON NOW (6)	1.25	2.50
□0366		WHO'LL BE THE NEXT IN LINE?/ EVERYBODY IS GONNA BE HAPPY (34)	1.50	2.50
□0379		SET ME FREE/I NEED YOU (23)	1.50	2.50
□0409		SEE MY FRIENDS/NEVER MET A GIRL LIKE YOU BEFORE	1.75	3.00

ISSUE #	LABEL	ARTIST/TITLE	VG	MINT
□0420		A WELL RESPECTED MAN/SUCH A SHAME (13)	1.25	2.50
□0454		TILL THE END OF THE DAY/WHERE HAVE ALL THE GOOD TIMES GONE (50)	1.50	2.50
□0471		DEDICATED FOLLOWER OF FASHION/ SITTING ON MY SOFA (36)	1.50	2.50
□0497		SUNNY AFTERNOON/I'M NOT LIKE EVERYONE ELSE (14)	1.25	2.50
□0540		DEADEND STREET/BIG BLACK SMOKE (73)	1.50	2.50
□0587		MR. PLEASANT/HARRY RAG (80)	1.50	2.50
□0612		WATERLOO SUNSET/TWO SISTERS	1.50	2.50
□0647		AUTUMN ALMANAC/DAVID WAITS	1.50	2.50
□0691		WONDERBOY/POLLY	1.50	2.50
□0743		LOLA/APEMAN	2.50	4.00
□0762		SHE'S GOT EVERYTHING/DAYS	1.50	2.50
□0806		STARSTRUCK/PICTURE BOOK	1.50	2.50
□0847		VILLAGE GREEN PRESERVATION SOCIETY/WALTER	1.50	2.50
□0863		VICTORIA/BRAINWASHED (62)	1.50	2.50
□0930		LOLA/MINDLESS CHILD OF MOTHERHOOD (9)	1.00	2.00
□0979		APEMAN/RATA (45)	1.25	2.00

LATER REPRISE SINGLES ARE WORTH UP TO $2.00 MINT

KINKS—ALBUMS

ISSUE #	LABEL	ARTIST/TITLE	VG	MINT
□6143 (M)	***REPRISE***	YOU REALLY GOT ME	6.00	10.00
□6143 (S)		YOU REALLY GOT ME	7.00	12.00
□6158 (M)		KINKS SIZE	5.00	8.00
□6158 (S)		KINKS SIZE	6.00	10.00
□6173 (M)		KINDA KINKS	5.00	8.00
□6173 (S)		KINDA KINKS	6.00	10.00
□6184 (M)		KINKDOM	3.50	6.00
□6184 (S)		KINKDOM	4.50	8.00
□6197 (M)		KINK KONTROVERSY	3.50	6.00
□6197 (S)		KINK KONTROVERSY	4.50	8.00
□6217 (M)		THE KINK'S GREATEST HITS	3.50	6.00
□6217 (S)		THE KINK'S GREATEST HITS	4.50	8.00

KNICKERBOCKERS

ISSUE #	LABEL	ARTIST/TITLE	VG	MINT
□59268	***CHALLENGE***	BITE BITE BARRACUDA/ALL I NEED IS YOU	1.75	3.00
□59293		JERKTOWN/ROOM FOR ONE MORE	1.50	2.50
□59321		LIES/THE COMING GENERATION (20)	1.00	2.00
□59326		ONE TRACK MIND/I MUST BE DOING SOMETHING RIGHT (46)	1.25	2.00
□59332		HIGH ON LOVE/STICK WITH ME (94)	1.25	2.00
□59335		CHAPEL IN THE FIELDS/JUST ONE GIRL	1.25	2.00
□59341		RUMORS, GOSSIP, WORDS UNTRUE/LOVE IS A BIRD	1.25	2.00

LATER CHALLENGE SINGES ARE WORTH UP TO $1.50 MINT

KNICKERBOCKERS—ALBUM

ISSUE #	LABEL	ARTIST/TITLE	VG	MINT
□622 (M)	***CHALLENGE***	LIES	3.50	6.00
□622 (S)		LIES	4.50	8.00

SONNY KNIGHT

ISSUE #	LABEL	ARTIST/TITLE	VG	MINT
□137	***VITA***	CONFIDENTIAL/JAIL BIRD	6.00	10.00
□15507	***DOT***	CONFIDENTIAL/JAIL BIRD (20)	1.50	3.00
□1	***STARLA***	DEDICATED TO YOU/SHORT WALK	2.50	4.00

ISSUE #	LABEL	ARTIST/TITLE	VG	MINT
		KNIGHTS		
☐5302	*CAPITOL*	HOT ROD HIGH/THEME FOR TEEN LOVE	2.00	3.50
		KNIGHTS—ALBUM		
☐2189 (M)	*CAPITOL*	HOT ROD HIGH	5.00	8.00
☐2189 (S)		HOT ROD HIGH	6.00	10.00

BUDDY KNOX

Happy, Texas? Yes, that was the birthplace of Buddy Knox on April 14, 1933. He became interested in music while a student at West Texas State College. He formed a college trio which included classmates Jimmy Bowen ("I'm Stickin' With You") and Donnie Lanier. As a trio they enjoyed local success. Later they added a drummer, a local disc jockey named Dave Alfred.

As the Rhythm Orchids the trio recorded two original songs at Norman Petty's New Mexico studio. The songs were then released on the small Triple D label but nothing happened. Newly formed Roulette Records in New York then bought the master tape and released both sides of the Triple D single. Knox's "Party Doll" hit No. 2 on the national charts. (Bowen's made the Top 20.) Buddy's hit won him an appearance on Ed Sullivan's television show and a cameo appearance in the movie "Jamboree".

Knox's Roulette hits later subsided, and then he signed with Liberty Records. There he saw strong sales with a cover version of the Clovers' "Lovey Dovey". Buddy later signed with other labels but found no commercial success.

ISSUE #	LABEL	ARTIST/TITLE	VG	MINT
		BUDDY KNOX		
□797	***TRIPLE D***	PARTY DOLL/I'M STICKIN' WITH YOU (Jimmy Bowen)	30.00	50.00
□4002	***ROULETTE***	PARTY DOLL/MY BABY'S GONE (2)	1.75	3.50
□4009		ROCK YOUR LITTLE BABY TO SLEEP/ DON'T MAKE ME CRY (23)	1.50	3.00
□4018		HULA LOVE/DEVIL WOMAN (12)	1.25	2.50
□4042		SWINGIN' DADDY/WHENEVER I'M LONELY (80)	1.50	2.50
□4082		SOMEBODY TOUCHED ME/C'MON BABY (22)	1.25	2.50
□4120		TEASABLE, PLEASABLE YOU/THAT'S WHY I CRY (85)	1.50	2.50
□4140		I THINK I'M GONNA KILL MYSELF/ TO BE WITH YOU (55)	1.50	2.50
□4179		I AIN'T SHARIN' SHARON/TASTE OF THE BLUES	1.50	2.50
□4262		LONG LONELY NIGHTS/STORM CLOUDS	1.50	2.50
□55290	***LIBERTY***	LOVEY DOVEY/I GOT YOU (25)	1.25	2.50
□55305		LING-TING-TONG/THE KISSES (65)	1.50	2.50
□55366		ALL BY MYSELF/THREE-EYED MAN	1.25	2.00
		LATER LIBERTY SINGLES ARE WORTH UP TO $1.50 MINT		
		BUDDY KNOX—EP		
□301	***ROULETTE***	BUDDY KNOX	7.00	12.00
		BUDDY KNOX—ALBUMS		
□25003 (M)	***ROULETTE***	BUDDY KNOX	20.00	30.00
□3251 (M)	***LIBERTY***	GOLDEN HITS	5.00	8.00
□7251 (S)		GOLDEN HITS	6.00	10.00
		KODOKS		
□1007	***FURY***	TEENAGER'S DREAM/LITTLE GIRL AND BOY	6.00	10.00
□1015		MAKE BELIEVE WORLD/OH GEE, OH GOSH	5.00	8.00
□1019		MY BABY AND ME/KINGLESS CASTLE	6.00	10.00
□1020		GUARDIAN ANGEL/RUNAROUND BABY	5.00	8.00
□1683	***J & S***	DON'T WANT NO TEASING/LOOK UP TO THE SKY	3.50	6.00
□1004	***WINK***	LET'S ROCK/TWISTA TWISTIN'	2.50	4.00
□1006		LOVE WOULDN'T MEAN A THING/MISTER MAGOO	3.50	6.00
		BILLY J. KRAMER AND THE DAKOTAS		
□55586	***LIBERTY***	DO YOU WANT TO KNOW A SECRET?/ I'LL BE ON MY WAY	3.00	5.00
□55626		BAD TO ME/I CALL YOUR NAME	2.50	4.00

ISSUE #	LABEL	ARTIST/TITLE	VG	MINT
☐ 55643		I'LL KEEP YOU SATISFIED/I KNOW	2.50	4.00
☐ 55667		DO YOU WANT TO KNOW A SECRET?/BAD TO ME . . .	1.75	3.00
☐ 66027	*IMPERIAL*	LITTLE CHILDREN/BAD TO ME (7)	1.00	2.50
☐ 66048		I'LL KEEP YOU SATISFIED/I KNOW (30)	1.25	2.50
☐ 66051		FROM A WINDOW/I'LL BE ON MY WAY (23)	1.25	2.50
☐ 66085		IT'S GOTTA LAST FOREVER/		
		THEY REMIND ME OF YOU (67)	1.50	2.50
☐ 66115		TRAINS AND BOATS AND PLANES/		
		THAT'S THE WAY I FEEL (42)	1.50	2.50
☐ 66135		IRRESISTABLE YOU/TWILIGHT TIME	1.50	2.50
☐ 66143		I'LL BE DOGGONE/NEON CITY	1.50	2.50
☐ 66210		TAKE MY HAND/YOU MAKE ME FEEL LIKE SOMEONE .	1.50	2.50
		BILLY J. KRAMER AND THE DAKOTAS—ALBUMS		
☐ 9267 (M)	*IMPERIAL*	LITTLE CHILDREN .	5.00	8.00
☐ 12267 (S)		LITTLE CHILDREN .	6.00	10.00
☐ 9273 (M)		I'LL KEEP YOU SATISFIED	3.50	6.00
☐ 12273 (S)		I'LL KEEP YOU SATISFIED	4.50	8.00
☐ 9291 (M)		TRAINS AND BOATS AND PLANES	3.50	6.00
☐ 12291 (S)		TRAINS AND BOATS AND PLANES	4.50	8.00

KUSTOM KINGS
PRODUCER: BRUCE JOHNSTON

☐ 1883	*SMASH*	CLUTCH RIDER/IN MY '40 FORD	2.50	4.00
		KUSTOM KINGS—ALBUM		
☐ 27051 (M)	*SMASH*	KUSTOM CITY, U.S.A. .	5.00	8.00
☐ 67051 (S)		KUSTOM CITY, U.S.A. .	6.00	10.00

ISSUE #	LABEL	ARTIST/TITLE	VG	MINT

LADDERS

☐ 2611	*HOLIDAY*	COUNTING THE STARS/I WANT TO KNOW	8.00	15.00

DENNY LAINE
SEE: MOODY BLUES

☐ 7509	*DERAM*	ASK THE PEOPLE/SAY YOU DON'T MIND	1.75	3.00
☐ 4340	*CAPITOL*	I'M LOOKIN' FOR SOMEONE TO LOVE/		
		IT'S SO EASY-LISTEN TO ME	1.75	3.00
☐ 4425		HEARTBEAT/MOONDREAMS	1.75	3.00

MAJOR LANCE

☐ 7175	*OKEH*	THE MONKEY TIME/MAMA DIDN'T KNOW (8)	1.00	2.00
☐ 7181		HEY LITTLE GIRL/CRYING IN THE RAIN (13)	1.00	2.00
☐ 7187		UM, UM, UM, UM, UM, UM/SWEET MUSIC (5)	1.00	2.00
☐ 7191		THE MATADOR/GONNA GET MARRIED (20)	1.25	2.00
☐ 7197		GIRLS/IT AIN'T NO USE (68)	1.25	2.00
☐ 7203		RHYTHM/PLEASE DON'T SAY NO MORE (24)	1.00	2.00
☐ 7209		SOMETIMES I WONDER/I'M SO LOST (64)	1.25	2.00
☐ 7216		COME SEE/YOU BELONG TO ME, MY LOVE (40)	1.25	2.00
☐ 7223		AIN'T IT A SHAME/GOTTA GET AWAY (91)	1.25	2.00
☐ 7226		TOO HOT TO HANDLE/DARK AND LONELY (93)	1.25	2.00

ISSUE #	LABEL	ARTIST/TITLE	VG	MINT
		MAJOR LANCE—ALBUMS		
☐ 12105 (M)	*OKEH*	MONKEY TIME	3.50	6.00
☐ 14105 (S)		MONKEY TIME	4.50	8.00
☐ 12106 (M)		UM, UM, UM, UM, UM, UM	3.50	6.00
☐ 14106 (S)		UM, UM, UM, UM, UM, UM	4.50	8.00
☐ 12110 (M)		GREATEST HITS	3.00	5.00
☐ 14110 (S)		GREATEST HITS	4.00	7.00
		JERRY LANDIS (PAUL SIMON)		
☐ 12822	*MGM*	ANNA BELLE/LONELINESS	8.00	15.00
☐ 522	*WARWICK*	SWANEE/TOOT TOOT TOOTSIE GOODBYE	6.00	10.00
☐ 552		JUST A BOY/SHY	5.00	8.00
☐ 588		JUST A BOY/I'D LIKE TO BE	4.00	7.00
☐ 619		PLAY ME A SAD SONG/IT MEANS A LOT TO THEM	3.50	6.00
☐ 130	*CANADIAN-AMERICAN*	I'M LONELY/I WISH I WEREN'T IN LOVE	6.00	10.00
☐ 875	*AMY*	THE LONELY TEEN RANGER/LISA (97)	4.00	7.00
		LARRY AND MIKE		
☐ 500	*PICADILLY*	QUEEN OF THE STARLIGHT DANCE/ WE FELL IN LOVE	2.50	4.00
		LAUGHING GRAVY		
		PRODUCER: DEAN TORRENCE		
☐ 261	*WHITE WHALE*	VEGETABLES/SNOW FLAKES	5.00	8.00
		ROD LAUREN		
☐ 7645	*RCA*	IF I HAD A GIRL/NO WONDER (31)	1.25	2.50
☐ 8020		WONDROUS PLACE/I DREAMED	1.50	2.50
☐ 1126	*CHANCELLOR*	I AIN'T GOT YOU/MEXICALI ROSE	1.25	2.00
☐ 1132		OH HOW I MISS YOU TONIGHT/ BLAME YOUR FRIENDS	1.25	2.00
☐ 1136		YESTERDAY'S LOVERS/I KNOW	1.25	2.00
☐ 1141		I WANNA KNOW/SEARCHER FOR LOVE	1.25	2.00
☐ 1146		LET ME TELL YOU 'BOUT MY BABY/ I CAN'T GET YOU OUT OF MY HEART	1.25	2.00
		ROD LAUREN—ALBUM		
☐ 2176 (M)	*RCA*	I'M ROD LAUREN	3.50	6.00
☐ 2176 (S)		I'M ROD LAUREN	4.50	8.00
		LINDA LAURIE		
☐ 290	*GLORY*	AMBROSE (PART 5)/OOH! WHAT A LOVER! (52)	1.75	3.00
☐ 294		FOREVER AMBROSE/WHEREVER HE GOES, I GO	2.00	3.50
		LEAVES		
☐ 207	*MIRA*	HEY JOE, WHERE YOU GONNA GO?/BE WITH YOU	2.50	4.00
☐ 213		YOU BETTER MOVE ON/A DIFFERENT STORY	2.00	3.50
☐ 222		HEY JOE/FUNNY LITTLE WORLD (31)	1.50	3.00
☐ 227		GIRL FROM THE EAST/TOO MANY PEOPLE	1.50	2.50
☐ 231		GIRL FROM THE EAST/GET OUT OF MY LIFE, WOMAN	1.25	2.50
		LEAVES—ALBUM		
☐ 3005 (M)	*MIRA*	HEY JOE	5.00	8.00
☐ 3005 (S)		HEY JOE	6.00	10.00

ISSUE #	LABEL	ARTIST/TITLE	VG	MINT
		LED ZEPPELIN		
		SEE: YARDBIRDS		
□2613	***ATLANTIC***	GOOD TIMES BAD TIMES/ COMMUNICATION BREAKDOWN (80)	2.50	4.00
□2690		WHOLE LOTTA LOVE/LIVING LOVING MAID (4)	1.00	2.00
□2777		IMMIGRANT SONG/HEY HEY, WHAT CAN I DO (16)	1.25	2.00
□2849		BLACK DOG/MISTY MOUNTAIN HOP (15)	1.25	2.00
□2865		ROCK AND ROLL/FOUR STICKS (47)	1.25	2.50
□2970		OVER THE HILLS AND FAR AWAY/ DANCING DAYS (51)	1.25	2.50
□2986		D'YER MAKER/THE CRUNGE (20)	1.00	2.00
□PR 175		STAIRWAY TO HEAVEN/STAIRWAY TO HEAVEN (dj release)	12.00	20.00
		BILLY LEE AND THE RIVIERAS		
		SEE: MITCH RYDER AND THE DETROIT WHEELS		
□3016	***HYLAND***	WON'T YOU DANCE WITH ME/YOU KNOW	3.50	6.00

BRENDA LEE

Brenda Mae Tarpley has been singing since she was four. (She was born December 11, 1944.) At the age of six she won top honors in a children's talent contest in her hometown of Atlanta, Georgia. That win aided her in getting a regular television show in the area.

The Tarpley family later moved to Augusta, Georgia. Brenda then began singing on a local radio station. When country singing star Red Foley came to Augusta on tour, Brenda met him and showed off her singing skills. Foley was overwhelmed by the little girl's skills and gusto and asked her to open his stage show for him.

When she entered her teens, Brenda began appearing on the "Ozark Jubilee" television show. Shortly thereafter Brenda Lee (her recording name was taken from the final syllable of her last name) earned minor chart success with "One Step At A Time", and her next single ("Dynamite") gave her the nickname of "Little Miss Dynamite".

As the 1960s began, Brenda experienced her first smash hit—"Sweet Nothin's". On the charts for half a year, "Sweet Nothin's" proved to be the first of ten Top 10 single winners, two of which went all the way to No. 1.

☐ 107 **JERRY LEE LEWIS—*THE GREAT BALL OF FIRE*** **$10.00**

☐ 1265 ***JERRY LEE'S GREATEST*** **$25.00**

□ 108 **JERRY LEE LEWIS—*(light blue cover—has 4 songs)* $10.00**

□ 109 **JERRY LEE LEWIS—*(yellow cover—has 4 songs)* $10.00**

☐1230 **JERRY LEE LEWIS—*(red cover—has 12 songs)*** **$15.00**

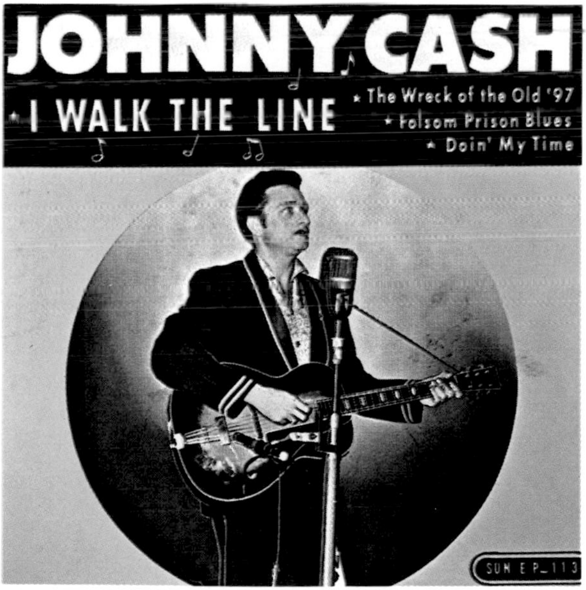

☐113 **JOHNNY CASH—*I WALK THE LINE*** **$7.50**

☐ 112 **JOHNNY CASH** **$7.50**

☐ 1220 **JOHNNY CASH—*HOT AND BLUE GUITAR*** **$10.00**

☐ 1235 **JOHNNY CASH—*THE SONGS THAT MADE HIM FAMOUS*** . **$10.00**

☐ 116 **JOHNNY CASH—*HOME OF THE BLUES*** **$7.50**

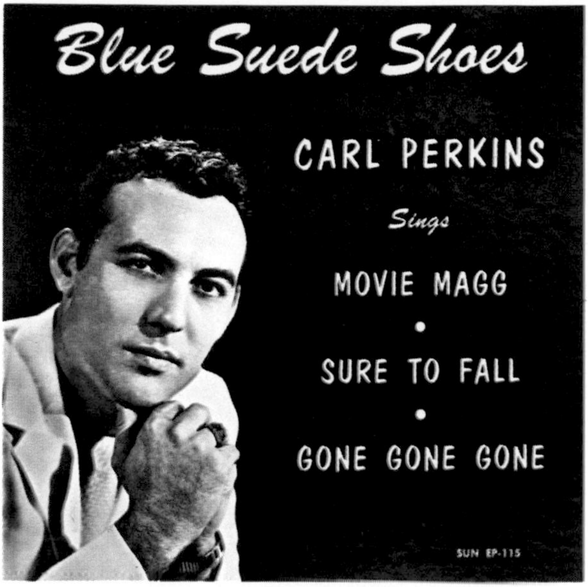

☐ 115 **CARL PERKINS—*BLUE SUEDE SHOES*** **$20.00**

☐ 1225 ***DANCE ALBUM OF CARL PERKINS*** **$100.00**

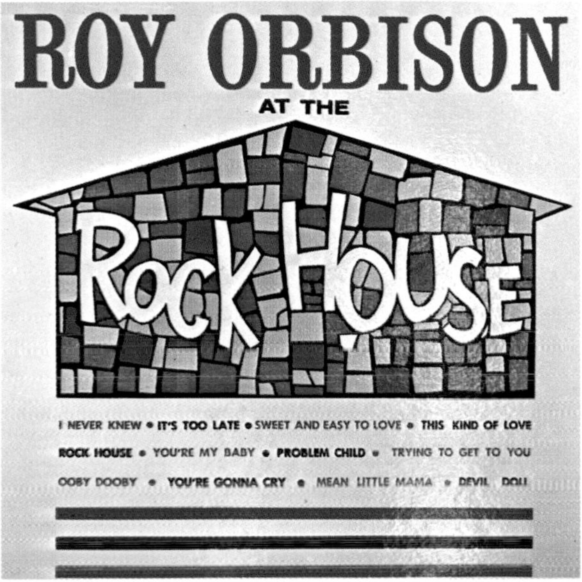

☐ 1260 ***ROY ORBISON AT THE ROCKHOUSE*** **$20.00**

☐ 1960 **CARL MANN—*LIKE MANN*** **20.00**

☐ 1950 **BILL JUSTIS—*CLOUD 9*** $15.00

☐ 1970 **CHARLIE RICH—*LONELY WEEKENDS*** $35.00

☐ 3532 **CHARLIE RICH—*WHIRLWIND*** **$6.00**

☐ 3559 **THE HAWK—*IN THE MOOD*** **$9.00**

□ 234 **CARL PERKINS—*BLUE SUEDE SHOES*** **$4.00**

□ 224 **CARL PERKINS—*GONE, GONE, GONE*** **$35.00**

☐ 209 **ELVIS PRESLEY—*THAT'S ALL RIGHT*** **$200.00**

☐ 210 **ELVIS PRESLEY—*GOOD ROCKIN' TONIGHT*** **$150.00**

☐223 **ELVIS PRESLEY—*MYSTERY TRAIN*** **$120.00**

☐215 **ELVIS PRESLEY—*MILKCOW BLUES BOOGIE*** **$200.00**

☐217 **ELVIS PRESLEY—*BABY LET'S PLAY HOUSE*** **$120.00**

☐211 **MALCOLM YELVINGTON—*DRINKIN' WINE SPODEE-O-DEE*** . . **$20.00**

☐300 **TOMMY BLAKE—*SWEETIE PIE*** **$100.00**

☐260 **BILLY RILEY—*FLYIN' SAUCERS ROCK & ROLL*** **$15.00**

☐ 281 **JERRY LEE LEWIS—*GREAT BALLS OF FIRE*** **$3.00**

☐ 267 **JERRY LEE LEWIS—*WHOLE LOT OF SHAKIN' GOING ON*** . . . **$3.00**

□242 **ROY ORBISON—*OOBY DOOBY*** **$8.00**

□251 **ROY ORBISON—*ROCKHOUSE*** **$8.00**

ISSUE #	LABEL	ARTIST/TITLE	VG	MINT
		BRENDA LEE		
☐30050	*DECCA*	JAMBALAYA/BIGELOW-6200	3.50	6.00
☐30107		CHRISTY CHRISTMAS/ I'M GONNA LASSO SANTA CLAUS	3.00	5.00
☐30198		ONE STEP AT A TIME/FAIRYLAND (43)	2.00	4.00
☐30333		DYNAMITE/LOVE YOU 'TIL I DIE (72)	2.50	4.00
☐30411		AIN'T THAT LOVE/ONE TEENAGER TO ANOTHER	2.00	3.50
☐30535		ROCK THE BOP/ROCK-A-BYE BABY BLUES	2.00	3.50
☐30673		RING-A MY PHONE/LITTLE JONAH	2.50	4.00
☐30776		ROCKIN' AROUND THE CHRISTMAS TREE/ PAPA NOEL (14)	1.25	2.50
☐30806		BILL BAILEY WON'T YOU PLEASE COME HOME/ HUMMIN' THE BLUES	2.00	3.50
☐30885		LET'S JUMP THE BROOMSTICK/ SOME OF THESE DAYS	2.00	3.50
☐30967		SWEET NOTHIN'S/WEEP NO MORE MY BABY (4)	1.25	2.50
☐31093		I'M SORRY/THAT'S ALL YOU GOTTA DO (1)	1.25	2.50
☐31149		I WANT TO BE WANTED/JUST A LITTLE (1)	1.25	2.50
☐31195		EMOTIONS/I'M LEARNING ABOUT LOVE (7)	1.00	2.50
☐31231		YOU CAN DEPEND ON ME/IT'S NEVER TOO LATE (6)	1.00	2.50
☐31272		DUM DUM/EVENTUALLY (4)	1.00	2.50
☐31309		FOOL NO. 1/ANYBODY BUT ME (3)	1.00	2.50
☐31348		BREAK IT TO ME GENTLY/SO DEEP (4)	1.00	2.50
☐31379		EVERYBODY LOVES ME BUT YOU/ HERE COMES THAT FEELIN' (6)	1.00	2.50
☐31407		HEART IN HAND/IT STARTED ALL OVER AGAIN (15)	1.00	2.00
☐31424		ALL ALONE AM I/ SAVE ALL YOUR LOVIN' FOR ME (3)	1.00	2.00
☐31454		YOUR USED-TO-BE/SHE'LL NEVER KNOW (32)	1.00	2.00
☐31478		LOSING YOU/HE'S SO HEAVENLY (6)	1.00	2.00
☐31510		MY WHOLE WORLD IS FALLING DOWN/ I WONDER (24)	1.25	2.00
☐31539		THE GRASS IS GREENER/ SWEET IMPOSSIBLE YOU (17)	1.25	2.00
☐31570		AS USUAL/LONELY LONELY LONELY ME (12)	1.25	2.00
☐31599		THINK/THE WAITING GAME (25)	1.25	2.00
☐31628		ALONE WITH YOU/MY DREAMS (48)	1.25	2.00
☐31654		WHEN YOU LOVED ME/ HE'S SURE TO REMEMBER ME (47)	1.25	2.00

LATER DECCA SINGLES ARE WORTH UP TO $2.00 MINT

ISSUE #	LABEL	ARTIST/TITLE	VG	MINT
		BRENDA LEE—EPs		
☐2661	*DECCA*	BRENDA LEE	5.00	8.00
☐2678		SWEET NOTHIN'S	4.00	7.00
☐2682		BRENDA LEE	3.50	6.00
☐2683		I'M SORRY	3.50	6.00
☐2702		BRENDA LEE	3.00	5.00
☐2704		LOVER, COME BACK TO ME	3.00	5.00
☐2712		BRENDA LEE	3.00	5.00
☐2716		BRENDA LEE	3.00	5.00
☐2725		EVERYBODY LOVES ME BUT YOU	3.00	5.00

ISSUE #	LABEL	ARTIST/TITLE	VG	MINT
		BRENDA LEE—ALBUMS		
☐4039 (M)	*DECCA*	BRENDA LEE	8.00	15.00
☐4082 (M)		THIS IS BRENDA	6.00	10.00
☐4082 (S)		THIS IS BRENDA	7.00	12.00
☐4104 (M)		EMOTIONS	5.00	8.00
☐4104 (S)		EMOTIONS	6.00	10.00
☐4176 (M)		ALL THE WAY	3.50	6.00
☐4176 (S)		ALL THE WAY	4.50	8.00
☐4216 (M)		SINCERELY, BRENDA LEE	3.50	6.00
☐4216 (S)		SINCERELY, BRENDA LEE	4.50	8.00
☐4326 (M)		THAT'S ALL	3.50	6.00
☐4326 (S)		THAT'S ALL	4.50	6.00
☐4370 (M)		ALL ALONE AM I	3.50	6.00
☐4370 (S)		ALL ALONE AM I	4.50	8.00
☐4439 (M)		LET ME SING	3.00	5.00
☐4439 (S)		LET ME SING	4.00	7.00
☐4509 (M)		BY REQUEST	3.00	5.00
☐4509 (S)		BY REQUEST	4.00	7.00
☐4583 (M)		MERRY CHRISTMAS FROM BRENDA LEE	3.00	5.00
☐4583 (S)		MERRY CHRISTMAS FROM BRENDA LEE	4.00	7.00
☐4626 (M)		TOP TEEN HITS	3.00	5.00
☐4626 (S)		TOP TEEN HITS	4.00	7.00

CURTIS LEE

SEE: C. L. AND THE PICTURES

ISSUE #	LABEL	ARTIST/TITLE	VG	MINT
☐7	*HOT*	I NEVER KNEW LOVE COULD DO/GOTTA HAVE YOU	6.00	10.00
☐1555	*WARRIOR*	WITH ALL MY HEART/PURE LOVE	5.00	8.00
☐517	*SABRA*	LET'S TAKE A RIDE/I'M ASKING FORGIVENESS	3.50	6.00
☐2001	*DUNES*	SPECIAL LOVE/D- IN LOVE	2.50	4.00
☐2003		PLEDGE OF LOVE/THEN I'LL KNOW	2.00	3.50
☐2007		PRETTY LITTLE ANGEL EYES/GEE HOW I WISH (7)	1.25	2.50
☐2008		UNDER THE MOON OF LOVE/BEVERLY JEAN (46)	1.50	3.00
☐2010		LET'S TAKE A RIDE/I'M ASKING FORGIVENESS	1.50	2.50
☐2012		A NIGHT AT DADDY GEE'S/JUST ANOTHER FOOL	1.50	2.50
☐2015		DOES HE MEAN THAT MUCH TO YOU?/THE WOBBLE	1.50	2.50
☐2017		MARY GO ROUND/AFRAID	1.50	2.50
☐2020		LONELY WEEKENDS/BETTER HIM THAN ME	1.50	2.50
☐2021		PICKIN' UP THE PIECES OF MY HEART/MR. MISTAKER	1.50	2.50
☐2023		THAT'S WHAT'S HAPPENING/I'M SORRY		

DICKIE LEE

SEE: SUN DISCOGRAPHY

ISSUE #	LABEL	ARTIST/TITLE	VG	MINT
☐131	*TAMPA*	STAY TRUE BABY/DREAM BOY	5.00	8.00
☐16087	*DOT*	WHY DON'T YOU WRITE ME?/ LIFE IN A TEENAGE WORLD	2.00	3.50
☐1758	*SMASH*	PATCHES/MORE OR LESS (6)	1.00	2.50
☐1791		I SAW LINDA YESTERDAY/ THE GIRL I CAN'T FORGET (14)	1.25	2.50
☐1808		DON'T WANNA THINK ABOUT PAULA/ JUST A FRIEND (68)	1.50	2.50
☐1822		I GO LONELY/TEN MILLION FACES	1.25	2.00

ISSUE #	LABEL	ARTIST/TITLE	VG	MINT
☐ 1844		SHE WANTS TO BE BOBBY'S GIRL/ THE DAY THE SAWMILL CLOSED DOWN	1.25	2.00
☐ 1871		TO THE AISLE/MOTHER NATURE	1.25	2.00
☐ 1913		ME AND MY TEARDROPS/ONLY TRUST IN ME	1.25	2.00
☐ 102	*TCF HALL*	LAURIE (STRANGE THINGS HAPPEN)/ PARTY DOLL (14)	1.00	2.50
☐ 111		THE GIRL FROM PEYTON PLACE/THE GIRL I USED TO KNOW (73)	1.25	2.00
☐ 118		GOOD GIRL GOIN' BAD/PRETTY WHITE DRESS	1.25	2.00
		DICKIE LEE—ALBUMS		
☐ 27020 (M)	*SMASH*	THE TALE OF PATCHES	3.50	6.00
☐ 67020 (S)		THE TALE OF PATCHES	4.50	8.00
☐ 8001 (M)	*TCF HALL*	LAURIE AND THE GIRL FROM PEYTON PLACE	3.00	5.00
☐ 8001 (S)		LAURIE AND THE GIRL FROM PEYTON PLACE	4.00	7.00
		LEFT BANKE		
☐ 2041	*SMASH*	WALK AWAY RENEE/I HAVEN'T GOT THE NERVE (5)	1.00	2.00
☐ 2074		PRETTY BALLERINA/LAZY DAY (15)	1.25	2.00
☐ 2089		AND SUDDENLY/IVY, IVY	1.25	2.00
☐ 2119		DESIREE/I'VE GOT SOMETHING ON MY MIND (98)	1.25	2.00
☐ 2197		BARTENDERS AND THEIR WIVES/ SHE MAY CALL YOU UP TONIGHT	1.25	2.00
		LEFT BANKE—ALBUMS		
☐ 27088 (M)	*SMASH*	WALK AWAY RENEE	5.00	8.00
☐ 67088 (S)		WALK AWAY RENEE	6.00	10.00
☐ 27113 (M)		TOO	4.00	7.00
☐ 67113 (S)		TOO	5.00	9.00
		LEVON AND THE HAWKS (THE BAND)		
☐ 6383	*ATCO*	THE STONES I THROW/HE DON'T LOVE YOU	3.00	5.00
☐ 6625		GO GO LISA JANE/HE DON'T LOVE YOU	2.50	4.00
		BOBBY LEWIS		
☐ 1002	*BELTONE*	TOSSIN' AND TURNIN'/OH YES, I LOVE YOU (1)	1.00	2.00
☐ 1012		ONE TRACK MIND/ARE YOU READY? (9)	1.25	2.00
☐ 1015		WHAT A WALK/CRY NO MORE (77)	1.25	2.00
☐ 1016		MAMIE IN THE AFTERNOON/YES, OH YES, IT DID	1.50	2.50
☐ 2018		A MAN'S GOTTA BE A MAN/ DAY BY DAY I NEED YOUR LOVE	1.25	2.00
☐ 2023		I'M TOSSIN' AND TURNIN' AGAIN/ NOTHIN' BUT THE BLUES (98)	1.50	2.50
☐ 2026		LONELY TEARDROPS/BOOM A CHICK CHICK	1.50	2.50
☐ 2035		INTERMISSION/NOTHIN' BUT THE BLUES	1.25	2.00
		BOBBY LEWIS—ALBUM		
☐ 4000 (M)	*BELTONE*	TOSSIN' AND TURNIN'	6.00	10.00

JERRY LEE LEWIS

"The Killer" was born in Ferriday, Louisiana, on September 29, 1935. At fourteen he made his professional debut, singing and playing for $9.00 at a local Ford dealer. Early in 1957 Jerry Lee signed with Sun Records. His first release was a plodding "Crazy Arms". The song failed and Lewis was puzzled. A friend then took Jerry Lee aside and convinced him that he should cast off all his inhibitions onstage.

Lewis' second single was the red-hot "Whole Lot Of Shakin' Going On". Jerry Lee Lewis then went on national television and created a furor with his dynamic stage presence and wildly flowing hair. Like "Shakin," Jerry Lee's "Great Balls Of Fire" and "Breathless" became million-sellers.

The career of Jerry Lee Lewis was in high gear by 1958, but news of his marriage (his third at age 22) to his thirteen-year-old cousin virtually ruined his rock-and-roll career. Undaunted, Lewis switched to country music, where today he is a superstar and is selling records almost as fast as he did during those frantic Sun days.

ISSUE #	LABEL	ARTIST/TITLE	VG	MINT
		JERRY LEE LEWIS		
		SEE: SUN DISCORAPHY		
		SEE: THE HAWK		
		JERRY LEE LEWIS—EPs		
□107	***SUN***	JERRY LEE LEWIS: THE GREAT BALL OF FIRE	6.00	10.00
□108		JERRY LEE LEWIS	6.00	10.00
□109		JERRY LEE LEWIS	6.00	10.00
□110		JERRY LEE LEWIS	6.00	10.00
		JERRY LEE LEWIS—ALBUMS		
□1230 (M)	***SUN***	JERRY LEE LEWIS	8.00	15.00
□1265 (M)		JERRY LEE'S GREATEST!	15.00	25.00
		WALLY LEWIS		
□117	***TALLY***	KATHLEEN/DONNA	3.50	6.00
□15705	***DOT***	KATHLEEN/DONNA	1.75	3.00
		LIL' JUNE AND THE JANUARYS		
□4009	***PROFILE***	OH, WHAT A FEELING/OH, MY LOVE	8.00	15.00
		KATHY LINDEN		
□106	***NATIONAL***	IT'S JUST MY LUCK TO BE FIFTEEN/TOUCH OF LOVE	2.50	4.00
□8510	***FELSTED***	BILLY/IF I COULD HOLD YOU IN MY ARMS (12)	1.25	3.00
□8521		YOU'D BE SURPRISED/WHY OH WHY (50)	1.50	3.00
□8554		SOMEBODY LOVES YOU/YOU WALKED INTO MY LIFE	1.75	3.00
□8571		GOODBYE JIMMY GOODBYE/ HEARTACHES AT SWEET SIXTEEN (11)	1.25	3.00
□8587		YOU DON'T KNOW GIRLS/ SO CLOSE TO MY HEART (92)	1.50	3.00
		KATHY LINDEN—ALBUM		
□7501 (M)	***FELSTED***	THAT CERTAIN BOY	8.00	15.00
		LIONS		
□10388	***EVEREST***	NO ONE (NO ONE BUT YOU)/GIGGLES	3.50	6.00
		LITTLE ANTHONY AND THE IMPERIALS		
□1552	***SAVOY***	MUST BE FALLING IN LOVE/YOU	3.00	6.00
□1027	***END***	TEARS ON MY PILLOW/TWO PEOPLE IN THE WORLD (5)	2.50	5.00
□1036		SO MUCH/OH YEAH (87)	2.50	4.00
□1038		THE DIARY/CHA CHA HENRY	2.50	4.00
□1039		WISHFUL THINKING/WHEN YOU WISH UPON A STAR (79)	2.00	3.50
□1047		A PRAYER AND A JUKE BOX/RIVER PATH (81)	2.00	3.50
□1053		I'M ALRIGHT/SO NEAR AND YET SO FAR	2.00	3.50
□1060		SHIMMY, SHIMMY, KO-KO-BOP/ I'M STILL IN LOVE WITH YOU (24)	1.50	3.00
□1067		MY EMPTY ROOM/BAYOU BAYOU BABY (86)	1.50	2.50
□1074		I'M TAKING A VACATION FROM LOVE/ ONLY SYMPATHY	1.50	2.50
□1080		LIMBO (PT. 1)/(PT. 11)	1.50	2.50
□1083		DREAM/FORMULA OF LOVE	1.50	2.50
□1086		PLEASE SAY YOU WANT ME/SO NEAR YET SO FAR	1.50	2.50
□1091		TRAVELING STRANGER/SAY YEAH	1.50	2.50
□1104		A LONELY WAY TO SPEND AN EVENING/DREAM	1.50	2.50

ISSUE #	LABEL	ARTIST/TITLE	VG	MINT
☐ 1104	*DCP*	I'M ON THE OUTSIDE (LOOKING IN)/PLEASE GO (15)	1.25	3.00
☐ 1119		GOIN' OUT OF MY HEAD/		
		MAKE IT EASY ON YOURSELF (6).............	1.25	2.50
☐ 1128		HURT SO BAD/REPUTATION (10)	1.25	2.50
☐ 1136		TAKE ME BACK/OUR SONG (16)	1.25	2.50
☐ 1149		I MISS YOU SO/GET OUT OF MY LIFE (34)	1.50	2.50
☐ 1154		HURT/NEVER AGAIN (51)	1.50	2.50

LITTLE ANTHONY AND THE IMPERIALS—EP

☐ 204	*END*	WE ARE THE IMPERIALS	5.00	8.00

LITTLE ANTHONY AND THE IMPERIALS—ALBUMS

☐ 303 (M)	*END*	WE ARE LITTLE ANTHONY AND THE IMPERIALS	12.00	20.00
☐ 3800 (M)	*DCP*	GOIN' OUT OF MY HEAD......................	3.00	5.00
☐ 6800 (S)		GOIN' OUT OF MY HEAD......................	4.00	7.00
☐ 3801 (M)		I'M ON THE OUTSIDE (LOOKING IN)...........	3.00	5.00
☐ 6801 (S)		I'M ON THE OUTSIDE (LOOKING IN)...........	4.00	7.00
☐ 3809 (M)		THE BEST OF LITTLE ANTHONY AND THE IMPERIALS	3.00	5.00
☐ 6809 (S)		THE BEST OF LITTLE ANTHONY AND THE IMPERIALS	4.00	7.00

LITTLE CAESAR AND THE ROMANS

☐ 4158	*DEL-FI*	THOSE OLDIES BUT GOODIES/FEVER	1.75	3.00
☐ 4158		THOSE OLDIES BUT GOODIES/		
		SHE DON'T WANNA DANCE (9)	1.00	2.00
☐ 4164		HULLY GULLY AGAIN/FRANKIE AND JOHNNY (54)..	1.25	2.50
☐ 4166		MEMORIES OF THOSE OLDIES BUT GOODIES/FEVER	1.50	2.50
☐ 4170		THE TEN COMMANDMENTS OF LOVE/C. C. RIDER ..	1.50	2.50
☐ 4176		POPEYE ONCE MORE/YOYO YO YOYO	1.25	2.00

LITTLE CAESAR AND THE ROMANS—ALBUM

☐ 1218 (M)	*DEL-FI*	MEMORIES OF THOSE OLDIES BUT GOODIES, VOL. 1	7.00	12.00

LITTLE CLYDIE AND THE TEENS

☐ 462	*RPM*	A CASUAL LOOK/OH ME	6.00	10.00

LITTLE DAVID
FEATURED: THE REGENTS

☐ 40	*SYMPHONY*	CALL ON ME/I WANT THE GOOD LIFE	5.00	8.00

LITTLE EVA

☐ 1000	*DIMENSION*	THE LOCO-MOTION/HE IS THE BOY (1)	1.25	2.50
☐ 1003		KEEP YOUR HANDS OFF MY BABY/		
		WHERE DO I GO? (12)	1.25	2.50
☐ 1006		LET'S TURKEY TROT/DOWN HOME (20)	1.50	2.50
☐ 1011		OLD SMOKEY LOCOMOTION/JUST A LITTLE GIRL (48) .	1.50	2.50
☐ 1013		THE TROUBLE WITH BOYS/WHAT I GOTTA DO	1.75	3.00
☐ 1019		PLEASE HURT ME/LET'S START THE PARTY AGAIN .	1.75	3.00
☐ 1021		THE CHRISTMAS SONG/		
		I WISH YOU A MERRY CHRISTMAS	1.50	2.50
☐ 1035		RUN TO HER/MAKIN' WITH THE MAGILLA	1.75	3.00
☐ 1042		WAKE UP JOHN/TAKIN' BACK WHAT I SAID	1.50	2.50
☐ 943	*AMY*	STAND BY ME/THAT'S MY MAN	1.50	2.50

LITTLE EVA—ALBUM

☐ 6000 (M)	*DIMENSION*	LOCOMOTION	7.00	12.00
☐ 6000 (S)		LOCOMOTION	8.00	15.00

ISSUE #	LABEL	ARTIST/TITLE	VG	MINT
		LITTLE JIMMY AND THE TOPS		
□ 102	*V-TONE*	PUPPY LOVE/SAY YOU LOVE ME	6.00	10.00
		LITTLE JOE AND THE THRILLERS		
□ 7075	*OKEH*	THIS I KNOW/LET'S DO THE SLOP	1.75	3.00
□ 7088		PEANUTS/LILLY LOU (23)	1.50	3.00
□ 7094		THE ECHOES KEEP CALLING ME/LONESOME	1.75	3.00
□ 7099		WHAT HAPPENED TO YOUR HALO?/ DON'T LEAVE ME ALONE	1.50	2.50
		LITTLE JOE AND THE THRILLERS—EP		
□ 7198	*EPIC*	LITTLE JOE AND THE THRILLERS	3.50	6.00
		LITTLE LOUIE AND THE LOVERS		
□ 102	*VISCOUNT*	SOMEDAY YOU'LL PAY/NOTHING BUT THE TWO-STEP	3.50	6.00

LITTLE RICHARD

Little Richard (Penniman), a legend in his own time, was born in Macon, Georgia, on December 5, 1932. He was the third in a family of fourteen children. As a youngster Richard sang and danced for coins on Macon street corners. In high school he was the lead singer in his father's church choir.

Winning a 1951 Atlanta talent show, Richard then signed a contract with RCA Records. With no success on that label, he drifted to Houston's Peacock label. Singles there also failed, so Richard returned to his old job—washing dishes at the Macon Greyhound bus depot.

Richard sent a demo tape to Art Rupe, owner of Specialty Records in Los Angeles. Summoned to Specialty, Little Richard recorded "Tutti Fruitti" as his initial single for that label.

Later a close call in an airplane was interpreted by Richard as a sign that rock-and-roll was evil and that he was being punished. Throwing away $20,000 worth of jewelry, Richard quit rock and became a minister. He later resolved his attitude and has returned to the stage as a headliner, belting out his many Specialty hits that have insured his name in the rock hall of fame.

ISSUE #	LABEL	ARTIST/TITLE	VG	MINT
		LITTLE RICHARD		
□4392	***RCA***	TAXI BLUES/EVERY HOUR	40.00	75.00
□4582		GET RICH QUICK/THINKIN' ABOUT MY MOTHER	35.00	60.00
□4722		WHY DID YOU LEAVE ME?/ AIN'T NOTHIN' HAPPENIN'	35.00	60.00
□5025		PLEASE HAVE MERCY ON ME/ I BROUGHT IT ALL ON MYSELF	30.00	50.00
□1616	***PEACOCK***	FOOL AT THE WHEEL/AIN'T THAT GOOD NEWS	12.00	20.00
□1628		RICE, RED BEANS AND TURNIP GREENS/ALWAYS	12.00	20.00
□1658		LITTLE RICHARD'S BOOGIE/ DIRECTLY FROM MY HEART	8.00	15.00
□1673		MAYBE I'M RIGHT/I LOVE MY BABY	0.00	10.00
□561	***SPECIALTY***	TUTTI FRUTTI/I'M JUST A LONELY GUY (21)	2.50	4.00
□572		LONG TALL SALLY/SLIPPIN' AND SLIDIN' (13)	2.00	3.50
□579		RIP IT UP/REDDY TEDDY (27)	2.50	4.00
□584		SHE'S GOT IT/HEEBIE JEEBIES	3.00	5.00
□591		THE GIRL CAN'T HELP IT/ ALL AROUND THE WORLD (49)	2.50	4.00
□598		LUCILLE/SEND ME SOME LOVIN' (27)	2.00	3.00
	FIRST-PRESSES OF THE ABOVE FEATURE A WAVY CENTER LINE			
□606		JENNY JENNY/MISS ANN (14)	1.50	3.00
□611		KEEP A KNOCKIN'/ CAN'T BELIEVE YOU WANNA LEAVE (8)	1.50	3.00
□624		GOOD GOLLY MISS MOLLY/HEY HEY HEY HEY (10)	1.50	3.00
□633		OOH! MY SOUL/TRUE, FINE MAMA (35)	1.50	2.00
□645		BABY FACE/I'LL NEVER LET YOU GO (41)	1.50	2.50
□652		SHE KNOWS HOW TO ROCK/EARLY ONE MORNING	1.50	2.50
□660		BY THE LIGHT OF THE SILVERY MOON/WONDERIN'	1.50	2.50
□664		KANSAS CITY/LONESOME AND BLUE (95)	1.50	2.50
□670		SHAKE A HAND/ALL NIGHT LONG	1.25	2.00
□680		WHOLE LOTTA SHAKIN' GOING ON/MAYBE I'M RIGHT	1.25	2.00
□681		I GOT IT/BABY	1.25	2.00
□686		DIRECTLY FROM MY HEART/THE MOST I CAN OFFER	1.25	2.00
□692		BAMA LAMA BAMA LOO/ANNIE'S BACK (82)	1.25	2.00
□697		KEEP A KNOCKIN'/BAMA LAMA BAMA LOO	1.00	1.50
		LITTLE RICHARD—EPs		
□400	***SPECIALTY***	HERE'S LITTLE RICHARD, VOL. 1	6.00	10.00
□401		HERE'S LITTLE RICHARD, VOL. 2	6.00	10.00
□402		HERE'S LITTLE RICHARD, VOL. 3	6.00	10.00
□403		LITTLE RICHARD, VOL. 1	5.00	8.00
□404		LITTLE RICHARD, VOL. 2	5.00	8.00
□405		LITTLE RICHARD, VOL. 3	5.00	8.00
		LITTLE RICHARD—ALBUMS		
□SP-100 (M)	***SPECIALTY***	HERE'S LITTLE RICHARD (yellow-and-white label)	12.00	20.00
□2100 (M)		HERE'S LITTLE RICHARD (gold label)	5.00	8.00
□2103 (M)		LITTLE RICHARD, VOL. 2	5.00	8.00
□2104 (M)		THE FABULOUS LITTLE RICHARD	5.00	8.00
		LITTLE SUNNY DAY		
□7001	***TANDEM***	LOU-ANN/BABY DOLL	5.00	8.00

ISSUE #	LABEL	ARTIST/TITLE	VG	MINT
		LIVELY ONES		
☐4189	***DEL-FI***	MISERLOU/LIVIN'	1.50	3.00
☐4196		SURF RIDER/SURFER'S LAMENT	1.50	2.50
☐4205		SURFER BOOGIE/RIC-A-TIC	1.50	2.50
☐4210		GOOFY FOOT/HIGH TIDE	1.50	2.50
☐4217		SURF CITY/TELSTAR SURF	1.50	2.50
		LIVELY ONES—ALBUMS		
☐1226 (M)	***DEL-FI***	SURF-RIDER	3.50	6.00
☐1226 (S)		SURF-RIDER	4.50	8.00
☐1231 (M)		SURF DRUMS	3.50	6.00
☐1231 (S)		SURF DRUMS	4.50	8.00
☐1237 (M)		THIS IS SURF CITY	3.50	6.00
☐1237 (S)		THIS IS SURF CITY	4.50	8.00
☐1238 (M)		GREAT SURF HITS	3.00	5.00
☐1238 (S)		GREAT SURF HITS	4.00	7.00
☐1240 (M)		SURFIN' SOUTH OF THE BORDER	3.50	6.00
☐1240 (S)		SURFIN' SOUTH OF THE BORDER	4.50	8.00
		LONNIE AND THE CRISIS		
☐103	***UNIVERSAL***	BELLS IN THE CHAPEL/SANTA TOWN, U.S.A.	6.00	10.00
		LOSERS		
☐711	***PARLEY***	SNAKE EYES/BALBOA PARTY	2.50	4.00
		LOVE		
☐45603	***ELEKTRA***	MY LITTLE RED BOOK/A MESSAGE TO PRETTY (52)	1.50	3.00
☐45605		7 AND 7 IS/NO, FOURTEEN (33)	1.50	2.50
☐45608		ORANGE SKIES/SHE COMES IN COLORS	1.75	3.00
☐45613		REVELATION/QUE VIDA	1.75	3.00
☐45629		ALONE AGAIN OR/A HOUSE IS NOT A MOTEL (99)	1.75	3.00
☐45633		YOUR MIND AND ME BELONG TOGETHER/ LAUGHING STOCK	1.75	3.00
☐45700		ALONE AGAIN OR/A HOUSE IS NOT A MOTEL	1.50	2.50
		LOVE—ALBUM		
☐4001 (M)	***ELEKTRA***	LOVE	3.50	6.00
☐74001 (S)		LOVE	4.50	8.00
		DARLENE LOVE		
		SEE: BLOSSOMS, BOB B. SOXX AND THE BLUE JEANS		
☐111	***PHILLIES***	(TODAY I MET) THE BOY I'M GONNA MARRY/ MY HEART BEAT A LITTLE BIT	3.00	5.00
☐111		(TODAY I MET) THE BOY I'M GONNA MARRY/ TAKE IT FROM ME (39)	2.00	3.50
☐114		WAIT 'TIL MY BOBBY GETS HOME/ TAKE IT FROM ME (26)	1.50	3.00
☐117		A FINE FINE BOY/NINO AND SONNY (53)	1.75	3.00
☐119		WINTER WONDERLAND/ CHRISTMAS BABY PLEASE COME HOME	3.00	5.00
☐123		HE'S A QUIET GUY/STUMBLED AND FELL	15.00	25.00
☐125		WINTER WONDERLAND/ CHRISTMAS BABY PLEASE COME HOME	2.50	4.00
		LOVE LETTERS		
☐714	***ACME***	WALKING THE STREETS ALONE/OWEE-NELLIE	20.00	35.00

ISSUE #	LABEL	ARTIST/TITLE	VG	MINT
		RONNIE LOVE		
□5001	***STARTIME***	CHILLS AND FEVER/PLEDGING MY LOVE	3.50	5.00
□16144	***DOT***	CHILLS AND FEVER/PLEDGING MY LOVE (72)	1.50	2.50
		LOVERS		
□2005	***LAMP***	DARLING IT'S WONDERFUL/ GOTTA WHOLE LOTTA LOVIN' (48)	2.50	4.00
		LUGEE AND THE LIONS		
		FEATURED: LOU CHRISTIE		
□112	***ROBBEE***	THE JURY/LITTLE DID I KNOW	6.00	10.00
		ROBIN LUKE		
□206	***INTERNATIONAL***	SUSIE DARLIN'/LIVING'S LOVING YOU	8.00	15.00
□208		MY GIRL/CHICKA CHICKA HONEY	3.50	6.00
□210		STROLLIN' BLUES/YOU CAN'T STOP ME FROM DREAMIN'	3.50	6.00
□212		FIVE MINUTES MORE/ WHO'S GONNA HOLD YOUR HAND?	3.50	6.00
□15781	***DOT***	SUSIE DARLIN'/LIVING'S LOVING YOU (5)	1.25	3.00
□15839		MY GIRL/CHICKA CHICKA HONEY	1.50	2.50
□15899		STROLLIN' BLUES/YOU CAN'T STOP ME FROM DREAMIN'	1.50	2.50
□15959		FIVE MINUTES MORE/ WHO'S GONNA HOLD YOUR HAND?	1.50	2.50
		ROBIN LUKE—EP		
□1092	***DOT***	SUSIE DARLIN'	6.00	10.00
		LULU		
□9678	***PARROT***	SHOUT/FORGET ME BABY (94)	1.50	3.00
□9714		HERE COMES THE NIGHT/I'LL COME RUNNING	1.50	3.00
□40021		SHOUT/WHEN HE TOUCHES ME (96)	1.50	2.50
		LULU—ALBUM		
□61016 (M)	***PARROT***	FROM LULU WITH LOVE	3.50	6.00
□71016 (S)		FROM LULU WITH LOVE	4.50	8.00
		BOB LUMAN		
□8311	***IMPERIAL***	RED CADILLAC AND A BLACK MUSTACHE/ ALL NIGHT CLEANUP	6.00	10.00
□8313		RED HOT/WHENEVER YOU'RE READY	8.00	15.00
□8315		MAKE UP YOUR MIND, BABY/YOUR LOVE	6.00	10.00
□4059	***CAPITOL***	PRECIOUS/SVENGALI	3.50	6.00
□5081	***WARNER BROTHERS***	CLASS OF '59/MY BABY WALKS ALL OVER ME	1.75	3.00
□5105		BUTTERCUP/DREAMY DOLL	1.75	3.00
□5172		LET'S THINK ABOUT LIVING/ YOU'VE GOT EVERYTHING (7)	1.25	2.50
		LATER WARNER BROTHERS SINGLES ARE WORTH UP TO $2.00 MINT		
		BOB LUMAN—EP		
□1396	***WARNER BROTHERS***	LET'S THINK ABOUT LIVING	3.50	6.00
		BOB LUMAN—ALBUM		
□1396 (M)	***WARNER BROTHERS***	LET'S THINK ABOUT LIVING	6.00	10.00
□1396 (S)		LET'S THINK ABOUT LIVING	7.00	12.00

ISSUE #	LABEL	ARTIST/TITLE	VG	MINT
		LARRY LUREX (QUEEN)		
□204	*ANTHEM*	I CAN HEAR MUSIC/GOIN' BACK................	6.00	10.00

FRANKIE LYMON AND THE TEENAGERS

The Teenagers were a New York City street-corner quintet formed in Harlem. After school hours the junior-high lads would gather to rehearse their singing, especially an original song called "Why Do Fools Fall In Love".

A music director for Rama Records heard the boys and expressed interest in their song. The Teenagers auditioned and won a recording contract. The boys used their lunch hours to rehearse at school, singing in an unoccupied music room.

On the day of the recording, the Teenagers' lead singer came down with a sore throat. Frankie Lymon, barely thirteen, then offered to sing the song—and belted out a powerful version to prove he was capable. The boys cut the record, which was released on Rama's new Gee label. It was listed as being by Frankie Lymon and the Teenagers.

"Why Do Fools Fall In Love" climbed into the Top 10. Lymon and his pals then left school and went on the road, proving themselves a major draw in England and Europe as well as in America.

Lymon, later a soloist, lost favor with recording companies and the public when his voice matured. Once instantly identifiable, Lymon later sounded like any other pop singer. He ended up begging for coins in the street and, in 1968, was found dead in his mother's Harlem apartment, the victim of a heroin overdose.

ISSUE #	LABEL	ARTIST/TITLE	VG	MINT
		FRANKIE LYMON AND THE TEENAGERS		
□1002	GEE	WHY DO FOOLS FALL IN LOVE/ PLEASE BE MINE (7)	2.00	4.00
□1012		I WANT YOU TO BE MY GIRL/ I'M NOT A KNOW IT ALL (17)	2.50	4.00
□1018		I PROMISE TO REMEMBER/WHO CAN EXPLAIN (57)	2.50	4.00
□1022		THE ABC'S OF LOVE/SHARE (77)	2.50	4.00
□1026		I'M NOT A JUVENILE DELINQUENT/BABY BABY	3.00	5.00
□1032		TEENAGE LOVE/PAPER CASTLES	2.50	4.00
□1035		LOVE IS A CLOWN/AM I FOOLING MYSELF AGAIN?	2.50	4.00
□1036		OUT IN THE COLD AGAIN/MIRACLE OF LOVE	2.50	4.00
□1039		GOODY GOODY/CREATION OF LOVE (22)	1.50	3.00
□1046		EVERYTHING TO ME/FLIP FLOP	2.00	3.50
□1052		GOODY GOODY GIRL/I'M NOT TOO YOUNG TO DREAM	1.75	3.00
		FRANKIE LYMON AND THE TEENAGERS—ALBUM		
□701 (M)	GEE	THE TEENAGERS FEATURING FRANKIE LYMON (red label)	12.00	20.00
		FRANKIE LYMON		
□4026	ROULETTE	MY GIRL/SO GOES MY LOVE	1.75	3.00
□4035		LITTLE GIRL/IT'S CHRISTMAS ONCE AGAIN	1.75	3.00
□4044		FOOTSTEPS/THUMB THUMB	1.75	3.00
□4068		MAMA DON'T ALLOW IT/ PORTABLE ON MY SHOULDER	1.75	3.00
□4093		ONLY WAY TO LOVE/MELINDA	1.75	3.00
□4128		NO MATTER WHAT YOU'VE DONE/ UP JUMPED A RABBIT	1.75	3.00
□4150		WHAT MOONLIGHT CAN DO/BEFORE I FELL ASLEEP	1.75	3.00
□4257		LITTLE BITTY PRETTY ONE/CREATION OF LOVE (58)	1.50	2.50
□4283		WAITIN' IN SCHOOL/BUZZ BUZZ BUZZ	1.50	2.50
□4310		SILHOUETTES/JAILHOUSE ROCK	1.50	2.50
□4348		CHANGE PARTNERS/SO YOUNG	1.50	2.50
□4391		I PUT THE BOMP/SO YOUNG	1.50	2.50
		FRANKIE LYMON—EP		
□304	ROULETTE	FRANKIE LYMON AT THE LONDON PALLADIUM	5.00	8.00
		FRANKIE LYMON—ALBUMS		
□25013 (M)	ROULETTE	FRANKIE LYMON AT THE LONDON PALLADIUM	8.00	15.00
□25036 (M)		ROCK AND ROLL	8.00	15.00

ISSUE #	LABEL	ARTIST/TITLE	VG	MINT
		LONNIE MACK		
☐906	*FRATERNITY*	MEMPHIS/DOWN IN THE DUMPS (5)	.75	2.00
☐912		WHAM!/SUSIE Q (25)	1.00	2.00
☐918		BABY, WHAT'S WRONG?/WHERE THERE'S A WILL (93)	1.25	2.00
☐920		LONNIE ON THE MOVE/SAY SOMETHING NICE TO ME	1.25	2.00
		LATER FRATERNITY SINGLES ARE WORTH UP TO $1.50 MINT		
		LONNIE MACK—ALBUM		
☐1014 (M)	*FRATERNITY*	THE WHAM OF THAT MEMPHIS MAN	3.50	6.00
		JOHNNY MADERA		
☐511	*BAMBOO*	A STORY UNTOLD/VACATION TIME	2.50	4.00
		JOHNNY MAESTRO		
		SEE: CRESTS		
☐527	*COED*	SAY IT ISN'T SO/THE GREAT PHYSICIAN (Johnny Masters)	3.00	5.00
☐545		MODEL GIRL/WE'VE GOT TO TELL HIM (20)	1.50	3.00
☐549		WHAT A SURPRISE!/THE WARNING VOICE (33)	1.50	3.00
☐552		MR. HAPPINESS/TEST OF LOVE (57)	1.75	3.00
☐557		THE WAY YOU LOOK TONIGHT/I.O.U.	2.50	4.00
☐562		BESAME BABY/IT MUST BE LOVE	2.00	3.50
☐987	*PARKWAY*	TRY ME/HEARTBURN	1.75	3.00
☐999		COME SEE ME/I CARE ABOUT YOU	1.75	3.00
☐118		MY TIME/IS IT YOU?	1.75	3.00
☐474	*UNITED ARTISTS*	BEFORE I LOVED HER/FIFTY MILLION HEARTACHES	3.50	6.00
☐25075	*APT*	SHE'S ALL MINE ALONE/ PHONE BOOTH ON THE HIGHWAY	3.00	5.00
☐256	*CAMEO*	I'LL BE THERE/OVER THE WEEKEND	3.00	5.00
☐305		LEAN ON ME/MAKE UP MY MIND	3.00	5.00
		MAJORS		
☐5855	*IMPERIAL*	A WONDERFUL DREAM/TIME WILL TELL (22)	1.25	2.50
☐5879		A LITTLE BIT NOW/SHE'S A TROUBLEMAKER (63)	1.50	2.50
☐5914		ANYTHING YOU CAN DO/WHAT IN THE WORLD	1.25	2.00
☐5936		TRA-LA-LA/WHAT HAVE YOU BEEN DOIN'?	1.25	2.00
☐5991		YOUR LIFE BEGINS/WHICH WAY DID SHE GO?	1.25	2.00
☐6009		I'LL BE THERE/OOH WEE BABY	1.50	2.50
		MAJORS—ALBUM		
☐9222 (M)	*IMPERIAL*	MEET THE MAJORS	3.50	6.00
☐12222 (S)		MEET THE MAJORS	4.50	8.00
		MANCHESTERS		
		FEATURED: DAVID GATES		
☐700	*VEE JAY*	I DON'T COME FROM ENGLAND/DRAGON FLY	2.50	4.00
		BARRY MANN		
☐5002	*JDS*	A LOVE TO LAST A LIFETIME/ ALL THE THINGS YOU ARE	3.00	5.00
☐10143	*ABC-PARAMOUNT*	COUNTING TEARDROPS/WAR PAINT	2.00	3.50

ISSUE #	LABEL	ARTIST/TITLE	VG	MINT
☐ 10180		HAPPY BIRTHDAY, BROKEN HEART/ THE MILLIONAIRE	1.75	3.00
☐ 10237		WHO PUT THE BOMP (IN THE BOMP, BOMP, BOMP?)/LOVE, TRUE LOVE (7)	1.25	2.50
☐ 10263		LITTLE MISS U.S.A./FIND ANOTHER FOOL	1.50	2.50
☐ 10356		HEY BABY, I'M DANCIN'/LIKE I DON'T LOVE YOU	1.50	2.50
☐ 10380		BLESS YOU/TEENAGE HAS-BEEN	1.75	3.00

BARRY MANN—ALBUM

ISSUE #	LABEL	ARTIST/TITLE	VG	MINT
☐ 399 (M)	*ABC-PARAMOUNT*	WHO PUT THE BOMP (IN THE BOMP, BOMP, BOMP?)	6.00	10.00
☐ 399 (S)		WHO PUT THE BOMP (IN THE BOMP, BOMP, BOMP?)	7.00	12.00

CARL MANN

ISSUE #	LABEL	ARTIST/TITLE	VG	MINT
☐ 502	*JASON*	GONNA ROCK AND ROLL TONIGHT/ROCKIN' LOVE	20.00	30.00
☐ 3539	*PHILLIPS INTERNATIONAL*	MONA LISA/FOOLISH ONE (25)	1.50	3.00
☐ 3546		PRETEND/ROCKIN' LOVE (57)	1.75	3.00
☐ 3550		SOME ENCHANTED EVENING/I CAN'T FORGET	2.00	3.50
☐ 3555		SOUTH OF THE BORDER/I'M COMIN' HOME	1.75	3.00
☐ 3564		THE WAYWARD WIND/BORN TO BE BAD	1.75	3.00
☐ 3569		I AIN'T GOT NO HOME/IF I COULD CHANGE YOU	2.00	3.50
☐ 3579		WHEN I GROW TOO OLD TO DREAM/MOUNTAIN DEW	1.75	3.00

CARL MANN—ALBUM

ISSUE #	LABEL	ARTIST/TITLE	VG	MINT
☐ 1960 (M)	*PHILLIPS INTERNATIONAL*	LIKE MANN	12.00	20.00

GLORIA MANN

ISSUE #	LABEL	ARTIST/TITLE	VG	MINT
☐ 100	*SOUND*	EARTH ANGEL/I LOVE YOU, YES I DO (24)	1.50	3.00
☐ 126		TEENAGE PRAYER/GYPSY LADY (21)	1.50	3.00
☐ 29832	*DECCA*	WHY DO FOOLS FALL IN LOVE/ PARTNERS FOR LIFE (59)	1.50	2.50

MANFRED MANN

ISSUE #	LABEL	ARTIST/TITLE	VG	MINT
☐ 2157	*ASCOT*	DO WAH DIDDY DIDDY/WHAT YOU GONNA DO? (1)	1.00	2.50
☐ 2165		SHA LA LA/JOHN HARDY (12)	1.25	2.50
☐ 2170		COME TOMORROW/WHAT DID I DO WRONG? (50)	1.50	2.50
☐ 2184		MY LITTLE RED BOOK/WHAT AM I DOING WRONG?	1.75	3.00
☐ 2194		IF YOU GOTTA GO, GO NOW/ONE IN THE MIDDLE	1.50	2.50
☐ 2210		SHE NEEDS COMPANY/HI LILI, HI LO	1.50	2.50
☐ 2241		I CAN'T BELIEVE WHAT YOU SAY/ MY LITTLE RED BOOK	1.50	2.50
☐ 55040	*UNITED ARTISTS*	PRETTY FLAMINGO/YOU'RE STANDING BY (29)	1.25	2.50
☐ 55066		WHEN WILL I BE LOVED?/DO YOU HAVE TO DO THAT?	1.75	3.00
☐ 72607	*MERCURY*	JUST LIKE A WOMAN/I WANNA BE RICH	1.75	3.00
☐ 72629		EACH AND EVERY DAY/ SEMI-DETACHED SUBURBAN MR. JONES	1.50	2.50
☐ 72675		HA HA, SAID THE CLOWN/FEELING SO GOOD	1.50	2.50
☐ 72770		QUINN THE ESKIMO/BY REQUEST- EDWIN GARVEY (original title)	1.75	3.00
☐ 72770		THE MIGHTY QUINN/BY REQUEST- EDWIN GARVEY (10)	1.00	2.00

ISSUE #	LABEL	ARTIST/TITLE	VG	MINT
☐ 72822		MY NAME IS JACK/THERE IS A MAN	1.50	2.50
☐ 72879		FOX ON THE RUN/TOO MANY PEOPLE (97)	1.50	2.50
☐ 72921		RAGAMUFFIN MAN/A B SIDE	1.50	2.50
		MANFRED MANN—ALBUMS		
☐ 13015 (M)	*ASCOT*	THE MANFRED MANN ALBUM	3.50	6.00
☐ 16015 (S)		THE MANFRED MANN ALBUM	4.50	8.00
☐ 13018 (M)		THE FIVE FACES OF MANFRED MANN	3.50	6.00
☐ 16018 (S)		THE FIVE FACES OF MANFRED MANN	4.50	8.00
☐ 13021 (M)		MY LITTLE RED BOOK OF WINNERS............	3.50	6.00
☐ 16021 (S)		MY LITTLE RED BOOK OF WINNERS............	4.50	8.00
☐ 13024 (M)		MANN MADE	3.00	5.00
☐ 16024 (S)		MANN MADE	4.00	7.00
☐ 3549 (M)	*UNITED ARTISTS*	PRETTY FLAMINGO	3.50	6.00
☐ 6549 (S)		PRETTY FLAMINGO	4.50	8.00
☐ 3551 (M)		MANFRED MANN'S GREATEST HITS	3.50	6.00
☐ 6551 (S)		MANFRED MANN'S GREATEST HITS	4.50	8.00

MANUEL AND THE RENEGADES

☐ 7000	*PIPER*	SURF WALK/WOODY WAGON	1.75	3.00
☐ 7001		REV-UP/TRANS-MISS-YEN	1.75	3.00

MARATHONS
SEE: JAYHAWKS, VIBRATIONS

☐ 5027	*ARVEE*	PEANUT BUTTER/TALKIN' TRASH (20)...........	1.50	3.00
		MARATHONS—ALBUM		
☐ 428 (M)	*ARVEE*	PEANUT BUTTER	7.00	12.00

MARCELS

☐ 186	*COLPIX*	BLUE MOON/GOODBYE TO LOVE (1)	1.25	3.00
☐ 196		SUMMERTIME/TEETER TOTTER LOVE (78)........	1.75	3.00
☐ 606		YOU ARE MY SUNSHINE/FIND ANOTHER FOOL	2.00	3.50
☐ 612		HEARTACHES/MY LOVE FOR YOU (7)	1.25	3.00
☐ 617		MERRY TWIST-MAS/DON'T CRY FOR ME THIS CHRISTMAS.........................	1.75	3.00
☐ 624		MY MELANCHOLY BABY/ REALLY NEED YOUR LOVE (58)	1.50	3.00
☐ 629		TWISTIN' FEVER/FOOTPRINTS IN THE SAND	1.75	3.00
☐ 640		HOLD UP/FLOWERPOT.......................	1.50	2.50
☐ 651		FRIENDLY LOANS/LOVED HER THE WHOLE WEEK THROUGH	1.50	2.50
☐ 665		ALL RIGHT, OKAY, YOU WIN/LOLLIPOP BABY	1.50	2.50
☐ 683		THAT OLD BLACK MAGIC/ DON'T TURN YOUR BACK ON ME	1.75	3.00
☐ 687		I WANNA BE THE LEADER/GIVE ME BACK YOUR LOVE .	1.50	2.50
☐ 694		ONE LAST KISS/TEETER TOTTER LOVE	1.75	3.00
☐ 694		ONE LAST KISS/YOU GOT TO BE SINCERE	1.75	3.00
		MARCELS—ALBUM		
☐ 416 (M)	*COLPIX*	BLUE MOON	8.00	15.00

(LITTLE) PEGGY MARCH

☐ 8107	*RCA*	LITTLE ME/PAGAN LOVE SONG	1.75	3.00
☐ 8139		I WILL FOLLOW HIM/WIND-UP DOLL (1)	1.00	2.50

ISSUE #	LABEL	ARTIST/TITLE	VG	MINT
☐ 8189		I WISH I WERE A PRINCESS/MY TEENAGE CASTLE (32)	1.25	2.50
☐ 8221		HELLO HEARTACHE, GOODBYE LOVE/BOY CRAZY (26) .	1.25	2.50
☐ 8267		THE IMPOSSIBLE HAPPENED/WATERFALL (57)	1.50	2.50
☐ 8302		EVERY LITTLE MOVE YOU MAKE/AFTER YOU (84) ..	1.50	2.50
☐ 8357		LEAVE ME ALONE/TAKIN' THE LONG WAY HOME...	1.25	2.00
☐ 8418		OH MY, WHAT A GUY/ONLY YOU COULD DO		
		THAT TO MY HEART	1.25	2.00
☐ 8460		WATCH WHAT YOU DO WITH MY BABY/		
		CAN'T STOP THINKING ABOUT HIM	1.25	2.00
☐ 8534		WHY CAN'T HE BE YOU/LOSIN' MY TOUCH	1.25	2.00
☐ 8605		LET HER GO/YOUR GIRL	1.25	2.00
☐ 8710		HEAVEN FOR LOVERS/HE COULDN'T CARE LESS ...	1.25	2.00
		(LITTLE) PEGGY MARCH—EP		
☐ 4376	*RCA*	I WISH I WERE A PRINCESS	3.00	5.00
		(LITTLE) PEGGY MARCH—ALBUM		
☐ 2732 (M)	*RCA*	I WILL FOLLOW HIM	3.50	6.00
☐ 2732 (S)		I WILL FOLLOW HIM	4.50	8.00

LEE MARENO

☐ 103	*NEW ART*	GODDESS OF LOVE/HE'S GONE	5.00	8.00

ERNIE MARESCA

☐ 107	*SEVILLE*	I DON'T KNOW WHY/LONESOME BLUES	1.50	2.50
☐ 117		SHOUT! SHOUT! (KNOCK YOURSELF OUT)/		
		CRYING LIKE A BABY (6)75	2.00
☐ 119		DOWN ON THE BEACH/MARY JANE.............	1.25	2.00
☐ 122		SOMETHING TO SHOUT ABOUT/HOW MANY TIMES?	1.25	2.00

LATER SEVILLE SINGLES ARE WORTH UP TO $1.50 MINT

MAR-KETS

☐ 501	*UNION*	SURFER'S STOMP/START....................	2.00	3.50
☐ 504		BALBOA BLUE/STOMPEDE	2.00	3.50
☐ 507		STOMPIN' ROOM ONLY/CANADIAN SUNSET	2.00	3.50
☐ 55401	*LIBERTY*	SURFER'S STOMP/START (31)	1.25	2.50
☐ 55443		BALBOA BLUE/STOMPEDE (48)................	1.50	2.50
☐ 5365	*WARNER*			
	BROTHERS	WOODY WAGON/COBRA	1.75	3.00
☐ 5391		OUTER LIMITS/BELLA DALENA (original title)	2.50	4.00
☐ 5391		OUT OF LIMITS/BELLA DALENA (3)	1.00	2.00
☐ 5423		VANISHING POINT/BOREALIS (90)	1.50	2.50
☐ 5468		LOOK FOR A STAR/COME SEE, COME SKA	1.75	2.50
☐ 5641		MIAMI BLUES/NAPOLEON'S GOLD	1.25	2.00
☐ 5670		READY, STEADY, GO/LADY IN THE CAGE	1.25	2.00
		MAR-KETS—ALBUMS		
☐ 3226 (M)	*LIBERTY*	SURFER'S STOMP	5.00	8.00
☐ 1870 (M)	*WORLD*			
	PACIFIC	SUN POWER.............................	3.50	6.00
☐ 21870 (S)		SUN POWER.............................	4.50	8.00
☐ 1509 (M)	*WARNER*			
	BROTHERS	TAKE TO WHEELS	3.00	5.00
☐ 1509 (S)		TAKE TO WHEELS	4.00	7.00
☐ 1537 (M)		OUT OF LIMITS	3.00	5.00
☐ 1537 (S)		OUT OF LIMITS	4.00	7.00

MARKSMEN (VENTURES)

ISSUE #	LABEL	ARTIST/TITLE	VG	MINT
☐ 6052	BLUE HORIZON	NIGHT RUN/SCRATCH	3.00	5.00

RITCHIE MARSH (SKY SAXON)

SEE: SEEDS

ISSUE #	LABEL	ARTIST/TITLE	VG	MINT
☐ 2203	SHEPHERD	THEY SAY/DARLING, I SWEAR THAT IT'S TRUE	6.00	10.00
☐ 412	ROSCO	THERE'S ONLY ONE GIRL/WHAT CHANCE HAVE I	3.50	6.00
☐ 125	ACAMA	BABY BABY BABY/HALF ANGEL	3.00	5.00
☐ 122	AVA	CRYING INSIDE MY HEART/GOODBYE	3.00	5.00

MARTHA AND THE VANDELLAS

ISSUE #	LABEL	ARTIST/TITLE	VG	MINT
☐ 7011	GORDY	I'LL HAVE TO LET HIM GO/ MY BABY WON'T COME BACK	1.75	3.00
☐ 7014		COME AND GET THESE MEMORIES/ JEALOUS LOVER (29)	1.25	2.50
☐ 7022		HEAT WAVE/A LOVE LIKE YOURS (4)	.75	2.00
☐ 7025		QUICKSAND/DARLING, I HUM OUR SONG (8)	.75	2.00
☐ 7027		LIVE WIRE/OLD LOVE (42)	1.00	2.00
☐ 7031		IN MY LONELY ROOM/A TEAR FOR THE GIRL (44)	1.00	2.00
☐ 7033		DANCING IN THE STREET/THERE HE IS (2)	.75	1.50
☐ 7036		WILD ONE/DANCING SLOW (34)	1.00	1.50
☐ 7039		NOWHERE TO RUN/MOTORING (8)	.75	1.50

LATER GORDY SINGLES ARE WORTH UP TO $1.50 MINT

MARTHA AND THE VANDELLAS—ALBUMS

ISSUE #	LABEL	ARTIST/TITLE	VG	MINT
☐ 902 (M)	GORDY	COME AND GET THESE MEMORIES	4.50	8.00
☐ 907 (M)		HEAT WAVE	3.50	6.00

GEORGE MARTIN

ISSUE #	LABEL	ARTIST/TITLE	VG	MINT
☐ 745	UNITED ARTISTS	RINGO'S THEME (THIS BOY)/AND LOVE HER (53)	1.25	2.50
☐ 750		A HARD DAY'S NIGHT/ I SHOULD HAVE KNOWN BETTER	1.50	2.50

JANIS MARTIN

ISSUE #	LABEL	ARTIST/TITLE	VG	MINT
☐ 6491	RCA	DRUG STORE ROCK AND ROLL/WILL YOU, WILLYUM?	5.00	8.00
☐ 6560		OOBY DOOBY/ONE MORE YEAR TO GO	6.00	10.00
☐ 6652		MY BOY ELVIS/LITTLE BIT	5.00	8.00
☐ 6983		LOVE AND KISSES/I'LL NEVER BE FREE	3.50	6.00
☐ 7318		BANG BANG/PLEASE BE MY LOVE	3.50	6.00

JANIS MARTIN—EP

ISSUE #	LABEL	ARTIST/TITLE	VG	MINT
☐ 4093	RCA	JUST SQUEEZE ME	12.00	20.00

MARVELETTES

Berry Gordy, Jr., supposedly borrowed $600 to start Motown during the late 1950s. (Prior to that he was a Ford assembly line worker.) By 1961 Gordy was on the lookout for a dynamic female vocal group to add to his fast-growing Tamla label. (One group of high school girls, the Primettes, had been dismissed by Gordy as being "giggly and unprofessional" when they approached him that year. They would later become known as the Supremes.)

Gordy was told of a quartet of girls singing at Inkster High School near his Detroit office. Gordy attended an Inkster talent show where the girls—who called themselves the Marvelettes—stole the show with their dynamic interpretations of current r & b hits. Gordy then approached the girls (all seventeen years old) and asked them to come to Motown for an audition.

The Marvelettes hit the No. 1 spot on both the r & b and rock charts with their maiden 1961 Tamla record, "Please Mr. Postman". (It later became a Carpenters hit.) After "Twistin' Postman" failed to cash in successfully on the twist craze, the Marvelettes returned to the Top 10 with the aggressive "Playboy" and scored another hit with the fine upbeat "Beechwood 4-5789".

ISSUE #	LABEL	ARTIST/TITLE	VG	MINT
		MARVELETTES		
☐54046	***TAMLA***	PLEASE MR. POSTMAN/SO LONG BABY (1)	1.25	2.50
☐54054		TWISTIN' POSTMAN/I WANT A GUY (34)	1.50	2.50
☐54060		PLAYBOY/ALL THE LOVE I'VE GOT (7)	1.25	2.50
☐54065		BEECHWOOD 4-5789/SOMEDAY, SOMEWAY (17)	1.25	2.50
		LATER TAMLA SINGLES ARE WORTH UP TO $2.00 MINT		
		MARVELETTES		
☐229 (M)	***TAMLA***	THE MARVELETTES SING	6.00	10.00
☐231 (M)		PLAYBOY	5.00	8.00
		MARVELS		
☐1916	***WINN***	FOR SENTIMENTAL REASONS/COME BACK	6.00	10.00
		MASCOTS		
☐107	***MERMAID***	BLUEBIRDS OVER THE MOUNTAIN/TIMBERLANDS	8.00	15.00
☐206	***BLAST***	ONCE UPON A LOVE/HEY LITTLE ANGEL	5.00	8.00
		BONNIE JO MASON (CHER)		
☐1001	***ANNETTE***	RINGO, I LOVE YOU/BEATLE BLUES	6.00	10.00
		MATADORS		
		FEATURED: JAN AND DEAN		
☐698	***COLPIX***	ACE OF HEARTS/PERFIDIA	2.50	4.00
☐718		I'VE GOTTA DRIVE/LA CORRIDA	2.50	4.00
☐741		C'MON, LET YOURSELF GO (PT. 1)/(PT. 11)	2.50	4.00
		DINO MATTHEWS		
☐16365	***DOT***	THAT GIRL THAT I LOVE/LENORE	8.00	15.00
		NATHANIEL MAYER		
☐542	***FORTUNE***	MY LAST DANCE WITH YOU/MY LITTLE DARLING	1.50	2.50
☐545		VILLAGE OF LOVE/I WANT A WOMAN (22) (also on Fortune 449)	1.25	2.50
☐550		WELL, I'VE GOT NEWS/MR. SANTA CLAUS	1.25	2.00
☐554		I HAD A DREAM/I'M NOT GONNA CRY	1.25	2.00
☐557		GOING BACK TO THE VILLAGE OF LOVE/ MY LAST DANCE WITH YOU	1.50	2.50
		NATHANIEL MAYER—ALBUM		
☐8014 (M)	***FORTUNE***	GOING BACK TO THE VILLAGE OF LOVE	6.00	10.00
		MC-5		
☐333	***A-SQUARE***	LOOKING AT YOU/BORDERLINE	7.00	12.00
☐45648	***ELEKTRA***	KICK OUT THE JAMS/MOTOR CITY IS BURNING (82)	1.75	3.00
☐2678	***ATLANTIC***	TONIGHT/LOOKING AT YOU	1.50	2.50
☐2724		AMERICAN RUSH/SHAKIN' STREET	1.50	2.50
		MC-5—ALBUMS		
☐74072 (S)	***ELEKTRA***	KICK OUT THE JAMS	6.00	10.00
☐8247 (S)	***ATLANTIC***	BACK IN THE U.S.A.	3.50	6.00
☐8285 (S)		HIGH TIME	3.50	6.00
		GENE McDANIELS		
☐55231	***LIBERTY***	IN TIMES LIKE THESE/ONCE BEFORE	1.50	2.50
☐55265		FACTS OF LIFE/THE GREEN DOOR	1.50	2.50
☐55308		A HUNDRED POUNDS OF CLAY/ TAKE A CHANCE ON LOVE (3)	1.00	2.00
☐55344		A TEAR/SHE'S COME BACK (31)	1.25	2.00

ISSUE #	LABEL	ARTIST/TITLE	VG	MINT
☐ 55371		TOWER OF STRENGTH/THE SECRET (5)	.75	2.00
☐ 55405		CHIP CHIP/ANOTHER TEAR FALLS	.75	2.00
☐ 55444		FUNNY/CHAPEL OF TEARS (99)	1.25	2.00
☐ 55480		POINT OF NO RETURN/WARMER THAN A WHISPER (21)	1.00	2.00
☐ 55510		SPANISH LACE/SOMEBODY'S WAITING (31)	1.00	2.00
☐ 55541		CRY BABY CRY/THE PUZZLE	1.25	2.00
☐ 55597		IT'S A LONELY TOWN/FALSE FRIENDS (64)	1.25	2.00

GENE McDANIELS—EP

ISSUE #	LABEL	ARTIST/TITLE	VG	MINT
☐ 1014	*LIBERTY*	GENE McDANIELS	3.00	5.00

GENE McDANIELS—ALBUMS

ISSUE #	LABEL	ARTIST/TITLE	VG	MINT
☐ 3146 (M)	*LIBERTY*	IN TIMES LIKE THESE	3.00	5.00
☐ 7146 (S)		IN TIMES LIKE THESE	4.00	7.00
☐ 3191 (M)		100 POUNDS OF CLAY	3.00	5.00
☐ 7191 (S)		100 POUNDS OF CLAY	4.00	7.00
☐ 3258 (M)		HIT AFTER HIT	3.00	5.00
☐ 7258 (S)		HIT AFTER HIT	4.00	7.00
☐ 3275 (M)		SPANISH LACE	3.00	5.00
☐ 7275 (S)		SPANISH LACE	4.00	7.00

BOB McFADDEN (ROD McKUEN)

ISSUE #	LABEL	ARTIST/TITLE	VG	MINT
☐ 55120	*BRUNSWICK*	FRANKIE AND IGOR AT A ROCK AND ROLL PARTY/ CHILDREN, CROSS THE BRIDGE	2.50	4.00
☐ 55140		THE MUMMY/THE BEAT GENERATION (39)	1.75	3.50

McQUIRE SISTERS

ISSUE #	LABEL	ARTIST/TITLE	VG	MINT
☐ 61187	*CORAL*	GOODNIGHT, SWEETHEART, GOODNIGHT/ HEAVENLY FEELING (1)	1.25	3.00
☐ 61323		SINCERELY/NO MORE (1)	1.25	3.00

ROD McKUEN

ISSUE #	LABEL	ARTIST/TITLE	VG	MINT
☐ 1407	*SPIRAL*	OLIVER TWIST/CELEBRITY TWIST (76)	1.50	2.50

TOMMY McLAIN

ISSUE #	LABEL	ARTIST/TITLE	VG	MINT
☐ 197	*JIN*	SWEET DREAMS/I NEED YOU SO	2.50	4.00
☐ 197	*MSL*	SWEET DREAMS/I NEED YOU SO (15)	1.00	2.50

CLYDE McPHATTER

SEE: DRIFTERS

ISSUE #	LABEL	ARTIST/TITLE	VG	MINT
☐ 1081	*ATLANTIC*	SEVEN DAYS/I'M NOT WORTHY OF YOU (44)	2.50	4.00
☐ 1092		TREASURE OF LOVE/WHEN YOU'RE SINCERE (22)	2.00	3.50
☐ 1117		WITHOUT LOVE (THERE IS NOTHING)/ I MAKE BELIEVE (38)	2.00	3.50
☐ 1133		JUST TO HOLD MY HAND/NO MATTER WHAT (30)	1.50	3.00
☐ 1149		LONG LONELY NIGHTS/HEARTACHES (49)	1.50	3.00
☐ 1199		A LOVER'S QUESTION/I CAN'T STAND UP ALONE (6)	1.00	2.00
☐ 2018		LOVEY DOVEY/MY ISLAND OF DREAMS (49)	1.25	2.00
☐ 2028		SINCE YOU'VE BEEN GONE/TRY, TRY BABY (38)	1.25	2.00
☐ 71941	*MERCURY*	LOVER PLEASE/LET'S FORGET ABOUT THE PAST (7)	1.00	2.00
☐ 71987		LITTLE BITTY PRETTY ONE/NEXT TO ME (25)	1.25	2.00

CLYDE McPHATTER—EPs

ISSUE #	LABEL	ARTIST/TITLE	VG	MINT
☐ 584	*ATLANTIC*	CLYDE McPHATTER	5.00	8.00
☐ 605		ROCK WITH CLYDE McPHATTER	3.50	6.00
☐ 618		CLYDE McPHATTER	3.50	6.00

ISSUE #	LABEL	ARTIST/TITLE	VG	MINT
		CLYDE McPHATTER—ALBUMS		
☐8024 (M)	***ATLANTIC***	LOVE BALLADS	8.00	15.00
☐8031 (M)		CLYDE	7.00	12.00
☐8077 (M)		THE BEST OF CLYDE McPHATTER	8.00	15.00
☐20711 (M)	***MERCURY***	LOVER PLEASE	3.50	6.00
☐60711 (S)		LOVER PLEASE	4.50	8.00
☐20783 (M)		GREATEST HITS	3.00	5.00
☐60783 (S)		GREATEST HITS	4.00	7.00

MELLO-KINGS

The Mello-Kings came from the city of Mount Vernon, New York. Two singing brothers decided to combine their efforts with three fellow New York vocalists. (All were in high school at the time.) They sang at parties and talent shows around Mount Vernon and soon found a growing following. They chose a name: The Mello-Tones.

They drove to New York City and got an audition with the r & b-oriented Herald Records. For their first song the Mello-Tones sang "Tonite-Tonite", a beautiful "do-wop" ballad. Herald liked the song and recorded it as the group's first single. After the initial pressing, though, the Mello-Tones made a startling discovery: another Mello-Tones group already existed! In fact, they had just released a song called "Rosie Lee" on the competitive Gee label. Later Herald singles of "Tonite-Tonite" then featured the group's new name, the Mello-Kings.

"Tonite-Tonite" became a national hit in 1957. The same song was re-released in 1961 and made the charts again. "Tonite-Tonite" proved to be the Mello-Kings' only hit.

ISSUE #	LABEL	ARTIST/TITLE	VG	MINT
		MELLO KINGS		
☐502	**HERALD**	TONITE-TONITE/DO BABY DO (Mello Tones)	20.00	30.00
☐502		TONITE-TONITE/DO BABY DO (77)	3.00	5.00
☐507		CHAPEL ON THE HILL/SASSAFRAS	2.50	4.00
☐518		VALERIE/SHE'S REAL COOL	2.50	4.00
		MELLO KINGS—EP		
☐451	**HERALD**	THE FABULOUS MELLO KINGS	7.00	12.00
		MELLO KINGS—ALBUM		
☐1013 (M)	**HERALD**	TONIGHT, TONIGHT	25.00	40.00
		MELLO-TONES		
☐1037	**GEE**	ROSIE LEE/I'LL NEVER FALL IN LOVE AGAIN (60)	2.50	4.00
☐1040		CA-SANDRA/RATTLESNAKE ROLL	2.00	3.50
		MERSEYBEATS		
☐1882	**FONTANA**	MISTER MOONLIGHT/I THINK OF YOU	1.75	3.00
☐1905		DON'T TURN AROUND/REALLY MYSTIFIED	1.50	2.50
☐1950		SEE ME BACK/LAST NIGHT	1.50	2.50
		MERSEYBEATS—ALBUM		
☐834 (M)	**ARC INTERNATIONAL**	ENGLAND'S BEST SELLERS	4.50	8.00
		JIM MESSINA AND THE JESTERS		
☐705	**ULTIMA**	DRAG BIKE BOOGIE/A-RAB	6.00	10.00
☐101	**FEATURE**	PANTHER POUNCE/TIGER TAIL	3.50	6.00
☐98	**AUDIO FIDELITY**	THE BREEZE AND I/STRANGE MAN	3.00	5.00
		JIM MESSINA AND THE JESTERS—ALBUM		
☐7037 (S)	**AUDIO FIDELITY**	THE DRAGSTERS	8.00	15.00

MICKEY AND SYLVIA

During the early 1950s New Yorker Sylvia Robinson recorded under the name of Little Sylvia. She saw no commercial success with her releases but was determimed to remain in the music business. An accomplished guitarist, Sylvia later teamed with Mickey "Guitar" Baker, a Kentucky-born session guitarist who had earned a good reputation for his skills.

Mickey and Sylvia signed with Groove—an RCA subsidiary—and recorded "Walking In the Rain". That single went nowhere. It wasn't until Mickey and Sylvia's second Groove release—"Love Is Strange"—that the duo found major success. The song became a Top 20 hit early in 1957. At the time Mickey was 31 and Sylvia was 20.

Mickey and Sylvia then moved to the Vik, Mickey and Sylvia dissolved their partnership.

In 1973 Sylvia briefly resurfaced. Her solo single of "Pillow Talk" went all the way to the No. 3 spot and stayed on the Top 100 for nearly half a year.

ISSUE #	LABEL	ARTIST/TITLE	VG	MINT
		MICKEY AND SYLVIA		
☐0164	GROOVE	WALKING IN THE RAIN/NO GOOD LOVER	3.00	5.00
☐0175		LOVE IS STRANGE/I'M GOING HOME (13)	2.00	4.00
☐0267	VIK	THERE OUGHT TO BE A LAW/DEAREST (47)	2.00	3.50
☐0280		LOVE WILL MAKE YOU FAIL IN SCHOOL/ TWO SHADOWS ON YOUR WINDOW	1.75	3.00
☐0290		LET'S HAVE A PICNIC/LOVE IS A TREASURE	1.75	3.00
☐0324		BEWILDERED/ROCK AND STROLL ROOM (57)	1.50	2.50
		MICKEY AND SYLVIA—EPs		
☐18	GROOVE	LOVE IS STRANGE	6.00	10.00
☐262	VIK	MICKEY AND SYLVIA	3.50	6.00
		MICKEY AND SYLVIA—ALBUM		
☐1102 (M)	VIK	NEW SOUNDS	7.00	12.00
		GARRY MILES		
		SEE: STATUES		
☐55261	LIBERTY	LOOK FOR A STAR/AFRAID OF LOVE (16)	1.25	2.50
☐55279		DREAM GIRL/WISHING WELL	1.50	2.50
☐55363		LOVE AT FIRST SIGHT/COMMANDMENTS OF LOVE	1.50	2.50
		GARY MILES—EP		
☐1005	LIBERTY	LOOK FOR A STAR	3.50	6.00
		GARRY MILLS		
☐5674	IMPERIAL	LOOK FOR A STAR (PT. 1)/(PT. 11) (26)	1.25	2.50
		HAYLEY MILLS		
☐385	VISTA	LET'S GET TOGETHER/COBBLER, COBBLER (8)	.75	2.00
☐395		JOHNNY JINGO/JEEPERS, CREEPERS (21)	1.00	2.00
☐401		SIDE BY SIDE/DING DING DING	1.25	2.00
☐408		CASTAWAY/SWEET RIVER	1.25	2.00
☐409		ENJOY IT/LET'S CLIMB	1.25	2.00
☐420		FLITTERIN'/BEAUTIFUL BEAULAH	1.25	2.00
		HAYLEY MILLS—ALBUM		
☐3311 (M)	BUENA VISTA	LET'S GET TOGETHER	3.50	6.00
		MINDBENDERS		
		SEE: WAYNE FONTANA AND THE MINDBENDERS		
☐1541	FONTANA	A GROOVY KIND OF LOVE/LOVE IS GOOD (2)	1.00	2.00
☐1555		ASHES TO ASHES/YOU DON'T KNOW ABOUT LOVE (55)	1.25	2.00
☐1620		BLESSED ARE THE LONELY/YELLOW BRICK ROAD	1.25	2.00
		MINDBENDERS—ALBUM		
☐27554 (M)	FONTANA	A GROOVY KIND OF LOVE	3.50	6.00
☐67554 (S)		A GROOVY KIND OF LOVE	4.50	8.00
		SAL MINEO		
☐9216	EPIC	START MOVIN'/LOVE AFFAIR (10)	1.00	2.50
☐9227		LASTING LOVE/YOU SHOULDN'T DO THAT (35)	1.25	2.50
☐9246		PARTY TIME/THE WORDS THAT I WHISPER (47)	1.25	2.50
☐9260		LITTLE PIGEON/CUTTIN' IN (47)	1.25	2.50
☐9327		MAKE BELIEVE BABY/YOUNG AS WE ARE	1.25	2.00
☐9345		I'LL NEVER BE MYSELF AGAIN/ WORDS THAT I WHISPER	1.25	2.00

ISSUE #	LABEL	ARTIST/TITLE	VG	MINT
		SAL MINEO—EPs		
□7187	*EPIC*	SAL MINEO	2.50	4.00
□7194		SAL	2.00	3.50
□7195		SAL	2.00	3.50
		MIRACLES		
		FEATURED: SMOKEY ROBINSON		
□1016	*END*	GOT A JOB/MY MAMA DONE TOLD ME	3.50	6.00
□1029		MONEY/I CRY	3.00	5.00
□1084		MONEY/I CRY	2.50	4.00
□1	*MOTOWN*	BAD GIRL/I LOVE YOU BABY	30.00	50.00
□1734	*CHESS*	BAD GIRL/I LOVE YOU BABY . (93)	2.00	5.00
□1768		I NEED A CHANGE/ALL I WANT	3.50	6.00
□54028	*TAMLA*	WAY OVER THERE/DEPEND ON ME	1.75	3.00
□54034		SHOP AROUND/WHO'S LOVIN' YOU (2)	1.00	2.50
□54036		AIN'T IT, BABY/THE ONLY ONE I LOVE (49)	1.25	2.50
□54044		MIGHTY GOOD LOVIN'/BROKEN HEARTED (51)	1.25	2.50
□54048		EVERYBODY'S GOTTA PAY SOME DUES/ I CAN'T BELIEVE (52)	1.25	2.50
□54053		WHAT'S SO GOOD ABOUT GOODBYE?/ I'VE BEEN GOOD TO YOU (35)	1.25	2.50
□54059		I'LL TRY SOMETHING NEW/ YOU NEVER MISS A GOOD THING (39)	1.25	2.50
□54069		WAY OVER THERE/ IF YOUR MOTHER ONLY KNEW (94)	1.50	2.50
□54073		YOU'VE REALLY GOT A HOLD ON ME/ HAPPY LANDING (8)	1.00	2.00
		LATER TAMLA SINGLES ARE WORTH UP TO $2.00 MINT		
		MIRACLES—ALBUMS		
□220 (M)	*TAMLA*	HI, WE'RE THE MIRACLES	8.00	15.00
□223 (M)		COOKIN' WITH THE MIRACLES	7.00	12.00
□224 (M)		SHOP AROUND	6.00	10.00
□230 (M)		I'LL TRY SOMETHING NEW	5.00	8.00
		MISFITS		
□7-10	*ARIES*	MIDNIGHT STAR/I DON'T KNOW	8.00	15.00
		MISTAKES		
□2312	*LO-FI*	CHAPEL BELLS/I GOT FIRED	3.50	6.00
		PAT MOLITTERI (FROM "AMERICAN BANDSTAND")		
□414	*TEEN*	THE U.S.A./SAY THAT YOU LOVE ME	8.00	15.00
		MONKEES		
□1001	*COLGEMS*	LAST TRAIN TO CLARKSVILLE/TAKE A GIANT STEP (1)	.75	2.00
□1002		I'M A BELIEVER/(I'M NOT YOUR) STEPPING STONE (1)	.75	2.00
□1004		A LITTLE BIT ME, A LITTLE BIT YOU/ THE GIRL I KNEW SOMEWHERE (2)	.75	2.00
□1007		PLEASANT VALLEY SUNDAY/WORDS (3)	.75	2.00
□1012		DAYDREAM BELIEVER/GOIN' DOWN (1)	.75	2.00
□1019		VALLERI/TAPIOCA TUNDRA (3)	.75	2.00
□1023		D. W. WASHBURN/IT'S NICE TO BE WITH YOU (19)	1.00	2.00
□1031		PORPOISE SONG/AS WE GO ALONG (62)	1.25	2.00
□5000		TEAR DROP CITY/A MAN WITHOUT A DREAM (56)	1.25	2.00

ISSUE #	LABEL	ARTIST/TITLE	VG	MINT
□ 5004		LISTEN TO THE BAND/SOMEDAY MAN (63)	1.25	2.00
□ 5005		GOOD CLEAN FUN/MOMMY AND DADDY (82)	1.50	2.50
□ 5011		OH MY MY/I LOVE YOU BETTER (98)	1.50	2.50
		MONKEES—ALBUMS		
□ 101 (M)	*COLGEMS*	MEET THE MONKEES	3.50	6.00
□ 101 (S)		MEET THE MONKEES	4.50	8.00
□ 102 (M)		MORE OF THE MONKEES	3.50	6.00
□ 102 (S)		MORE OF THE MONKEES	4.50	8.00
□ 103 (M)		HEADQUARTERS	3.50	6.00
□ 103 (S)		HEADQUARTERS	4.50	8.00
□ 104 (M)		PISCES, AQUARIUS, CAPRICORN AND JONES, LTD.	4.00	7.00
□ 104 (S)		PISCES, AQUARIUS, CAPRICORN AND JONES, LTD.	5.00	9.00
□ 109 (M)		THE BIRDS, THE BEES, AND THE MONKEES	4.00	7.00
□ 109 (S)		THE BIRDS, THE BEES, AND THE MONKEES	5.00	9.00
□ 113 (S)		INSTANT REPLAY	5.00	9.00
□ 115 (S)		GREATEST HITS	6.00	10.00
□ 117 (S)		THE MONKEES PRESENT	7.00	12.00
□ 5008 (S)		HEAD	8.00	15.00
□ 1001 (S)		A BARREL FULL OF MONKEES	7.00	12.00
		MONOTONES		
□ 124	*MASCOT*	BOOK OF LOVE/YOU NEVER LOVED ME	12.00	20.00
□ 5290	*ARGO*	BOOK OF LOVE/YOU NEVER LOVED ME (5)	2.00	4.00
		CHRIS MONTEZ		
□ 500	*MONOGRAM*	ALL YOU HAD TO DO (WAS TELL ME)/LOVE ME	1.75	3.00
□ 505		LET'S DANCE/YOU'RE THE ONE (4)	1.00	2.50
□ 507		SOME KINDA FUN/TELL ME (43)	1.25	2.50
□ 513		MY BABY LOVES TO DANCE/IN AN ENGLISH TOWNE	1.50	2.50
□ 517		ALL YOU HAD TO DO (WAS TELL ME)/LOVE ME (with Kathy Young)	1.75	3.00
		CHRIS MONTEZ—ALBUM		
□ 100 (M)	*MONOGRAM*	LET'S DANCE/SOME KINDA FUN	7.00	12.00
		MOODY BLUES		
		FEATURED: DENNY LAINE		
□ 9726	*LONDON*	GO NOW!/LOSE YOUR MONEY (10)	1.25	2.50
□ 9764		FROM THE BOTTOM OF MY HEART/ MY BABY'S GONE (93)	1.50	3.00
□ 9799		YOU DON'T/EV'RY DAY	1.75	3.00
□ 9810		STOP!/BYE BYE BIRD (98)	1.50	2.50
□ 20030		FLY ME HIGH/I REALLY HAVEN'T GOT THE TIME	1.50	2.50

LATER DERAM SINGLES ARE WORTH UP TO $2.00 EACH

MOONGLOWS

The quintet formed in 1951 in Louisville, Kentucky. They sang at parties, dances and small clubs but never bothered to settle on a permanent name. A year after they formed, the group became aware of the growing importance of Cleveland disc jockey Alan Freed, reportedly the first white radio personality to refuse to play white "cover" versions of hits made originally by black artists.

They visited Freed at the WJW studios in Cleveland, and Freed suggested they take on the name of the Moonglows. (Freed's radio program was called "Moondog's Rock and Roll Party".) Freed steered the Moonglows to a solitary single on Champagne, then five discs on the Chance label. He then negotiated a contract with the Chess label in Chicago. Supposedly Freed promised the Moonglows good airplay in return for inclusion of his name as a co-writer on their songs. Words has it that Freed never really wrote anything.

The Moonglows saw their biggest commercial success on Chess, although their original version of the classic "Sincerely" went to No. 1 as a "cover" version by the saccharine McGuire Sisters.

ISSUE #	LABEL	ARTIST/TITLE	VG	MINT
		MOONGLOWS		
□1581	CHESS	SINCERELY/TEMPTING	6.00	10.00
□1589		MOST OF ALL/SHE'S GONE	6.00	10.00
□1611		IN MY DIARY/LOVER LOVE ME	5.00	8.00
□1619		WE GO TOGETHER/CHICKIE UM BAH	5.00	8.00
□1629		SEE SAW/WHEN I'M WITH YOU (28)	2.00	4.00
□1646		OVER AND OVER AGAIN/I KNEW FROM THE START	3.50	6.00
□1705		TEN COMMANDMENTS OF LOVE/MEAN OLD BLUES (with Harvey) (22)	2.50	5.00
		MOTHERS OF INVENTION		
		FEATURED: FRANK ZAPPA		
		SEE: BABY RAY AND THE FERNS, BOB GUY, RON ROMAN, RUBEN AND THE JETS, FRANK ZAPPA		
□10418	VERVE	HOW COULD I BE SUCH A FOOL/HELP, I'M A ROCK	3.50	6.00
□10458		WHO ARE THE BRAIN POLICE?/ TROUBLE COMIN' EVERY DAY	3.00	5.00
□10513		BIG LEG EMMA/WHO DON'T YOU DO ME RIGHT?	3.50	6.00
□10570		MOTHER PEOPLE/LONELY LITTLE GIRL	3.00	5.00
□840	BIZARRE	DOG BREATH/MY GUITAR	3.00	5.00
□967		WOULD YOU GO ALL THE WAY?/ TELL ME YOU LOVE ME	3.00	5.00
□1052		JUNIOR MINTZ BOOGIE/TEARS BEGAN TO FALL	3.00	5.00
□1127		EAT THAT QUESTION/ CLERIUS AWREETUS-AWRIGHTUS	3.00	5.00
		MUGWUMPS (MAMAS AND PAPAS)		
□5471	WARNER BROTHERS	I'LL REMEMBER TONIGHT/I DON'T WANNA KNOW	1.75	3.00
□7018		SEARCHIN'/HERE IT IS, ANOTHER DAY	1.75	3.00
□900	SIDEWALK	JUG BAND MUSIC/BALD-HEADED WOMAN	1.75	3.00
□000		SEASON OF THE WITCH/MY GAL	1.75	3.00
		MUGWUMPS (MAMAS AND PAPAS)—ALBUM		
□1697 (M)	WARNER BROTHERS	THE MUGWUMPS	3.50	6.00
		MURMAIDS		
□628	CHATTAHOOCHEE	POPSICLES AND ICICLES/BLUE DRESS	1.75	3.00
□628		POPSICLES AND ICICLES/HUNTINGTON FLATS (3)	1.00	2.50
□636		HEARTBREAK AHEAD/HE'S GOOD TO ME	1.25	2.00
□650		WILD AND WONDERFUL/BULL TALK	1.25	2.00
		MUSIC EXPLOSION		
□1404	ATTACK	LITTLE BLACK EGG/STAY BY MY SIDE	2.50	4.00
□3380	LAURIE	LITTLE BIT O' SOUL/I SEE THE LIGHT (2)	.75	2.00
□3400		SUNSHINE GAMES/CAN'T STOP NOW (63)	1.25	2.00
□3414		HEARTS AND FLOWERS/WE GOTTA GO HOME	1.25	2.00
□3429		ROAD RUNNER/WHAT YOU WANT	1.25	2.00
□3440		FLASH/WHERE ARE WE GOING?	1.25	2.00
		LATER LAURIE SINGLES ARE WORTH UP TO $1.50 MINT		
		MUSIC EXPLOSION—ALBUM		
□2040 (S)	LAURIE	LITTLE BIT O' SOUL	4.00	7.00

ISSUE #	LABEL	ARTIST/TITLE	VG	MINT
		MUSIC MACHINE		
☐61	**ORIGINAL SOUND**	TALK TALK/COME ON IN (15)	1.25	2.50
☐67		THE PEOPLE IN ME/MASCULINE INTUITION (66) . . .	1.25	2.50
☐71		DOUBLE YELLOW LINE/ABSOLUTELY POSITIVELY . .	1.50	2.50
		MUSIC MACHINE—ALBUM		
☐5015 (M)	**ORIGINAL SOUND**	TURN ON THE MUSIC MACHINE	3.50	6.00
☐8875 (S)		TURN ON THE MUSIC MACHINE	4.50	8.00
		MYSTERIANS		
		SEE: ? AND THE MYSTERIANS		
☐040	**JOX**	IS IT A LIE?/WHY SHOULD I LOVE YOU?	3.50	6.00
		MYSTICS		
☐3028	**LAURIE**	HUSHABYE/ADAM AND EVE (20)	1.50	3.00
☐3038		DON'T TAKE THE STARS/SO TENDERLY (98)	1.75	3.00
☐3047		ALL THROUGH THE NIGHT/		
		I BEGIN (TO THINK OF YOU AGAIN)	1.75	3.00
☐3058		WHITE CLIFFS OF DOVER/BLUE STAR	2.00	3.50
☐3086		STAR-CROSSED LOVERS/GOODBYE MR. BLUES	1.75	3.00
☐3104		A SUNDAY KIND OF LOVE/DARLING, I KNOW	2.00	3.50

ISSUE #	LABEL	ARTIST/TITLE	VG	MINT
		NASHVILLE TEENS		
☐9689	**LONDON**	TOBACCO ROAD/I LIKE IT LIKE THAT (14)	1.25	2.50
☐9712		T.N.T./GOGGLE EYE .	1.50	2.50
☐9736		FIND MY WAY BACK HOME/DEVIL-IN-LAW (98)	1.50	2.50
☐13357	**MGM**	LITTLE BIRD/WHATCHA GONNA DO	1.25	2.00
☐13406		I KNOW HOW IT FEELS TO BE LOVED/		
		SOON FORGOTTEN .	1.25	2.00
☐13483		THE HARD WAY/UPSIDE DOWN	1.25	2.00
		NASHVILLE TEENS—ALBUM		
☐3407 (M)	**LONDON**	TOBACCO ROAD .	3.50	6.00
☐407 (S)		TOBACCO ROAD .	4.50	8.00
		JERRY NAYLOR (FORMER CRICKET)		
☐1118	**SKYLA**	STOP YOUR CRYING/YOU'RE THIRTEEN	2.00	3.50
☐1123		JUDEE MALONE/I'M TIRED	1.75	3.00
		JERRY NEAL (CAPEHART)		
		GUITAR: EDDIE COCHRAN		
☐15810	**DOT**	SCRATCHIN'/I HATES RABBITS	6.00	10.00

RICKY NELSON

Ricky Nelson's parents starred in the hit radio show "The Adventures Of Ozzie and Harriet". Ricky joined the show in 1949 when he was nine years old. (His birthday was May 8, 1940.) Later the show became a television hit.

One night on the television show young Nelson imitated Elvis Presley. In that episode Ricky was dressed as Elvis and was headed to a costume party. Although he sang only a couple of lines of "Love Me Tender", over 10,000 letters poured in the next week. Ricky—with Ozzie as his manager—then went to Verve Records. His first single was a two-sided winner: "A Teenager's Romance"/I'm Walkin' ".

After Nelson's second Verve disc, Imperial Records' president Lew Chudd found that Ricky had no written contract with Verve. Young Nelson was then signed to a long-term Imperial contract. With his good looks, weekly television exposure and some of the best songwriters available, Ricky Nelson became one of the best-selling rock artists of the 1950s.

After nearly a dozen Top 10 Imperial hits, he signed with Decca. There Rick (he changed his name when he turned 21) had only two million-sellers.

ISSUE #	LABEL	ARTIST/TITLE	VG	MINT
		RICKY NELSON		
□ 10047	***VERVE***	A TEENAGER'S ROMANCE/I'M WALKIN' (8)	2.00	4.00
□ 10070		YOU'RE MY ONE AND ONLY LOVE/HONEY ROCK (16)	3.50	6.00
□ 5463	***IMPERIAL***	BE BOP BABY/HAVE I TOLD YOU LATELY THAT I LOVE YOU? (5)	2.00	3.50
□ 5483		STOOD UP/WAITIN' IN SCHOOL (5)	1.75	3.00
□ 5503		BELIEVE WHAT YOU SAY/ MY BUCKET'S GOT A HOLE IN IT (8)	1.75	3.00
□ 5528		POOR LITTLE FOOL/DON'T LEAVE ME THIS WAY (1)	1.50	3.00
□ 5545		LONESOME TOWN/I GOT A FEELING (7)	1.50	3.00
□ 5565		NEVER BE ANYONE ELSE BUT YOU/IT'S LATE (6)	1.50	3.00
□ 5595		SWEETER THAN YOU/JUST A LITTLE TOO MUCH (9)	1.50	3.00
□ 5614		I WANNA BE LOVED/MIGHTY GOOD (20)	1.25	2.50
□ 5663		YOUNG EMOTIONS/RIGHT BY MY SIDE (12)	1.25	2.50
□ 5685		I'M NOT AFRAID/YES SIR, THAT'S MY BABY (27)	1.50	2.50
□ 5707		YOU ARE THE ONLY ONE/MILK COW BLUES (25)	1.50	2.50
□ 5741		TRAVELIN' MAN/HELLO MARY LOU (1)	1.25	2.50
□ 5770		A WONDER LIKE YOU/EVERLOVIN' (11)	1.50	2.50
□ 5805		YOUNG WORLD/SUMMERTIME (5)	1.25	2.50
□ 5864		TEEN AGE IDOL/I'VE GOT MY EYES ON YOU (5)	1.25	2.50
□ 5901		IT'S UP TO YOU/I NEED YOU (6)	1.25	2.50
□ 5910		THAT'S ALL/I'M IN LOVE AGAIN (48)	1.50	2.50
□ 5935		OLD ENOUGH TO LOVE/IF YOU CAN'T ROCK ME (94)	1.50	2.50
□ 5958		A LONG VACATION/MAD, MAD WORLD	1.50	2.50
□ 5985		TIME AFTER TIME/THERE'S NOT A MINUTE	1.50	2.50
□ 66004		TODAY'S TEARDROPS/THANK YOU DARLIN' (54)	1.50	2.50
□ 66017		CONGRATULATIONS/ONE MINUTE TO ONE (63)	1.50	2.50
□ 66039		LUCKY STAR/EVERYBODY BUT ME	1.50	2.50
□ 31475	***DECCA***	YOU DON'T LOVE ME ANYMORE/I GOT A WOMAN (47)	1.50	2.50
□ 31495		STRING ALONG/GYPSY WOMAN (25)	1.25	2.50
□ 31533		FOOLS RUSH IN/DOWN HOME (12)	1.25	2.50
□ 31574		FOR YOU/THAT'S ALL SHE WROTE (6)	1.00	2.00
□ 31612		THE VERY THOUGHT OF YOU/I WONDER (26)	1.25	2.00
□ 31656		THERE'S NOTHING I CAN SAY/LONELY CORNER (47)	1.25	2.00
□ 31703		A HAPPY GUY/DON'T BREATHE A WORD (82)	1.25	2.00
□ 31756		MEAN OLD WORLD/WHEN THE CHIPS ARE DOWN (96)	1.25	2.00
□ 31800		YESTERDAY'S LOVE/COME OUT DANCIN'	1.25	2.00
□ 31845		LOVE AND KISSES/SAY YOU LOVE ME	1.25	2.00
□ 31900		YOUR KIND OF LOVIN'/FIRE-BREATHIN' DRAGON	1.25	2.00
□ 31956		LOUISIANA MAN/YOU JUST CAN'T QUIT	1.25	2.00
□ 32026		THINGS YOU GAVE ME/ALONE	1.25	2.00
□ 32055		TAKE A BROKEN HEART/THEY DON'T GIVE MEDALS	1.25	2.00
□ 32120		I'M CALLED LONELY/TAKE A CITY BRIDE	1.25	2.00
□ 32176		SUZANNE ON A SUNDAY MORNING/MOONSHINE	1.25	2.00
□ 32222		DREAM WEAVER/BABY CLOSE ITS EYES	1.25	2.00
□ 32284		PROMENADE IN GREEN/ DON'T BLAME IT ON YOUR WIFE	1.25	2.00
□ 32298		DON'T MAKE PROMISES/BAREFOOT BOY	1.25	2.00
□ 32550		SHE BELONGS TO ME/PROMISES (33)	1.25	2.00
□ 32635		EASY TO BE FREE/COME ON IN (48)	1.25	2.00
□ 32676		I SHALL BE RELEASED/IF YOU GOTTA, GO, GO NOW	1.25	2.00

ISSUE #	LABEL	ARTIST/TITLE	VG	MINT
□32711		WE GOT SUCH A LONG WAY TO GO/LOOK AT MARY	1.25	2.00
□32739		HOW LONG?/DOWN ALONG THE BAYOU COUNTRY	1.25	2.00
□32779		LIFE/CALIFORNIA	1.25	2.00
□32860		SING ME A SONG/THANK YOU, LORD	1.25	2.00
□32906		LOVE MINUS ZERO-NO LIMIT/GYPSY PILOT	1.50	2.50
□32980		GARDEN PARTY/SO LONG MAMA (6)	.75	1.50
		RICKY NELSON—EPs		
□5048	***VERVE***	RICKY	12.00	20.00
□153	***IMPERIAL***	RICKY	5.00	8.00
□154		RICKY	5.00	8.00
□155		RICKY	5.00	8.00
□156		RICKY NELSON	4.00	7.00
□157		RICKY NELSON	4.00	7.00
□158		RICKY NELSON	4.00	7.00
□159		RICKY SINGS AGAIN	3.50	6.00
□160		RICKY SINGS AGAIN	3.50	6.00
□161		RICKY SINGS AGAIN	3.50	6.00
□162		SONGS BY RICKY	3.00	5.00
□163		SONGS BY RICKY	3.00	5.00
□164		SONGS BY RICKY	3.00	5.00
□165		RICKY SINGS SPIRITUALS	3.00	5.00
		RICKY NELSON—ALBUMS		
□2083 (M)	***VERVE***	TEEN TIME	15.00	25.00
□9048 (M)	***IMPERIAL***	RICKY	8.00	15.00
□9050 (M)		RICKY NELSON	7.00	12.00
□9061 (M)		RICKY SINGS AGAIN	7.00	12.00
□9082 (M)		SONGS BY RICKY	7.00	12.00
□9122 (M)		MORE SONGS BY RICKY	6.00	10.00
□9152 (M)		RICK IS 21	6.00	10.00
□9167 (M)		ALBUM SEVEN BY RICK	6.00	10.00
□9218 (M)		BEST SELLERS	5.00	8.00
□74419 (M)	***DECCA***	FOR YOUR SWEET LOVE	3.50	6.00
□4419 (S)		FOR YOUR SWEET LOVE	4.50	8.00
□74479 (M)		RICK NELSON SINGS FOR YOU	3.50	6.00
□4479 (S)		RICK NELSON SINGS FOR YOU	4.50	8.00
□74559 (M)		THE VERY THOUGHT OF YOU	3.00	5.00
□4559 (S)		THE VERY THOUGHT OF YOU	4.00	7.00
□74608 (M)		SPOTLIGHT ON RICK	3.00	5.00
□4608 (S)		SPOTLIGHT ON RICK	4.00	7.00
STEREO AND MONO ALBUMS HAVE THE SAME VALUE FOR THE FOLLOWING:				
□74660 (M)		BEST ALWAYS	3.50	6.00
□74678 (M)		LOVE AND KISSES	3.50	6.00
□74779 (M)		BRIGHT LIGHTS AND COUNTRY MUSIC	4.00	7.00
□74836 (M)		ON THE FLIP SIDE	3.50	6.00
□74837 (M)		COUNTRY FEVER	3.50	6.00
□75014 (M)		PERSPECTIVE	3.00	5.00

SANDY NELSON

ISSUE #	LABEL	ARTIST/TITLE	VG	MINT
□5	***ORIGINAL SOUND***	TEEN BEAT/BIG JUMP (4)	1.25	2.50
□5630	***IMPERIAL***	DRUM PARTY/BIG NOISE FROM WINNETKA	1.50	2.50
□5648		PARTY TIME/THE WIGGLE	1.50	2.50

ISSUE #	LABEL	ARTIST/TITLE	VG	MINT
□5672		BOUNCY/LOST DREAMS	1.50	2.50
□5708		COOL OPERATOR/JIVE TALK	1.50	2.50
□5745		BIG NOISE FROM THE JUNGLE/GET WITH IT	1.50	2.50
□5775		LET THERE BE DRUMS/QUITE A BEAT (7)	1.00	2.00
□5809		DRUMS ARE MY BEAT/THE BIRTH OF THE BEAT (29)	1.25	2.00
□5829		DRUMMIN' UP A STORM/DRUM STOMP (67)	1.25	2.00
□5860		ALL NIGHT LONG/ROMPIN' AND STOMPIN' (75)	1.25	2.00
□5870		AND THEN THERE WERE DRUMS/LIVE IT UP (65)	1.25	2.00
□5884		TEENAGE HOUSE PARTY/DAY TRAIN	1.25	2.00
□5904		LET THE FOUR WINDS BLOW/BE BOP BABY	1.25	2.00
□5932		OOH POO PAH DOO/FEEL SO GOOD	1.25	2.00
		LATER IMPERIAL SINGLES ARE WORTH UP TO $1.50 MINT		
		SANDY NELSON—ALBUMS		
□9044 (M)	*IMPERIAL*	SANDY NELSON PLAYS TEEN BEAT	6.00	10.00
□9136 (M)		HE'S A DRUMMER BOY	4.50	8.00
□9159 (M)		LET THERE BE DRUMS	3.50	6.00
□9168 (M)		DRUMS ARE MY BEAT	3.50	6.00
□9189 (M)		DRUMMIN' UP A STORM	3.00	5.00
		NEONS		
□444	*TETRA*	ANGEL FACE/KISS ME QUICKLY	5.00	8.00
□4449		ROAD TO ROMANCE/MY CHICKADEE	7.00	12.00
		NERVOUS NORVUS		
		SEE: FOUR JOKERS		
□15470	*DOT*	TRANSMISSION/DIG (13)	2.50	4.00
□15485		APE CALL/WILD DOG OF KENTUCKY (28)	3.00	5.00
□15500		THE FANG/THE BULLFROG HOP	4.00	7.00
		THE ABOVE FIRST-ISSUES WERE ON A MAROON LABEL		
□117	*EMBEE*	STONEAGE WOO/I LIKE GIRLS	6.00	10.00
		MIKE NESMITH		
		SEE: MONKEES		
□1001	*EDAN*	JUST A LITTLE LOVE/CURSON TERRACE	8.00	15.00
		NEWBEATS		
□1269	*HICKORY*	BREAD AND BUTTER/TOUGH LITTLE BUGGY (2)	1.00	2.00
□1282		EVERYTHING'S ALRIGHT/PINK DALLY RUE (16)	1.25	2.00
□1290		BREAK AWAY (FROM THAT BOY)/HEY-O, DADDY-O (40)	1.25	2.00
□1305		THE BIRDS ARE FOR THE BEES/ BETTER WATCH YOUR STEP (50)	1.25	2.00
□1332		RUN BABY RUN/MEAN WOOLIE WILLY (12)	1.00	2.00
□1366		SHAKE HANDS/TOO SWEET TO BE FORGOTTEN (92)	1.25	2.00
		NEWBEAT—ALBUM		
□120 (M)	*HICKORY*	BREAD AND BUTTER	4.50	8.00
□122 (M)		BIG BEAT SOUNDS	4.00	7.00
□128 (M)		RUN BABY RUN	4.00	7.00
		TED NEWMAN		
□3505	*REV*	PLAYTHING/UNLUCKY ME (45)	1.50	2.50
□3511		I DOUBLE DARE YOU/NONE OF YOUR TEARS	1.25	2.00
		NEWPORTERS		
		SEE: WALKER BROTHERS		
□500	*SCOTCHTOWN*	LOOSE BOARD/ADVENTURES IN PARADISE	3.00	5.00

ISSUE #	LABEL	ARTIST/TITLE	VG	MINT
		WAYNE NEWTON		
		FEATURED: BRUCE JOHNSTON, TERRY MELCHER (BRUCE AND TERRY)		
□5338	*CAPITOL*	COMIN' ON TOO STRONG/ LOOKING THROUGH A TEAR (65)	4.00	7.00
		OLIVIA NEWTON-JOHN		
□55281	*UNI*	IF NOT FOR YOU/THE BIGGEST CLOWN (25)	1.25	2.00
□55304		BANKS OF THE OHIO/ IT'S HARD TO SAY GOODBYE (94)	1.50	2.50
□55317		WHAT IS LIFE/IN A SMALL AND LONELY LIGHT	1.50	2.50
□55348		JUST A LITTLE TOO MUCH/MY OLD MAN'S GOT A GUN	1.50	2.50
□40043	*MCA*	TAKE ME HOME, COUNTRY ROADS/ SAIL INTO TOMORROW	1.25	2.00
		LATER MCA SINGLES ARE WORTH UP TO $1.50 MINT		
		NICKIE AND THE NITELITES		
□55155	*BRUNSWICK*	TELL ME YOU CARE/I'M LONELY	7.00	12.00
		NICKY AND THE NOBLES		
□1098	*END*	SCHOOL BELLS/SCHOOL DAY CRUSH	3.50	6.00
□5039	*GONE*	SCHOOL BELLS/SCHOOL DAY CRUSH	2.50	4.00
□1	*TIMES SQUARE*	TING-A-LING/POOR ROCK 'N' ROLL	3.00	5.00
□12		CRIME DON'T PAY/DARKNESS	3.00	5.00
□33		WHY BE A FOOL/THE SEARCH	2.50	4.00
□37		SCHOOL BELLS/SCHOOL DAY CRUSH	2.00	3.50
		NIGHTCRAWLERS		
□1012	*LEE*	LITTLE BLACK EGG/IF I WERE YOU	3.00	5.00
□709	*KAPP*	LITTLE BLACK EGG/IF I WERE YOU (85)	1.50	2.50
		NIGHTCRAWLERS—ALBUM		
□1520 (M)	*KAPP*	THE LITTLE BLACK EGG	5.00	8.00
		NINO AND THE EBB TIDES		
□405	*RECORTE*	PUPPY LOVE/YOU MAKE ME WANT TO ROCK AND ROLL	6.00	10.00
□408		PURPLE SHADOWS/ THE REAL MEANING OF CHRISTMAS	8.00	15.00
□409		I'M CONFESSIN'/TELL THE WORLD I DO	6.00	10.00
□413		DON'T LOOK AROUND/I LOVE GIRLS	7.00	12.00
		JACK NITZSCHE		
□20202	*REPRISE*	THE LONELY SURFER/ SONG FOR A SUMMER NIGHT (39)	1.50	2.50
□20225		RUMBLE/THEME FOR A BROKEN HEART (91)	1.50	2.50
		JACK NITZSCHE—ALBUM		
□6101 (M)	*REPRISE*	THE LONELY SURFER	5.00	8.00
□6101 (S)		THE LONELY SURFER	6.00	10.00
		NOBLETONES		
□182	C & M	I'M REALLY TOO YOUNG/I LOVE YOU	8.00	15.00
□438		I'M CRYING/MAMBO BOOGIE	5.00	8.00

ISSUE #	LABEL	ARTIST/TITLE	VG	MINT
		NORTONES		
□ 5065	***WARNER BROTHERS***	SUSIE JONES/THAT'S THE WAY THE COOKIE CRUMBLES	3.50	6.00
□ 5115		SMILE, JUST SMILE/BOY	3.00	5.00
		NUMBERS		
□ 101	***BONNEVILLE***	MY PILLOW/BIG RED	7.00	12.00
		NUTMEGS		
□ 452	***HERALD***	A STORY UNTOLD/MAKE ME LOSE MY MIND	4.00	7.00
□ 459		SHIP OF LOVE/ROCK ME, SQUEEZE ME	3.50	6.00
		NUTMEGS—EP		
□ 452	***HERALD***	THE NUTMEGS	5.00	8.00
		LAURA NYRO		
□ 5024	***VERVE FORECAST***	WEDDING BELL BLUES/STONEY END	1.50	2.50
□ 5051		AND WHEN I DIE/FLIM FLAM MAN	1.50	2.50
□ 44531	***COLUMBIA***	ELI'S COMIN'/SWEET BLINDNESS	1.50	2.50

THESE ARE ORIGINAL VERSIONS OF SONGS THAT WERE LATER TO BECOME MAJOR HITS FOR OTHER SINGERS AND GROUPS.

ISSUE #	LABEL	ARTIST/TITLE	VG	MINT
		OLYMPICS		
□ 1508	***DEMON***	WESTERN MOVIES/WELL (8)	1.25	3.00
□ 1512		DANCE WITH THE TEACHER/ EV'RYBODY NEEDS LOVE (71)	1.50	3.00
□ 1514		CHICKEN/YOUR LOVE	1.75	3.00
□ 562	***ARVEE***	(BABY) HULLY GULLY/PRIVATE EYE (72)	1.75	3.00
□ 595		BIG BOY PETE/THE SLOP (50)	1.50	3.00
□ 5006		SHIMMY LIKE KATE/WORKIN' HARD (42)	1.50	3.00
□ 5020		DANCE BY THE LIGHT OF THE MOON/DODGE CITY (47)	1.50	3.00
□ 5023		LITTLE PEDRO/BULL FIGHT (76)	1.50	2.50
□ 5031		DOOLEY/STAY WERE YOU ARE (94)	1.50	2.50
□ 5044		STOMP/MASH THEM 'TATERS	1.50	2.50
□ 5051		EVERYBODY LIKES TO CHA-CHA-CHA/TWIST	1.50	2.50
□ 5056		BABY IT'S HOT/THE SCOTCH	1.50	2.50
		OLYMPICS—EP		
□ 423	***ARVEE***	DOIN' THE HULLY GULLY	3.00	5.00
		OLYMPICS—ALBUMS		
□ 423 (M)	***ARVEE***	DOIN' THE HULLY GULLY	7.00	12.00
□ 424 (M)		DANCE BY THE LIGHT OF THE MOON	6.00	10.00

ROY ORBISON

Born in the Texas town of Vernon on April 21, 1936, Roy Orbison and his family soon moved to the village of Wink. As a boy, the talented Roy mastered the guitar and harmonica in a fairly short time.

After finishing high school, Roy entered North Texas State College. It was there that classmate Pat Boone encouraged Orbison to pursue a singing career. (At the time Roy was a geology major.) Roy Orbison formed a band—the Teen Kings—and cut a solitary disc for Je-Wel Records. The song was "Ooby Dooby" and was co-written by a college professor of English. The Je-Wel single failed to sell, so Orbison and his group auditioned for Sun Records. They re-cut "Ooby Dooby" and it became a fair-sized hit.

Roy Orbison hit the Top 10 in 1960 with "Only the Lonely" on Monument. Eight more Monument best-sellers followed, with a pair going to No. 1. Roy later signed with MGM Records, but by then his career was on the wane.

Orbison was also a talented songwriter and penned such hits as the Everly Brothers' "Claudette". The song was written for his wife, who died in a motorcycle accident. Roy would later lose two of his three children in a tragic house fire.

ISSUE #	LABEL	ARTIST/TITLE	VG	MINT
		ROY ORBISON		
☐101	*JE-WEL*	OOBY DOOBY/TRYING TO GET TO YOU	80.00	150.00
THE JE-WEL VERSION DIFFERS FROM THE SUN VERSION OF "OOBY DOOBY"				
		SEE SUN DISCOGRAPHY		
☐7381	*RCA*	SWEET AND INNOCENT/SEEMS TO ME	3.50	6.00
☐7447		ALMOST EIGHTEEN/JOLIE	5.00	8.00
☐409	*MONUMENT*	PAPER BOY/WITH THE BUG	2.50	4.00
☐412		UP TOWN/PRETTY ONE (72)	1.75	3.00
☐421		ONLY THE LONELY/ HERE COMES THAT SONG AGAIN (2)	1.25	2.50
☐425		BLUE ANGEL/TODAY'S TEARDROPS (9)	1.25	2.50
☐433		I'M HURTIN'/I CAN'T STOP LOVING YOU (27)	1.50	2.50
☐438		RUNNING SCARED/LOVE HURTS (1)	1.00	2.50
☐447		CRYIN'/CANDY MAN (2)	1.00	2.50
☐456		DREAM BABY/THE ACTRESS (4)	1.00	2.50
☐461		THE CROWD/MAMA (26)	1.50	2.50
☐467		LEAH/WORKIN' FOR THE MAN (25)	1.50	2.50
☐806		IN DREAMS/SHAHDAROBA (7)	1.00	2.00
☐815		FALLING/DISTANT DRUMS (22)	1.25	2.00
☐824		MEAN WOMAN BLUES/BLUE BAYOU (5)	1.00	2.00
☐830		PRETTY PAPER/BEAUTIFUL DREAMER (15)	1.25	2.00
☐837		IT'S OVER/INDIAN WEDDING (9)	1.00	2.00
☐851		OH, PRETTY WOMAN/YO TE AMO MARIA (1)	1.00	2.00
☐873		GOODNIGHT/ONLY WITH YOU (21)	1.25	2.00
☐891		(SAY) YOU'RE MY GIRL/SLEEPY HOLLOW (39)	1.25	2.00
☐906		LET THE GOOD TIMES ROLL/DISTANT DRUMS (81)	1.25	2.00
☐939		LANA/OUR SUMMER SONG	1.25	2.00
		ROY ORBISON—ALBUMS		
☐1260 (M)	*SUN*	ROY ORBISON AT THE ROCKHOUSE	12.00	20.00
☐4002 (M)	*MONUMENT*	LONELY AND BLUE	7.00	12.00
☐14002 (S)		LONELY AND BLUE	8.00	15.00
☐4007 (M)		CRYING	6.00	10.00
☐14007 (S)		CRYING	7.00	12.00
☐4009 (M)		GREATEST HITS	3.50	6.00
☐14009 (S)		GREATEST HITS	4.50	8.00
☐8003 (M)		IN DREAMS	4.00	7.00
☐18003 (S)		IN DREAMS	5.00	9.00
☐8023 (M)		EARLY ORBISON	3.50	6.00
☐18023 (S)		EARLY ORBISON	4.50	8.00
☐8024 (M)		MORE OF ROY ORBISON'S GREATEST HITS	4.00	7.00
☐18024 (S)		MORE OF ROY ORBISON'S GREATEST HITS	5.00	9.00
		ORIOLES		
☐5122	*JUBILEE*	CRYING IN THE CHAPEL/ DON'T YOU THINK I OUGHT TO KNOW (11)	5.00	10.00
☐5154		IN THE CHAPEL IN THE MOONLIGHT/TAKE THE LORD	7.00	12.00

TONY ORLANDO

Michael Anthony Orlando Cassivitis quit school in 1958 after completing only the eighth grade. (Birthdate: April 3, 1944). Both his mother and step-father worked in the evenings, and young Cassivitis was left in the care of his severely retarded step-sister. The compassionate boy's soft crooning had a sedating effect on the infant. Tony paid the price, though; he often fell asleep during class and had no time for homework at night.

Tony managed to convince Don Kirshner, then a fast-rising music publisher, to hire him as a demo singer. (Kirshner also had Carole King and Paul Simon working for him as demo vocalists.) While he usually had Tony cut songs for other, established artists, Kirshner did release several Tony Orlando singles. Only two broke the Top 40. Orlando was pleased (a previous Milo single had done nothing) but was overweight and reluctant to tour to promote his records. As a result his career declined.

Tony later sang under different names. In 1970 "Candida", a song done by Tony as a demo for a friend, appeared on Bell Records as being by Dawn (really Tony and two unknown Motown session singers). Orlando went on a diet, lost 98 pounds, toured and enjoyed great success during the early 1970s.

ISSUE #	LABEL	ARTIST/TITLE	VG	MINT
		TONY ORLANDO		
		SEE: BERTELL DACHE, BILLY SHIELDS, WIND		
□101	*MILO*	DING DONG/YOU AND ONLY YOU	8.00	15.00
□9441	*EPIC*	HALFWAY TO PARADISE/LONELY TOMORROWS (39)	1.50	3.00
□9452		BLESS YOU/AM I THE GUY (15)	1.25	3.00
□9476		HAPPY TIMES ARE HERE TO STAY/LONELY AM I (82)	1.50	3.00
□9491		MY BABY'S A STRANGER/TALKIN' ABOUT YOU	1.50	2.50
□9502		LOVE ON YOUR LIPS/I'D NEVER FIND ANOTHER YOU	1.50	2.50
□9519		CHILLS/AT THE EDGE OF TEARS	1.75	3.00
□9562		THE LONELIEST/BEAUTIFUL DREAMER	1.50	2.50
□9570		SHIRLEY/JOANIE	1.50	2.50
□9622		I'LL BE THERE/WHAT AM I GONNA DO?	1.75	3.00
□9668		SHE DOESN'T KNOW ME/TELL ME, WHAT CAN I DO?	1.50	2.50
□9715		TO WAIT FOR LOVE/ACCEPTED	1.50	2.50
□6376	*ATCO*	THINK BEFORE YOU ACT/ SHE LOVES ME (FOR WHAT I AM)	1.75	3.00
□471	*CAMEO*	SWEET, SWEET/MANUELITO	1.75	3.00
		TONY ORLANDO—ALBUM		
□3808 (M)	*EPIC*	BLESS YOU	8.00	15.00
□611 (S)		BLESS YOU	12.00	20.00
		ORLONS		
□198	*CAMEO*	I'LL BE TRUE/HEART DARLING ANGEL	2.00	3.50
□211		MR. 21/PLEASE LET IT BE ME	1.75	3.00
□218		THE WAH WATUSI/HOLIDAY HILL (2)	1.00	2.00
□231		DON'T HANG UP/THE CONSERVATIVE (4)	1.00	2.00
□243		SOUTH STREET/THEM TERRIBLE BOOTS (3)	1.00	2.00
□257		NOT ME/MY BEST FRIEND (12)	1.00	2.00
□273		CROSSFIRE!/IT'S NO BIG THING (19)	1.00	2.00
□287		BON-DOO-WAH/DON'T THROW YOUR LOVE AWAY (55)	1.25	2.00
□295		SHIMMY SHIMMY/EVERYTHING NICE (66)	1.25	2.00
□319		RULES OF LOVE/HEARTBREAK HOTEL (66)	1.25	2.00
□332		KNOCK KNOCK (WHO'S THERE?)/GOIN' PLACES (64)	1.25	2.00
		LATER CAMEO SINGLES ARE WORTH UP TO $1.50 MINT		
		ORLONS—ALBUMS		
□1041 (M)	*CAMEO*	SOUTH STREET	3.00	5.00
□1054 (M)		NOT ME	3.00	5.00
□1061 (M)		BIGGEST HITS	3.00	5.00
		OUR GANG		
		FEATURED: LEON RUSSELL, DEAN TORRENCE		
□001	*BR'ER BIRD*	SUMMERTIME, SUMMERTIME/ THEME FROM LEON'S GARAGE	25.00	40.00
		OUTSIDERS		
□5573	*CAPITOL*	TIME WON'T LET ME/WAS IT REALLY REAL? (5)	1.00	2.00
□5646		GIRL IN LOVE/WHAT MAKES YOU SO BAD? (21)	1.25	2.00
□5701		RESPECTABLE/LOST IN MY WORLD (15)	1.25	2.00
□5759		HELP ME GIRL/YOU GOTTA LOOK (37)	1.25	2.00
□5843		I'LL GIVE YOU TIME/I'M NOT TRYIN' TO HURT YOU	1.25	2.00
□5892		I JUST CAN'T SEE YOU ANYMORE/ GOTTA LEAVE US ALONE	1.25	2.00

ISSUE #	LABEL	ARTIST/TITLE	VG	MINT
☐ 5955		AND NOW YOU WANT MY SYMPATHY/		
		I'LL SEE YOU IN THE SUMMERTIME	1.25	2.00
☐ 2055		LITTLE BIT OF LOVIN'/I WILL LOVE YOU	1.25	2.00
☐ 2216		OH, HOW IT HURTS/WE AIN'T GONNA MAKE IT	1.00	1.50
		OUTSIDERS—ALBUMS		
☐ 2501 (M)	*CAPITOL*	TIME WON'T LET ME .	3.50	6.00
☐ 2501 (S)		TIME WON'T LET ME .	4.50	8.00
☐ 2568 (M)		ALBUM #2 .	3.00	5.00
☐ 2568 (S)		ALBUM #2 .	4.00	7.00

OVATIONS

☐ 101	*BARRY*	THE DAY WE FELL IN LOVE/MY LULLABY	3.50	6.00

ISSUE #	LABEL	ARTIST/TITLE	VG	MINT

PALISADES
FEATURED: CAROLE KING

☐ 4401	*CHAIRMAN*	MAKE THE NIGHT A LITTLE LONGER/		
		IT'S HEAVEN BEING WITH YOU	5.00	8.00

PARADONS

☐ 2003	*MILESTONE*	DIAMONDS AND PEARLS/I WANT LOVE (18)	1.25	2.50

PARAMOUNTS

☐ 524	*CARLTON*	TRYING/GIRL FRIEND .	3.50	6.00
☐ 16201	*DOT*	WHEN YOU DANCE/YOU'RE SEVENTEEN	3.50	6.00
☐ 1099	*EMBER*	SHEDDING TEARDROPS/IN A DREAM	3.00	5.00
☐ 3201	*LAURIE*	JUST TO BE WITH YOU/ONE MORE FOR THE ROAD	3.50	6.00

PARAMOURS (RIGHTEOUS BROTHERS)

☐ 214	*MOONGLOW*	THAT'S ALL I WANT TONIGHT/THERE SHE GOES . . .	4.00	7.00
☐ 214		THAT'S ALL I WANT TONIGHT/THERE SHE GOES		
		(colored wax) .	6.00	10.00

PARIS SISTERS

☐ 5465	*IMPERIAL*	OLD ENOUGH TO CRY/TELL ME MORE	2.00	3.50
☐ 5487		SOME DAY/MY ORIGINAL LOVE	2.00	3.50
☐ 2	*GREGMARK*	BE MY BOY/I'LL BE CRYING TOMORROW (56)	1.75	3.00
☐ 6		I KNOW HOW YOU LOVE ME/		
		ALL THROUGH THE NIGHT (5)	1.25	2.50
☐ 10		HE KNOWS I LOVE HIM TOO MUCH/		
		A LONELY GIRL'S PRAYER (34)	1.50	2.50
☐ 12		LET ME BE THE ONE/WHAT AM I TO DO (87)	1.50	2.50
☐ 13		ONCE UPON A WHILE AGO/YES, I LOVE YOU	1.50	2.50
☐ 13236	*MGM*	DREAM LOVER/LONELY GIRL (91)	1.25	2.00
		PARIS SISTERS—ALBUM		
☐ 5906 (M)	*SIDEWALK*	GOLDEN HITS OF THE PARIS SISTERS	5.00	8.00

BILL PARSONS

☐ 835	*FRATERNITY*	THE ALL AMERICAN BOY/RUBBER DOLLY (2)	1.50	3.00
☐ 838		EDUCATED ROCK AND ROLL/CAREFREE WANDERER	1.75	3.00

ISSUE #	LABEL	ARTIST/TITLE	VG	MINT
		PASSIONS		
☐102	***AUDICON***	JUST TO BE WITH YOU/OH MELANCHOLY ME (69)	3.00	5.00
☐105		I ONLY WANT YOU/THIS IS MY LOVE	2.50	4.00
☐106		GLORIA/JUNGLE DRUMS	3.50	6.00
☐108		BEAUTIFUL DREAMER/ONE LOOK IS ALL IT TOOK	3.00	5.00
☐112		MADE FOR LOVERS/YOU DON'T LOVE ME ANYMORE	4.00	7.00
☐146	***DIAMOND***	SIXTEEN CANDLES/THE THIRD FLOOR	3.00	5.00
☐5406	***JUBILEE***	LONELY ROAD/ONE LOOK IS ALL IT TOOK	2.50	4.00
		PASTEL SIX		
☐102	***ZEN***	CINNAMON CINDER/BANDIDO (25)	1.25	2.50
☐101	***DOWNEY***	TWITCHIN'/OPEN HOUSE AT THE CINDER	1.75	3.00
☐101		TWITCHIN'/WINO STOMP	1.50	2.50
		PAUL AND PAULA		
		SEE: JILL AND RAY		
☐40084	***PHILIPS***	HEY PAULA/BOBBY IS THE ONE (1)	1.00	2.00
☐40096		YOUNG LOVERS/BA-HAY-BE (6)	1.00	2.00
☐40114		FIRST QUARREL/SCHOOL IS THRU (27)	1.25	2.00
☐40130		SOMETHING OLD, SOMETHING NEW,/ FLIPPED OVER YOU (77)	1.25	2.00
☐40142		FIRST DAY BACK AT SCHOOL/A PERFECT PAIR (60)	1.25	2.00
☐40158		HOLIDAY FOR TEENS/HOLIDAY HOOTENANNY	1.25	2.00
		LATER PHILIPS SINGLES ARE WORTH UP TO $2.00 MINT		
		PAUL AND PAULA—ALBUM		
☐200078 (M)	***PHILIPS***	PAUL AND PAULA SING FOR YOUNG LOVERS	3.50	6.00
☐600078 (S)		PAUL AND PAULA SING FOR YOUNG LOVERS	4.50	8.00
		GARY PAXTON		
☐44108	***GARPAX***	YOUR PAST IS BACK AGAIN/ DUAL HUMP CAMEL NAMED ROBERT E. LEE	1.75	3.00
☐44177		HOW TO BE A FOOL/THE SCAVENGER	1.75	3.00
☐8691	***FELSTED***	KANSAS CITY/SWEET SENORITA FROM SANTA FE	1.75	3.00
☐55584	***LIBERTY***	SPOOKY MOVIES (PT. 1)/(PT. 11)	1.50	2.50
☐5208	***LONDON***	SUPER TORQUE/CUTE LITTLE COLT	1.75	3.00
		PENDLETONS		
		FEATURED: GARY USHER		
☐16511	***DOT***	BAREFOOT ADVENTURE/BOARD PARTY	2.00	3.50
		PENGUINS		
☐348	***DOOTONE***	EARTH ANGEL/HEY SENORITA (8)	6.00	12.00

CARL PERKINS

Carl Perkins came from the Tennessee farming town of Jackson, where he was born on April 9, 1932. Being from the South, Carl grew up hearing both the sounds of country music and that of r & b songs. He soon began to play the guitar and make up songs of his own.

Not wanting to become a farmer as his ancestors had been, Perkins went to Memphis to look up Sam Phillips, the owner of Sun Records. At that time Elvis Presley—a former Sun artist—had just become the first rock-and-roll superstar. Sam Phillips hoped to create a new Presley in the form of lanky Carl Perkins.

A first single flopped, but Carl's second release of "Blue Suede Shoes" became a Top 10 smash and stands today as a true rockabilly classic. Carl had been at a dance and overheard someone say "Don't step on my blue suede shoes!" At home Perkins wrote the lyrics to the future million-seller on a paper shopping bag. (The family had no writing paper, Perkins later said.)

Carl Perkins' career failed to gain momentum when he was hurt in a car wreck and was unable to tour to promote his later Sun singles. Perkins later switched to Columbia but had little success.

ISSUE #	LABEL	ARTIST/TITLE	VG	MINT
		CARL PERKINS		
☐501	*FLIP*	MOVIE MAGG/TURN AROUND	125.00	200.00
		SEE SUN DISCOGRAPHY		
☐41131	*COLUMBIA*	PINK PEDAL PUSHERS/JIVE AFTER FIVE (91)	3.00	5.00
☐41207		LEVI JACKET/POP, LET ME HAVE THE CAR	2.50	4.00
☐41379		POINTED TOE SHOES/HIGHWAY OF LOVE (93)	3.00	5.00
☐42061		ANYWAY THE WIND BLOWS/THE UNHAPPY GIRLS	2.50	4.00
☐45107		ALL MAMA'S CHILDREN/STEP ASIDE	2.50	4.00
☐45347		RED HEADED WOMAN/ME WITHOUT YOU	2.50	4.00
		CARL PERKINS—EPs		
☐115	*SUN*	CARL PERKINS	12.00	20.00
☐12341	*COLUMBIA*	WHOLE LOTTA SHAKIN'	8.00	15.00
		CARL PERKINS—ALBUMS		
☐1225	*SUN*	DANCE ALBUM (shoes on cover)	60.00	100.00
☐1225		TEEN BEAT-THE BEST OF CARL PERKINS (without shoes)	40.00	70.00
☐1234 (M)	*COLUMBIA*	WHOLE LOTTA SHAKIN'	25.00	40.00
		PERSIANS		
☐114	*RSVP*	TEARS OF LOVE/DANCE NOW	3.50	6.00
☐1	*GOLDISC*	TEARDROPS ARE FALLING/VAULT OF MEMORIES	2.50	4.00
☐17		WHEN YOU SAID LET'S GET MARRIED/ LET'S MONKEY AROUND	2.00	3.50
		PAUL PETERSON		
☐620	*COLPIX*	SHE CAN'T FIND HER KEYS/VERY UNLIKELY (19)	1.25	2.50
☐632		KEEP YOUR LOVE LOCKED/ BE EVERYTHING TO ANYONE YOU LOVE (58)	1.50	2.50
☐649		LOLLIPOPS AND ROSES/PLEASE MR. SUN (54)	1.50	2.50
☐663		MY DAD/LITTLE BOY SAD (6)	1.25	2.50
☐676		AMY/GOODY GOODY (65)	1.50	2.50
☐697		GIRLS IN THE SUMMERTIME/ MAMA, YOUR LITTLE BOY FELL	1.50	2.50
☐707		THE CHEER LEADER/ POLKA DOTS AND MOON BEAMS (78)	1.50	2.50
☐720		SHE RIDES WITH ME/POOREST BOY IN TOWN	3.50	6.00
		PRODUCER ON COLPIX 720: BRIAN WILSON		
		PAUL PETERSON—ALBUMS		
☐429 (M)	*COLPIX*	LOLLIPOPS AND ROSES	3.50	6.00
☐429 (S)		LOLLIPOPS AND ROSES	4.50	8.00
☐442 (M)		MY DAD	3.50	6.00
☐442 (S)		MY DAD	4.50	8.00
		RAY PETERSON		
☐7098	*RCA*	FEVER/WE'RE OLD ENOUGH TO CRY	1.75	3.00
☐7165		LET'S TRY ROMANCE/SHIRLEY PURLY	1.75	3.00
☐7255		SUDDENLY/TAIL LIGHT	1.75	3.00
☐7303		MY BLUE-EYED BABY/PATRICIA	1.75	3.00
☐7336		DREAM WAY/I'LL ALWAYS WANT YOU NEAR	1.75	3.00
☐7404		RICHER THAN I/LOVE IS A WOMAN	1.75	3.00
☐7513		THE WONDER OF YOU/I'M GONE (25)	1.50	2.50
☐7578		MY BLUE ANGEL/COME AND GET IT	1.50	2.50

ISSUE #	LABEL	ARTIST/TITLE	VG	MINT
□7635		GOODNIGHT MY LOVE/TILL THEN (64)	1.50	2.50
□7703		ANSWER ME, MY LOVE/WHAT DO YOU WANT TO MAKE THOSE EYES AT ME FOR?	1.50	2.50
□7745		TELL LAURA I LOVE HER/WEDDING DAY (7)	1.25	2.50
□7779		TEENAGE HEARTACHE/I'LL ALWAYS WANT YOU NEAR	1.50	2.50
□7845		MY BLUE ANGEL/I'M TIRED	1.25	2.00
□8333		THE WONDER OF YOU/I'M GONE (70)	1.25	2.00
□2002	*DUNES*	CORINNA, CORINNA/BE MY GIRL (9)	1.25	2.50
□2004		SWEET LITTLE KATHY/YOU DIDN'T CARE (100)	1.50	2.50
□2006		MISSING YOU/YOU THRILL ME (29)	1.50	2.50
□2009		I COULD HAVE LOVED YOU SO WELL/ WHY DON'T YOU WRITE ME (57)	1.50	2.50
□2013		YOU KNOW ME MUCH TOO WELL/YOU DIDN'T CARE	1.50	2.50
□2018		IF ONLY TOMORROW/YOU DIDN'T CARE	1.25	2.00
□2019		IS IT WRONG?/SLOWLY	1.25	2.00
□2022		I'M NOT JIMMY/A LOVE TO REMEMBER	1.25	2.00
□2024		WHERE ARE YOU?/DEEP ARE THE ROOTS	1.25	2.00
□2025		GIVE US YOUR BLESSING/WITHOUT LOVE (70)	1.50	2.50
□2027		BE MY GIRL/I FORGOT WHAT IT WAS LIKE	1.25	2.00
□2030		SWEET LITTLE KATHY/ PROMISES YOU MADE ARE BROKEN	1.25	2.00
		RAY PETERSON—EP		
□4367	*RCA*	TELL LAURA I LOVE HER	3.50	6.00
		RAY PETERSON—ALBUM		
□2297 (M)	*RCA*	TELL LAURA I LOVE HER	6.00	10.00
□2297 (S)		TELL LAURA I LOVE HER	7.00	12.00

NORMAN PETTY TRIO

GUITAR: BUDDY HOLLY

□41039	*COLUMBIA*	MOONDREAMS/TOY BOY	7.00	12.00

PHAETONS

FEATURED: DEAN TORRENCE

□103	*SAHARA*	THE BEATLE WALK/FRANTIC	2.00	3.50

PHAROAHS

□1006	*CLASS*	TEENAGER'S LOVE SONG/WATUSI	12.00	20.00

PHAROS

PRODUCER: BRUCE JOHNSTON

□1327	*DONNA*	TENDER TOUCH/HEADS UP, HIGH HOPES OVER YOU	3.50	6.00
□4208	*DEL-FI*	RHYTHM SURFER/PINTOR	2.50	4.00

PHIL PHILLIPS

□711	*KHOURY'S*	SEA OF LOVE/JUELLA	25.00	40.00
□71465	*MERCURY*	SEA OF LOVE/JUELLA (2)	1.25	2.50

BOBBY "BORIS" PICKETT

□44167	*GARPAX*	MONSTER MASH/MONSTER MASH PARTY (1)	1.00	2.50
□44171		MONSTER'S HOLIDAY/MONSTER MOTION (30)	1.25	2.50
□44175		GRADUATION DAY/THE HUMPTY DUMPTY (88)	1.50	2.50

VITO PICONE

SEE: ELEGANTS

□103	*ADMIRAL*	I LIKE TO RUN/THE SONG FROM MOULIN ROUGE	3.00	5.00
□302		STILL WATERS RUN DEEP/BOLT OF LIGHTNING	4.00	7.00

ISSUE #	LABEL	ARTIST/TITLE	VG	MINT
		PILTDOWN MEN		
□ 4414	*CAPITOL*	BRONTOSAURUS STOMP/McDONALD'S CAVE (75)	2.00	3.50
□ 4460		PILTDOWN RIDES AGAIN/BUBBLES IN THE TAR	1.75	3.00
□ 4501		GOODNIGHT MRS. FLINTSTONE/ THE GREAT IMPOSTER	1.75	3.00
□ 4581		FOSSIL ROCK/GARGANTUA	1.75	3.00
□ 4703		BIG LIZARD/A PRETTY GIRL IS LIKE A MELODY	1.75	3.00
		GENE PITNEY		
		SEE: BILLY BRYAN		
□ 25002	*FESTIVAL*	PLEASE COME BACK/I'LL FIND YOU	4.00	7.00
□ 1002	*MUSICOR*	LOVE MY LIFE AWAY/ I LAUGHED SO HARD I CRIED (39)	1.50	3.00
□ 1006		LOUISIANA MAN/TAKE ME TONIGHT	1.75	3.00
□ 1009		TOWN WITHOUT PITY/ AIR MAIL SPECIAL DELIVERY (13)	1.00	2.50
□ 1011		EVERY BREATH I TAKE/ MR. MOON, MR. CUPID AND I (42)	1.50	3.00
□ 1020		LIBERTY VALANCE/TAKE IT LIKE A MAN (4)	1.00	2.50
□ 1022		ONLY LOVE CAN BREAK A HEART/ IF I DIDN'T HAVE A DIME (2)	1.00	2.50
□ 1026		HALF HEAVEN-HALF HEARTACHE/TOWER TALL (12)	1.00	2.50
□ 1028		MECCA/TEARDROP BY TEARDROP (12)	1.00	2.50
□ 1032		TRUE LOVE NEVER RUNS SMOOTH/ DONNA MEANS HEARTBREAK (21)	1.25	2.50
□ 1034		TWENTY-FOUR HOURS FROM TULSA/ LONELY NIGHT DREAMS (17)	1.25	2.50
□ 1036		THAT GIRL BELONGS TO YESTERDAY/ WHO NEEDS IT? (49)	1.25	2.00
□ 1038		YESTERDAY'S HERO/CORNFLOWER BLUE (64)	1.25	2.00
□ 1040		IT HURTS TO BE IN LOVE/HAWAII (7)	.75	2.00
□ 1045		I'M GONNA BE STRONG/ALADDIN'S LAMP (9)	.75	2.00
□ 1045		I'M GONNA BE STRONG/E SE DOMANI (9)	.75	2.00
□ 1070		I MUST BE SEEING THINGS/MARIANNE (31)	1.25	2.00
□ 1093		LAST CHANCE TO TURN AROUND/ SAVE YOUR LOVE (13)	.75	1.50
		LATER MUSICOR SINGLES ARE WORTH UP TO $1.50 MINT		
		GENE PITNEY—ALBUMS		
□ 2001 (M)	*MUSICOR*	THE MANY SIDES OF GENE PITNEY	3.50	6.00
□ 2001 (S)		THE MANY SIDES OF GENE PITNEY	4.50	8.00
□ 2003 (M)		ONLY LOVE CAN BREAK A HEART	3.00	5.00
□ 2003 (S)		ONLY LOVE CAN BREAK A HEART	4.00	7.00
□ 2004 (M)		GENE PITNEY SINGS JUST FOR YOU	3.00	5.00
□ 2004 (S)		GENE PITNEY SINGS JUST FOR YOU	4.00	7.00
□ 2005 (M)		WORLD WIDE WINNERS	3.00	5.00
□ 2005 (S)		WORLD WIDE WINNERS	4.00	7.00

PLATTERS

The Platters began as a Los Angeles r & b quartet. Tony Williams, the Platters' founder and lead singer, met with local songwriter and group manager Buck Ram. The Platters sang for Ram, who agreed to manage the group. Before long the Platters were signed to the Federal label.

The Platters saw no real success with Federal, so Ram sought another label. Ram also managed the Penguins, who had just recorded the 1954 smash of "Earth Angel". Mercury Records, believing the Penguins to be the next major vocal group, was eager to sign the former Dootone artists. However, Ram insisted that Mercury could sign the Penguins only if they agreed to sign the Platters as well. Mercury had no interest in the Platters but reluctantly signed them in order to get the Penguins. The result: the Penguins never had another hit, and the Platters became the most popular vocal group of the 1950s.

Seven Platters singles reached the Top 10, with four going all the way to the top. The Platters' last major hit—"Harbor Lights"—came in 1960.

ISSUE #	LABEL	ARTIST/TITLE	VG	MINT
		PLATTERS		
☐12244	***FEDERAL***	ONLY YOU/YOU MADE ME CRY	50.00	80.00
☐70633	***MERCURY***	ONLY YOU/BARK, BATTLE AND BALL (5)	2.50	5.00
☐70753		THE GREAT PRETENDER/ I'M JUST A DANCING PARTNER (1)	2.50	5.00
☐70819		THE MAGIC TOUCH/WINNER TAKE ALL (4)	2.25	4.50
☐70893		MY PRAYER/HEAVEN ON EARTH (1)	2.00	4.00
☐70948		YOU'LL NEVER NEVER KNOW/IT ISN'T RIGHT (14)	2.00	3.50
☐71011		ON MY WORD OF HONOR/ONE IN A MILLION (27)	2.00	3.50
☐71032		I'M SORRY/HE'S MINE (19)	2.00	3.50
☐71093		MY DREAM/I WANNA (26)	2.00	3.50
☐71184		ONLY BECAUSE/THE MYSTERY OF YOU (65)	1.75	3.00
☐71246		HELPLESS/INDIFF'RENT (56)	1.75	3.00
☐71289		TWILIGHT TIME/OUT OF MY MIND (1)	1.50	3.00
☐71320		YOU'RE MAKING A MISTAKE/MY OLD FLAME (51)	1.75	3.00
☐71353		I WISH/IT'S RAINING OUTSIDE (42)	1.75	3.00
☐71383		SMOKE GETS IN YOUR EYES/ NO MATTER WHAT YOU ARE (1)	1.50	3.00
☐71427		ENCHANTED/THE SOUND AND THE FURY (12)	1.25	2.50
☐71467		REMEMBER WHEN/LOVE OF A LIFETIME (41)	1.50	2.50
☐71502		WHERE/WISH IT WERE ME (44)	1.50	2.50
☐71538		MY SECRET/WHAT DOES IT MATTER?	1.75	2.50
☐71563		HARBOR LIGHTS/SLEEPY LAGOON (8)	1.25	2.50
		LATER MERCURY SINGLES ARE WORTH UP TO $2.00 MINT		
		PLATTERS—EPs		
☐3336	***MERCURY***	THE PLATTERS	5.00	8.00
☐3341		THE FLYING PLATTERS	3.50	6.00
☐3343		THE PLATTERS	3.00	5.00
☐3344		THE PLATTERS	3.00	5.00
☐3345		THE PLATTERS	3.00	5.00
☐3353		THE FLYING PLATTERS	3.00	5.00
☐3354		THE FLYING PLATTERS	3.00	5.00
☐3355		THE FLYING PLATTERS	3.00	5.00
☐3393		TWILIGHT TIME	3.00	5.00
		PLATTERS—ALBUMS		
☐549 (M)	***FEDERAL***	PLATTERS	25.00	40.00
☐20146 (M)	***MERCURY***	THE PLATTERS	7.00	12.00
☐20216 (M)		THE PLATTERS, VOL. 2	6.00	10.00
☐20298 (M)		THE FLYING PLATTERS	5.00	8.00
☐20366 (M)		AROUND THE WORLD WITH THE FLYING PLATTERS	5.00	8.00
☐60043 (S)		AROUND THE WORLD WITH THE FLYING PLATTERS	6.00	10.00
☐20481 (M)		REFLECTIONS	3.50	6.00
☐60160 (S)		REFLECTIONS	4.50	8.00
☐20543 (M)		ENCORE OF GOLDEN HITS	4.00	7.00
☐60243 (S)		ENCORE OF GOLDEN HITS	5.00	9.00
		PLAYMATES		
☐4003	***ROULETTE***	BAREFOOT GIRL/PRETTY WOMAN	2.00	3.50
☐4022		DARLING IT'S WONDERFUL/ISLAND GIRL	2.00	3.50
☐4022		DARLING IT'S WONDERFUL/MAGIC SHOES	2.00	3.50
☐4037		JO-ANN/YOU CAN'T STOP ME FROM DREAMING (20)	1.50	3.00

ISSUE #	LABEL	ARTIST/TITLE	VG	MINT
□4056		LET'S BE LOVERS/GIVE ME ANOTHER CHANCE (87)	1.75	3.00
□4072		DON'T GO HOME/CAN'T YOU GET IT THROUGH YOU HEAD? (36)	1.50	3.00
□4100		THE DAY I DIED/ WHILE THE RECORD GOES AROUND (81)	1.75	3.00
□4115		BEEP BEEP/YOUR LOVE (4)	1.25	2.50
□4136		STAR LOVE/THE THING-A-MA-JIG (75)	1.50	2.50
□4160		WHAT IS LOVE?/I AM (15)	1.25	2.50
□4200		FIRST LOVE/A CIU-E	1.50	2.50
□4211		ON THE BEACH/THE SONG EVERYBODY'S SINGING	1.50	2.50
□4227		THESE THINGS I OFFER YOU/SECOND CHANCE	1.50	2.50
□4252		OUR WEDDING DAY/PARADE OF PRETTY GIRLS	1.50	2.50
□4276		WAIT FOR ME/THE EYES OF AN ANGEL (37)	1.25	2.00
□4322		LITTLE MISS STUCK-UP/REAL LIFE (70)	1.25	2.00
		LATER ROULETTE SINGLES ARE WORTH UP TO $1.50 MINT		
		PLAYMATES—ALBUMS		
□25001 (M)	*ROULETTE*	CALYPSO	6.00	10.00
□25043 (M)		AT PLAY WITH THE PLAYMATES	5.00	8.00
□25059 (M)		ROCK AND ROLL RECORD HOP	5.00	8.00
□25139 (M)		WAIT FOR ME	3.50	6.00
□25139 (S)		WAIT FOR ME	4.50	8.00
		PLEDGES		
		SEE: SKIP AND FLIP		
□3517	*REV*	BERMUDA SHORTS/BETTY JEAN	3.50	6.00
		PONI-TAILS		
□9846	*ABC-PARAMOUNT*	IT'S JUST MY LUCK TO BE FIFTEEN/ WILD EYES AND TENDER LIPS	2.00	3.50
□9934		BORN TOO LATE/COME ON, JOEY, DANCE WITH ME (7)	1.50	3.00
□9969		SEVEN MINUTES IN HEAVEN/CLOSE FRIENDS (85)	1.50	2.50
□9995		FATHER TIME/EARLY TO BED	1.50	2.50
□10027		MOODY/OO-PAH POLKA	1.25	2.00
		PORTRAITS		
□928	*SIDEWALK*	A MILLION TO ONE/LET'S TELL THE WORLD	3.50	6.00
□935		OVER THE RAINBOW/RUNAROUND GIRL	3.50	6.00
		JOEY POWERS		
□892	*AMY*	MIDNIGHT MARY/WHERE DO YOU WANT THE WORLD DELIVERED? (10)	1.00	2.00
□898		BILLY OLD BUDDY/EARLY IN THE MORNING, GLORIA	1.25	2.00
□903		LOVE IS A REASON/YOU COMB HER HAIR	1.25	2.00
□914		TEARS KEEP FALLING/WHERE DID THE SUMMER GO?	1.25	2.00
		JOEY POWERS—ALBUM		
□8001 (M)	*AMY*	MIDNIGHT MARY	5.00	8.00

ELVIS PRESLEY

Born on January 8, 1935, in Tupelo, Mississippi, Elvis Aaron Presley was the only surviving child of Vernon and Gladys Presley. A twin, Jesse Garon, was born dead.

At an early age Elvis was exposed to gospel music, as his parents were very religious. The energetic singing style and stage movements of the gospel singers had a profound impact on Presley's stage mannerisms later on. Elvis also spent many lonely hours in his bedroom listening to country and r & b music.

Vernon Presley moved his family to Memphis in hopes of a better life. He went to work packing paint cans into boxes. Mrs. Presley took on a menial hospital job, and Elvis worked as a theater usher during his high-school days. At Memphis's Humes High Elvis was a loner and labeled an oddball because of his flashy clothes and uncommonly long hair. A C- student, Elvis graduated in 1953.

Elvis paid $4.00 to cut his first disc at Sun Records, his first recording home. Sun issued five commercial Presley singles, two of which made the Country Top 10. Colonel Tom Parker, Elvis's manager, offered Presley's contract to Capitol Records for $35,000. They turned it down. RCA then took a chance on the youngster from the South.

The greatest rock-and-roll star of all time, Elvis Presley died of a heart attack on August 16, 1977, at the age of 42.

ISSUE #	LABEL	ARTIST/TITLE	VG	MINT
		ELVIS PRESLEY *SEE SUN DISCOGRAPHY*		
☐6357	***RCA***	MYSTERY TRAIN/ I FORGOT TO REMEMBER TO FORGET	8.00	15.00
☐6380		THAT'S ALL RIGHT/BLUE MOON OF KENTUCKY	8.00	15.00
☐6381		GOOD ROCKIN' TONIGHT/ I DON'T CARE IF THE SUN DON'T SHINE	8.00	15.00
☐6382		MILKCOW BLUES BOOGIE/YOU'RE A HEARTBREAKER	8.00	15.00
☐6383		BABY LET'S PLAY HOUSE/ I'M LEFT, YOU'RE RIGHT, SHE'S GONE	8.00	15.00
☐6420		HEARTBREAK HOTEL/I WAS THE ONE (1)	2.50	5.00
☐6540		I WANT YOU, I NEED YOU, I LOVE YOU/ MY BABY LEFT ME (3)	2.50	5.00
☐6604		DON'T BE CRUEL/HOUND DOG (1)	2.00	4.00
☐6636		BLUE SUEDE SHOES/TUTTI FRUITTI	8.00	15.00
☐6637		I GOT A WOMAN/I'M COUNTIN' ON YOU	8.00	15.00
☐6638		I'M GONNA SIT RIGHT DOWN AND CRY OVER YOU/ I'LL NEVER LET YOU GO	8.00	15.00
☐6639		TRYIN' TO GET TO YOU/I LOVE YOU BECAUSE	8.00	15.00
☐6640		BLUE MOON/JUST BECAUSE	8.00	15.00
☐6641		MONEY HONEY/ONE-SIDED LOVE AFFAIR	8.00	15.00
☐6642		SHAKE, RATTLE AND ROLL/LAWDY MISS CLAWDY	8.00	15.00
☐6643		LOVE ME TENDER/ANYWAY YOU WANT ME (1)	2.00	4.00
☐6800		TOO MUCH/PLAYING FOR KEEPS (2)	2.00	4.00
☐6870		ALL SHOOK UP/ THAT'S WHEN YOUR HEARTACHES BEGIN (1)	2.00	4.00
☐7000		TEDDY BEAR/LOVING YOU (1)	1.75	3.50
☐7035		JAILHOUSE ROCK/TREAT ME NICE (1)	1.75	3.50
☐7150		DON'T/I BEG OF YOU (1)	1.75	3.50
☐7240		WEAR MY RING AROUND YOUR NECK/ DONCHA THINK IT'S TIME (3)	1.75	3.50
☐7280		HARD HEADED WOMAN/DON'T ASK MY WHY (2)	1.75	3.50
☐7410		ONE NIGHT/I GOT STUNG (4)	1.75	3.50
☐7506		A FOOL SUCH AS I/I NEED YOUR LOVE TONIGHT (2)	1.75	3.50
☐7600		A BIG HUNK O' LOVE/MY WISH CAME TRUE (1)	1.75	3.00
☐7740		STUCK ON YOU/FAME AND FORTUNE (1)	1.50	3.00
☐7740		STUCK ON YOU/FAME AND FORTUNE (stereo single)	35.00	60.00
☐7777		IT'S NOW OR NEVER/A MESS OF BLUES (1)	1.50	3.00
☐7777		IT'S NOW OR NEVER/A MESS OF BLUES (stereo single)	40.00	70.00
☐7810		ARE YOU LONESOME TONIGHT?/I GOTTA KNOW (1)	1.50	3.00
☐7810		ARE YOU LONESOME TONIGHT?/I GOTTA KNOW (stereo single)	40.00	70.00
☐7850		SURRENDER/LONELY MAN (1)	1.50	3.00
☐7850		SURRENDER/LONELY MAN (stereo single)	60.00	100.00
☐7880		I FEEL SO BAD/WILD IN THE COUNTRY (5)	1.50	3.00
☐7880		I FEEL SO BAD/WILD IN THE COUNTRY (stereo single)	60.00	100.00
☐7908		HIS LATEST FLAME/LITTLE SISTER (4)	1.50	3.00
☐7968		CAN'T HELP FALLING IN LOVE/ ROCK-A-HULA BABY (2)	1.25	2.50

ISSUE #	LABEL	ARTIST/TITLE	VG	MINT
□ 7992		GOOD LUCK CHARM/ ANYTHING THAT'S PART OF YOU (1)	1.25	2.50
□ 8041		SHE'S NOT YOU/JUST TELL HER JIM SAID HELLO (5)	1.25	2.50
□ 8100		RETURN TO SENDER/WHERE DO YOU COME FROM? (2)	1.25	2.50
□ 8134		ONE BROKEN HEART FOR SALE/ THEY REMIND ME TOO MUCH OF YOU (11)	1.25	2.50
□ 8188		DEVIL IN DISGUISE/PLEASE DON'T DRAG THAT STRING AROUND (3)	1.25	2.50
□ 8243		BOSSA NOVA BABY/WITCHCRAFT (8)	1.25	2.50
□ 8307		KISSIN' COUSINS/IT HURTS ME (12)	1.25	2.50
□ 8360		WHAT'D I SAY/VIVA LAS VEGAS (21)	1.25	2.50
□ 8400		SUCH A NIGHT/NEVER ENDING (16)	1.25	2.50
□ 8440		ASK ME/AIN'T THAT LOVING YOU BABY (12)	1.25	2.50
□ 8500		DO THE CLAM/YOU'LL BE GONE (21)	1.25	2.50
□ 8585		(SUCH AN) EASY QUESTION/IT FEELS SO RIGHT (11)	1.25	2.50
□ 8740		TELL ME WHY/BLUE RIVER (33)	1.50	2.50
□ 8780		FRANKIE AND JOHNNY/ PLEASE DON'T STOP LOVING ME (25)	1.25	2.50
□ 8870		LOVE LETTERS/COME WHAT MAY (19)	1.25	2.50
□ 8941		SPINOUT/ALL THAT I AM (40)	1.50	2.50
□ 8950		IF EVERY DAY WAS LIKE CHRISTMAS/ HOW WOULD YOU LIKE TO BE	2.50	4.00
□ 9056		INDESCRIBABLY BLUE/FOOLS FALL IN LOVE (33)	1.50	2.50
□ 9115		LONG LEGGED GIRL/ THAT'S SOMEONE YOU NEVER FORGET (63)	1.50	2.50
□ 9287		THERE'S ALWAYS ME/JUDY (56)	1.50	2.50
□ 9341		BIG BOSS MAN/YOU DON'T KNOW ME (38)	1.50	2.50
□ 9425		GUITAR MAN/HIGH HEELED SNEAKERS (43)	1.50	2.50
□ 9465		U.S. MALE/STAY AWAY JOE (28)	1.50	2.50
□ 9547		LET YOURSELF GO/ YOUR TIME HASN'T COME YET BABY (71)	1.50	2.50
□ 9600		YOU'LL NEVER WALK ALONE/WE CALL ON HIM (90)	1.50	2.50
□ 9610		A LITTLE LESS CONVERSATION/ ALMOST IN LOVE (69)	1.50	2.50
□ 9670		IF I CAN DREAM/EDGE OF REALITY (12)	1.00	2.00
□ 9731		MEMORIES/CHARRO (35)	1.25	2.00
□ 9741		IN THE GHETTO/ANY DAY NOW (3)	1.00	2.00

LATER RCA SINGLES ARE WORTH UP TO $2.00 MINT

ELVIS PRESLEY—GOLD STANDARD SINGLES

ISSUE #	LABEL	ARTIST/TITLE	VG	MINT
□ 0639	***RCA***	KISS ME QUICK/SUSPICION (34)	1.75	3.00
□ 0643		CRYING IN THE CHAPEL/ I BELIEVE IN THE MAN IN THE SKY (3)	1.25	2.50
□ 0647		BLUE CHRISTMAS/SANTA CLAUS IS BACK IN TOWN	2.50	4.00
□ 0650		PUPPET ON A STRING/WOODEN HEART (14)	1.25	2.50
□ 0651		JOSHUA FIT THE BATTLE/KNOWN ONLY TO HIM	2.50	4.00
□ 0652		SWING DOWN SWEET CHARIOT/MILKY WHITE WAY	2.50	4.00
□ 0720		BLUE CHRISTMAS/WOODEN HEART	1.75	3.00
□ 0130		HOW GREAT THOU ART/HIS HAND IN MINE	4.00	7.00

ISSUE #	LABEL	ARTIST/TITLE	VG	MINT
		ELVIS PRESLEY—EPs		
☐ 1254	***RCA***	ELVIS PRESLEY (double-pocket)	60.00	100.00
☐ 747		ELVIS PRESLEY (24)	6.00	12.00
☐ 821		HEARTBREAK HOTEL (76)	7.00	12.00
☐ 830		ELVIS PRESLEY (55)	7.00	12.00
☐ 940		THE REAL ELVIS	7.00	12.00
☐ 965		ANYWAY YOU WANT ME	7.00	12.00
☐ 4006		LOVE ME TENDER (35)	6.00	12.00
☐ 992		ELVIS, VOL. 1 (6)	6.00	12.00
☐ 993		ELVIS, VOL. 2 (47)	7.00	12.00
☐ 994		STRICTLY ELVIS	7.00	12.00
☐ 1-1515		LOVING YOU, VOL. 1	7.00	12.00
☐ 2-1515		LOVING YOU, VOL. 2	7.00	12.00
☐ 4041		JUST FOR YOU	7.00	12.00
☐ 4054		PEACE IN THE VALLEY (39)	6.00	12.00
☐ 4108		ELVIS SINGS CHRISTMAS SONGS	7.00	12.00
☐ 4114		JAILHOUSE ROCK	7.00	12.00
☐ 4319		KING CREOLE, VOL. 1	7.00	12.00
☐ 4321		KING CREOLE, VOL. 2	7.00	12.00
☐ 4325		ELVIS SAILS	12.00	20.00
☐ 4340		CHRISTMAS WITH ELVIS	8.00	15.00
☐ 4368		FOLLOW THAT DREAM (15)	4.00	8.00
☐ 4371		KID GALAHAD (30)	4.00	8.00
☐ 4382		EASY COME, EASY GO (92)	6.00	10.00
☐ 4383		TICKLE ME (70)	6.00	10.00
☐ 5088		A TOUCH OF GOLD, VOL. 1 (maroon label)	20.00	30.00
☐ 5088		A TOUCH OF GOLD, VOL. 1 (black label)	7.00	12.00
☐ 5120		THE REAL ELVIS (reissue) (maroon label)	20.00	30.00
☐ 5120		THE REAL ELVIS (reissue) (black label)	6.00	10.00
☐ 5121		PEACE IN THE VALLEY (reissue) (maroon label)	20.00	30.00
☐ 5121		PEACE IN THE VALLEY (reissue) (black label)	6.00	10.00
☐ 5122		KING CREOLE, VOL. 1 (reissue) (maroon label)	20.00	30.00
☐ 5122		KING CREOLE, VOL. 1 (reissue) (black label)	6.00	10.00
☐ 5101		A TOUCH OF GOLD, VOL. 2 (maroon label)	20.00	30.00
☐ 5101		A TOUCH OF GOLD, VOL. 2 (black label)	7.00	12.00
☐ 5141		A TOUCH OF GOLD, VOL. 3 (maroon label)	20.00	30.00
☐ 5141		A TOUCH OF GOLD, VOL. 3 (black label)	7.00	12.00
☐ 5157		ELVIS SAILS (reissue) (maroon label)	25.00	40.00
☐ 5157		ELVIS SAILS (reissue) (black label)	7.00	12.00
		ELVIS PRESLEY—COMPACT 33's		
☐ 37-7850	***RCA***	SURRENDER/LONELY MAN	30.00	50.00
☐ 37-7880		I FEEL SO BAD/WILD IN THE COUNTRY	50.00	80.00
☐ 37-7908		HIS LATEST FLAME/LITTLE SISTER	50.00	80.00
☐ 37-7968		CAN'T HELP FALLING IN LOVE/ ROCK-A-HULA BABY	50.00	80.00
☐ 37-7992		GOOD LUCK CHARM/ANYTHING THAT'S PART OF YOU	50.00	80.00
☐ 37-8041		SHE'S NOT YOU/JUST TELL HER JIM SAID HELLO	70.00	120.00
☐ 37-8100		RETURN TO SENDER/WHERE DO YOU COME FROM?	70.00	120.00

ISSUE #	LABEL	ARTIST/TITLE	VG	MINT
		ELVIS PRESLEY—ALBUMS		
		THE ALBUMS BELOW WERE FIRST ISSUED ONLY IN MONO		
☐ 1254 (M)	***RCA***	ELVIS PRESLEY	15.00	25.00
☐ 1382 (M)		ELVIS	15.00	25.00
☐ 1515 (M)		LOVING YOU	12.00	20.00
☐ 1035 (M)		ELVIS' CHRISTMAS ALBUM (double-pocket)	60.00	100.00
☐ 1707 (M)		ELVIS' GOLDEN RECORDS	12.00	20.00
☐ 1884 (M)		KING CREOLE	10.00	18.00
☐ 1951 (M)		ELVIS' CHRISTMAS ALBUM (reissue) (photos on back)	12.00	20.00
☐ 1990 (M)		FOR LP FANS ONLY	15.00	25.00
☐ 2011 (M)		A DATE WITH ELVIS (double pocket)	25.00	40.00
☐ 2011 (M)		A DATE WITH ELVIS (single pocket)	12.00	20.00
☐ 2075 (M)		ELVIS' GOLDEN RECORDS, VOL. 2	10.00	18.00
		THE ALBUMS BELOW HAVE EQUIVALENT VALUE IN MONO AND STEREO		
☐ 2231 (M)		ELVIS IS BACK	7.00	12.00
☐ 2256 (M)		G. I. BLUES	7.00	12.00
☐ 2328 (M)		HIS HAND IN MINE	8.00	15.00
☐ 2370 (M)		SOMETHING FOR EVERYBODY	7.00	12.00
☐ 2436 (M)		BLUE HAWAII	7.00	12.00
☐ 2523 (M)		POT LUCK	7.00	12.00
☐ 2621 (M)		GIRLS! GIRLS! GIRLS!	7.00	12.00
☐ 2697 (M)		IT HAPPENED AT THE WORLD'S FAIR	12.00	20.00
☐ 2756 (M)		FUN IN ACAPULCO	7.00	12.00
☐ 2765 (M)		ELVIS' GOLDEN RECORDS, VOL. 3	7.00	12.00
☐ 2894 (M)		KISSIN' COUSINS	7.00	12.00
☐ 2999 (M)		ROUSTABOUT	7.00	12.00
☐ 3338 (M)		GIRL HAPPY	7.00	12.00
☐ 3450 (M)		ELVIS FOR EVERYONE	7.00	12.00
☐ 3468 (M)		HARUM SCARUM (with enclosed photo)	12.00	20.00
☐ 3553 (M)		FRANKIE AND JOHNNY	12.00	20.00
☐ 3643 (M)		PARADISE, HAWAIIAN STYLE	8.00	15.00
☐ 3702 (M)		SPINOUT	12.00	20.00
☐ 3758 (M)		HOW GREAT THOU ART	7.00	12.00
☐ 3787 (M)		DOUBLE TROUBLE	10.00	18.00
		THE ALBUMS BELOW HAVE A HIGHER VALUE IN MONO		
☐ 3893 (M)		CLAMBAKE	20.00	35.00
☐ 3893 (S)		CLAMBAKE	10.00	18.00
☐ 3921 (M)		ELVIS' GOLDEN RECORDS, VOL. 4	20.00	30.00
☐ 3921 (S)		ELVIS' GOLDEN RECORDS, VOL. 4	7.00	12.00
☐ 3989 (M)		SPEEDWAY	50.00	80.00
☐ 3989 (S)		SPEEDWAY	6.00	10.00

JOHNNY PRESTON

☐ 71474	***MERCURY***	RUNNING BEAR/MY HEART KNOWS (1)	1.25	2.50
☐ 71528		CRADLE OF LOVE/CITY OF TEARS (7)	1.25	2.50
☐ 71651		FEEL SO FINE/I'M STARTING TO GO STEADY (14)	1.25	2.50
☐ 71691		UP IN THE AIR/CHARMING BILLY	1.50	2.50
☐ 71728		ROCK AND ROLL GUITAR/NEW BABY FOR CHRISTMAS	1.50	2.50
☐ 71761		LEAVE MY KITTEN ALONE/TOKEN OF LOVE (73)	1.25	2.00

LATER MERCURY SINGLES ARE WORTH UP TO $2.00 MINT

ISSUE #	LABEL	ARTIST/TITLE	VG	MINT
		JOHNNY PRESTON—EP		
□ 3397	***MERCURY***	RUNNING BEAR	4.00	7.00
		JOHNNY PRESTON—ALBUM		
□ 20592 (M)	***MERCURY***	RUNNING BEAR	8.00	15.00

LLOYD PRICE

Lloyd Price was born on March 9, 1933, in Fats Domino's hometown of New Orleans, Louisiana. Lloyd was one of eleven children. His parents were musically inclined; Lloyd learned the piano from his mother and the guitar from his father.

While in his late teens Lloyd wrote "Lawdy Miss Clawdy", which was first used on a radio commercial in New Orleans. (Fats Domino played piano on the song.) Art Rupe, the owner of Specialty Records, heard the song, looked up Price and offered him a Specialty contract. Later the song became an r & b hit but failed to reach a large mass audience.

After two years in the military, Lloyd Price formed his own record company but had no success. He then wrote and recorded "Just Because", which was released by ABC-Paramount Records. The song was a moderate hit but nothing like the one that would come a year later. "Stagger Lee" skyrocketed to No. 1 on both the r & b and rock charts. It was Price's biggest hit ever and was followed by other Top 10 hits such as "Personality" and "I'm Gonna Get Married".

ISSUE #	LABEL	ARTIST/TITLE	VG	MINT
		LLOYD PRICE		
□9792	***ABC-PARAMOUNT***	JUST BECAUSE/WHY (29)	1.50	3.00
□9972		STAGGER LEE/YOU NEED LOVE (1)	1.25	3.00
□9997		WHERE WERE YOU (ON OUR WEDDING DAY?)/ IS IT REALLY LOVE (23)	1.25	2.50
□10018		PERSONALITY/HAVE YOU EVER HAD THE BLUES? (2)	1.00	2.50
□10032		I'M GONNA GET MARRIED/THREE LITTLE PIGS (3)	1.00	2.50
□10062		COME INTO MY HEART/WON'TCHA COME HOME (20)	1.25	2.50
□10075		LADY LUCK/NEVER LET ME GO (14)	1.25	2.50
□10102		NO IF'S-NO AND'S/FOR LOVE (40)	1.50	2.50
□10123		QUESTION/IF I LOOK A LITTLE BLUE (19)	1.25	2.50
□10139		JUST CALL ME/WHO COULD HAVE TOLD YOU (79)	1.25	2.00
		LATER ABC-PARAMOUNT SINGLES ARE WORTH UP TO $2.00 MINT.		
		LLOYD PRICE—EPs		
□A-272	***ABC-PARAMOUNT***	THE EXCITING LLOYD PRICE	3.00	5.00
□B-272		THE EXCITING LLOYD PRICE	3.00	5.00
□C-272		THE EXCITING LLOYD PRICE	3.00	5.00
□315		MR. PERSONALITY SINGS THE BLUES	2.50	4.00
		LLOYD PRICE—ALBUMS		
□277 (M)	***ABC-PARAMOUNT***	THE EXCITING LLOYD PRICE	6.00	10.00
□297 (M)		MR. PERSONALITY	5.00	8.00
□315 (M)		MR. PERSONALITY SINGS THE BLUES	4.00	7.00
□324 (M)		MR. PERSONALITY'S BIG 15	4.00	7.00
		P. J. PROBY		
□55367	***LIBERTY***	THERE STANDS THE ONE/TRY TO FORGET HER	1.75	3.00
□55505		WATCH ME WALK AWAY/THE OTHER SIDE OF TOWN	1.75	3.00
□55588		I CAN'T TAKE IT LIKE YOU CAN/SO DO I	1.75	3.00
□55757		SOMEWHERE/JUST LIKE HIM (91)	1.50	2.50
□55777		ROCKIN' PNEUMONIA/I APOLOGIZE	1.50	2.50
□55791		MISSION BELL/STAGGER LEE	1.50	2.50
□55850		MARIA/GOOD THINGS ARE COMING MY WAY	1.50	2.50

· ISSUE #	LABEL	ARTIST/TITLE	VG	MINT
☐ 55875		MY PRAYER/WICKED WOMAN..................	1.50	2.50
☐ 55936		NIKI HOKEY/GOOD THINGS ARE COMING MY WAY (23)	1.25	2.00

LATER LIBERTY SINGLES ARE WORTH UP TO $2.00 MINT.

P. J. PROBY—ALBUMS

☐ 3406 (M)	*LIBERTY*	SOMEWHERE.............................	3.50	6.00
☐ 7406 (S)		SOMEWHERE.............................	4.50	8.00
☐ 3421 (M)		P. J. PROBY.............................	3.50	6.00
☐ 7421 (S)		P. J. PROBY.............................	4.50	8.00

PRIMETTES (SUPREMES)

☐ 120	*LUPINE*	TEARS OF SORROW/PRETTY BABY.............	12.00	20.00

PYRAMIDS

☐ 13001	*BEST*	PYRAMID STOMP/PAUL	1.75	3.00
☐ 13002		PENETRATION/HERE COMES MARSHA (18)	1.25	2.50
☐ 13005	*CEDWICKE*	MIDNIGHT RUN/CUSTOM CARAVAN.............	1.50	2.50
☐ 13006		CONTACT/PRESSURE	1.50	2.50

PYRAMIDS—ALBUM

☐ 1001 (M)	*BEST*	PENETRATION	6.00	10.00

_ ISSUE #	LABEL	ARTIST/TITLE	VG	MINT

QUEEN
SEE: LARRY LUREX, SMILE

? AND THE MYSTERIANS
SEE: MYSTERIANS

☐ 102	*PA-GO-GO*	96 TEARS/MIDNIGHT HOUR	15.00	25.00
☐ 441		I NEED SOMEBODY/''8'' TEEN	5.00	8.00
☐ 467		CAN'T GET ENOUGH OF YOU, BABY/SMOKES......	4.00	7.00
☐ 479		GIRL (YOU CAPTIVATE ME)/GOT TO	3.00	5.00
☐ 496		DO SOMETHING TO ME/LOVE ME BABY	3.00	5.00
☐ 428	*CAMEO*	96 TEARS/MIDNIGHT HOUR (1)................	1.00	2.50
☐ 441		I NEED SOMEBODY/''8'' TEEN (22)	1.25	2.50
☐ 467		CAN'T GET ENOUGH OF YOU, BABY/SMOKES (56) ..	1.50	2.50
☐ 479		GIRL (YOU CAPTIVATE ME)/GOT TO (98)..........	1.50	2.50
☐ 496		DO SOMETHING TO ME/LOVE ME BABY	1.50	2.50

? AND THE MYSTERIANS—ALBUMS

☐ 2004 (M)	*CAMEO*	96 TEARS...............................	3.50	6.00
☐ 2004 (S)		96 TEARS...............................	4.50	8.00
☐ 2006 (M)		ACTION	4.00	7.00
☐ 2006 (S)		ACTION	5.00	9.00

QUICK
FEATURED: ERIC CARMEN
SEE: CHOIR, CYRUS ERIE

☐ 10516	*EPIC*	AIN'T NOTHIN' GONNA STOP ME/		
		SOUTHERN COMFORT	3.50	6.00

ISSUE #	LABEL	ARTIST/TITLE	VG	MINT
		QUIN-TONES		
☐ 1009	*GEE*	STRANGE AS IT SEEMS/I'M WILLING	40.00	75.00
		QUIN-TONES		
☐ 1685	*CHESS*	I TRY SO HARD/DING DONG	3.00	5.00
☐ 108	*RED TOP*	DOWN THE AISLE OF LOVE/PLEASE DEAR	3.50	6.00
☐ 321	*HUNT*	DOWN THE AISLE OF LOVE/PLEASE DEAR (20)	1.75	3.00
☐ 322		WHAT AM I TO DO?/ THERE'LL BE NO SORROW	1.75	3.00
		EDDIE QUINTEROS		
☐ 7009	*BRENT*	COME DANCE WITH ME/VIVIAN	3.00	5.00
☐ 7012		LOOKIN' FOR MY BABY/PLEASE DON'T GO	3.50	6.00
☐ 7014		SLOW DOWN SANDY/LINDA LOU	5.00	8.00
		QUOTATIONS		
☐ 10245	*VERVE*	IMAGINATION/ALA-MEN-SA-AYE	3.00	5.00
☐ 10252		THIS LOVE OF MINE/ WE'LL REACH HEAVEN TOGETHER	5.00	8.00
☐ 10261		SEE YOU IN SEPTEMBER/SUMMERTIME GOODBYES	5.00	8.00

R

ISSUE #	LABEL	ARTIST/TITLE	VG	MINT
		RACHEL AND THE REVOLVERS		
		PRODUCER: BRIAN WILSON		
☐ 16392	*DOT*	THE REVO-LUTION/NUMBER ONE	8.00	15.00
		RAINDROPS		
		FEATURED: JEFF BARRY, ELLIE GREENWICH		
☐ 5444	*JUBILEE*	WHAT A GUY/IT'S SO WONDERFUL (41)	1.50	2.50
☐ 5455		THE KIND OF BOY YOU CAN'T FORGET/ EVEN THOUGH YOU CAN'T DANCE (15)	1.25	2.50
☐ 5466		THAT BOY JOHN/HANKY PANKY (66)	1.50	2.50
☐ 5469		BOOK OF LOVE/I WON'T CRY (62)	1.50	2.50
☐ 5475		LET'S GET TOGETHER/YOU GOT WANT I LIKE	1.50	2.50
☐ 5487		ONE MORE TEAR/ANOTHER BOY LIKE MINE (97)	1.50	2.50
☐ 5497		DON'T LET GO/MY MAMA DON'T LIKE HIM	1.50	2.50
		RAINDROPS—ALBUM		
☐ 5023 (M)	*JUBILEE*	RAINDROPS	5.00	8.00
☐ 5023 (S)		RAINDROPS	6.00	10.00
		RAINY DAZE		
☐ 404	*CHICKORY*	THAT ACAPULCO GOLD/IN MY MIND LIVES A FOREST	4.00	7.00
☐ 55002	*UNI*	THAT ACAPULCO GOLD/ IN MY MIND LIVES A FOREST (70)	1.25	2.00
		RALLY PACKS		
		FEATURED: JAN AND DEAN		
☐ 66035	*IMPERIAL*	MOVE OUT LITTLE MUSTANG/BUCKET SEATS	3.00	5.00

ISSUE #	LABEL	ARTIST/TITLE	VG	MINT
		RAMRODS		
□813	*AMY*	(GHOST) RIDERS IN THE SKY/ZIG ZAG (30)	1.25	2.00
□817		TAKE ME BACK TO MY BOOTS AND SADDLE/ LOCH LOMOND ROCK	1.25	2.00
□846		WAR CRY/BOING	1.25	2.00

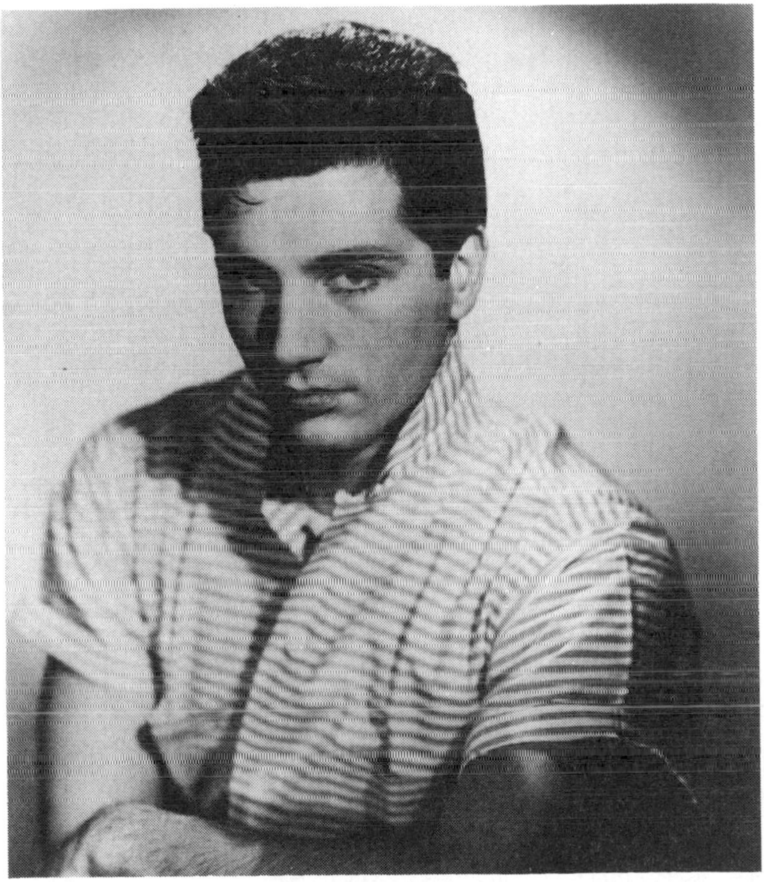

TEDDY RANDAZZO

Theodore (Teddy) Randazzo was born in New York City on May 20, 1937. Teddy's grandfather was musically inclined and helped steer his grandson toward a musical career. Young Randazzo took up the accordian and had mastered it by the age of twelve.

During the 1950s Teddy appeared in the Alan Freed movie "Rock Rock Rock". Randazzo and two friends later formed a singing group which they dubbed the Three Chuckles. Teddy sang lead and played the accordian when the Three Chuckles first began recording.

In 1957 Randazzo struck out on his own in pursuit of a solo career; the Three Chuckles consequently disbanded. As a solo artist Teddy had no luck with his maiden Vik single of "Next Stop Paradise", but did fairly well with his second effort, "Little Serenade". Teddy's fifth ABC-Paramount single in 1960—"The Way Of A Clown"—became Teddy Randazzo's only reasonable-sized hit.

A few years later Teddy began to work with Little Anthony and the Imperials when their career was rejuvenated at DCP (Don Costa Productions) Records. Randazzo wrote, among other songs, the hit single of "Goin' Out Of My Head".

ISSUE #	LABEL	ARTIST/TITLE	VG	MINT
		TEDDY RANDAZZO		
		SEE: THREE CHUCKLES		
□ 0277	**VIK**	NEXT STOP PARADISE/HOW COULD YOU KNOW?	2.00	3.50
□ 0330		LITTLE SERENADE/ BE MY KITTEN, LITTLE CHICKEN (66)	1.50	3.00
□ 9998	**ABC-PARAMOUNT**	YOU ARE ALWAYS IN MY HEART/PAPITO	1.50	2.50
□ 10014		LAUGHING ON THE OUTSIDE/AWKWARD AGE	1.50	2.50
□ 10043		I'M ON A MERRY-GO-ROUND/LIES	1.50	2.50
□ 10068		YOU DON'T CARE ANYMORE/HOW I NEED YOU	1.50	2.50
□ 10088		THE WAY OF A CLOWN/CHERIE (44)	1.50	2.50
		TEDDY RANDAZZO—EPs		
□ 281	**VIK**	I'M CONFESSIN'	2.50	4.00
□ 300		MISTER ROCK AND ROLL	2.50	4.00
□ 301		MISTER ROCK AND ROLL	2.50	4.00
		TEDDY RANDAZZO—ALBUMS		
□ 1121 (M)	**VIK**	I'M CONFESSIN'	7.00	12.00
□ 352 (M)	**ABC-PARAMOUNT**	JOURNEY TO LOVE	5.00	8.00
□ 352 (S)		JOURNEY TO LOVE	6.00	10.00
		RAN-DELLS		
□ 4403	**CHAIRMAN**	MARTIAN HOP/FORGIVE ME DARLING (16)	1.25	2.50
□ 4407		SOUND OF THE SUN/COME ON AND LOVE ME TOO	1.50	2.50
		RANDY AND THE RAINBOWS		
		SEE: DIALTONES		
□ 5059	**RUST**	DENISE/COME BACK (10)	1.00	2.00
□ 5073		WHY DO KIDS GROW UP?/SHE'S MY ANGEL (97)	1.25	2.00
□ 5080		HAPPY TEENAGER/DRY YOUR EYES	1.25	2.00
□ 5091		LITTLE STAR/SHARIN'	1.50	2.50
□ 5101		JOYRIDE/LITTLE HOT ROD SUZIE	1.25	2.00
		RATIONALS		
□ 101	**A-SQUARE**	LOOK WHAT YOU'RE DOIN'/GAVE MY NAME	3.00	5.00
□ 103		LITTLE GIRLS CRY/FEELIN' LOST	3.00	5.00

ISSUE #	LABEL	ARTIST/TITLE	VG	MINT
☐ 104		RESPECT/LEAVIN' HERE	3.50	6.00
☐ 107		I NEED YOU/OUT IN THE STREETS	3.00	5.00
		RAYS		
☐ 1613	*CHESS*	TIPPITY TOP/MOO-GOO-GAI-PAN	6.00	10.00
☐ 1678		HOW LONG MUST I WAIT?/SECOND FIDDLE	5.00	8.00
☐ 117	*CAMEO*	SILHOUETTES/DADDY COOL (3)	1.50	3.00
☐ 128		RENDEZVOUS/TRIANGLE	1.50	2.50
☐ 133		RAGS TO RICHES/THE MAN ABOVE	1.50	2.50
☐ 605	*XYZ*	MEDITERRANEAN MOON/IT'S A CRYIN' SHAME (95)	1.50	2.50
☐ 607		MAGIC MOON/LOUIE HOO HOO (49)	1.25	2.50
		RAYS—EP		
☐ 5120	*CHESS*	THE RAYS	5.00	8.00
		REBELS		
		SEE: BUFFALO REBELS, ROCKIN' REBELS		
☐ 0094	*MARLEE*	WILD WEEKEND/WILD WEEKEND CHA CHA	6.00	10.00
☐ 4125	*SWAN*	WILD WEEKEND/WILD WEEKEND CHA CHA (8)	1.25	2.00
		EIVETS REDNOW (STEVIE WONDER)		
☐ 7076	*GORDY*	ALFIE/MORE THAN A DREAM (66)	1.50	2.50
		REDWOODS		
☐ 9447	*EPIC*	SHAKE SHAKE SHERRY/THE MEMORY LINGERS ON	3.50	6.00
☐ 9473		NEVER TAKE IT AWAY/UNEMPLOYMENT INSURANCE	3.00	5.00
☐ 9505		WHERE YOU USED TO BE/PLEASE MR. SCIENTIST	3.00	5.00
		REFLECTIONS		
☐ 9	*GOLDEN WORLD*	ROMEO AND JULIET/ CAN'T YOU TELL BY THE LOOK IN MY EYES (6)	1.25	2.50
☐ 12		LIKE COLUMBUS DID/LONELY GIRL (96)	1.50	2.50
☐ 15		TALKIN' 'BOUT MY GIRL/OOWEE WOW	1.50	2.50
☐ 16		DON'T DO THAT TO ME/A HENPECKED GUY	1.50	2.50
☐ 19		YOU'RE MY BABY/SHABBY LITTLE HUT	1.50	2.50
☐ 20		POOR MAN'T SON/COMIN' AT YOU (55)	1.50	2.50
		REFLECTIONS—ALBUM		
☐ 300 (M)	*GOLDEN WORLD*	JUST LIKE ROMEO AND JULIET	5.00	8.00
		REGENTS		
☐ 1002	*COUSINS*	BARBARA-ANN/I'M SO LONELY	15.00	25.00
☐ 1065	*GEE*	BARBARA-ANN/I'M SO LONELY (13)	1.50	2.50
☐ 1071		RUNAROUND/LAURA MY DARLING (28)	1.75	3.00
☐ 1073		DON'T BE A FOOL/LIAR	1.75	3.00
☐ 1075		LONESOME BOY/OH BABY	1.75	3.00
		REGENTS—ALBUM		
☐ 706 (M)	*GEE*	BARBARA-ANN	7.00	12.00
☐ 706 (S)		BARBARA-ANN	8.00	15.00
		KEITH RELF		
		SEE: YARDBIRDS		
☐ 10044	*EPIC*	MR. ZERO/KNOWING	1.75	3.00
☐ 10110		SHAPES IN MY MIND/BLUE SANDS	3.00	5.00

ISSUE #	LABEL	ARTIST/TITLE	VG	MINT
		DIANE RENAY		
☐ 456	***20TH FOX***	NAVY BLUE/UNBELIEVABLE GUY (6)	1.00	2.00
☐ 477		KISS ME SAILOR/SOFT SPOKEN GUY (29)	1.25	2.00
☐ 514		WAITIN' FOR JOEY/GROWIN' UP TOO FAST	1.25	2.00
☐ 533		A PRESENT FROM EDDIE/IT'S IN YOUR TEARS	1.25	2.00
		DIANE RENAY—ALBUM		
☐ 3133 (M)	***20TH FOX***	NAVY BLUE	4.00	7.00
		RENEGADES		
		FEATURED: BRUCE JOHNSTON, SANDY NELSON, KIM FOWLEY		
☐ 537	***AMERICAN INTERNATIONAL***	CHARGE!/GERONIMO	5.00	8.00
		REPARTA AND THE DELRONS		
☐ 1036	***WORLD ARTISTS***	WHENEVER A TEENAGER CRIES/HE'S MY GUY (60)	1.50	2.50
☐ 1051		TOMMY/MAMA DON'T ALLOW (92)	1.50	2.50
☐ 1062		THE BOY I LOVE/I FOUND MY PLACE	1.50	2.50
☐ 1075		HE'S THE GREATEST/SUMMER THOUGHTS	1.50	2.50
		REPARTA AND THE DELRONS—ALBUM		
☐ 2006 (M)	***WORLD ARTISTS***	WHENEVER A TEENAGER CRIES	5.00	8.00
		JOHNNY RESTIVO		
☐ 7559	***RCA***	THE SHAPE I'M IN/YA YA (80)	1.50	2.50
☐ 7601		DEAR SOMEONE/I LIKE GIRLS	1.25	2.00
		JOHNNY RESTIVO—ALBUM		
☐ 2149 (M)	***RCA***	OH JOHNNY!	5.00	8.00
		PAUL REVERE AND THE RAIDERS		
☐ 106	***GARDENA***	BEATNIK STICKS/ORBIT	5.00	8.00
☐ 115		PAUL REVERE'S RIDE/UNFINISHED 5TH	3.50	6.00
☐ 116		LIKE LONG HAIR/SHARON (38)	2.50	4.00
☐ 118		LIKE CHARLESTON/MIDNIGHT RIDE	3.00	5.00
☐ 124		ALL NIGHT LONG/GROOVY	3.00	5.00
☐ 127		LIKE BLUEGRASS/LEATHERNECK	3.00	5.00
☐ 131		SHAKE IT UP (PT. 1)/(PT. 11)	3.00	5.00
☐ 137		TALL COOL ONE/ROAD RUNNER	3.00	5.00
☐ 807	***JERDEN***	SO FINE/BLUES STAY AWAY	4.00	7.00
☐ 101	***SANDE***	LOUIE LOUIE/NIGHT TRAIN	3.00	5.00
☐ 42814	***COLUMBIA***	LOUIE LOUIE/NIGHT TRAIN	1.75	3.00
☐ 43008		HAVE LOVE, WILL TRAVEL/LOUIE GO HOME	1.75	3.00
☐ 43114		OVER YOU/SWIM	1.75	3.00
☐ 43273		OO POO PAH DO/SOMETIMES	1.75	3.00
☐ 43375		STEPPIN' OUT/BLUE FOX (46)	1.50	2.50
☐ 43461		JUST LIKE ME/B.F.D.R.F. BLUES (11)	1.25	2.00
☐ 43556		KICKS/SHAKE IT UP (4)	1.00	2.00
☐ 43678		HUNGRY/THERE SHE GOES (6)	1.00	2.00
☐ 43810		THE GREAT AIRPLANE STRIKE/ IN MY COMMUNITY (20)	1.25	2.00
☐ 43907		GOOD THING/UNDECIDED MAN (4)	1.00	2.00
☐ 44018		UPS AND DOWNS/LESLIE (22)	1.25	2.00
☐ 44094		HIM OR ME-WHAT'S IT GONNA BE/ LEGEND OF PAUL REVERE (5)	1.00	2.00

ISSUE #		LABEL	ARTIST/TITLE	VG	MINT
☐ 44227			I HAD A DREAM/UPON YOUR LEAVING (17)	1.25	2.00
☐ 44335			PEACE OF MIND/DO UNTO OTHERS (42)	1.25	2.00
☐ 44444			TOO MUCH TALK/HAPPENING '68 (19)	1.25	2.00
☐ 44553			DON'T TAKE IT SO HARD/ OBSERVATION FROM FLIGHT 285 (27)	1.25	2.00
☐ 44655			CINDERELLA SUNSHINE/IT'S HAPPENING (58)	1.25	2.00
☐ 44744			MR. SUN, MR. MOON/WITHOUT YOU (18)	1.00	1.50
☐ 44854			LET ME/I DON'T KNOW (20)	1.00	1.50
			LATER COLUMBIA SINGLES ARE WORTH UP TO $1.50 MINT		
			PAUL REVERE AND THE RAIDERS—ALBUMS		
☐ 1000	(M)	***GARDENA***	LIKE LONG HAIR	25.00	40.00
☐ 7004	(M)	***JERDEN***	IN THE BEGINNING	5.00	8.00
☐ 1001	(M)	***SANDE***	PAUL REVERE AND THE RAIDERS	35.00	60.00
☐ 2307	(M)	***COLUMBIA***	HERE THEY COME	3.50	6.00
☐ 9107	(S)		HERE THEY COME	4.50	8.00
☐ 2451	(M)		JUST LIKE ME	3.50	6.00
☐ 9251	(S)		JUST LIKE ME	4.50	8.00
☐ 2508	(M)		MIDNIGHT RIDE	3.00	5.00
☐ 9308	(S)		MIDNIGHT RIDE	4.00	7.00
☐ 2595	(M)		THE SPIRIT OF '67	3.00	5.00
☐ 9395	(S)		THE SPIRIT OF '67	4.00	7.00
☐ 2662	(M)		GREATEST HITS	3.00	5.00
☐ 9462	(S)		GREATEST HITS	4.00	7.00
			JODY REYNOLDS		
☐ 1507		***DEMON***	ENDLESS SLEEP/TIGHT CAPRIS (5)	1.25	3.00
☐ 1509			FIRE OF LOVE/DAISY MAE (66)	1.50	2.50
☐ 1511			CLOSIN' IN/ELOPE WITH ME	1.50	2.50
☐ 1515			GOLDEN IDOL/BEULAH LEE	1.50	2.50
☐ 1519			PLEASE REMEMBER/THE STORM	1.50	2.50

CHARLIE RICH

Colt, Arkansas, was the birthplace of Charlie Rich on the 12th of December in 1932. As a lover of music during his adolescense, Charlie joined a combo. After graduating from high school, he entered the University of Arkansas as a music major, concentrating on the piano.

Later he enlisted in the air force. There Rich formed his own group, which he called the Velvetones. They played around the base but broke up when Charlie was discharged.

Charlie Rich returned to Arkansas and began farming. Still, music was in his blood. He managed to get some weekend bookings around the Memphis area, and at a small club was heard by a talent scout for Phillips International Records. Rich was signed, but only as a session pianist for Judd Records. (Judd Phillips was the brother of Sam Phillips.) Sam later heard Rich's singing and signed him as a vocalist/pianist to the Phillips International label.

After a trio of singles Rich hit it big with "Lonely Weekends" in 1960. He continued making records for Phillips International, but it wasn't until his move to Smash Records that Charlie Rich found chart success again with the 1965 rocker, "Mohair Sam".

Today Rich is a highly successful country artist for Epic Records.

ISSUE #	LABEL	ARTIST/TITLE	VG	MINT
		CHARLIE RICH		
		SEE: BOBBY SHERIDAN		
☐3532	***PHILLIPS INTERNATIONAL***	WHIRLWIND/PHILADELPHIA BABY	3.50	6.00
☐3542		BIG MAN/REBOUND	2.00	4.00
☐3552		LONELY WEEKENDS/EVERYTHING I DO IS WRONG (22)	1.50	3.00
☐3560		GONNA BE WAITING/SCHOOL DAYS	2.00	3.50
☐3562		STAY/ON MY KNEES	2.00	3.50
☐3566		WHO WILL THE NEXT FOOL BE?/ CAUGHT IN THE MIDDLE	2.00	3.50
☐3572		JUST A LITTLE SWEET/IT'S TOO LATE	2.00	3.50
☐3576		MIDNIGHT BLUES/EASY MONEY	2.00	3.50
☐3582		SITTIN' AND THINKIN'/FINALLY FOUND OUT	2.00	3.50
☐3584		THERE'S ANOTHER PLACE I CAN'T GO/ I NEED YOUR LOVE	2.00	3.50
☐1993	***SMASH***	MOHAIR SAM/I WASHED MY HANDS IN MUDDY WATER (21)	1.25	2.50
☐2012		THE DANCE OF LOVE/I CAN'T GO ON	1.25	2.00
☐2022		SOMETHING JUST CAME OVER ME/HAWG JAW	1.25	2.00
☐2038		TEARS AGO/NO HOME	1.25	2.00
		CHARLIE RICH—ALBUMS		
☐1970 (M)	***PHILLIPS INTERNATIONAL***	LONELY WEEKENDS	20.00	35.00
☐27070 (M)	***SMASH***	MANY NEW SIDES OF CHARLIE RICH	3.50	6.00
☐67070 (S)		MANY NEW SIDES OF CHARLIE RICH	4.50	8.00
		CLIFF RICHARD		
☐10042	***ABC-PARAMOUNT***	LIVING DOLL/APRIL STRINGS (30)	1.50	3.00
☐10066		DYNAMITE/TRAVELING LIGHT	1.50	2.50
☐10093		DON'T BE MAD AT ME/A VOICE IN THE WILDERNESS	1.50	2.50
☐10109		FALL IN LOVE WITH YOU/CHOPPIN' AND CHANGIN'	1.50	2.50
☐10136		WHERE IS MY HEART?/PLEASE DON'T TEASE	1.50	2.50
☐10175		CATCH ME, I'M FALLING/"D" IN LOVE	1.50	2.50
☐10195		THEME FOR A DREAM/MUMBLIN' MOSIE	1.50	2.50
☐9597	***EPIC***	LUCKY LIPS/NEXT TIME (62)	1.50	2.50
☐9633		IT'S ALL IN THE GAME/ I'M LOOKING OUT OF THE WINDOW (25)	1.25	2.50
☐9670		I'M THE LONELY ONE/ I ONLY HAVE EYES FOR YOU (92)	1.50	2.50
☐9691		BACHELOR BOY/TRUE TRUE LOVIN' (99)	1.50	2.50
☐9737		LOOK IN MY EYES/I DON'T WANNA LOVE YOU	1.50	2.50
☐9757		THE MINUTE YOU'RE GONE/AGAIN	1.50	2.50
☐9810		ON MY WORD/I COULD EASILY FALL IN LOVE WITH YOU	1.50	2.50
☐9839		THE TWELFTH OF NEVER/PARADISE LOST	1.50	2.50
☐9867		WIND ME UP/EYE OF A NEEDLE	1.50	2.50
		CLIFF RICHARD—ALBUMS		
☐321 (M)	***ABC-PARAMOUNT***	CLIFF SINGS	3.50	6.00
☐321 (S)		CLIFF SINGS	4.50	8.00

ISSUE #	LABEL	ARTIST/TITLE	VG	MINT
□ 391 (M)		LISTEN TO CLIFF	3.50	6.00
□ 391 (S)		LISTEN TO CLIFF	4.50	8.00
□ 24063 (M)	EPIC	HITS FROM THE SOUND TRACK OF "SUMMER HOLIDAY"	3.50	6.00
□ 26063 (S)		HITS FROM THE SOUND TRACK OF "SUMMER HOLIDAY"	4.50	8.00
□ 24089 (M)		IT'S ALL IN THE GAME	3.50	6.00
□ 26089 (S)		IT'S ALL IN THE GAME	4.50	8.00
		JAPE RICHARDSON (BIG BOPPER)		
□ 71219	MERCURY	BEGGAR TO A KING/CRAZY BLUES	3.50	6.00
□ 71312		TEENAGE MOON/THE MONKEY SONG	3.50	6.00
		RICK AND THE KEENS		
□ 721	LE CAM	PEANUTS/I'LL BE HOME	3.50	6.00
□ 1705	SMASH	PEANUTS/I'LL BE HOME (60)	1.50	2.50
		RICK AND THE MASTERS		
□ 101	TABA	FLAME OF LOVE/HERE COMES NANCY	6.00	10.00
□ 226	CAMEO	FLAME OF LOVE/HERE COMES NANCY	3.00	5.00
		RICK AND THE RAIDERS (McCOYS)		
□ 76234	SONIC	I KNOW THAT I LOVE YOU/WHAT CAN I DO?	3.00	5.00
		RIGHTEOUS BROTHERS *SEE: PARAMOURS*		
□ 215	MOONGLOW	LITTLE LATIN LUPE LU/I'M SO LONELY (49)	1.50	3.00
□ 220		I NEED A GIRL/HOT TAMALE (Bobby Hatfield)	1.75	3.00
□ 223		MY BABE/FEE-FI-FIDDILY-I-OH (75)	1.50	2.50
□ 224		KO KO JOE/B FLAT BLUES	1.50	2.50
□ 231		TRY TO FIND ANOTHER MAN/I STILL LOVE YOU	1.50	2.50
□ 234		BRING YOUR LOVE TO ME/ IF YOU'RE LYING YOU'LL BE CRYING (83)	1.50	2.50
□ 235		THIS LITTLE GIRL OF MINE/ IF YOU'RE LYING YOU'LL BE CRYING	1.50	2.50
□ 238		FANNIE MAE/BRING YOUR LOVE TO ME	1.50	2.50
□ 239		YOU CAN HAVE HER/LOVE OR MAGIC (67)	1.50	2.50
□ 242		JUSTINE/IN THAT GREAT GETTIN' UP MORNIN' (85)	1.50	2.50
□ 243		FOR YOUR LOVE/GOTTA TELL YOU HOW I FEEL	1.50	2.50
□ 244		GEORGIA ON MY MIND/MY TEARS WILL GO AWAY (62)	1.50	2.50
□ 245		I NEED A GIRL/BRING YOUR LOVE TO ME	1.25	2.00
□ 124	PHILLES	YOU'VE LOST THAT LOVIN' FEELIN' (1)	1.25	2.50
□ 127		JUST ONCE IN MY LIFE/THE BLUES (9)	1.25	2.50
□ 129		UNCHAINED MELODY/HUNG ON YOU (4)	1.25	2.50
□ 130		EBB TIDE/FOR SENTIMENTAL REASONS (5)	1.25	2.50
□ 132		WHITE CLIFFS OF DOVER/SHE'S MINE, ALL MINE	1.75	3.00
□ 10383	VERVE	(YOU'RE MY) SOUL AND INSPIRATION/ B SIDE BLUES (1)	1.00	2.00
□ 10403		RAT RACE/GREEN ONIONS	1.25	2.00
□ 10406		HE/HE WILL BREAK YOUR HEART (18)	1.25	2.00
□ 10425		SOMETHING'S SO WRONG/ THIS IS A LOVE SONG (Bill Medley)	1.25	2.00
□ 10430		GO AHEAD AND CRY/ THINGS DIDN'T GO YOUR WAY (30)	1.25	2.00

ISSUE #	LABEL	ARTIST/TITLE	VG	MINT
☐ 10449		ON THIS SIDE OF GOODBYE/ A MAN WITHOUT A DREAM (47)	1.25	2.00

LATER VERVE SINGLES ARE WORTH UP TO $1.50 MINT

RIGHTEOUS BROTHERS—EP

☐ 1004	*MOONGLOW*	GREATEST HITS .	3.00	5.00

RIGHTEOUS BROTHERS—ALBUMS

☐ 1001 (M)	*MOONGLOW*	RIGHT NOW .	4.00	7.00
☐ 1002 (M)		SOME BLUE-EYED SOUL .	3.50	6.00
☐ 1003 (M)		THIS IS THE RIGHTEOUS BROTHERS	3.50	6.00
☐ 1004 (M)		BEST OF THE RIGHTEOUS BROTHERS	3.00	5.00
☐ 4007 (M)	*PHILLIES*	YOU'VE LOST THAT LOVIN' FEELIN'	5.00	8.00
☐ 4007 (S)		YOU'VE LOST THAT LOVIN' FEELIN'	6.00	10.00
☐ 4008 (M)		JUST ONCE IN MY LIFE .	3.50	6.00
☐ 4008 (S)		JUST ONCE IN MY LIFE .	4.50	8.00
☐ 4009 (M)		BACK TO BACK .	3.50	6.00
☐ 4009 (S)		BACK TO BACK .	4.50	8.00
☐ 5004 (M)	*VERVE*	GO AHEAD AND CRY .	3.00	5.00
☐ 5004 (S)		GO AHEAD AND CRY .	4.00	7.00
☐ 5010 (M)		SAYIN' SOMETHIN' .	3.00	5.00
☐ 5010 (S)		SAYIN' SOMETHIN' .	4.00	7.00
☐ 5020 (M)		THE RIGHTEOUS BROTHERS' GREATEST HITS	3.00	5.00
☐ 5020 (S)		THE RIGHTEOUS BROTHERS' GREATEST HITS	4.00	7.00

RINKY-DINKS
FEATURED: BOBBY DARIN

☐ 6121	*ATCO*	EARLY IN THE MORNING/NOW WE'RE ONE (24)	2.00	3.50
☐ 6128		MIGHTY MIGHTY MAN/YOU'RE MINE	3.00	5.00

RIP CHORDS
FEATURED: BRUCE JOHNSTON, TERRY MELCHER (BRUCE AND TERRY)

☐ 42687	*COLUMBIA*	HERE I STAND/KAREN (51)	1.50	3.00
☐ 42812		GONE/SHE THINKS I STILL CARE (88)	1.50	3.00
☐ 42921		HEY LITTLE COBRA/THE QUEEN (4)	1.25	2.50
☐ 43035		THREE WINDOW COUPE/HOT ROD U.S.A. (28)	1.50	2.50
☐ 43093		ONE-PIECE TOPLESS BATHING SUIT/ WAH-WAHINI (96) .	1.50	3.00
☐ 43221		DON'T BE SCARED/BUNNY HILL	1.75	3.00

RIP CHORDS—ALBUMS

☐ 2151 (M)	*COLUMBIA*	HEY LITTLE COBRA .	6.00	10.00
☐ 8951 (S)		HEY LITTLE COBRA .	7.00	12.00
☐ 2216 (M)		THREE WINDOW COUPE .	6.00	10.00
☐ 9016 (S)		THREE WINDOW COUPE .	7.00	12.00

RITUALS
FEATURED: ARNIE GINSBERG (OF JAN AND ARNIE)
PRODUCER: BRUCE JOHNSTON

☐ 120	*ARWIN*	GIRL IN ZANZIBAR/GUITARRO	3.50	6.00
☐ 127		THIS IS PARADISE/GONE .	3.50	6.00
☐ 128		SURFERS RULE/GONE .	3.00	5.00

JOHNNY RIVERS

Johnny was born in New York City on November 7, 1942. Soon his family moved to the Louisiana capitol of Baton Rouge. Rivers was fourteen when he organized his first band, which played at school functions and parties around Baton Rouge.

After high school Johnny set out to make a name for himself. He drifted from label to label—some large, some small—but never found success during those early scuffling days. Feeling that his career might take a turn for the better in southern California, Johnny Rivers moved there in 1962. Before long he established himself at the popular dance club Whiskey-A-Go-Go in Hollywood.

After signing with Imperial Records (his eleventh label), Johnny finally hit it big during the summer of 1964 with "Memphis". Even against British chart dominance, he managed to "cover" a multitude of previous hits which accounted for half a dozen winners before turning to newer material such as "Secret Agent Man" and "Poor Side Of Town", which he wrote.

ISSUE #	LABEL	ARTIST/TITLE	VG	MINT
		JOHNNY RIVERS		
□5026	***GONE***	BABY COME BACK/LONG, LONG WALK	4.00	7.00
□9047	***CUB***	EVERY DAY/DARLING, TALK TO ME	3.50	6.00
□9058		ANSWER ME, MY LOVE/THE CUSTOMARY THING	3.50	6.00
□239	***DEE DEE***	THAT'S MY BABE/YOUR FIRST AND LAST LOVE	3.50	6.00
□3037	***ERA***	CALL ME/ANDERSONVILLE	3.00	5.00
□2033	***GUYDEN***	YOU'RE THE ONE/HOLE IN THE GROUND	3.00	5.00
□1070	***CHANCELLOR***	KNOCK THREE TIMES/I GET SO DOGGONE LONESOME	2.50	4.00
□1096		BLUE SKIES/THAT SHOULD BE ME	2.50	4.00
□1108		TO BE LOVED/TOO GOOD TO LAST	2.50	4.00
□4850	***CAPITOL***	LONG BLACK VEIL/THIS COULD BE THE ONE	2.50	4.00
□4913		IF YOU WANT IT I'VE GOT IT/ MY HEART IS IN YOUR HANDS	2.50	4.00
□5232		LONG BLACK VEIL/DON'T LOOK NOW	2.00	3.50
□13266	***MGM***	ANSWER ME, MY LOVE/THE CUSTOMARY THING	1.75	3.00
□62425	***CORAL***	THAT'S MY BABE/YOUR FIRST AND LAST LOVE	1.75	3.00
□4565	***ROULETTE***	BABY COME BACK/LONG, LONG WALK	1.75	3.00
□66032	***IMPERIAL***	MEMPHIS/IT WOULDN'T HAPPEN WITH ME (2)	1.00	2.00
□66056		MAYBELLENE/WALK MYSELF ON HOME (12)	1.25	2.00
□66075		MOUNTAIN OF LOVE/MOODY RIVER (9)	1.00	2.00
□66087		MIDNIGHT SPECIAL/CUPID (20)	1.25	2.00
□66112		SEVENTH SUN/UN-SQUARE DANCE (7)	1.00	2.00
□66133		WHERE HAVE ALL THE FLOWERS GONE/ LOVE ME WHILE YOU CAN (26)	1.25	2.00
□66144		UNDER YOUR SPELL AGAIN/LONG TIME MAN (35)	1.25	2.00
□66159		SECRET AGENT MAN/YOU DIG (3)	.75	2.00
□66175		(I WASHED MY HANDS IN) MUDDY WATER/ ROOGALATOR (19)	1.00	2.00
□66205		POOR SIDE OF TOWN/A MAN CAN CRY (1)	.75	1.50
□66227		BABY, I NEED YOUR LOVIN'/ GETTIN' READY FOR TOMORROW (3)	.75	1.50
□66244		THE TRACKS OF MY TEARS/REWIND MEDLEY (10)	1.00	1.50
□66267		SUMMER RAIN/MEMORY OF THE COMING GOOD (14)	1.00	1.50
		JOHNNY RIVERS—ALBUMS		
□2161 (M)	***CAPITOL***	THE SENSATIONAL JOHNNY RIVERS	5.00	8.00
□9264 (M)	***IMPERIAL***	JOHNNY RIVERS AT THE WHISKY A-GO-GO	3.50	6.00
□12264 (S)		JOHNNY RIVERS AT THE WHISKY A-GO-GO	4.50	8.00
□9274 (M)		HERE WE A-GO-GO AGAIN	3.00	5.00
□12274 (S)		HERE WE A-GO-GO AGAIN	4.00	7.00
□9280 (M)		IN ACTION	3.00	5.00
□12280 (S)		IN ACTION	4.00	7.00
□9284 (M)		MEANWHILE BACK AT THE WHISKY A-GO-GO	3.00	5.00
□12284 (S)		MEANWHILE BACK AT THE WHISKY A-GO-GO	4.00	7.00
□9293 (M)		JOHNNY RIVERS ROCKS THE FOLK	3.00	5.00
□12293 (S)		JOHNNY RIVERS ROCKS THE FOLK	4.00	7.00
□9307 (M)		AND I KNOW YOU WANNA DANCE	3.00	5.00
□12307 (S)		AND I KNOW YOU WANNA DANCE	4.00	7.00
□9324 (M)		JOHNNY RIVERS' GOLDEN HITS	3.00	5.00
□12324 (S)		JOHNNY RIVERS' GOLDEN HITS	4.00	7.00

ISSUE #	LABEL	ARTIST/TITLE	VG	MINT
		RIVIERAS		
□503	***COED***	COUNT EVERY STAR/ TRUE LOVE IS HARD TO FIND (73)	3.00	5.00
□508		MOONLIGHT SERENADE/ NEITHER RAIN NOR SNOW (47)	2.00	3.50
□522		SINCE I MADE YOU CRY/ ELEVENTH HOUR MELODY (93)	2.00	3.50
□529		MOONLIGHT COCKTAILS/BLESSING OF LOVE	2.50	4.00
		RIVIERAS		
□1401	***RIVIERA***	CALIFORNIA SUN/H.B. GOOSE STEP (5)	1.00	2.00
□1402		LITTLE DONNA/LET'S HAVE A PARTY (93)	1.25	2.00
□1403		ROCKIN' ROBIN/BATTLE LINE (96)	1.25	2.00
□1405		WHOLE LOTTA SHAKIN'/RIP IT UP	1.25	2.00
		RIVIERAS—ALBUM		
□701 (M)	***RIVIERA***	CAMPUS PARTY	6.00	10.00
		RIVINGTONS		
□55427	***LIBERTY***	PAPA-OOM-MOW-MOW/DEEP WATER (48)	1.25	2.50
□55513		KICKAPOO JOY JUICE/MY REWARD	1.50	2.50
□55528		MAMA-OOM-MOW-MOW/WAITING	1.50	2.50
□55553		THE BIRD'S THE WORD/I'M LOSING MY GRIP (52)	1.25	2.50
□55585		THE SHAKY BIRD (PT. 1)/(PT. 11)	1.50	2.50
□55610		LITTLE SALLY WALKER/CHERRY	1.50	2.50
□55671		WEEJEE WALK/FAIRY TALES	1.50	2.50
		RIVINGTONS—ALBUM		
□3282 (M)	***LIBERTY***	DOIN' THE BIRD	6.00	10.00
□7282 (S)		DOIN' THE BIRD	7.00	12.00
		ROADSTERS		
		PRODUCER: GARY USHER		
□1390	***DONNA***	MAG RIMS/CANDYMATIC	2.00	3.50
□486	***20TH FOX***	JOY RIDE/DRAG	1.75	3.00
		ROBINS		
		SEE: COASTERS		
□103	***SPARK***	RIOT IN CELL BLOCK #9/WRAP IT UP	8.00	15.00
□107		LOOP DE LOOP MAMBO/FRAMED	12.00	20.00
□122		SMOKEY JOE'S CAFE/JUST LIKE A FOOL	8.00	15.00
□6059	***ATCO***	SMOKEY JOE'S CAFE/JUST LIKE A FOOL (79) (maroon label)	3.00	5.00
		ROBBINS AND PAXTON		
		FEATURED: GARY "FLIP" PAXTON		
□704	***RORI***	TEEN ANGEL/STRANGE RAIN	2.50	4.00
		ROBERT AND JOHNNY		
□1021	***OLD TOWN***	I BELIEVE IN YOU/TRAIN TO PARADISE	3.50	6.00
□1047		WE BELONG TOGETHER/WALKIN' IN THE RAIN (33)	2.50	4.00
□1052		I BELIEVE IN YOU/MARRY ME (93)	2.00	3.50
		FLOYD ROBINSON		
□7529	***RCA***	MAKIN' LOVE/MY GIRL (20)	1.25	2.50
□7637		LET IT BE ME/TONIGHT YOU BELONG TO ME	1.25	2.00
□7693		TATTLETALE/I BELIEVE IN LOVE	1.25	2.00

ISSUE #	LABEL	ARTIST/TITLE	VG	MINT
		FLOYD ROBINSON—EP		
☐4350	*RCA*	MAKIN' LOVE	3.00	5.00
		FLOYD ROBINSON—ALBUM		
☐2162 (M)	*RCA*	FLOYD ROBINSON	5.00	9.00
☐2162 (S)		FLOYD ROBINSON	7.00	12.00
		ROCK-A-TEENS		
☐3515	*DORAN*	WOO-HOO/UNTRUE	7.00	12.00
☐4192	*ROULETTE*	WOO-HOO/UNTRUE (16)	1.25	2.50
☐4217		TWANGY/DOGGONE IT BABY	1.50	2.50
		ROCK-A-TEENS—ALBUM		
☐25109 (M)	*ROULETTE*	WOO-HOO	12.00	20.00
☐25109 (S)		WOO-HOO	18.00	30.00
		ROCKAWAYS (JAY AND THE AMERICANS)		
☐10-005	*RED BIRD*	DON'T CRY/TOP DOWN TIME	2.50	4.00
		ROCKIN' REBELS		
		SEE: BUFFALO REBELS, REBELS		
☐4140	*SWAN*	ROCKIN' CRICKETS/HULLY GULLY ROCK (87)	1.25	2.00
☐4150		ANOTHER WILD WEEKEND/HAPPY POPCORN	1.25	2.00
		ROCKIN' REBELS—ALBUM		
☐509 (M)	*SWAN*	WILD WEEKEND	7.00	12.00
		TOMMY ROE		
☐1018	*JUDD*	CAVEMAN/I GOTTA GIRL	5.00	8.00
☐1022		SHEILA/PRETTY GIRL	8.00	12.00
☐10329	*ABC-PARAMOUNT*	SHEILA/SAVE YOUR KISSES (1)	1.00	2.50
☐10362		SUSIE DARLIN'/PIDDLE DE PAT (35)	1.25	2.50
☐10379		TOWN CRIER/RAINBOW	1.50	2.50
☐10389		DON'T CRY DONNA/GONNA TAKE A CHANCE	1.50	2.50
☐10423		THE FOLK SINGER/COUNT ON ME (84)	1.50	2.50
☐10454		KISS AND RUN/WHAT MAKES THE BLUES	1.50	2.50
☐10478		EVERYBODY/SORRY I'M LATE, LISA (3)	1.00	2.00
☐10515		COME ON/THERE WILL BE BETTER YEARS (36)	1.25	2.00
☐10543		CAROL/BE A GOOD LITTLE GIRL (61)	1.25	2.00
☐10604		PARTY GIRL/OH, HOW COULD I LOVE YOU (85)	1.25	2.00
☐10762		SWEET PEA/MUCH MORE LOVE (8)	.75	1.50
☐10852		HOORAY FOR HAZEL/NEED YOUR LOVE (6)	.75	1.50
☐10888		IT'S NOW WINTER'S DAY/KICK ME, CHARLIE (23)	1.00	1.50
☐10908		SING ALONG WITH ME/NIGHTTIME (91)	1.00	1.50
☐10945		LITTLE MISS SUNSHINE/THE YOU I NEED (99)	1.00	1.50
☐11164		DIZZY/THE YOU I NEED (1)	.75	1.50
☐11211		HEATHER HONEY/MONEY IS MY PAY (29)	1.00	1.50
☐11229		JACK AND JILL/TIP TOE TINA (53)	1.00	1.50
☐11247		JAM UP AND JELLY TIGHT/MOONTALK (8)	.75	1.50
		LATER ABC SINGLES ARE WORTH UP TO $1.50 MINT		
		TOMMY ROE—ALBUMS		
☐432 (M)	*ABC-PARAMOUNT*	SHEILA	3.50	6.00
☐432 (S)		SHEILA	4.50	8.00
☐467 (M)		SOMETHING FOR EVERYBODY	3.00	5.00

ISSUE #	LABEL	ARTIST/TITLE	VG	MINT
☐467 (S)		SOMETHING FOR EVERYBODY	4.00	7.00
☐575 (M)		SWEET PEA	3.00	5.00
☐575 (S)		SWEET PEA	4.00	7.00
☐594 (M)		IT'S NOW WINTER'S DAY	3.00	5.00
☐594 (S)		IT'S NOW WINTER'S DAY	4.00	7.00
☐610 (S)		PHANTASY	3.50	6.00
☐683 (S)		DIZZY	3.00	5.00
☐700 (S)		12 IN A ROE (greatest hits)	3.00	5.00
		KENNETH ROGERS (KENNY ROGERS)		
☐454	*CARLTON*	THAT CRAZY FEELING/ WE'LL ALWAYS HAVE EACH OTHER	2.50	4.00
☐468		I'VE GOT A LOT TO LEARN/FOR YOU ALONE	2.50	4.00
		TIMMIE ROGERS		
☐116	*CAMEO*	BACK TO SCHOOL AGAIN/ I'VE GOT A DOG WHO LOVES ME (36)	1.50	2.50
☐131		TAKE ME TO YOUR LEADER/FLA-GA-LA-PA	1.25	2.00
		ROGUES		
		PRODUCER: BRUCE JOHNSTON		
☐43190	*COLUMBIA*	EVERYDAY/ROGUE'S REEF	2.50	4.00
☐43253		COME ON LET'S GO/ROGUE'S REEF, PART 2	2.50	4.00

ROLLING STONES

One night in 1962 Brian Jones—who played harmonica, sax and clarinet—jammed onstage with a London band called Little Boy Blue and the Blue Boys. The group consisted of two lifelong pals, Mick Jagger and Keith Richard, as well as drummer Charlie Watts.

The group later broke up, and the new quartet (as yet unnamed) moved into a cheap apartment, where they lived solely on mashed potatoes and fried eggs. Bassist Bill Wyman came into the group, and the quintet took on the name of the Rolling Stones, from the 1950 disc "Rollin' Stone Blues" by Muddy Waters.

They played cheap bars and pubs and gained a reputation as a rowdy r & b band. The Stones' first American-released single was "Stoned", which had virtually no sales because of the drug-reference title. (Oddly enough, the song was an instrumental.) Their second American release from London was "I Wanna Be Your Man", although the flip side of "Not Fade Away" (the Crickets oldie and flip of "Oh, Boy!") became the stronger side. The first group to dress sloppily and act surly onstage, the Rolling Stones later gained a permanent place in the annals of rock-and-roll history.

ISSUE #	LABEL	ARTIST/TITLE	VG	MINT
		ROLLING STONES		
□ 9641	*LONDON*	STONED/I WANNA BE YOUR MAN	30.00	50.00
□ 9657		NOT FADE AWAY/I WANNA BE YOUR MAN (48)	2.50	4.00
□ 9682		TELL ME/I JUST WANT TO MAKE LOVE TO YOU (24)	2.00	4.00
□ 9687		IT'S ALL OVER NOW/GOOD TIMES, BAD TIMES (26)	2.00	4.00
□ 9708		TIME IS ON MY SIDE/CONGRATULATIONS (6)	1.75	3.50
□ 9725		HEART OF STONE/WHAT A SHAME (19)	2.00	3.50
□ 9741		THE LAST TIME/PLAY WITH FIRE (9)	1.50	3.00
□ 9766		SATISFACTION/UNDER ASSISTANT WEST COAST PROMOTION MAN (1)	1.25	2.50
□ 9792		GET OFF OF MY CLOUD/I'M FREE (1)	1.25	2.50
□ 9808		AS TEARS GO BY/GOTTA GET AWAY (6)	1.25	2.50
□ 9823		19TH NERVOUS BREAKDOWN/SAD DAY (2)	1.25	2.50
□ 901		PAINT IT, BLACK/STUPID GIRL (1)	1.25	2.50
□ 902		MOTHER'S LITTLE HELPER/LADY JANE (8)	1.25	2.50
□ 903		HAVE YOU SEEN YOUR MOTHER, BABY, STANDING IN THE SHADOW/WHO'S DRIVING YOUR PLANE (9)	1.25	2.50
□ 904		RUBY TUESDAY/ LET'S SPEND THE NIGHT TOGETHER (1)	1.25	2.50
□ 905		DANDELION/WE LOVE YOU (14)	1.25	2.50
□ 906		SHE'S A RAINBOW/ 2,000 LIGHT YEARS FROM HOME (25)	1.50	2.50
□ 907		IN ANOTHER LAND/THE LANTERN (Bill Wyman) (87)	1.75	3.00
□ 908		JUMPIN' JACK FLASH/CHILD OF THE MOON (3)	1.00	2.00
□ 909		STREET FIGHTING MAN/NO EXPECTATIONS (48)	1.50	2.50
□ 910		HONKY TONK WOMEN/YOU CAN'T ALWAYS GET WHAT YOU WANT (1)	1.00	2.00
		LATER SINGLES ON ROLLING STONES ARE WORTH UP TO $1.50 MINT		
		ROLLING STONES—ALBUMS		
□ 3375 (M)	*LONDON*	THE ROLLING STONES	6.00	10.00
□ 3402 (M)		12 X 5	5.00	8.00
□ 3420 (M)		THE ROLLING STONES NOW	5.00	8.00
□ 3429 (M)		OUT OF OUR HEADS	5.00	8.00
□ 3451 (M)		DECEMBER'S CHILDREN	5.00	8.00
□ 3476 (M)		AFTERMATH	4.00	7.00
□ 3493 (M)		GOT LIVE IF YOU WANT IT	4.00	7.00
□ 3499 (M)		BETWEEN THE BUTTONS	4.00	7.00
□ 3509 (M)		FLOWERS	4.00	7.00
		(STEREO COPIES OF THE ABOVE ALBUMS HAVE A SLIGHTLY LOWER VALUE)		
□ NPS-2 (S)		THEIR SATANIC MAJESTIES' REQUEST (with 3-D cover)	7.00	12.00
□ 539 (S)		BEGGAR'S BANQUET	3.00	5.00
□ NPS-3 (S)		THROUGH THE PAST DARKLY	3.00	5.00
□ NPS-4 (S)		LET IT BLEED	3.00	5.00
□ NPS-5 (S)		GET HER YA-YA'S OUT	3.50	6.00
		RON ROMAN (FRANK ZAPPA)		
□ 101	*DAANI*	LOVE IS MY LIFE/TELL ME	12.00	20.00

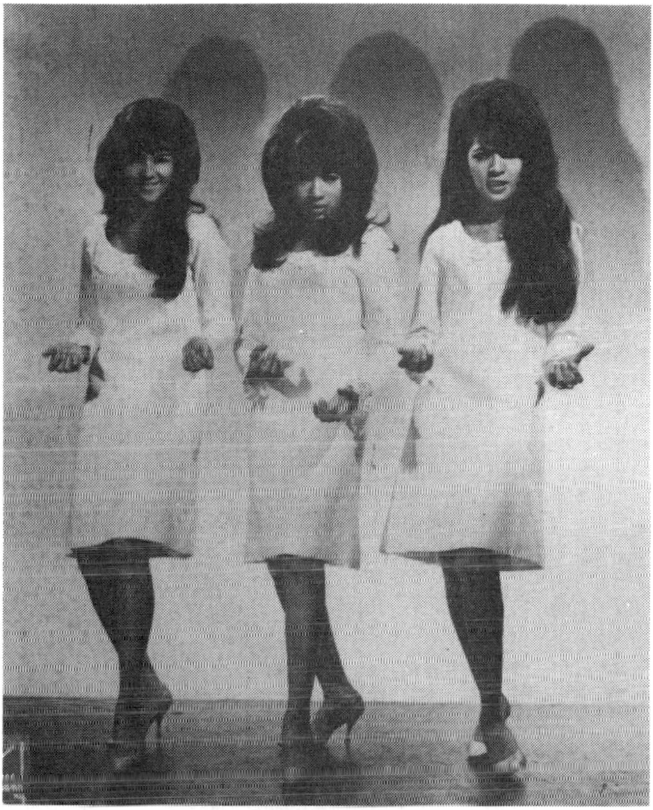

RONETTES

Ronie and Estelle Bennett, two New York City sisters, formed a group in 1959 with their first cousin, Nedra Talley. They spent much after-school time (they were in junior high at the time) rehearsing a tight, sexy, "little girl" sound. During the early 1960s they began getting gigs at such places as the Peppermint Lounge, where they worked as a warmup act for Joey Dee and the Starliters.

In 1963 record-production genius Phil Spector was in New York in search of new talent. Impressed with the trio, Spector signed the girls (who had recorded flops on Colpix and May) to his red-hot Philles label. By the end of the summer, the Ronettes were rapidly climbing the charts with "Be My Baby", a song that went all the way to No. 2. This was followed by such later hits as "Baby, I Love You", "(The Best Part Of) Breakin' Up", "Do I Love You" and the now-classic "Walking In the Rain".

In 1968 Phil Spector married Ronnie Bennett, but they were divorced six years later.

ISSUE #	LABEL	ARTIST/TITLE	VG	MINT

RONETTES

SEE: BONNIE AND THE TREASURES, RONNIE AND THE RELATIVES, RONNIE SPECTOR, VERONICA

ISSUE #	LABEL	ARTIST/TITLE	VG	MINT
☐646	**COLPIX**	I'M GONNA QUIT WHILE I'M AHEAD/ I'M ON THE WAGON	6.00	10.00
☐114	**MAY**	SILHOUETTES/YOU BET I WOULD	5.00	8.00
☐138		GOOD GIRLS/MEMORY	5.00	8.00
☐116	**PHILLES**	BE MY BABY/TEDESCO AND PITTMAN (2)	1.50	3.00
☐118		BABY, I LOVE YOU/MISS JOAN AND MR. SAM (24)	1.75	3.00
☐120		(THE BEST PART OF) BREAKIN' UP/BIG RED (39)	1.75	3.00
☐121		DO I LOVE YOU/BEBE AND SUSU (34)	1.75	3.00
☐123		WALKING IN THE RAIN/HOW DOES IT FEEL? (23)	1.75	3.00
☐126		BORN TO BE TOGETHER/BLUES FOR MY BABY (52)	2.00	3.50
☐128		IS THIS WHAT I GET FOR LOVING YOU?/ OH, I LOVE YOU (75)	2.00	3.50
☐133		I CAN HEAR MUSIC/WHEN I SAW YOU (100)	2.50	4.00

RONETTES—ALBUMS

ISSUE #	LABEL	ARTIST/TITLE	VG	MINT
☐486 (M)	**COLPIX**	THE RONETTES FEATURING VERNOICA	7.00	12.00
☐4006 (M)	**PHILLES**	PRESENTING THE FABULOUS RONETTES	20.00	30.00
☐4006 (S)		PRESENTING THE FABULOUS RONETTES	30.00	50.00

RONNIE AND THE RELATIVES (RONETTES)

ISSUE #	LABEL	ARTIST/TITLE	VG	MINT
☐601	**COLPIX**	SWEET SIXTEEN/I WANT A BOY	6.00	10.00
☐111	**MAY**	MY GUIDING ANGEL/ I'M GONNA QUIT WHILE I'M AHEAD	7.00	12.00

RONNY AND THE DAYTONAS

ISSUE #	LABEL	ARTIST/TITLE	VG	MINT
☐481	**MALA**	G.T.O./HOT ROD BABY (4)	1.25	2.50
☐490		CALIFORNIA BOUND/HEY LITTLE GIRL (72)	1.50	2.50
☐492		BUCKET "T"/LITTLE RAIL JOB (54)	1.50	2.50
☐497		LITTLE SCRAMBLER/TEENAGE YEARS	1.50	2.50
☐503		NO WHEELS/BEACH BOY	1.50	2.50
☐513		SANDY (vocal)/SANDY (instrumental) (27)	1.25	2.00
☐525		GOODBYE BABY/SOMEBODY TO LOVE ME	1.25	2.00
☐531		ANTIQUE '32 STUDEBAKER DICTATOR COUPE/ THEN THE RAINS CAME	1.50	2.50
☐542		I'LL THINK OF SUMMER/LITTLE SCRAMBLER	1.25	2.00

RONNY AND THE DAYTONAS—ALBUMS

ISSUE #	LABEL	ARTIST/TITLE	VG	MINT
☐4001 (M)	**MALA**	G.T.O.	5.00	8.00
☐4002 (M)		SANDY	4.00	7.00

LINDA RONSTADT

ISSUE #	LABEL	ARTIST/TITLE	VG	MINT
☐937	**SIDEWALK**	EVERBODY HAS THEIR OWN IDEAS/SO FINE	5.00	8.00
☐5838	**CAPITOL**	ALL THE BEAUTIFUL THINGS/ SWEET SUMMER BLUE AND GOLD	2.50	4.00
☐5910		EVERGREEN/ONE FOR ALL	2.50	4.00
☐2004		DIFFERENT DRUM/I'VE GOT TO KNOW (13) (Stone Poneys)	1.25	2.50
☐2110		UP TO MY NECK IN MUDDY WATER/ CARNIVAL BEAT (93)	1.50	2.50
☐2195		SOME OF SHELLY'S BLUES/HOBO (MORNING GLORY)	1.50	2.50
☐2438		DOLPHINS/LONG WAY AROUND	1.50	2.50

ISSUE #	LABEL	ARTIST/TITLE	VG	MINT
☐2767		WILL YOU LOVE ME TOMORROW/LOVESICK BLUES	1.50	2.50
☐2846		LONG LONG TIME/NOBODYS (25)	1.25	2.00
☐3021		(SHE'S A) VERY LOVELY WOMAN/ LONG WAY AROUND (70)	1.50	2.50
☐3210		I FALL TO PIECES/CAN IT BE TRUE	1.50	2.50
☐3273		ROCK ME ON THE WATER/CRAZY ARMS (85)	1.25	2.00
		ROOMATES		
		SEE: CATHY JEAN AND THE ROOMATES		
☐008	*VALMOR*	GLORY OF LOVE/NEVER KNEW (49)	1.50	3.00
☐13		MY FOOLISH HEART/ MY KISSES FOR YOUR THOUGHTS	1.75	3.00
☐40105	*PHILIPS*	ANSWER ME, MY LOVE/GEE	1.50	2.50
☐40153		THE NEARNESS OF YOU/PLEASE DON'T CHEAT ON ME	1.50	2.50
☐40161		THE NEARNESS OF YOU/PLEASE DON'T CHEAT ON ME	1.25	2.00
		ROSIE AND THE ORIGINALS		
☐1011	*HIGHLAND*	ANGEL BABY/GIVE ME LOVE (5)	1.25	2.50
		ROSIE		
☐55205	*BRUNSWICK*	LONELY BLUE NIGHTS/WE'LL HAVE A CHANCE (66)	2.00	3.50
☐55213		MY DARLIN' FOREVER/THE TIME IS NEAR	2.50	4.00
		ROSIE—ALBUM		
☐54102 (M)	*BRUNSWICK*	LONE BLUE NIGHTS	6.00	10.00
		BILLY JOE ROYAL		
☐21009	*FAIRLANE*	NEVER IN A HUNDRED YEARS/ WE HAVEN'T A MOMENT TO LOSE	1.75	3.00
☐21013		DARK GLASSES/PERHAPS	1.75	3.00
☐401	*ALL WOOD*	IF IT WASN'T FOR A WOMAN/WAIT FOR ME BABY	1.75	3.00
☐1	*PLAYERS*	I'M SPECIALIZED/REALLY YOU	1.75	3.00

SINGLES ON COLUMBIA ARE WORTH UP TO $1.50 MINT

ROYAL TEENS

A group of New Jersey high-school lads formed an instrumental quintet in 1957. At first they called themselves the Royal Tones, but soon changed to the Royal Teens.

They recorded two unsuccessful singles for a small local label called Power. ABC-Paramount expressed interest in their second Power flop, "Short Shorts". The Royal Teens signed with ABC-Paramount Records, which released the master under its own logo. The song became a hit and sold over a million copies.

Later ABC-Paramount singles failed to maintain the momentum of the group's first hit. The Royal Teens then went with Capitol Records and, as with ABC-Paramount, found success in their first release. "Believe Me", a satin-smooth ballad, reached the Top 30. But it was to be the last chart winner for the Royal Teens. After a pair of singles on the Mighty label, the Royal Teens disbanded.

Some members of the Royal Teens later appeared in other groups. Al Kooper was instrumental in establishing Blood, Sweat and Tears. Bob Gaudio became an important creative force with the Four Seasons.

ISSUE #	LABEL	ARTIST/TITLE	VG	MINT
		ROYAL TEENS		
☐113	*POWER*	SITTIN' WITH MY BABY/MAD GRASS	6.00	10.00
☐215		SHORT SHORTS/PLANET ROCK	8.00	15.00
☐9882	*ABC-PARAMOUNT*	SHORT SHORTS/PLANET ROCK (3)	1.25	3.00
☐9918		BIG NAME BUTTON/SHAM ROCK	1.75	3.00
☐9945		HARVEY'S GOT A GIRL FRIEND/ HANGIN' 'ROUND (78)	1.50	3.00
☐9955		MY KIND OF DREAM/OPEN THE DOOR	1.75	3.00
☐4261	*CAPITOL*	BELIEVE ME/LITTLE CRICKET (26)	1.50	3.00
☐4335		THE MOON'S NOT MEANT FOR LOVERS/ WAS IT A DREAM?	2.00	3.50
☐4402		IT'S THE TALK OF THE TOWN/WITH YOU	2.00	3.50
☐111	*MIGHTY*	ROYAL BLUE/LEOTARDS	1.50	2.50
☐200		MY MEMORIES OF YOU/LITTLE TRIXIE	1.50	2.50
		ROYALTONES		
☐5338	*JUBILEE*	POOR BOY/WAIL! (17)	1.25	2.50
☐5362		SEESAW/LITTLE BO	1.25	2.00
☐3004	*GOLDISC*	BIG WHEEL/SHORT LINE	1.25	2.00
☐3011		FLAMINGO EXPRESS/TACOS (82)	1.25	2.00
☐3016		DIXIE CUP/BUTTERSCOTCH	1.25	2.00
		RUBEN AND THE JETS *FEATURED: FRANK ZAPPA*		
☐10632	*VERVE*	JELLY ROLL GUM DROP/ANYWAY THE WIND BLOWS	3.00	5.00
☐73381	*MERCURY*	IF I COULD BE YOUR LOVE AGAIN/WEDDING BELLS	2.50	4.00
		RUMBLERS		
☐1026	*HIGHLAND*	INTERSECTION/STOMPING TIME	3.00	5.00
☐103	*DOWNEY*	BOSS/I DON'T NEED YOU NO MORE	2.50	4.00
☐106		BOSS STRIKES BACK/SORRY	2.00	3.50
☐107		ANGRY SEA/BUGGED	2.00	3.50
☐111		IT'S A GASS/TOOTENANNY	1.75	3.00
☐114		HIGH OCTANE/NIGHT SCENE	1.75	3.00
☐127		SOULFUL JERK/HEY-DID-A-DA-DA	1.75	3.00
☐16421	*DOT*	BOSS/I DON'T NEED YOU NO MORE (87)	1.50	2.50
☐16455		BOSS STRIKES BACK/SORRY	1.75	2.50
☐16480		ANGRY SEA/BUGGED	1.75	2.50
☐10292		IT'S A GASS/TOOTENANNY	1.75	2.50
		RUMBLER—ALBUMS		
☐1001 (M)	*DOWNEY*	BOSS!	7.00	12.00
☐1001 (S)		BOSS!	8.00	15.00
☐3509 (M)	*DOT*	BOSS!	5.00	8.00
☐25509 (S)		BOSS!	6.00	10.00
		RUNAROUNDS (REGENTS)		
☐1004	*COUSINS*	MASHED POTATO MARY/I'M ALL ALONE	3.50	6.00
☐116	*KC*	UNBELIEVABLE/HOORAY FOR LOVE	3.00	5.00
☐8704	*FELSTED*	CARRIE (YOU'RE AN ANGEL)/SEND HER BACK	2.50	4.00
		LEE RUSSELL (LEON RUSSELL)		
☐4049	*ROULETTE*	HONKY TONK WOMAN/RAINBOW AT MIDNIGHT	3.00	5.00

BOBBY RYDELL

Robert Lewis Ridarelli was born on April 26, 1942, in the South Philadelphia area. He showed an early interest in show business by mimicking television entertainers. Bobby's father encouraged the boy to pursue a music career. By the age of six, Young Rydell was banging away on a set of drums purchased by his dad. Within a year the elementary-school student was appearing in night clubs, imitating his idol Gene Krupa and establishing himself as a local child star.

During the early 1950s Bobby became a regular on Paul Whiteman's television show. Whiteman came up with the idea of shortening Bobby's last name to something easier to remember.

As a high-school boy Bobby became a drummer with a local rock band called Rocco and the Saints, which at one time had featured a trumpeteer named Frankie Avalon.

Bobby signed with a couple of small local record companies but had no success. He then went with Cameo-Parkway. Thanks in part to "American Bandstand" exposure, Rydell became a major teen star after the sucess of "Kissin' Time", his first Cameo winner.

ISSUE #	LABEL	ARTIST/TITLE	VG	MINT
		BOBBY RYDELL		
☐201	***VENISE***	FATTY FATTY/HAPPY HAPPY	6.00	10.00
☐731	***VEKO***	FATTY FATTY/DREAM AGE	4.00	7.00
☐160	***CAMEO***	PLEASE DON'T BE MAD/MAKIN' TIME	6.00	10.00
☐164		ALL I WANT IS YOU/FOR YOU, FOR YOU	6.00	10.00
☐167		KISSIN' TIME/YOU'LL NEVER TAME ME (11)	1.50	2.50
☐169		WE GOT LOVE/I DIG GIRLS (6)	1.50	2.50
☐171		WILD ONE/ITTY BITTY GIRL (2)	1.25	2.50
☐175		SWINGIN' SCHOOL/DING A LING (5)	1.25	2.50
☐179		VOLARE/I'LL DO IT AGAIN (4)	1.25	2.50
☐182		SWAY/GROOVY TONIGHT (14)	1.25	2.00
☐186		GOOD TIME BABY/CHERIE (11)	1.25	2.00
☐190		THAT OLD BLACK MAGIC/DON'T BE AFRAID (21)	1.25	2.00
☐192		THE FISH/THE THIRD HOUSE (25)	1.25	2.00
☐201		I WANNA THANK YOU/THE DOOR TO PARADISE (21)	1.25	2.00
☐209		I'VE GOT BONNIE/LOSE HER (18)	1.25	2.00
☐217		I'LL NEVER DANCE AGAIN/ GEE, IT'S WONDERFUL (14)	1.25	2.00
☐228		THE CHA-CHA-CHA/THE BEST MAN CRIED	1.25	2.00
☐242		BUTTERFLY BABY/LOVE IS BLIND (23)	1.25	2.00
☐252		WILDWOOD DAYS/WILL YOU BE MY BABY (17)	1.25	2.00
☐265		LITTLE QUEENIE/THE WOODPECKER SONG	1.50	2.50
☐272		LET'S MAKE LOVE TONIGHT/ CHILDHOOD SWEETHEART (98)	1.25	2.00
☐280		FORGET HIM/LOVE, LOVE, GO AWAY (4)	1.00	2.00
☐309		MAKE ME FORGET/ LITTLE GIRL, I'VE HAD A BUSY DAY (43)	1.25	2.00
☐320		A WORLD WITHOUT LOVE/OUR FADED LOVE (80)	1.25	2.00
☐361		CIAO CIAO BAMBINO/VOCE DE LA NOTTE	1.50	2.50
☐1070		FORGET HIM/A MESSAGE FROM BOBBY	.75	1.50
		CAPITOL SINGLES ARE WORTH UP TO $1.50 MINT		
		BOBBY RYDELL—ALBUMS		
☐1006 (M)	***CAMEO***	WE GOT LOVE	5.00	8.00
☐1007 (M)		BOBBY SINGS	4.00	7.00
☐1009 (M)		BIGGEST HITS	5.00	8.00
☐1010 (M)		BOBBY RYDELL SALUTES THE GREAT ONES	4.00	7.00
☐1011 (M)		RYDELL AT THE COPA	4.00	7.00
☐1019 (M)		ALL THE HITS BY BOBBY RYDELL	4.00	7.00
☐1028 (M)		BIGGEST HITS, VOL. 2	4.00	7.00
		BOBBY RYDELL AND CHUBBY CHECKER		
☐205	***CAMEO***	JINGLE BELL ROCK/ JINGLE BELL ROCK IMITATIONS (21)	1.25	2.00
☐214		TEACH ME TO TWIST/SWINGIN' TOGETHER	1.50	2.50
		BOBBY RYDELL AND CHUBBY CHECKER—ALBUM		
☐1013 (M)	***CAMEO***	BOBBY RYDELL AND CHUBBY CHECKER	4.00	7.00
		MITCH RYDER AND THE DETROIT WHEELS		
		SEE: BILLY LEE AND THE RIVIERAS		
☐801	***NEW VOICE***	I NEED HELP/I HOPE	1.75	3.00
☐806		JENNY TAKE A RIDE!/BABY JANE (10)	1.25	2.00
☐808		LITTLE LATIN LUPE LU/I HOPE (17)	1.25	2.00

ISSUE #	LABEL	ARTIST/TITLE	VG	MINT
□811		BREAK OUT/I NEED HELP (62)	1.25	2.00
□814		TAKIN' ALL I CAN GET/YOU GET YOUR KICKS (100)	1.50	2.00
□817		DEVIL WITH A BLUE DRESS ON/I HAD IT MADE (4)	1.00	2.00
□820		SOCK IT TO ME-BABY!/I NEVER HAD IT BETTER (6)	1.00	2.00
□822		TOO MANY FISH IN THE SEA/ ONE GRAIN OF SAND	1.25	2.00
□824		JOY/I'D RATHER GO TO JAIL (41)	1.25	2.00
□826		YOU ARE MY SUNSHINE/WILD CHILD (88)	1.50	2.00
□828		COME SEE ABOUT ME/FACE IN THE CROWD	1.50	2.00
□830		RUBY BABY-PEACHES ON A CHERRY TREE/ YOU GET YOUR KICKS	1.50	2.00
		MITCH RYDER AND THE DETROIT WHEELS—ALBUMS		
□2000 (M)	***NEW VOICE***	JENNY TAKE A RIDE	5.00	8.00
□2002 (M)		BREAKOUT	4.00	7.00
□2002 (S)		BREAKOUT	5.00	8.00
□2003 (M)		SOCK IT TO ME	3.50	6.00
□2003 (S)		SOCK IT TO ME	4.50	8.00
□2004 (M)		ALL MITCH RYDER HITS	3.50	6.00
□2004 (S)		ALL MITCH RYDER HITS	4.50	8.00
		MITCH RYDER		
□901	***DYNO VOICE***	WHAT NOW MY LOVE/BLESSING IN DISGUISE (30)	1.25	2.00
□905		PERSONALITY-CHANTILLY LACE/ I MAKE A FOOL OF MYSELF (87)	1.50	2.00
□916		THE LIGHTS OF NIGHT/I NEED LOVING YOU	1.00	1.50
□934		RING YOUR BELL/BABY I NEED YOUR LOVING— THEME FOR MITCH	1.00	1.50
		MITCH RYDER—ALBUM		
□31901 (M)	***DYNO VOICE***	WHAT NOW MY LOVE	3.50	6.00
□31901 (S)		WHAT NOW MY LOVE	4.50	8.00

SAFARIS

The Safaris formed in 1959 in Los Angeles, California. Lead singer Jim Stephens had just graduated, but three other members were still attending high school. Thanks to the smooth, well-developed voice of Stephens, the Safaris soon became local favorites, appearing at school dances and at small L. A. night spots.

After little success in trying to convince larger record companies of their abilities, the Safaris found the doors of the small Eldo label open to them. They recorded an original song, "Image Of a Girl". Their only major hit, the Safaris saw the single reach the Top 10 during the summer of 1960.

Their second single, the excellent "Girl With The Story In Her Eyes" (backed by an equally good flip of "Summer Nights"), failed to make the Safaris more than a one-hit group. In desperation they turned from original material to such proven r & b oldies as "In the Still Of the Night" and "Soldier Of Fortune". While both were fine interpretations of the originals, the Safaris were never again to be heard of. In 1961 they decided to call it quits and broke up.

ISSUE #	LABEL	ARTIST/TITLE	VG	MINT
		SAFARIS		
☐ 101	ELDO	IMAGE OF A GIRL/4 STEPS TO LOVE (6)	1.25	3.00
☐ 105		GIRL WITH THE STORY IN HER EYES/ SUMMER NIGHTS (85)	1.50	3.00
☐ 110		IN THE STILL OF THE NIGHT/SHADOWS	2.50	4.00
☐ 113		SOLDIER OF FORTUNE/GARDEN OF LOVE	2.00	3.50
		SAGITTARIUS		
		FEATURED: BRUCE JOHNSTON, TERRY MELCHER (BRUCE AND TERRY), GARY USHER, GLEN CAMPBELL		
☐ 44163	COLUMBIA	MY WORLD FELL DOWN/LIBRA (70)	1.50	3.00
☐ 44289		HOTEL INDISCREET/VIRGO	2.00	3.50
☐ 44398		ANOTHER TIME/PISCES	2.00	3.50
☐ 105	TOGETHER	IN MY ROOM/NAVAJO GIRL (85)	1.50	3.50
☐ 122		I CAN STILL SEE YOUR FACE/ I GUESS THE LORD MUST BE IN NEW YORK CITY	1.75	3.00
		SAGITTARIUS—ALBUMS		
☐ 9644 (S)	COLUMBIA	PRESENT TENSE	5.00	8.00
☐ 1002 (S)	TOGETHER	THE BLUE MARBLE	5.00	8.00
		DOUG SAHM		
		SEE: SIR DOUGLAS QUINTET		
☐ 107	HARLEM	WHY OH WHY/IF YOU EVER NEED ME	3.50	6.00
☐ 625	SWINGIN'	WHY OH WHY/IF YOU EVER NEED ME	2.50	4.00
☐ 3505	PERSONALITY	BABY, WHAT'S ON YOUR MIND?/ CRAZY, CRAZY FEELING	3.50	6.00
☐ 212	RENNER	MAKES NO DIFFERENCE/BIG HAT	3.00	5.00
☐ 215		BABY, WHAT'S ON YOUR MIND?/ CRAZY, CRAZY FEELING	2.50	4.00
☐ 226		JUST BECAUSE/TWO HEARTS IN LOVE	3.00	5.00
☐ 240		LUCKY ME/A YEAR AGO TODAY	3.00	5.00
		CRISPIAN ST. PETERS		
☐ 1309	JAMIE	NO NO NO/AT THIS MOMENT	1.50	2.50
☐ 1310		YOU WERE ON MY MIND/WHAT I'M GONNA BE (36)	1.50	2.50
☐ 1320		THE PIED PIPER/SWEET DAWN, MY TRUE LOVE (4)	1.00	2.00
☐ 1324		CHANGES/MY LITTLE BROWN EYES (57)	1.25	2.00
☐ 1328		YOUR EVER-CHANGIN' MIND/BUT SHE'S UNTRUE	1.25	2.00
☐ 1334		ALMOST PERSUADED/YOU HAVE GONE	1.25	2.00
☐ 1344		FREE SPIRIT/I'M ALWAYS CRYING	1.25	2.00
☐ 1359		PLEASE TAKE ME BACK/LOOK INTO MY TEARDROPS	1.25	2.00
		CRISPIAN ST. PETERS—ALBUM		
☐ 3027 (M)	JAMIE	THE PIED PIPER	5.00	8.00
		SAM THE SHAM AND THE PHAROAHS		
☐ 2982	TUPELO	BETTY AND DUPRESS/MAN CHILD	3.50	6.00
☐ 001	DINGO	HAUNTED HOUSE/ HOW DOES A CHEATING WOMAN FEEL?	3.00	5.00
☐ 905	XL	THE SIGNIFYING MONKEY/JUIMONOS	3.00	5.00
☐ 906		WOOLY BULLY/AIN'T GONNA MOVE	8.00	15.00
☐ 13322	MGM	WOOLY BULLY/AIN'T GONNA MOVE (2)	1.00	2.00
☐ 13364		JU JU HAND/BIG CITY LIGHTS (26)	1.25	2.00
☐ 13397		RING DANG DOO/DON'T TRY IT (33)	1.25	2.00

ISSUE #		LABEL	ARTIST/TITLE	VG	MINT
□ 13452			RED HOT/A LONG LONG WAY (82)	1.25	2.00
□ 13506			LIL' RED RIDING HOOD/ LOVE ME LIKE BEFORE (2)	1.00	2.00
□ 13581			THE HAIR ON MY CHINNY CHIN CHIN/ THE OUT CROWD (22)	1.25	2.00
□ 13649			HOW DO YOU CATCH A GIRL?/ THE LOVE YOU LEFT BEHIND (27)	1.25	2.00
□ 13713			OH THAT'S GOOD, NO THAT'S BAD/ TAKE WHAT YOU CAN GET (54)	1.25	2.00
□ 13747			BLACK SHEEP/MY DAY'S GONNA COME (68)	1.25	2.00
			LATER MGM SINGLES ARE WORTH UP TO $1.50 MINT		
			SAM THE SHAM AND THE PHAROAHS—ALBUMS		
□ 4297	(M)	*MGM*	WOOLY BULLY	3.50	6.00
□ 4297	(S)		WOOLY BULLY	4.50	8.00
□ 4314	(M)		THEIR SECOND ALBUM	4.00	5.00
□ 4314	(S)		THEIR SECOND ALBUM	4.00	7.00
□ 4347	(M)		ON TOUR	3.00	5.00
□ 4347	(S)		ON TOUR	4.00	7.00
□ 4407	(M)		LIL' RED RIDING HOOD	3.00	5.00
□ 4407	(S)		LIL' RED RIDING HOOD	4.00	7.00
□ 4422	(M)		THE BEST OF SAM THE SHAM AND THE PHAROAHS	3.00	5.00
□ 4422	(S)		THE BEST OF SAM THE SHAM AND THE PHAROAHS	4.00	7.00

TOMMY SANDS

Tommy Sands first saw life on August 27, 1937, in Chicago, Illinois. Influenced by his piano-playing father, young Sands started singing before he reached his tenth birthday. While he had first learned music on the piano, Tommy later took up the guitar.

The family moved to Houston, Texas. Tommy Sands, then a twelve-year-old seventh grader, landed a job as an afternoon disc jockey on a small Houston radio station. He worked there until his graduation from high school in 1955. Tommy soon left Houston and made appearances on Tennessee Ernie Ford's television show.

Sands' career blossomed when he landed the part of a rock-and-roll singer on NBC's "Kraft Television Theater" in 1957. The show on which Tommy appeared was called "The Singing Idol", and the twenty-year-old rocker sang two songs, "Hep Dee Hootie" and "Teenage Crush". Response to Sands' appearance was so great that Capitol Records signed him to record "Teenage Crush" immediately. The song became a smash and Tommy Sands' only million-seller.

ISSUE #	LABEL	ARTIST/TITLE	VG	MINT
		TOMMY SANDS		
□ 3639	*CAPITOL*	TEEN-AGE CRUSH/HEP DEE HOOTIE (3)	1.50	3.00
□ 3690		RING-A-DING-A-DING/MY LOVE SONG (50)	1.50	2.50
□ 3723		GOIN' STEADY/RING MY PHONE (19)	1.25	2.50
□ 3867		SING BOY SING/CRAZY 'CAUSE I LOVE YOU (46)	1.50	2.50
□ 3953		TEENAGE DOLL/HAWAIIAN ROCK (81)	1.50	2.50
□ 3985		AFTER THE SENIOR PROM/BIG DATE	1.75	2.50
□ 4036		BLUE RIBBON BABY/I LOVE YOU BECAUSE (50)	1.50	2.50
□ 4082		THE WORRYIN' KIND/BIGGER THAN TEXAS (69)	1.50	2.50
□ 4259		I'LL BE SEEING YOU/THAT'S THE WAY I AM (51)	1.50	2.50
□ 4405		THE OLD OAKEN BUCKET/ THESE ARE THE THINGS YOU ARE (73)	1.50	2.50
		TOMMY SANDS—EPs		
□ 1-848	*CAPITOL*	STEADY DATE WITH TOMMY SANDS	2.50	4.00
□ 2-848		STEADY DATE WITH TOMMY SANDS	2.50	4.00
□ 3-848		STEADY DATE WITH TOMMY SANDS	2.50	4.00
□ 851		TEENAGE CRUSH	2.50	4.00
		TOMMY SANDS—ALBUMS		
□ 848 (M)	*CAPITOL*	STEADY DATE WITH TOMMY SANDS	7.00	12.00
□ 1009 (M)		TEENAGE ROCK	6.00	10.00
□ 1081 (M)		SANDS STORM	5.00	8.00
		SANTO AND JOHNNY		
□ 103	*CANADIAN-AMERICAN*	SLEEP WALK/ALL NIGHT DINER (1)	1.50	3.00
□ 107		TEAR DROP/THE LONG WALK HOME (23)	1.75	3.00
□ 111		CARAVAN/SUMMERTIME (48)	1.50	2.50
□ 115		THE BREEZE AND I/LAZY DAY	1.75	2.50
□ 120		TWISTIN' BELLS/BULLSEYE (49)	1.50	2.50
□ 124		HOP SCOTCH/SEA SHELLS (90)	1.50	2.50
□ 132		TWISTIN' BELLS/CHRISTMAS DAY (with Linda Scott)	1.25	2.00
□ 137		SPANISH HARLEM/STAGE TO CIMARRON	1.25	2.00
□ 144		MISERLOU/TOKYO TWILIGHT	1.25	2.00
□ 164		IN THE STILL OF THE NIGHT/ SONG FOR ROSEMARY (58)	1.25	2.00
□ 167		A THOUSAND MILES AWAY/ROAD BLOCK	1.25	2.00
		SANTO AND JOHNNY—ALBUMS		
□ 1001 (M)	*CANADIAN-AMERICAN*	SANTO AND JOHNNY	6.00	10.00
□ 1002 (M)		ENCORE	3.50	6.00
□ 1002 (S)		ENCORE	4.50	8.00
□ 1014 (M)		IN THE STILL OF THE NIGHT	3.50	6.00
□ 1014 (S)		IN THE STILL OF THE NIGHT	4.50	8.00
□ 1017 (M)		THE BEATLES' GREATEST HITS	3.00	5.00
□ 1017 (S)		THE BEATLES' GREATEST HITS	4.00	7.00
		SAPPHIRES		
□ 4143	*SWAN*	YOUR TRUE LOVE/WHERE IS JOHNNY NOW?	1.50	2.50
□ 4162		WHO DO YOU LOVE/OH SO SOON (25)	1.25	2.00
□ 4177		I'VE GOT MINE, YOU BETTER GET YOURS/ I FOUND OUT TOO LATE	1.50	2.50

ISSUE #	LABEL	ARTIST/TITLE	VG	MINT
☐ 4184		GOTTA BE MORE THAN FRIENDS/ SONG FROM MOULIN ROUGE	1.50	2.50
		SAPPHIRES—ALBUM		
☐ 513 (M)	***SWAN***	WHO DO YOU LOVE	6.00	10.00
		SKY SAXON		
		SEE: RITCHIE MARSH, SEEDS		
☐ 777	***CONQUEST***	THEY SAY/GO AHEAD AND CRY	3.50	6.00
		JACK SCOTT		
☐ 9818	***ABC-PARAMOUNT***	BABY SHE'S GONE/ YOU CAN BET YOUR BOTTOM DOLLAR	8.00	15.00
☐ 9860		TWO TIMIN' WOMAN/I NEED YOUR LOVE	15.00	25.00
☐ 10843		BEFORE THE BIRD FLIES/INSANE	8.00	15.00
☐ 462	***CARLTON***	MY TRUE LOVE/LEROY (3)	2.00	4.00
☐ 483		WITH YOUR LOVE/GERALDINE (28)	2.50	4.00
☐ 493		GOODBYE BABY/SAVE MY SOUL (8)	2.00	4.00
☐ 504		I NEVER FELT LIKE THIS/BELLA (78)	2.00	3.50
☐ 514		THE WAY I WALK/MIDGIE (35)	1.75	3.50
☐ 519		THERE COMES A TIME/BABY MARIE (71)	1.75	3.00
☐ 209	***GUARANTEED***	WHAT AM I LIVING FOR?/INDIANA WALTZ	2.50	4.00
☐ 211		GO WILD, LITTLE SADIE/NO ONE WILL EVER KNOW	5.00	8.00
☐ 2028	***TOP RANK***	WHAT IN THE WORLD'S COME OVER YOU?/ BABY, BABY (5)	1.50	3.00
☐ 2041		BURNING BRIDGES/OH LITTLE ONE (3)	1.50	3.00
☐ 2055		IT ONLY HAPPENED YESTERDAY/COOL WATER (38)	1.75	3.00
☐ 2075		PATSY/OLD TIME RELIGION (65)	1.50	2.50
☐ 2093		IS THERE SOMETHING ON YOUR MIND?/ FOUND A WOMAN (89)	1.50	2.50
☐ 4554	***CAPITOL***	A LITTLE FEELING CALLED LOVE/NOW THAT I (91)	2.50	4.00
☐ 4597		MY DREAM COME TRUE/STRANGE DESIRE (83)	2.00	3.50
☐ 4637		STEPS 1 AND 2/ONE OF THESE DAYS (86)	2.00	3.50
☐ 4689		CRY, CRY, CRY/GRIZZLY BEAR	2.50	4.00
☐ 4738		THE PART WHERE I CRY/ YOU ONLY SEE WHAT YOU WANT TO SEE	2.50	4.00
☐ 4796		SAD STORY/ I CAN'T HOLD YOUR LETTERS (IN MY ARMS)	2.50	4.00
☐ 4855		IF ONLY/GREEN, GREEN VALLEY	2.00	3.50
☐ 4903		STRANGERS/LAUGH AND THE WORLD LAUGHS WITH YOU	2.00	3.50
☐ 4955		ALL I SEE IS BLUE/ME-O MY-O	2.00	3.00
		JACK SCOTT—EPs		
☐ 1070	***CARLTON***	JACK SCOTT	6.00	10.00
☐ 1071		JACK SCOTT	6.00	10.00
☐ 1072		JACK SCOTT SINGS	6.00	10.00
☐ 1073		STARRING JACK SCOTT	6.00	10.00
☐ 1001	***TOP RANK***	WHAT IN THE WORLD'S COME OVER YOU?	7.00	12.00
		JACK SCOTT—ALBUMS		
☐ 107 (M)	***CARLTON***	JACK SCOTT	25.00	40.00
☐ 107 (S)		JACK SCOTT	30.00	50.00
☐ 122 (M)		WHAT AM I LIVING FOR?	30.00	50.00
☐ 122 (S)		WHAT AM I LIVING FOR?	40.00	60.00

ISSUE #	LABEL	ARTIST/TITLE	VG	MINT
☐ 319 (M)	*TOP RANK*	I REMEMBER HANK WILLIAMS	20.00	35.00
☐ 619 (S)		I REMEMBER HANK WILLIAMS	25.00	40.00
☐ 326 (M)		WHAT IN THE WORLD'S COME OVER YOU?	25.00	45.00
☐ 626 (S)		WHAT IN THE WORLD'S COME OVER YOU?	30.00	50.00
☐ 348 (M)		THE SPIRIT MOVES ME	20.00	35.00
☐ 648 (S)		THE SPIRIT MOVES ME	25.00	40.00
☐ 2035 (M)	*CAPITOL*	BURNING BRIDGES	8.00	15.00
☐ 2035 (S)		BURNING BRIDGES	12.00	20.00

JOEL SCOTT

☐ 101	*PHILLES*	HERE I STAND/YOU'RE MY ONLY LOVE	3.00	5.00

LINDA SCOTT

☐ 123	*CANADIAN-*			
	AMERICAN	I'VE TOLD EVERY LITTLE STAR/THREE GUESSES (3)	1.25	2.50
☐ 127		DON'T BET MONEY HONEY/		
		STARLIGHT, STARBRIGHT (9)	1.25	2.50
☐ 129		I DON'T KNOW WHY/IT'S ALL BECAUSE (12)	1.25	2.50
☐ 132		CHRISTMAS DAY/TWISTIN' BELLS		
		(with Santo and Johnny)	1.25	2.00
☐ 133		COUNT EVERY STAR/LAND OF STARS (41)	1.50	2.50
☐ 134		BERMUDA/LONELY FOR YOU (70)...............	1.25	2.00
☐ 101	*CONGRESS*	YESIREE/TOWN CRIER (60)	1.25	2.00
☐ 103		NEVER IN A MILLION YEARS/		
		THROUGH THE SUMMER (56)	1.25	2.00
☐ 106		I LEFT MY HEART IN THE BALCONY/		
		LOPSIDED LOVE AFFAIR (74)	1.25	2.00
☐ 108		LONELIEST GIRL IN TOWN/		
		I'M SO AFRAID OF LOSING YOU	1.25	2.00

LATER CONGRESS SINGLES ARE WORTH UP TO $1.50 MINT

LINDA SCOTT—ALBUMS

☐ 1005 (M)	*CANADIAN-*			
	AMERICAN	STARLIGHT, STARBRIGHT	5.00	8.00
☐ 1005 (S)		STARLIGHT, STARBRIGHT	6.00	10.00
☐ 1007 (M)		GREAT SCOTT - HER GREATEST HITS	3.50	6.00
☐ 1007 (S)		GREAT SCOTT - HER GREATEST HITS	4.50	8.00

JIMMY SEALS (PRE-SEALS AND CROFTS)

☐ 9153	*CHALLENGE*	WISH FOR YOU, WANT FOR YOU, WAIT FOR YOU/		
		RUNAWAY HEART	2.50	4.00
☐ 9200		LADY HEARTBREAK/GROUNDED	2.50	4.00
☐ 59270		EVERYBODY'S DOIN' THE JERK/WA-HOO	3.00	4.50

SEARCHERS

☐ 55646	*LIBERTY*	SUGAR AND SPICE/SAINTS AND SINNERS	2.00	3.50
☐ 55689		SUGAR AND SPICE/SAINTS AND SINNERS	1.75	3.00
☐ 27	*KAPP*	LOVE POTION NUMBER NINE/HI-HEEL SNEAKERS (3) .	1.25	2.50
☐ 49		BUMBLE BEE/A TEAR FELL (21)	1.50	2.50
☐ 577		NEEDLES AND PINS/AIN'T THAT JUST LIKE ME (13)	1.50	2.50
☐ 593		DON'T THROW YOUR LOVE AWAY/		
		I PRETEND I'M WITH YOU (16)...............	1.50	2.50
☐ 609		SOME DAY WE'RE GONNA LOVE AGAIN/		
		NO ONE ELSE COULD LOVE ME (34)...........	1.25	2.00

ISSUE #	LABEL	ARTIST/TITLE	VG	MINT
☐ 618		WHEN YOU WALK IN THE ROOM/ I'LL BE MISSING YOU (35)	1.25	2.00
☐ 644		WHAT HAVE THEY DONE TO THE RAIN?/ THIS FEELING INSIDE (29)	1.25	2.00
☐ 658		GOODBYE MY LOVER GOODBYE/ TILL I MEET YOU (52)	1.25	2.00
☐ 686		HE'S GOT NO LOVE/SO FAR AWAY (79)	1.25	2.00
☐ 706		YOU CAN'T LIE TO A LIAR/DON'T KNOW WHY	1.25	2.00
☐ 729		TAKE ME FOR WHAT I'M WORTH/ TOO MANY MILES (76)	1.25	2.00
☐ 783		HAVE YOU EVER LOVED SOMEBODY?/ IT'S JUST THE WAY (94)	1.25	2.00
☐ 811		LOVERS/POPCORN DOUBLE FEATURE	1.25	2.00
		SEARCHERS—ALBUMS		
☐ 3363 (M)	*KAPP*	MEET THE SEARCHERS	6.00	10.00
☐ 3412 (M)		THE NEW SEARCHERS' LP	5.00	8.00
☐ 1409 (M)		THIS IS US	4.00	7.00
☐ 1449 (M)		SEARCHERS NO. 4	3.00	5.00
☐ 1477 (M)		TAKE ME FOR WHAT I'M WORTH	3.00	5.00

NEIL SEDAKA

Sedaka grew up in Brooklyn, New York, where he was born in 1939 on March 13th. As a youngster Neil showed great skill on the piano and was writing songs by the time he entered his teens. Neil later formed a singing group from his high school math class. They called themselves the Tokens, and would later have a No. 1 winner with "The Lion Sleeps Tonight".

When Neil was seventeen he played a piano selection on New York's WQXR, a classical music station. As a result he won a scholarship to Juillard School of Music. However, young Sedaka frequently cut classes to spend the day peddling his original r & b songs to groups hanging out at the Apollo Theater.

Sedaka first recorded for the Decca, Legion and Guyden labels without success. Convinced that Neil Sedaka had talent, RCA Records gambled on Sedaka and had him record an original composition called "The Diary". The song became a major 1959 hit.

Neil Sedaka later recorded "Oh! Carol" for neighborhood pal Carole Klein (now known as Carole King). Neil's biggest hit was "Breaking Up Is Hard To Do", a Top 10 hit for him both in 1962 and 1976.

ISSUE #	LABEL	ARTIST/TITLE	VG	MINT
		NEIL SEDAKA		
□ 30520	***DECCA***	LAURA LEE/SNOWTIME	7.00	12.00
□ 133	***LEGION***	RING-A-ROCKIN'/FLY DON'T FLY ON ME	6.00	10.00
□ 2004	***GUYDEN***	RING-A-ROCKIN'/FLY DON'T FLY ON ME	6.00	10.00
□ 7408	***RCA***	THE DIARY/NO VACANCY (14)	1.50	3.00
□ 7473		I GO APE/MOON OF GOLD (42)	1.75	3.00
□ 7530		YOU GOTTA LEARN YOUR RHYTHM AND BLUES/ CRYING MY HEART OUT FOR YOU	2.00	3.50
□ 7597		OH! CAROL/ONE WAY TICKET (9)	1.50	3.00
□ 7709		STAIRWAY TO HEAVEN/FORTY WINKS AWAY (9)	1.50	3.00
□ 7781		YOU MEAN EVERYTHING TO ME/ RUN SAMPSON RUN (17)	1.50	2.50
□ 7829		CALENDAR GIRL/THE SAME OLD FOOL (4)	1.25	2.50
□ 7874		LITTLE DEVIL/I MUST BE DREAMING (1))	1.25	2.50
□ 7922		SWEET LITTLE YOU/I FOUND MY WORLD IN YOU (59)	1.50	2.50
□ 7957		HAPPY BIRTHDAY, SWEET SIXTEEN/ DON'T LEAD ME ON (6)	1.00	2.50
□ 8007		KING OF CLOWNS/WALK WITH ME (45)	1.50	2.50
□ 8046		BREAKING UP IS HARD TO DO/ AS LONG AS I LIVE (1)	1.00	2.00
□ 8086		NEXT DOOR TO AN ANGEL/I BELONG TO YOU (5)	1.25	2.00
□ 8137		ALICE IN WONDERLAND/CIRCULATE (17)	1.25	2.00
□ 8169		LET'S GO STEADY AGAIN/WAITING FOR NEVER (26)	1.25	2.00
□ 8209		THE DREAMER/LOOK INSIDE YOUR HEART (47)	1.25	2.00
□ 8254		BAD GIRL/WAIT 'TIL YOU SEE MY BABY (33)	1.25	2.00
		LATER RCA SINGLES ARE WORTH UP TO $1.50 MINT		
		NEIL SEDAKA—EPs		
□ 4334	***RCA***	I GO APE	3.50	6.00
□ 4353		OH! CAROL	3.50	6.00
		NEIL SEDAKA—ALBUMS		
□ 2317 (M)	***RCA***	CIRCULATE	5.00	8.00
□ 2317 (S)		CIRCULATE	6.00	10.00
□ 2421 (M)		LITTLE DEVIL	3.50	6.00
□ 2421 (S)		LITTLE DEVIL	4.50	8.00
□ 2627 (M)		NEIL SEDAKA SINGS HIS GREATEST HITS	3.00	5.00
□ 2627 (S)		NEIL SEDAKA SINGS HIS GREATEST HITS	4.00	7.00
		SEEDS		
		FEATURED: SKY SAXON		
□ 354	***GNP-CRESCENO***	I CAN'T SEEM TO MAKE YOU MINE/DAISY MAE (41)	1.50	2.50
□ 372		PUSHIN' TOO HARD/TRY TO UNDERSTAND (36)	1.50	2.50
□ 383		MR. FARMER/NO ESCAPE (86)	1.75	2.50
□ 394		A THOUSAND SHADOWS/ MARCH OF THE FLOWER CHILDREN (72)	1.75	2.50
□ 398		THE WIND BLOWS YOUR HAIR/SIX DREAMS	2.00	3.50
□ 408		900 MILLION PEOPLE DAILY (MAKING LOVE)/ SATISFY YOU	2.00	3.50
		SEEDS—ALBUMS		
□ 2023 (M)	***GNP-CRESCENDO***	THE SEEDS	5.00	8.00
□ 2033 (M)		A WEB OF SOUND	4.00	7.00
□ 2038 (M)		FUTURE	4.00	7.00

ISSUE #	LABEL	ARTIST/TITLE	VG	MINT
☐ 2040 (M)		A SPOONFUL OF SEEDY BLUES		
		(Sky Saxon's Blues Band)	5.00	8.00
☐ 2043 (S)		MERLIN'S MUSIC BOX	3.50	6.00

BOB SEGER
SEE: BEACH BUMS, UNDERDOGS

☐ 1013	HIDEOUT	EAST SIDE STORY (vocal)/		
		EAST SIDE STORY (instrumental)	3.50	6.00
☐ 1014		CHAIN SMOKIN'/PERSECUTION SMITH	3.50	6.00
☐ 438	CAMEO	EAST SIDE STORY (vocal)/		
		EAST SIDE STORY (instrumental)	2.00	3.50
☐ 444		SOCK IT TO ME, SANTA/FLORIDA TIME	2.00	3.50
☐ 465		CHAIN SMOKIN'/PERSECUTION SMITH	2.00	3.50
☐ 473		VAGRANT WINTER/VERY FEW.............	2.00	3.50
☐ 494		HEAVY MUSIC (PT. 1)/(PT. 11)...............	2.00	3.50

BOB SEGER SYSTEM

☐ 2143	CAPITOL	2 PLUS 2 EQUALS WHAT?/DEATH ROW	1.75	3.00
☐ 2297		RAMBLIN' GAMBLIN' MAN/TALES OF LUCY BLUE (17)	1.25	2.50
☐ 2480		IVORY/THE LAST SONG (97)	1.50	2.50
☐ 2576		NOAH/LENNIE JOHNSON....................	1.25	2.00
☐ 2640		LONELY MAN/INNERVENUS EYES	1.25	2.00
		LATER CAPITOL SINGLES ARE WORTH UP TO $2.00 MINT		

RONNIE SELF

☐ 40989	COLUMBIA	AIN'T I'M A DOG/ROCKY ROAD BLUES	5.00	8.00
☐ 41101		BOP-A-LENA/I AIN'T GOIN' NOWHERE (63)	2.50	4.00
☐ 41166		BIG BLON' BABY/DATE BAIT	3.50	6.00
		### RONNIE SELF—EP		
☐ 2149	COLUMBIA	AIN'T I'M A DOG	25.00	40.00

SHADOWS OF KNIGHT

☐ 116	DUNWICH	GLORIA/STANDING AT MY DOOR (10)............	1.25	2.50
☐ 122		OH YEAH/LIGHT BULB BLUES (39)	1.50	2.50
☐ 128		BAD LITTLE WOMAN/GOSPEL ZONE (91)	1.50	2.50
☐ 141		I'M GONNA MAKE YOU MINE/		
		I'LL MAKE YOU SORRY (90)..................	1.50	2.50
☐ 151		THE BEHEMOTH/WILLIE JEAN	1.50	2.50
		### SHADOWS OF KNIGHT—ALBUMS		
☐ 666 (M)	DUNWICH	GLORIA.............................	5.00	8.00
☐ 666 (S)		GLORIA.............................	6.00	10.00
☐ 667 (M)		BACK DOOR MEN	3.50	6.00
☐ 667 (S)		BACK DOOR MEN	4.50	8.00

SHANGRI-LAS

☐ 1866	SMASH	SIMON SAYS/SIMON SPEAKS..................	2.00	3.50
☐ 4006	SPOKANE	WISHING WELL/HATE TO SAY I TOLD YOU SO	2.50	4.00
☐ 10-]]8	RED BIRD	REMEMBER (WALKIN' IN THE SAND)/		
		IT'S EASIER TO CRY (5)	1.50	2.50
☐ 10-014		LEADER OF THE PACK/WHAT IS LOVE (1)	1.25	2.50
☐ 10-018		GIVE HIM A GREAT BIG KISS/		
		TWIST AND SHOUT (18)	1.50	2.50
☐ 10-019		MAYBE/SHOUT (91)	1.75	3.00

ISSUE #	LABEL	ARTIST/TITLE	VG	MINT
□ 10-025		OUT IN THE STREETS/THE BOY (53)	1.50	2.50
□ 10-030		GIVE US YOUR BLESSINGS/ HEAVEN ONLY KNOWS (29)	1.50	2.50
□ 10-036		RIGHT NOW AND NOT LATER/ TRAIN FROM KANSAS CITY (92)	1.75	3.00
□ 10-043		I CAN NEVER GO HOME ANYMORE/ SOPHISTICATED BOOM BOOM (6)	1.25	2.50
□ 10-043		I CAN NEVER GO HOME ANYMORE/BULLDOG (6)	1.25	2.50
□ 10-048		LONG LIVE OUR LOVE/ SOPHISTICATED BOOM BOOM (33)	1.50	2.50
□ 10-053		HE CRIED/DRESSED IN BLACK (65)	1.50	2.50
□ 10-068		PAST, PRESENT AND FUTURE/PARADISE (59)	1.50	2.50
		SHANGRI-LAS—ALBUMS		
□ 101 (M)	***RED BIRD***	LEADER OF THE PACK	6.00	10.00
□ 104 (M)		I CAN NEVER GO HOME ANYMORE	7.00	12.00

DEL SHANNON

Before his days of fame and fortune, Del Shannon went by his real name of Charles Westover. He was born on December 30, 1939, in the Michigan city of Grand Rapids.

Del first begun playing guitar in 1954. Three years later he graduated from high school and joined the army. There he sharpened his musical skills and appeared in some military stage shows.

After a 1960 discharge, Shannon returned to Michigan to begin singing and playing in local clubs around Ann Arbor. A disc jockey friend soon introduced Shannon to two executives of Embee Records in Detroit. Liking what they saw and heard, the businessmen signed Del to record "Runaway", the first rock record to use a mellotron. Shannon's first single, "Runaway" became a No. 1 hit on the Big Top label.

After four more hits, Shannon went to England. There he headlined over a rising Liverpool band called the Beatles. Del Shannon consequently became the first American to record a Beatles song when he saw "From Me To You" become his last Big Top chart single in 1963.

He moved on to other labels but never repeated the success of his earlier days.

ISSUE #	LABEL	ARTIST/TITLE	VG	MINT
		DEL SHANNON		
□3067	*BIG TOP*	RUNAWAY/JODY (1)	1.25	2.50
□3075		HATS OFF TO LARRY/ DON'T GILD THE LILY, LILY (5)	1.25	2.50
□3083		SO LONG BABY/THE ANSWER TO EVERYTHING (28)	1.50	2.50
□3091		HEY! LITTLE GIRL/I WON'T CARE ANYMORE (38)	1.50	2.50
□3098		GINNY IN THE MIRROR/I WON'T BE THERE	1.75	3.00
□3112		CRY MYSELF TO SLEEP/I'M GONNA MOVE ON (99)	1.75	3.00
□3117		THE SWISS MAID/YOU NEVER TALKED ABOUT ME (64)	1.50	2.50
□3131		LITTLE TOWN FLIRT/THE WAMBOO (12)	1.25	2.50
□3143		TWO KINDS OF TEARDROPS/KELLY (50)	1.50	2.50
□3152		FROM ME TO YOU/TWO SILHOUETTES (77)	2.50	4.00
□501	*BERLEE*	SUE'S GOTTA BE MINE/NOW SHE'S GONE (71)	1.50	2.50
□502		THAT'S THE WAY LOVE IS/TIME OF THE DAY	1.75	3.00
□897	*AMY*	STAINS ON MY LETTER/MARY JANE	1.75	3.00
□905		HANDY MAN/GIVE HER LOTS OF LOVIN' (22)	1.50	2.50
□911		DO YOU WANT TO DANCE/ THIS IS ALL I HAVE TO GIVE (45)	1.50	2.50
□915		KEEP SEARCHIN'/BROKEN PROMISES (9)	1.25	2.50
□919		STRANGER IN TOWN/OVER YOU (30)	1.50	2.50
□925		BREAK UP/WHY DON'T YOU TELL HIM (95)	1.75	2.50
□937		SHE STILL REMEMBERS TONY/MOVE IT ON OVER	1.75	2.50
		LIBERTY SINGLES ARE WORTH UP TO $2.00 MINT		
		DEL SHANNON—ALBUMS		
□1303 (M)	*BIG TOP*	RUNAWAY	8.00	15.00
□1308 (M)		LITTLE TOWN FLIRT	7.00	12.00
□8003 (M)	*AMY*	HANDY MAN	6.00	10.00
□8003 (S)		HANDY MAN	7.00	12.00
□8004 (M)		DEL SHANNON SINGS HANK WILLIAMS	5.00	8.00
□8004 (S)		DEL SHANNON SINGS HANK WILLIAMS	6.00	10.00
□8006 (M)		1,661 SECONDS OF DEL SHANNON	5.00	8.00
□8006 (S)		1,661 SECONDS OF DEL SHANNON	6.00	10.00
		JACKIE SHANNON (JACKIE DeSHANNON)		
□290	*SAGE*	JUST ANOTHER LIE/CAJUN BLUES	3.00	5.00
□15928	*DOT*	JUST ANOTHER LIE/CAJUN BLUES	2.00	3.50

DEE DEE SHARP

Her real name was Dionne LaRue, but she became known to the world as Dee Dee Sharp during the early 1960s. Born September 9, 1945, in Philadelphia, Pennsylvania, Dee Dee began her vocal career by singing in her father's church choir. She also learned to play the piano.

By 1961 Dee Dee had gained enough confidence to answer a newspaper ad for the local Cameo Records outfit. They were, according to the ad, seeking a girl who could sing, play the piano and read music. Dee Dee was hired after a brief audition.

She was first heard on two records released at the same time. She was an uncredited backup vocalist for Chubby Checker on his hit of "Slow Twistin' ". (Checker reportedly flew into a rage when told a girl would accompany him on his newest dance single.) Dee Dee also hit big with her own 45 of "Mashed Potato Time".

She scored three more Top 10 hits while the dance mania of the early 1960s was sweeping America. Her career later diminished, although she records to this day as Dee Dee Sharp. She is now the wife of multimillionaire record producer Kenny Gamble of he Gamble-Huff team, a major force in the production of soul discs.

ISSUE #	LABEL	ARTIST/TITLE	VG	MINT
		DEE DEE SHARP		
□212	*CAMEO*	MASHED POTATO TIME/ SET MY HEART AT EASE (2)	1.00	2.00
□219		GRAVY/BABY CAKES (9)	1.00	2.00
□230		RIDE!/THE NIGHT (5)	1.00	2.00
□244		DO THE BIRD/LOVER BOY (10)	1.25	2.00
□260		ROCK ME IN THE CRADLE OF LOVE/ YOU'LL NEVER BE MINE (43)	1.25	2.00
□274		WILD!/WHY DONCHA ASK ME (33)	1.25	2.00
□296		WHERE DID I GO WRONG?/ WILLYAM, WILLYAM (82)	1.25	2.00
□375		I REALLY LOVE YOU/ STANDING IN THE NEED OF LOVE (78)	1.25	2.00
		DEE DEE SHARP—ALBUMS		
□1018 (M)	*CAMEO*	IT'S MASHED POTATO TIME	4.00	7.00
□1022 (M)		SONGS OF FAITH	4.00	7.00
□1027 (M)		ALL THE HITS	4.00	7.00
□1032 (M)		ALL THE HITS BY DEE DEE SHARP	3.50	6.00
□1032 (S)		ALL THE HITS BY DEE DEE SHARP	4.00	7.00
□1050 (M)		DO THE BIRD	3.50	6.00
□1050 (S)		DO THE BIRD	4.00	7.00
□1074 (M)		DOWN MEMORY LANE	3.00	5.00
□1074 (S)		DOWN MEMORY LANE	3.50	6.00
		RAY SHARPE		
□1128	*JAMIE*	LINDA LU/MONKEY'S UNCLE	1.75	3.00
□1128		LINDA LU/RED SAILS IN THE SUNSET (46)	1.50	2.50
□1138		LONG JOHN/T. A. BLUES	1.25	2.00
□1149		GONNA LET IT GO THIS TIME/BERMUDA	1.25	2.00
□1155		FOR YOU MY LOVE/RED SAILS IN THE SUNSET	1.00	1.50
		SHELLS		
□104	*JOHNSON*	BABY OH BABY/ANGEL EYES (21)	1.50	3.00
		SHEP AND THE LIMELITES (HEARTBEATS)		
□740	*HULL*	DADDY'S HOME/THIS I KNOW (2)	1.25	2.50
□742		READY FOR YOUR LOVE/YOU'LL BE SORRY (42)	1.50	2.50
□747		THREE STEPS FROM THE ALTAR/ OH, WHAT A FEELING (58)	1.50	2.50
□748		OUR ANNIVERSARY/WHO TOLD THE SANDMAN (59)	1.50	2.50
□751		WHAT DID DADDY DO?/TEACH ME HOW TO TWIST (94)	1.50	2.50
		LATER HULL SINGLES ARE WORTH UP T $2.00 MINT		
		SHEP AND THE LIMELITES (HEARTBEATS)—ALBUM		
□25350	*ROULETTE*	OUR ANNIVERSARY	8.00	15.00
		BOBBY SHERIDAN (CHARLIE RICH)		
□354	*SUN*	RED MAN/SAD NEWS	1.75	3.00
		TONY SHERIDAN AND THE BEAT BROTHERS (BEATLES)		
□31382	*DECCA*	MY BONNIE/THE SAINTS (dj copy) (pink)	175.00	300.00
□31382		MY BONNIE/THE SAINTS (regular release) (black)	500.00	800.00
		BOBBY SHERMAN		
□31672	*DECCA*	YOU MAKE ME HAPPY/MAN OVERBOARD	1.75	3.00
□31741		IT HURTS ME/GIVE ME YOUR WORD	1.75	3.00
□31779		HEY LITTLE GIRL/WELL, ALL RIGHT	1.75	3.00
□967	*PARKWAY*	ANYTHING YOUR LITTLE HEART DESIRES/ GOODY GALUM-SHUS	1.75	3.00

ISSUE #	LABEL	ARTIST/TITLE	VG	MINT
☐10181	*EPIC*	THINK OF RAIN/COLD GIRL	1.75	3.00
☐1002	*CONDOR*	TELEGRAMS/I'LL NEVER TELL YOU	2.00	3.50
		SHERRYS		
☐2068	*GUYDEN*	POP POP POP-PIE/YOUR HAND IN MINE (35)	1.50	2.50
☐2077		SLOP TIME/LET'S STOMP AGAIN (97)	1.50	2.50
		SHERRYS—ALBUM		
☐503 (M)	*GUYDEN*	AT THE HOP WITH SHERRYS	5.00	8.00
		SHIELDS		
☐513	*TENDER*	YOU CHEATED/THAT'S THE WAY IT'S GONNA BE	7.00	12.00
☐15805	*DOT*	YOU CHEATED/THAT'S THE WAY IT'S GONNA BE (15)	1.50	3.00
		BILLY SHIELDS (TONY ORLANDO)		
☐304	*HARBOUR*	I WAS A BOY/MOMENTS FROM NOW, TOMORROW	3.50	6.00

SHIRELLES

The four girls hailed from the city of Passaic, New Jersey. As high-school students they were influenced by the vocal stylings of the Chantels. When the girls decided to join forces as a singing quartet, they used the first half of lead singer Shirley Alston's name to come up with the name Shirelles. They sang at several talent shows and parties around their area in order to build a name.

The mother of a classmate had just begun a small record label called Tiara. At her daughter's insistence the lady heard the Shirelles perform at school. She was favorably impressed and asked the girls to record a song called "I Met Him On A Sunday". Since Tiara had no way of promoting the single on a national basis, the master was leased to Decca Records.

"I Met Him On A Sunday" made the Top 50 in 1958, but a pair of follow-up Decca discs did nothing. The Shirelles then went to the Scepter label. Their first single there was "Dedicated To the One I Love". As a 1959 release it did little, but as a 1961 re-release the two-year-old single became a Top 5 follow-up to "Will You Love Me Tomorrow", the Shirelles' blockbuster No. 1 single from late 1960.

During their career the Shirelles hit the Top 10 half a dozen times.

ISSUE #	LABEL	ARTIST/TITLE	VG	MINT

SHIRELLES

ISSUE #	LABEL	ARTIST/TITLE	VG	MINT
☐6112	***TIARA***	I MET HIM ON A SUNDAY/ I WANT YOU TO BE MY BOYFRIEND	35.00	60.00
☐30588	***DECCA***	I MET HIM ON A SUNDAY/ I WANT YOU TO BE MY BOYFRIEND (50)	2.50	5.00
☐30669		MY LOVE IS A CHARM/SLOP TIME	2.50	4.00
☐30761		I GOT THE MESSAGE/STOP ME	2.50	4.00
☐1203	***SCEPTER***	DEDICATED TO THE ONE I LOVE/ LOOK-A-HERE BABY (3)	1.25	2.50
☐1205		A TEARDROP AND A LOLLIPOP/DOIN' THE RONDE	1.75	3.00
☐1207		PLEASE BE MY BOYFRIEND/I SAW A TEAR	1.75	3.00
☐1208		TONIGHT'S THE NIGHT/THE DANCE IS OVER (39)	1.50	2.50
☐1211		WILL YOU LOVE ME TOMORROW/BOYS (1)	1.25	2.50
☐1217		MAMA SAID/BLUE HOLIDAY (4)	1.25	2.50
☐1220		A THING OF THE PAST/ WHAT A SWEET THING THAT WAS (41)	1.50	2.50
☐1223		BIG JOHN/TWENTY-ONE (21)	1.50	2.50
☐1227		BABY IT'S YOU/THE THINGS I WANT TO HEAR (8)	1.25	2.50
☐1228		SOLDIER BOY/LOVE IS A SWINGIN' THING (1)	1.00	2.00
☐1234		WELCOME HOME BABY/ MAMA, HERE COMES THE BRIDE (22)	1.25	2.00
☐1237		STOP THE MUSIC/ IT'S LOVE THAT REALLY COUNTS (36)	1.25	2.00
☐1243		EVERYBODY LOVES A LOVER/I DON'T THINK SO (19)	1.25	2.00
☐1248		FOOLISH LITTLE GIRL/NOT FOR ALL THE MONEY (4)	1.00	2.00
☐1255		DON'T SAY GOODNIGHT AND MEAN GOODBYE/ I DIDN'T MEAN TO HURT YOU (26)	1.25	2.00

LATER SCEPTER SINGLES ARE WORTH UP TO $2.00 MINT

SHIRELLES—ALBUMS

ISSUE #	LABEL	ARTIST/TITLE	VG	MINT
☐501 (M)	***SCEPTER***	TONIGHT'S THE NIGHT	8.00	15.00
☐502 (M)		SHIRELLES SING TO TRUMPETS AND STRINGS	6.00	10.00
☐504 (M)		BABY IT'S YOU	6.00	10.00
☐505 (M)		SHIRELLES AND KING CURTIS GAVE A TWIST PARTY	5.00	8.00
☐507 (M)		GREATEST HITS	5.00	8.00

SHIRLEY AND LEE

ISSUE #	LABEL	ARTIST/TITLE	VG	MINT
☐3325	***ALADDIN***	LET THE GOOD TIMES ROLL/ DO YOU MEAN TO HURT ME? (27)	2.50	5.00
☐3338		I FEEL GOOD/NOW THAT IT'S OVER (38)	2.50	4.00
☐3362		THAT'S WHAT I WANNA DO/WHEN I SAW YOU	3.00	5.00

TROY SHONDELL

ISSUE #	LABEL	ARTIST/TITLE	VG	MINT
☐161	***GOLDCREST***	THIS TIME/GIRL AFTER GIRL	5.00	8.00
☐55353	***LIBERTY***	THIS TIME/GIRL AFTER GIRL (6)	1.00	2.00

SHOWMEN

ISSUE #	LABEL	ARTIST/TITLE	VG	MINT
☐632	***MINIT***	IT WILL STAND/COUNTRY FOOL (61)	1.50	3.00
☐66033	***IMPERIAL***	IT WILL STAND/COUNTRY FOOL (80)	1.50	2.50
☐56166	***LIBERTY***	IT WILL STAND/COUNTRY FOOL	1.25	2.00

ISSUE #	LABEL	ARTIST/TITLE	VG	MINT
		SILHOUETTES		
□1029	EMBER	GET A JOB/I AM LONELY (1)	1.50	3.00
□1032		HEADIN' FOR THE POOR HOUSE/MISS THING	2.50	4.00
□1037		VOODOO EYES/BING BONG	7.00	12.00
		SILKIE		
□1525	FONTANA	YOU'VE GOT TO HIDE YOUR LOVE AWAY/ CITY WINDS (10)	1.25	2.00
□1536		LEAVE ME TO CRY/KEYS TO MY SOUL	1.50	2.50
□1551		BORN TO BE WITH YOU/I'M SO SORRY	1.75	3.00
		SILKIE—ALBUM		
□27548 (M)	FONTANA	YOU'VE GOT TO HIDE YOUR LOVE AWAY	3.50	6.00
□67548 (S)		YOU'VE GOT TO HIDE YOUR LOVE AWAY	4.50	8.00
		SILVA-TONES		
□5281	MONARCH	THAT'S ALL I WANT FROM YOU/ ROSES ARE BLOOMING	3.50	6.00
□5281	ARGO	THAT'S ALL I WANT FROM YOU/ ROSES ARE BLOOMING (86)	1.75	3.00
		JUMPIN' GENE SIMMONS		
		SEE: SUN DISCOGRAPHY		
□1027	SANDY	WAITING GAME/SHENENDOAH WALTZ	3.00	5.00
□2034	HI	TEDDY BEAR/YOUR TRUE LOVE	1.50	2.50
□2050		CALDONIA/BE HER NUMBER ONE	1.50	2.50
□2076		HAUNTED HOUSE/HEY HEY LITTLE GIRL (11)	1.00	2.00
□2080		THE DODO/THE JUMP (83)	1.25	2.00
		JUMPIN' GENE SIMMONS—ALBUM		
□12018 (M)	HI	JUMPIN' GENE SIMMONS	3.50	6.00
□32018 (S)		JUMPIN' GENE SIMMONS	4.50	8.00
		PAUL SIMON		
		SEE: PAUL KANE, JERRY LANDIS, TRUE TAYLOR, TICO AND THE TRIUMPHS		
□128	TRIBUTE	HE WAS MY BROTHER/CARLOS DOMINGUEZ	2.50	4.00
		SIMON SISTERS		
		FEATURED: CARLY SIMON		
□586	KAPP	WINKIN' BLINKIN' AND NOD/SO GLAD I'M HERE (73)	1.50	2.50
□624		CUDDLE BUG/NO ONE TO TALK MY TROUBLES TO	1.75	3.00
		SIMON SISTERS—ALBUM		
□1359 (M)	KAPP	SIMON SISTERS	5.00	8.00
		SIR DOUGLAS QUINTET		
		SEE: DOUG SHAM		
□8308	TRIBE	SHE'S ABOUT A MOVER/WE'LL TAKE OUR LAST WALK TONIGHT (13)	1.25	2.50
□8310		THE TRACKER/BLUE NORTHER	1.75	3.00
□8312		THE STORY OF JOHN HARDY/IN TIME	1.75	3.00
□8314		THE RAINS CAME/BACON FAT (31)	1.50	2.50
□8317		QUARTER TO THREE/SHE'S GOTTA BE BOSS	1.75	3.00
		SINGLES ON SMASH ARE WORTH UP TO $1.50 MINT		
		SIR DOUGLAS QUINTET—ALBUM		
□37001 (M)	TRIBE	BEST OF THE SIR DOUGLAS QUINTET	4.00	7.00
□47001 (S)		BEST OF THE SIR DOUGLAS QUINTET	5.00	9.00

ISSUE #	LABEL	ARTIST/TITLE	VG	MINT
		SIXPENCE (STRAWBERRY ALARM CLOCK)		
□1025	***IMPACT***	YOU'RE THE LOVE/WHAT TO DO	3.00	5.00

SIX TEENS

In 1955 a group of six Los Angeles, California, youngsters—three boys and three girls—decided to form a singing group. Under the leadership of member Ed Wells, they became known first as the Sweeteens. Lead vocal chores were delegated to Trudy Williams, a fourteen-year-old with a fine, high-pitched voice.

The group began recording for Flip Records, a small r & b label in Los Angeles. The Sweeteens' first record was a fine ballad called "Don't Worry About A Thing". But it failed to sell. Then the group changed its name and its luck. Their second Flip single (and their first as the Six Teens) was the classic "A Casual Look". Beginning as an L. A. hit, "A Casual Look" quickly became a national hit—and the only Flip record to ever make the Top 50.

Although later Six Teens singles were excellent offerings, the group never again achieved a major hit. While songs such as "Only Jim" deserved to be winners, only "Arrow Of Love" made the charts after the demise of "A Casual Look".

ISSUE #	LABEL	ARTIST/TITLE	VG	MINT
		SIX TEENS		
☐311	*FLIP*	DON'T WORRY ABOUT A THING/ FOREVER MORE (by the Sweeteens)	8.00	15.00
☐315		A CASUAL LOOK/TEEN AGE PROMISE (48)	1.50	3.00
☐317		AFAR INTO THE NIGHT/SEND ME FLOWERS	2.00	3.50
☐320		ONLY JIM/MY SPECIAL GUY	2.00	3.50
☐322		ARROW OF LOVE/WAS IT A DREAM OF MINE? (80)	1.75	3.00
☐326		BABY YOU'RE DYNAMITE/MY SURPRISE	1.75	3.00
☐329		MY SECRET/STOP PLAYING PING PONG (WITH MY HEART)	1.75	3.00
☐333		DANNY/LOVE'S FUNNY THAT WAY	1.75	3.00

SKIP AND FLIP

They were really Clyde Batton and Gary Paxton. During the late 1950s Skip (Batton) and Flip (Paxton) were college classmates at the University of Arizona. They became friends while playing in a rock band called the Pledges. Skip, who also worked part-time as a disc jockey in Tuscon, soon convinced Flip to leave the Pledges behind and try to make it on record with him as a ballad-oriented duo.

They taped a song Skip had written called "It Was I". Skip was later put in touch with a man from L. A.'s Brent Records. He expressed interest in the song, and it was released on Brent during the summer of 1959. Many laughed at the seeming awkwardness of the title "It Was I", but it proved to be grammatically correct.

The pair's second single, "Fancy Nancy", saw little success. Skip and Flip's third outing, however, became as big a hit as "It Was I". Originally done by r & b balladeers Marvin and Johnny, "Cherry Pie" became Skip and Flip's second hit and their last go at the charts. Later Brent singles went nowhere.

Paxton later joined the Hollywood Argyles ("Alley Oop") and then formed Garpax (Gary + Paxton) Records, which had a 1962 million-seller with Bobby "Boris" Pickett's "Monster Mash".

ISSUE #	LABEL	ARTIST/TITLE	VG	MINT
		SKIP AND FLIP *FEATURED: GARY "FLIP" PAXTON* *SEE: GARY AND CLYDE, PLEDGES*		
☐7002	***BRENT***	IT WAS I/LUNCH HOUR (11)	1.50	3.00
☐7005		FANCY NANCY/IT COULD BE (71)	1.75	3.00
☐7010		CHERRY PIE/CRYIN' OVER YOU (11)	1.50	3.00
☐7013		TEENAGE HONEYMOON/HULLY GULLY CHA CHA CHA	1.50	2.50
☐7017		WILLOW TREE/GREEN DOOR	1.50	2.50

SKYLINERS

Originally from Pittsburgh, Pennsylvania, the Skyliners were formed from two different local groups, the Crescents and the El Rios. They retained the name Crescents after they merged until their manager renamed them the Skyliners. The inspiration had been an old Charlie Barnett song, "Skyliner'.

The quintet (led by Jimmie Beaumont) and an outside friend wrote "Since I Don't Have You". Thumbing through the Pittsburgh phone book, the group came across the name of Calico Records. As it turned out, Calico was on the lookout for a hot act and eagerly signed the Skyliners to record.

"Since I Don't Have You" was one of the first rock ballads to use an orchestra. The song became a major hit early in 1959. And the Skyliners' second single—"This I Swear"—reached the Top 20. It too featured lush strings and brass. However, it was to take three more singles before the Skyliners found their way into the Top 30 again, this time with the upbeat "Pennies From Heaven".

Recording for two other labels produced only one minor chart single.

ISSUE #	LABEL	ARTIST/TITLE	VG	MINT
		SKYLINERS		
		FEATURED: JIMMIE BEAUMONT		
□ 103	*CALICO*	SINCE I DON'T HAVE YOU/ ONE NIGHT, ONE NIGHT (12)	1.50	3.00
□ 106		THIS I SWEAR/TOMORROW (26)	1.75	2.50
□ 109		IT HAPPENED TODAY/LONELY WAY (59)	1.50	2.50
□ 114		HOW MUCH/LORRAINE FROM SPAIN	1.75	2.50
□ 117		PENNIES FROM HEAVEN/I'LL BE SEEING YOU (24)	1.25	2.50
□ 120		BELIEVE ME/HAPPY TIME	1.75	2.50
□ 188	*COLPIX*	I'LL CLOSE MY EYES/THE DOOR IS STILL OPEN	1.50	2.50
□ 613		OUR LOVE WILL LAST/CLOSE YOUR EYES	1.50	2.50
□ 5506	*JUBILEE*	THE LOSER/EVERYTHING IS FINE (72)	1.50	2.50
□ 5512		WHO DO YOU LOVE/GET YOURSELF A BABY	1.75	2.50
□ 5520		I RUN TO YOU/DON'T HURT ME BABY	1.75	2.50
		SKYLINERS—ALBUM		
□ 3000 (M)	*CALICO*	SKYLINERS	12.00	20.00
		SLADES		
□ 500	*DOMINO*	YOU CHEATED/THE WADDLE (42)	2.50	4.00
□ 1000		SUMMERTIME/YOU MUST TRY	2.00	3.50
		SMALL FACES		
□ 9826	*PRESS*	SHA-LA-LA-LA-LEE/GROW YOUR OWN	2.50	4.00
□ 5007		HEY GIRL/ALMOST GROWN	2.50	4.00
□ 501	*IMMEDIATE*	ITCHYKOO PARK/I'M ONLY DREAMING (16)	1.25	2.00
□ 5003		TIN SOLDIER/I FEEL MUCH BETTER (73)	1.50	2.00
		SMALL FACES—ALBUM		
□ 52002 (M)	*IMMEDIATE*	HERE ARE BUT FOUR SMALL FACES	5.00	8.00
		SMILE (PRE-QUEEN)		
□ 72977	*MERCURY*	EARTH/STEP ON ME	8.00	15.00
		HEY "PIANO" SMITH AND THE CLOWNS		
□ 521	*ACE*	LITTLE LIZA JANE/EVERYBODY'S WAILIN'	2.50	4.00
□ 530		ROCKIN' PNEUMONIA AND THE BOOGIE WOOGIE FLU (PT. 1)/(PT. 11) (52)	1.75	3.00
□ 538		JUST A LONELY CLOWN/ FREE, SINGLE AND DISENGAGED	1.75	3.00
□ 545		DON'T YOU JUST KNOW IT/ HIGH BLOOD PRESSURE (9)	1.50	3.00
□ 548		HAVIN' A GOOD TIME/WE LIKE BIRDLAND	1.75	3.00
□ 533		DON'T YOU KNOW YOCKOMO/ WELL, I'LL BE JOHN BROWN (56)	1.50	2.50
		HUEY "PIANO" SMITH AND THE CLOWNS—EP		
□ 104	*ACE*	HAVING FUN WITH HUEY "PIANO" SMITH	5.00	8.00
		HUEY "PIANO" SMITH AND THE CLOWNS—ALBUM		
□ 1004 (M)	*ACE*	HAVING A GOOD TIME	12.00	20.00
		RAY SMITH		
		SEE: SUN DISCOGRAPHY		
□ 1016	*JUDD*	ROCKIN' LITTLE ANGEL/THAT'S ALL RIGHT (22)	1.75	3.00
□ 1017		PUT YOUR ARMS AROUND ME HONEY/ MARIA ELENA (91)	2.00	3.50
□ 1019		MAKES ME FEEL GOOD/ONE WONDERFUL LOVE	2.00	3.50
□ 1021		BLONDE HAIR, BLUE EYES/YOU DON'T WANT ME	2.00	3.50

ISSUE #	LABEL	ARTIST/TITLE	VG	MINT
		RAY SMITH—ALBUM		
☐701 (M)	*JUDD*	TRAVELIN' WITH RAY	25.00	40.00
		RONNY SOMMERS (SONNY BONO)		
☐1001	*SWAMI*	DON'T SHAKE MY TREE/ (MAMA) COME GET YOUR BABY BOY	3.00	5.00
		JIMMY SOUL		
☐3300	*S.P.Q.R.*	TWISTIN' MATILDA/ I CAN'T HOLD OUT ANY LONGER (22)	1.25	2.50
☐3302		WHEN MATILDA COMES BACK/SOME KINDA NUT	1.50	2.50
☐3305		IF YOU WANNA BE HAPPY/DON'T RELEASE ME (1)	1.00	2.00
☐3310		TREAT 'EM TOUGH/ CHURCH STREET IN THE SUMMERTIME	1.25	2.00
☐3312		EVERYBODY'S GONE APE/GO 'WAY, CHRISTINA	1.25	2.00
		JIMMY SOUL—ALBUM		
☐16001 (M)	*S.P.Q.R.*	IF YOU WANNA BE HAPPY	5.00	8.00
		SPANIELS		
☐107	*VEE JAY*	GOODNIGHT SWEETHEART GOODNIGHT/ YOU DON'T MOVE ME	7.00	12.00
		SPARROW (STEPPENWOLF)		
☐43755	*COLUMBIA*	TOMORROW'S SHIP/ISN'T IT STRANGE?	3.50	6.00
☐43960		GREEN BOTTLE LOVER/DOWN GOES YOUR LOVE LIFE	3.00	5.00
		SPATS		
☐1268	*ENITH*	GATOR TAILS AND MONKEY RIBS/THE ROACH	2.50	4.00
☐10585	*ABC-PARAMOUNT*	GATOR TAILS AND MONKEY RIBS/THE ROACH (96)	1.25	2.00
		SPATS—ALBUM		
☐502 (M)	*ABC-PARAMOUNT*	COOKIN' WITH THE SPATS	3.00	5.00
☐502 (S)		COOKIN' WITH THE SPATS	4.00	7.00
		RONNIE SPECTOR		
		SEE: RONETTES, VERONICA		
☐1832	*APPLE*	TRY SOME, BUY SOME/TANDOORI CHICKEN (77)	1.50	2.50
☐0409	*WARNER-SPECTOR*	WHEN I SAW YOU/PARADISE	1.75	3.00
		SPECTORS THREE		
		PRODUCER: PHIL SPECTOR		
☐3001	*TREY*	I KNOW WHY/I REALLY DO	2.50	4.00
☐3005		MY HEART STOOD STILL/MR. ROBIN	2.50	4.00
		BENNY SPELLMAN		
☐644	*MINIT*	LIPSTICK TRACES/FORTUNE TELLER (80)	1.75	3.00

SPIDERS

New Orleans has long been known as the birthplace of many blues and jazz products. So it was during the mid-1950s that the Spiders got together. Led by vocalist Chuck Garbo—a longtime blues fan—the Spiders developed an unusual rhythm-and-blues sound known as "down-tempo blues".

Imperial Records' president Lew Chudd had discovered Fats Domino in a small new Orleans club during the late 1940s. Chudd later hoped to discover another hot talent in New Orleans. Chudd undoubtedly felt that the Spiders' unusual sound would help Imperial sell a great many blues ballads.

The Spiders recorded thirteen singles for Imperial, and all but the second one ("Tears Began To Flow") sold well in the r & b markets. The Spiders' biggest hit was "Witchcraft". It was played on progressive rock-and-roll stations during the mid-1950s but failed to break the Top 100 lists. The Spiders' ninth single, "Witchcraft" was to later become a hit for such diverse talents as Frank Sinatra and Elvis Presley.

The Spiders were never able to duplicate the success of "Witchcraft" and broke up in 1957.

ISSUE #	LABEL	ARTIST/TITLE	VG	MINT
		SPIDERS		
☐5366	***IMPERIAL***	WITCHCRAFT/IS IT TRUE	3.00	5.00
		SPIDERS		
		FEATURED: ALICE COOPER		
☐003	***SANTA CRUZ***	DON'T BLOW YOUR MIND/NO PRICE TAG	25.00	40.00
		SPRING (HONEYS)		
		PRODUCER: BRIAN WILSON		
		SEE: AMERICAN SPRING		
☐50848	***UNITED ARTISTS***	NOW THAT EVERYTHING'S BEEN SAID/AWAKE	3.00	5.00
☐50907		GOOD TIME/SWEET MOUNTAIN	3.00	5.00
		SPRINGFIELDS		
		FEATURED: DUSTY SPRINGFIELD		
☐40038	***PHILIPS***	SILVER THREADS AND GOLDEN NEEDLES/ AUNT RHODY (20)	1.25	2.00
☐40072		DEAR HEARTS AND GENTLE PEOPLE/ GOTTA TRAVEL ON (95)	1.25	2.00
☐40099		ISLAND OF DREAMS/FOGGY MOUNTAIN TOP	1.00	2.00
		SPRINGFIELDS—ALBUM		
☐200052 (M)	***PHILIPS***	SILVER THREADS AND GOLDEN NEEDLES	3.50	6.00
☐600052 (S)		SILVER THREADS AND GOLDEN NEEDLES	4.50	8.00
		TERRY STAFFORD		
☐101	***CRUSADE***	SUSPICION/JUDY (3)	1.25	2.50
☐105		I'LL TOUCH A STAR/PLAYING WITH FIRE (25)	1.50	2.50
☐109		FOLLOW THE RAINBOW/ARE YOU A FOOL LIKE ME?	1.75	2.50
☐110		A LITTLE BIT BETTER/HOPING	1.75	2.50
		TERRY STAFFORD—ALBUM		
☐1001 (M)	***CRUSADE***	SUSPICION	5.00	8.00
☐1001 (S)		SUSPICION	6.00	10.00
		STANDELLS		
☐185	***TOWER***	DIRTY WATER/RORI (11)	1.25	2.50
☐257		SOMETIMES GOOD GUYS DON'T WEAR WHITE/ WHY DID YOU HURT ME (43)	1.50	2.50
☐282		WHY PICK ON ME?/MR. NOBODY (54)	1.50	2.50
☐310		POOR SHELL OF A MAN/TRY IT	1.75	2.50
☐312		DON'T TELL ME WHAT TO DO/WHEN I WAS A COWBOY	1.75	2.50
☐314		RIOT ON SUNSET STRIP/BLACK HEARTED WOMAN	1.75	2.50
☐348		CAN'T HELP BUT LOVE YOU/ NINETY-NINE-AND-A-HALF	1.50	2.50
☐398		ANIMAL GIRL/SOUL DRIPPIN'	1.75	2.00
		STANDELLS—ALBUMS		
☐5027 (M)	***TOWER***	DIRTY WATER	5.00	8.00
☐5027 (S)		DIRTY WATER	6.00	10.00
☐5044 (M)		WHY PICK ON ME?	4.00	7.00
☐5044 (S)		WHY PICK ON ME?	5.00	9.00
☐5049 (M)		HOT ONES	3.50	6.00
☐5049 (S)		HOT ONES	4.50	8.00

ISSUE #	LABEL	ARTIST/TITLE	VG	MINT
		PAT STANLEY		
		GUITAR: EDDIE COCHRAN		
☐011	***ZEPHYR***	PUSHIN'/MARKET PLACE	5.00	8.00
☐012		MY LOVIN' BABY/LOVE CHARMS	6.00	10.00
		STATUES		
		FEATURED: GARRY MILES		
☐55245	***LIBERTY***	BLUE VELVET/ KEEP THE HALL LIGHT BURNING (84)	2.00	3.50
☐55292		WHITE CHRISTMAS/ JEANNIE WITH THE LIGHT BROWN HAIR	2.50	4.00
		STEREOS		
☐9095	***CUB***	I REALLY LOVE YOU/PLEASE COME BACK TO ME (29)	1.50	2.50
		CAT STEVENS		
☐5872	***DERAM***	PORTOBELLO ROAD/I LOVE MY DOG	2.00	3.50
☐7505		MATTHEW AND SON/GRANNY	2.50	4.00
☐85006		SCHOOL IS OUT/I'M GONNA GET ME A GUN	2.00	3.50
☐85015		BAD NIGHT/LAUGHING APPLE	1.75	3.00
		CONNIE STEVENS		
☐5092	***WARNER BROTHERS***	WHY DO I CRY FOR JOEY?/APOLLO	1.75	3.00
☐5137		SIXTEEN REASONS/LITTLE SISTER (3)	1.00	2.50
☐5159		TOO YOUNG TO GO STEADY/A LITTLE KISS (71)	1.50	2.50
☐5217		MAKE-BELIEVE LOVER/AND THIS IS MINE	1.75	2.50
☐5265		WHY'D YOU WANNA MAKE MY CRY/ JUST ONE KISS (52)	1.50	2.50
☐5289		MR. SONGWRITER/I COULDN'T SAY NO (43)	1.50	2.50
☐5318		NOBODY'S LONESOME FOR ME/HEY GOOD LOOKIN'	1.75	2.50
		CONNIE STEVENS—ALBUMS		
☐1208 (M)	***WARNER BROTHERS***	CONCHETTA	5.00	8.00
☐1382 (M)		CONNIE STEVENS (FROM "HAWAIIAN EYE")	3.50	6.00
☐1382 (S)		CONNIE STEVENS (FROM "HAWAIIAN EYE")	4.50	8.00
☐1431 (M)		CONNIE STEVENS	3.00	5.00
☐1431 (S)		CONNIE STEVENS	4.00	7.00

DODIE STEVENS

Until she was twelve, this Temple City, California, girl was known as Geraldine Ann Pasquale. Born on February 17, 1947, Dodie moved to California from Illinois in 1950.

She was a natural singing and dancing talent and performed at several army and navy hospitals as well as a number of U. S. O. shows.

It was not surprising, therefore, that she was eventually put in touch with a record company. Dodie Stevens' first recording home was the small Crystalette label in Los Angeles. At the time they were seeking an answer to Vista Records' teen rocker Annette. Dodie passed her audition with flying colors and was given a song to record. "Pink Shoe Laces", cut when Dodie was a barely-twelve-year-old seventh grader, became a million-seller. It was on the charts within three weeks and easily went to the Top 5.

The dynamic Dodie then scored in a minor way with her second release, "Yes-Sir-Ee". She later signed with Dot Records and cut four singles for them. Two minor Dot records failed to reproduce the impact of "Pink Shoe Laces".

ISSUE #	LABEL	ARTIST/TITLE	VG	MINT
		DODIE STEVENS		
□724	***CRYSTALLETTE***	PINK SHOE LACES/COMING OF AGE (3)	1.25	3.00
□728		YES-SIR-EE/THE FIVE PENNIES (79)	1.50	2.50
□16002	***DOT***	STEADY EDDY/MAIRZY DOATS	1.25	2.00
□16103		NO/A-TISKET-A-TASKET (73)	1.25	2.00
□16139		AM I TOO YOUNG?/SO LET'S DANCE	1.25	2.00
□16167		YES, I'M LONESOME TONIGHT/TOO YOUNG (60)	1.25	2.00
		DODIE STEVENS—ALBUMS		
□3212 (M)	***DOT***	DODIE STEVENS	3.50	6.00
□25212 (S)		DODIE STEVENS	4.50	8.00
□3323 (M)		OVER THE RAINBOW	3.00	5.00
□25323 (S)		OVER THE RAINBOW	4.00	7.00
□3371 (M)		PINK SHOELACES	3.00	5.00
□25371 (S)		PINK SHOELACES	4.00	7.00
		ROD STEWART		
		SEE: PYTHON LEE JACKSON		
□9722	***PRESS***	GOOD MORNING, LITTLE SCHOOLGIRL/ I'M GONNA MOVE TO THE OUTSKIRTS OF TOWN	3.50	6.00
		GARY STITES		
□508	***CARLTON***	LONELY FOR YOU/SHINE THAT RING (24)	1.50	3.00
□516		A GIRL LIKE YOU/HEY LITTLE GIRL (80)	1.75	3.00
□521		STARRY EYED/WITHOUT YOUR LOVE (77)	1.75	3.00
□525		LAWDY MISS CLAWDY/ DON'T WANNA SAY GOODBYE (47)	1.75	3.00
□529		GLORIA LEE/ HEY, HEY	1.75	3.00
		GARY STITES—ALBUM		
□120 (M)	***CARLTON***	LONELY FOR YOU	3.50	6.00
□120 (S)		LONELY FOR YOU	4.50	8.00
		GALE STORM		
□15412	***DOT***	I HEAR YOU KNOCKING/NEVER LEAVE ME (2)	1.25	3.00
□15436		TEEN AGE PRAYER/ MEMORIES ARE MADE OF THIS (9)	1.25	2.50
□15448		WHY DO FOOLS FALL IN LOVE/I WALK ALONE (15)	1.50	2.50
□15458		IVORY TOWER/I AIN'T GONNA WORRY (10)	1.25	2.50
□15474		TELL MY WHY/DON'T TREAT ME THAT WAY (52)	1.50	2.50
□15493		A CASUAL LOOK/COTTON PICKIN' KISSES	1.75	2.50
□15539		LUCKY LIPS/ON TREASURE ISLAND (74)	1.50	2.50
□15558		DARK MOON/A LITTLE TOO LATE (5)	1.00	2.00
□15606		LOVE BY THE JUKEBOX LIGHT/ON MY MIND AGAIN	1.25	2.00
		GALE STORM—EPs		
□1050	***DOT***	GALE STORM	2.00	4.00
□1051		GALE STORM	2.00	4.00
□1052		GALE STORM	2.00	4.00
□1074		GALE'S GREAT HITS	2.50	5.00
		GALE STORM—ALBUMS		
□3011 (M)	***DOT***	GALE STORM	6.00	10.00
□3017 (M)		SENTIMENTAL ME	5.00	8.00
□3098 (M)		GALE STORM HITS	6.00	10.00

ISSUE #	LABEL	ARTIST/TITLE	VG	MINT
		STRAWBERRY ALARM CLOCK		
		SEE: SIXPENCE		
☐373	***ALL AMERICAN***	INCENSE AND PEPPERMINTS/ BIRDMAN OF ALKATRASH	5.00	8.00
☐55018	***UNI***	INCENSE AND PEPPERMINTS/ BIRDMAN OF ALKATRASH (1)	.75	1.50
		BARRETT STRONG		
☐1111	***ANNA***	MONEY/OH, I APOLOGIZE (23)	2.00	3.50
☐1116		YOU KNOWS WHAT I WANT TO DO/ YES, NO, MAYBE SO	1.75	3.00
☐54029	***TAMLA***	YOU KNOWS WHAT I WANT TO DO/ YES, NO, MAYBE SO	1.50	2.50
		GENE SUMMERS		
☐100	***JAN***	SCHOOL OF ROCK 'N ROLL/STRAIGHT SKIRT	7.00	12.00
☐102		GOTTA LOTTA THAT/NERVOUS	6.00	10.00
		SUNRAYS		
☐101	***TOWER***	CAR PARTY/OUT OF GAS	2.50	4.00
☐148		I LIVE FOR THE SUN/BYE BABY BYE (51)	1.50	3.00
☐191		ANDREA/YOU DON'T PLEASE ME (41)	1.50	3.00
☐224		STILL/WHEN YOU'RE NOT HERE (93)	1.50	2.50
☐256		DON'T TAKE YOURSELF TOO SERIOUSLY/ I LOOK, BABY, BUT I CAN'T SEE	1.50	2.50
		SUNRAYS—ALBUM		
☐5017 (M)	***TOWER***	ANDREA	6.00	10.00
		SUPER STOCKS		
		FEATURED: GARY USHER		
☐5153	***CAPITOL***	THUNDER ROAD/WHEEL STANDS	1.75	3.00
☐2113		MIDNIGHT RUN/SANTA BARBARA	1.75	3.00
		SUPER STOCKS—ALBUMS		
☐2060 (M)	***CAPITOL***	THUNDER ROAD	5.00	8.00
☐2060 (S)		THUNDER ROAD	6.00	10.00
☐2113 (M)		SURF ROUTE 101	3.50	6.00
☐2113 (S)		SURF ROUTE 101	4.50	8.00

SUPREMES

Diana Ross, Florence Ballard and Mary Wilson were Detroit friends who formed a singing trio during their high-school days. Calling themselves the Primettes, the girls became neighborhood celebrities and even cut a record, the unsuccessful "Tears Of Sorrow" on the small Lupine label.

Raising their sights and hopes, the Primettes then approached Motown's Berry Gordy, Jr., who found the auditioning girls "giggly and unprofessional". He told them to return after they finished high school. In 1962 the girls graduated and returned to Gordy, who had forgotten them. Florence Ballard (who later died on welfare) suggested the Primettes become the Supremes. Leader Diana Ross agreed to the name change.

After a pair of flop Tamla singles, the Supremes' career went into high gear on the Motown label. Their fourth Motown outing of "When the Lovelight Starts Shining Through His Eyes" broke into the national Top 30. In time the Supremes became the world's most successful vocal group, scoring no less than a dozen No. 1 hits within five years.

After Diana Ross's 1969 departure, the Supremes recorded few hits, while Diana went to even greater fame and fortune in both recording and films.

ISSUE #	LABEL	ARTIST/TITLE	VG	MINT

SUPREMES
FEATURED: DIANA ROSS
SEE: PRIMETTES

☐ 54038	*TAMLA*	I WANT A GUY/NEVER AGAIN	7.00	12.00
☐ 54045		BUTTERED POPCORN/WHO'S LOVING YOU	6.00	10.00

THE ABOVE PRICES APPLY TO FIRST-PRESS TAMLA LABELS WITH LINES

☐ 1027	*MOTOWN*	YOUR HEART BELONGS TO ME/(HE'S) SEVENTEEN (95).	1.75	3.00
☐ 1034		LET ME GO THE RIGHT WAY/		
		TIME CHANGES THINGS (90)	1.75	3.00
☐ 1040		YOU BRING BACK MEMORIES/		
		MY HEART CAN'T TAKE IT NO MORE	2.00	3.50
☐ 1044		A BREATH-TAKING GUY/		
		ROCK AND ROLL BANJO BAND (75)	1.50	2.50
☐ 1051		WHEN THE LOVELIGHT STARTS SHINING THROUGH		
		HIS EYES/STANDING AT THE CROSSROADS		
		OF LOVE (23)	1.00	2.00
☐ 1054		RUN, RUN, RUN/I'M GIVING YOU YOUR FREEDOM (93)	1.25	2.00

LATER MOTOWN SINGLES ARE WORTH UP TO $1.50 MINT

SUPREMES—ALBUM

☐ 606 (M)	*MOTOWN*	MEET THE SUPREMES (girls on stools)	8.00	15.00
☐ 606 (M)		MEET THE SUPREMES (girls' faces)	4.50	0.00

SURFARIS

☐ 11/12	*DFS*	WIPEOUT/SURFER JOE	25.00	40.00
☐ 50	*PRINCESS*	WIPEOUT/SURFER JOE	6.00	10.00
☐ 16479	*DOT*	WIPEOUT/SURFER JOE (2)	1.25	2.00
☐ 16966		SHOW BIZ/CHICAGO GREEN75	1.50
☐ 31538	*DECCA*	POINT PANIC/WAIKIKI RUN (49)	1.50	2.50
☐ 31561		SANTA'S SPEED SHOP/SURFER'S CHRISTMAS LIST	1.75	2.50
☐ 31581		SCATTER SHIELD/		
		I WANNA TAKE A TRIP TO THE ISLANDS	1.75	2.50
☐ 31641		BOSS BARRACUDA/DUNE BUGGY	1.75	2.50
☐ 31682		HOT ROD HIGH/KAREN	1.75	2.50

SURFARIS—ALBUMS

☐ 3535 (M)	*DOT*	WIPE OUT.....................................	5.00	8.00
☐ 25535 (S)		WIPE OUT....................................	6.00	10.00
☐ 4470 (M)	*DECCA*	THE SURFARIS................................	3.50	6.00
☐ 74470 (S)		THE SURFARIS................................	4.50	8.00
☐ 4487 (M)		HIT CITY '64	3.50	6.00
☐ 74487 (S)		HIT CITY '64	4.50	8.00

SURFETTES
FEATURED: CAROL CONNORS

☐ 3001	*MUSTANG*	SAMMY THE SIDEWALK SURFER/BLUE SURF	2.50	4.00

SURVIVORS (BEACH BOYS)

☐ 5120	*CAPITOL*	PAMELA JEAN/AFTER THE GAME	15.00	25.00

SWINGING BLUE JEANS

☐ 66021	*IMPERIAL*	HIPPY HIPPY SHAKE/NOW I MUST GO (24)........	1.25	2.50
☐ 66030		GOOD GOLLY MISS MOLLY/SHAKING FEELING (43)...	1.50	2.50
☐ 66049		YOU'RE NO GOOD/SHAKE, RATTLE AND ROLL (97) ...	1.75	2.50
☐ 66059		TUTTI FRUITTI/PROMISE YOU'LL TELL HER.......	1.75	2.50

ISSUE #	LABEL	ARTIST/TITLE	VG	MINT
		SWINGING BLUE JEANS—ALBUM		
☐9261 (M)	IMPERIAL	HIPPY HIPPY SHAKE	3.50	6.00
☐12261 (S)		HIPPY HIPPY SHAKE	4.50	8.00
		SWINGIN' MEDALLIONS		
☐002	4 SALE	DOUBLE SHOT/HERE IT COMES AGAIN	4.00	7.00
☐2033	SMASH	DOUBLE SHOT/HERE IT COMES AGAIN (17)	1.25	2.00
		SYNDICATE OF SOUND		
☐228	HUSH	LITTLE GIRL/YOU	5.00	8.00
☐640	BELL	LITTLE GIRL/YOU (8)	1.00	2.00
☐646		RUMORS/THE UPPER HAND (55)	1.25	2.00
☐655		KEEP IT UP/GOOD TIME MUSIC	1.25	2.00
		SYNDICATE OF SOUND—ALBUM		
☐6001 (M)	BELL	LITTLE GIRL	3.50	6.00
☐6001 (S)		LITTLE GIRL	4.50	8.00

T

ISSUE #	LABEL	ARTIST/TITLE	VG	MINT
		LARRY TAMBLYN		
☐601	FARO	DEAREST/PATTY ANN	2.50	4.00
☐603		THE LIE/MY BRIDE TO BE	2.50	4.00
☐612		THIS IS THE NIGHT/DESTINY	2.50	4.00
		TASSELS		
☐117	MADISON	TO A SOLDIER BOY/THE BOY FOR ME (55)	1.50	2.50
☐121		TO A YOUNG LOVER/MY GUY AND I	1.50	2.50
☐11	GOLDISC	THE TWELFTH OF NEVER/SINCE YOU WENT AWAY	1.50	2.50
		AUSTIN TAYLOR		
☐3067	LAURIE	PUSH PUSH/A HEART THAT'S TRUE (90)	1.75	3.00
☐3082		LOVIN' HANDS/I DON'T WANT TO LOVE YOU	1.50	2.50
☐3095		I LOVE BEING LOVED BY YOU/TOGETHER FOREVER	1.50	2.50
		TRUE TAYLOR (PAUL SIMON)		
☐614	BIG	TRUE OR FALSE/TEENAGE FOOL	8.00	15.00
		TEDDY BEARS		
		FEATURED: PHIL SPECTOR		
☐503	DORE	TO KNOW HIM, IS TO LOVE HIM/ DON'T YOU WORRY MY PRETTY PET (1)	1.50	3.00
☐520		WONDERFUL, LOVEABLE YOU/TILL YOU'LL BE MINE	2.50	4.00
☐5562	IMPERIAL	OH WHY/I DON'T NEED YOU ANYMORE (91)	2.00	3.50
☐5581		IF YOU ONLY KNEW/YOU SAID GOODBYE	2.50	4.00
☐5594		DON'T GO AWAY/SEVEN LONELY DAYS	2.50	4.00
		TEDDY BEARS—ALBUM		
☐9067 (M)	IMPERIAL	TEDDY BEARS	12.00	20.00
☐12067 (S)		TEDDY BEARS	18.00	30.00

ISSUE #	LABEL	ARTIST/TITLE	VG	MINT
		TEENAGERS		
		SEE: FRANKIE LYMON AND THE TEENAGERS		
☐ 1046	***GEE***	FLIP FLOP/EVERYTHING TO ME	2.50	4.00
☐ 4086	***ROULETTE***	MY BROKEN HEART/MAMA WANNA ROCK	2.00	3.50
☐ 42054	***COLUMBIA***	WHAT'S ON YOUR MIND?/THE DRAW	1.75	3.00
☐ 43094		SOMEWHERE/SWEET AND LOVELY	1.75	3.00
☐ 1071	***END***	TONIGHT'S THE NIGHT/CRYING	2.00	3.50
☐ 1076		CAN YOU TELL ME?/A LITTLE WISER NOW	1.75	3.00
		TEENAGERS—EP		
☐ 602	***GEE***	THE TEENAGERS GO ROMANTIC	5.00	8.00
		TEMPOS		
☐ 199	***KAPP***	THE PRETTIEST GIRL IN SCHOOL/NEVER YOU MIND	1.75	3.00
☐ 102	***CLIMAX***	SEE YOU IN SEPTEMBER/BLESS YOU MY LOVE (23)	1.50	2.50
☐ 105		CROSSROADS OF LOVE/WHATEVER HAPPENS	1.75	3.00

TEMPTATIONS

Eddie Kendricks was a native of Birmingham, Alabama, where he organized an r & b group called the Primes during the early 1960s. When the group disbanded, Kendricks motored north to Detroit in hopes of getting together an even better group.

In Detroit Kendricks met with Mississippi-born David Ruffin who, like Kendricks, had come from a gospel-music background. With three other soul singers, the Temptations quintet auditioned for Berry Gordy, Jr., who signed them to his Gordy label. To the Tempatations this was a major breakthrough; two failed records for the small Miracle label in Detroit hadn't advanced their career.

After four unsuccessful singles, the Temptations hit the mark with a smooth Motown soul product—"The Way You Do the Things You Do"—that crossed over from the soul to the rock charts and sold over a million discs. The Temptations later went on to record an incredible 23 singles that made the national Top 20, with four going all the way to the top chart spot.

In 1968 lead singer David Ruffin left for a successful solo career; in 1972 Eddie Kendricks did the same.

ISSUE #	LABEL	ARTIST/TITLE	VG	MINT
		TEMPTATIONS		
☐5	*MIRACLE*	OH MOTHER OF MINE/ROMANCE WITHOUT FINANCE .	3.50	6.00
☐12		YOUR WONDERFUL LOVE/CHECK YOURSELF	2.50	4.00
☐7001	*GORDY*	DREAM COME TRUE/ISN'T SHE PRETTY	1.75	3.00
☐7010		PARADISE/SLOW DOWN HEART	1.75	3.00
☐015		THE FURTHER YOU LOOK/I WANT A LOVE I CAN SEE	1.75	3.00
☐7020		MAY I HAVE THIS DANCE?/FAREWELL MY LOVE ...	1.75	3.00
☐7028		THE WAY YOU DO THE THINGS YOU DO/ JUST LET ME KNOW (11)	1.25	1.50
		LATER GORDY SINGLES ARE WORTH UP TO $1.50 MINT		
		TEMPTATIONS—ALBUM		
☐911 (M)	*GORDY*	MEET THE TEMPTATIONS	3.50	6.00
☐911 (S)		MEET THE TEMPTATIONS	4.50	8.00
		TEMPTATIONS		
☐3001	*GOLDISC*	BARBARA/SOMEDAY (29)	1.50	3.00
☐3007		LETTER OF DEVOTION/FICKLE LITTLE GIRL	1.75	3.00
☐3019		BALLAD OF LOVE/TONIGHT MY HEART SHE IS CRYING	1.75	3.00
		TERRACE TONES		
☐25016	*APT*	WORDS OF WISDOM/THE RIDE OF PAUL REVERE ...	8.00	15.00
		CHUCK THARP		
		FEATURED: FIREBALLS		
☐0012	*LUCKY*	LONG LONG PONYTAIL/LET THERE BE LOVE.......	3.00	5.00
☐77020	*JARO*	LONG LONG PONYTAIL/LET THERE BE LOVE.......	2.50	4.00
		THEE MIDNITERS		
☐666	*CHATTAHOOCHEE*	LAND OF A THOUSAND DANCES/BALL O' TWINE (67) .	1.50	2.50
☐675		SAD GIRL/HEAT WAVE	1.50	2.50
☐684		WHITTIER BOULEVARD/EVIL LOVE	1.50	2.50
☐693		I NEED SOMEONE/EMPTY HEART	1.25	2.00
		THEE MIDNITERS—ALBUM		
☐1001 (M)	*CHATTAHOOCHEE*	THE MIDNITERS	5.00	8.00
		THEM		
		FEATURED: VAN MORRISON		
☐356	*PARROT*	GLORIA/IF YOU AND I COULD BE AS TWO	5.00	8.00
☐9702		DON'T START CRYING NOW/ONE, TWO BROWN EYES .	3.50	6.00
☐9727		GLORIA/BABY PLEASE DON'T GO (71)	1.50	2.50
☐9749		HERE COMES THE NIGHT/ALL FOR MYSELF (24) ...	1.25	2.50
☐9784		GONNA DRESS IN BLACK/IT WON'T HURT	1.75	2.50
☐9796		MYSTIC EYES/IF YOU AND I COULD BE AS TWO (33) ..	1.25	2.50
☐9819		CALL MY NAME/BRING 'EM ON IN	1.75	2.50
☐3003		DON'T YOU KNOW/RICHARD CORY	1.75	2.50
☐3006		DON'T START CRYING NOW/ I CAN ONLY GIVE YOU EVERYTHING	1.50	2.50
		THEM—ALBUMS		
☐61005 (M)	*PARROT*	THEM (FEATURING "HERE COMES THE NIGHT") ...	3.50	6.00
☐71005 (S)		THEM (FEATURING "HERE COMES THE NIGHT") ...	4.50	8.00
☐61008 (M)		THEM AGAIN	3.50	6.00
☐71008 (S)		THEM AGAIN	4.50	8.00

ISSUE #	LABEL	ARTIST/TITLE	VG	MINT
		THIRTEENTH FLOOR ELEVATORS		
☐10002	*ZERO*	YOU'RE GONNA MISS ME/WE SELL SOUL	50.00	80.00
☐492	*HBR*	YOU'RE GONNA MISS ME/TRIED TO HIDE	18.00	30.00
☐5269	*CONTACT*	YOU'RE GONNA MISS ME/TRIED TO HIDE	8.00	15.00
☐107	*INTERNATIONAL ARTISTS*	YOU'RE GONNA MISS ME/TRIED TO HIDE (55)	2.50	4.00
☐111		REVERBERATION/FIRE ENGINE	3.00	5.00
☐113		BEFORE YOU ACCUSE ME/I'VE GOT LEVITATIONS	3.00	5.00
☐121		SHE LIVES IN A TIME OF HER OWN/BABY BLUE	3.00	5.00
		THIRTEENTH FLOOR ELEVATORS—ALBUMS		
☐1 (M)	*INTERNATIONAL ARTISTS*	13TH FLOOR ELEVATORS	8.00	15.00
☐5 (M)		EASTER EVERYWHERE	8.00	15.00
☐8 (M)		LIVE	8.00	15.00
		B. J. THOMAS		
☐231	*PACEMAKER*	MAMA/WENDY	3.00	5.00
☐253		BABY CRIED/I'M NOT A FOOL ANYMORE	2.50	4.00
☐103	*BRAGG*	BILLY AND SUE/NEVER TELL	3.00	5.00
☐5491	*WARNER BROTHERS*	BILLY AND SUE/NEVER TELL	2.00	3.50
		B. J. THOMAS—ALBUM		
☐3001 (M)	*PACEMAKER*	I'M SO LONESOME I COULD CRY	6.00	10.00
		GENE THOMAS		
☐1429	*VENUS*	SOMETIME/EVERY NIGHT	3.50	6.00
☐1441		LAMP OF LOVE/TWO LIPS	2.50	4.00
☐338	*UNITED ARTISTS*	SOMETIME/EVERY NIGHT (53)	1.50	2.50
☐418		THAT'S WHAT YOU ARE TO ME/MYSTERIES OF LOVE	1.75	2.50
☐501		IT'S MAKE-BELIEVE/SO WRONG	1.75	2.50
☐583		PEACE OF MIND/THE PUPPET	1.75	2.50
☐640		BABY'S GONE/STAND-BY LOVE (84)	1.50	2.50
		SUE THOMPSON		
☐1153	*HICKORY*	SAD MOVIES (MAKE ME CRY)/ NINE LITTLE TEARDROPS (5)	1.00	2.00
☐1159		NORMAN/NEVER LOVE AGAIN (3)	1.00	2.00
☐1166		TWO OF A KIND/IT HAS TO BE (42)	1.25	2.00
☐1174		HAVE A GOOD TIME/IF THE BOY ONLY KNEW (31)	1.25	2.00
☐1183		JAMES (HOLD THE LADDER STEADY)/MY HERO (17)	1.25	2.00
☐1196		WILLIE CAN/TOO MUCH IN LOVE (78)	1.25	2.00
☐1284		PAPER TIGER/ MAMA, DON'T CRY AT MY WEDDING (23)	1.25	2.00
		THREE CHUCKLES		
		FEATURED: TEDDY RANDAZZO		
☐100	*BOULEVARD*	AT LAST YOU UNDERSTAND/RUN AROUND	7.00	12.00
☐0066	*X*	AT LAST YOU UNDERSTAND/RUN AROUND	2.00	3.50
☐0095		FOOLISHLY/IF YOU SHOULD LOVE AGAIN	2.00	3.50
☐0134		SO LONG/YOU SHOULD HAVE TOLD ME	2.00	3.50
☐0150		BLUE LOVER/REALIZE	2.00	3.50

ISSUE #	LABEL	ARTIST/TITLE	VG	MINT
□0162		TIMES TWO, I LOVE YOU/ STILL THINKING OF YOU (67)	1.75	3.00
□0186		THE FUNNY LITTLE THINGS WE USED TO DO/ ANYWAY	2.00	3.50
□0186	*VIK*	THE FUNNY LITTLE THINGS WE USED TO DO/ ANYWAY	1.75	3.00
□0194		AND THE ANGELS SING/TELL ME (70)	1.50	2.50
□0116		GYPSY IN MY SOUL/WE'RE STILL HOLDING HANDS	1.50	2.50
□0232		MIDNIGHT 'TIL DAWN/FALLEN OUT OF LOVE	1.50	2.50
□0244		WON'T YOU GIVE ME A CHANCE/ WE'RE GONNA ROCK TONIGHT	1.50	2.50
		THREE CHUCKLES—EPs		
□192	*RCA*	THE THREE CHUCKLES	2.50	4.00
□193		THE THREE CHUCKLES	2.50	4.00
□194		THE THREE CHUCKLES	2.50	4.00
		THE THREE CHUCKLES—ALBUM		
□1067 (M)	*RCA*	THE THREE CHUCKLES	8.00	15.00
		THREE FRIENDS		
□500	*LIDO*	BLANCHE/BABY I'LL CRY	2.50	4.00
□504		NOW THAT YOU'RE GONE/CHINESE TEA ROOM	2.50	4.00
		THREE G'S		
□41175	*COLUMBIA*	LET'S GO STEADY FOR THE SUMMER/WILD MAN (55)	1.50	2.50
□41292		THESE ARE THE LITTLE THINGS/WONDER	1.50	2.50
□41513		BARBARA/DON'T CRY KATHY	1.50	2.50
		THYME		
□201	*A-SQUARE*	SHAME, SHAME/SOMEHOW	2.50	4.00
□202		TIME OF THE SEASON/I FOUND A LOVE	3.00	5.00
		TICO AND THE TRIUMPHS *FEATURED: PAUL SIMON*		
□169	*MADISON*	MOTORCYCLE/I DON'T BELIEVE THEM	3.50	6.00
□835	*AMY*	MOTORCYCLE/I DON'T BELIEVE THEM (99)	2.50	4.00
□845		EXPRESS TRAIN/WILDFLOWER	3.00	5.00
□860		CRY, LITTLE BOY, CRY/GET UP AND DO THE WONDER	3.00	5.00
□876		CARDS OF LOVE/NOISE	4.00	7.00
		JOHNNY TILLOTSON		
□1353	*CADENCE*	DREAMY EYES/WELL, I'M YOUR MAN (63)	2.00	3.50
□1364		TRUE TRUE HAPPINESS/LOVE IS BLIND (54)	1.75	3.00
□1372		WHY DO I LOVE YOU SO/NEVER LET ME GO (42)	1.75	3.00
□1377		EARTH ANGEL/PLEDGING MY LOVE (57)	1.75	3.00
□1384		POETRY IN MOTION/PRINCESS, PRINCESS (2)	1.25	2.50
□1391		JIMMY'S GIRL/HIS TRUE LOVE SAID GOODBYE (25)	1.50	2.50
□1404		WITHOUT YOU/CUTIE PIE (7)	1.25	2.50
□1409		DREAMY EYES/WELL, I'M YOUR MAN (35)	1.50	2.50
□1418		IT KEEPS RIGHT ON A-HURTIN'/ SHE GAVE SWEET LOVE TO ME (3)	1.00	2.00
□1424		SEND ME THE PILLOW YOU DREAM ON/ WHAT'LL I DO? (17)	1.25	2.00
□1432		I CAN'T HELP IT/ I'M SO LONESOME I COULD CRY (24)	1.25	2.00

ISSUE #	LABEL	ARTIST/TITLE	VG	MINT
☐1434		OUT OF MY MIND/EMPTY FEELIN' (24)	1.25	2.00
☐1437		YOU CAN NEVER STOP ME LOVING YOU/ JUDY JUDY JUDY (18)	1.25	2.00
☐1441		FUNNY HOW THE TIME SLIPS AWAY/ GOOD YEAR FOR GIRLS (50)	1.25	2.00
		JOHNNY TILLOTSON—EP		
☐114	*CADENCE*	JOHNNY TILLOTSON	3.00	5.00
		JOHNNY TILLOTSON—ALBUMS		
☐3052 (M)	*CADENCE*	JOHNNY TILLOTSON'S BEST	8.00	15.00
☐25052 (S)		JOHNNY TILLOTSON'S BEST	12.00	20.00
☐3058 (M)		IT KEEPS RIGHT ON A-HURTIN'	6.00	10.00
☐25058 (S)		IT KEEPS RIGHT ON A-HURTIN'	7.00	12.00
☐3067 (M)		YOU CAN NEVER STOP ME LOVING YOU	3.50	6.00
☐25067 (S)		YOU CAN NEVER STOP ME LOVING YOU	4.50	8.00

TOKENS

SEE: BUDDIES, DARREL AND THE OXFORDS, FOUR WINDS

ISSUE #	LABEL	ARTIST/TITLE	VG	MINT
☐615	*WARWICK*	TONIGHT I FELL IN LOVE/ I'LL ALWAYS LOVE YOU (15)	1.50	2.50
☐658		TASTE OF A TEAR/NEVER TILL NOW (Johnny and the Tokens)	2.50	4.00
☐7896	*RCA*	WHEN I GO TO SLEEP/DRY YOUR EYES	1.75	3.00
☐7925		SINCERELY/WHEN THE SUMMER IS THROUGH	1.75	3.00
☐7954		THE LION SLEEPS TONIGHT/TINA (1)	1.25	2.50
☐7991		B'WA NINA/WEEPING RIVER (55)	1.50	2.50
☐8052		LA BAMBA/A TOKEN OF LOVE (85)	1.50	2.50
☐8089		I'LL DO MY CRYING TOMORROW/ DREAM ANGEL, GOODNIGHT	1.75	2.50
☐8114		A BIRD FLIES OUT OF SIGHT/WISHING	1.75	2.50
☐8148		TONIGHT I MET AN ANGEL/HINDU LULLABY	1.75	2.50
☐8210		HEAR THE BELLS/ABC-123 (94)	1.50	2.50
☐8309		LET'S GO TO THE DRAG STRIP/2 CARS	1.75	2.50
☐500	*B. T. PUPPY*	A GIRL NAMED ARLENE/SWING	1.75	2.50
☐502		HE'S IN TOWN/OH CATHY (43)	1.50	2.50
☐504		YOU'RE MY GIRL/HAVIN' FUN	1.75	2.50
☐518		I HEAR TRUMPETS BLOW/DON'T CRY, SING ALONG WITH THE MUSIC (30)	1.25	2.00
☐5900	*WARNER BROTHERS*	PORTRAIT OF MY LOVE/SHE COMES AND GOES (36)	1.25	2.00
☐7056		IT'S A HAPPENING WORLD/HOW NICE (69)	1.25	2.00
		TOKENS—ALBUMS		
☐2514 (M)	*RCA*	THE LION SLEEPS TONIGHT	6.00	10.00
☐2514 (S)		THE LION SLEEPS TONIGHT	7.00	12.00
☐2631 (M)		WE SING FOLK	5.00	8.00
☐2631 (S)		WE SING FOLK	6.00	10.00
☐2886 (M)		WHEELS	3.50	6.00
☐2886 (S)		WHEELS	4.50	8.00
☐3685 (M)		THE TOKENS AGAIN	3.50	6.00
☐3685 (S)		THE TOKENS AGAIN	4.50	8.00
☐1000 (M)	*B. T. PUPPY*	I HEAR TRUMPETS BLOW	3.50	6.00
☐1000 (S)		I HEAR TRUMPETS BLOW	4.50	8.00
☐1006 (M)		TOKENS OF GOLD	3.00	5.00
☐1006 (S)		TOKENS OF GOLD	5.00	7.00

TOM AND JERRY

In 1957 two New York City high school juniors formed a singing duo. As Everly Brothers soundalikes, they became popular at assemblies and talent shows at their Flushing high school. They were, in reality, Paul Simon and Art Garfunkel, but they felt that the use of their real names would only provoke laughter. As a result they adopted the name of Tom and Jerry, after the popular cartoon characters.

They recorded a single for the local Big label. The song—"Hey, Schoolgirl"—got good airplay on the East Coast but nationally was not a huge success. Three follow-up Big singles failed to make the charts. Tom and Jerry then saw some of their later Big tracks released on larger labels, but again songs failed to sell. They signed with ABC-Paramount Records, again without success.

Both college graduates by the mid-1960s, Paul and Art recorded an album of folk songs. One track ("Sounds Of Silence") began getting airplay, so Columbia Records sweetened "Sounds Of Silence" with electric guitars and drums and released it as a single. It went to No. 1 near the end of 1965 and Simon and Garfunkel—using their real names this time—began a long string of folk-rock hits.

ISSUE #	LABEL	ARTIST/TITLE	VG	MINT
		TOM AND JERRY (SIMON AND GARFUNKEL)		
□613	*BIG*	HEY, SCHOOLGIRL/DANCIN' WILD (54)	2.50	5.00
□616		OUR SONG/TWO TEENAGERS	3.50	6.00
□618		THAT'S MY STORY/DON'T SAY GOODBYE	3.50	6.00
□621		BABY TALK/TWO TEENAGERS	7.00	12.00
□319	*HUNT*	THAT'S MY STORY/DON'T SAY GOODBYE	6.00	10.00
□120	*BELL*	BABY TALK/I'M GOING TO GET MARRIED (Ronnie Lawrence)	8.00	15.00
□5167	*KING*	HEY, SCHOOLGIRL/DANCIN' WILD	5.00	8.00
□10363	*ABC-PARAMOUNT*	SURRENDER, PLEASE SURRENDER/FIGHTING MAD	6.00	10.00
□10788		THAT'S MY STORY/TIA-JUANA BLUES	5.00	8.00
		TONETTES		
□103	*DOT*	HE LOVES ME, HE LOVES ME NOT/UH-OH	3.50	6.00
		TORNADOES		
□9561	*LONDON*	TELSTAR/JUNGLE FEVER (1)	1.25	2.50
□9579		LIKE LOCOMOTION/GLOBETROTTIN'	1.75	2.50
□9581		RIDIN' THE WIND/THE BREEZE AND I (63)	1.50	2.50
□9599		LIFE ON VENUS/ROBOT	1.50	2.50
		TORNADOES—ALBUM		
□3279 (M)	*LONDON*	TELSTAR	3.50	6.00
		TORNADOES		
		SEE: HOLLYWOOD TORNADOES		
□100	*AERTAUN*	BUSTIN' SURFBOARDS/BEYOND THE SURF	1.75	3.00
□103		PHANTOM SURFER/SHOOTIN' BEAVERS	1.75	3.00
		TORNADOES—ALBUM		
□4005 (M)	*JOSIE*	BUSTIN' SURFBOARDS	7.00	12.00
		MITCHELL TOROK		
□30230	*DECCA*	PLEDGE OF LOVE/WHAT'S BEHIND THAT STRANGE DOOR? (26)	1.50	2.50
□2018	*GUYDEN*	CARIBBEAN/HOOTCHY KOOTCHY HENRY (27)	1.50	3.00
□2028		YOU ARE THE ONE/MEXICALLI JOE	1.75	3.00
□2032		GUARDIAN ANGEL/I WANT TO KNOW EVERYTHING	1.75	3.00
□2034		PINK CHIFFON/WHAT YOU DON'T KNOW (60)	1.50	2.50
		MITCHELL TOROK—ALBUM		
□502 (M)	*GUYDEN*	CARIBBEAN	5.00	9.00
□502 (S)		CARIBBEAN	7.00	12.00
		TRADE WINDS (VIDELS)		
□10-020	*RED BIRD*	NEW YORK'S A LONELY TOWN/CLUB SEVENTEEN (32)	1.25	2.50
□10-028		ROCK AND ROLL SHOW IN TOWN/GIRL FROM GREENWICH VILLAGE	1.50	2.50
□10-033		SUMMERTIME GIRL/THE PARTY STARTS AT NINE	1.50	2.50
□212	*KAMA SUTRA*	MIND EXCURSION/LITTLE SUSAN'S DREAMIN' (51)	1.25	2.00
□218		I BELIEVE IN HER/CATCH ME IN THE MEADOW	1.25	2.00
□234		MIND EXCURSION/ONLY WHEN I'M DREAMIN'	1.00	2.00

ISSUE #	LABEL	ARTIST/TITLE	VG	MINT
		TRADE WINDS (VIDELS)—ALBUM		
☐8057 (M)	*KAMA SUTRA*	EXCURSIONS	3.00	5.00
☐8057 (S)		EXCURSIONS	4.00	7.00
		TRAMPS		
☐548	*ARVEE*	RIDE ON/YOU'RE A SQUARE	3.50	6.00
☐570		YOUR LOVE/MIDNIGHT FLYER	3.50	6.00
		TRASHMEN		
☐4002	*GARRETT*	SURFIN' BIRD/KING OF THE SURF (4)	1.25	2.50
☐4003		BIRD DANCE BEAT/A-BONE (30)	1.50	2.50
☐4005		ON THE MOVE/BAD NEWS	1.50	2.50
☐4010		PEPPERMINT MAN/NEW GENERATION	1.50	2.50
		TRASHMEN—ALBUM		
☐200 (M)	*SOMA*	SURFIN' BIRD	6.00	10.00
		TREMELOES		
☐10075	*EPIC*	GOOD DAY SUNSHINE/WHAT A STATE I'M IN	1.25	2.00
		LATER EPIC SINGLES ARE WORTH UP TO $1.50 MINT		
		TRENTONS		
☐2204	*SHEPHERD*	ALL ALONE/STAR BRIGHT	5.00	8.00
		TROGGS		
☐6415	*ATCO*	WILD THING/WITH A GIRL LIKE YOU (1)	1.00	2.00
☐6415		WITH A GIRL LIKE YOU/I WANT YOU	2.50	4.00
☐6444		I CAN'T CONTROL MYSELF/ GONNA MAKE YOU MINE (43)	1.25	2.00
☐1548	*FONTANA*	WILD THING/FROM HOME (1)	1.00	2.00
☐1552		WITH A GIRL LIKE YOU/I WANT YOU (29)	1.50	2.50
☐1557		I CAN'T CONTROL MYSELF/ GONNA MAKE YOU MINE (43)	1.50	2.50
☐1607		LOVE IS ALL AROUND/ WHEN WILL THE RAIN COME? (7)	1.00	2.00
		TROGGS—ALBUMS		
☐193 (M)	*ATCO*	WILD THING	5.00	8.00
☐67556 (S)	*FONTANA*	WILD THING	3.50	6.00
☐67576 (S)		LOVE IS ALL AROUND	3.00	5.00
		TROJANS		
☐518	*TENDER*	DON'T ASK ME TO BE LONELY/ ALONE IN THIS WORLD	7.00	12.00

TUNE WEAVERS

During the 1950s a former soldier asked his sister to join him as a singing team in the Boston area. However, the lady's husband objected until he was asked to join the group also. After the inclusion of a cousin, the family quartet established themselves as the Tone Weavers. At a dance one night they were wrongly introduced as the Tune Weavers but decided to keep that as their new name.

The Tune Weavers' club fare usually included the standard hits of the day, but occasionally they would sing an original composition. One of the most favorably received was a song called "Happy Happy Birthday Baby", written by lead vocalist Margo Sylvia five years earlier when she was sixteen.

A night-club customer heard the song and asked the Tune Weavers if he could become their manager. They agreed and were soon signed to the small Casa Grande label. The single flopped. Nearly a year later a Philadelphia disc jockey played the song by accident. When telephone response proved overwhelming, the disc jockey referred the Tune Weavers to Checker Records. The Tune Weavers sold a million with "Happy Happy Birthday Baby" but were never to be heard from again.

ISSUE #	LABEL	ARTIST/TITLE	VG	MINT
		TUNE WEAVERS		
☐4037	***CASA GRANDE***	HAPPY HAPPY BIRTHDAY BABY/OL' MAN RIVER ...	5.00	8.00
☐872	***CHECKER***	HAPPY HAPPY BIRTHDAY BABY/OL' MAN RIVER (5)	1.50	3.50
		IKE AND TINA TURNER		
☐730	***SUE***	A FOOL IN LOVE/THE WAY YOU LOVE ME (27)	1.50	3.00
☐735		I IDOLIZE YOU/LETTER FROM TINA (82)	2.00	3.50
☐749		IT'S GONNA WORK OUT FINE/ WON'T YOU FORGIVE ME (14)	1.25	2.50
☐131	***PHILLES***	RIVER DEEP-MOUNTAIN HIGH/ I'LL KEEP YOU HAPPY (88)	2.00	3.50
☐134		A MAN IS A MAN IS A MAN/TWO TO TANGO	2.50	4.00
☐135		I'LL NEVER NEED MORE THAN THIS/ THE CASHBOX BLUES	2.50	4.00
☐136		HOLD ON BABY/A LOVE LIKE YOURS	2.50	4.00
		IKE AND TINA TURNER—ALBUMS		
☐2007 (M)	***SUE***	IT'S GONNA WORK OUT FINE..................	6.00	10.00
☐2007 (M)	***PHILLIES***	RIVER DEEP-MOUNTAIN HIGH	20.00	35.00
☐2007 (S)		RIVER DEEP-MOUNTAIN HIGH	25.00	40.00
		JOE TURNER		
☐1026	***ATLANTIC***	SHAKE, RATTLE AND ROLL/YOU KNOW I LOVE YOU .	3.00	5.00
☐1053		FLIP, FLOP AND FLY/TI-RI-LEE	2.50	4.00
☐1088		CORRINE CORRINA/ BOOGIE WOOGIE COUNTRY GIRL (41)...........	2.00	3.50
☐1100		LIPSTICK, POWDER AND PAINT/ROCK A WHILE	2.00	3.50

CONWAY TWITTY

His real name is Harold Lloyd Jenkins. Born in Friars Point, Mississippi, on September 1, 1935, he learned how to play the guitar from his father, a Mississippi riverboat captain. The family later moved to Helena, Arkansas, where Twitty—then ten years old—formed his first band, the Phillips Country Ramblers.

Conway planned on becoming a minister, so music was initially just a hobby for him, as was playing baseball. But after high-school graduation Twitty was offered a contract with the Philadelphia Philles. He wanted a car first, though, and turned down the offer in favor of a factory job. Shortly after buying a 1948 Buick, Conway Twitty was drafted into the army. There he formed a second group called the Cimarrons.

Twitty's name was born in his manager's office, and was gleaned from the towns of Conway, Arkansas, and Twitty, Texas, both found on a pair of road maps.

Two Mercury singles paved the way for Conway's first MGM hit, the Elvis-flavored "It's Only Make Believe", a No. 1 winner. On MGM Twitty ran up a sales record of seven Top 30 hits before becoming a successful country artist on MCA Records.

ISSUE #	LABEL	ARTIST/TITLE	VG	MINT
		CONWAY TWITTY		
□ 71086	*MERCURY*	I NEED YOUR LOVIN'/ BORN TO SING THE BLUES (93)	5.00	8.00
□ 71384		DOUBLE TALK BABY/ WHY CAN'T I GET THROUGH TO YOU	6.00	10.00
□ 12677	*MGM*	IT'S ONLY MAKE BELIEVE/I'LL TRY (1)	1.50	3.00
□ 12748		THE STORY OF MY LOVE/ MAKE ME KNOW YOU'RE MINE (28)	1.50	3.00
□ 12785		HEY LITTLE LUCY/WHEN I'M NOT WITH YOU (87)	1.75	3.00
□ 12804		MONA LISA/HEAVENLY (29)	1.50	2.50
□ 12826		DANNY BOY/HALFWAY TO HEAVEN (10)	1.50	2.50
□ 12857		LONELY BLUE BOY/STAR SPANGLED HEAVEN (6)	1.25	2.50
□ 12886		WHAT AM I LIVING FOR?/ THE HURT IN MY HEART (26)	1.50	2.50
□ 12911		IS A BLUE BIRD BLUE/SHE'S MINE (35)	1.50	2.50
□ 12962		WHOLE LOT OF SHAKIN' GOING ON/THE FLAME (55)	1.25	2.00
□ 12969		C'EST SI BON/DON'T YOU DARE LET ME DOWN (22)	1.25	2.00
□ 12998		THE NEXT KISS (IS THE LAST GOODBYE)/ MAN ALONE (72)	1.25	2.00
		CONWAY TWITTY—EPs		
□ 1623	*MGM*	IT'S ONLY MAKE BELIEVE	5.00	8.00
□ 1640		CONWAY TWITTY SINGS	4.00	7.00
□ 1641		CONWAY TWITTY SINGS	4.00	7.00
□ 1642		CONWAY TWITTY SINGS	4.00	7.00
□ 1678		SATURDAY NIGHT WITH CONWAY TWITTY	3.50	6.00
□ 1679		SATURDAY NIGHT WITH CONWAY TWITTY	3.50	6.00
□ 1680		SATURDAY NIGHT WITH CONWAY TWITTY	3.50	6.00
□ 1071		LONELY BLUE BOY	3.50	6.00
		CONWAY TWITTY—ALBUMS		
□ 3744 (M)	*MGM*	CONWAY TWITTY SONGS	8.00	15.00
□ 3786 (M)		SATURDAY NIGHT WITH CONWAY TWITTY	7.00	12.00
□ 3786 (S)		SATURDAY NIGHT WITH CONWAY TWITTY	8.00	15.00
□ 3818 (M)		LONELY BLUE BOY	6.00	10.00
□ 3818 (S)		LONELY BLUE BOY	7.00	12.00
□ 3849 (M)		CONWAY TWITTY'S GREATEST HITS	5.00	8.00
□ 3849 (S)		CONWAY TWITTY'S GREATEST HITS	6.00	10.00
		TYMES		
□ 871-A	PARKWAY	SO IN LOVE/ROSCOE JAMES McLAIN	1.75	3.00
□ 871-C		SO MUCH IN LOVE/ROSCOE JAMES McLAIN (1)	1.00	2.00
□ 884		WONDERFUL! WONDERFUL!/ COME WITH ME TO THE SEA (7)	1.00	2.00
□ 891		SOMEWHERE/VIEW FROM MY WINDOW (19)	1.25	2.00
□ 908		TO EACH HIS OWN/WONDERLAND OF LOVE (78)	1.25	2.00
□ 919		THE MAGIC OF OUR SUMMER LOVE/ WITH ALL MY HEART (99)	1.25	2.00
□ 924		HERE SHE COMES/MALIBU (92)	1.25	2.00
		TYMES—ALBUM		
□ 7038 (M)	*PARKWAY*	THE SOUND OF THE WONDERFUL TYMES	3.00	5.00
□ 7038 (S)		THE SOUND OF THE WONDERFUL TYMES	4.00	7.00

ISSUE #	LABEL	ARTIST/TITLE	VG	MINT
		UNDERDOGS		
		FEATURED: BOB SEGER		
□1001	*HIDEOUT*	THE MAN IN THE GLASS/JUDY BE MINE	2.50	4.00
□1004		DON'T PRETEND/LITTLE GIRL	2.50	4.00
□1011		SUNRISE/GET DOWN ON YOUR KNEES	2.50	4.00
		UNIQUES		
□219	*PAULA*	NOT TOO LONG AGO/FAST WAY OF LIVING (66)	1.50	2.50
□222		TOO GOOD TO BE TRUE/NEVER BEEN IN LOVE	1.25	2.00
□227		LADY'S MAN/BOLIVAR	1.25	2.00
□231		STRANGE/YOU AIN'T TUFF	1.25	2.00
□238		ALL THESE THINGS/TELL ME WHAT TO DO (97)	1.25	2.00
		UNIQUES—ALBUM		
□2190 (M)	*PAULA*	UNIQUELY YOURS	3.50	6.00
		UNIT FOUR PLUS TWO		
□9732	*LONDON*	SORROW AND PAIN/WOMAN FROM LIBERIA	1.75	3.00
□9751		CONCRETE AND CLAY/WHEN I FALL IN LOVE (28)	1.50	2.50
□9761		YOU'VE NEVER BEEN IN LOVE LIKE THIS BEFORE/ TELL SOMEBODY YOU KNOW	1.25	2.00
□9790		STOP WASTING YOUR TIME/HARK	1.25	2.00
		UNIT FOUR PLUS TWO—ALBUM		
□3427 (M)	*LONDON*	UNIT FOUR PLUS TWO	3.50	6.00
□427 (S)		UNIT FOUR PLUS TWO	4.50	8.00
		UNTOUCHABLES		
□128	*MADISON*	POOR BOY NEEDS A PREACHER/NEW FAD	3.00	5.00
□134		GOODNIGHT SWEETHEART GOODNIGHT/VICKIE LEE	2.50	4.00
□139		SIXTY MINUTE MAN/EVERYBODY'S LAUGHIN'	2.50	4.00
□147		RAISIN' SUGAR CANE/DO YOUR BEST	2.00	3.50
		PHILIP UPCHURCH COMBO		
□3398	*BOYD*	YOU CAN'T SIT DOWN (PT. 1)/(PT. 11) (29)	1.25	2.50
		PHILIP UPCHURCH COMBO—ALBUM		
□389 (M)	*BOYD*	YOU CAN'T SIT DOWN	3.50	6.00
		UPTONES		
□6225	*LUTE*	I'LL BE THERE/NO MORE	2.50	4.00
□6229		DREAMIN'/BE MINE	3.00	5.00
		GARY USHER		
		PRODUCER: BRIAN WILSON		
□5128	*CAPITOL*	THE BEETLE/JODY	3.50	6.00
□5193		SACRAMENTO/THAT'S THE WAY I FEEL	6.00	10.00
□16518	*DOT*	THREE SURFER BOYS/THE MILKY WAY	5.00	8.00

RITCHIE VALENS

His real name was Richard Valenzuela, but the world knew him briefly as Richie Valens. Born in the Los Angeles, California, suburb of Pacoima on May 13, 1941, he organized a band called the Silhouettes while in junior high.

The band stayed together into high school. One night Bob Keane, who owned the small Del Fi label, saw and heard Valens at a dance. Ritchie was singing an original song, the hard-driving "Come On, Let's Go". A few days later Ritchie Valens was a Del Fi artist.

"Come On, Let's Go" became a moderate hit. For his second single, Valens wrote a song called "Donna" for his sixteen-year-old girl friend, Donna Ludwig. Ritchie later said that he knew the song would be a hit for one reason: Donna cried when the song was sung to her over the telephone. A smash hit, "Donna" would have made the No. 1 chart spot late in 1958 had it not been for "The Chipmunk Song".

Ritchie Valens, the first Mexican-American rock success, died on February 3, 1959, along with Buddy Holly and the Big Bopper, when their chartered plane crashed into an Iowa pasture.

ISSUE #	LABEL	ARTIST/TITLE	VG	MINT
		RITCHIE VALENS		
		SEE: ARVEE ALLENS		
□4106	*DEL-FI*	COME ON, LET'S GO/FRAMED (42)	2.50	4.00
□4110		DONNA/LA BAMBA (2)	2.00	3.50
□4114		THAT'S MY LITTLE SUZIE/IN A TURKISH TOWN (55)	2.00	3.50
□4117		LITTLE GIRL/WE BELONG TOGETHER (92)	2.50	4.00
□4128		STAY BESIDE ME/BIG BABY BLUES	2.00	3.50
□4133		CRY, CRY, CRY/PADDIWACK SONG	2.00	3.50
		RITCHIE VALENS—EPs		
□101	*DEL-FI*	RITCHIE VALENS	6.00	10.00
□111		RITCHIE VALENS	6.00	10.00
		RITCHIE VALENS—ALBUMS		
□1201 (M)	*DEL-FI*	RITCHIE VALENS	12.00	20.00
□1206 (M)		RITCHIE	15.00	25.00
□1214 (M)		IN CONCERT AT PACOIMA JR. HIGH	25.00	40.00
□1225 (M)		HIS GREATEST HITS	7.00	12.00
□1247 (M)		GREATEST HITS, VOL. 2	15.00	25.00
		FRANKIE VALLEY (VALLI)		
□1234	*CORONA*	MY MOTHER'S EYES/THE LAUGH'S ON ME	60.00	100.00
		FRANKY VALLEY AND THE TRAVELERS (VALLI)		
□70381	*MERCURY*	FORGIVE AND FORGET/ SOMEBODY ELSE TOOK HER NAME	20.00	35.00
		FRANKIE VALLE AND THE ROMANS (FOUR SEASONS)		
□3012	*CINDY*	COME SI BELLA/REAL	18.00	30.00
		FRANKIE VALLY (VALLI)		
□30994	*DECCA*	PLEASE TAKE A CHANCE/IT MAY BE WRONG	18.00	30.00
		VANITY FAIR		
□7067	*BRENT*	SALT WATER TAFFY/PETER WHO?	1.50	2.50
□027	*PAGE ONE*	EARLY IN THE MORNING/ YOU MADE ME LOVE YOU (12)	1.25	2.00
□029		HITCHIN' A RIDE/MAN CHILD (5)	1.00	2.00
□033		(I REMEMBER) SUNDAY MORNING/MEGOWD (98)	1.25	2.00
		VANITY FAIR—ALBUM		
□2502 (S)	*PAGE ONE*	EARLY IN THE MORNING	3.50	6.00

BOBBY VEE

Bobby Vee (real name Vellene) was born on April 30, 1943, in Fargo, North Dakota. He came from a musical family and began playing the guitar as a high-school freshman. Later Bobby, his brother and two classmates formed a rock-and-roll group called the Shadows.

On February 3, 1959, Bobby Vee was only one of hundreds of stunned Fargo residents who learned that Buddy Holly, Ritchie Valens and the Big Bopper had all been killed on their way to Fargo to play a show that night. Young Vee, who sounded a great deal like his idol Holly, was asked to have his Shadows group fill in as the show's opening act.

The Shadows later drove to the Minneapolis, Minnesota, home of Soma Records. There they recorded a Vee original called "Suzie Baby" on a four-track recorder. The song began getting Midwestern airplay and Liberty picked up the Soma master, signing Bobby Vee as a solo artist.

His fourth Liberty single was "Devil Or Angel", a remake of the Clovers' 1955 r & b classic. Bobby Vee, age seventeen, then saw his own version climb into the Top 10, sell a million copies and become the first of many Liberty hits he would record.

ISSUE #	LABEL	ARTIST/TITLE	VG	MINT
		BOBBY VEE		
☐ 1110	*SOMA*	SUZIE BABY/FLYIN' HIGH	8.00	15.00
☐ 55208	*LIBERTY*	SUZIE BABY/FLYIN' HIGH (77)	3.00	5.00
☐ 55234		WHAT DO YOU WANT/MY LOVE LOVES ME (93)	2.50	4.50
☐ 55251		ONE LAST KISS/LAURIE	3.00	5.00
☐ 55270		DEVIL OR ANGEL/SINCE I MET YOU BABY (6)	1.25	2.50
☐ 55287		RUBBER BALL/EVERYDAY (6)	1.25	2.50
☐ 55296		STAYIN' IN/MORE THAN I CAN SAY (33)	1.50	2.50
☐ 55325		HOW MANY TEARS/BABY FACE (63)	1.50	2.50
☐ 55354		TAKE GOOD CARE OF MY BABY/BASHFUL BOB (1)	1.00	2.50
☐ 55388		RUN TO HIM/WALKIN' WITH MY ANGEL (2)	1.00	2.50
☐ 55419		PLEASE DON'T ASK ABOUT BARBARA/ I CAN'T SAY GOODBYE (15)	1.25	2.50
☐ 55451		SHARING YOU/IN MY BABY'S EYES (15)	1.25	2.50
☐ 55479		PUNISH HER/SOMEDAY (20) (with the Crickets)	1.25	2.50
☐ 55521		THE NIGHT HAS A THOUSAND EYES/ ANONYMOUS PHONE CALL (3)	.75	2.00
☐ 55530		CHARMS/BOBBY TOMORROW (13)	1.00	2.00
☐ 55581		BE TRUE TO YOURSELF/A LETTER FROM BETTY (34)	1.25	2.00
☐ 55636		YESTERDAY AND YOU/NEVER LOVE A ROBIN (55)	1.25	2.00
☐ 55654		STRANGER IN YOUR ARMS/1963 (83)	1.25	2.00
☐ 55670		I'LL MAKE YOU MINE/SHE'S SORRY (52)	1.25	2.00
☐ 55700		HICKORY, DICK AND DOC/ I WISH YOU WERE MINE AGAIN (63)	1.25	2.00
☐ 55726		WHERE IS SHE/HOW TO MAKE A FAREWELL	1.50	2.00
☐ 55751		EV'RY LITTLE BIT HURTS/ PRETEND YOU DON'T SEE HER (84)	1.25	2.00
☐ 55761		CROSS MY HEART/THIS IS THE END (99)	1.25	2.00
☐ 55790		YOU WON'T FORGET ME/KEEP ON TRYING (85)	1.50	2.00
		LATER LIBERTY SINGLES ARE WORTH UP TO $2.00 MINT		
		BOBBY VEE—EPs		
☐ 1006	*LIBERTY*	DEVIL OR ANGEL	3.50	6.00
☐ 1010		BOBBY VEE'S HITS	3.00	5.00
☐ 1013		BOBBY VEE	3.00	5.00
		BOBBY VEE—ALBUMS		
☐ 3165 (M)	*LIBERTY*	DEVIL OR ANGEL	7.00	12.00
☐ 7165 (S)		DEVIL OR ANGEL	8.00	15.00
☐ 3181 (M)		BOBBY VEE	6.00	10.00
☐ 7181 (S)		BOBBY VEE	7.00	12.00
☐ 3186 (M)		WITH STRINGS AND THINGS	3.50	6.00
☐ 7186 (S)		WITH STRINGS AND THINGS	4.50	8.00
☐ 3205 (M)		HITS OF THE ROCKIN' 50'S	3.50	6.00
☐ 7205 (S)		HITS OF THE ROCKIN' 50'S	4.50	8.00
☐ 3211 (M)		TAKE GOOD CARE OF MY BABY	3.50	6.00
☐ 7211 (S)		TAKE GOOD CARE OF MY BABY	4.50	8.00
☐ 3228 (M)		BOBBY VEE MEETS THE CRICKETS	3.50	6.00
☐ 7228 (S)		BOBBY VEE MEETS THE CRICKETS	4.50	8.00
☐ 3232 (M)		A BOBBY VEE RECORDING SESSION	3.50	6.00
☐ 7232 (S)		A BOBBY VEE RECORDING SESSION	4.50	8.00
☐ 3245 (M)		GOLDEN GREATS	3.00	5.00
☐ 7245 (S)		GOLDEN GREATS	4.00	7.00

ISSUE #	LABEL	ARTIST/TITLE	VG	MINT

VELAIRES

☐1198	JAMIE	ROLL OVER BEETHOVEN/BRAZIL (51)	1.50	2.50
☐1203		STICKS AND STONES/DREAM	1.25	2.00
☐1211		UBANGI STOMP/IT'S ALMOST TOMORROW	1.25	2.00

VELVETS

☐435	MONUMENT	THAT LUCKY OLD SUN/TIME AND AGAIN	2.00	3.50
☐441		TONIGHT (COULD BE THE NIGHT)/SPRING FEVER (26)	1.50	2.50
☐448		LAUGH/LANA (90)	1.75	3.00
☐458		DON'T LET HIM TAKE MY BABY/THE LOVE EXPRESS	1.75	3.00
☐464		LET THE GOOD TIMES ROLL/THE LIGHTS GO ON, THE LIGHTS GO OFF	1.75	3.00

VENTURES

SEE: MARKSMEN

☐100	BLUE HORIZON	THE REAL McCOY/COOKIES AND COKE	3.50	6.00
☐101		WALK-DON'T RUN/HOME	5.00	8.00
☐25	DOLTON	WALK-DON'T RUN/HOME (2)	1.25	2.50
☐28		PERFIDIA/NO TRESPASSING (15)	1.50	2.50
☐32		RAM-BUNK-SHUSH/LONELY HEART (29)	1.50	2.50
☐41		LULLABY OF THE LEAVES/GINCHY (69)	1.25	2.00
☐44		(THEME FROM) SILVER CITY/BLUER THAN BLUE (83)	1.25	2.00
☐47		BLUE MOON/LADY OF SPAIN (54)	1.25	2.00
☐50		YELLOW JACKET/GENESIS	1.50	2.00
☐55		INSTANT MASHED/MY BONNIE	1.50	2.00
☐60		LOLITA YA-YA/LUCILLE (61)	1.25	2.00
☐67		THE 2,000 POUND BEE (PT. 1)/(PT. 11) (91)	1.25	2.00
☐68		SKIP TO M'LIMBO/EL CUMBANCHERO	1.25	2.00
☐78		THE NINTH WAVE/DAMAGED GOODS	1.25	2.00
☐85		THE CHASE/THE SAVAGE	1.25	2.00
☐91		JOURNEY TO THE STARS/WALKIN' WITH PLUTO	1.25	2.00
☐94		FUGITIVE/SCRATCHIN'	1.25	2.00
☐96		WALK-DON'T RUN '64/THE CRUEL SEA (8)	.75	1.00

VENTURES—EP

☐503	DOLTON	WALK-DON'T RUN	3.50	6.00

VENTURES—ALBUMS

☐2003 (M)	DOLTON	WALK-DON'T RUN	5.00	8.00
☐8003 (S)		WALK-DON'T RUN	6.00	10.00
☐2004 (M)		THE VENTURES	4.00	7.00
☐8004 (S)		THE VENTURES	5.00	9.00
☐2006 (M)		ANOTHER SMASH	3.50	6.00
☐8006 (S)		ANOTHER SMASH	4.50	8.00
☐2008 (M)		THE COLORFUL VENTURES	3.00	5.00
☐8008 (S)		THE COLORFUL VENTURES	4.00	7.00
☐2010 (M)		TWIST WITH THE VENTURES	3.00	5.00
☐8010 (S)		TWIST WITH THE VENTURES	4.00	7.00

VERONICA (RONNIE SPECTOR)

SEE: RONETTES

☐1	PHIL SPECTOR	SO YOUNG/LARRY L.	2.50	4.00
☐2		WHY DON'T THEY LET US FALL IN LOVE/ CHUBBY DANNY D.	2.50	4.00

ISSUE #	LABEL	ARTIST/TITLE	VG	MINT
		VIBRATIONS		
		SEE: JAYHAWKS, MARATHONS		
☐969	***CHECKER***	THE WATUSI/WALLFLOWER (25)	1.25	2.50
☐982		STRANDED IN THE JUNGLE/DON'T SAY GOODBYE	1.50	2.50
☐5389	***ARGO***	PEANUT BUTTER/DOWN IN NEW ORLEANS	1.50	2.50
☐2221	***ATLANTIC***	MY GIRL SLOOPY/DADDY WOO-WOO (26)	1.25	2.00
		VIDELS		
		SEE: TRADE WINDS		
☐5004	***JDS***	MR. LONELY/I'LL FORGET YOU (73)	2.00	3.50
☐5005		NOW THAT SUMMER IS HERE/ SHE'S NOT COMING HOME	2.50	4.00
☐361	***KAPP***	I'LL KEEP WAITING/STREETS OF LOVE	1.75	3.00
☐495		A LETTER FROM ANNE/THIS YEAR'S MISTER NEW	1.75	3.00

GENE VINCENT

On February 11, 1935, Gene Vincent (Vincent Eugene Craddock) was born in the Virginia city of Norfolk. At twelve Gene bought his first guitar. Four years later he quit school and joined the navy. While stationed in Korea he was injured in a motorcycle accident. Doctors wanted to amputate Gene's left leg but he refused. He spent a year in a naval hospital and endured pain he rest of his life.

Returning to Virginia, Gene formed a group called the Blue Caps. One song they did was a Vincent original called "Be Bop A Lula", supposedly inspired by a Little Lulu comic book Gene was reading one night when he was drunk. Capitol Records, smarting after passing up a chance to sign Elvis Presley before RCA got him, thought Vincent could be another Elvis. They flew Gene and his Blue Caps to Hollywood and had them record "Be Bop A Lula", an instant hit around the world.

When Gene Vincent's popularity declined, he gained a large British following. However, he eventually lost favor there due in part to his constant drinking to ease the pain of his shattered leg.

On October 12, 1971, Gene Vincent died in poverty at a military hospital in Saugus, California.

ISSUE #	LABEL	ARTIST/TITLE	VG	MINT
		GENE VINCENT		
		FEATURED: THE BLUE CAPS		
☐3450	*CAPITOL*	BE-BOP-A-LULU/WOMAN LOVE (9)	2.00	4.00
☐3530		RACE WITH THE DEVIL/GONNA BACK UP BABY (96)	3.00	5.00
☐3558		BLUEJEAN BOP/WHO SLAPPED JOHN	2.50	4.00
☐3617		CRAZY LEGS/IMPORTANT WORDS	2.50	4.00
☐3678		FIVE DAYS, FIVE DAYS/BI-BICKEY-BI-BO-BO-GO	2.50	4.00
☐3763		LOTTA LOVIN'/WEAR MY RING (14)	2.00	4.00
☐3839		DANCE TO THE BOP/I GOT IT (43)	2.50	5.00
☐3874		WALKIN' HOME FROM SCHOOL/I GOT A BABY	2.00	3.50
☐3959		BABY BLUE/TRUE TO YOU	2.00	3.50
☐4010		ROCKY ROAD BLUES/YES, I LOVE YOU BABY	2.00	3.50
☐4051		LITTLE LOVER/GIT IT	2.00	3.50
☐4105		BE BOP BOOGIE BABY/SAY MAMA	2.00	3.50
☐4153		WHO'S PUSHIN' YOUR SWING?/OVER THE RAINBOW	2.00	3.50
☐4237		RIGHT NOW/THE NIGHT IS SO LONELY	2.00	3.50
☐4313		WILD CAT/RIGHT HERE ON EARTH	2.00	3.50
☐4442		ANNA-ANNABELLE/PISTOL PACKIN' MAMA	2.00	3.50
☐4525		IF YOU WANT MY LOVIN'/MISTER LONELINESS	2.00	3.50
☐4665		LUCKY STAR/BABY DON'T BELIEVE HIM	2.00	3.50
		GENE VINCENT—EPs		
☐1-764	*CAPITOL*	BLUEJEAN BOP	7.00	12.00
☐2-764		BLUEJEAN BOP	7.00	12.00
☐3-764		BLUEJEAN BOP	7.00	12.00
☐1-811		GENE VINCENT AND HIS BLUE CAPS	7.00	12.00
☐2-811		GENE VINCENT AND HIS BLUE CAPS	7.00	12.00
☐3-811		GENE VINCENT AND HIS BLUE CAPS	7.00	12.00
☐1-970		GENE VINCENT ROCKS	7.00	12.00
☐2-970		GENE VINCENT ROCKS	7.00	12.00
☐3-970		GENE VINCENT ROCKS	7.00	12.00
☐985		HOT ROD GANG (soundtrack)	12.00	20.00
☐1-1059		A GENE VINCENT RECORD DATE	7.00	12.00
☐2-1059		A GENE VINCENT RECORD DATE	7.00	12.00
☐3-1059		A GENE VINCENT RECORD DATE	7.00	12.00
		GENE VINCENT—ALBUMS		
☐764 (M)	*CAPITOL*	BLUEJEAN BOP	25.00	40.00
☐811 (M)		GENE VINCENT AND HIS BLUE CAPS	20.00	35.00
☐970 (M)		GENE VINCENT ROCKS AND THE BLUE CAPS ROLL	25.00	40.00
☐1059 (M)		A GENE VINCENT RECORD DATE	25.00	40.00
☐1207 (M)		SOUNDS LIKE GENE VINCENT	18.00	30.00
☐1342 (M)		CRAZY TIMES	18.00	30.00
		BOBBY VINTON		
☐50	*ALPINE*	YOU'LL NEVER FORGET/FIRST IMPRESSION	3.00	5.00
☐59		THE SHIEK/A FRESHMAN AND A SOPHOMORE	3.00	5.00
☐121	*DIAMOND*	I LOVE YOU THE WAY YOU ARE/ YOU'RE MY GIRL (38)	1.50	3.00
☐9417	*EPIC*	TORNADO/POSIN'	1.50	2.50
☐9440		CORRINA, CORRINA/LITTLE LOVELY ONE	1.50	2.50
☐9469		WELL, I ASK YA/HIP-SWINGING, HIGH-STEPPING DRUM MAJORETTE	1.50	2.50

LATER EPIC SINGLES ARE WORTH UP TO $1.50 MINT

ISSUE #	LABEL	ARTIST/TITLE	VG	MINT
		VIRTUES		
□ 501	*SURE*	GUITAR BOOGIE SHUFFLE/GUITAR IN ORBIT	4.00	7.00
□ 1733		GUITAR BOOGIE SHUFFLE TWIST/ GUITAR BOOGIE STOMP (96)	1.75	3.00
□ 1779		TELSTAR GUITAR/JERSEY BOUNCE	1.75	3.00
□ 324	*HUNT*	GUITAR BOOGIE SHUFFLE/GUITAR IN ORBIT (5)	1.50	3.00
□ 327		SHUFFLIN' ALONG/FLIPPIN' IN	1.50	2.50
□ 328		VIRTUES' BOOGIE WOOGIE/PICKIN' THE STROLL	1.50	2.50
		VIRTUES—ALBUM		
□ 1061 (M)	*STRAND*	GUITAR BOOGIE SHUFFLE	6.00	10.00
□ 1061 (S)		GUITAR BOOGIE SHUFFLE	7.00	12.00
		VISCOUNTS		
□ 123	*MADISON*	HARLEM NOCTURNE/DIG (52)	1.50	2.50
□ 129		CHUG-A-LUG/THE TOUCH	1.75	2.50
□ 133		NIGHT TRAIN/SUMMERTIME (82)	1.50	2.50
□ 140		WABASH BLUES/SO SLOW (77)	1.50	2.50
□ 940	*AMY*	HARLEM NOCTURNE/DIG (30)	1.25	2.00
□ 949		NIGHT TRAIN/WHEN THE SAINTS GO MARCHING IN	1.25	2.00
		VISCOUNTS—ALBUMS		
□ 1001 (M)	*MADISON*	THE VISCOUNTS	7.00	12.00
□ 8008 (M)	*AMY*	HARLEM NOCTURNE	3.50	6.00
□ 8008 (S)		HARLEM NOCTURNE	4.50	8.00
		VITO AND THE SALUTATIONS		
□ 5002	*KRAN*	YOUR WAY/HEY, HEY BABY	7.00	12.00
□ 583	*HERALD*	UNCHAINED MELODY/HEY, HEY BABY (66)	1.50	3.50
□ 586		EENIE MEENIE/EXTRAORDINARY GIRL	2.50	4.00
□ 5009	*RAYNA*	GLORIA/LET'S UNTWIST THE TWIST	3.50	6.00
□ 1001	*RED BOY*	SO WONDERFUL (MY LOVE)/I'D BEST BE GOING	2.00	3.50
□ 103	*SANDBAG*	SO WONDERFUL (MY LOVE)/I'D BEST BE GOING	1.75	3.00
		VOGUES		
□ 15798	*DOT*	LOVE'S A FUNNY LITTLE GAME/ WHICH WITCH DOCTOR	2.00	3.50
□ 15859		FALLING STAR/TRY, BABY, TRY	1.75	3.00
		VOGUES		
□ 1029	*ASTRA*	YOU'RE THE ONE/GOODNIGHT MY LOVE	6.00	10.00
□ 229	*BLUE STAR*	YOU'RE THE ONE/SOME WORDS	4.00	7.00
□ 229	*CO & CE*	YOU'RE THE ONE/SOME WORDS (4)	.75	1.50
		LATER CO & CE SINGLES ARE WORTH UP TO $1.50 MINT.		
		VOGUES—ALBUM		
□ 1229 (M)	*CO & CE*	YOU'RE THE ONE	3.00	5.00
□ 1229 (S)		YOU'RE THE ONE	4.00	7.00

W

ISSUE #	LABEL	ARTIST/TITLE	VG	MINT
		WAILERS		
☐518	***GOLDEN CREST***	TALL COOL ONE/ROAD RUNNER (36) (1959-photo on label)	1.50	3.00
☐518		TALL COOL ONE/ROAD RUNNER (38) (1964-plain label)	1.00	2.00
☐526		MAU MAU/DIRTY ROBBER (68)	1.50	2.50
☐532		WAILIN'/SHANGHIED	1.25	2.00
☐545		SCRATCHIN'/LUCILLE	1.25	2.00
		WAILERS—ALBUM		
☐3075 (M)	***GOLDEN CREST***	THE FABULOUS WAILERS	7.00	12.00
		WALKER BROTHERS		
☐1952	***SMASH***	PRETTY GIRLS EVERYWHERE/DOIN' THE JERK	1.50	2.50
☐1976		SEVENTH DAWN/LOVE HER	1.50	2.50
☐2000		MKAE IT EASY ON YOURSELF/DO THE JERK	1.50	2.50
☐2009		MAKE IT EASY ON YOURSELF/BUT I DO (16)	1.00	2.00
☐2016		MY SHIP IS COMIN' IN/ YOU'RE ALL AROUND ME (63)	1.25	2.00
☐2032		THE SUN AIN'T GONNA SHINE (ANYMORE)/ AFTER THE LIGHTS GO OUT (13)	1.00	2.00
☐2048		YOU DON'T HAVE TO TELL ME BABY/ THE YOUNG MAN CRIED	1.25	2.00
☐2063		ANOTHER TEAR FALLS/SADDEST NIGHT IN THE WORLD	1.25	2.00
		WALKER BROTHERS—ALBUMS		
☐27076 (M)	***SMASH***	INTRODUCING THE WALKER BROTHERS	3.50	6.00
☐67076 (S)		INTRODUCING THE WALKER BROTHERS	4.50	8.00
☐27082 (M)		THE SUN AIN'T GONNA SHINE ANYMORE	3.00	5.00
☐67082 (S)		THE SUN AIN'T GONNA SHINE ANYMORE	4.00	7.00
		JERRY WALLACE		
☐1003	***CHALLENGE***	BLUE JEAN BABY/FOOL'S HALL OF FAME	2.50	4.00
☐59000		THE OTHER ME/GOOD AND BAD	2.00	3.50
☐59013		HOW THE TIME FLIES/WITH THIS RING (11)	1.75	3.00
☐59027		DIAMOND RING/ALL MY LOVE BELONGS TO YOU (78)	1.75	3.00
☐59040		A TOUCH OF PINK/OFF STAGE (92)	1.75	3.00
☐59047		PRIMROSE LANE/BY YOUR SIDE (8)	1.25	2.50
☐59060		LITTLE COCO PALM/MISSION BELL BLUES (36)	1.50	2.50
☐59072		KING OF THE MOUNTAIN/YOU'RE SINGING OUR LOVE SONG TO SOMEONE ELSE	1.75	2.50
☐59082		SWINGIN' DOWN THE LANE/ TEARDROPS IN THE RAIN (79)	1.50	2.50
☐59098		THERE SHE GOES/ANGEL ON MY SHOULDER (26)	1.25	2.00
☐9107		LIFE'S A HOLIDAY/I CAN SEE AN ANGEL WALKING (91)	1.25	2.00
		LATER CHALLENGE SINGLES ARE WORTH UP TO $2.00 MINT		
		JERRY WALLACE—EPs		
☐7103	***CHALLENGE***	JERRY WALLACE	3.00	5.00
☐7104		THERE SHE GOES	3.00	5.00

ISSUE #	LABEL	ARTIST/TITLE	VG	MINT
		JERRY WALLACE—ALBUMS		
☐606 (M)	*CHALLENGE*	JUST JERRY	7.00	12.00
☐612 (M)		THERE SHE GOES	5.00	8.00
☐612 (S)		THERE SHE GOES	6.00	10.00
		BILLY WARD AND HIS DOMINOES		
☐55071	*LIBERTY*	STAR DUST/LUCINDA (13)	1.50	3.00
☐55099		DEEP PURPLE/DO IT AGAIN (22)	1.75	3.00
☐55111		SOMEONE GREATER THAN I/ MY PROUDEST POSSESSION	1.50	2.50
☐55126		SWEETER AS THE YEARS GO BY/SOLITUDE	1.50	2.50
☐55136		JENNIE LEE/MUSIC, MAESTRO, PLEASE (55)	1.50	3.00
☐55181		PLEASE DON'T SAY NO/BEHAVE, HULA GIRL	1.50	2.50
		BILLY WARD AND HIS DOMINOES—EPs		
☐1-3056	*LIBERTY*	SEA OF GLASS	3.00	5.00
☐2-3056		SEA OF GLASS	3.00	5.00
☐3-3056		SEA OF GLASS	3.00	5.00
☐1-2083		YOURS FOREVER	2.50	4.00
☐2-2083		YOURS FOREVER	2.50	4.00
☐3-3083		YOURS FOREVER	2.50	4.00
		BILLY WARD AND HIS DOMINOS—ALBUMS		
☐3056 (M)	*LIBERTY*	SEA OF GLASS	7.00	12.00
☐3083 (M)		YOURS FOREVER	6.00	10.00
		DALE WARD		
☐16520	*DOT*	LETTER FROM SHERRY/OH JULIE (25)	1.50	2.50
☐16590		CRYING FOR LAURA/I'VE GOT A GIRL FRIEND	1.75	2.50
☐16632		I'LL NEVER LOVE AGAIN/ YOUNG LOVERS AFTER MIDNIGHT	1.75	2.50
☐16672		ONE LAST KISS, CHERIE/THE FORTUNE	1.75	2.50
☐118	*BOYD*	BIG DALE TWIST/HERE'S YOUR HAT	1.75	3.00
☐150		SHAKE, RATTLE AND ROLL/YOU GOTTA LET ME KNOW	1.75	3.00
☐152		LIVING ON COAL/I TRIED	1.75	3.00
		ROBIN WARD		
☐37	*SONGS UNLIMITED*	LOSER'S LULLABY/LOLLY TOO DUM	1.75	3.00
☐16530	*DOT*	WONDERFUL SUMMER/DREAM BOY (14)	1.00	2.00
☐16578		BOBBY/WINTER'S HERE	1.25	2.00
☐16599		JOHNNY, COME AND GET ME/ WHERE THE BLUE MEETS THE GOLD	1.25	2.00
☐16624		IN HIS CAR/WISHING	1.25	2.00
		ROBIN WARD—ALBUM		
☐3555 (M)	*DOT*	WONDERFUL SUMMER	3.50	6.00
☐25555 (S)		WONDERFUL SUMMER	4.50	8.00
		THOMAS WAYNE		
☐109	*FERNWOOD*	TRAGEDY/SATURDAY DATE (5)	1.50	3.00
☐111		ETERNALLY/SCANDALIZING MY NAME (92)	1.50	2.50
☐113		GONNA BE WAITIN'/JUST BEYOND	1.50	2.50
☐122		THE GIRL NEXT DOOR/BECAUSE OF YOU	1.50	2.50
☐71454	*MERCURY*	YOU'RE THE ONE THAT DONE IT/THIS TIME	8.00	15.00

ISSUE #	LABEL	ARTIST/TITLE	VG	MINT
		WE FIVE		
□770	*A & M*	YOU WERE ON MY MIND/SMALL WORLD (3)	.75	1.50
□784		LET'S GET TOGETHER/ CAST YOUR FATE TO THE WIND (31)	1.25	2.00
□793		SOMEWHERE BEYOND THE SEA/ YOU LET A LOVE BURN OUT	1.25	2.00
□800		SOMEWHERE/THERE STANDS THE DOOR	1.25	2.00
□820		HIGH-FLYING BIRD/WHAT DO I DO NOW?	1.25	2.00
		WE FIVE—ALBUMS		
□111 (M)	*A & M*	YOU WERE ON MY MIND	3.50	6.00
□4111 (S)		YOU WERE ON MY MIND	3.00	5.00
□138 (M)		MAKE SOMEONE HAPPY	3.50	6.00
□4138 (S)		MAKE SOMEONE HAPPY	3.00	5.00
		MARY WELLS		
□1003	*MOTOWN*	BYE BYE BABY/PLEASE FORGIVE ME (45)	2.00	3.50
□1011		I DON'T WANT TO TAKE A CHANCE/ I'M SO SORRY (33)	1.75	3.00
□1016		COME TO ME/STRANGE LOVE	1.75	3.00
□1024		THE ONE WHO REALLY LOVES YOU/ I'M GONNA STAY (8)	1.00	2.00
□1032		YOU BEAT ME TO THE PUNCH/OLD LOVE (9)	1.00	2.00
□1035		TWO LOVERS/OPERATOR (7)	.75	1.50
		LATER MOTOWN SINGLES ARE WORTH UP TO $1.50 MINT		
		MARY WELLS—ALBUMS		
□600 (M)	*MOTOWN*	BYE BYE BABY	7.00	12.00
□605 (M)		ONE WHO REALLY LOVES YOU	6.00	10.00
		IAN WHITCOMB		
□120	*TOWER*	THIS SPORTING LIFE/FIZZ (100)	1.75	3.00
□134		YOU TURN ME ON/POOR BUT HONEST (8)	1.00	2.50
□155		N-E-R-V-O-U-S/THE END (59)	1.50	2.50
□170		18 WHITCOMB STREET/FIZZ	1.00	2.00
□189		BE MY BABY/NO TEARS FOR JOHNNY	1.25	2.00
□192		HIGH BLOOD PRESSURE/GOOD HARD ROCK	1.25	2.00
□251		YOU WON'T SEE ME/ PLEASE DON'T LEAVE ME ON THE SHELF	1.25	2.00
□274		WHERE DID ROBINSON CRUSOE GO WITH FRIDAY ON SATURDY NIGHT/POOR LITTLE BIRD	1.75	3.00
		IAN WHITCOMB—ALBUMS		
□5004 (M)	*TOWER*	YOU TURN ME ON	5.00	8.00
□5004 (S)		YOU TURN ME ON	6.00	10.00
□5042 (M)		IAN WHITCOMB'S MOD, MOD MUSIC HALL	3.50	6.00
□5042 (S)		IAN WHITCOMB'S MOD, MOD MUSIC HALL	4.50	8.00
		WHO		
		SEE: HIGH NUMBERS		
□31725	*DECCA*	I CAN'T EXPLAIN/BALD HEADED WOMAN (93)	2.00	3.50
□31801		ANYWAY, ANYWHERE, ANYHOW/ DADDY ROLLING STONE	3.00	5.00
□31801		ANYWAY, ANYWHERE, ANYHOW/ ANYTIME YOU WANT ME	3.00	5.00

ISSUE #	LABEL	ARTIST/TITLE	VG	MINT
□31877		MY GENERATION/OUT IN THE STREET (74)	1.75	3.00
□31988		THE KIDS ARE ALRIGHT/A LEGAL MATTER	2.00	3.50
□32058		I'M A BOY/IN THE CITY	2.00	3.50
□32114		HAPPY JACK/WHISKEY MAN (24)	1.25	2.50
□32156		PICTURES OF LILY/DOCTOR, DOCTOR (51)	1.50	2.50
□32206		I CAN SEE FOR MILES/ MARY-ANNE WITH THE SHAKEY HANDS (9)	1.00	2.00
□32288		CALL ME LIGHTNING/DR. JEKYLL AND MR. HYDE (40)	1.25	2.00
□32362		MAGIC BUS/SOMEONE'S CRYING (25)	1.00	2.00
□32465		PINBALL WIZARD/DOGS, PART 1 (19)	1.00	2.00
□32519		I'M FREE/WE'RE NOT GONNA TAKE IT (37)	1.25	2.00
□32670		THE SEEKER/HERE FOR MORE (44)	1.25	2.00
□32708		SUMMERTIME BLUES/HEAVEN AND HELL (27)	1.25	2.00
□32729		SEE ME, FEEL ME/OVERTURE FROM TOMMY (12)	1.00	2.00

LATER DECCA SINGLES ARE WORTH UP TO $1.50 MINT

WHO—ALBUMS

□4664 (M)	***DECCA***	THE WHO SINGS "MY GENERATION"	7.00	12.00
□4892 (M)		HAPPY JACK	6.00	10.00
□4950 (M)		THE WHO SELL OUT	6.00	10.00

LARRY WILLAIMS

□597	***SPECIALTY***	JUST BECAUSE/LET ME TELL YOU, BABY	2.50	4.00
□608		SHORT FAT FANNIE/HIGH SCHOOL DANCE (6)	1.50	3.00
□615		BONY MORONIE/YOU BUG ME BABY (18)	1.50	3.00
□626		DIZZY, MISS LIZZY/SLOW DOWN (69)	1.75	3.00

LARRY WILLIAMS—ALBUM

□2109 (M)	***SPECIALTY***	HERE'S LARRY WILLIAMS	8.00	15.00

MAURICE WILLIAMS AND THE ZODIACS

□552	***HERALD***	STAY/DO YOU REMEMBER (1)	1.25	2.50
□556		I REMEMBER/ALWAYS (86)	1.50	2.50
□559		COME ALONG/DO I (83)	1.50	2.50
□563		COME AND GET IT/SOMEDAY	1.50	2.50

CHUCK WILLIS

□1130	***ATLANTIC***	C. C. RIDER/EASE THE PAIN (12)	2.00	3.50
□1168		BETTY AND DUPREE/MY CRYING EYES (33)	2.50	3.50
□1179		WHAT AM I LIVING FOR/HANG UP MY ROCK AND ROLL SHOES (15)	2.00	3.50

CHUCK WILLIS—ALBUM

□8018 (M)	***ATLANTIC***	CHUCK WILLIS-THE KING OF THE STROLL	12.00	20.00

BRIAN WILSON

SEE: BEACH BOYS

□5610	***CAPITOL***	CAROLINE, NO/SUMMER MEANS NEW LOVE (32)	1.50	2.50

JACKIE WILSON

Born in Detroit, Michigan, on June 9, 1934, Jackie Wilson grew up listening to such r & b wailers as the great Roy Brown. At sixteen Wilson won the Golden Gloves award and set his sights on the boxing world. Three years later, though, he appeared at Detroit's Fox Theater one afternoon. Billy Ward was seeking a replacement for Clyde McPhatter, who had recently left Ward's group, the Dominoes. The brash Wilson stated that he was simply a better singer than Clyde—and belted out a soulful rocker to prove his point. Jackie Wilson was then hired on the spot.

He sang lead on the Dominoes' 1956 hit of "St. Therese Of the Roses", but a year later went on his own. He signed with Brunswick Records; his debut song for that label was the dynamic "Reet Petite". It had been composed by a struggling songwrither and former factory worker, Berry Gordy, Jr.

After a long string of hits, Wilson ended up touring as a headliner with Dick Clark's traveling oldies revue. In October of 1975, Jackie suffered a near-fatal heart attack onstage at the Latin Casino in Cherry Hill, New Jersey. He is now unable to communicate in any way and spends his days in a New Jersey convalescent hospital.

ISSUE #	LABEL	ARTIST/TITLE	VG	MINT
		JACKIE WILSON		
☐55024	***BRUNSWICK***	REET PETITE/BY THE LIGHT OF THE SILVERY MOON (62)	2.50	4.00
☐55052		TO BE LOVED/COME BACK TO ME (22)	2.00	3.50
☐55070		AS LONG AS I LIVE/I'M WANDERIN'	2.00	3.50
☐55086		WE HAVE LOVE/SINGING A SONG (93)	1.75	3.00
☐55105		LONELY TEARDROPS/ IN THE BLUE OF THE EVENING (7)	1.50	3.00
☐55121		THAT'S WHY/LOVE IS ALL (13)	1.50	3.00
☐55100		I'LL BE SATISFIED/ASK (20)	1.50	3.00
☐55149		YOU BETTER KNOW IT/NEVER GO AWAY (37)	1.50	2.50
☐55165		TALK THAT TALK/ONLY YOU AND ONLY ME (34)	1.50	2.50
☐55166		NIGHT/DOGGIN' AROUND (4)	1.25	2.50
☐55167		ALL MY LOVE/A WOMAN, A LOVER, A FRIEND (12)	1.25	2.50
☐55170		ALONE AT LAST/AM I THE MAN? (8)	1.25	2.50
☐55201		MY EMPTY ARMS/TEAR OF THE YEAR (9)	1.25	2.50
☐55208		PLEASE TELL ME WHY/ YOUR ONE AND ONLY LOVE (20)	1.25	2.00
☐55216		I'M COMING ON BACK TO YOU/LONELY LIFE (19)	1.25	2.00
☐55219		YEARS FROM NOW/ YOU DON'T KNOW WHAT IT MEANS (37)	1.25	2.00
☐55220		THE WAY I AM/ MY HEART BELONGS TO ONLY YOU (58)	1.25	2.00
☐55221		THE GREATEST HURT/ THERE'LL BE NO NEXT TIME (34)	1.25	2.00
☐55225		HEARTS/SING (58)	1.25	2.00
☐55229		I JUST CAN'T HELP IT/MY TALE OF WOE (70)	1.25	2.00
☐55233		FOREVER AND A DAY/BABY THAT'S ALL (82)	1.25	2.00
☐55239		BABY WORKOUT/I'M GOING CRAZY (5)	1.00	2.00
		LATER BRUNSWICK SINGLES ARE WORTH UP TO $2.00 MINT		
		JACKIE WILSON—EPs		
☐71040	***BRUNSWICK***	THE VERSATILE JACKIE WILSON	4.00	7.00
☐71042		JUMPIN' JACK	3.50	6.00
☐71045		THAT'S WHY	3.50	6.00
☐71046		TALK THAT TALK	3.50	6.00
☐71047		MR. EXCITEMENT	3.50	6.00
☐71048		JACKIE WILSON	3.00	5.00
☐71049		JACKIE WILSON	3.00	5.00
		JACKIE WILSON—ALBUMS		
☐54042 (M)	***BRUNSWICK***	HE'S SO FINE	12.00	20.00
☐54045 (M)		LONELY TEARDROPS	8.00	15.00
☐54050 (M)		SO MUCH	5.00	8.00
☐754050 (S)		SO MUCH	6.00	10.00
☐54058 (M)		MY GOLDEN FAVORITES	5.00	8.00
☐754058 (S)		MY GOLDEN FAVORITES	6.00	10.00
		J. FRANK WILSON		
☐722	***LE CAM***	LAST KISS/CARLA	6.00	10.00
☐761	***TAMLA***	LAST KISS/THAT'S HOW MUCH I LOVE YOU	5.00	8.00

(LE CAM AND TAMARA VERSIONS OF "LAST KISS" ARE DIFFERENT)

ISSUE #	LABEL	ARTIST/TITLE	VG	MINT
☐ 923	*JOSIE*	LAST KISS/THAT'S HOW MUCH I LOVE YOU (2)	1.25	2.50
☐ 926		HEY LITTLE ONE/SPEAK TO ME (85)	1.50	2.50
☐ 929		SIX BOYS/SAY IT NOW	1.50	2.50
☐ 931		DREAMS OF A FOOL/OPEN YOUR EYES	1.50	2.50

J. FRANK WILSON—ALBUM

☐ 4006 (M)	*JOSIE*	LAST KISS	5.00	8.00
☐ 4006 (S)		LAST KISS	6.00	10.00

WIND
FEATURED: TONY ORLANDO

☐ 200	*LIFE*	MAKE BELIEVE/GROOVIN' WITH MR. BLOE (28)....	1.50	3.00
☐ 202		TEENY BOPPER/I'LL HOLD OUT MY HAND	2.50	4.00

WIND—ALBUM

☐ 20000 (S)	*LIFE*	MAKE BELIEVE..........................	6.00	10.00

(LITTLE) STEVIE WONDER

☐ 54061	*TAMLA*	I CALL IT PRETTY MUSIC (BUT OLD PEOPLE CALL IT THE BLUES) (PT. 1)/(PT. 11)	3.50	6.00
☐ 54070		LA LA LA LA LA/LITTLE WATER BOY.............	3.00	5.00
☐ 54074		CONTRACT ON LOVE/SUNSET.................	3.00	5.00
☐ 54080		FINGERTIPS (PT. 1)/(PT. 11) (1)	1.25	2.50
☐ 54086		WORKOUT STEVIE, WORKOUT/MONKEY TALK (33) .	1.50	2.50
☐ 54090		CASTLES IN THE SAND/TO THANK YOU (52)	1.50	2.50
☐ 54096		HEY HARMONICA MAN/THIS LITTLE GIRL (29)	1.50	2.50
☐ 54103		SAD BOY/HAPPY STREET	1.75	3.00
☐ 54114		TEARS IN VAIN/KISS ME, BABY	1.75	3.00
☐ 54119		HIGH HEEL SNEAKERS/MUSIC NOTES (59)	1.50	2.50
☐ 54124		UPTIGHT (EVERYTHING'S ALRIGHT)/ PURPLE RAINDROPS (3).....................	1.25	2.00

LATER TAMLA SINGLES ARE WORTH UP TO $2.00 MINT
(LITTLE) STEVIE WONDER—ALBUMS

☐ 232 (M)	*TAMLA*	TRIBUTE TO UNCLE RAY	7.00	12.00
☐ 233 (M)		JAZZ SOUL................................	7.00	12.00
☐ 240 (M)		THE 12-YEAR-OLD GENIUS	6.00	10.00
☐ 248 (M)		WORKOUT STEVIE, WORKOUT.................	5.00	8.00
☐ 268 (M)		UPTIGHT	4.00	7.00

LINK WRAY
FEATURED: WRAYMEN

☐ 1347	*CADENCE*	RUMBLE/THE SWAG (16)	1.75	3.50
☐ 9300	*EPIC*	RAW-HIDE/DIXIE DOODLE (23)	1.75	3.00
☐ 9321		COMANCHE/LILLIAN.........................	1.50	2.50
☐ 9343		SLINKY/RENDEZVOUS	1.50	2.50
☐ 9419		AIN'T THAT LOVIN' YOU BABY/MARY ANN	1.50	2.50
☐ 1000	*RUMBLE*	JACK THE RIPPER/THE STRANGER	3.50	6.00
☐ 4137	*SWAN*	JACK THE RIPPER/THE BLACK WIDOW (64)	1.75	2.50
☐ 4154		TURNPIKE U.S.A./WEEKEND	1.50	2.50
☐ 4163		RUN CHICKEN RUN/THE SWEEPER..............	1.50	2.50

LINK WRAY—ALBUMS

☐ 3661 (M)	*EPIC*	LINK WRAY AND HIS WRAYMEN	12.00	20.00
☐ 510 (M)	*SWAN*	JACK THE RIPPER	8.00	15.00

ISSUE #	LABEL	ARTIST/TITLE	VG	MINT
		YARDBIRDS		
		SEE: LED ZEPPELIN, KEITH RELF		
☐9709	*EPIC*	I WISH YOU WOULD/A CERTAIN GIRL	7.00	12.00
☐9709		I WISH YOU WOULD/I AIN'T GOT YOU	7.00	12.00
☐9790		FOR YOUR LOVE/GOT TO HURRY (6)	1.50	3.00
☐9823		HEART FULL OF SOUL/STEELED BLUES (9)	1.50	3.00
☐9857		I'M A MAN/STILL I'M SAD (17)	1.75	3.00
☐9891		SHAPES OF THINGS/I'M NOT TALKING	3.50	6.00
☐10006		SHAPES OF THINGS/NEW YORK CITY BLUES (11)	1.50	3.00
☐10006		SHAPES OF THINGS/ YOU'RE A BETTER MAN THAN I (11)	1.50	3.00
☐10035		OVER UNDER SIDEWAYS DOWN/JEFF'S BOOGIE (13)	1.50	3.00
☐10094		HAPPENINGS TEN YEARS TIME AGO/ THE NAZZ ARE BLUE (30)	1.75	3.50
☐10094		HAPPENINGS TEN YEARS TIME AGO/ PSYCHO DAISIES (30)	1.75	3.50
☐10156		LITTLE GAMES/PUZZLES (51)	2.00	3.50
☐10204		HA HA SAID THE CLOWN/ TINKER, TAILOR, SOLDIER, SAILOR (45)	2.00	3.50
☐10248		TEN LITTLE INDIANS/DRINKIN' MUDDY WATER (96)	2.50	4.00
☐10303		GOODNIGHT SWEET JOSEPHINE/THINK ABOUT IT	3.00	5.00
		YARDBIRDS—ALBUMS		
☐24167 (M)	*EPIC*	FOR YOUR LOVE	6.00	10.00
☐26167 (S)		FOR YOUR LOVE	7.00	12.00
☐24177 (M)		HAVING A RAVE-UP WITH THE YARDBIRDS	6.00	10.00
☐26177 (S)		HAVING A RAVE-UP WITH THE YARDBIRDS	7.00	12.00
☐24210 (M)		OVER UNDER SIDEWAYS DOWN	6.00	10.00
☐26210 (S)		OVER UNDER SIDEWAYS DOWN	7.00	12.00
☐24313 (M)		LITTLE GAMES	7.00	12.00
☐26313 (S)		LITTLE GAMES	8.00	15.00
☐30615 (S)		LIVE YARDBIRDS FEATURING JIMMY PAGE	15.00	25.00
		YELLOW BALLOON		
		PRODUCER: DEAN TORRENCE		
☐508	*CANTERBURY*	YELLOW BALLOON/NOOLLAB WOLLEY (25)	1.25	2.00
		YELLOW BALLOON—ALBUM		
☐1502 (M)	*CANTERBURY*	THE YELLOW BALLOON	6.00	10.00
		RUSTY YORK		
☐100	*P. J.*	SUGAREE/RED ROOSTER	5.00	8.00
☐10021	*NOTE*	SUGAREE/RED ROOSTER	3.00	5.00
☐1730	*CHESS*	SUGAREE/RED ROOSTER (77)	2.50	4.00

KATHY YOUNG

During the summer of 1960 Wink Martindale (then a Los Angeles disc jockey) broadcast a live dance show every Saturday night from an oceanfront amusement park. One night a fifteen-year-old Long Beach school-girl named Kathy Young approached Wink and asked him how she might go about making a record. Wink suggested she look up his friend Jim Lee, the head of a small Los Angeles record label called Indigo.

Lee had signed another group—the Innocents—to his label, and they had scored a Top 30 winner with the haunting ballad "Honest I Do". Jim was impressed with Kathy Young when she auditioned, so he decided to team her up with the Innocents. The result was a million-selling "cover" of the Rivileers' "A Thousand Stars" in the fall of 1960.

Born in Long Beach on October 21, 1945, Kathy often sang at parties and school talent shows and assemblies. She eventually gained enough confidence to seek a recording contract. After "A Thousand Stars" faded, Kathy hit the Top 30 with "Happy Birthday Blues". Her last Indigo chart hit—and probably her best single ever— was "Magic Is the Night".

ISSUE #	LABEL	ARTIST/TITLE	VG	MINT
		KATHY YOUNG		
		FEATURED: INNOCENTS		
☐ 108	*INDIGO*	A THOUSAND STARS/EDDIE MY DARLING (3)	1.25	2.50
☐ 115		HAPPY BIRTHDAY BLUES/SOMEONE TO LOVE (30)	1.50	2.50
☐ 121		OUR PARENTS TALKED IT OVER/JUST AS	1.75	3.00
☐ 125		MAGIC IS THE NIGHT/DU DU'NT DU (80)	1.50	3.00
☐ 127		BABY OH BABY/THE GREAT PRETENDER	1.75	3.00
☐ 146		LONELY BLUE NIGHTS/		
		I'LL HANG MY LETTERS OUT TO DRY	1.75	3.00
☐ 147		DREAM AWHILE/SEND HER AWAY	1.75	3.00
☐ 506	*MONOGRAM*	DREAM BOY/I'LL LOVE THAT MAN	1.75	3.00
☐ 517		ALL YOU HAD TO TO (WAS TELL ME)/		
		LOVE ME (with Chris Montez)	1.75	3.00
		KATHY YOUNG—EP		
☐ 1001	*INDIGO*	KATHY YOUNG	5.00	8.00
		KATHY YOUNG—ALBUM		
☐ 504 (M)	*INDIGO*	THE SOUND OF KATHY YOUNG	7.00	12.00
		YOUNGTONES		
☐ 104	*X-TRA*	IT'S OVER NOW/YOU I ADORE	15.00	25.00
☐ 110		BY THE CANDLEGLOW/PATRICIA	15.00	25.00
☐ 120		CAN I COME OVER?/GONNA GET TOGETHER AGAIN	15.00	25.00
		TIMI YURO		
☐ 55343	*LIBERTY*	HURT/I APOLOGIZE (4)	1.00	2.50
☐ 55375		SMILE/SHE REALLY LOVES YOU (42)	1.25	2.00
☐ 55410		LET ME CALL YOU SWEETHEART/		
		SATAN NEVER SLEEPS (66)	1.25	2.00
☐ 55432		COUNT EVERYTHING/I KNOW	1.25	2.00
☐ 55469		WHAT'S A MATTER BABY/THIRTEENTH HOUR (12)	.75	1.50
☐ 55519		THE LOVE OF A BOY/I AIN'T GONNA CRY NO MORE (44)	1.25	2.00
☐ 55552		INSULT TO INJURY/JUST ABOUT THE TIME (81)	1.00	1.50
☐ 55587		MAKE THE WORLD GO AWAY/LOOK DOWN (24)	.75	1.50
☐ 55634		GOTTA TRAVEL ON/DOWN IN THE VALLEY (64)	1.00	1.50
		TIMI YURO—ALBUMS		
☐ 3208 (M)	*LIBERTY*	HURT	3.50	6.00
☐ 7208 (S)		HURT	4.50	8.00
☐ 3263 (M)		WHAT'S A MATTER BABY	3.00	5.00
☐ 7263 (S)		WHAT'S A MATTER BABY	4.00	7.00
☐ 3286 (M)		THE BEST OF TIMI YURO	3.00	5.00
☐ 7286 (S)		THE BEST OF TIMI YURO	4.00	7.00

ISSUE #	LABEL	ARTIST/TITLE	VG	MINT
		JOHN ZACHERLE		
☐ 130	*CAMEO*	DINNER WITH DRAC (PT. 1)/(PT. 11) (6)	1.25	3.00
☐ 139		LUNCH WITH MOTHER GOOSE/82 TOMBSTONES	1.75	3.00
☐ 145		I WAS A TEENAGE CAVEMAN/DUMMY DOLL	1.75	3.00
☐ 853	*PARKWAY*	DINNER WITH DRAC/HURRY BURY HURRY	1.50	2.50

ISSUE #	LABEL	ARTIST/TITLE	VG	MINT
☐45013	***ELEKTRA***	COOLEST LITTLE MONSTER/ RING-A-DING ORANGOUTANG	2.00	3.50
		JOHN ZACHERLE—ALBUMS		
☐7018 (M)	***PARKWAY***	MONSTER MASH	7.00	12.00
☐7023 (M)		SCARY TALES	6.00	10.00
☐190 (M)	***ELEKTRA***	SPOOK ALONG WITH ZACHERLE	4.00	7.00
☐7190 (S)		SPOOK ALONG WITH ZACHERLE	5.00	9.00
		ZAGER AND EVANS		
☐8082	***TRUTH***	IN THE YEAR 2525/LITTLE KIDS	4.00	7.00
☐0174	***RCA***	IN THE YEAR 2525/LITTLE KIDS (1)	.75	1.50
		ZAGER AND EVANS—ALBUM		
☐1077 (S)	***RCA***	IN THE YEAR 2525	3.00	5.00
		ZANIES		
☐1080	***RCA***	THE BLOB/DO YOU DIG ME, MR. PYGMY	5.00	8.00
☐509	***DORE***	THE BLOB/DO YOU DIG ME, MR. PYGMY	3.00	5.00
		FRANK ZAPPA		
		SEE: BABY RAY AND THE FERNS, BOB GUY, MOTHER OF INVENTION, RON ROMAN, RUBEN AND THE JETS		
☐889	***BIZARRE***	LITTLE UMBRELLAS/PEACHES EN REGALIA	1.75	3.00
☐967		WOULD YOU GO ALL THE WAY FOR THE U.S.A./ TELL ME YOU LOVE ME	1.75	3.00
☐58057	***UNITED ARTISTS***	MAGIC FINGERS/ DADDY, DADDY, DADDY	1.75	3.00
☐1312	***DISCREET***	DON'T EAT THE YELLOW SNOW/COSMIK DEBRIS (86)	3.00	5.00
☐214		SHE'S MINE/BICYCLE RIDE	3.00	5.00
☐215		DON'T MISS THE BOAT/YES MY LOVE	3.00	5.00
☐5006	***ROTATE***	THERE'S SOMETHING ABOUT YOU/SHE'S LOST YOU	3.00	5.00
☐5009		WONDER WHAT I'M GONNA DO/ LET ME LOVE YOU BABY	3.00	5.00
		BEN ZEPPA		
☐577	***SPECIALTY***	A FOOLISH FOOL/BABY I NEED (TING A LING)	6.00	10.00
☐278	***TOP (EP)***	WHY DO FOOLS FALL IN LOVE (+ various artists and songs)	5.00	8.00
		ZOMBIES		
☐9695	***PARROT***	SHE'S NOT THERE/YOU MAKE ME FEEL SO GOOD (2)	1.25	2.50
☐9723		TELL HER NO/LEAVE ME BE (6)	1.25	2.50
☐9747		SHE'S COMING HOME/I MUST MOVE (58)	1.50	2.50
☐9769		I WANT YOU BACK AGAIN/ONCE UPON A TIME (95)	1.75	3.00
☐9797		JUST OUT OF REACH/REMEMBER YOU	1.75	3.00
☐9821		DON'T GO AWAY/IS THIS THE DREAM?	1.75	3.00
☐3004		HOW WE WERE BEFORE/INDICATION	1.75	3.00
☐1604	***DATE***	TIME OF THE SEASON/I'LL CALL YOU MINE	1.75	3.00
☐1612		THIS WILL BE YOUR YEAR/BUTCHER'S TALE	1.50	2.50
☐1628		TIME OF THE SEASON/FRIENDS OF MINE (3)	1.00	2.00
☐1644		CONVERSATION ON FLORAL STREET/ IMAGINE THE SWAN	1.25	2.00
☐1648		IF IT DON'T WORK OUT/DON'T CRY FOR ME	1.25	2.00
		ZOMBIES—ALBUMS		
☐61001 (M)	***PARROT***	ZOMBIES	5.00	8.00
☐4013 (S)	***DATE***	ODYSSEY AND ORACLE	3.50	6.00

SUN RECORDS

It was located at the corner of Union and Marshall Avenues and was partially obscured by a used-car lot. The brick-covered Memphis studios was owned and operated by Sam Phillips, a high school dropout and former Southern disc jockey with an uncanny business sense and an ear for what would sell. Phillips' motto over the sign of MEMPHIS RECORDING SERVICE was "We Record Anything-Anywhere-Anytime."

The number of future country, rockabilly and rock-and-roll stars who passed through the whitewashed doors at 706 Union Avenue stands as a tribute to Phillips' sense of talent. Conway Twitty, David Houston and Charlie Rich began their careers at Sun, as did the fabled Jerry Lee Lewis, Johnny Cash, Carl Perkins and Roy Orbison. And Sun Records is where Elvis Aaron Presley walked in one summer day during his lunch hour and paid $4.00 to cut a single of "That's When Your Heartaches Begin" as a surprise gift for his mother, Gladys. That disc, undoubtedly locked away in the Presley family archives, would stand as the world's most prized rock-and-roll collection item. Its value: priceless.

An obscure building with an 18' X 30' studio, Sun Records is without question the most significant independent label of the 1950s. The musical contributions from this small outfit cannot be fully appreciated until one surveys the impressive roster of artists and discs that emerged from that tiny building in a sleazy area of Memphis, Tennessee.

SUN RECORDS SINGLES DISCOGRAPHY

ISSUE #	LABEL	ARTIST/TITLE	VG	MINT
		JACKIE BOY AND LITTLE WALTER		
☐174		SELLIN' MY WHISKEY/BLUES IN MY CONDITION...	80.00	150.00
		(KNOWN ONLY TO EXIST ON ACETATE)		
		JOHNNY LONDON		
☐175		DRIVIN' SLOW/FLAT TIRE	30.00	50.00
		WALTER BRADFORD AND THE BIG CITY FOUR		
☐176		DREARY NIGHT/NUTHIN' BUT THE BLUES	40.00	70.00
		HANDY JACKSON		
☐177		GOT MY APPLICATION BABY/ TROUBLE (WILL BRING YOU DOWN)	30.00	50.00
		JOE HILL LOUIS		
☐178		WE ALL GOTTA GO SOMETIME/SHE MAY BE YOURS	30.00	50.00
		WILLIE NIX-THE MEMPHIS BLUES BOY		
☐179		SEEMS LIKE A MILLION YEARS/BARBER SHOP BOOGIE	25.00	40.00
		(THE FIRST SIX SUN SINGLES WERE PRESSED ONLY ON 78 RPM)		
		JIMMY AND WALTER		
☐180		EASY/BEFORE LONG	60.00	100.00
		RUFUS "HOUND DOG" THOMAS, JR.		
☐181		BEARCAT (THE ANSWER TO HOUND DOG)/ WALKIN' IN THE RAIN	15.00	25.00
		(LATER PRESSINGS OMITTED "THE ANSWER TO HOUND DOG")		
		DUSTY BROOKS AND HIS TONES		
☐182		TEARS AND WINE/HEAVEN OR FIRE	20.00	35.00
		D. A. HUNT		
☐183		LONESOME OL' JAIL/GREYHOUND BLUES	150.00	250.00
		(NOT KNOWN IF 45 RPM EXISTS; 78 PRICE WOULD BE HALF OF ABOVE)		
		BIG MEMPHIS MARAINEY-ONZIE HORNE COMBO		
☐184		CALL ME ANYTHING BUT CALL ME/NO MEANS NO	75.00	120.00
		JIMMY DEBERRY		
☐185		TAKE A LITTLE CHANCE/TIME HAS MADE A CHANGE	40.00	70.00
		PRISONAIRES		
☐186		JUST WALKIN' IN THE RAIN/BABY PLEASE	12.00	20.00
		LITTLE JUNIOR'S BLUE FLAMES		
☐187		FEELIN' GOOD/FUSSIN' AND FIGHTIN' BLUES	8.00	15.00
		RUFUS THOMAS, JR.		
☐188		TIGER MAN (KING OF THE JUNGLE)/ SAVE THAT MONEY	12.00	20.00
		PRISONAIRES		
☐189		MY GOD IS REAL/SOFTLY AND TENDERLY	8.00	15.00
		RIPLEY COTTON CHOPPERS		
☐190		SILVER BELLS/BLUES WALTZ	75.00	120.00
		("HILLBILLY" STAMPED IN RED ON LABEL)		

ISSUE #	LABEL	ARTIST/TITLE	VG	MINT
		PRISONAIRES		
☐191		A PRISONER'S PRAYER/I KNOW	18.00	30.00
		LITTLE JUNIOR'S BLUE FLAMES		
☐192		MYSTERY TRAIN/LOVE MY BABY	8.00	15.00
		DOCTOR ROSS		
☐193		COME BACK BABY/CHICAGO BREAKDOWN	30.00	50.00
		LITTLE MILTON		
☐194		BEGGIN' MY BABY/SOMEBODY TOLD ME	12.00	20.00
		BILLY "THE KID" EMERSON		
☐195		NO TEASING AROUND/IF LOVIN' IS BELIEVING	12.00	20.00
		HOT SHOT LOVE		
☐196		WOLF CALL BOOGIE/HARMONICA JAM	60.00	100.00
		EARL PETERSON-MICHIGAN'S SINGING COWBOY		
☐197		BOOGIE BLUES/IN THE DARK	15.00	25.00
		("HILLBILLY" STAMPED IN RED ON LABEL)		
		HOWARD SERATT		
☐198		TROUBLESOME WATERS/I MUST BE SAVED	75.00	120.00
		JAMES COTTON		
☐199		MY BABY/STRAIGTEN UP BABY	50.00	80.00
		LITTLE MILTON		
☐200		IF YOU LOVE ME/ALONE AND BLUE	15.00	25.00
		HARDROCK GUNTER		
☐201		GONNA DANCE ALL NIGHT/FALLEN ANGEL	75.00	120.00
		DOUG POINDEXTER AND STARLITE WRANGLERS		
☐202		MY KIND OF CARRYIN' ON/ NOW SHE CARES NO MORE FOR ME	60.00	100.00
		("HILLBILLY" STAMPED IN RED ON LABEL)		
		BILLY (THE KID) EMERSON		
☐203		I'M NOT GOING HOME/THE WOODCHUCK	25.00	40.00
		RAYMOND HILL		
☐204		BOURBON STREET JUMP/THE SNUGGLE	30.00	50.00
		HARMONICA FRANK		
☐205		ROCKIN' CHAIR DADDY/ THE GREAT MEDICAL MENAGERIST	125.00	200.00
		JAMES COTTON		
☐206		HOLD ME IN YOUR ARMS/COTTON CROP BLUES	60.00	100.00
		PRISONAIRES		
☐207		THERE IS LOVE IN YOU/WHAT'LL YOU DO NEXT	125.00	200.00
		BUDDY CUNNINGHAM		
☐208		RIGHT OR WRONG/WHO DO I CRY	25.00	40.00

ISSUE #	LABEL	ARTIST/TITLE	VG	MINT
		ELVIS PRESLEY-SCOTTY AND BILL		
☐209		THAT'S ALL RIGHT/BLUE MOON OF KENTUCKY	125.00	200.00
		ELVIS PRESLEY-SCOTTY AND BILL		
☐210		GOOD ROCKIN' TONIGHT/I DON'T CARE IF THE SUN DON'T SHINE	80.00	150.00
		MALCOLM YELVINGTON AND STAR RHYTHM BOYS		
☐211		DRINKIN' WINE SPODEE-O-DEE/ JUST ROLLING ALONG	12.00	20.00
		DOCTOR ROSS		
☐212		THE BOOGIE DISEASE/JUKE BOX BOOGIE	60.00	100.00
		THE JONES BROTHERS		
☐213		EVERY NIGHT/LOOK TO JESUS	125.00	200.00
		(NOT KNOWN IF 45 RPM EXISTS; 78 PRICES WOULD BE LESS THAN HALF THAN THOSE LISTED ABOVE)		
		BILLY (THE KID) EMERSON		
☐214		MOVE BABY MOVE/WHEN IT RAINS IT POURS	12.00	20.00
		ELVIS PRESLEY-SCOTTY AND BILL		
☐215		MILKCOW BLUES BOOGIE/YOU'RE A HEARTBREAKER	125.00	200.00
		SLIM RHODES		
☐216		DON'T BELIEVE/UNCERTAIN LOVE	12.00	20.00
		ELVIS PRESLEY-SCOTTY AND BILL		
☐217		BABY LET'S PLAY HOUSE/ I'M LEFT, YOU'RE RIGHT, SHE'S GONE	75.00	120.00
		SAMMY LEWIS-WILLIE JOHNSON COMBO		
☐218		SO LONG BABY/I FEEL SO WORRIED	6.00	10.00
		BILLY "THE KID" EMERSON		
☐219		RED HOT/NO GREATER LOVE	10.00	18.00
		LITTLE MILTON		
☐220		LOOKIN' FOR MY BABY/HOMESICK FOR MY BABY	35.00	60.00
		JOHNNY CASH AND THE TENNESSEE TWO		
☐221		HEY PORTER/CRY! CRY! CRY!	3.00	5.00
		THE FIVE TINOS		
☐222		SITTING BY MY WINDOW/DON'T DO THAT	80.00	150.00
		ELVIS PRESLEY-SCOTTY AND BILL		
☐223		MYSTERY TRAIN/I FORGOT TO REMEMBER TO FORGET	70.00	120.00
		CARL PERKINS		
☐224		LET THE JUKE BOX KEEP ON PLAYING/ GONE GONE GONE	20.00	35.00
		SLIM RHODES		
☐225		THE HOUSE OF SIN/ARE YOU ASHAMED OF ME	8.00	15.00
		EDDIE SNOW		
☐226		AIN'T THAT RIGHT/BRING YOU LOVE BACK HOME	12.00	20.00

ISSUE #	LABEL	ARTIST/TITLE	VG	MINT
		ROSCOE GORDON		
□ 227		JUST LOVE ME BABY/WEEPING BLUES	7.00	12.00
		(ALSO RELEASED ON FLIP 227 WITH SAME VALUE)		
		SMOKEY JOE		
□ 228		THE SIGNIFYING MONKEY/LISTEN TO ME BABY	6.00	10.00
		(ALSO RELEASED ON FLIP 228; DOUBLE VALUE FROM ABOVE)		
		MAGGIE SUE WIMBERLY		
□ 229		HOW LONG/DAYDREAMS COME TRUE	6.00	10.00
		THE MILLER SISTERS		
□ 230		THERE'S NO RIGHT WAY TO DO ME WRONG/ YOU CAN TELL ME	12.00	20.00
		(ALSO RELEASED ON FLIP 230 WITH SAME VALUE)		
		CHARLIE FEATHERS		
□ 231		DEFROST YOUR HEART/WEDDING GOWN OF WHITE	80.00	150.00
		(ALSO RELEASED ON FLIP 231 WITH SAME VALUE)		
		JOHNNY CASH		
□ 232		FOLSOM PRISON BLUES/SO DOGGONE LONESOME	2.50	4.00
		BILLY "THE KID" EMERSON		
□ 233		LITTLE FINE HEALTHY THING/ SOMETHING FOR NOTHING	4.00	7.50
		CARL PERKINS		
□ 234		BLUE SUEDE SHOES/HONEY DON'T (4)	2.00	4.00
		CARL PERKINS		
□ 235		SURE TO FALL/TENNESSEE		
		(UNISSUED)		
		JIMMY HAGGETT		
□ 236		NO MORE/THEY CALL OUR LOVE A SIN	125.00	200.00
		ROSCO GORDON		
□ 237		"THE CHICKEN" (DANCE WITH YOU)/ LOVE FOR YOU BABY	3.00	5.00
		(ALSO RELEASED ON FLIP 237 WITH SAME VALUE)		
		SLIM RHODES		
□ 238		GONNA ROMP AND STOMP/BAD GIRL	8.00	15.00
		WARREN SMITH		
□ 239		ROCK 'N' ROLL RUBY/ I'D RATHER BE SAFE THAN SORRY	6.00	10.00
		JACK EARLS AND THE JIMBOS		
□ 240		SLOW DOWN/A FOOL FOR LOVIN' YOU	8.00	15.00
		JOHNNY CASH AND THE TENNESSEE TWO		
□ 241		I WALK THE LINE/GET RHYTHM (19)	1.75	3.00
		ROY ORBISON AND THE TEEN KINGS		
□ 242		OOBY DOOBY/GO, GO, GO (59)	5.00	8.00

ISSUE #	LABEL	ARTIST/TITLE	VG	MINT
		CARL PERKINS		
☐243		BOPPIN' THE BLUES/ALL MAMA'S CHILDREN (70)	2.50	4.00
		JEAN CHAPEL		
☐244		I WON'T BE ROCKIN' TONIGHT/ WELCOME TO THE CLUB	3.00	5.00
		BILLY RILEY		
☐245		TROUBLE BOUND/ROCK WITH ME BABY	8.00	15.00
		MALCOLM YELVINGTON		
☐246		ROCKIN' WITH MY BABY/IT'S ME BABY	7.00	12.00
		SONNY BURGESS		
☐247		RED HEADED WOMAN/WE WANNA BOOGIE	6.00	10.00
		RHYTHM ROCKERS		
☐248		FIDDLE BOP/JUKE BOX, HELP ME FIND MY BABY	6.00	10.00
		CARL PERKINS		
☐249		DIXIE FRIED/I'M SORRY, I'M NOT SORRY	2.50	4.00
		WARREN SMITH		
☐250		UBANGI STOMP/BLACK JACK DAVID	5.00	8.00
		ROY ORBISON-TEEN KINGS		
☐251		ROCKHOUSE/YOU'RE MY BABY	5.00	8.00
☐252		UNISSUED		
		BARBARA PITMAN		
☐253		I NEED A MAN/NO MATTER WHO'S TO BLAME	3.50	6.00
		RAY HARRIS		
☐254		COME ON LITTLE MAMA/ WHERE'D YOU STAY LAST NIGHT	12.00	20.00
		MILLER SISTERS		
☐255		TEN CATS DOWN/FINDERS KEEPERS	15.00	25.00
		SLIM RHODES FEATURING SANDY BROOKS		
☐256		TAKE AND GIVE/DO WHAT I DO	3.50	6.00
		ROSCO GORDON		
☐257		SHOOBIE OOBIE/CHEESE AND CRACKERS	1.75	3.00
		JOHNNY CASH AND TENNESSEE TWO		
☐258		TRAIN OF LOVE/THERE YOU GO	1.75	3.00
		JERRY LEE LEWIS		
☐259		CRAZY ARMS/END OF THE ROAD	3.00	5.00
		BILLY RILEY AND HIS LITTLE GREEN MEN		
☐260		FLYIN' SAUCERS ROCK & ROLL/I WANT YOU BABY	8.00	15.00
		CARL PERKINS		
☐261		YOUR TRUE LOVE/MATCHBOX (67)	2.50	4.00
		ERNIE CHAFFIN		
☐262		LONESOME FOR MY BABY/FEELIN' LOW	1.75	3.00

ISSUE #	LABEL	ARTIST/TITLE	VG	MINT
		SONNY BURGESS		
□ 263		RESTLESS/AIN'T GOT A THING	5.00	8.00
		GLENN HONEYCUTT		
□ 264		I'LL BE AROUND/I'LL WAIT FOREVER	2.50	4.00
		ROY ORBISON AND THE ROSES		
□ 265		DEVIL DOLL/SWEET AND EASY	3.50	6.00
		JOHNNY CASH AND THE TENNESSEE TWO		
□ 266		NEXT IN LINE/DON'T MAKE ME GO (99)	1.25	2.00
		JERRY LEE LEWIS		
□ 267		WHOLE LOT OF SHAKIN' GOING ON/IT'LL BE ME (3)	1.50	3.00
		WARREN SMITH		
□ 268		SO LONG I'M GONE/MISS FROGGIE (72)	5.00	8.00
		WAKE AND DICK THE COLLEGE KIDS		
□ 269		BOP BOP BABY/DON'T NEED YOUR LOVIN' BABY	2.50	4.00
		JIM WILLIAMS		
□ 270		PLEASE DON'T CRY OVER ME/ THAT DEPENDS ON YOU	1.75	3.00
		RUDI RICHARDSON		
□ 271		FOOL'S HALL OF FAME/WHY SHOULD I CRY	1.75	3.00
		RAY HARRIS		
□ 272		GREENBACK DOLLAR, WATCH AND CHAIN/ FOOLISH HEART	6.00	10.00
		MACK SELF		
□ 273		EASY TO LOVE/EVERY DAY	1.75	3.00
		CARL PERKINS		
□ 274		FOREVER YOURS/THAT'S RIGHT	2.50	4.00
		ERNIE CHAFFIN		
□ 275		I'M LONESOME/LAUGHIN' AND JOKIN'	1.75	3.00
		EDWIN BRUCE		
□ 276		ROCK BOPPIN' BABY/MORE THAN YESTERDAY	1.75	3.00
		BILLY RILEY-LITTLE GREEN MEN		
□ 277		RED HOT/PEARLY LEE	2.50	4.00
		TOMMY BLAKE-RHYTHM REBELS		
□ 278		FLAT FOOT SAM/LORDY HOODY	3.00	5.00
		JOHNNY CASH AND THE TENNESSEE TWO		
□ 279		HOME OF THE BLUES/GIVE MY LOVE TO ROSE (88)	1.75	3.00
		DICKEY LEE AND THE COLLEGIATES		
□ 280		MEMORIES NEW GROW OLD/GOOD LOVIN'	1.75	3.00
		JERRY LEE LEWIS		
□ 281		GREAT BALLS OF FIRE/YOU WIN AGAIN (2)	1.50	3.00

ISSUE #	LABEL	ARTIST/TITLE	VG	MINT
		DICK PENNER		
☐ 282		YOUR HONEY LOVE/CINDY LOU	3.00	5.00
		JOHNNY CASH AND THE TENNESSEE TWO		
☐ 283		BALLAD OF A TEENAGE QUEEN/BIG RIVER (16)	1.50	3.00
		ROY ORBISON		
☐ 284		CHICKEN-HEARTED/I LIKE LOVE	3.00	5.00
		SONNY BURGESS		
☐ 285		MY BUCKET'S GOT A HOLE IN IT/SWEET MISERY	3.50	6.00
		WARREN SMITH		
☐ 286		I'VE GOT LOVE IF YOU WANT IT/I FEEL IN LOVE	3.50	6.00
		CARL PERKINS		
☐ 287		GLAD ALL OVER/LEND ME YOUR COMB	1.75	3.00
		JERRY LEE LEWIS		
☐ 288		BREATHLESS/DOWN THE LINE (7)	1.50	3.00
		BILLY RILEY-THE LITTLE GREEN MEN		
☐ 289		WOULDN'T YOU KNOW/BABY PLEASE DON'T GO	3.00	5.00
		RUDY GRAYZELL		
☐ 290		JUDY/I THINK OF YOU	3.50	6.00
		JACK CLEMENT		
☐ 291		TEN YEARS/YOUR LOVER BOY	1.25	2.00
		EDWIN BRUCE		
☐ 292		SWEET WOMAN/PART OF MY LIFE	2.50	4.00
		THE SUN-RAYS		
☐ 293		THE LONELY HOURS/LOVE IS A STRANGER	1.75	3.00
		MAGEL FRIESMAN		
☐ 294		I FEEL SO BLUE/MEMORIES OF YOU	1.75	3.00
		JOHNNY CASH AND THE TENNESSEE TWO		
☐ 295		GUESS THINGS HAPPEN THAT WAY/ COME IN STRANGER (11)	1.50	3.00
		JERRY LEE LEWIS		
☐ 296		HIGH SCHOOL CONFIDENTIAL/FOOLS LIKE ME (21)	1.75	3.00
		DICKEY LEE		
☐ 297		FOOL, FOOL, FOOL/DREAMY NIGHTS	1.75	3.00
		RAY SMITH		
☐ 298		RIGHT BEHIND YOU BABY/SO YOUNG	3.00	5.00
		GENE SIMMONS		
☐ 299		DRINKIN' WINE/I DONE TOLD YOU	8.00	15.00
		TOMMY BLAKE		
☐ 300		SWEETIE PIE/I DIG YOU BABY	60.00	100.00
		GEORGE AND LOUIS		
☐ 301		THE RETURN OF JERRY LEE/LEWIS BOOGIE	2.50	4.00

ISSUE #	LABEL	ARTIST/TITLE	VG	MINT
		JOHNNY CASH AND THE TENNESSEE TWO		
□ 302		THE WAYS OF A WOMAN IN LOVE/ YOU'RE THE NEAREST THING TO HEAVEN (24) . . .	1.50	3.00
		JERRY LEE LEWIS		
□ 303		BREAK-UP/I'LL MAKE IT ALL UP TO YOU (52)	1.75	3.00
		SONNY BURGESS		
□ 304		ITCHY/THUNDERBIRD	8.00	15.00
		ROSCO GORDON		
□ 305		SALLY JO/TORRO	1.75	3.00
		JIMMY ISLE		
□ 306		I'VE BEEN WAITING/DIAMOND RING	1.75	3.00
		ERNIE CHAFFIN		
□ 307		MY LOVE FOR YOU/BORN TO LOSE	1.75	3.00
		RAY SMITH		
□ 308		WHY, WHY, WHY/YOU MADE A HIT	1.75	3.00
		JOHNNY CASH AND THE TENNESSEE TWO		
□ 309		IT'S JUST ABOUT TIME/I JUST THOUGHT YOU'D LIKE TO KNOW (47)	1.25	2.00
		VERNON TAYLOR		
□ 310		BREEZE/TODAY IS BLUE DAY	1.75	3.00
		JACK CLEMENT		
□ 311		THE BLACK HAIRED MAN/WRONG	1.25	2.00
		JERRY LEE LEWIS		
□ 312		I'LL SAIL MY SHIP ALONE/IT HURT ME SO (93)	1.75	3.00
		BILL RILEY		
□ 313		DOWN BY THE RIVERSIDE/NO NAME GIRL	1.75	3.00
		WARREN SMITH		
□ 314		SWEET, SWEET GIRL/GOODBYE MR. LOVE	2.50	4.00
		ONIE WHEELER		
□ 315		JUMP RIGHT OUT OF THIS JUKE BOX/TELL 'EM OFF	2.50	4.00
		JOHNNY CASH AND THE TENNESSEE TWO		
□ 316		THANKS A LOT/LUTHER PLAYED THE BOOGIE	1.75	3.00
		JERRY LEE LEWIS		
□ 317		LOVIN' UP A STORM/BIG BLON' BABY	1.75	3.00
		JIMMY ISLE		
□ 318		TIME WILL TELL/WITHOUT A LOVE	1.75	3.00
		RAY SMITH		
□ 319		ROCKIN' BANDIT/SAIL AWAY	1.75	3.00
		ERNIE CHAFFIN		
□ 320		DON'T EVER LEAVE ME/MIRACLE OF YOU	1.75	3.00

ISSUE #	LABEL	ARTIST/TITLE	VG	MINT
		JOHNNY CASH AND THE TENNESSEE TWO		
□ 321		KATY TOO/I FORGOT TO REMEMBER TO FORGET (66)	1.50	3.00
		BILL RILEY		
□ 322		GOT THE WATER BOILING/ONE MORE TIME	5.00	8.00
		ALTON AND JIMMY		
□ 323		HAVE FAITH IN MY LOVE/ NO MORE CRYING THE BLUES	3.00	5.00
		JERRY LEE LEWIS		
□ 324		LET'S TALK ABOUT US/BALLAD OF BILLY JOE.....	1.75	3.00
		VERNON TAYLOR		
□ 325		MYSTERY TRAIN/SWEET AND EASY TO LOVE......	3.00	5.00
		JERRY McGILL AND THE TOP COATS		
□ 326		I WANNA MAKE SWEET LOVE/LOVE STRUCK	2.50	4.00
		JOHNNY POWERS		
□ 327		WITH YOUR LOVE, WITH YOUR KISS/ BE MINE, ALL MINE	7.00	12.00
		SHERRY CRANE		
□ 328		WILLIE, WILLIE/WINNIE THE PARAKEET	1.25	2.00
		WILL MERCER		
□ 329		YOU'RE JUST MY KIND/BALLAD OF ST. MARKS ...	1.25	2.00
		JERRY LEE LEWIS		
□ 330		LITTLE QUEENIE/I COULD NEVER BE ASHAMED OF YOU.	1.75	3.00
		JOHNNY CASH AND THE TENNESSEE TWO		
□ 331		GOODBYE, LITTLE DARLING/YOU TELL ME........	1.25	2.00
		JIMMY ISLE		
□ 332		WHAT A LIFE/TOGETHER.....................	1.25	2.00
		RAY B. ANTHONY		
□ 333		ALICE BLUE GOWN/ST. LOUIS BLUES	1.25	2.00
		JOHNNY CASH AND THE TENNESSEE TRIO		
□ 334		STRAIGHT A'S IN LOVE/I LOVE YOU BECAUSE (84) .	1.25	2.00
		TRACY PENDARVIS AND THE SWAMPERS		
□ 335		A THOUSAND GUITARS/IS IT TOO LATE	1.25	2.00
		MACK OWEN		
□ 336		WALKIN' AND TALKIN'/SOMEBODY JUST LIKE YOU	1.25	2.00
		JERRY LEE LEWIS		
□ 337		OLD BLACK JOE/BABY, BABY BYE BYE...........	1.75	3.00
		PAUL RICKY		
□ 338		LEGEND OF THE BIG STEEPLE/ BROKEN HEARTED WILLIE	1.25	2.00
		RAYBURN ANTHONY		
□ 339		THERE'S NO TOMORROW/WHOSE GONNA SHINE YOUR PRETTY LITTLE FEET.............	1.25	2.00

ISSUE #	LABEL	ARTIST/TITLE	VG	MINT
		BILL JOHNSON		
☐ 340		BOBALOO/BAD TIMES AHEAD	1.25	2.00
		SONNY WILSON		
☐ 341		THE GREAT PRETENDER/I'M GONNA TAKE A WALK	1.25	2.00
		BOBBIE JEAN		
☐ 342		YOU BURNED THE BRIDGES/CHEATERS NEVER WIN	1.25	2.00
		JOHNNY CASH AND THE TENNESSEE TWO		
☐ 343		DOWN THE STREET TO 301/ THE STORY OF A BROKEN HEART (85)	1.25	2.00
		JERRY LEE LEWIS		
☐ 344		JOHN HENRY/HANG UP MY ROCK AND ROLL SHOES	1.75	3.00
		TRACY PENDARVIS		
☐ 345		IS IT ME/SOUTHBOUND LINE	1.25	2.00
		BILL STRENGTH		
☐ 346		I GUESS I'D BETTER GO/SENORITA	1.25	2.00
		JOHNNY CASH AND THE TENNESSEE TWO		
☐ 347		MEAN EYED CAT/PORT OF LONELY HEARTS	1.75	3.00
		LANCE ROBERTS		
☐ 348		THE GOOD GUY ALWAYS WIN/THE TIME IS RIGHT	1.25	2.00
		TONY ROSSINI		
☐ 349		I GOTTA KNOW WHERE I STAND/IS IT TOO LATE	1.25	2.00
		THE ROCKIN' STOCKINGS		
☐ 350		YULESVILLE U.S.A./ROCKIN' OLD LANG SYNE	1.75	3.00
		IRA JAY II		
☐ 351		YOU DON'T LOVE ME/MORE THAN ANYTHING	1.25	2.00
		JERRY LEE LEWIS		
☐ 352		WHEN I GET PAID/LOVE MADE A FOOL OF ME	1.75	3.00
		ROY ORBISON		
☐ 353		DEVIL DOLL/SWEET AND EASY TO LOVE	2.50	4.00
		BOBBY SHERIDAN		
☐ 354		RED MAN/SAD NEWS	1.75	3.00
		(BOBBY SHERIDAN WAS REALLY CHARLIE RICH)		
		JOHNNY CASH AND THE TENNESSEE TWO		
☐ 355		OH, LONESOME ME/LIFE GOES ON (93)	1.25	2.00
		JERRY LEE LEWIS		
☐ 356		WHAT'D I SAY/LIVIN' LOVIN' WRECK (30)	1.50	3.00
☐ 357		UNISSUED		
		GEORGE KLEIN		
☐ 358		U. T. PARTY (PT. 1)/(PT. 11)	1.25	2.00
		TRACY PENDARVIS		
☐ 359		BELL OF THE SUWANEE/ETERNALLY	1.25	2.00

ISSUE #	LABEL	ARTIST/TITLE	VG	MINT
		WADE CAGLE AND THE ESCORTS		
☐360		GROOVEY TRAIN/HIGHLAND ROCK	1.75	3.00
		ANITA WOOD		
☐361		I'LL WAIT FOREVER/I CAN'T SHOW HOW I FEEL	1.25	2.00
		HAROLD DORMAN		
☐362		THERE THEY GO/I'LL STICK BY YOU	1.25	2.00
		JOHNNY CASH AND THE TENNESSEE TRIO		
☐363		MY TREASURE/SUGAR TIME	1.25	2.00
		JERRY LEE LEWIS		
☐364		IT WON'T HAPPEN WITH ME/COLD, COLD HEART	1.75	3.00
		SHIRLEY SISK		
☐365		I FORGOT TO REMEMBER TO FORGET/OTHER SIDE	1.25	2.00
		TONY ROSSINI		
☐366		WELL I ASK YA/DARLENA	1.25	2.00
		JERRY LEE LEWIS		
☐367		SAVE THE LAST DANCE FOR ME/AS LONG AS I LIVE	1.75	3.00
		DON HOSEA		
☐368		SINCE I MET YOU/U HUH UNH	1.25	2.00
		BOBBY WOOD		
☐369		EVERYBODY'S SEARCHIN'/HUMAN EMOTIONS	1.75	3.00
		HAROLD DORMAN		
☐370		UNCLE JONAH'S PLACE/JUST ONE STEP	1.25	2.00
		JERRY LEE LEWIS		
☐371		MONEY/BOBBIE B	1.75	3.00
		RAY SMITH		
☐372		TRAVELIN' SALESMAN/I WON'T MISS YOU (TIL YOU'RE GONE)	1.75	3.00
		RAYBURN ANTHONY		
☐373		HOW WELL I KNOW/BIG DREAM	1.25	2.00
		JERRY LEE LEWIS		
☐374		I'VE BEEN TWISTIN'/RAMBLIN' ROSE	1.75	3.00
		RAY SMITH		
☐375		CANDY DOLL/HEY, BOSS MAN	1.75	3.00
		JOHNNY CASH AND THE TENNESSEE TWO		
☐376		BLUE TRAIN/BORN TO LOSE	1.75	3.00
		HAROLD DORMAN		
☐377		WAIT TIL' SATURDAY NIGHT/IN THE BEGINNING	1.25	2.00
		TONY ROSSINI		
☐378		(MEET ME) AFTER SCHOOL/ JUST AROUND THE CORNER	1.25	2.00

ISSUE #	LABEL	ARTIST/TITLE	VG	MINT
		JERRY LEE LEWIS		
□379		SWEET LITTLE SIXTEEN/ HOW'S MY EX TREATING YOU? (95)	1.75	3.00
		TONY ROSSINE AND THE CHIPPERS		
□380		YOU MAKE IT SOUND SO EASY/NEW GIRL IN TOWN	1.25	2.00
		THE FOUR UPSETTERS		
□381		CRAZY ARMS/MIDNIGHT SOIREE	1.25	2.00
		JERRY LEE LEWIS		
□382		GOOD GOLLY, MISS MOLLY/ I CAN'T TRUST ME (IN YOUR ARMS)	1.75	3.00
□383		UNISSUED		
		JERRY LEE LEWIS		
□384		TEENAGE LETTER/SEASONS OF MY HEART (with Linda Gail Lewis)	1.75	3.00
□385		UNISSUED		
		THE FOUR UPSETTERS		
□386		WABASH CANNONBALL/SURFIN' CALLIOPE	1.25	2.00
		TONY ROSSINI		
□387		MOVED TO KANSAS CITY/NOBODY	1.25	2.00
		THE TEENANGELS		
□388		AIN'T GONNA LET YOU/TELL ME MY LOVE (dj only)	6.00	10.00
		BILLY ADAMS		
□389		BETTY AND DUPREE/GOT MY MOJO WORKIN'	1.25	2.00
		BILL YATES AND HIS T-BIRDS		
□390		DON'T STEP ON MY DOG/STOP, WAIT, LISTEN	1.25	2.00
		DILLY ADAMS		
□391		TROUBLE IN MIND/LOOKIN' FOR MARY ANN	1.25	2.00
		JOHNNY CASH		
□392		WIDE OPEN ROAD/BELSHAZAR	1.75	3.00
		SMOKEY JOE		
□393		SIGNIFYING MONKEY/LISTEN TO ME BABY	2.50	4.00
		BILLY ADAMS		
□394		RECONSIDER BABY/RUBY JANE	1.25	2.00
		RANDY AND THE RADIANTS		
□395		PEEK-A-BOO/MOUNTAIN HIGH	1.25	2.00
		JERRY LEE LEWIS		
□396		CARRY ME BACK TO OLD VIRGINIA/ I KNOW WHAT IT MEANS	1.75	3.00
		GORGEOUS BILL		
□397		CARLEEN/TOO LATE TO RIGHT MY WRONG	1.25	2.00
		RANDY AND THE RADIANTS		
□398		MY WAYS OF THINKING/TRUTH FROM MY EYES	1.25	2.00

ISSUE #	LABEL	ARTIST/TITLE	VG	MINT
		BILL YATES		
☐ 399		BIG, BIG WORLD/I DROPPED MY M AND M'S	1.25	2.00
		THE JESTERS		
☐ 400		MY BABE/CADILLAC MAN	2.50	4.00
		BILLY ADAMS		
☐ 401		OPEN THE DOOR RICHARD/ROCK ME BABY	1.25	2.00
		DANE STINIT		
☐ 402		DON'T KNOCK WHAT YOU DON'T UNDERSTAND/ ALWAYS ON THE GO	1.25	2.00
		DAVID HOUSTON		
☐ 403		SHERRY'S LIPS/MISS BROWN	1.75	3.00
		THE CLIMATES		
☐ 404		NO YOU FOR ME/BREAKING UP AGAIN	1.25	2.00
		DANE STINIT		
☐ 405		SWEET COUNTRY GIRL/THAT MUDDY OLE RIVER	1.25	2.00
		GOSPEL SERIES: BROTHER JAMES ANDERSON		
☐ 406		I'M GONNA MOVE IN THE ROOM WITH THE LORD/ MY SOUL NEEDS RESTING	2.50	4.00
		"LOAD OF MISCHIEF"		
☐ 407		BACK IN MY ARMS AGAIN/I'M A LOVER	2.50	4.00

COLLECTORS DIRECTORY

WHILE YOU'RE THINKING OF IT and to make sure you are listed in the next edition of the COLLECTOR'S DIRECTORY, send us your name, address, and phone number, whether you are a collector or a dealer and what area of collecting you are interested in. PLEASE INCLUDE A CHECK FOR $5.00. We will print all information as submitted, so please check for accuracy. Mail to: HOUSE OF COLLECTIBLES, Dept. RR-105, 773 KIRKMAN ROAD, #120, ORLANDO, FL 32811

ALABAMA

MIKE GILL, 2426 29th ST., BIRMINGHAM, 35208
R/R 45's (1955-64), Buddy Holly .... (205) 788-8628
H. A. HYCHE, 529 CAMBRIDGE ST., BIRMINGHAM, 35224
S. G. JOHNSON, P. O. BOX 63, DECATUR, 35602
R/R, C/W (1950-60) .... (205) 353-7989
KING BEE RECORDS, 1472 TOMAHAWK RD., BIRMINGHAM, 35214
JOE O. RAY, 1618 S. CULLOM ST., BIRMINGHAM, 35205
Folk Albums & 45's .... (205) 324-8893
RHODA THORN, R #6, BOX 174, RUSSELLVILLE, 35653
MAGS, LP's, 45's, PHOTOS

ALASKA

SAM S. CORWIN, 4218 CHECKMATE DR., ANCHORAGE, 99504
JERRY HITE, 1401 HYDER ST., ANCHORAGE, 99501
2,000 LP's (1950-) & 2,000 45's (1950-60) to Trade

ARIZONA

ALBUM'S OF TUCSON (DAVID CANTERMAN), 1043 E. SIXTH ST., TUSCON, 85719
.... (602) 622-0201
HARVEY BOND, 4728 E. POLK, PHOENIX, 85008
GRANT BOYD, BOX 1988, PHOENIX, 85001
R/R, JAZZ .... (602) 264-0325
DUANE EDDY CIRCLE, USA (DAVE ACKER), 4527 E. RIVERSIDE, PHOENIX, 85040
Fee; $2.00 year; $10.00 life (double for overseas). Write for details.
WARREN ERICKSON, 1645 W. PAMPA AVE., MESA, 85202
R/R, Beatles, Beach Boys, Jan & Dean
PHYLLIS FRENCH, 6407 W. CLOUSE DR., PHOENIX, 85033
N. GRASSI, 2731 N. ALVERNON, TUSCON, 85712
78's, 45's & LP's & 33⅓ LP's
TOM JACKSON, 1617 N. McALLISTER, AVE., TEMPE, 85281
.... (602) 947-6438

PAUL R. JANESIK, 6817 W. PALM LN., PHOENIX, 85035
R/R & PHOTOS, Jackie DeShannon, Tommy Jones, Del Shannon, Jan & & Dean & Gene Vincent . . . . (602) 849-4048
JOLLY ROGER TRADES, 1024 A S. McCLINTOCK, TEMPE, 85281
45's (1950-) . . . . (602) 967-2517
TOM KOEHLER, BOX 27737, TEMPE, 85282
R/R, MOTOWN, (1950-60), Bob Dylan . . . . (602) 838-2816
J. LINDSAY, RT. 3, LOT 66, FLAGSTAFF, 86001 . . . . (602) 526-0169
THE "MAD DADDY", 4213 W. VALENCIA, TUCSON, 85706
R/R, R/B, C/W . . . . (601) 883-6076
RORY MUSIL, BOX 2313, MESA, 85204 . . . . (602) 969-9793
WILLIAM PAGEL, P. O. BOX 27796, TEMPE, 85282
Dylan
JOHN RHEA, 3410 W. JOAN DE ARC, PHOENIX, 85029
Conway Twitty MGM, Pat Boone DOT, Tommy Sands CAP, Narvel Felts (45's & LP's), Brenda Lee, Bobby Darin, Ventures, Bobby Vee, Billy Vaughn . . . . (602) 942-3176
WILLIAM SCHUH, P. O. BOX 1572, SCOTTSDALE, 85252
45's (1956-70)
BILL SHAVER, 5233 N. 67th DR., GLENDALE, 85303
Johnny Cash, 45's, EP's & 78's . . . . (602) 846-7347
DWAYNE WITTEN, 541 W. HOLLY ST., PHOENIX, 85003

ARKANSAS

RECORD WORLD, 703 N. WEST AVE., EL DORADO, 71730
CHARLES R. WOMBLE, 8215 2nd St. N., LITTLE ROCK, 72117
R/R & C/W . . . . (501) 835-0839

CALIFORNIA

ALEX ABERBOM, 22364 CASS AVE., WOODLAND HILLS, 91364
R/R, (1950-60)
JERRY ABRAHAM, 375 DRAKELEY AVE., ATWATER, 95301
C/W, ROCK, JAZZ
ROBERT ABRAMOWITZ, 18620 PALO VERDE, APT. A, CERRITOS, 90701
Beatles
ACORNS RECORDS & TAPES, 1465 N. VAN NESS, FRESNO, 93728 233-3149
WILLIAM ANTHONY, 954 HENDERSON AVE. #63, SUNNYVALE, 94086
Elvis 45's, 78's, LP's & COVERS. Brenda Lee 45's & LP's
RICHARD WESLEY BALL, 935 'A' ALICE LANE, MENLO PARK, 94025
Beatle
STAN BAUMRUK, 436 ALTA ISTA BLVD., L.A., 90036
C/W, R/R . . . . (213) 935-1606
CAROL BERGER, P. O. BOX J, FILROY, 95020
Bobby Vinton

L. JOHN BERTELSEN, 2210 W. 34th ST., SAN PEDRO, 90732
R/B, Black Artists (1931-'51) .... (213) 832-6892
BOB BERTRAM STUDIOS, 1069-D SHARY CR., CONCORD, 94518
All Speeds and all Categories of Records
BOOGIE BOY RECORDS (JEFF STOLPER), P. O. BOX 1196, PACIFIC PALISADES, 90272
R/B VOCAL GROUPS, ROCKABILY
FRANK BRANDON, 1322 E. HOME AVE., APT. B., FRESNO, 93728
BOB BREWER, 16761 VIEW POINT LANE #330, HUNTINGTON BEACH, 92647
LARRY BUCK, 240 BELLE MILL RD., SP. 7, RED BLUFF, 96080
45 RPM's (1950)
EVERETT CALDWELL, 1135 OAKMONT ST., ORANGE, 92667
45's, LP's & EP's (1950-70)
MICHAEL K. CARLTON, 1095 DAVIDS RD., PERRIS, 92370
CENTURY COMMERCIAL CORP. (MARK S. RANDELL),
600 S. COMMONWEALTH AVE., #1100, L.A., 90005
CHARISMA, 1110 BURLINGAME AVE., BURLINGAME, 94010
ROCK RECORDS, (1950-60), Beatle & Elvis .... (415) 344-7555
CHIMAERA RECORDS, 405 KIPLING, PALO ALTO, 94301
JIM CLARKE, 15701½ CORNUTA, BELLFLOWER, 90706
R/B, R/B 45's, LP's, Beatles .... (213) 866-8336
MIKE DANIELS, 44 CREEK RD., FAIRFAX, 94930
MR. WARREN DEBENHAM, 143 ARLINGTON, BERKELEY, 94707
THE DISC TRIP, 25 W. 25th AVE. (IN THE PATIO), SAN MATEO, 94402
78's, 45's & LP's .... (415) 345-4009
DINO'S OLDIES, P. O. BOX 074, SAN DIEGO, 92115
45's (1940-60) .... (714) 264-1467
RICHARD ELLIOTT, 2548 SAPRA ST., THOUSAND OAKS, 91360
ELVIS PRESLEY APPRECIATION CLUB, P. O. BOX 201, SUN VALLEY, 91352
The Elvis Memory. No Membership Fee. Buy, Sell, Trade Elvis Items (1956-). Support National Elvis Presley Day, Write for Details .... (213) 899-1719
ENCORE RECORDS, 4593 EL CAJON BLVD., SAN DIEGO, 92115
45's (1950-) .... (714) 280-6834
GEORGE A. FARRIS, 3815 HILLCREST DR., EL SOBRANTE, 94803
W. R. FIELDER, P. O. BOX 758, BIGGS, 95917
COMEDY (1920-60)
STEVE FODOR, P. O. BOX 25884, L.A., 90025
R/B & C/W 45's (1950) .... (213) 820-2215
PAUL FREEMAN, 116 W. 43rd AVE., SAN MATEO, 94403
Rick Nelson .... (415) 574-0173
MIKE GARNESE, 945 FREMONT ST., SANTA CLARA, 95050
ROCK (1960-70), Beatles .... (408) 246-1754
LOU "SPEEDY" GONZALES, 3101 DELTA AVE., MODESTO, 95355
Big Bands .... (209) 527-0642
CARL A. GUIDO, 9215 GUESS ST., ROSEMEAD, 91770
Doors
JIM HARKEY, 2011 GISLER AVE., OXNARD 93030
Beatles

JOHN HARMER, 5001 REYNARD, LA CRESCENTA, 91214
TOM HAYDON, 1083 EL CAMINO REAL, MENLO PARK, 94025
BLUES LP's . . . . (415) 321-1333
EDDIE HOOVER, 21142 ASPEN AVE., CASTRO VALLEY, 94546
MRS. JAMES HOWARD, 4260 RUTHELMA, PALO ALTO, 94306
78's, 45's, 33's (1890-1970)
JOHN F. HOWARD, P. O. BOX 1214, PALO ALTO, 93032
LP's, POP VOCALISTS . . . . (805) 486-6235
CONRAD & LORRIE JANCA, 165 W. ELMWOOD, APT. F, BURBANK, 91502
45's (1950-70)
MARK KALMAN, 6181 WOOSTER AVE., L.A., 90056
ROCK & SURF (1960), Beach Boys, Beatles, Bob Dylan & Elvis
DAVID KLAYMAN, 14535 CLARK ST., #102, VAN NUYS, 91411
ROCK 45's & LP's, Top 40 Charts . . . . (213) 981-2279
BERNARD KLEIN, 2852 BRIMHALL DR., ROSSMOOR, 90720
Beatle . . . . (213) 431-6414
DAVID KONJOYAN, 25 SARAH LN., MORAGA, 94556
45's
MICHAEL A. LANG, 6519 ALDEA AVE., VAN NUYS, 91406
R/B, R/R, JAZZ, CLASSICAL
DON LEITE, 2049 W. HEDDING ST., SAN JOSE, 95128
R/B 45's & LP's (1950-60)
JOE A. LEWIS, 4604 EXCUELA CT., RICHMOND, 94804
C/W, R/B . . . . (415) 529-0912
DENNIS R. LIFF, 19439 LEMAY ST., RESEDA, 91335
R/R (1956-), Bob Dylan . . . . (213) 345-5380
ROBERT E. LOPEZ, JR., 8123 OTIS #A, SO. GATE, 90280
C/W & (1950-), ROCK 45's & LP's
KAREN LOWRY, 155 FLYING CLOUD ISLE, FOSTER CITY, 94404
ACID ROCK (1960-)
JON MANOUSOS, 7001 EASTSIDE RD., UKIAH, 95482
R/R, R/B (1940-60)
ALLAN MASON, 125 OCEAN PARK BLVD., SANTA MONICA, 90405
LP's & 45's (1950-), R/R & R/B (CIRCA 1976-78)
TOM McMARUS, P. O. BOX 38, SAN JACINTO, 92383
R/B & COMEDY
JORGE HERNANDEZ MELGAR, 900 TOYON DR. #1, BURLINGAME, 94010
Beatles LP's & 45's
JIM NORMAN, 307 W. ELM, LODI, 95240
R/R, R/B, C/W, LP's, 45's, 78's
STEVE PAHNKE, 24 SOLA AVE., SAN FRANCISCO, 94116
R/B (1950-60) . . . . (415) 566-3193
CHRIS PEAKE, 6526 HOMEWOOD, HOLLYWOOD, 90028
POP (1960)
JOHN PETERS, 8 DALE CT., ORINDA, 94563
LP's Black Vocal, R/B (1940) . . . . (415) 376-1252
LANCE PHILLIPS, 5353 YOSEMITE OAKS RD., MARIPOSA, 95338
POSTWAR BLUES (1960), British

MICHAEL PLAYTOND, 5534 W. 78th ST., L.A., 90045
JAZZ, BLUES & DANCE BANDS
DONALD H. PRATER, 1746 MIDDLEFIELD, STOCKTON, 95204
C/W, R/R, R/B, 30,000 45's, Beatles, Presley .... (209) 464-8494
PRELUDE ENTERPRISES, 5730 PARK CREST DR., SAN JOSE, 95118 (408) 269-4209
NORMAN S. PRESLEY, P. O. BOX 59118, L.A., 90059
R/B, POP, C/W 45's
BRAD PUESCHEL, 839 COLBY ST., SAN FRANCISCO, 94134
ROCK & POP 45's
WILLIAM C. PURVIANCE, 20149 S. MAPES, CERRITOS, 90701
Elvis 33's, 45's, 78's, RCA, SUN and Boots. R/B, COMEDY & R/R .... (213) 924-2947
R & T ENTERPRISES, 2720 SO. HARBOR BLVD. UNIT A, SANTA ANA, 92704
RECORD COLLECTORS STUDIO, 2240 MAIN ST. UNIT 4, CHULA VISTA 92011
Records, Tapes & Collectibles of all Categories .... (714) 424-7861
RECORD TOWN, 1851 W. LaHABRA BLVD., LaHABRA, 90631
R/R, R/B .... (213) 691-6216
REMEMBER WHEN MUSIC, 760 MARKET #315, SAN FRANCISCO, 94102
REPERTOIRE RENDEZVOUS, 3032 4th ST., CERES, 95307
R/R, R/B LP's & 45's .... (209) 537-9694
LARRY KEVIN ROBERTS, 563 LA MIRADA AVE., PASADENA, 91108
NON-ROCK 45's
JESSE & ALICE ROGERS, 10940 DENSMORE AVE., GRANADA HILLS 91344
Specialty if Out-of-Print RECORDS .... (213) 365-1735
RIC ROSS, 132 S. RODEO DR. #600, BEVERLY HILLS, 90212
Sinatra .... (213) 278-6700
SANTEE SWAP-A-TAPE, 10251 MAST BLVD., SUITE S, SANTEE 92071
Elvis
BOB SASSAMAN, 12062 MOORPARK, STUDIO CITY, 91604
C/W, ROCK
HERBERT N. SCHOTT, 34 GRANHAM CT., PACIFICA, 94044
R/R, R/B, ROCKABILY .... (415) 359-5633
JOHN SIAMAS, 5523 MASONIC AVE., OAKLAND, 94618
R/B, BLUES, R/R (1947-62)
BILL SMITH, 3711 J ST., SACRAMENTO, 95816
PAT SMITH, P. O. BOX 291, SUN VALLEY, 91352
R/B, Elvis
J. ANTHONY SPICER, 818 ACACIA DR., BURLINGAME, 94010
L. R. STILLMAN, 437 BANDON AVE., VALINDA 91744
45's
RICHARD E. STRONG. 725 NORD AVE. #108, CHICO, 95926
Elvis, Beatles, Beach Boys
JAMES L. SUTTON, 1900 E. OCEAN #402, LONG BEACH, 90802
Beatle & Elvis LP's
PETE TAUSCHER, 212 WHELLER AVE., REDWOOD CITY, 94061
LP's, 45's, Buddy Holly, Big Bopper, Eddie Cochran, Beatles, Rolling Stones, Richie Valens
CROFTY THORP, 4520 HIGHLAND AVE., SAN DIEGO, 92115
R/B Groups, 45's & LP's (1950)

GEORGE W. TWEEDY, P. O. BOX 2505, VAN NUYS, 91404
R/B, ROCKABILY, C/W, ROCK . . . . (213) 785-6989
TOM ULLBERG, 426 DUNSVIEW, VALINDA, 91744
ROCK, Linda Ronstadt, Stone Poneys, Olivia Newton-John
DON MAGNO VILLANUEVA, 6516 ARIZONA AVE., L.A., 90045
S'TRACK & R/R
THE VINYL JUNKIE, 4520 HIGHLAND AVE., SAN DIEGO, 92115 . . . (714) 280-7745
JIM WALROTH, 232 MILLER #10, MILL VALLEY, 94941
Prewar & Postwar BLUES, GOSPEL, R/B, JAZZ, ROCKABILY
KENNETH WARWICK, P. O. BOX 976, STOCKTON, 95201
R/B, Beatles, Elvis
KEN WATTS, P. O. BOX 801, NOVATO, 94947
ROCKABILY, R/R, R/B (1950-60) . . . . (415) 897-8703
JONATHON WEBER, P. O. BOX 674, MALIBU, 90265
R/R (1960)
DAN L. WELLS, 2390 JETTER ST., CASTRO VALLEY, 94546
Perry Como 45's, 78's, LP's. Bing Crosby, Patti Page, Dinah Shore, Roy Rogers
JIM WHITE, 2144 SIERRAWOOD DR., SAN JOSE, 95132
R/R (1950-60), Jack Scott, Elvis, P. Anka, F. Cannon, Del Shannon, B. Holly, R. Valens . . . . (408) 263-5127
CLIFF YAMASAKI, P. O. BOX 27648, SAN FRANCISCO, 94127
Beatles . . . . (415) 334-4166
DAN YOUNG, 419 SUNNYVALE, HEALDSBURG, 95448
Bob Dylan, Grateful Dead, SF Groups, Comedy . . . . (707) 433-4300

COLORADO

MIKE BACZUK, 709 13th ST., GREELEY, 80631
R/R (1950), Surfing, Drag: Elvis, Beatles, Beach Boys, James Dean
M. D. COLVIN, 85 GARLAND ST., DENVER, 80226
45 Oldies Listed in J. Whitburn's Top Pop Records (1955-70) Billboard Book.
DUKE OF DISCS, P. O. BOX 26544 A, LAKEWOOD, 80226
Auction Catalog of Orig. Oldie 45's & LP's: POP ROCK, C/W
MARTIN HAUGEN, 6288 UNION ST., ARVADA, 80004
ROCK, BOP, R/B
JOHN MARSH, P. O. BOX 9663, DENVER, 80209
Stones & Joe Walsh, R/R

MAYO McNEAL, BOX 6434, DENVER, 80206
KEN MOHR, 1635 DOVER ST., BROOMFIELD, 80020
Buddy Holly, Moody Blues
JOE PARKER, BOX 818, EATON 80615
R/R (1960), Beatles
RECORD ReUNION, 675 S. UNION AVE., PUEBLO, 81004
ROCK, POP & SOUL, C/W
RECYCLE RECORDS, 2501 SHERIDAN BLVD., DENVER, 80214
Specializing in Rare & Colored Wax LP's & 45's
PETER REUM, P. O. BOX 1523, GREELY, 80631
Beach Boys ....(303) 356-6298
MIKE STEARNS, 2775 S. FEDERAL #304, DENVER, 80236
Beatle LP's, 45's, Films, Posters, Buttons
WES WORLD RECORDS, 4125 N. ACADEMY, COLO. SPRINGS, 80907

CONNECTICUT
BRAD BROWNE, 67 LEDGEBROOK DR., NORWALK, 06854
British Groups & Surf Sounds
LEES BROWNE, 67 LEDGEBROOK DR., NORWALK, 06854
Bubblegum Rock, Novelty, Chubby Checker, Raiders, Jan & Dean
BUDDY HOLLY MEMORIAL SOCIETY (BILL GRIGGS), 75 BELCHER RD., WETHERSFIELD, 06109
All Speeds of any Records or Materials that pertain to Buddy Holly in any way. I Buy, Sell & Trade. I also collect Cover Records of Buddy Holly Material, as well as Tributes. Write for Details about Joining the Society.
DAVE COOK, 121 OAK ST., SOUTHINGTON, 06489
COUNTRY, BLUEGRASS & WESTERN (1940-50)
PHILLIP M. DeVOE, 217 BURNSIDE AVE. E., HARTFORD, 06100
R/R, R/B, S'TRACKS: Buddy Holly, Gene Vincent, Ritchie Valens, Eddie Cochran, Elvis, Beatles, Rick Nelson, Everly Bros.
DAVID FORD, 142 TAFT LANE, WINDSOR LOCKS, 06096
R/R, ROCKABILY, POP (1950).................................(203) 623-0084
RICHARD HEGHINIAN, 76 WENDY DR., S. WINDSOR, 06074
WAYNE JONES, 7 ELLINGTON RD., E. HARTFORD, 06108
HALVARD LJONQUIST, 59 LEWIS AVE., WOLCOTT, 06716
Postwar Blues, R/B, C/W, JAZZ, 45's, 78's & LP's

ROBERT E. O'LOUGHLIN, P. O. BOX 3533, BRIDGEPORT 06605
R/B, R/R, 45's & LP's (1958-60)
DAVID PONAK, RT. 3 BOX 201, POMFRET CENTER, 06259
Rolling Stones, Beach Boys
LISA PONAK, RFD 2 BOX 201, POMFRET CENTER, 06259
R/R, C/W, LP's & 45's, Beatles, Jimi Hendrix, Dylan, Donovan . (203) 974-1086
ALVIN E. RUDA, 42 HIGHVIEW TERR. APT. 26D, HAMDEN, 06514
ROBERT RYMARZICK, 38 WRIGHTS LANE, GLASTONBURY, 06033
R/R, R/B . . . . (203) 633-2385
JIMMY SMITH, 7 CAROLINA PL., GREENWICH, 06830
ACID ROCK, Rod Stewart & Peter Frampton
ROCK STAMBERG, MEADOW LN., GREENWICH, 06830
R/B, Doowop Sounds & Sam the Sham
L. G. STEFANO, 232 S. WATER ST., G7, WAREHOUSE POINT, 06088
R/R, BLUES 45's (1955-65), Billie Holiday, Curtis Lee, Haley Mills, Paul Peterson, Early Paul Anka Hits, Del-Viking . . . . (203) 623-5487

DELAWARE
DISC COLLECTOR PUBLICATIONS, P. O. BOX 169, CHESWOLD, 19936
C/W, LP's, 45's
JOEL GLAZIER, 705 W. 38th ST., WILMINGTON, 19802
Beatles
BUDDY LOVEALL, 100 KENTUCKY AVE., WILMINTON, 19804
Beatles . . . . (303) 994-6475
JAMES L. NORMAN, P. O. BOX 11, MAIN ST., DAGSBORO 19939
ROCK-45's, 45 EP's (1950), Elvis, Gene Vincent, Jack Scott, Larry Hall, Timmie Rogers, Virginia Lowe, Bell Notes, Impalas, Eddie Cochran, Nervous Norvous

DISTRICT OF COLUMBIA (WASHINGTON)
CHIP BISHOP, 901 SIXTH ST., SW, APT. 605, 20024
R/R, R/B, 45's (1950-70)
ROSSER B. MADDOX, 1101 NEW HAMPSHIRE AVE. NW #1007, 20037
LP's
MISS BARBARA MARVIN, 4629 TILDEN ST., NW, 20016
Vocal of Swing Era (1930-45)
MR. DANIEL MEDINA, 1418 HOPKIN ST., NW #1, 20037
CHARLES SANDERS, 58 ALLISON ST., NE, 20011
R/R, R/B, 45's & LP's (1950-60)

FLORIDA
SID ARTHUR, 8265 W. SUNRISE BLVD., PLANTATION, 33322
R/B, C/W, JAZZ, ORIG. CASTS, S'TRACKS, Elvis
THE BOOK STORE, 739 E. SILVER SPRINGS, BLVD., OCALA, 32670
. . . . (904) 622-7812 OR 629-0903

THOMAS A. BUBY, 5611 NEWBERRY RD., GAINESVILLE, 32607
LP's, 45's (1970), ROCK & JAZZ (1950-60) ROCK
DAVE BUSHBY, P. O. BOX 15883, ORLANDO, 32808
R/B GROUPS, ROCK, 45's .... (305) 299-5282
CHARLOTTE'S OLD RECORD GALLERY, 2920 HARBORVIEW RD., TAMPA, 33611
JAZZ, SWING, BLUES, C/W
LARRY & LYNN COOPER, RT. 2 BOX 580, THONOTOSASSA, 33592
.... (813) 936-3698
THOMAS DEUBER, 1501 E. 142nd AVE. #6, TAMPA, 33612
R/B, R/R, 78's (1950), RARE LP's (R/R & Hard Rock) (1960-70), R/B, R/R, 45's (1940-50)
BOB GRASSO, 9020 NW 24 CT., FT. LAUDERDALE, 33322
R/B GROUPS, SUN LABEL, BLUES
ELSIE HINE, 1147 DELPHINIUM DR., ORLANDO, 32807
R/R, C/W, OLD 78's, LP's
HYDE & ZEKE RECORD EXCHANGE, 919 W. UNIVERSITY, GAINESVILLE, 32601
CHARLES KEEBLER, 19911 HOLIDAY RD., MIAMI, 33157
Buddy Holly, Jim Croce
RON KIRCHER, P. O. BOX 9202, PANAMA CITY, 32407
Recording (1939-65)
RON LeBOW, 2128 W. 58th AVE., FT. LAUDERDALE, 33313
R/R (1950-), Surfing Vocals .... (305) 733-2485
LOUBE'S NOSTALGIA BOOK STORE, 4802 E. BUSCH BLVD., TAMPA, 33617
JAZZ, R/B, R/R, C/W .... (813) 985-3743
JOHN MILLER, P. O. BOX 640116, WETABR., MIAMI, 33164
White Vocal Groups (Doowop), Surfing, Novelty
RICHARD MINOR, 9415 S.W. 42nd ST., MIAMI, 33165
R/R, C/W, R/B, BLUES, ROCK (1950-60), Beatles, Elvis, Buddy Holly
PHOENIX RECORDS, 1642 W. UNIVERSITY, GAINESVILLE, 32603 (904) 377-5215
RECORDS, RT. 2 BOX 194, CRYSTAL RIVER, 32629
R/R, R/B, ROCK, 78's, 45's, LP's (1960-), ... *(904) 795-3809 or 795-7512*
LOU RALLO, BOX 47, ORANGE PARK, 32073
R/B, GOSPEL, R/R, BLUES, 45's, 78's, LP's (1940-70)
BOBBY SALERNO, 10264 GULF BLVD., TREASURE ISLAND, 33706
R/R (1950-60), Elvis, Beatles, Surf, Beach Boys
JIM SHELBY, 12240 SW 187 TERR., MIAMI, 33177
LP's ONLY, ROCKABILY, BLUES, C/W, FOLK, R/B, Oldtime R/R and some POP & JAZZ
BOB SINK, 1208 BARONWOOD PLACE, BRANDON, 33511
R/R, Beatles
JOSEPH WEEKS/BRIAN SOUTHARD, 7200 SW 83 ST., PLAZA 3-117, MIAMI, 33143
*MOTOWN, Mary Wells, Leslie Gore, Shirelles, Crystals, Ronettes, Chiffons, Shangri Las, Vandells, Marvellets. Also early 60's, R/R***DAN WELLS,** 8730 5th WAY N., ST. PETERSBURG, 33702
R/R, R/B (1950-) .... (813) 576-4125
BOB WOOD, P. O. BOX 2394, PENSACOLA, 32503

GEORGIA

RONALD W. BONDS, 1948 GLENMAR DR., DECATUR, 30032
Bizarre/Straight, ESP, etc., Beefheart, Zappa
"THE BOOGIE MAN", 944 SHARON CIR., SMYRNA, 30080
45's, R/B, R/R, C/W
BRIAN S. CADY, BOX 128, REED HALL, U. OF G., ATHENS, 30602
(1964-), Who, Beatles .... (404) 542-4432
FANTASYLAND BOOKS & RECORDS, 2817 PEACHTREE RD., NE, ATLANTA, 30305
ROCK (1960-70), Beatles .... (404) 237-3193
MIKE HALL, 2 EXCHANGE PL., SUITE 2264, CHAMBLEE, 30338
MIKE JONES, R #2, RANDAL RD., CAVE SPRING, 30124
R/R, POP ROCK, C/W, ALBUMS, 45's, S'TRACKS (1950-60)
LAWRENCE LONG, JR., BOX 555 B, RT. 4, MARTINEZ, 30907
45's & LP's, Buddy Holly, Elvis Presley, Big Bands, Beatles, Haley & Comets (Crickets)
A. RAYE SMITH, 2023 DUG GAP RD., DALTON, 30720
BRITISH & U.S. ROCK, Beatles .... (404) 278-8980
WUXTRY, 201 COLLEGE AVE., ATHENS, 30601
I Pay $1.00 and Up for Used & Out-of-Print LP's .... (404) 543-3739

HAWAII

GOIN' BACK ENTERPRISES, P. O. BOX 7161, HONOLULU, 96821
ROCK (1960-70)
WILLIAM A. KUESTER, 95-019 WAIHONU ST., APT. B202, WAHIWA, 96786
LP's, PICTURES, PHOTOS, Loretta Lynn & Wanda Jackson, & Teresa Brewer
MOM N' POPS RECORDS, 2915 KAPIOLANI BLVD., HONOLULU, 96826
R/R, JAZZ, R/B
DAVID B. THOMPSON, 1103 A CORNET AVE., HICKAM A.F.B., 96553
R/B, R/R, LP's (1950-60)
RICHARD YOUNG, 1056 12th AVE., HONOLULU, 96816

IDAHO

MIKE FEENEY, 2136 2nd ST., LEWISTON, 83501
R/R, R/B & ROCK (1950)
RICHARD OCHOA, 1206 N. 15th ST., COEUR D'ALENE, 83814
R/R (1960-64), R/B, C/W, ROCKABILY (1940-77), Elvis, W. Jennings, B. Knox, Chess, Checker & 2,000 LP'sSend Wants.

ILLINOIS

A. LEVIN RARE RECORDS, 454 CENTRAL AVE., HIGHLAND PARK, 60035
45's, LP's, R/B, R/R (1950-60)
CHUCK ARGABRITE, 10474 ETHEL CT., ROSEMONT 60018
SUN, POP, ROCK, C/W

GARY BERNSTEIN, 1921 N. KEYSTONE, CHICAGO, 60639
45's, LP's 78's, EP's, Elvis, Buddy Holly, Jack Scott, G. Vincent, Janis Martin & Four Lovers .... (312) 276-1380
FRANK BLACK, 108 WEBSTER APTS., CLINTON, 61727
GEORGE BLESKIN, 5935 W. GIDDINGS, CHICAGO, 60630
TYLER-TRAVIS BOLDEN, P. O. BOX 1164, EFFINGHAM, 62401
33⅓, 45's, EP's, Beatles .... (217) 342-3079
MR. GEORGE IRA BOEREMA, 34W888 N. JAMES DR., ST. CHARLES, 60174
GARY G. BOWMAN, 611 CORNELIA ST., JOLIET, 60435
R/B, ROCKABILY, 45's, 78's .... (815) 723-5775
BUFFALO RECORDS, 1423 9th ST., ROCKFORD, 61104
ROCK & POP VOCALS (1950-60), Elvis, Beatles
MICHAEL CAIN, 906 WILSON, CT., ZION, 60099
Beatle .... (312) 872-2820
WILLIAM C. CHAPMAN, 403 BIRCHWOOD LN., DeKALB, 60115
R/R
COWBOY CARL RECORDS, P. O. BOX 116, PARK FOREST, 60456
C/W, ROCK, R/R
BRUCE EDELSON, 8139 KILPATRICK, SKOKIE, 60076
BRITISH ROCK, PUNK & 60's ROCK .... (312) 674-2203
DEVIN FORD, 4710 W. 83rd ST., CHICAGO, 60652
BRITISH INVASION & ROCK (1900)
WILLIAM J. KINCAID, 7406 W. RANDOLPH-APT. 3A, FOREST PARK, 60130
ROCK, SUN, ACE & All MEMPHIS LABELS (1950), Presley, Jerry Lee Lewis
BETTY LACEY, 14349 LAWNDALE, MIDLOTHIAN, 60445
C/W, Patsy Cline
ROBERT A. LATTIN, 7813 S. LUNA AVE., BURBANK, 60459
LP's, Nugent, Amboy Dukes, Rory Gallagher, Cactus
DON LEGO, 410 ILLINOIS ST., JOLIET, 60436
BILL MANLEY, 262 TAYLOR AVE., GLEN ELLYN, 60137
45's, ALBUMS, Monkees
KEN MILLER, 727 36th ST., CAIRO, 62914
R/R, R/B, C/W, 45's, LP's (1950-60) .... (618) 734-4228
BOB NOVY, 408 S. PHELPS, ARLINGTON HTS., 60004
Phil Spector, British Invasion, Punk & Surf
ROBERT PRUTER, 576 STRATFORD AVE., ELMHURST, 60126
DOOWOPS (1950), SOUL, BLUES, CHICAGO R/B (1960-)
JOHN L. RINALDO, 2510 BORDEAUX DR., ROCKFORD, 61111
R/R (1960), Beach Boys .... (815) 877-3337
JOHNNY TRACY, 1560 FLORENCE AVE., GALESBURG, 61401
C/W, 45's, 78's ON LP's
RICK TYLER, 1138 LORENA AVE., WOOD RIVER 62095
KIM URBAN, 1309 S. GLENWOOD, SPRINGFIELD, 62704
R/B (1950-70)
RON VAIL, 706 S. CLAYTON ST., BLOOMINGDALE, 61701
S'TRACKS, R/R, LP's .... (309) 829-4011
VICTROLA, 202 N. LAFAYETTE, MACOMB, 61455 .... (309) 837-3720

V. L. WALSH, 619 E. 2nd, CENTRALIA, 62801
NOVELTY, C/W, LP's, Loretta Lynn
BRIAN WICHMAN, 576 DARA JAMES, DES PLAINES, 60016
ACID/HARD ROCK, British Invasion
NANCY WINTERS, 7 N. MAPLE AVE., FOX LAKE, 60020
LP's, EP's, 45's, ROCK MAGS (1960-70), Stones

INDIANA
JOHN P. BRIGGS, BRIGGS FARM, GENEVA, 46740
ROCKABILY, COUNTRY-ROCK, Punk, Beatles, Stones, Dylan .... (219) 368-7289
FRED CALHOUN, 616 E. NORTH, KOKOMO, 46901
BLUES, R/B, BOOGIE WOOGIE, JAZZ, 78's, 45's, LP's (1940-70)
GOLDEN MEMORIES RECORDS, INC., P. O. BOX 217, MOORESVILLE, 46158
10,000 Different Older LP's
FLOYD HAAS, JR., 2209 E. CARTER RD., KOKOMO, 46901
JOHN HIATT, 7801 ST. RD. 227 N., RICHMOND, 47374
45's, LP's, Jack Scott, Buddy Holly, Patience & Prudence, Fats Domino
TOM PETERSEN, 1018 HARRISON AVE., APT. 3A, DYER, 46311
R/R, 45's, LP's, CLASSICAL (1950-1970)
KENNETH L. SCHILLING, 1313 W. RIDGE RD., HOBART, 46342
RICHARD W. WELCH, 102 MARQUETTE AVE., SOUTH BEND 46617
Sun, Phillips International and Flip Records

IOWA
DOYLE D. HASKELL, 113 S. WASHINGTON, BLOOMFIELD, 52537 . . (515) 664-9512
MEMORY LANE, 113 S. WASHINGTON, BLOOMFIELD, 52537
STEVE PARROTT, 525 TERRACE RD., IOWA CITY, 52240
DANNY SAWHILL, P. O. BOX 2749, DES MOINES, 50315
R/B, C/W, R/R, ROCK, 45's (1950-60)

KANSAS
JIMMIE APPLEBEE, 317 E. WASHINGTON, OSBORNE, 67473
C/W (1950-60), R/R
DONALD L. KUHN, 1113 DOWNING AVE., HAYS, 67601
R/R (1950-60), Annette, Dale Ward, Dickey Lee, Glen Campbell .... (913) 625-5858
JERRY LEE LETCHER, 817 SANDUSKY, KANSAS CITY, 66101
Elvis Presley, Frankie & Johnnie .... (913) 281-1719
LARRY WAGGONER, 9030 SUNCREST, WICHITA, 67212
POPULAR FOLK MUSIC, COUNTRY (1950-60), ROCK, ALBUMS, SINGLES (1950)

KENTUCKY

DON C. COPHER, RT. 3, OWINGSVILLE, 40360
Elvis

STEVE MALLORY, 3051 KIRKLEVINGTON DR., #S, LEXINGTON, 40502
Beatles .... (606) 272-9761

C. RICHARD MATTHEWS, BOX 589, PINEVILLE, 40977
Johnnie Ray

RAY WATKINS, 6810 SEBREE DR. APT. 4, FLORENCE, 41042
R/R, POP, ENGLISH ROCK, 45's, LP's

LOUISIANA

BILL DELLE, 2625 N. BENGAL RD., METAIRIE, 70002
R/B, R/R (1950) .... (504) 729-3129

HEL-LO RECORD CO., INC., 710 ARIS AVE., BOX 9447, METAIRIE 70005
45's, LP's

TERRY PATTISON, BOX 19702-MID CITY, NEW ORLEANS, 70179
R/B, 45's, 78's, LP's

MICHAEL SALLINGER, SR., 933 BEECHGROVE BLVD., APT. D., WESTWEGO, 70094

MAINE

DIS-COLLECTORS OF MAINE, P. O. BOX 1056, N. WINDHAM, 04062

NELSON GARDNER, BOX 1082, PORTLAND, 04104
C/W, ROCKABILY (1950), Elvis Presley

LARRY GRAY, 12 CLEVELAND ST., CALAIS, 04619
(1960-70)

LEE F. RAND, P. O. BOX 134, OLD TOWN, 04468

GREG SCHULZ, BOX 37, LEWISTON, 04240
ROCK, LP's (1960)

KENNETH TURNER, 66 BRAMHALL ST., PORTLAND, 04102

ROBERT W. VIGUE, 35 PROSPECT ST., SPRINGVALE, 04083

RICHARD WOOD, P. O. BOX 145, KENNEBUNK, 04043
LP's, EP's, Beatles

MARYLAND

EDWARD ALLAN, 118 HEDGEWOOD RD., LUTHERVILLE, 21093
R/R, R/B, ROCK, Elvis

CLIFFORD D. ALPER, 1029 FLAGTREE LN., BALTIMORE, 21208
C/W, R/R, 33's, 45's, 78's of POP

HAROLD E. BAGG, JR., 2906 GOODWOOD RD., BALTIMORE, 21214

EDWARD M. BAYES, 544 VALLEYWOOD RD., MILLERSVILLE, 21108
R/B, R/R, ROCK; Janis Martin, Del Vikings, Mickey & Sylvia .... (301) 987-5478

ROBERT W. BECKER, JR., 50 KING HENRY CT., BALTIMORE, 21237
R/R, R/B, POP, C/W & ROCK (1950-60)
LARRY BLACK, 4808 GUILFORD RD., COLLEGE PARK, 20740
R/B, R/R (1950-60) . . . . (301) 277-2555
ANNE BORTNER, 1416 CATLYN PL., ANNAPOLIS, 21401
Four Seasons
TED GOETZ, 5814 BERKELEY AVE., BALTIMORE, 21215
45's (1950), R/B, Whirlin Disc, Onyx, Rama, Aladdin, Federal, Red Robin
LOUIS HOWARD, 3821 INGLESIDE ST., OLNEY, 20832
HARRY JONES, 11700 OLD COLUMBIA DR., #2017, SILVER SPRINGS, 20904
R/R, R/B, ROCKABILY, SUN 45's, 78's . . . . (301) 622-2344
JAMES S. KING, 2313 MT. HEBRON DR., ELLICOTT CITY, 21043
ROCK, R/B, R/R, 45's, LP's; Elvis, Heartbeats, Five Keys, Bobby Rydell, Jimmy Clanton . . . . (301) 465-7329
MARTIN R. METTEE, JR., 1225 TEN OAKS RD., ARBUTUS, 21227
ENGLISH ROCK, SURF, BLUES, R/B, LP's, 45's, 78's (1960)
CHARLES N. SCHEMM, 7763 TIEKNACK RD., PASADENA, 21122
POP, C/W, R/R (1940-50), Kay Starr, R. Clooney, Hank Snow
DAVID L. SCOTT, 1278 RIVERSIDE AVE., BALTIMORE, 21230
Elvis, Johnny Crawford, Janis Martin, Bay City Rollers, Kiss
MARK V. STEIN, 2202 MILRIDGE DR., OWINGS MILLS, 21117
James Taylor, Bill Joel, Jesse Colin Young, Youngbloods, Beautiful Day, Little Feat
ROBERT H. TIERNEY, BOX 175, RT. 2, HANOVER, 21076
R/R, R/B (1950-60), Little Eva, Del Shannon, Dimension & Mohawk Labels . . . . (301) 799-7871
AL TELGHMAN, S. ELLAMONT ST., BALTIMORE, 21229
R/B, JAZZ, 78's, 45's, LP's
BRIAN WEINSTEIN, 4225 ROUNDHILL RD., WHEATON, 20906

MASSACHUSETTS

MR. TIMOTHY AHERN, 6 LEDGE RD., SEEKONK, 02771
SEVY ALEXANDER (KING OF THE OLDIES), 408 PONT ST., FRANKLIN, 02308
BARON RECORDS, 11 DELL AVE., MELROSE, 02176
BILL BRUNO, 161 SOUTH ST., FOXBORO, 02035
R/B, R/R 45's, LP's & EP's (1950-)
WARREN R. CAREY, 3 MARION DR., TEWKSBURY, 01876
45's OF R/R, POP, R/B, C/W, (1940), EP's, LP's, ... (617) 851-9165
ROGER D. COFSKY, 4 UPTON ST., MILLBURY, 01527 . . . . (617) 755-9343
TONY COLAO, 2904 VILLAGE RD., WEST, NORWOOD, 02062
LP's, ROCK & POP (1950) . . . . (617) 731-0500

ROBERT CORTESE, 35 CARLETON ST., HAVERHILL, 01830
ROCK, BLUES, R/R
GENE DIAS, 116 BISHOP ST., FALL RIVER, 02721
(1950) R/R, R/B, ROCK, Elvis
MIKE FLANAGAN, 44 CEDAR AVE., RANDOLPH, 02368
45's & LP's (1960) .... (617) 963-4677
JACK FITZPATRICK, 16 PRATT PL. #23, REVERE, 02151
Phil Spector, Ronettes/Ronnie Spector, Diana Ross
CHUCK GREGORY, 17 CHAVENSON ST., FALL RIVER, 02723
R/B, R/R, POP, (1948-64), 78's, 45's, LP's
GENE GUZIK, 1 UPLAND RD., HOLYOKE, 01040
Phil Spector, Paris Sisters, Shangri-Las, Roy Orbison, Neil Diamond, ...
.... (413) 533-4510
FRED A. JOHNSON, 48 W. SCHOOL, WESTFEILD, 01085
Joni Mitchell
JACK FITZPATRICK, 16 PRATT PL. #23, REVERE, 02151
Phil Spector, Ronettes/Ronnie Spector, Diana Ross/Supremes, Beach Boys, Orbison, Pitney
ROGER KIRK, BOX 806, LAWRENCE, 01842
R/B, ROCK, (1950-)
ED LINDBACK, 24 VINTON ST., RANDOLPH, 02368
45's, POP, (1950-) .... (617) 963-4508
RON MARTIN, 563 KING PHILIP ST., FALL RIVER, 02724
R/R, R/B, Elvis 45's, EP's, LP's
JON McAULIFFE, 24 BOWEN ST., NEWTON, 02159
Elvis Presley LP's, BLUES LP's, ROCK LP's, (1950-70) ROCK & POP LP's
GERALD M. MELLO, 24 BARNES ST., FALL RIVER, 02723
LP's, 45's, EP's, Buddy Holly .... (617) 678-2595
MICHAEL MICHEL, P.O. BOX 505, KENMORE, STN., BOSTON, 02215
(1950) Uptemps, R/B Vocal Groups, 45's (1950-63)
GEORGE A MOONOGAIN, 197 BROADWAY, HAVERHILL, 01830
R/B (1940-57)
JOHN H. MORAN, 121 STEBBINS ST., CHICOPEE, 01020
THE MUSIC MACHINE, BOX 262, SHREWSBURY, 01545
KEITH JOSEPH O'CONNOR, 70 VERMONT ST., HOLYOKE, 01040
Monkees, Herman's Hermits, Dave Clark Five
DAVID OKSANEN, 220 BEDFORD ST., BRIDGEWATER, 02324
Elvis, (1960) R/R
VICTOR PEARLIN, P.O. BOX 199A GREENDALT STN., WORCRESTER, 01606
(1950) R/B
DOUGLAS PEDERSON, 11 EMERSON DR., LITTLETON, 01460
KIP PUIIA, 8 WESTGATE DR., #207, WOBURN, 01801
(1963-66) British Releases

RANDOLPH MUSIC CENTER, INC., 340 N. MAIN ST., RANDOLPH, 02368
LP's & 45's R/R (1950-60)
THE RECORD CORNER, 66 CINTRAS ST., IPSWICH, 01938
LP's, 45's, R/R (1950-70)
DENNIS RICHARD, 152 GILBERT ST., LAWRENCE, 01943
Beatles, Stones, Kinks, Who, Tom Rush
MIKE RICHARD, BOX 434 GARDNER RD., HUBBARDSTON, 01452
(1950-60) R/R, Buddy Holly, Ritchie Valens, Big Bopper & Info on the Crash . . . . (617) 928-3344
JACK SHADOIAN, RFD #3, AMHERST, 01002
(1940-50) ROCK, BLUES
WESLEY A. SMITH, 290 S. MAIN ST., PALMER 01069
(1950-60), R/R, LP's & 45's. Champs, Ventures, Fireballs, Shadows, Phil Spector . . . . (413) 283-6901
WATHAM RECORD SHOP, 20 LEXINGTON ST., WALTHAM, 02154
DAVID A. YEAGER, 67 PARKSIDE ST., LONGMEADOW, 01106
ROCK, POP, R/B, SOUL (1964-69)

MICHIGAN
BLACK KETTLE RECORDS (FRED REIF), 542 GRATIOT AVE., SAGINAW, 48602
ALLEN E. BROWN, P.O. BOX 188, MARNE, 49435
45's OF R/B, R/R & C/W (1950-60)
MARK A. BROWN, RT. 1, BOX 382-D, BERRIEN SPRINGS, 49103
45's OF R/R, R/B, COUNTRY (1958-68) . . . . (616) 471-2146
MICHAEL BROZOVIC, 6633 SHADOWLAWN, DEARBORN HEIGHTS, 48127
TOM CEDERBERG, 2203 32ND. ST., BAY CITY, 48706
(1950) R/R, Elvis, C/W (1950-)
MARIANNE DE NEVE, RT. 1, BOX 8, QUINNESEC, 49876
Bobby Rydell, Rick Nelson
JEANETTE ESSER, 30740 AVONDALE, WESTLAND, 48185
45's (1950-69) Soul Groups
FANTASTICO COLLECTORS CONVENTIONS & PUBLICATIONS (STU SHARPIRO), 17106 RICHARD, SOUTHFIELD, 48075 . . . . (313) 557-8819
CRAIG V. GORDON, RT. #1, BOX 89, EDWARDSBURG, 49112
Chicago Blues Artists, Dylan
JACK HARPER, 2356 BUCHANAN, SW, GRAND RAPIDS, 49507
(1922-50) C & W . . . . (616) 452-4104
DENNIS M. JOHNS, 4013 MOORLAND DR., MIDLAND, 48640
Top 40 (1955-65), Philies, Motown, Cameo & Parkway Labels
BILL KROHN, RT. 2, PAW PAW, 49079
LOONEY TUNES, 1516 W. MICHIGAN AVE., KALAMAZOO, 49007

DIANE OTIS, 5741 RIDGEWAY DRIVE, #10, HASLETT, 44840
BLUES & ROCK (1950-60)
JIM PASHKOT, 26769 W. HILLS DR. INKSTER, 48141
R/B, R/B .... (313) 563-9350
ED PASHULLEWICH, 11310 ASPEN DR., PLYMOUTH, 48170
(1950-60) 45's
WARREN PEACE, 316 STUART #1, KALAMAZOO
Beatles, Yardbirds, ROCK, BLUES, "The Record Man".
PAUL W. PORTER, 4172 HI HILL DR. LAPEER, 48446
45's
M. RADOFSKI, 3238 HARRIS, FERNDALE, 48220
Beatles & Bob Dylan
JERRY L. RATHBUN, 706 BEUIAH, LANSING, 48910
45's & LP's (1950)
CRAIG SIGWORTH, 146 W. HICKORY GROVE, BLOOMFIELD HILLS, 48013
BRITISH ROCK, LP's
ERIC J. STIMAC, 3839 JENNINGS DR., KALAMAZOO, 49001
R/R (1960-70) Beatles, Lennon & Yardbirds .... (616) 342-5520
FRANK D. YOWORSKI, 505 S. VAN BUREN, BAY CITY, 48706

MINNESOTA

GARY D. BAHR, 1727 HODGONRD., N. MANKATO, 56001
R/R 45's, LP's (1960-) .... (507) 387-0926
WAYNE BLESSING, 573 LAUREL AVE. #7, ST. PAUL, 55102
C/W, (1950) R/R
HOWIE RUTLER, 2343 E. LARPENTEUR, ST. PAUL, 55109
POP, BLUES, JAZZ, (-1960) R/R. Tone Arden, Otis, Rush, Sonny Rollins, Elvis, Fats, Jerry Lee
JERRY CHAMBERLAIN, 3704 AUGER AVE., WHITE BEAR LADE, 55110
R/B & R/R 45's (1950-60) .... (612) 429-7851
WILLIAM A. CONRAD, P.O. BOX 6545, ST. PAUL, 55106
POP, C/W, R/B, 45's, LP's
GARY LEE SCHWARTZ, 11014 CO. RD., 15 MINNEAPOLIS, 55441
C/W, BLUES, ROCK, LP's, 45's, 78's .... (612) 545-8727

MISSISSIPPI

BOBBY W. GOFF, JR., P.O. BOX 56, BILOXI, 39533
R/B, POP
KATE PEART, 456 HANGING MOSS CR., JACKSON, 39206
Sinatra

MISSOURI

VANCE DE LOZIER, BOX 541, WARRENSBURG, 64093
(1950-60) POP (Mainly 45's)

GLADYS DILEY, 2143 SHIMOOR LN., ST. LOUIS, 63141
R/R, ROCK (1950-60) - 45's ONLY . . . . (314) 434-4121
ENCORE RECORDS, P.O. BOX 12585, ST. LOUIS, 63141
(1950-60) 45's . . . . (314) 434-4121
HARRY HILBURN, BOX 308, W. PLAINS, 65775
R/R 45's, Elvis . . . . (417) 256-0797
GREG JONES, P.O. BOX 22413, SAPPINGTON, 63126
Petula Clark, Diana Ross, Supremes, Beach Boys, Bruce Johnston . . . . (314) 842-2815
TOM KELLY, 707 WASHINGTON, ST. LOUIS, 63101
R/B, 45's, 78's (-1960)
TOM MIX, 6 S. EULCID, ST. LOUIS, 63108 . . . . (314) 361-7353
TIM NEELEY, 2519 LEMAY FERRY RD., ST. LOUIS, 63125 . . . . (314) 892-1394
RICHARD A. PORTER, 8004 BROOKLYN, KANSAS CITY, 64132
Elvis 45's & LP's . . . . (816) 363-2090
ROCKIN' RECORDS, P.O. BOX 6012, KANSAS CITY, 64110
R/R, R/B, ROCKABILLY, POP, C/W
GARY SONGER, 1702 WESTMINSTER, MEXICO, 65265
45's, LP's, & 78's (1950), Elvis, Ral Donner, Cochran, Vincent . . . . (314) 581-6587
CHUCK TURMAN, 4438 FORREST, KANSAS CITY, 64110
(1950-60) R/R, R/B, Elvis
CHUCK M. VOGEL, 4363 MIAMI ST., ST. LOUIS, 63116
Beatles, British Invasion, Jan & Dean, Beach Boys, (1960) 45's
BARON YAMA, BOX 62, SAVANNAH, 64485
ROCKABILLY, R/R, R/B: 45's & LP's Only

MONTANA
L & C RECORDS, STAR ROUTE BOX 432, BRADY, 59416
POP, ROCK, C/W, 45's, LP's (1950-70)

NEBRASKA
MIKE HALL, 2601 WINTHROP RD., LINCOLN, 68502
Beatles, Jimi Hendrix, Cream, Bubble Puppy, Mountain, West, Bruce / Laing, Ted Nugent, Queen & Wishbone Ash
MICHAEL J. MAJESKI, 515 S. 31st ST., #1, OMAHA, 68105
ROCK, LP's, SINGLES (1964-), Jefferson Airplane, Starship, Grateful Dead, Zappa, Mothers
DAVE "OZ" OSBORN, 9666 "V" PLAZA #18, OMAHA, 68127

NEVADA
WM. R. FELLOWS, 5800 PEBBLE BEACH, LAS VEGAS, 89108
R/R, LP's, 45's (1960)

JIM HENRY, 645-C DENSLOWE DR., RENO, 89512
COUNTRY, 78's, 45's & Pre-Beatles R/R 45's
LES M. KASTEN, 3805 HADDOCK AVE., LAS VEGAS, 89110
Jan & Dean, Jan & Arnie, Jan Berry, The Marcels .... (702) 452-4365
BILL MANSFIELD, 2648 VIKING WAY, CARSON CITY, 89701
R/R, R/B, 45's, LP's, PIC Sleeves of C/W
EVERETT H. YOCAM, 2725 KIETZKE LN. SP. 31A, RENO, 89502
C/W

NEW HAMPSHIRE

JOHN C. BANKS, BOX 697, S. DANVILLE, 03881
R/R; Lou Christie, Johnny Horton
BRUCE DUMAIS, 1 MEMORIAL DR., SOMERSWORTH, 03878
POP 45's, R/B (1954-63) .... (603) 692-5173
JACK WARNER, 77 MARYLAND AVE., MANCHESTER, 03104
Little Richard .... (603) 625-6779

NEW JERSEY

LOU ANTONICELLO, 95 STUYVESANT AVE., JERSEY CITY, 07306
ROCK, Elvis, Duane Eddy, Jack Scott .... (201) 451-4717
WENDY BLUME, 764 SCOTLAND RD. #35, SOUTH ORANGE, 07079
Rolling Stones
JOSEPH BOZZA, JR., 55 MILTON AVE., NUTLEY, 07110
(1960), Beach Boys, Jan & Dean
CHEAP THRILLS, LTD., 382 GEORGE ST., NEW BRUNSWICK, 08001
ROCK (1960), Beatles, Shadows of Knight, Beau Brummels
DUANE CHRISTIE, 637 SEMINARY AVE., RAHWAY, 07065
Buddy Holly, Elvis, Eddie Cochran, Roy Orbison, Crickets, Jerry Lee Lewis, Carl Perkins, Jape Richardson, Gene Vincent
L. J. CHELSON, 17 CHADOWLAWN DR., LIVINGSTON, 07039
R/R: (1950), ROCK, INSTRUMENTS, (1960) Surfing Vocal & Instrumental, British Rock, (1970) Heavy Metal
FRANK J. CHOLOSKI, 16 FONTAINE AVE., BLOOMFIELD, 07003
LP's, 45's (1950-60)
TOM COOK, 2 VINCENT PLACE, BRIDGEWATER 08807
R/B, R/R (1950-60)
JOHN A. DI ROCCO, P. O. BOX 222, MAPLE SHADE, 08052
R/R, R/B, 45's, 33's, 78's
CATHY DIPPEL, P. O. BOX 212, EDGEWATER, 07020
Beatle
THE DOO WOP SHOP, P. O. BOX 2261, EDISON, 08817
R/B, R/R .... (201) 738-7666
TOM DOW, 137 JULIA AVENUE, TRENTON, 08610

DONALD D. DUNN, 170 BEECH ST., PATERSON, 07501
Elvis 45's, LP's
STEVE FREEDMAN, BOX 2054, EAST ORANGE, 07019
Beatles, Elvis, POP
ED GOFDON, LOT 9-B KARL-LEMOBILE MANOR, CARDIFF, 09232
R/R (1950-60), ROCKABILY, INSTRUMENTAL R/R . . . . (609) 646-6744
JAMES GRACZYK, 12 QUINCY LN., BERGENFIELD, 07621
HARD ROCK (1950-60), Stones, Yardbirds, Who . . . . (201) 384-2306
J. RONALD GRAU, 407 S. UNION AVE., CRANFORD, 07016
R/B, POP, LP's . . . . (201) 276-0140
TOM KENNEDY, P. O. BOX 347, ABSECON, 08201
Elvis
RAYMOND B. HOMISKI, 464 FOURTH AVE., ELIZABETH, 07206
Elvis & Beatles (1950-60)
JOE KIVAK, P. O. BOX 679, ELIZABETH, 07207
Dylan & Springsteen
ROBERT KORDISH, BOX 496 STATE HOME RD., JAMESBURG, 08831
R/B, R/B, ROCK (1950-60) . . . . (201) 521-2760
RON KUSHNER, 58 SHERMAN PL., IRVINGTON, 07111
R/R
PETER MALLOY, 8 WOODMONT DR., CHATHAM TWSP, 07928
JAMES F. McNABOE, 235 PROSPECT AVE., HACKENSACK, 07601
R/R, R/B
MR. RECORDS, P. O. BOX 764, HILLSIDE, 07205
NEVER GONE RECORDS, 926 GRANDVIEW AVE., UNION 07083
RUSS NUGENT, 138-A TIERNEY DR., CEDAR GROVE 07009
45's, Fontane Sisters, Crew-Cuts, Ella Mae Morse, Pat Boone, McGuire Sisters, Georgia Biggs, Gale Storm, Teresa Brewer, Four Aces, Chordettes, De Castro Sisters, Laurie Sisters, De John Sisters & Elvis . . . . (201) 239-2218
THE OLDE TYME MUSIC SCENE, 915 MAIN ST., BOONTON, 07005
"Everything from Edison to Elvis"
LINDA PARENTI, 196 MILL ST., APT. 3, BELLEVILLE 07109
Frankie Valle, Four Seasons, Four Lovers . . . . (201) 759-5868
CHESTER F. PIELL, P. O. BOX 107, FLEMINGTON, 08822
ROCK, Cliff Richard, Rick Nelson . . . . (201) 996-4291
SCOTT PISKIN, 741 AVENUE C., BAYONNE, 07002
45's, Grateful Dead, Hot Tuna, Airplane
PLATTER WORLD, P. O. BOX 234, GARFIELD, 07026
EDDIE PLUNGIS, JR., 701 TUXEDO PL., LINDEN, 07036
ROCK (1960-70), Yardbirds, Bubble Puppy, etc. . . . . (201) 925-6902
CLIFFORD PRIGA, 1300 EDGEWOOD AVE., WESTVILLE, 08093
R/B, R/R (1950-60)
FRED RATHYEN, JR., 41 JAMES AVE., CLARK, 07066
EP's, 45's, 78's, LP's; Frankie Valli & The Four Seasons
THE RECORD EXCHANGE (LES MARELLA), 113 A CHESTER AVE., W. BERLIN, 08091
RECORDS & ROCK MAGS (1950-60), R/R . . . . (609) 627-0841
EDWARD T. REILLY, 501 WASHINGTON ST., EATONTOWN, 07730

MARK RESTIVO, 64 EASTON AVE., NEW BRUNSWICK, 08901
(1960), British Rock, Kinks, Beach Boys
LOUIS ROATCHE, 5419 GAUMER AVE., PENNSAUKEN, 08109
R/B, R/R, 45's, LP's
RICK SALIERNO, P. O. BOX 1606, BLOOMFIELD, 07003
ROCK (1960-70), David Bowie
EDWARD P. SANSEVERINO, 16A WOODMERE APTS./W. COUNTY LINE RD., JACKSON, TWP, 08527
JOHN J. SCHUMITTA, 409 BRICK BLVD. APT. 26A, BRICKTOWN, 08723
Elvis 45's, ALBUMS .... (201) 920-1964
MARK A. TESORO, 6 LYNN DR., TOMS RIVER, 08723
45's (1930-50)
KEN THOMPSON, 2802 BUCHANAN ST., WALL, 07719
R/B GROUPS, DOOWOPS, 45's, LP's .... (201) 681-2450
JOSEPH P. M. TRAPANI, 253 ANDOVER DR., WAYNE, 07470
GROUPS, LP's (1950-60)
STEVE VIOLA, 6110 JOHNSON PL., W. NEW YORK, 07093
Elvis, ROCKABILY, Beatles, Beach Boys, EP's .... (201) 868-1482
ANN M. WALTON, 4 WEXFORD RD., GIBBSBORO, 08026
SHEET MUSIC, 45's, 33's, 78's, DISCOGROPHYS

NEW MEXICO

ROGER J. BERNARD, 3908 DOUGLAS MacARTHUR NE, ALBUQUERQUE, 87110
R/B RECORDS
JUDY PETRUNGARO, 1436 CAMINO CERRITO SE, ALBUQUERQUE, 87123
MR. VAL WYSZYNSKI, NMSU ELEC. MUSIC LAB., BOX 188, LAS CRUCES, 88001
EARLY ROCK, C/W, 78's, 45's

NEW YORK

ART ARF, P. O. BOX 755, COOPER STN., NEW YORK, 10003
45's, (1950-). .... (212) 243-6484
ROBERT BALDWIN, 79 OAKDALE AVE., NEW HARTFORD, 13413
R/R, 45's, 33's (1950-60)
WILLIAM D. BALDWIN, 400 SEMLOH DR., SYRACUSE, 13219
ROCK (1960)
SCOTT BARREY, 103 S. NINTH ST., OLEAN, 14760
R/B, R/R, ROCKABILY 45's, C/W, POP 45's .... (716) 372-7041
BURT BELKNAP, 183 PALMDALE DR., #4, WILLIAMSVILLE, 14221
ROCKABILY, R/B LP's, 45's (1950-60) .... (716) 634-8147
CHARLES R. BERGER, 164 GRAHAM AVE., STATEN ISLAND, 10314
POP (1950-55), F. Lanie, Hilltoppers, Four Aces, P. Page, K. Starr, etc. .... (212) 761-4756
CHIP CHAPMAN, P. O. BOX 492, CHADWICKS, 13319
ROCK (1960)

ROY H. COHEN, 130-11 60 AVE., FLUSHING, 11355
R/R, R/B, 45's, 78's, LP's, Elvis, Sinatra
BILL & JEFF COLLINS, 98-25 65th AVE., #5A, REGO PARK, 11374
Neil Diamond
DUANE F. COUGHENOUR, 4168 W. SENECA TPKE,. SYRACUSE, 13215
R/R, R/B, (1960-) .... (315) 492-3006
BOB COUSE, 113 LENA TERRACE, N. SYRACUSE, 13212
Gerry & Pacemakers, Bobby Vee, Del Shannon, Doors, Hollies, Searchers, Jan & Dean .... (315) 458-5174
TONY D'ANGELO, P. O. BOX 432, E. ELMHURST, QUEENS, 11369
Elvis Presley, STEREO 45's, LP's (1950-60)
TONY DeLUCA, 570 WESTMINSTER RD., BROOKLYN, 11230
FRED DE POALO, 30 S. COLE AVE., SPRING VALLEY, 10977
R/R, R/B, ROCKABILY, DOO WOPS, (1950-60), Elvis
DENNIS A. DIOGUARDI, P. O. BOX 56-ROSEBANK, STATEN ISLAND, 10305
Beatles, Dion, Valli & Four Seasons, Holly, J. Maestro, P. Anka, Elegants, Del Satins, British Rock
MAX DIAMOND, 1701 HERTEL AVE., BUFFALO 14216
BRUCE PROMS, 1216 TRACY AVE., SCHENECTADY, 12309
R/R, R/B
EL ENGEL, 45-10 KISSENA BLVD., FLUSHING, 11355
Four Seasons, Tokens, Earls, Regents, The Elegants
FLASHBACK RECORDS, 412 9th ST., (OFF 1st AVE.), N.Y.C., 10003
COLLECTORS ROCK, LP's, 45's (1960-70) .... (212) 260-8363
DAN FRIEDLANDER, 145 N. RAILROAD AVE., BABYLON, 11702
R/B, R/R, 45's, Cleftones, Flamingoes, Clovers
ROLD GALUPO, 69-63 ALDERTON ST., REGO PARK 11374
DOOWOPS, DISCO
R. GETREUER, 798 BROOKRIDGE DR., APT. 33, VALLEY COTTAGE, 10989
DOO WOP GROUP, 45's (1950-)
PHILLIP GRABASH, 345 E. 80th ST., NEW YORK, 10021
R/R, 45's, LP's (1950) .... (212) 535-7192
ANDRE GRABOWICZ, P. O. BOX 1881, BROOKLYN, 11202
Out-of-Print ROCK, JAZZ, FOLK .... (212) 499-8598
JOHN GRAY, 14 CADDY PL., ROCKY POINT, 11778
R/B, R/R, 78's, 45's .... (516) 744-7937
BENJY GREENBERY, 9 RICHARD PL., RYE, 10580
Worlds No. 1 Beatlemaniac
RAY GREENBERG, 50-35 184th ST., FLUSHING, 11365
C/W, R/R, LP's, 78's
STEVEN L. GUBLER, HYDE PARK ESTATES, APT. 6C, HYDE PARK, 12538
Beatles & Frank Ifield
JOHN HERGULA, 105-33 OTIS AVE., NEW YORK, 11368
R/B, 45's, LP's (1950-) .... (212) 592-6580
GARY C. HUESTED, 4170 SLUGA DR., NEWBURGH, 12550
Annette, Dion & Belmonts, Crests, James Daren, Elegants, Buzz Clifford, Johnny Preston, Del Shannon, Phil Spector, Gale Storm, Curtis Lee, Ray Peterson

ROBERT S. HYDE, 229 E. 28th ST. 1E, NEW YORK, 10016
ROCKABILY (1960), Jan & Dean . . . . (212) 532-9115
THE JIMI HENDRIX ARCHIVES (TOM RICHARDS), 4700 W. LAKE RD., CANANDAIGUA, 14424
LP's, EP's, 45's, no 78's (1960), Hendrix, Yardbirds, Beatles, British, Texas
CARL P. KIRSCHENBAUM, 27 PETTIBONE, DR., ALBANY, 12205
45's, British Sound, Instrumental Surf, Billboard Top 100
ROCKY KREAMER, 30 FAIRWAY RD., CORNING, 14830
R/R, Beatle
JOHN KURTZ, 110 BEMENT AVE., STATEN ISLAND, 10310
R/R, C/W, ROCKABILY
ARTHUR LANE, P. O. BOX 1187, NEW YORK, 13201
R/B, VOCAL GROUPS (1950-60) . . . . (315) 422-2452
LARRY LAPKA, 11 WENDY LN., MASSAPEQUA, 11762
R/R, LP's, Monkees & Dave Clark Five . . . . (516) 541-8454
HOWARD L. LENT, 151-75 22nd AVE., WHITESTONE, 11357
MINT R/R & R/B (1950-64) ESP. EP's & 45's
JOSEPH M. LOGLISCI, 4200 AVE. K #1HH, BROOKLYN, 11210
R/R, R/B, ROCK (1960), Phil Spector, Surf, Beach Boys, Four Seasons
CRAIG LONG, 776 WESTBROOK DR., N. TONAWANDA, 14120
POP, R/R, R/B
DAVID MICHALAK, 26 CARHART AVE., JOHNSON CITY, 13790
RUSS MASON, 82 BENSON RD., FREEVILLE, 13068
POP, R/R, 45's, LP's (1955-65) . . . . (607) 257-7765
PAUL L. MICHEL, 9 WOODHALL LN., CLIFTON PARK, 12065
R/B, VOCAL GROUPS (1950-60)
MIKE MONNAT, 15 DICKENSON AVE., BINGHAMPTON, 13901
RECORDS, EARLY R/B (1950-60)
JAMES M. MOYER, 380 HARTFORD RD., APT. 1-C, AMHERST, 14226
(1950-60), Annette, Spike Jones, Edd (Kookie) Byrnes
ROBERT M. MURRAY, RR#1 LAKE SHORE DR., S. SALEM, 10590
R/B, R/R, 45's, DOOWOP, Bill Haley, Buddy Holly, Fats Domino
WILLIAM PRICE, BOX 356, ELBRIDGE, 13060
R/B GROUPS, Early BLUES, Very Early POP
THE RECORD ARCHIVE, 762 MONROE AVE., ROCHESTER, 14607
Out-of-Print Records . . . . (716) 473-3820
MIKE REDMOND, 12 HAMPTON ST., HAUPPAUGE, 11787
R/R, R/B, 45's & LP's. (Pre-1956) R/B VOCAL GROPUS . . . . (516) 234-3216
JAY REPOLEY, 45 SCARBORO AVE., STATEN ISLAND, 10305
R/B GROUPS, 45's, LP's, 78's. R/B (1930-40). MELLOW ROCK LP's & ROCK LP's (MOODY BLUES, EARLY STONES, BEATLES, DOORS, ETC.). . 981-2550
MARTIN ROSEN, 2410 BARKER AVE., BRONX, 10467
RICHARD R. ROSEN, BOX 42, HOMECREST STATION, BROOKLYN, 11229
R/B, R/R, DOOWOPS (1950-60) . . . . (212) 253-1869
GARY ROSENOWITZ, 902 E. 56th ST., BROOKLYN, 11234
Out-of-Print LP's
MARIE E. SADLO, 9 FAYE AVE., NEW WINDSOR, 12550

VINCENT SANSONE, 47-61 196th ST., FLUSHING, 11358
Beatles, Elvis, ROCK, American & British (1960) POP & ROCK, Left Banke, Shadows of Knight, New Colony Six, Spanky & Our Gang
PETER T. SANTACROCE, BOX 1592, SOUTHAMPTON COLL., SOUTHAMPTON, 11968
LP's OF JAZZ, ROCK, FOLK
MR. JACK SCHNUR, 41-42 LITTLE NECK PKWY, LITTLE NECK, 11363
Sinatra
JOE SCHIAVONE, 181 C EDGEWATER PARK, NEW YORK, 10465
STUART SCHNEIDER, 208 E. BROADWAY, NEW YORK, 10002
ROCKABILY, 45's .... (212) 533-3861
RICK SHAW DWA (DOO WOPS ANONYMOUS), 44 STRAWBERRY HILL LN., WEST NYACK, 10994
ROCK, DOO WOP, BLUES, POP FOLK, 45's, LP's (1950-1960)
DAVID SHLOSH, 570 WESTMINSTER RD., BROOKLYN, 11230
ROCK, POP (1950-70), BLACK VOCAL
ALAN SHUTRO, 140 S. ASH AVE., FLUSHING, 11355
LP's (1950-); R/R, SOUL ROCK, SURF, R/R .... (212) 961-4927
TEDD SIVRAIS, 12 SLAUSON AVE., BINGHAMTON, 13905
Phil Spector, Crystals, Ronettes, Chiffons, Darlene Love
DONNA SLATING, 10 COCHOCTON ST., NAPLES, 14512
WALTER SNYDER, 224 JEFFERSON AVE., MINEOLA, 11501
R/B (1950-60), BLACK GROUP
MR. WESLEY TILLMAN, 474 W. 158th ST. APT. 44, NEW YORK, 10032
R/R, R/B, POP & SOUL, LP's, 45's (1950-60)
STEPHEN J. TOKASH, G.P.O. BOX 2302, NEW YORK, 10001
Elvis
FRANK TURNER, 149-36 DELAWARE AVE., FLUSHING, 11355
ROCKABILY, R/B, R/R, C/W, Southern & Chicago BLUES, 45's
ANTONIO VASQUEZ, 1330 WM. FLOYD PKWY., SHIRLEY, 11967
R/B, Early ROCK, 78's, 45's (1950-) .... (516) 281-2027
GREG F. WADE, 297 OLEAN ST., E. AURORA, 14052
MOVIE POSTERS, ROCK & BLUES Only, 45's, 78's, LP's ..... (716) 652-4382
MARCUS WALDMAN, 120-18 ELGAR PL., BRONX, 10475
R/B Single Artists & Groups (1955-65), JACKIE Wilson, Sam Cooke, Clyde McPhatter, Cadillacs, Flamingoes, Elvis, LP's, EP's, 45's .... (212) 320-0261
WHIRLIN' DISC RECORDS, 230 MAIN ST., FARMINGDALE, 11735
MELANIE WILSON, 15 WOODS RD., ISLIP TERRACE, 11752
Glen Campbell, Barry Manilow, Groucho Mark on DECCA & Imported Ace of Hearts. (AH-103) .... (516) 277-9750
D. WIUR, 41 LOCUST AVE., BETHPAGE, 11714
Walker Bros., Yoko Ono, Beefheart, Nico
JACK WOLAK, STAR RT., DEPEYSTER, 13633
T-REX 45's. EP's; Dylan 45's, EP's
EDWART ZLOTNICK, 300 W. 55th ST., RM. 16R, NEW YORK, 10019
LP's, EP's, 45's (1950-), Beatles, Buddy Holly

NORTH CAROLINA

RUSSELL BATTEN, P. O. BOX 516, THOMASVILLE, 27360
Bob Dylan .... (919) 475-9233
WESLEY BROOKS, 680 BRENTWOOD CT., WINSTON-SALEM, 27104
R/R, R/B, (1950); Big Bands (1940-50); C/W .... (919) 765-2537
ROBERT S. DEAN, 243 BEDFORD DR., EDEN, 27288
WILLIAM H. MELTON, 469 ROCK CREEK RD., RALEIGH, 27612
R/R, C/W, ROCKABILY, R/B, 45's
RICK SCOGGINS, BOX 12274, CHARLOTTE, 28205
Beatles .... (704) 568-6488
THURMAN SHOCKLEY, 1437 NEW FAGGE RD., EDEN, 27288
C/W, R/R (1950-60) .... (919) 627-4513
JOHN STYERS, RT. 1 BOX B-540, STATESVILLE, 28677
Beatles, Beach Boys & Surfing Music
JOHN SWAIN, 1220 BANBURY RD., RALEIGH 27607
R/B, ROCKABILY & (Pre-1956) C/W
MIKE VALLE, P. O. BOX 2687, BURLINGTON, 27215
R/R, R/B, GROUP, ROCKABILY, C/W, BLUES, POP (1950-60) .. (919) 584-0096
BILL WALL, 309 TAFT ST., EDEN, 27288
R/R, R/B, ROCKABILY LP's

NORTH DAKOTA

DAVE BAKER, 1102 E. 4th, W. FARGO, 58078
ROCK, ROCKABILY, R/B (1950-60)
ANGELINE KADY, 2018 UNIVERSITY AVE., GRAND FORKS, 58201
C/W, POP, ROCK, 70's (1930-50)

OHIO

TERRY ALEXANDER, 3361 E. HIGH ST., SPRINGFIELD, 45505
POP, EP's (1950-70), Annette, Olivia Newton-John, Bee Gees .... (513) 325-8457
SANDOLL ANDROMEDA, 5048 HARBOR BLVD., COLUMBUS, 43227
Beatles
GEORGE BELDEN, 613 DAVID DR., STREETSBORO, 44240
Live Concert Recordings
TED DESPRES, 5523 PARKVILLE ST., COLUMBUS, 43229
POP, R/R, HARD ROCK, C/W (1950-) .... (614) 891-9353
E. ROBBIE DUMOULIN, 1580 RUTH DR., WOOSTER, 44691
DUSTY DISC RECORDS (CHRIS DODGE), P. O. BOX 310, MIDDLETOWN, 45042
R/R, ROCKABILY, 45's (1950-) .... (513) 422-7090
MIKE GREENFIELD, 148 S. WHITNEY ST., YOUNGSTOWN, 44509
POP (1960), Beatles

DANIEL E. HOWE, 423 PARK LN., WALBRIDGE, 43465
R/B, R/R, DOOWOP
WILLIAM JOHNS, 554 KAPPLER RD., HEATH, 43055
R/R, R/B (1950)
J. P. KEHOE, 6593 BEVERLY DR., PARMA HEIGHTS, 44130
LP's, Dion, Beatles
ROBERT KOTABISH, 5667 MEADOW LANE, BEDFORD HEIGHTS, 44146
Four Seasons, Frankie Valli, Jay & the Americans, Johnny Rivers
JEFF KREITER, RT. 2 BOX 113B, BELLAIRE, 43906
45's (1955-63) BLACK VOCAL
JERRY LADD, 7255 JETHIVE LN., CINCINNATI, 45243
R/R (1950-60), ELVIS, Annette .... (513) 271-0570
LENNY MAJOR RECORDS, P. O. BOX 706, ASHTABULA, 44004
45's, ALBUMS, Auction Lists
DAN LIBERATORE, 4266 NOBLE ST., BELLAIRE, 43906
DOOWOPS, R/B, 45's (1955-63)
JOHN MARSH, 5163 SOUTH AVE., TOLEDO, 43615
Freddy Cannon, Flying Saucers
JOHN McCARTHY, 4002 GROVE AVE., CINCINNATI, 45227
R/R, R/B, ROCKABILY, C/W, BOOGIE, 45's, LP's
*Beatles***BOB McGUINNES,** 4305-B COX DR., STOW, 44224
KEN McPECK, 2131 NORWOOD BLVD., ZANESVILLE, 43701
ROCK, BOOKS, MAGS: Jan & Dean, Duane Eddy, Rick Nelson, Johnny & Hurricanes, Fabian, Frankie Avalon, Bobby Rydell
MARLENE J. MILLER, 461 HARMONY LN., CAMPBELL, 44405
Frank Sinatra .... (216) 755-3451
MARY NEER, 1916 PERKINS DR., SPRINGFIELD, 45505
45's, LP's & One-Sided 78's
PHILIP J. PEACHOCK, 435 LANSING AVE., YOUNGSTOWN, 44506
STEVE PETRYSZYN, 4347 PEARL RD., CLEVELAND, 44109
R/B, Sedaka, Manilow, Five Satins
ROBERT & COMPANY, 1910 LOCKBOURNE RD., COLUMBUS, 43207
DONALD SCHROCK, 161 W. 10th AVE., COLUMBUS, 43201
ROCK INSTRUMENTAL, LP's, 45's (1950)
JAMES L. SCOTT, 12716 SPEEDWAY OVERLOOK, E. CLEVELAND, 44112
R/B (1960-70)
2ND TIME AROUND, RECORD & TAPE EXCHANGE, 1133 BROWN ST., DAYTON, 45409
ROCK, 10,000 LP's .... (513) 228-6399
LARRY SKILLMAN, 337 E. WATER ST., NEW LEXINGTON, 43764
R/R, 45's, LP's, Beatles
JOE SLOAT, BOX 242, MID CITY STATION, DAYTON, 45402
DAVE SPRAGUE, 4103 W-58, CLEVELAND, 44144
JERRY VILLING, 8439 LIVINGTON RD., CINCINNATI, 45239
ROCKABILY, R/B, 45's .... (513) 385-9733
VINCE WALDRON, P. O. BOX 426, YELLOW SPRINGS, 45387
WINFRED WILHOIT, 6553 ELVIN LN., HAMILTON, 45011
R/R, C/W, S'TRACKS

DENNY WRIGHT, 1776 DEPOT RD., SALEM, 44460
BLUES, R/R, ROCKABILY .... (216) 332-1252
DOUG YOUNG, 6117 LARCHWAY, TOLEDO, 43613
R/B GROUP, TREAT & CHANCE LABELS

OKLAHOMA
TOM BIDDLE, 1150 N. TOLEDO, TULSA, 74115
R/B, 45's, 78's (1950), R/R, 45's (-1965) .... (918) 835-8782
STEVE HOVIS, 402 SW 24th ST., LAWTON, 73505
Elvis, Jack Scott, ROCKABILY
JACK L. JONES, 2009 N. OSAGE, PONCA CITY, 74601
R/R, ROCKABILY, C/W (1950-60), DOOWOP .... (405) 762-6134
KERRY KUDLACEK, 4909 S. BRADEN, 13-E, TULSA, 74135
LP's, ROCK, COMEDY
CLIFF ROBNETT, 7600 NW 25 TERR., BETHANY, 73008
(1950-60), DOOWOP, Beatles, Beach Boys, Elvis, Carl Perkins ....
.... (405) 787-6703

OREGON
KEN COSTELLO, 2840 RIVER RD., EUGENE, 97404
50,000 Records For Sale .... (503) 688-5590
BERNE GREENE, 1833 S.E. 7th AVE., PORTLAND, 97214
ROCK & SOUL, POP, 45's, LP's. 40,000 Records in Stock ..... (503) 232-5964
VAN KENNEL, 600 FLORENCE AVE., ASTORIA, 97103
BUTCH MacKIMMIE, 208 N. EVANS, McMINNVILLE, 97128
ROCK, Beatles
CRAIG MOERER, P. O. BOX 13247, PORTLAND, 97213
ROCKABILY, C/W
MARK K. O'NEIL, 5518 S.E. 4th AVE., PORTLAND, 97206
Out-of-Print LP's .... (503) 774-1411
KEITH PRIDIE, 6685 SW SAGERT #94, TUALATIN, 97062
Beatles
RICHARD L. REESE, 11403 S.E. STANLEY, MILWAUKEE, 97222
R/R (1954-70), Rick Nelson, Elvis, Beach Boys, Jan & Dean, Beatles
SHIRLEY VOIT, BOX 804, 305 E. ST. APT. #3, EUGENE, 97477

PENNSYLVANIA
ARNOLD AMBER, P. O. BOX 153, LEMONT FURNACE, 15456
(1959-63), The Lettermen, Four Seasons, Beach Boys
ARBORIA-USED BOOKS & RECORDS, 151 S. ALLEN ST., STATE COLLEGE, 16801
R/R, LP's .... (814) 237-7624

FRANK ARMBRUSTER, 306 GRANT ST., OLYPHANT, 18447
R/R, R/B, C/W ....(717) 489-8991
RICK BALSLEY, 435 N. WALNUT ST., WERNERSVILLE, 19565
R/R, R/B, 45's, Beatles, Elvis
ROBERT M. BROWN, P. O. BOX 124, HIGHSPIRE, 17034
C/W, BIG BANDS, LP ALBUMS
JIM BURLEIGH, 207 WILLIAMS ST., TOWMAND, 18848
BOB & PATTY CAMPBELL, 157 WINDSOR AVE., LANSDOWNE, 19050
Beatles
JOSEPH CONTI, 514 BRIARWOOD RD., GLENSIDE, 19038
ROCK (1960), Rolling Stones, Beach Boys, Phil Spector, Garland Jeffries, Denny Laine
KEN CLEE, STAK-O-WAX, P. O. BOX 11412, PHILADELPHIA, 19111
R/R, R/B, DOOWOPS, 45's (1950-60)
FLOYD COPELAND, 13 BRIARWOOD RD., SHREWBURY, 71361
R/B, R/R, ROCKABILY (1950-64)
BOB COWAN, P. O. BOX 8803, PITTBURGH, 15221
R/R, R/B, 45's ONLY (1953-60)
ANNE CRAMER, 223 ELBRIDGE ST., PHILADELPHIA, 19111
45's, LP's (1950-60)
FRANK CZURI, 11403 ALTHEA RD., PITTSBURGH, 15235
MALE R/B GROUP (-1960)
EDWARD J. DEEM, JR., RD. #1, P. O. BOX 73, INDUSTRY, 15052
R/R, R/B, LP's, 45's (1960-70), Beatles
THE DUKE, 256 MARTSOFF AVE., PITTSBURGH, 15229
FOR SALE: Rare, Out-of-Print, Mint & Used LP's. Most Categories. $5.00 each plus postage. Catalog $1.00 (Refundable with order). U.S. Only
LAWRENCE R. ECKERT, 28 ELMWOOD ST., PITTSBURGH, 15205
ROCK (1950), Buddy Holly, Eddy Cochran, Gene Vincent, etc.
BOB EMERY, 92 CAROL LN., RICHBORO, 18954
R/B, R/R, ROCKABILY, 45's (1950-60), Guy Mitchell, Marty Robbins 45's
JOHN EVANS, 2113 DALTON ST., McKEESPORT, 15132
Anything on Aerosmith, The Runaways, The Chain Reaction . (412) 678-1251
WALT FISCH, 712 PICNIC LN., SELLINSGROVE, 17870
Anything from 50's & 60's. R/B VOCAL GROUPS & Beatles .... (717) 784-2065
RUSSEL FORSYTHE, 428 EBERHART RD., BUTLER, 16001
ROCK GROUPS, SOLO ARTISTS, 45's, ALBUMS (1960-70)
JAMES E. FRIES, 2206 EVERGREEN RD., PITTSBURGH, 15209
ROCKABILY, R/R SOUNDS (1950), ELVIS BEATLES
BOB GALLO, P. O. BOX 246, HATFIELD, 19440
New Orleans R/B, R/R GROUPS, ROCKERS, ROCKABILY, BLUES ....
....(215) 855-6074
EDWARD F. GARDNER, 5 RODNEY RD., ROSEMONT 19010
RICH GAZAK, 312 STEVENS ST., PHILADELPHIA, 19111
Elvis, Beatles, DJ Copies of any R/R, R/B ARTIST (1950-60), Philly & New York Groups, DOOWOP
GALEN GEORGE, 709 NAPOLEON ST., JOHNSTOWN, 15905
Orig. 45's & 78's (1950-60), R/R, R/B GROUPS

ROBERT GIBSON, 6325 GREENE ST., PHILADELPHIA, 19144
(Boxer, Blind Faith), MOVIES STARS (Jane, Marilyn, Gina, etc.), BOP, but mainly R/B & R/R OF BLACK & WHITE ARTISTS

LARRY M. GOLDSTEIN, 307 RIDGEWAY ST., PHILADELPHIA, 19116

MARK HENNESSY, 53 E. CHELTON RD., PARKSIDE, 19015
R/R (1950-62), 45's Only

TED HESBACHER, 3007 ELLIOTT AVE., WILLOW GROVE, 19090
R/R, R/B, LP's (1950-60)

WAYNE HINSLEY, 226 N. MAIN ST., BUTLER, 16001
Slow R/B, Basically 45's, 78's. DJ Stormy Weather, Five Sharps 45's .... (412) 283-9065

C. E. HOCKENBROHT, P. O. BOX 484, SUNBURY, 17801
Music from 30's to 50's. Anything on Spike Jones

ROBERT E. HOSIE, 139 CRANBROOKE DR., CORAOPOLIS, 15108
45's, LP's, 78's all types, J. Mathis, Tommy Edwards, Joni James

GARY JAFFE, BOX 18085, PHILADELPHIA, 19148
R/R, R/B (1950-60)

CARL JANUSEK, 1123 GRANT AVE., DUQUESNE, 15110
R/B VOCAL GROUPS (1950). POP Groups also: Hilltoppers, Four Aces, Four Voices, Four Lads .... (412) 466-7211

PETER JENSEN, FRANKFORD STATION, RT. 14, PHILADELPHIA, 19124
R/R, BEBOP (1950-), Charlie Parker, Dizzy Trombone Records, Little Richard, Elvis, Jerry Lee, SUN Label

MICHAEL H. JOHNSON, 15 GRANT ST., COKEBURG, 15324

ROBERT JUNCKNEWICH, 685 RICHMOND DR., SHARON, 16146
C/W, ROCK, INSTRU. OLDIES, LP's, 45's. ESP. Ral Donner, Jack Scott, Hank Snow, Johnny Maddox .... (412) 081-2794

TED KACMARIK, 1523 ONEIDA DR., CLARITON, 15025
R/R, R/B, 45's, EP's, LP's

DAVID LEE KLEES, 89 DRINKER ST., BLOOMSBURG, 17815
R/R, JAZZ, BLUES; ESP. (Pre 1964 ROCK, British Invasion, R/B, POP (1920-30), JAZZ .... (717) 784-2004

ROBERT G. KOKSTEIN, 4905 QUINCE DR., READING, 19606
45's, LP's (1950-60), Phil Spector, J. Scott, Wanda Jackson, Randy/Rainbows

LARRY'S RECORDS, BOX 86, SOUDERSBURG, 17577
R/B, R/R GROUPS, 45's, 78's (1950-60)

SHERRY McCABE, 2 PIERCE ST., WELLSBORO, 16901
Bee Gees, Andy Gibb, Inc.

ARCHIE McCOY, 1509 KINSDALE, ST., PHILADELPHIA, 19126
R/B VOCAL GROUPS & JAZZ SINGERS

THOMAS MERKEL, R.D. #1 BOX 180, NEW HOPE, 18938
R/B, R/R (1950-1960)

MRS. LESLEY I. MINNIG, 695 CHERRY TREE RD., ASTON, 19014

JOSEPH A. MORINELLI, 901 FAIRFAX RD., DREXEL HILL, 19026
R/B Singles & Promotional DISCO Releases

MR. & MRS. WILLIAM F. MULLER, 2156 GARFIELD AVE., WEST LAWN, 19609
R/B, R/R (1951-65)

LEE NICHOLS, 1714 NEVADA ST., PITTSBURGH, 15218
U.S., BRITISH BLUES/ ROCK, Clapton, Buchanan . . . . (412) 243-0882
PAUL NOWICKI, 520 LANCASTER AVE., LANCASTER, 17603
Elvis, Beatles, 45's (1950-60), POP, R/B, R/R. Vogue Picture Records, 78's
JOHN OKOLOWICZ, 836 SUNNYSIDE AVE., AUDUBON, 19407
TONY PALLATTO, 1013 LARIMER AVE., EXT, TURTLE CREEK, 15145
R/B, LP's (1950-60)
J. A. PANARELLO, 442 BLVD. AVE., DICKSON CITY, 18519
JOHN POLITIS, 966 N. RANDOLPH, PHILADELPHIA, 19123
CHARLES REINHART, 1616 ROBERT RD., LANCASTER, 17601
ROCK & SOUL, 45's, LP's; Beatles, Apple Records . . . . (717) 299-4275
REVOLVER (MAX SHENK), 304 GLENDALE ST., CARLISLE, 17013
LP's, 45's, POST-'65, Beatles, Beach Boys, Capitol & Reprise Singles, Jan & Dean, Jan Berry, Jan & Dean on Dore, I Publish "Revolver" A Beatles Fanzine . . . . (717) 243-4361
FOSTER J. RITCHIE, JR., 62 SEMINARY PL., FORTY FORT, 18704
Old LP's & Singles by the Ventures & any 12" DISCO 45 Singles
CRAIG SATINSKY, 1029 FANSHAWE ST., PHILADELPHIA, 19111
1,000's of LP's, (1950-70) . . . . (215) 725-1948
TONY SBERNA, 4057 CABINET ST., PITTSBURGH, 15224
45's (1950-60), Flamingoes, Hank Ballard, Bo Diddley, Coasters
PAUL SCHWARTZ, 6024 N. WARNOCK ST., PHILADELPHIA, 19141
R/B, ROCKABILY (1950)
MAX H. SHENK, 304 GLENDALE ST., CARLISLE, 17013
(Post '66), Beatles, Beach Boys & Beatles/Beach Boys, Elvis EP's . . . . (717) 243-4361
HARRIS SHERMAN, 1211 VALLEY RD., LANCASTER, 17603
Beatles, Monkees
ALICE & JESSE SIMON, P. O. BOX 152, FRIEDENS, 15541
ANDREW P. SMITH, R.D. 3 BOX 268, DILLSBURG, 17019
SPENCER SMITH, BOX 139, R.D. #4, MOUNTAIN TOP, 18707
Buddy Holly, Elvis, Johnny Maestro, Ray Eterson
MARILYN SONTHEIMER, 3532 HAZEL, ERIE, 16508
Elvis Presley
JOSEPH STOKES, P. O. BOX 1323, MECHANICSBURG, 17055
45's, LP's (1950-60)
HENRY SULNER, RD #2, LANDFILL RD., FELTON, 17322
R/R, R/B, 45's
KEN SWEIGART, BOX 29, PARADISE, 17562
POP, R/B, C/W (1920-incl) . . . . (717) 687-6414
SAM VETOVICH, 1308 W. WILLOW ST., SHAMOKIN, 17872
David Cassidy, Elton John, Tanya Tucker, John Denver, Lesley Duncan, Jim Croce, Olivia Newton-John, Too Morros & La Costa
JERRY WASSERMAN, 4712 HOLLY CIRCLE, HARRISBURG, 17110
TOM WELCOMER, 143 NISSLEY STR., MIDDLETOWN, 17057
Elvis

ROBERT WIELGUS, 1233 S. 7th ST., PHILADELPHIA, 19147
Beach Boys, Four Seasons, Annette
BILL WOLF, P. O. BOX 426, TREXLERTOWN, 18087
BRITISH ROCK (1960-70), Beatles
MIKE ZAHORCHAK, RD #3, GARVIN RD., EVANS CITY, 16033
R/R, R/B, 45's, 78's (1950-60)

RHODE ISLAND
DICK CHESTER, 15 CENTENNIAL ST., WARWICK, 02886
R/B, R/R, 45's (1950-60) .... (401) 738-7253
GARY MONNIER, 20 SHADY LEA RD., NORTH KINGSTOWN, 02852
Frankie Valli/Four Seasons International Organization
HARVEY S. SIMON, 83 NINTH ST., PROVIDENCE, 02906
R/B, ROCKABILY (1950-60), R/R
FRANK A. WATSON, 575 DYER AVE., APT. M59, CRANSTON, 02920

SOUTH CAROLINA
JAMES C. DAVIS, 110 LANCEWAY DR., MAULDIN, 29662
R/B, ROCKABILY 45's, LP's, EP's .... (803) 288-0424
LARRY JONES, 48 APPALOOSA DR., GREENVILLE, 29611
Oldies (1950), Elvis .... (803) 295-1374
KEN NEILSON, 614 PERIWINKLE CT., SUMTER, 29150
LP's, Bob Dylan, Frank Zappa & Jimi Hendrix
HAROLD J. NEWTON, 7 JUNE LN., GREENVILLE, 29605
RICH'S RECORD EXCHANGE, 4812 MAIN ST., COLUMBIA, 29203
RECORD SHOWCASE, P. O. BOX 146, GOOSE CREEK, 29445
R/R, R/B, ROCKABILY (1950-60), Elvis .... (803) 553-1991
HAROLD L. SWAFFORD, 1413 CALHOUN ST., COLUMBIA, 29201
R/B, LP's .... (803) 779-5057 or 754-7903
DAVE WERNICK, P. O. BOX 28485, FURMAN UNIVERSITY, GREENVILLE, 29613
R/B, ROCKABILY, 45's Looking for 50's

TENNESSEE
PATRICIA A. BAILEY, 324 WATERLOO ST., LAWRENCEBURG, 38464
Elvis .... (615) 762-4423
CHRISTOPHER ECKERT, 241 CHEROKEE RD., NASHVILLE 37205
Beatle .... (615) 297-0721
GENERAL S. GENTRY, RT. #1, NORRIS FREEWAY, POWELL, 37849
C/W .... (615) 922-8653

THE GREAT ESCAPE, 1919 DIVISION, NASHVILLE, 37203
Beatles, Presley, Orlons, Marcels
BARRY MAYER, P. O. BOX 23504, NASHVILLE, 37202
BRITISH & U.S. ROCK LP's (1960-), Kinks, Beau Brummels, Left Bank, 10CC, Beatles, Beach Boys, Bee Gees, Easybeats, Harpers Bizarre
ED. F. RUPP, GREENWOOD DR., RT. 10, FAIRVIEW HTS., MARYVILLE, 37801
(1950-60) Top Forty. American Bandstand Music
SHILOH MUSIC CENTER, 5001 LEBANON RD., OLD HICKORY, 37138
LP RECORDS .... (615) 758-9437
ERNEST TUCKER, BOX 251, FAYETTEVILLE, 37334

TEXAS

JEAN BROWN, 3114 REDFIELD, PASADENA, 77503
ROCKABILY, R/B, R/R (1950) .... (713) 472-0952
BILLY BUCK, 4805 STEVENS, FT. WORTH, 76114
ROCKABILY, R/B, R/R .... (817) 737-5992
J. J. CANTINI, JR., 7301-BROADWAY #B-102, GALVESTON, 77550
CHART (45's) & OBSCURE, (Post '60) LP's
EDY J. CHANDLER, BOX 20664, HOUSTON, 77025
Beatles, Rolling Stones, Led Zeppelin
RALPH DeWITT, 4423 38th ST., LUBBOCK, 79414
R/R, LP's, 45's (1950-60) 792-0837
L. R. DOCKS, P. O. BOX 13685, SAN ANTONIO, 78213
C/W, R/R, R/B, ROCKABILY .... (512) 341-0978
ZENDA EBY, P. O. BOX 6220, LUBBOCK, 79413
78's (1904-56) & R/R, POP, C/W, 45's
THOMAS C. GOODALL, 6505 WESTHEIMER #357, HOUSTON, 77057
National & Regional Chart Records (1950-) .... (713) 781-7557
R. B. GRIFFITH, 2633 BROOKVIEW, PLANO, 75074
R/B (1950)
FRANK HAECKER, 423 WOODCREST DR. (45-2), SAN ANTONIO, 78209
ROCK RECORD RARITIES
HOWELL'S NOSTAGIC ANTIQUES (MR. & MRS. ARTHUR HOWELL)
BOX 179-HIGHWAY 90, NOME, 77629
OLD TIME 78's, 10" & 12", NEW/O,S
CATHY HUDSON, P. O. BOX 574, WINNSBORO, 75494
R/R, C/W, Waylon Jennings, Johnny Paycheck, Glaser Brothers, Buddy Holly & Crickets, Ray Price .... (214) 342-5679
JERRY KNIGHT, RT. 3 BOX 343 K, FT. WORTH, 76140
R/B, POP, C/W, 45's (1950-65)
RICHARD A. LATTANZI, P. O. BOX 3672, ARLINGTON, 76010
R/R, R/B, ROCKABILY (1950-65)
GILBERT LOPEZ, 819 SALDANA, SAN ANTONIO, 78225
W. STANTON MEALS, 202 BELLEVUE DR., CLEBURNE, 76031
POP (1930-50), R/B, R/R (1950-60) .... (817) 645-7839

SCOTT MOSELEY, 9203 KRISTIN DR., HOUSTON, 77031
Elvis & 4 Other ROCKABILY & R/R ARTISTS .....(713) 771-6299 or 945-6078
JIM MORRIS, 322 RECOLETA AVE., APT. 417, SAN ANTONIO, 78216
R/B, ROCK, SURF, S'TRACKS, POSTERS, LP's, 45's, 78's ....(512) 826-3464
OLYMPIC RECORDS, BOX 1323, ALVIN, 77511
We Have Auction & Set Sale Lists ....(713) 331-1326
TERRY A. PARKENING, U OF T MEDICAL BRANCH, BOX 129, GALVESTON, 77550
R/B, R/R, ROCKABILY, 45's, EP's, LP's (1950-60), Buddy Holly, Eddie Cochran, D. Hawkins, Vincent, D. Eddy, Vocal Groups, C. Berry, F. Domino
RAM ROCHA, 4001 WOODCRAFT, HOUSTON, 77025........(713) 661-4414
GERRY ROSAMOND, 122 S. WESTMORELAND, DALLAS, 75211
POP, R/R, 78's, 45's, LP's (1950-65)
SCOTT SAYERS, 7219 COLGATE, DALLAS, 75225
Sinatra
SINATRA SOCIETY OF AMERICA, P. O. BOX 10512, DALLAS, 75207
New Members Welcomed. Dues $7.00 U.S., $8.50 Foreign. Bi-Monthly Newsletter, Annual Convention
ED SMITH, P. O. BOX 3380, EL PASO, 79923
JOE SPECHT, BOX 237, McMUEEY STATION, ABILENE, 79605
C/W, 45's, LP's (1940-), R/R (1950-60) ....(915) 677-5178
JOHN I. TAYLOR, 3317 REED ST., FT. WORTH, 76119
ROBERT W. WHITBY, 421 CELESTE ST., EVERMAN, 76140...(817) 293-4106
EVELYN WRAY, 925 BEACHUM ST., ARLINGTON, 76011
ROCK & COUNTRY, 45's, LP's (1950-60) ....(817) 275-2294
WAYNE ZOTOPEK, P. O. BOX 598, HURST, 76053
R/R, C/W, BLUES, ROCKABILY

UTAH

BARBARA McGURK, 3347 PLAZA WAY, SALT LAKE CITY, 84109
R/B, DOOWOP

VIRGINIA

ROBERT MIKE ARBOGAST, P. O. BOX 483, COVINGTON, 24426
R/R, ROCKABILY, DOOWOP: Buddy Holly, Elvis, Earls, Dion & Belmonts
DAVID BERNARD, 5269 BALFOR DR., VIRGINIA BEACH, 23462
R/B, 78's (1940-50), VOCAL GROUP
LARRY BLEVINS, 8436 RUGBY RD., MANASSAS, 22110
C/W, R/R (1950), Jack Scott, Terry Stafford & Johnny Rivers
ED CAFFEY, 3rd, 1830 BANNING RD., NORFOLK, 23518
JIMMY COLE & THE ROADMASTERS, 13408 BRISTOL RD., NOKESVILLE, 22123 ....(703) 791-3307
DeLOATCH MUSIC SERVICES, P. O. BOX 724, PORTSMOUTH, 23705
R/B, 78's, 45's, LP's. 10,000 78's, 45's. 5,000 LP's

GAY K. DOOLEY, 2604 HILLCREST AVE. NW, ROANOKE, 24012
DAVID E. DZULA, RT. 1, BOX 155F, WEST POINT, 23181
Rolling Stones
DON GLEASON, P. O. BOX 166, SPOTSYLVANIA, 22553
Elvis, Johnny Cash on SUN .... (703) 972-7620
MRS. FRANCY GLESSNER, GREENVIEW FARM RT. 2, WARRENTON, 22186
Elvis .... (703) 439-8646
GINA GUSTIN, 9008 ROBSON DR., MANASSAS, 22110
Jethro Tull .... (703) 361-4735
MIKE HANLON, 13448 NYSTOM CT., WOODBRIDGE, 22193
ROCKABILY: SUN & PHILLIPS. 78's, 45's .... (703) 590-5064
MARK F. HOBACK, 937 N. MADISON ST., ARLINGTON, 22205
MARANATHA MEMORY LANE RECORDS, 12592 WARWICK BLVD., NEWPORT NEWS, 23606
200,000 45's, 78's, LP's in Stock .... (804) 595-5709
HENRY L. McCORLE, 1121 FIRST ST., SW #11, ROANOKE, 24016
R/B, 12" & 10" LP's: Ink Spots, Mills Bros., Deep River Boys, Red Caps, Delta Rhythm Boys & Others
LYNN McCUTCHEON, 753 OLD WATERLOO RD., WARRENTON, 22186
R/B, 45's, LP's .... (703) 347-7618
SANDI LEE McFADDEN, 14582D OLDE COURT HOUSE, NEWPORT NEWS, 23602
THOMAS A. NORRIS, 2624 MEMORIAL ST., ALEXANDRIA, 22306
R/R, C/W (1950-60)
AUSTIN PANKEY, 203 WESTBURG DR., LYNCHBURG, 24502
R/R, R/B from Late '50's .... (804) 237-3365
C. R. PERDUE, SR., 3551 OVER BROOK DR., SW, ROANOKE, 24018
SUN RECORDS, MOVIE POSTERS (1930-50) For Sale
THE RECORD BOX INTERNATIONAL, P. O. BOX 4008, PETERSBURG, 23803
R/R, R/B, C/W, JAZZ
RECORD & TAPE EXCHANGE, 821 N. TAYLOR ST., ARLINGTON, 22203
DAN RISWICK, 1105-GASTON CT., CHESAPEAKE, 23323
Buddy Holly, Rock & Surf Instrumentals & Atlantic Label
ROBERT BRUCE TAYLOR, 2514 N. 12 ST., ARLINGTON CO., 22201
C/W, R/R
DON THORE, 3200 JACKSON RD., HOPEWELL, 23860
Anything on SUN Label. C/W, 78's
DENNIS W. WEST, P. O. BOX 489, ROANOKE, 24153
BLUES, ROCKABILY (1950) .... (703) 389-1982
ERNIE WHITE, BOX 9637, RICHMOND, 23228
CHARLES D. YOUNG, 185 COLBURN DR., MANASSAS PARK, 22110
R/R, LP's, 45's: Mugwumps, Beefeaters, Hawks, Lovin' Spoonful .... (703) 361-7762

WASHINGTON

TIMOTHY B. ANDERSON, 71 HARBOR VW PL., FRIDAY HARBOR, 98250
Allman to Zappa

KIP AYERS, 205 A N. 63rd AVE., YAKIMA, 98908
Elvis, Beatles & Beach Boys
BEATLES FOR SALE, U.S.A., P. O. BOX 132, SPOKANE, 99211
Apple Records, Beatles, 45's
HARRY L. BALISURE, 4634 B. REDWOOD, TACOMA, 98439
Beatle & Apple Records, 45's . . . . (206) 584-6047
RICK CLARK, P. O. BOX 4722, VANCOUVER, 98662
R/R (1960-70), Led Zeppelin, Yardbirds
VICKY COLGROVE, 27822 PACIFIC HWY, KENT, 98031
LES DERBY, 4546 S. 7th ST., TACOMA, 98405
R/R, R/B, ROCKABILY (1950-60), Elvis and DOOWOP . . . . (206) 752-0636
JOHN FISHER, 9219 40th AVE., E., TACOMA, 98446
SUE FREDERICK, #3, 13703 J. ST., S., TACOMA, 98444
ROCK (1950), Buddy Holly, Valens, Bopper, Crickets, Doors
WES GEESMAN, 4141 UNIVERSITY WAY, NE, SEATTLE, 98105
100,000 Records For Sale
ED Y. GUANCO, 15113 122nd CT., NE, KIRKLAND, 98033
BILL HANSEN, P. O. BOX 7113, TACOMA, 98407
Paul McCartney & Wings
GERALD B. JOHNSON, 11416 RAINIER AVE., S., LOT 1, SEATTLE, 98178
Beatle
KARAVAN RECORDS, W416 GRETA, SPOKANE, 99208
R/R, R/B, COUNTRY, 45's, LP's
DON KIRSCH, 806 S. FIFE, TACOMA, 98405
ROCKABILY, R/R
RICH KOCH, 19302 AUROA DR., E., SPANAWAY, 98387
ROCK, R/R, POP
LARRY J. LONG, 11504 20th ST., NE, LAKE STEVENS, 98258
R/R (1955-), Frankie Avalon to Led Zeppelin
THOMAS J. MEENACH III, E 1721-58th, SPOKANE, 99205
Beatle Collector . . . . (509) 448-1814
MR. RANDALL C. NUTTER, P. O. BOX 2130, SPOKANE, 99210
THE OLD CURIOSITY SHOP, N 705 MONROE, SPOKANE, 99201
R/R (1950), Elvis
GARY OSWOLD, 10715 24 SW, SEATTLE, 90140
Elvis, Fats Domino . . . . (206) 246-2916
BOB PEGG, 8420 S. 16th ST., TACOMA, 98465
Beach Boys & Four Seasons
SKIP PIACQUAEIO, JR., 13826 116th PL., NE, KIRLAND, 98033
R/R, R/B: Buddy Holly
MARK PLUMMER, 1666 LARCH DR., OAK HARBOR, 98277
R/R, Jan & Dean, Beach Boys
R. ROBBINS, 1104 GRANT ST. BELLINGHAM, 98225
(1960-70) ROCK LP's. Send for free list.
JIM SCHANTZ, 2037 13TH WAY, SEATTLE, 98502
ROCK, Peter Green, Toe Fat, Yardbirds, Johnny Burnette Trio . . . .
. . . . (206) 285-4288

DICK SCHMITT, 10350 INTERLAKE NO. SEATTLE, 98133
Elvis & R/R 78's & EP's
2ND TIME AROUND RECORDS, 4141 UNIVERSITY WAY NE, SEATTLE, 98105 .... (206) 632-1698
DEAN SILVERSTONE (GOLDEN OLDIES), 1835 McGILVRA BLVD., EAST, SEATTLE, 98112
45's (1950-70)
SHIRLEY C. STEARNS, 22904-86th PL., WEST, EDMONDS, 98020
C/W, 45's & Albums (1950-) .... (207) 775-6923
CHRIS TRANT, 421 E. 34th, TACOMA, 98404
Elvis Records

WEST VIRGINIA

WILLIAM DAVIS, 100 22nd ST., DUNBAR, 25064
ROCKABILY & DOOWOP
JIM FIORILLI, 103-19th ST., WHEELING, 26003
R/R, R/B, Four Seasons, Token's, Surf Music, Jimmy Boyd, Rose Murphy
JAMES WILLARD GRIMMETTE, MOD 11 CN, HAMPDEN, 25623
C/W, 78's, 33⅓'s, 45's
DICK NEWMAN, 14 CAMPBELL LN., HARBOURSVILLE, 25504 .... (304) 736-5380

WISCONSIN

WILLIAM J. BLUMENBERG, 2845 No. 84th ST., MILWAUKEE, 53222
RICHARD J. CONRARDY, 2114 N. 23rd ST. SHEBOYGAN, 53081
R/R (1950-60)
BUCK HAFEMAN, 1603 W. COLLEGE AVE., APPLETON, 54911
ROCK 45's, (1955-65), Elvis .... (414) 733-7668
STEVE & TINA HASLEHURST, RT. 9, NORTH RD., APPLETON, 54911
JERRY HILDESTAD, 1809 KROPF AVE., MADISON, 53704
R/B, Elvis .... (608) 249-3967
LEE HYLINGIRL, ROOM 384C, DHSS, 1 WEST WILSON, MADISON, 53702
STEVE JOHNSON, P. O. BOX 843, MILWAUKEE, 53201
Elvis, Rolling Stones & Beatles
PAUL JUSZCZAK, 2413 E. VAN NORMAN, MILWAUKEE, 53207
Olivia Newton-John
STEVE KRUPP, BOX 7, PRINCETON, 54968
Juke Boxes .... (414) 295-3972
RON LOFMAN, P. O. BOX 2242, MADISON, 53701
ROCK, LP's (1950)
CAROL MACE, P. O. BOX 468, 221 CAPITOL ST., WISCONSIN DELLS, 53965
Elvis

MEAN MOUNTAIN MUSIC, P. O. BOX 04352, MILWAUKEE, 53204
ROCKABILY 45's, 78's; R/R, BLUES, R/B, C/W 45's, 78's (1950-)
PHILIP MEDVED, 3010 5th AVE., #28, S. MILWAUKEE, 53172
ROCKABILY, 45's ....(414) 764-5141
BRUCE A. OZANICH, 1208 S. 29th ST., MILWAUKEE, 53215
R/R, C/W, ROCK, R/B, 45's, EP's, LP's (1950-60)
DOUGLAS RAY, 309 N. PELHAM ST., RHINELANDER, 54501 ....(715) 362-4734
RICHARD ROMMICH, 4251 S. 122nd ST., GREENFIELD, 53228
R/R, R/B, POP
GEORGE J. RUBATT, RT. 1 BOX 168, FOXBORO, 54836
R/R, 45's, LP's (1950-), Jack Scott, Elvis, Beatles
DICK TISHKEN, 1441 OAKES RD. #3, RACINE, 53406
R/R, R/B, Beach Boys, Beatles, Rick Nelson & Ventures ......(414) 886-0827
JAMES TRIEB, 920 SECOND ST., HUDSON, 54016
DONALD E. WETTSTEIN, 1149 CHERRY, GREEN BAY, 54301
C/W, R/B (1961-77), LP's (1945-77)

- ✓ *RECORD DIGEST* GIVES YOU THE SLICK PROFESSIONAL FEATURES OF A MAGAZINE, COUPLED WITH THE SPEED AND DEPENDABILITY OF A NEWSPAPER. THE WORLD'S MUSIC NEWS AT YOUR FINGERTIPS, BIWEEKLY!
- ✓ WHETHER YOU'RE LOOKING TO BUILD YOUR COLLECTION, SELL YOUR COLLECTION, OR JUST LEARN MORE ABOUT YOUR COLLECTION, *RECORD DIGEST* IS ESSENTIAL! THOUSANDS OF RARE RECORDS ARE BOUGHT AND SOLD THROUGH THE PAGES OF THE *DIGEST*.
- ✓ *RECORD DIGEST* IS ACKNOWLEDGED AS THE MOST AUTHORATATIVE MUSIC PUBLICATION IN THE WORLD. EDITOR JERRY OSBORNE (AUTHOR OF NUMEROUS BOOKS AND MAGAZINES SERVING RECORD COLLECTING) AND HIS WORLD-WIDE STAFF OF PROFESSIONAL CORRESPONDENTS ARE DEVOTED TO KEEPING YOU TOTALLY INFORMED!
- ✓ *RECORD DIGEST* IS MAILED BIWEEKLY (THE MOST FREQUENTLY PUBLISHED RECORD COLLECTOR'S PUBLICATION IN THE WORLD) AND THERE HAS NEVER BEEN AN ISSUE MAILED LATE! OUR DEPENDABILITY IS UNMATCHED. YOU'LL LEARN OF NEW RELEASES WHILE THEY ARE STILL AVAILABLE; WHETHER IT'S A COLORED VINYL ISSUE FROM THAILAND, A PICTURE DISC FROM ENGLAND, A BOOTLEG FROM NEW YORK, OR SPECIAL PROMO RELEASE!
- ✓ JOIN THOUSANDS OF INFORMED COLLECTORS, FROM NEARLY EVERY COUNTRY ON EARTH, BEGIN YOUR *RECORD DIGEST* SUBSCRIPTION NOW!

NOW IN IT'S 2ND BIG YEAR! SEE WHY RECORD DIGEST IS THE FAVORITE OF THE FANS!

SUBSCRIBE NOW!

★

RECORD DIGEST IS THE MUSIC & RECORD LOVER'S TOTAL INFORMATION SOURCE!

*COMPLETE COVERAGE OF THE MUSIC OF THE 50's, 60's & 70's!

RECORD DIGEST —Without It....You're Not With It!

Send To: RECORD DIGEST · GROOM CREEK · PRESCOTT, AZ. 86301

U.S. RATES

1 Yr (24 Issues) · $19.00 • 6 Mo (12 Issues) · $11.00 • 3 Mo (6 Issues) · $6.00
FOR AIR MAIL/FIRST CLASS: ADD 41 CENTS PER ISSUE TO ABOVE RATES

CANADA

1 Yr (24 Issues) · $25.00 • 6 Mo (12 Issues) · $14.00 • 3 Mo (6 Issues) · $7.50
FOR AIR MAIL/FIRST CLASS: ADD 41 CENTS PER ISSUE TO ABOVE RATES

OVERSEAS

FOR AIR MAIL – $2.00 PER ISSUE (TOTAL COST)
FOR SURFACE MAIL – SAME AS CANADIAN SURFACE RATES
*All funds in U. S. currency please

MAILED ON THE 1ST & 15TH – NEVER MAILED LATE!

NAME ____________________

ADDRESS ____________________

CITY __________ STATE __________ ZIP __________

Check or Money Order Enclosed in the Amount of __________ for __________ Issues

Credit Card No. __________ Exp. Date __________

_____ MASTRCHG _____ BAC (VISA) Signature __________